A History of Israel to Bar Kochba

H. Jagersma

A History of Israel
to Bar Kochba

Part I
The Old Testament Period

Part II
From Alexander the Great
to Bar Kochba

SCM PRESS LTD

Part I translated by John Bowden from the Dutch
Geschiedenis van Israël in het Oudtestamentische Tijdvak,
published 1979 by Uitgevermaatschappij J. H. Kok, Kampen.

Part II translated by John Bowden from the Dutch
Geschiedenis van Israël van Alexander de Grote tot Bar Kochba,
published 1985 by Uitgeversmaatschappij J. H. Kok, Kampen.

0 334 02577 X

Part I first published 1982 as *A History of Israel in the
Old Testament Period* and Part II first published 1985 as
A History of Israel from Alexander the Great to Bar Kochba
by SCM Press Ltd

This edition first published in one volume 1994
by SCM Press Ltd
26–30 Tottenham Road, London N1 4BZ

Printed in Great Britain by
Biddles Ltd, Guildford and King's Lynn

Part I

The Old Testament Period

CONTENTS

ABBREVIATIONS

AAASH	Acta Antiqua Academiae Scientiarum Hungaricae, Budapest
AASOR	Annual of the American Schools of Oriental Research, New Haven
AB	The Anchor Bible, Garden City
ABR	*The Australian Biblical Review*, Melbourne
ADPV	Abhandlungen des Deutschen Palästina-Vereins, Wiesbaden
AFLNW	Veröffentlichungen der Arbeitsgemeinschaft für Forschung des Landes Nordrhein-Westfalen, Köln-Opladen
AHW	W. von Soden, *Akkadisches Handwörterbuch*, Wiesbaden 1965
AJBA	*Australian Journal of Biblical Archaeology*, Sydney
AJBI	*Annual of the Japanese Biblical Institute*, Tokyo
ANET	*Ancient Near Eastern Texts relating to the Old Testament*, ed. J. B. Pritchard, Princeton ³1969
AOAT	Alter Orient und Altes Testament, Neukirchen-Vluyn
AOT	*Altorientalische Texte zum Alten Testament*, ed. H. Gressmann, Berlin and Leipzig ²1926
AOTS	*Archaeology and Old Testament Study*, ed. D. Winton Thomas, Oxford 1969
APAW	Abhandlungen der Preussischen Akademie der Wissenschaften
ARM(T)	*Archives Royales de Mari (Transcriptions et Traductions)*, ed. A. Parrot and G. Dossin, 15 vols, Paris 1946–76
ArOr	Archiv Orientálni, Prague
ATD	Das Alte Testament Deutsch, Göttingen
AUSS	Andrews University Seminary Studies, Michigan
B	Texts cited following J. Bottéro, *Le Problème des Habiru*, Paris 1954
BA	*Biblical Archaeologist*, New Haven

BASOR	*Bulletin of the American Schools of Oriental Research*, New Haven
BBB	Bonner Biblische Beiträge, Bonn
BeO	R. de Vaux, *Bible et Orient*, Paris 1967
BETL	Bibliotheca Ephemeridum Theologicarum Lovaniensium, Louvain
BHW	*Biblisch-historisches Wörterbuch*, ed. B. Reicke and L. Rost, Göttingen
BiOr	Bibliotheca Orientalis, Leiden
BJRL	*Bulletin of the John Rylands Library*, Manchester
BKAT	Biblischer Kommentar Altes Testament, Neukirchen-Vluyn
BMB	*Bulletin du Musée de Beyrouth*, Paris
BOT	De Boeken van het Oude Testament, Roermond and Maaseik
BR	Biblical Research, Amsterdam
BRL	*Biblisches Reallexikon*, Tübingen
BWANT	Beiträge zur Wissenschaft vom Alten und Neuen Testament, Stuttgart
BZ	*Biblische Zeitschrift*, Paderborn
BZAW	Beihefte zur *Zeitschrift für die Alttestamentliche Wissenschaft*, Berlin and New York
CAD	*The Assyrian Dictionary of the Oriental Institute of the University of Chicago*, Chicago 1956
CAH	*The Cambridge Ancient History*, Cambridge 1971
CAT	Commentaire de l'Ancien Testament, Neuchâtel
CB	The Century Bible, London and Edinburgh
CBQ	*Catholic Biblical Quarterly*, Washington
CH	*Codex Hammurabi*
CHME	F. M. Cross, *Canaanite Myth and Hebrew Epic*, Cambridge, Mass. and London ²1975
COT	Commentaar op het Oude Testament, Kampen
CTM	*Concordia Theological Monthly*, St Louis
D	Deuteronomy
Dtr	Deuteronomist/Deuteronomistic history work
DOTT	*Documents from Old Testament Times*, ed. D. Winton Thomas, London 1958
DTT	*Dansk Teologisk Tidsskrift*, Copenhagen
E	Elohist
EA	J. A. Knudtzon, *Die El-Amarna Tafeln*, Leipzig 1915

EAEHL	*Encyclopedia of Archaeological Excavations in the Holy Land*, I, II, III, ed. M. Avi Yonah (and E. Stern), London 1975, 1976, 1977
EHI	R. de Vaux, *The Early History of Israel*, London 1978
EI	*Eretz Israel*, Jerusalem
EOTHR	A. Alt, *Essays on Old Testament History and Religion*, Oxford 1966
ETL	Ephemerides Theologicae Lovanienses, Louvain
EvTh	*Evangelische Theologie*, Munich
FRLANT	Forschungen zur Religion und Literatur des Alten und Neuen Testaments, Göttingen
FWCJS	Fourth World Congress of Jewish Studies, Jerusalem 1967
G	Texts quoted following M. Greenberg, *The Hab/piru*, New Haven 1955
GS	Gesammelte Studien
HAT	Handbuch zum Alten Testament, Tübingen
HI	John Bright, *History of Israel*, Philadelphia and London ²1972
HIOTT	S. Herrmann, *A History of Israel in Old Testament Times*, London and Philadelphia ²1981
HTR	*Harvard Theological Review*, Cambridge, Mass.
HUCA	*Hebrew Union College Annual*, Cincinnati
IEJ	*Israel Exploration Journal*
IH	A. Lemaire, *Inscriptions Hébraïques, Tome I, Les Ostraca*, Paris 1977
IJH	*Israelite and Judaean History*, ed. J. H. Hayes and J. Maxwell Miller, OTL, London and Philadelphia 1977
J	Yahwist
JANES	*Journal of the Ancient Near Eastern Society of Columbia University*, New York
JAOS	*Journal of the American Oriental Society*, Baltimore
JBL	*Journal of Biblical Literature*, Missoula, Montana
JBR	*Journal of Bible and Religion*, Boston, Mass.
JCS	*Journal of Cuneiform Studies*, New Haven, Conn.
JEOL	*Jaarbericht van het Vooraziatisch-Egyptisch Genootschap Ex Oriente Lux*, Leiden
JNES	*Journal of Near Eastern Studies*, Chicago
JNSL	*Journal of Northwest Semitic Languages*, Leiden
JRT	*Journal of Religious Thought*, Washington DC
JSJ	*Journal for the Study of Judaism in the Persian, Hellenistic and Roman Period*, Leiden
JSOT	*Journal for the Study of the Old Testament*, Sheffield

JSS	*Journal of Semitic Studies*, Manchester
JTS	*Journal of Theological Studies*, Oxford
KAI	H. Donner and W. Röllig, *Kanaanäische und aramäische Inschriften*, I–III, Wiesbaden ³1971, ²1968, ²1969
KAT	Kommentar zum Alten Testament, Gütersloh
KBL	L. Köhler and W. Baumgartner, *Hebräisches und Aramäisches Lexikon zum Alten Testament*, Leiden 1967
KS	Kleine Schriften
KTU	M. Dietrich, O. Loretz and J. Sammartin, Die *keilalphabetischen Texte aus Ugarit*, Neukirchen-Vluyn 1976
LOI	T. C. Vriezen and A. S. van der Woude, *De literatuur van oud-Israël*, Wassenaar ⁴1973
LXX	Septuagint
MT	Massoretic text
NF (NS)	Neue Folge (New Series)
NKZ	*Neue kirchliche Zeitschrift*, Erlangen
NTT	*Nederlands Theologisch Tijdschrift*, Wageningen and The Hague
OBL	*Orientalia et biblica Lovaniensia*, Louvain
OLZ	*Orientalische Literaturzeitung*, Berlin
OTL	Old Testament Library, London and Philadelphia
OTS	*Oudtestamentische Studiën*, Leiden
OTWSA	Die Ou-Testamentiese Werkgemeenschap in Suid-Afrika, Pretoria
P	Priestly Writing
PEQ	*Palestine Exploration Quarterly*, London
PJB	*Palästinajahrbuch*, Berlin
POT	Die Prediking van het Oude Testament, Nijkerk
POTT	*Peoples of Old Testament Times*, ed. D. J. Wiseman, Oxford 1973
PRU	C. Virolleaud, *Le Palais Royal d'Ugarit*, II and V, Paris 1957, 1965
RA	*Revue d'Assyriologie et d'Archéologie Orientale*, Paris
RAI	*Rencontre Assyriologique Internationale*, Paris
RB	*Revue Biblique*, Paris
RGG	*Die Religion in Geschichte und Gegenwart*, Tübingen
RHPR	*Revue d'Histoire et de Philosophie Religieuses*, Paris
RS	Ras Shamra
RSO	*Rivista degli Studi Orientali*, Rome
RVV	*Religionsgeschichtliche Versuche und Vorarbeiten*, Berlin
SBS	Stuttgarter Bibelstudien, Stuttgart

SBT	Studies in Biblical Theology, London
SHI	M. A. Beek, *A Short History of Israel*, London 1963
SNVAO	Skrifter utgitt av Det Norske Videnskaps-Akademi i Oslo
ST	Studia Theologica, Oslo
SVT	Supplements to *Vetus Testamentum*, Leiden
Targ	Targum
TGI	K. Galling, *Textbuch zur Geschichte Israels*, Tübingen ²1968
THAT	*Theologisches Handwörterbuch zum Alten Testament*, I, II, ed. E. Jenni and C. Westermann, Munich and Zurich 1971, 1976
TLZ	*Theologische Literaturzeitung*, Leipzig
ThR	*Theologische Rundschau*, Tübingen
ThT	*Theology Today*, Princeton, New Jersey
TSTS	Toronto Semitic Texts and Studies, Toronto
UF	*Ugarit-Forschungen*, Neukirchen-Vluyn
VDI	*Vestnik Drevnej Istorii*
VoxTh	*Vox Theologica*, Assen and Zwolle
VT	*Vetus Testamentum*, Leiden
VuF	*Verkündigung und Forschung*, Munich
Vulg	Vulgate
WMANT	Wissenschaftliche Monographien zum Alten und Neuen Testament, Neukirchen-Vluyn
WUS	J. Aistleitner, *Wörterbuch der ugaritischen Sprache*, Berlin ⁴1974
WZMLUHW	*Wissenschaftliche Zeitschrift der Martin-Luther-Universität*, Halle-Wittenberg
WZUL	*Wissenschaftliche Zeitschrift Universitäts Leipzig*
ZA	*Zeitschrift für Assyriologie*, Leipzig and Berlin
ZAW	*Zeitschrift für die alttestamentliche Wissenschaft*, Berlin
ZDMG	*Zeitschrift der Deutschen Morgenländischen Gesellschaft*, Wiesbaden
ZDPV	*Zeitschrift des Deutschen Palästina-Vereins*, Wiesbaden
ZdZ	Zeichen der Zeit, Berlin
ZEE	*Zeitschrift für evangelische Ethik*, Gütersloh
ZTK	*Zeitschrift für Theologie und Kirche*, Tübingen

Chapter 1

Introduction

1.1 *An explanation*

The books of the Old Testament are religious writings. In the first place they consist of confessions of faith, in which pride of place is taken by the acts of God and not the words and deeds of human beings. Above all, they were written with the intention of demonstrating that these acts of God have a lasting significance for the present and the future. In other words, the Old Testament 'tells stories and bears witness, sings and meditates, instructs and raises questions' and is by no means to be understood as a historical account.[1]

All this means that the Old Testament does not give us an exact account of historical events or a precise report of particular facts from the past. That is not its concern. The Old Testament – and indeed the Bible as a whole – is not a history book, although many people from a great variety of groups have been constantly inclined to reduce the Bible, and with it the Old Testament, to this level. We can see this simply from the fact that there is constant discussion as to whether this or that feature of the Bible did or did not happen, with no sign of any realization that there can be other and indeed deeper forms of truth than historical truth.

It follows from what I have just said that we should not expect from the Old Testament any first-hand information about the history of Israel in the Old Testament period. Of course the Old Testament was written, and came into being, within the framework of particular historical events. In the same way, we can find in it numerous reflections on different historical facts and particular structures.

Anyone who is interested in the history of Israel will therefore seek to reconstruct it on the basis of these considerations. Furthermore, in many cases the Old Testament seems to be not only the most important source, but even the only source at our disposal. However, alongside that we can often refer to sources which come from the ancient Near East, or to particular results which have been produced by archaeological investigations.[2]

On numerous occasions, however, it will transpire that all this information is not enough to give us an assured and trustworthy picture of the history of Israel in the Old Testament period. The further back into this history we go, the more hypothetical this picture becomes. That is true above all for the patriarchal period, but in fact we have little certain knowledge about any of the history of Israel in the pre-exilic period.

Still, hitherto people have taken it for granted that we can talk of a history of Israel in the Old Testament period, and that is the title of this book. However, a number of objections can be made to it. In the first place, it will become increasingly clear during the course of this book that we are dealing not with the history of a single people, but at least with that of two, namely Israel and Judah. In view of this, I could well have considered some such title as 'A History of Israel and Judah in the Old Testament Period'. However, there would then be at least a second problem, concerning the name Israel. It seems that this name can have different significances in the Old Testament.[3] Furthermore, only at a much later stage can we truly speak of a people 'Israel' and a people 'Judah', whereas here we are concerned with the earliest stages of their history, from the time of the patriarchs on. I finally chose the present title after some heart-searching, simply because it is the title usually given to a work of this kind in the scholarly field, and another title could give rise to just as many problems – albeit of a different kind.[4]

These preliminary remarks should already have made clear the aim of this book. It begins with the preliminaries to the history of Israel, in the patriarchal period, and then continues by describing the history of Israel and Judah down to about 330 BC. I have tried to write this history as far as possible in association with the history of the ancient Near East. This means that I have also laid great emphasis on political, social and economic problems and structures. These particular factors seem increasingly to be of the utmost importance for historical and religious developments in Israel and Judah.

The following sections will discuss the question of the sources that are at our disposal and the way in which these can be used.

1.2 *Sources*

This section will describe in succession the most important sources for the history of Israel deriving from the Old Testament and the ancient Near East; it will also discuss the archaeological material which is important in this connection.

First of all, I should point out that there is a clear difference between these groups of sources. Unlike the texts from the ancient Near East, those from the Old Testament are all based on copies from a later period.[5] Furthermore, they go back to texts or textual units which are certainly not to be taken as contemporaneous or as eye-witness accounts. Rather, they are the result of a final redaction from a time later than the events described. Of course, this does not in any way imply that these textual units cannot be authentic or cannot contain old material. They are, though, characterized by theological presuppositions and particular emphases which are especially characteristic of those who produced the final edition of the material. Thus one and the same event is often reported from a different perspective or on the basis of other, later theological considerations.[6]

After these general reflections, let us now turn our attention to the sources as such.

1.2.1 *The Old Testament*

Within the Old Testament, the principal sources for our knowledge of the history of Israel in the Old Testament period are the Pentateuch, the Deuteronomistic and Chronistic history works, and the prophetic literature.

In the Pentateuch it is usual to distinguish four series of traditions: J, the Yahwist; E, the Elohist; D, the Deuteronomist; and P, the Priestly Writing.[7] These were composed in different periods and were gradually collected together to form a whole. The Yahwist (*c.* 900 BC) is regarded as the earliest; then come the Elohist (*c.* 750 BC), the Deuteronomist (*c.* 600 BC), and the Priestly Writing (from the period of the exile in Babylon and shortly thereafter). The Yahwist is thought to come from the south (Judah), while the origins of the Elohist and the Deuteronomist (Deuteronomy) are sought in the north. Whereas the Yahwist, so-called because he uses Yahweh throughout as the name for God, displays a universalist attitude, with the Elohist, who uses the Name Elohim for God, we find a more prominent nationalistic sense, and the universalism fades into the background. In Deuteronomy, great stress is laid on the centralization of the cult in Jerusalem, whereas the Priestly Writing consists chiefly of material in which worship and cultic institutions play an important role. This probably comes from ancient temple archives.

In recent years, however, there have been some changes in these assessments. The Yahwist has been the focal point of interest in this connection.[8] In particular, people have begun to think in terms of a much later date than has been assumed hitherto. Thus van Seters[9] and Schmid[10] want to put the Yahwist much closer to the time in which the Deuteronomic/ Deuteronomistic tradition was shaped and given its final form. While Rendtorff[11] does not make specific comments on the question of date, he does begin from the assumption that in the Pentateuch we find no extensive redactional work from the period before Deuteronomy and the Deuteronomistic history work. Neither does he see the Yahwist as an author or a theologian. An important argument in this connection is that there is no mention of the patriarchs and the promises given to them either in Exodus or in Numbers, in what have hitherto been regarded as ancient sources. According to Rendtorff, had the Yahwist been a theologian, he would certainly have carried this theme right through.[12] Schmid wants to see 'the Yahwist' as the name for a process of redaction and interpretation, rather than as a collector, author and theologian.[13]

An important conclusion that it would seem possible to draw from these recent studies is that different parts of the Pentateuch, like the patriarchal narratives, the oppression in Egypt, the exodus, and so on, must be regarded rather as originally quite independent traditions, and also must be evaluated and studied as such.

The two other large works from the Old Testament are the Deuteronomistic and Chronistic history works,[14] which in all probability can be dated *c.* 550 BC and at the end of the fourth century BC respectively. According to Noth, the former work comprises the books from Deuteronomy up to and including II Kings,[15] while the latter is composed of the books of Chronicles, Ezra and Nehemiah.

The main aim of the Deuteronomistic history work is evidently to give an explanation of the divine judgment of 587/586. Previous history is seen and described in this light. Alongside this, the centralization of the cult in Jerusalem plays an important role, above all in the books of Kings.

Whereas Noth was still thinking principally of one author in the case of the Deuteronomistic history work, most recently the notion has come strongly to the fore that we can distinguish at least three important redactions: DtrG, in which history has a central role; DtrP, in which prophecy and the rise of the prophets occupy the foreground; and a DtrN, in which the Deuteronomic law plays a central part.[16]

The figure of David and the temple at Jerusalem are a central concern of the Chronistic history work.[17] In this connection it is important to realize that the Chronicler, who in Chronicles largely covers the same period of the history of Israel as Samuel and Kings, clearly has a different perspective from the Deuteronomist. This aspect is constantly expressed in the way in which the different accounts are narrated.

The books of the latter prophets are also an important source of our knowledge of the history of Israel. They not only provide supplements to the information given in the works mentioned above, but also sometimes offer more or less information about the events or aspects which we come across in them. This is important above all because we know that in many cases the prophets themselves saw to it that their prophecies were written down.[18]

1.2.2 *The ancient Near East*

I shall now go on to describe briefly the most important sources from the ancient Near East which are significant for the history of Israel in the period which I shall be describing.

Ebla. Since 1964 an Italian expedition under the direction of P. Matthiae and G. Pettinato has been occupied with excavations in the tumulus Tell Mardik, about sixty kilometres south-west of Aleppo; at a very early stage it proved possible to identify this with Ebla, an important royal city in Northern Syria in about 2400 BC.[19] From 1974 onwards a large number of cuneiform texts were discovered, coming from a period which must be somewhere between 2500 and 2250 BC. In the future these texts may prove to be of great importance for our understanding of the historical background and the language of the Old Testament. However, at present we still await a reliable scholarly edition of the relevant text material.[20]

Sinuhe. This is the story of an Egyptian court official who had to flee from Egypt in about 1950 BC and then spent a long time in Syria and Palestine.[21] However, it must be handled with the greatest possible care as a source of historical information.[22]

The 'Execration Texts'. These Egyptian texts, which seem to come from a somewhat later period,[23] contain lists of hostile rulers, tribes, countries and so on. Names from Canaan and thereabouts also appear in them.[24]

Mari. This was a city lying on the right bank of the Euphrates, in present-day Syria near the border with Iraq. A large number of texts were found here, dating from the eighteenth century BC. These texts give us a vast amount of information about the life of the nomads of this period, the rise of Hammurabi, and certain names and places which are mentioned in the Old Testament. They are also important for the understanding of early prophecy[25] in Israel.[26]

Nuzu. This city was a Hurrian centre in Mesopotamia, about thirteen kilometres south-west of Kirkuk (Iraq). About four thousand texts were found here, dating from the fifteenth and fourteenth centuries BC. They are chiefly important for their mentions of various legal usages which also appear in connection with the patriarchs.[27]

Amarna. In its day this was the capital of Pharaoh Amenophis IV (Akhenaten), which was situated on the east bank of the Nile, about 140 kilometres south of Cairo. A large number of texts were found here, proably belonging to the archive of Amenophis III and IV and dating from the fourteenth century BC. They also include a number of letters containing the correspondence between the Pharaohs and their vassals from the city states in Syria, Phoenicia and Palestine. These letters give us a picture of the political and social situation in these areas which at that time were within the Egyptian sphere of influence.[28]

Ugarit. This was an ancient Syrian port on the Mediterranean, about ten kilometres north of Latakia. Here, in the old tumulus of Ras es-Shamra, since 1929 a great deal of material has been found including temple archives, palaces archives and various private libraries. The texts which they contain can be dated to the time between 1500 and 1200 BC. Among other things, they are of particular importance for our knowledge of the religion and early history of Israel. They give us a great deal more insight into the worship of Baal, which is mentioned only in a fragmentary way in the Old Testament, and then in a polemical context.[29]

Egyptian royal inscriptions. These are inscriptions in hieroglyphic writing, put up, for example, on temple walls, which contain accounts of Egyptian expeditions and thus corresponding lists of conquered cities.[30] One example is the well-known Israel stele of Merneptah (*c.* 1220 BC),[31] together with a number of inscriptions found on the walls of a temple in Thebes, which describe the fight of Ramses III against the Sea Peoples in about 1180 BC.[32]

Assyrian and Babylonian sources. Among other things, these inscriptions contain lists and accounts of the expeditions of Assyrian, Babylonian and Persian kings. For Syria and Palestine they provide information from about 950 BC down to the period after the Babylonian captivity.[33]

Elephantine. From 1890 onwards a number of papyri were discovered, written in Aramaic, which seem to come from an Israelite military colony which at that time was settled at Jeb-Syene (Elephantine), an island in the Nile. These papyri, which can be dated to the fifth century BC, provide us (among other things) with information about forms of government during the period of Persian rule and about the religious situation in this period.[34]

That brings us to the end of this short survey of the most important sources which are of major significance for the understanding of the history of Israel. Of course it would be possible to think of a great deal of further material in this connection.[35] Here one should include at least collections of laws[36] and wisdom literature.

1.2.3 *The evidence of archaeology*

This evidence has to be handled with the greatest possible care. Thus earlier conclusions should constantly be tested in the light of more recent developments and discoveries. Furthermore, all archaeological investigations always involve a good deal of subjectivity and intuition.[37]

Of the available archaeological material, the remains of buildings earthworks, tools, weapons and the like give us the most general information.

However, the historian usually derives most profit from the written sources, though we do well to remember that this material comes from obviously 'well-to-do' circles, and provides us with very one-sided information. So it need not surprise us that the written sources usually come to light from temple and palace archives. Consequently we shall only hear anything about, say, nomads, when these come into contact, in one way or another, with groups who practise the art of writing and make mention of such contacts.

I shall now mention some of the most important archaeological discoveries, as I did the most important sources from the ancient Near East, without attempting any kind of completeness.[38]

The Mesha Inscription (Moabite Stone). This inscription, from about 850 BC, gives us an indication of the relationship between Moab and Israel in the time of the dynasty of Omri.[39]

The Siloam Inscription. This was discovered in the Siloam tunnel, which was constructed in about 700 BC, in the time of Hezekiah. It tells how some of the work turned out.[40]

The Deir 'Alla texts. These texts were discovered in Jordan in 1967, in an excavation under the direction of H. J. Franken. The fragments, which are of great significance above all for the study of Aramaic, include a prophecy which is ascribed to Balaam the son of Beor (cf. Num. 22–24).[41]

Hebrew and Aramaic ostraca. 'Ostraca' is the term usually applied to potsherds, fragments of earthenware, which have been used as writing material. In the ancient Near East these were used for various purposes, such as sending reports, and for literature. Many of these ostraca have also been found in Palestine. They come from a variety of places and periods. The Hebrew ostraca, of which those from Samaria, Lachish and Arad are the most important, date from the period of *c.* 1000–587 BC.[42] Those from a later period are written in Aramaic.

Royal seals. Round about eight hundred seals have been found in more than twenty different places in Judah. These seals, which probably date from the time of Hezekiah and Josiah, were attached to jars which contained provisions for fortresses in Judah. Since most of the places in which they were found can be located on the frontiers of Judah, they give us some idea of the extent and internal administration of the state of Judah in the period concerned.[43]

The Dead Sea Scrolls. Since 1947, a large number of manuscripts or fragments of manuscripts have been found in the wilderness of Judah to the west of the Dead Sea. These writings, which for the most part come from the period round about the beginning of the Christian era, are principally of importance for the study of the period between the testaments.[44]

Although in the strictest sense they do not belong under this heading, I would like finally to mention the works of **Flavius Josephus**.[45] In his *Jewish Antiquities* and *The Jewish War*, Josephus describes the history of the Jewish people from the creation up to and including the Jewish revolt against the Romans in AD 66–70. However, this account is often very tendentious and shows many legendary traits, so that it needs to be handled with the greatest possible care.[46]

1.3 *The land and the people*

1.3.1 *The land*

The name Canaan appears for the first time on an inscription of Idrimi, a king of Alalakh, from the fifteenth century BC.[47] This name is probably connected with the Akkadian word *kinaḫḫu*, 'reddish purple', and is perhaps in the first instance meant to indicate the area where this reddish purple came from. This was chiefly in the coastal regions of Syria. Consequently, from the fifteenth century BC down to the Hellenistic period, the name Canaan was often used for the Syrian coastal regions and their hinterland, as far as Upper Galilee.

However, from the Amarna period until Merneptah, Canaan in the broader sense refers to the territory governed by Egypt which, in addition to what was later Palestine, also comprised Phoenicia and part of Syria.[48] In this connection it is interesting to see that in the Old Testament Canaan is called a son of Ham.[49] Now in some places in the Old Testament Ham is identified with Egypt,[50] while in others Canaan is called a younger brother of Egypt.[51] Both traditions seem to point to an original supremacy of Egypt over Canaan.

In a later period Canaan is a term for the land promised by Yahweh.[52]

In addition, yet other names are used for the area which will be our chief concern in this book. Thus we also find the term 'land of Israel' (see I Sam. 13.19). However, Palestine is one of the best known names, though this dates from a much later period. It is derived from 'Philistia', and was originally the name for the coastal plain occupied by the Philistines. The word is used by Herodotus in this sense.[53] After the Bar Kochba revolt (AD 132–135), it became the name of a Roman province which embraced the land to the west of the Jordan as well as the coastal plain.

1.3.2 *The people*

When we are discussing the history of Israel in the Old Testament period, we cannot talk of a single people. This will already become evident when we go on to subject the significance of the name Israel to closer investigation.

After the name for God (Yahweh), the name Israel is the most frequent word in the Old Testament (it occurs about 2500 times). Its etymology is uncertain, and it is still impossible to be completely sure of its exact meaning.[54] However, we can say that in form it belongs to the earliest types of names which occur in the Old Testament.

Perhaps we already find the name in Ebla;[55] at all events, it is certainly on the Israel stele of Merneptah (*c.* 1220 BC), mentioned above. There Israel is mentioned alongside a number of cities in Canaan like Ashkelon, Gezer and Jenoam. It is because of that that this monument, discovered in Thebes, has been called the 'Israel stele'.

Now it is striking that all the names in this Egyptian text have been provided with the ideogram for 'land', apart from Israel, which is given that for 'people'. If this is not a scribal error, Israel in this text could therefore refer to a group of people in Canaan.[56]

After these introductory remarks, we must now turn our attention to the Old Testament. It is clear that the name Israel there is not always used in the same sense. It can represent both a person (the patriarch Jacob) and a group of tribes, as is the case after the settlement in Canaan. Furthermore, this name can also denote a political entity: the monarchy in the time of Saul and the northern kingdom after the death of Solomon.[57]

In addition to the meanings mentioned above, we also find the name Israel in the Old Testament in the sense of a religious entity.[58] This last meaning comes strongly to the fore above all after the fall of the northern kingdom, and increases especially in the period of the Babylonian exile and thereafter. During this period the term 'Jews' also comes increasingly to the fore in more or less the same sense.

From all that has been said, it is already clear that when the name Israel is used in the Old Testament, we certainly cannot think of a political entity which embraces the whole of the population of Canaan during the period of the monarchy. At least from the time when David became king there were clearly two kingdoms, Israel and Judah. Nor can we ever speak of an entity from an ethnic point of view. In this respect the population in both kingdoms was very heterogeneous in composition, though this was probably true to a greater degree of Israel than of Judah. All this was the result of a long process in which – as we shall see later – other groups of people, and many Canaanites, were increasingly taken up and integrated into these two kingdoms.

Excursus I

'Apiru and Hebrews

In ancient Near Eastern literature from the second millennium BC there is constant mention of individuals and groups who in Sumerian, Assyrian, Babylonian and Hittite texts are indicated by the ideogram SA.GAZ and by Ḫapiru or Ḫabiru,[1] in Egyptian by 'Apiru, and in Ugaritic by 'aprm.[2]

Of course it is impossible within the framework of this book to discuss in detail all the facts which the extra-biblical sources offer in this respect, and it is not strictly necessary.[3] I shall content myself here with a few remarks which may perhaps be important in arriving at a better understanding of the word 'Hebrew' in the Old Testament.

It seems virtually certain that the words SA.GAZ, Ḫabiru, 'Apiru and 'aprm are equivalents, and that the authentic form of the name is 'Apiru.[4] So for the sake of brevity, I shall go on to speak only of 'Apiru. There is much less certainty about the etymology of these words. Attempts to arrive at a solution in this respect have not met with general assent.[5]

Another important question is whether the 'Apiru are an ethnological entity or a social grouping. There is still considerable disagreement about this question, too, though in this connection the majority of scholars think in terms of a social grouping.[6] De Vaux expresses hesitations, and he prefers to keep the matter open.[7] His judgment might well be endorsed, though it should be added that nevertheless the bulk of the material available favours seeing the 'Apiru as a social grouping.[8]

Given all this, it therefore seems best to concentrate our attention on the most important facts which the extra-biblical texts offer us about the 'Apiru. We shall do that in the hope that these facts will prove useful in those places where the Old Testament talks of a Hebrew or of Hebrews.

I shall now go through these facts in more or less chronological order.

SA.GAZ appears in the earliest texts[9] with the meaning 'robber' or 'plunderer'. However, it is not certain here whether we can substitute 'Apiru for SA.GAZ.

In a letter written in Old Assyrian[10] from about the nineteenth century BC and coming from Cappadocia, the 'Apiru seem to be prisoners in the service of a prince, who are, however, in a position to buy themselves free. Babylonian texts from about the eighteenth century BC[11] show us 'Apiru who serve the state for payment (usually in kind). In the Mari letters[12] 'Apiru seems to indicate a kind of mercenary soldier; these soldiers often move from the service of one lord to that of another, and go on the rampage in armed groups, above all to the north and north-west of Mari.

In a text from Alalakh (eighteenth century BC)[13] we hear that the king of this land makes 'peace' with the 'Apiru and enlists them as regular troops in his army. It also emerges from a Hittite text[14] that the king of the Hittites can call upon 'Apiru as regular troops. In later texts from Alalakh (fifteenth century BC),[15] the 'Apiru are evidently soldiers who are encamped or settled in certain places under their own leaders. At the same time it also emerges from these texts that they form an important group and that some of them even have very prominent functions.

A number of texts from Nuzi speak of 'Apiru who serve the royal court[16] or a well-to-do person[17] for pay – again, usually in kind. These conditions of service can relate to both soldiers and work-people. In many instances it seems possible to characterize the 'Apiru in these texts as people who have a rather higher status than that of a slave.[18] Here this status of 'Apiru often seems to have been acquired by people who come from another city or from another land.[19]

In a number of places in the Amarna letters 'Apiru seems to refer to armed groups who are hostile to the Pharaoh and his vassal princes.[20] Cities in Canaan are often mentioned in this connection, including Hazor (*EA* 148), Megiddo (*EA* 243), Jerusalem (*EA* 287) and Shechem (*EA* 289).[21]

A couple of Egyptian texts from the thirteenth century BC[22] speak of 'Apiru who are prisoners, put to work in Egypt in the service of Pharaoh.

The 'Apiru are also repeatedly mentioned in the texts from Ugarit.[23] Here the 'Apiru are regarded as aliens and evidently have a bad name.[24] By contrast, however, a Hittite text from about the same period as those from Ugarit gives us the impression that the 'Apiru are beginning finally to settle.[25]

A number of features emerge from this survey of the extra-biblical texts in which the 'Apiru are mentioned. First of all, attention should be drawn to the militant attitude which the 'Apiru seem so often to display. Furthermore, they are almost everywhere, and apparently settle as aliens of unknown origin. Next, we should note the phenomenon that these 'Apiru are often in the service of a king, the state or a person – perhaps as prisoners.[26] Finally, we should note the fact that the 'Apiru are very widely distributed not only geographically, but also chronologically.

Given all this, we shall now try to see whether these facts about the 'Apiru can also tell us anything about the use and the significance of the words 'Hebrew' and 'Hebrews' in the Old Testament.

First of all, we should note a number of texts deriving from different traditions[27] which are connected with the sojourn in Egypt. In all these cases the word 'Hebrews' is used whenever an Israelite speaks with an Egyptian or in order to distinguish the Israelites from the Egyptians.[28] In all these places the Hebrews are evidently people who settled in Egypt as aliens and there were at work either as slaves[29] or in forced labour.[30]

We find another group of texts in I Samuel, where the Philistines use the word 'Hebrews' of the Israelites, or it is used to distinguish the Israelites from the Philistines.[31] Here the word 'Hebrews' always appears in a military context.[32] It is possible that the Philistines use this designation to characterize the Israelites as aliens who pose a threat to the Philistine coastland from the hinterland. On the other hand, we note that a distinction is made here between Hebrews and Israelites, which is evident in I Sam. 13.6f.; 14.21. Clearly the Hebrews here are people who serve in the armies of others, for example of the Philistines (cf. I Sam. 14.21; 29.3).

Is there any connection between the Hebrews in the Old Testament and the 'Apiru mentioned in the extra-biblical sources? Some reject any connection,[33] whereas others see a clear link.[34]

Quite apart from a linguistic similarity, against which there seem to be few objections,[35] there are a number of other points which could indicate a link between these two groups. This especially applies to texts connected with the sojourn in Egypt and those which deal with the wars against the Philistines in the time of Saul. Features like being aliens or warriors seem to point in this direction.

All this could indicate a direct historical relationship, though it is just as possible that this designation 'Hebrew' or 'Hebrews' arose at a later period precisely because of these affinities. It is equally possible, too, that the terms were later interpreted as being the name for a people at a time when it was still not possible to speak of a people of Israel. The Old Testament itself does not give us any guidance in this respect.

The same also applies to a derivation of the word 'Hebrews' from the name Eber in Gen. 10 and 11.[36] It is impossible to see Eber as the ancestor of the Hebrews or of what was later Israel, because a number of peoples were thought to be descended from him.[37]

In view of all this – and without ruling out the possibility of a later intepretation as mentioned above – I think that most of the evidence points to an original relationship between the 'Apiru and the people in the Old Testament who are called Hebrews. Here I am thinking specially of the Hebrews mentioned in the texts connected with the sojourn in Egypt and the fight against the Philistines at the time of Saul, and those texts which speak of Hebrew slaves.[38]

We cannot therefore exclude the possibility that some of the ancestors of what later became 'Israel' belonged to the group called 'Apiru in many extra-biblical texts.

Chapter 2

The Patriarchs

2.1 *Origins*

In this section we shall be investigating the facts presented in the Old Testament which relate to the origins of the patriarchs. At the same time, we shall look at a number of important hypotheses about them.

2.1.1 *Ur of the Chaldaeans*

Four passages in the Old Testament, and only four, say that Abraham came from Ur of the Chaldaeans.[1] This reference raises a number of problems.

In the first place, the Old Testament tradition is not unanimous in this respect. In all these passages the Septuagint has 'the region of the Chaldaeans'. Albright has therefore suggested, referring to Jubilees 2.3, that in both MT and the Septuagint we have an abbreviated sentence construction and that the original text will have read, 'Ur in the land of the Chaldaeans'.[2] However, given the fact that the Samaritan Pentateuch and other versions, including the Vulgate, correspond with MT, there is little reason to doubt the latter.

The location of Ur presents another problem. The addition 'of the Chaldaeans' is only of limited help, because in the Old Testament 'Chaldaeans' is always the name for Babylon or its inhabitants. However, in cuneiform texts from the eleventh century BC there is mention for the first time of a people called the 'Chaldaeans'.[3] It is therefore very probable that the reference to 'Chaldaeans' in the Old Testament is meant to indicate that Abram came from the area which was inhabited by the Chaldaeans at the time when these stories were set down in writing.

In that case, it is clear that Ur is to be located in Mesopotamia. However, in antiquity as in our own time, several places might bear the same name. This was also the case with Ur. We are still far from general agreement on the location of the 'Ur of the Chaldaeans' mentioned in the Old Testament, but it can at least be said that most scholars would place it in southern Mesopotamia (see Map 1).[4]

Now the existence of a city of Ur in southern Mesopotamia is virtually established for about 2700 BC, by texts dating from that period.[5] Consequently, it was here above all that intensive excavations were carried on in a search for information about the figure of Abraham. The most important of these, which were directed by Sir Leonard Woolley, produced a good deal of important material.[6] However, nothing was found which could be regarded as direct evidence that Abraham and his kin lived in the city or that would rule out that possibility.

Now in addition to this place in southern Mesopotamia, there are also a number in northern Mesopotamia which bear the same name.[7] According to Gordon, it can be argued convincingly that Abraham's 'Ur' can be identified with Ur(a), which must have been somewhere in the region of Haran.[8] Gordon was also led to this conclusion by an Ugaritic text which speaks of merchants from the city of Ura.[9] However, it is by no means certain whether the place Ura mentioned in this text did in fact lie in the region of Haran.[10]

From what has been said above, it is evident that we cannot be certain of the location of 'Ur of the Chaldaeans', which in the Old Testament is mentioned only in connection with Abraham's descent. The only thing that can perhaps be said with any certainty is that the place was probably in Mesopotamia.

2.1.2 *'Beyond the River'*

We find another piece of biblical evidence which might perhaps suggest a Mesopotamian background for Abraham and his kin in Josh. 24.2–3, 14–15.

Joshua mentions their 'fathers' in a speech to the people. In vv. 2, 14, he then goes on to say that these 'fathers' originally dwelt 'beyond the River'.[11] The chapter in which these verses occur seems to go back to an old tradition.[12] At all events, it is certain that the tradition that 'the fathers' dwelt 'beyond the River' is an old one.

The question is, however, what 'beyond the River' means in these passages. In Josh. 24 the phrase is in all probability a reference to the land east of the Euphrates,[13] i.e. Mesopotamia. If that is correct, then this piece of information from Josh. 24 would also indicate that the remembrance that the patriarchs originally came from Mesopotamia still lived on strongly in certain circles.

2.1.3 *Haran and its surroundings*

In Gen. 11.31–32 we are told that Abram and his kin went from 'Ur of the

Chaldaeans' to Haran. In Gen. 12.4b–5 we are then told that Abram left Haran and went to Canaan. These texts from Genesis, all of which are assigned to the Priestly writing, do not give us any information about how long Abram stayed in Haran. We may assume that this must have been for quite a long time. This assumption might be taken to be a certainty if we could prove that the information in Gen. 12.5, which says that Abram left Haran 'with the persons that they had gotten in Haran', meant that Abraham had formed a religous group there. To do anything of that kind would certainly have taken time. Although we have no proof, the existence of a community of this kind centred on Abraham may perhaps be regarded as a historical possibility.[14]

However, it is also quite conceivable that we should not think so much in terms of a long-stay of Abraham and his kin in Haran; perhaps our starting point should be that they all came from there. A strong argument in favour of this is that while Ur is mentioned only sporadically in this connection, Haran and its region is regularly associated in the Old Testament with Abraham's origins.

Both Isaac and Jacob get wives belonging to the family of Abram who, according to Gen. 24.10; 27.43;[15] 28.1–2 (=P), lived in Aram-naharaim, Haran and Paddan-aram respectively.[16] According to Abraham's words in Gen. 24.4 (which in any case must be assigned to the same cycle of traditions as v. 10), Abraham himself came from Aram-naharaim.[17] This is a place which we should locate in the general area of Haran, in the region of the Balikh and the Habor, and therefore in northern Mesopotamia. There are two views about the location of Paddan-aram. According to one, Paddan-aram was another name for Haran;[18] according to the other, it was a name for the region in which Haran was situated.[19]

Mention should also be made in this connection of the genealogy of Shem (Gen. 11.10–26). In this list of Abraham's ancestors we find a collection of names which also appear in non-biblical texts as the names of cities or territories around Haran.[20]

On the basis of all this it is therefore possible that several ancient traditions have been preserved in the Old Testament, in which remembrance was strong that the patriarchs came from the region of Haran or had stayed there for a long time. However, nothing has come to light through extra-biblical sources or archaeological excavations to confirm these Old Testament data.

2.1.4 'A wandering Aramaean was my father'[21]

The words quoted above from Deut. 26.5 are part of a prayer whose form and content show it to be older than the literary context in which it has now been placed.[22] This prayer connects the patriarchs – Deut. 26.5 clearly must have been thinking of Jacob[23] – with the Aramaeans.

In addition to Deut. 26.5, there are several traditions in the Old Testament which suggest such a relationship. For example, the wives of Isaac and Jacob, taken from the circle of Abraham's kinsfolk, were regarded as the daughters of an Aramaean (Gen. 25.20 P; 28.5 P; 31.20, 24 E). Furthermore, the name Aram also appears in names like Aram-Naharaim and Paddan-Aram, which (as I remarked earlier) are also mentioned in connection with the origins of the patriarchs.

Now with the exception of a few places where it appears as a proper name,[24] the word Aram is always used in the Old Testament as a designation for the Aramaeans and the area (Syria) in which they live. In the tradition about Jacob which we find in Gen. 29–31 we even get the strong impression that the territory of these Aramaeans extended as far as Transjordan. Jacob goes 'to the land of the people of the east' (29.1=E),[25] and Jacob and Laban make a covenant in which Gilead, in Transjordan, is clearly established as the border between the Aramaeans and Jacob and his descendants (31.23,46–52). However, one problem here is that the words Aram and Aramaean in these passages in the Old Testament must almost certainly represent a nomenclature from a later period.

The only certain evidence for this designation outside the Bible is in an Assyrian text from the twelfth century BC.[26] A place name Aram appears in some texts from the twenty-third century BC, but it is questionable whether we should connect this name with the later Aramaeans.[27] The same is true of the use of the proper name Aram in e.g. the Mari letters.[28] So in fact neither of these pieces of non-biblical evidence provide any support for the view that the patriarchs might be descended from those who at a later date were called 'Aramaeans'.

However, there is yet more to be said on this question. An etymological argument has been suggested to the effect that names of people and places in northern Mesopotamia, and also the Mari letters, contain many Aramaisms.[29] All this, coupled with the fact that the kindred of Abraham and Jacob are called Aramaeans (see above), led Noth[30] and de Vaux[31] – the latter with rather more reservations – to call the patriarchs proto-Aramaeans. However, this hypothesis does not seem to have been established either. The linguistic evidence which has been adduced in this connection is not at all convincing.[32]

Another approach refers to Amos 9.7 (cf. II Kings 16.9; Isa. 22.6; Amos 1.5) as a piece of evidence which could suggest an affinity between the patriarchs and the Aramaeans. According to Amos 9.7 the Aramaeans lived in Kir. Some scholars in fact think that Kir is identical with the city of Ur in southern

Mesopotamia.[33] However, there is not sufficient evidence to make this identification.

2.1.5 'Abram the Hebrew'

In Gen. 14.13, Abram is called 'the Hebrew'. Not only is this the first occasion on which the word occurs in the Old Testament; it is also the only occasion on which it is used in connection with the patriarchs. Of course the words Hebrew and Hebrews appear in the Old Testament, but only to a very limited extent.[34]

After what has already been said in the excursus preceding this chapter about the 'Apiru and Hebrews, here we need consider only the use of the word 'Hebrew' in Gen. 14.13.[35]

From its form, the word 'Hebrew' in this text can be regarded as a *gentilicium*,[36] but the same can also be said of the designation 'Amorite' attached to Mamre in Gen. 14.13. Elsewhere, though, the inhabitants of Mamre (Hebron) are called Hittites (Gen. 23) or Canaanites (Judg. 1.20). It is therefore very much open to question whether we can accept the *gentilicium* 'Hebrew' in Gen. 14.13 as a historical fact. Furthermore, the tradition here is not of one mind. The Septuagint, which usually agrees with the MT in the rendering of the word 'Hebrew', here has 'who comes from the other side' instead of 'Hebrew', thus seeing the term as a geographical designation. This last may be an indication of a later interpretation, but it could equally well go back to an earlier tradition. Such a geographical interpretation of the word 'Hebrew' could also very well support a relationship with the 'Apiru. However, in view of the fact that the word only occurs once in the framework of the patriarchal narratives, it seems impossible to arrive at any conclusions from it in connection with the patriarchs. .

2.1.6 *The names of the patriarchs*

The names Abram, Abraham and Jacob appear as West Semitic personal names in various texts from the second millennium BC.[37] The name Isaac has still to be found outside the Bible. However, the first names mentioned do not give us any information at all about the origins of the patriarchs. The geographical spread of the non-biblical parallels to these names is so wide that they do not help us in any way.

2.1.7 *Conclusion*

Outside the Bible we do not have a single reference to either the existence or the origins of the patriarchs. All the traditions in the Old Testament[38] which mention the origins of the patriarchs are agreed in their view that the patriarchs were not originally natives of Canaan but came there from elsewhere. Most of these traditions point towards Mesopotamia as their place of origin.

We know that all these traditions come from a much later period and have undergone a process of interpretation (above all theological interpretation). However, in particular the fact that there is unanimity that the origin of the patriarchs lay outside Canaan is an indication that at least among some groups in what was to become Israel there was a strong recollection that their ancestors once came to Canaan from elsewhere.

2.2 *Patterns of life*

The popular idea is still that the patriarchs were nomads. For that reason alone we must begin by investigating what nomads actually are (2.2.1; 2.2.2). After that, we shall briefly consider the widely accepted theory, put forward by Albright and Gordon, that the patriarchs were caravan traders. At the same time we shall attempt to establish what can be said about the life-style of the patriarchs on the basis of the evidence which we have from the Old Testament and from extra-biblical sources.

2.2.1 *Nomads*

It is very difficult for us to form a clear picture of the role of nomads in the history of the ancient Near East. This is largely because the texts from this period which we have almost all derive from a settled population living in cities. Consequently these texts only mention nomads whenever the nomads come into contact with the settled population in one way or another – and the encounters are usually hostile.[39] The result is that we have a very one-sided picture of nomads in this period, because the settled population was not very sympathetic towards them.

No wonder, then, that a great deal has been written about nomads from the second millennium BC[40] and that there is still much dispute as to what precisely we mean by nomads.

Taking account of all these factors I shall now try to say something about nomads in connection with the patriarchal narratives. According to most recent research, complete nomadism is a later development.[41] The true nomad cannot exist without camels. The camel allows the nomad to cover long distances and to cross deserts. However, it is striking that whereas the texts from Mari, Amarna and Ugarit seem to say a great deal about nomads, they never say anything about camels. True, camel bones have been discovered in archaeological excavations, which indicate the use of these animals in the third and second millennnia BC.[42] Such finds are difficult to interpret, but we can hardly establish a frequent use of domesticated camels with any certainty before the end of the second millennium BC.

If we compare all this with what Genesis tells us about the patriarchs, it is clear that the patriarchs cannot in any way be described as complete nomads. Of course camels are mentioned in these stories, but only to a very limited degree: on two occasions in the Abraham stories,[43] never in connection with Isaac and only five times in connection with Jacob.[44] Furthermore, it is possible that the mention of camels in these accounts is an anachronism.[45]

At all events, on the basis of the texts in Genesis we may certainly conclude that the camel did not play any great part in the life of the patriarchs.

2.2.2. *Tenders of livestock*

Those who are principally concerned with tending livestock, sheep and goats, can also be called nomads. Albright describes this group as 'ass nomads' to distinguish them from the group mentioned in the previous section, who were principally concerned with breeding camels.[46] However, this term 'ass nomads' seems somewhat inaccurate, because it suggests that those who are described in this way were involved in breeding great herds of asses. Another term widely used in this connection is 'semi-nomads', but this too is open to criticism, because it begins from the presupposition that this group is occupied in settling down permanently in a specific place.[47] These people who tended herds of livestock, and who generally used the ass as a beast of burden, differ in many respects from the nomads discussed in 2.2.1.

For example, those tending flocks were not in a position to cover any great distances. They also found it hard to live in the desert, because their flocks had to drink regularly and needed better pastures than could be found there. Consequently they often stayed in areas round the edge of the desert,[48] near to water and not far from cities.

The texts from Mari give us a very good idea of the life-style of these groups.[49] Here we learn of shepherds who have their flocks in the *nāwum*. This word *nāwum* means not only pasture but also herd and even camp.[50] The shepherds have goats as well as sheep. The ass is their means of transport.[51] We often also hear that a tribe or part of a tribe has settled more or less definitively in the region of a city.[52]

It is clear that some similarities can be seen between the features of the Mari texts brought out above and some aspects of patriarchal life as they come down to us in Genesis.

The picture of the patriarchs that we have in Genesis does not give us the impression that they regularly covered long distances with their flocks. The only exception to this is the account of Abraham's journey from Ur via Haran to Canaan (Gen. 11.31—12.6), and even there we are not told explicitly that he took flocks with him. The travels of Abram narrated in Gen. 12.10–20 and those of Jacob mentioned in Gen. 46.1ff. cannot be seen as a normal pattern of life, as they were the result of a famine. Usually the patriarchs remained in the same area, and in the vicinity of cities. Abram and Isaac were in the south, the Negeb, and Jacob was more to the north, in the area around Shechem.

Thus for the most part the patriarchs lived in areas not really very different from the wilderness which lay close by. In this connection it is also important to note that, for example, they never settled on the coastal plain, which had probably already come under cultivation at a very early stage.[53]

The livestock of the patriarchs is also usually presented to us as consisting of sheep and goats. Only once do we hear of larger animals, at the announcement of Isaac's birth in Gen. 18.7. Furthermore, they are only mentioned in lists of animals, for example in Gen. 26.14 and in the Joseph stories in connection with Joseph's arrival in Egypt (Gen. 45.10; 46.32; 47.1). Van Seters has pointed out that the livestock possessed by the patriarchs was not in fact different from that of a well-to-do Jewish peasant farmer at the time of the late monarchy.[54] For support he refers to lists of animals in the annals of Sennacherib,[55] as mentioned on the occasion of his expedition into Judah.

However, this list also mentions animals like horses which the patriarchs certainly did not own. Furthermore, there is only scant mention in the patriarchal narratives of larger animals like camels and oxen (see above), so these certainly did not form an important part of their livestock. In addition, we can very well suppose that these large animals, which never appear separately – except in Gen. 18.7 – but are always included in a list later in these texts, which have a long tradition behind them, are in fact additions.

Some passages in Genesis, like Gen. 26.12, where we are told that Isaac sows and reaps, and Gen. 37.7, Joseph's dreams about the sheaves of corn, give the impression that at least Isaac and Jacob were already beginning to settle in the country. However, these sparse allusions are insufficient for us to be able to draw any conclusions in this direction. The information given in Genesis leads us mainly to suppose that the patriarchs still cannot be said to have had settled dwellings, as was probably the case to some degree with the herdsmen of Mari.

One important distinction between the patriarchs and the herdsmen of

Mari seems to be that the latter evidently formed part of a larger group or tribe. In the case of the patriarchs, on the other hand – apart perhaps from a later period, in the case of Jacob – we can talk only in terms of a small group or perhaps even a family or clan.

2.2.3 *Caravan traders?*

Both Albright[56] and Gordon[57] have defended the theory that the patriarchs can be seen as caravan traders. Albright's references in this connection include Gen. 14.14–15 and the appearance of a verb *shr*[58] in these stories, which according to him must mean 'travel round as a merchant'.

Although to begin with this view put forward by Albright and Gordon found some acceptance,[59] it now seems to be slowly being discarded. Consequently there is little point in discussing it at length here, especially as it has meanwhile been adequately refuted by scholars like Weippert[60] and Thompson.[61]

2.2.4 *Conclusion*

The picture that we get in Genesis of the life-style of the patriarchs shows that they can best be characterised as pastors looking after flocks of sheep – and goats.[62] This picture also largely corresponds with what is known to us about the life-style of herdsmen in Mari about the eighteenth century BC. In just one instance it seems that the patriarchs are making a permanent settlement. There are differences from the facts known from Mari as well as similarities.

Finally, it is impossible now to be certain how far the history of the tradition has played its part in affecting this picture of the patriarchs in Genesis.

2.3 *Customs*

In this section I shall investigate some of the customs which are mentioned in the patriarchal narratives in Genesis and then try to establish whether there is also evidence of them in a particular period of ancient Near Eastern history. Here we are particularly concerned with the question whether in fact there is some correspondence between certain legal usages among the patriarchs and those which we have discovered in the Nuzu texts.[63] We shall consider some of the most important features of this kind, like adoption, the significance of household gods, marriage, the right of the firstborn and some economic customs.

2.3.1 *Adoption*

In this connection, mention should first be made of Gen. 15.2–3. In these verses Abram, who is childless, names Eliezer, one of his slaves, as his future heir. Many people think that here we have a form of adoption which also appears in the Nuzu texts.[64]

However, in the relevant Nuzu texts, which are often mentioned in this connection, the adopted person is never a slave, but is always free. Furthermore, Gen. 15.2b, which plays an important part in this connection, raises many problems of both interpretation and translation,[65] to such a degree that there is no definite indication that the text is in fact concerned with adoption. Consequently many scholars see little occasion to talk here of any connection with the Nuzu texts.[66]

Apart from Gen. 15.2–3, people have thought that in a number of places in Gen. 29; 30 there is also mention of adoption, and that there is also a connection between these passages and the texts found at Nuzu. The context here is the relationship between Laban and Jacob. Because there is talk of Laban's sons towards the end of Jacob's stay with him, it has been supposed[67] that Laban at first had no sons and therefore at that time adopted Jacob as his son. In that case we would also have a so-called *errubu* wedding here, i.e. a wedding in which the adopted son marries the daughter of the man who adopted him. The favourite references for adoption are then Gen. 29.13–14; 31.43.

This view also raises many difficulties.[68] Thus Laban never calls Jacob 'his son', nor does Jacob call Laban 'his father', though this happens in the relevant Nuzu texts.[69]

2.3.2 *The significance of household gods*

In Gen. 31.19 we are told that on Jacob's journey to Canaan, Rachel stole the teraphim[70] from her father. Now in a contract of adoption from Nuzu it seems that on the death of the father, these teraphim passed into the possession of the son. When there were no natural sons, they passed over to the adopted son. This information from Nuzu is also used to give an explanation of Rachel's theft. The possession of these teraphim is said to imply Jacob's right to Laban's heritage.[71]

This view has proved equally untenable. In the first place, Laban was still alive when Rachel took these teraphim; and in the second place, even if Jacob was in fact adopted by Laban, he would never have inherited from him because according to the contracts of adoption from Nuzu any sons born to Laban later would have had precedence over him.[72]

2.3.3 *Marriage*

In three narratives we are told that a patriarch seeks to pass his wife off as his sister. In Gen. 12.10–20 (=J) and 20 (=E), Abraham does this with Sarah, and in Gen. 26.1–11 (=J) Isaac does the same thing with Rebekah. Speiser[73] in particular has sought to demonstrate that this action by Abraham and Isaac is illuminated by a particular Hurrian marriage custom which is recorded in texts from Nuzu. What we are supposed to have here is a custom – practised above all in higher society – according to which a man at the same time adopted his wife as his sister. In this way the wife achieved a higher social and legal position.

This view of Speiser's has aroused some opposition; van Seters, in particular, has pointed out that there is no support for the hypothesis from the Nuzu documents.[74]

It is evident from the Nuzu texts that after the death of his father, a brother has an obligation to arrange a wedding for his sister. Perhaps something of this kind is to be found in Gen. 24, where Laban plays an important part in connection with Rebekah's marriage.[75] Furthermore, there is evidence for this custom not only in Nuzu but also in texts from the early and late Babylonian period and in the Elephantine papyri from the fifth century BC.[76]

Scholars have also claimed to be able to find parallels with the Nuzu texts in the marriages of Isaac and Jacob.[77] In both cases it is thought to be clear that, as in Nuzu, there was a custom among the patriarchs that after the wedding the husband lived in the home of his wife's parents. This is said to be suggested at least by Gen. 24.5, where Abraham's servant asks whether he is to take Isaac to his bride's house if the bride refuses to go with him. The fact that Jacob continues to live with Laban after marrying Leah and Rachel is also thought to point in the same direction.

However, conclusions of this kind cannot be sustained, given the fact that Abraham refuses to let Isaac go (Gen. 24.6), and that as we know (see Gen. 27.44; 28.1–4), Jacob never intended to stay permanently with Laban after his wedding.

Finally, I should mention here a few passages in Genesis where there is marriage to a slave girl. These are Gen. 16.1ff. (Abraham and Hagar); Gen. 30.3ff., 9ff. (Jacob and the two girls Bilhah and Zilpah).

Following Speiser,[78] many scholars[79] again see clear parallels here with certain customs from the Nuzu texts. However, closer investigation has shown that conclusions of this kind cannot stand up to close comparison with the relevant material in the texts.[80]

2.3.4 *The right of the firstborn*

In the patriarchal narratives the right of the firstborn never goes to the oldest son, but always to the younger.[81] It is understandable that parallels to this right of the firstborn have been sought outside the Bible. However, there is a problem. In Genesis we are never told the precise connection between the right of the firstborn and inheritance, but the latter plays a prominent role in the extra-biblical texts. Still, these texts are far from being uniform. Thus in the Codex Hammurabi[82] all children seem to have had an equal share, whereas in the texts from Mari, Nuzu and Assyria towards the end of the second millennium BC the oldest son seems to have had a double share,[83] though at least in some Nuzu texts the father can decide otherwise and give all children an equal share.[84] The striking thing is, of course, that the patriarchs do not know any provision of this kind,[85] or at any rate do not put it into practice.

2.3.5 *Economic practices*

Genesis 30.28–34 and 31.38–40 have often been compared with similar texts from extra-biblical sources dating from the second millennium BC. A main point of comparison is given by the conditions under which Jacob entered the service of Laban as a herdsman.[86] According to van Seters, there is more similarity between the Genesis passage mentioned above and texts from the early and late Babylonian periods.[87] However, the Hebrew word for recompense which is used in Gen. 31.39, and there only in the Old Testament, could go back to a very old legal term.[88]

Another transaction which is constantly recalled in this connection is the purchase of the cave of Machpelah in Gen. 23. One of the first problems here is the designation 'sons of Heth'. That this is a reference to Hittites is usually denied.[89] The conclusion is based on the fact that the names Ephron and Zohar, mentioned in Gen. 23, are pure Semitic names. This seems to be a strong argument.

The most important problem in Gen. 23, however, relates to the way in which the business deal between Abraham and Ephron comes about. M. Lehman has compared this with similar transactions in Hittite laws, and has come to the conclusion that in Gen. 23 we find a good deal that is strongly reminiscent of Hittite legislation.[90] However, this conclusion has been vigorously challenged by the Hittite scholar H. A. Hoffner and many others.[91] It is clear that, to say the least, there are as many parallels with purchasing contracts from a much later period, as there are with Hittite contracts from quite an early date.[92]

2.3.6 *Conclusion*

A comparison between legal usages among the patriarchs and those in the texts from Nuzu and other documents from the ancient Near East shows that at all events they give us no grounds for confidence in placing the patriarchs in a particular historical context.

2.4 *Religion*

Over the years, a good deal has been written about patriarchal worship.[93] I shall discuss some of its aspects here.

2.4.1 *The God of the fathers*

In 1929 a study by A. Alt was published under the title 'The God of the Fathers'.[94] This work was a milestone in the investigation of the religion of the patriarchs. According to Alt, the earliest element in this worship is belief in the God of one's ancestors. This is expressed in certain designations of God like the 'God of my fathers', the 'God of Abraham', the 'God of Isaac', the 'God of Jacob', the *paḥad yiṣḥaq* (the fear of Isaac) and the *'abbīr ya 'aqōb* (the mighty one of Jacob).[95] According to Alt,[96] these designations of God are an old tradition which goes back to the time before Moses. Their characteristic feature is that they indicate a relationship with a person, the patriarch, in contrast to the way in which the *'ēlīm*, the deities worshipped in Canaan, are connected with a particular place of worship.

At the same time, one can detect a parallel between the 'God of the fathers' and Yahweh, of whom it is said very emphatically at a later period that he is bound to people rather than places. At a later stage, in Ex. 3; 6, Yahweh would then have been identified with the 'God of the fathers'.

With some modifications, this theory of Alt's has found a wide following. For Noth, too, the patriarchs established cults and received promises about the land and about future descendants. In his view, after the patriarchs had settled in Canaan, there was an amalgamation of the 'God of the fathers' with the already existing local sanctuaries.[97] Gemser differs from Alt in seeing the designation 'God of the fathers' as referring not to many gods, but to one.[98]

Despite the great success enjoyed by Alt's hypothesis, there have also been a number of criticisms of it.[99] In Holland these have been expressed above all by Hoftijzer, who argues in particular that it is impossible to claim that only in Ex. 3.14 is there an identification of the 'God of the fathers' with Yahweh. The two are identified from the very beginning.[100] This seems to me to be correct. As they have come down to us, the Old Testament texts do not allow of any other possibility. We can no longer discover what led up to the final redaction of these texts, but it is quite possible that this identification had not yet been made in the traditions which were incorporated in them.

2.4.2 *El and the 'God of the fathers'*

In the book of Genesis we often find God referred to as El. This was not only a generic name for 'god', but also the name of a specific deity. In Ugarit, El is the name of the god who stands at the head of the pantheon.[101] The name also appears in Genesis, often in connection with other divine names like Elyon, Shaddai and Olam.[102] At present there is general agreement that these designations of God do not relate to local Canaanite deities but are representations of the one God El.

On the basis of all this Eissfeldt has defended the theory[103] that to begin with the patriarchs worshipped the 'God of the fathers' (see 2.4.1), but that at a second stage they sought to be more closely connected with El religion. Cross has argued strongly for the view that patriarchal religion was essentially an El religion.[104]

However, we must note Westermann's's[105] serious reservations about the views of Cross and Eissfeldt; he argues that these are based only on research into the names of God. The investigation has been only into part of patriarchal religion and not into that religion as a whole. In this connection it can be pointed out that patriarchal religion clearly differs at many points from the religion of Ugarit. We hear nothing in the patriarchal narratives of many cultic practices which were current in Ugarit. Furthermore, we may note that the patriarchs are not on the same high cultural level that we find in Ugaritic religion, with its feast, temples, priests and so on.[106] In short, if in this connection we can already describe Ugaritic religion as an institution, we can as yet find nothing of the sort among the patriarchs.

So it is virtually certain that on the basis of the texts which have come down to us in Genesis we cannot describe patriarchal religion as El religion like that to be found in Ugarit. It is also striking that whereas the Old Testament texts as they have come down to us often have fierce polemic against Baal, designations like El and the names of other Canaanite deities seem to have been handed down almost uncritically. This might signify that when the patriarchal narratives were included in a wider context, the patriarchs were not regarded as worshippers of alien gods, but that these names were regarded as designations of the one God (Yahweh)·.[107] How this development came about in the tradition underlying these texts we can no longer discover.

However, the fact that the Old Testament tradition connects the patriarchs

very naively with El and other divine names from Canaan might suggest that
their religion differed from that of a later period, at least in its names for God.
In the next section we shall see that this was also the case in other respects.

2.4.3 'Religious institutions' among the patriarchs

From what I have said so far it will already be evident that patriarchal religion
certainly cannot be termed institutional. For that reason we can hardly talk of
'religious institutions' among the patriarchs. In this respect also it is clearly
different from the religion of later Israel.

Outside Gen. 14.18[108] we never hear of priests in the patriarchal narratives,
though there were probably large numbers of them in Israel from the time of
the early monarchy on. The patriarchs themselves perform functions, like
offering sacrifices,[109] which were later restricted to priests.

The patriarchs also build altars; usually, however, they do this not to offer
sacrifices but to express the fact that the place concerned, usually a sanctuary,
falls under the jurisdiction of Yahweh.[110] At a later date, altars in Israel were
used primarily for the offering of sacrifices.[111]

Furthermore, the patriarchal narratives speak quite naturally about sacred
stones (*maṣṣēbōth*) and 'trees' (*'ēlōne*).[112] Thus for example we hear that Jacob
erects a *maṣṣēbāh* in Bethel (Gen. 28.18) and by Rachel's tomb (Gen. 35.20).
However, such *maṣṣēbōth* were seen by Hosea, and in Deuteronomic and
Deuteronomistic circles, as symbols of Baal, and as such were severely
condemned.[113]

The *'ēlōne* ('trees') are chiefly mentioned in the narratives about Abraham.
Abraham's first stopping place in Canaan is by 'the tree' of Moreh (Gen. 12.6),
and later there is regular mention of Abraham living by the 'trees' of Moreh
(Gen. 13.18; 14.13; 18.1). There is also is mention of such a 'tree' in connection
with Jacob (Gen. 35.4,8). There is no further association with these 'trees'
anywhere else in the Old Testament; outside the patriarchal narratives neither
the tree of Moreh nor that of Mamre is ever mentioned again.

Finally, mention should be made here of circumcision. In Gen. 17 we hear
that Abraham and e.g. also Ishmael are circumcised, and the circumcision of
Isaac is mentioned in Gen. 21.4. The Priestly tradition in Gen. 17 describes
this 'operation' as a sign of the covenant which God made with Abraham.
According to Gen. 34.13–24, this custom continued among the patriarchs.
However, the text of the Old Testament as it has come down to us shows that
the religious significance of circumcision became a firm tradition in Israel only
very gradually. Passages like Ex. 4.24–26 (the circumcision of the son of
Moses) and Josh. 5.5 (all the Israelites born in the wilderness were circumcised) show that circumcision of the newborn was not always a firm rule.

Furthermore, pericopae like Gen. 34.13–24 perhaps go back to an ancient and original rite or initiation in connection with marriage.[114]

Thus it seems certain that circumcision was only made a sign of the covenant with God at a much later date, and that it did not yet have an integral function in patriarchal religion. And this is to leave out of account consideration of the influence that later editing by the Priestly tradition may have had on texts like Gen. 17; 21.4.

2.4.4 *Conclusion*

In conclusion, we may say that there were some elements in patriarchal religion (see above all 2.4.3) which point to forms and usages which either did not appear at a later period, or, if they did, appeared in a quite different framework.

The same is also true of the divine designations which we also find in the patriarchal narratives. It is striking that there is no mention in these narratives of a typical vegetation god like Baal (see n. 106). Unlike settled peasant farmers, those who tended livestock (see 2.2.2) will not have attached much importance to such a deity.

All this suggests very strongly that in many respects patriarchal religion had quite a different character from that of later times.

2.5 *Dating*

Scholars who have concerned themselves with dating the patriarchs have usually arrived at very different solutions.[115] Generally speaking we can distinguish between two groups here: those who date the patriarchs very early, even at the beginning of the second millennium BC, and those who put them in a later period, round about the middle of the second millennium BC. Thompson[116] occupies a special position in putting the 'historical background' to the patriarchs in the early Israelite period, given that this was the time when the ancient traditions were shaped and in which the geographical and ethnic picture outlined in Genesis seems to be most appropriate. Van Seters should be mentioned alongside Thompson, though he follows a different method.[117] According to him, no historical context can be found for the Genesis narratives in the second millennium BC.[118]

In the next sections I shall discuss this question in detail; we shall also have to return once again to Gen. 14.

2.5.1 *Early dating*

One of the arguments for putting the patriarchs in an early period, say between 1900 and 1700, is based on the so-called 'Amorite hypothesis'.

The starting point for this hypothesis is that there is a connection between the patriarchs and 'nomadic' groups which entered northern Mesopotamia and Syria-Palestine round about 2000 BC. These 'nomads' are called Amorites, 'Westerners', in Sumerian and Akkadian texts of the third and second millennium BC.[119]

Albright in particular[120] has argued that Abraham's move to Canaan must be seen in connection with the Amorite invasion mentioned above. Following him, many scholars have therefore called this 'the patriarchal period'.[121] This Amorite hypothesis is based above all on archaeological discoveries. Thus K. M. Kenyon,[122] especially, has tried to demonstrate from archaeological material like diggings and earthworks that there is a clear break between two cultures in the period between 2000 and 1800 BC. This is all said to be the result of the Amorite invasion. Such a view has not lacked critics.[123] Thus the so-called Amorite invasion rests entirely on a particular interpretation of the non-biblical texts mentioned above which is certainly not impregnable. Furthermore, it is difficult to connect it with the picture of the patriarchs presented by Genesis. We hear that Abraham already comes into contact with cities, and with one exception (Gen. 14; 34), the patriarchal period is described in Genesis as a peaceful one. Furthermore, we can find no evidence in these narratives that might indicate a violent invasion on the part of the Amorites.

Another argument that might be adduced in favour of an early dating of the patriarchs is connected with the information given in I Kings 6.1. Here the time between the exodus and the building of Solomon's temple is put at 480 years. Furthermore, in Ex. 12.40 the period of the stay in Egypt is set at 430 years. Now if we can put the building of the temple at roughly 1000 BC, the patriarchs could in fact be dated around 2000–1800 BC. However, quite apart from the fact that different figures are given elsewhere in the Bible,[124] the figure 480 in I Kings 6.1 indicates very clearly that we are not dealing with exact figures, but have to think in terms of an artificially constructed chronological system, which regards the time between the exodus and the building of the temple and that between the building of the temple and the return from captivity as in each instance representing the same number of generations[125] (12×40).[126]

In addition to all this, reference is made to the names[127] and the lifestyle of the patriarchs and to the (legal) customs with which they are familiar as facts which should support an early dating. However, it should have become quite clear from the previous sections that these cannot be used as proof in connection with dating.

2.5.2 *Late dating*

Only a few scholars have argued for a late dating, compared with the supporters of an early date. It is striking, though, that Gordon, who like Albright saw Abraham as a caravan trader, arrived at a late dating, while Albright argued for an early dating.

According to Gordon, Abraham must have been born about the end of the fifteenth century, and Jacob towards the end of the fourteenth century BC.[128] He also comes to this conclusion on the basis of what he sees as links between various legal customs in Nuzu and among the patriarchs.[129] Consequently he puts Abraham in the Amarna period.

Fohrer puts the arrival of the patriarchs in Canaan after the sixteenth century BC and does so primarily from parallels with the Nuzu texts.[130] In so doing he stresses that the legal customs which appear in those texts are parallel only with the patriarchs and do not appear elsewhere in the Old Testament.

Herrmann also argues for a late dating of the patriarchs; he suggests towards the end of the second millennium BC. The rise of the Aramaean tribes seems to fit best with the genealogical system[131] which we find in the book of Genesis.[132]

2.5.3 *Genesis 14*

This chapter would be of the utmost importance in dating the patriarchs were it not that this particular part of Genesis poses the greatest problems to scholars.

It is impossible within the scope of the present book to go into all the problems in detail.[133] I shall therefore content myself with making just a few comments. Although Gen. 14 does not seem to belong to any particular source of the Pentateuch, and perhaps must even be seen as a late composition, the chapter may well contain very early material. In this connection one might point e.g. to a large number of words and names (about twenty-five of them) which appear only here and nowhere else in the Old Testament. It is also striking that certain place names, etc., are often explained by other, clearly later, names. Thus in v. 3 we have a mention of the 'Valley of Siddim', with the addition 'that is the Salt Sea'.[134] Furthermore, in Gen. 14 Mamre, Aner and Eshcol are personal names, whereas elsewhere in the Old Testament they are names of places. In addition, one might point out that in Gen. 14 the Rephaim, Zuzim and Emim are evidently still seen as extant peoples or groups, whereas in later tradition they increasingly acquire a legendary character or vanish altogether.[135] Finally, it can probably be demonstrated through the Ebla texts[136] that the cities mentioned in Gen. 14.2 in any event lay in this region in the third millennium BC.

However, one great problem is that there is no period known to us from the history of the ancient Near East when these cities (Sodom, Gomorrah, Admah, Zeboiim and Zoar) were conquered by a king of Elam, much less a time when there is mention of a treaty between four kings (who were perhaps quite powerful) with the king of Elam at their head. Furthermore, research into the proper names in Gen. 14 has so far produced no results whatsoever. The identification of Amraphel with Hammurabi of Babylon, which was taken for granted over a long period, has now proved untenable and in practice has been almost entirely abandoned. These few comments should be enough to show that it is impossible to use Gen. 14 to place Abraham, and with him the patriarchs, in a specific historical context. It can, however, be said with some certainty that the names and vocabulary of Gen. 14, in particular, may go back to a very early period.

2.5.4 *Conclusion*

From what I have said above, it will be clear that in fact it is impossible to be more precise about the dating of the patriarchs on the basis of non-biblical texts and archaeology. The works of Thompson and van Seters, above all, warn us to proceed with the utmost caution in this respect.[137]

But does that mean that we must put the historical background to the patriarchal narratives only a short while before the first formation of the tradition (J), in the tenth or ninth century BC or even later? That seems highly improbable. Of course the patriarchal narratives are literary and theological reconstructions which were made centuries after the events they describe. However, that does not mean that the patriarchs are entirely the creation of the imagination of those who collected these stories together. We do find a good deal of authentic material in these accounts, like old names which do not appear again later.[138] Furthermore, we should also note the different names for God and the mention of 'holy trees' in connection with the patriarchs in a way which does not seem to cause any embarrassment.[139] Nor do we hear anything of Baal in the patriarchal narratives. If the historical background to the patriarchal narratives was in fact that of the ninth century BC or even later, we would expect to see at least some polemic against Baal or the worship of Baals. So the lack of any reference to Baal as a vegetation deity in the patriarchal narratives could well be an indication that they are a very early tradition. An important argument in this direction is that in the texts we have from Ugarit, Baal begins to play a dominant role only from about 1500 BC, whereas in the earlier period El is much more in the foreground.[140]

Chapter 3

The Sojourn in Egypt and the Exodus

3.1 *The Joseph narrative*

Within the framework of the Joseph narrative we are told of the arrival of Jacob and his sons in Egypt. In this section we shall be primarily concerned with the biblical and extra-biblical data relating to this account. First we shall consider the information given in Gen. 37; 39—50; then the position of Joseph in Egypt; and finally the arrival of Joseph and his sons in Egypt.

3.1.1 *The information in Gen. 37; 39—50*

The Joseph story as handed down to us in the last part of the book of Genesis may be regarded as a literary climax in the Old Testament. In its present form, the probability is that it should be seen as the work of a writer who was not only familiar with conditions in Egypt, but in his work also collected and revised early traditions. What emerged is akin to the earliest wisdom literature in the Old Testament.

We find the theme of the Joseph story above all in two passages in which Joseph says to his brothers, 'So it was not you who sent me here, but God' (Gen. 45.8), and, 'As for you, you meant evil against me; but God meant it for good, to bring it about that many people should be kept alive' (Gen. 50.20). These words above all make us think of the wisdom teachers. Many people argue that such a composition is inconceivable before the time of Solomon.[1]

I shall now leave this question largely on one side in order to concentrate on the main purpose of this study, i.e. on the question whether it is also possible to point to early elements in this composition which can shed some light on a period in which Israelite tribes might have been compelled by circumstances to seek temporary refuge in Egypt.

In this connection it is important to note the many attempts which have been made to employ Egyptology as an aid towards arriving at specific conclusions.[2] Pride of place here must be given to the work of J. Vergote.[3] His book may be taken to be one of the most extensive Egyptological commentaries on the Joseph stories, and as such has gained a considerable reputation.[4] However, much of what Vergote takes to be specifically Egyptian in these narratives can just as legitimately be explained from a wider ancient Near Eastern background, and sometimes even from the Old Testament itself.[5] Vergote is most open to criticism for his view that the earliest form of the Joseph story may go back to the time of Ramses II.[6] Redford is one scholar who arrives at a completely opposed view on the basis of the same data: he concludes that the seventh century BC must be seen as the *terminus a quo* for the Egyptian background to the Joseph narratives.[7]

All this does not yet mean that the narratives about Joseph's arrival in Egypt and his stay there may not go back to one historical event or another.[8] At all events it is clear that strong memories of an episode of this kind lived on in Israel, and that they must have been preserved in more than one group. This is shown by the fact that at least two traditions have been worked together in the Joseph stories. For example, when Joseph is sold as a slave into Egypt, both Ishmaelites[9] and Midianites[10] are said to have been involved as intermediaries in the transaction. Furthermore, Reuben is only mentioned at first as protagonist, after which this role is taken over by Judah. Also we find an alternation between the names Jacob and Israel. Consequently de Vaux speaks here of an Israel–Judah–Ishmaelites tradition and a Jacob–Reuben–Midianites tradition.[11] In that case the latter must derive from central Canaan, where the Joseph tribes had settled, and the former from the south, where the tribe of Judah came to occupy a predominant position. If it is supposed that the Joseph stories underwent a final redaction in the period of Solomon or even later, then the last mentioned of these two traditions must be the oldest.[12]

Thus the biblical evidence provides us with firm points of contact which make it possible to suppose that Joseph did in fact spend some time in Egypt.

3.1.2 *The position of Joseph in Egypt*

Another question which arises is whether the position which Joseph occupied in Egypt is also within the realm of historical possibility.

It is in fact well-known that foreigners, including Semites, often occupied eminent positions in Egypt. This was the case, for example, during the Middle Kingdom,[13] at the time of the Hyksos,[14] and during the New Kingdom.[15] Roughly speaking, this covers the period from about 2000 BC to 950 BC. However, of all the functionaries who are mentioned in this connection over this long period of time, there is none who really suggests to us the figure of Joseph from the book of Genesis. The only conclusion which can be drawn from this extra-biblical data (scant as it is) is that it does not rule out the possibility that Joseph spent some time in Egypt and even came to hold a prominent position there.

3.1.3 *The arrival of Jacob and his sons in Egypt*

In the book of Genesis, the earliest form of the tradition of Joseph's arrival in Egypt and his sojourn there (see 3.1.1) is indissolubly connected with another tradition, namely the arrival of his kinsfolk in Egypt as well.[16] The circumstances in which this happened are very plausible. The fertility of Egypt seems to have been well known throughout antiquity, and there is often mention in Egyptian texts of groups which journeyed to Egypt with their livestock in times of famine and were in fact allowed entry. Of course at an early period the Egyptians had taken measures against groups which might enter the land for other, far from peaceful, reasons. This was why the so-called 'Prince's Wall' was built as early as the beginning of the second millennium BC: it served to protect the frontier against invaders of this kind. There were crossing points on this wall at which investigations were first made into the reasons why groups wanted to enter Egypt.[17] The report sent by a frontier official to Pharaoh Merneptah is interesting in this connection. This official reports that he has admitted a tribe Shasu from Edom with their cattle.[18] This was clearly a group which was driven by hunger to seek refuge in Egypt.

This information does not amount to support from Egyptian texts that Jacob and his kinsfolk entered Egypt and stayed there. The texts simply illustrate the circumstances envisaged by the narratives in Genesis and show that they are plausible.

3.2 *The oppression*

The link between the Joseph stories in Genesis and the events described at the beginning of Exodus is in fact provided by the information given in Ex. 1.8: 'Now there arose a new king over Egypt, who did not know Joseph.' According to Exodus, from this moment on there was a radical change in the Egyptian attitude towards the descendants of Jacob.

3.2.1 *The information in Exodus 1.15–22*

In this section[19] we learn how Pharaoh commands that all the newborn children of the Hebrews are to be killed. It is striking that, apart from the connection with Moses in Ex. 2.1ff., this measure of Pharaoh's is mentioned only here in Ex. 1.15–22. There is no further reference to it of any kind in the rest of the Old Testament. This is in contrast to the forced labour in Egypt, which is one of the most important themes in the Old Testament and Judaism. However, it seems possible to find an old tradition in this account in the names of the two women mentioned in Ex. 1.15. The name Shiprah appears as early as an Egyptian text of the eighteenth century BC,[20] and that of Puah in the texts from Ugarit.[21] According to de Vaux,[22] both are representative of a very early type of Semitic personal name.

It is also striking that in this pericope we hear nothing of Israelites, but exclusively of Hebrews. This, coupled with the fact that the Old Testament does not take any further account of the measure mentioned here, might indicate that the Pharaoh's action applied only to one group in Egypt at one particular time. However, certainty is very hard to come by in this respect.

In its present context this part chiefly acts as an introduction (see especially v. 22) to the account of the miraculous rescue of Moses in Ex. 2.1–10.

3.2.2 *Forced labour in Egypt*

Exodus 1.8–14; 5.6–21 report that the Israelites were subjected to forced labour in Egypt. According to Ex. 1.11, this forced labour was connected with the fortified cities of Pithom and Raamses.[23] This information is among the few facts in Exodus which make it possible to arrive at a historical reconstruction of the sojourn in Egypt and the oppression there. On the basis of the present text which mentions these cities, many scholars are inclined to regard Ramses II (*c.* 1290–1224) as the Pharaoh of the oppression.[24] It will, of course, be clear that such a conclusion is based on a very scanty foundation. However, there is also information from an extra-biblical source which seems to provide confirmation. An Egyptian text from the time of Rameses II speaks of 'Apiru who are compelled to bring stones for the building of fortifications.[25] Now something of this kind is also reported in texts from the time of Ramses III and IV,[26] but the name of the city of Raamses disappears from Egyptian texts before the accession of Ramses III.[27]

Thus there are some indications from outside the Bible that Ramses II should be regarded as the Pharaoh of the oppression. However, we should be well aware that the information here is purely indirect. Outside the Old Testament we cannot find any direct evidence which might confirm views either about the Pharaoh of the exodus or about the oppression in Egypt of the ancestors of those who were later to become Israelites. Still, the vivid memory of the oppression and the liberation from Egypt which keeps coming to the foreground in the Old Testament seems to be a strong argument for regarding this detail in Exodus as a historical reality.

The question which of the later Israelite tribes had ancestors in Egypt who were subjected to forced labour there is a separate problem. In this respect the central role played by the figure of Joseph in Egypt points to those tribes which later inhabited central Canaan. However, Judah, Benjamin and Simeon also come into the foreground, which points towards groups from southern Canaan. Furthermore, there is still the figure of Moses and the eminent tribe of Levi which is akin to him. Some typical Egyptian names seem to occur especially in this group. As well as the name Moses, these also include Hophni, Merari and Phinehas. These too could point to an association with Egypt and a stay there.[28] Above all the fact that Moses, who played such a decisive role in the religion of Israel, did not bear a specifically Israelite name, must go back to historical reality. It is hard to imagine how he, and no one else, could have been given an Egyptian name afterwards.

All this makes it probable that the kinsfolk of a number of later tribes (see above) were in Egypt.[29]

3.3 *Moses*

In this section we shall be primarily concerned with the episode of Moses' stay in Midian, his appearance in Egypt in connection with events which precede the exodus, and the institution of the passover. First, however, we shall direct our attention to the information in Ex. 1—15.

3.3.1 *Exodus 1—15*

The biblical account of the sojourn in Egypt is almost exclusively devoted, after the Joseph narratives, to the activity of Moses. Generally speaking, this covers chapters 1–15 of Exodus.

The story of Moses begins with the account of his birth and rescue in Ex. 2.1–10.[30] This is followed by the stories of his flight to Midian, his call, the confrontation with Pharaoh, the institution of the passover and the exodus.

This complex of narratives presents anyone concerned to reconstruct the history of Israel with countless problems. It is immediately clear that we cannot speak here of a homogeneous and identical tradition.[31]

All this led Pedersen to regard Ex. 1—15 as a festal legend of the celebration of the passover,[32] thus in fact abandoning any connection between these chapters and history. However, while they evidently had this function in the cult at a later stage, that certainly does not mean that they also originated in the cult. Rather, the complex character of the narratives shows that here we have a compilation and redaction of various ancient traditions.

All this, of course, makes a historical reconstruction of the events described here extremely difficult. On the other hand, however, the very fact that there are different traditions seems to make it possible to reconstruct some things with a reasonable degree of certainty.

3.3.2 *Moses' stay in Midian*

What has just been said applies first of all to Moses' contacts with the Midianites, which are mentioned especially in Ex. 2.16–22; 4.18ff. The fact that Moses' father-in-law is referred to by two different names (Reuel and Jethro) indicates that here we have to do with more than one version of the tradition. This fact argues strongly that the contacts mentioned here have a historical background.

This seems all the more likely when we consider that at a later period we often hear of a hostile attitude towards the Midianites.[33] Consequently it seems less likely that a later tradition would naturally make Moses have good contacts with the Midianites. So this tradition must not only be old, but also go back to a historical background.[34] Whether in this connection we may even go so far as to suppose that in Midian Moses came into contact with Yahwism and that we must therefore look here for the origin of Yahwism in Israelite religion seems highly improbable.[35] This so-called Kenite hypothesis has a very weak foundation, since apart from one allusion in the Old Testament, we in fact know absolutely nothing of the religion of the Midianites or the Kenites. Furthermore, it is far from certain whether there is evidence for the divine name Yahweh outside Israel before the time of Moses.[36]

3.3.3 *Moses' appearance in Egypt*

According to Exodus, after his call and return to Egypt, Moses appears as the leading character who argues for the oppressed before Pharaoh and leads them out of Egypt in the exodus.

All these events, as also the later journey through the wilderness, and so on, call as it were for a strong personality who lay behind them. In the first place, that would indicate someone who was familiar with the Egyptian court and problems in Egypt, and at the same time could identify with those who were being oppressed there. The figure of Moses fulfils all these conditions, and this makes the biblical tradition about these events, in which Moses plays an important role, extremely credible.[37]

There is neither support nor contradiction of this in the fact that Egyptian texts maintain complete silence over all the events, like the ten plagues and the drowning of Pharaoh and his army, which according to the book of Exodus caused a great uproar in Egypt. Matters of this kind are not mentioned in this category of texts. Defeats and reverses are concealed, if not omitted altogether.

Thus the fact that there is no record of these events in the Egyptian texts need not mean that they did not happen at all.[38]

3.3.4 *The institution of the Passover*

The Passover is an ancient feast, celebrated annually by shepherds in the spring, by night, at the time of the first full moon. This was when the flocks were brought to their summer pastures. On that occasion a young animal was sacrificed for the well-being and fertility of the flocks. The blood of this animal, which was sprinkled on the tent-posts, served to drive away evil powers, personified as the 'exterminator'.[39]

We can now see that in its present context, Ex. 12–13, this feast is connected with the exodus and that the blood of the sacrificial animal provides a link between the Passover and the tenth plague.

All this seems to preserve a remembrance of a historical event, an account of how the exodus took place under Moses' leadership at the time when the Passover was being celebrated.[40] It is quite conceivable that a plague did in fact ravage Egypt in this period and made such a departure easier.

At all events, it is certain that a number of traditions[41] knew of this relationship between the exodus and this feast and handed it on.

3.4 *The exodus*

The account of the liberation and exodus from Egypt was of decisive importance for Israelite faith and religion. Furthermore, there are references or allusions to such an event in a variety of ways in the Old Testament.[42] Above all in the book of Exodus we have the impression that this is an ancient tradition which has been handed down in different versions.

First of all we shall discuss that fact. Then we shall consider the question what might have happened in this exodus from Egypt.

3.4.1 *The character of the exodus*

When we read in Exodus about the events which preceded the departure from Egypt or took place after it, we can hardly escape the notion that here we have a number of traditions.

In Ex. 3.18 Moses receives a commission to go to Pharaoh and ask that the Israelites be allowed to go for three days into the wilderness to offer a sacrifice there to Yahweh. The first nine plagues are then a consequence of Pharaoh's refusal to grant this request.

However, not a word is mentioned about this question in another context.

Thus in Ex. 5.24b[43] it is announced that Pharaoh will drive *them* (definitive) out of Egypt.[44] This event is closely bound up with the tenth plague.

That seems to indicate that we have two different accounts of the exodus which were perhaps already woven together at an early stage. According to de Vaux, it is quite conceivable that these two recensions are two narratives about the exodus coming from two different groups. A first group will have been driven out of Egypt and a second group will have fled under the leadership of Moses.[45]

A view of this kind seems quite plausible, but of course adequate proof cannot be given. We lack sufficient evidence to arrive at a reconstruction of the events connected with the exodus which cannot be challenged. The only source at our disposal here is the Old Testament, and, as has often been pointed out, the aim of that is not to give a historical account of facts and events. Other sources, like those from Egypt, are in every respect silent about the exodus from Egypt and the events connected with it.

Of course, it is striking that the sequel goes on to give two different routes for the exodus – and this gives considerable support to de Vaux's view: some narratives lay considerable stress on a period in Kadesh,[46] others on a time at Sinai. Furthermore, for the entry into Canaan we hear of a route from the south and one through Transjordan.

On the basis of this information de Vaux[47] therefore arrives at the following reconstruction: the group which was driven out of Egypt left the country northwards and after a stay in Kadesh entered Canaan in the south; the second group fled from Egypt by the eastern frontier, spent some time in Sinai and subsequently went through Transjordan into Canaan.

Given the information which the Old Testament offers, this does in fact seem to be a very acceptable reconstruction.[48] Be this as it may, one thing seems certain. A tradition like this, which clearly lived on very vividly in the memories of the people and therefore is firmly rooted in Israelite religion, must go back in one way or another to a historical event.

3.4.2 *Who came out from Egypt?*

The question raised in the title of this section has already largely been answered in 3.2.2. In that context I referred to groups, akin to tribes, which later lived in the south and centre of Canaan. At the same time, I should stress once again that on the basis of the information available to us from the Old Testament, it is impossible to give a precise answer to the question with which we are concerned. It is, however, certain – and here there is a very great deal of agreement[49] – that we are talking in terms of a relatively small group of people

who were oppressed in Egypt and that these did not include all the ancestors of
the tribes which settled later in Canaan.

In all probability, one indication of the small size of this group is the
information in Ex. 1, where we are told that there were only two midwives for
all the Hebrews living in Egypt.

It seems undeniable that the figure of Moses was involved in so
fundamental an event as the exodus. A happening of this kind clearly requires
a leader and organizer. In this connection there is no reason to look for any
other figure than the one which every section of the tradition mentions, i.e.
Moses.[50]

3.5 *The crossing of the sea*

In this section I shall discuss three aspects of this crossing: the place where it
happened, the textual tradition and the relationship of it to the crossing of the
Jordan.

3.5.1 *The place of the crossing*

In Ex. 13.18 the sea which is crossed is called the *yam sūph*. These words are
usually translated by modern scholars as 'Reed Sea', but this rendering is
uncertain, given that there is no firm evidence for the exact meaning of the
second word, *sūph* (usually rendered 'reed').

However, even if this translation was correct, it would not give us much help
in providing an exact location for this 'sea'. At any rate, it is conceivable that
several stretches of water could have been characterized, e.g., by a reed bed,
and then given this name.

The geographical data in Ex. 14.2 could be of some help in arriving at a more
exact location: the places mentioned here are Migdol and Baal-zephon. The
first-mentioned already occurs in Egyptian texts before and during the period of
the Ramessids[51] and can be placed in the region of present-day El-qantara, by
the Suez canal. On the basis of his research, which includes the study of Ugaritic
texts, Eissfeldt[52] has also been able to put Baal-zephon in this area. According to
Eissfeldt, the 'sea' referred to is then the Sirbonian Sea. However, there is no
general agreement on this question and it is unlikely that such agreement will
ever be reached. This is not least because of the problem of the route that might
have been followed on the exodus from Egypt to Sinai.

Those who support the theory of the 'southern route' differ from those who
support the 'northern route' in their location of this 'sea'. The latter follow
Eissfeldt in thinking of the Sirbonian Sea. In addition, there are yet others who

reject both these theories and look for this 'sea' somewhere else again.[53] Futhermore the exact location of Sinai, so familiar a name from the wilderness period, is completely unknown. Quite apart from this group of problems, yet another question arises in connection with this issue. Ex. 14.2 (=P) belongs to a late tradition and is certainly not to be regarded as contemporary information. Furthermore, Noth has rightly pointed out[54] that the possibility that the geographical information here is secondary must certainly be taken into consideration. That is all the more likely since after the end of the state of Judah – and probably even earlier – it is clear that Israelites and Judaeans often travelled to and from Egypt.[55]

However, the fact that we cannot arrive at an exact location of the 'sea' of the exodus need not cause us any surprise. There was no scope for such a geographical localization in Israelite religion, so it was hardly relevant for the tradition through which these texts of Exodus were handed down. All the emphasis was made to fall on the liberating act of God.

3.5.2 *The information in Exodus*

The passage through the sea narrated in Ex. 13.17—14.31 and celebrated in song in Ex. 15.1b–18, 20–21 is the main theme of the exodus. Both sections form the climax of the narrative in which we are told of Yahweh's greatest act in the history of Israel, the liberation from Egypt. However, both the narrative and the hymn present scholars with great problems.

It seems that at least two traditions can be demonstrated in Ex. 13.17—14.31.[56] In one tradition the dividing of the sea is described as a natural phenomenon (caused by the east wind)[57] (Ex. 14.21=J), while the other stresses the marvellous act of God by which the waters stand up like a wall when Moses raises his rod over the sea (Ex. 14.16=E). Kaiser[58] thinks that the second of the two traditions is the earlier. However, it seems more likely that this second tradition rests on later theological reflection and that the first-mentioned can be regarded as the earlier and most authentic tradition.

The description of this event given in the hymn Ex. 15.1b–18 seems to be earlier still. According to Cross[59] this hymn could be dated as early as the twelfth or eleventh century BC. However, particular expressions, like the one concerning the temple in v. 17, point rather to the late period of the monarchy, though passages of this kind could just as well be a later addition.

Along with Ex. 15.1b–18 a short song has been handed down in Ex. 15.20–21 which also relates to the deliverance at the time of the exodus. The brevity of this second song might suggest that it is extremely old.[60]

Even more important than the question of antiquity is the fact that here we have several traditions about the exodus and the deliverance at the sea. This implies that the event made a deep impression. The same thing is also indicated by the numerous other quotations and allusions to this event in the Old Testament.[61] Something of the kind seems inconceivable unless all these go back to a historical event. However, it is impossible to discover precisely what this event entailed and what in fact happened. In this connection the tradition is by no means agreed. It is striking that in Ex. 13.17—14.31 the Egyptians are drowned as the waters of the sea flow back, while in the two hymns in Ex. 15 it is said that Yahweh threw them into the 'sea'.

3.5.3 *The connection with the crossing of the Jordan*

It has been argued[62] that the account of the crossing of the sea has subsequently been influenced by the account of the crossing of the Jordan. As a result it is thought that this narrative, which was originally part of the wilderness tradition, later found a place in the exodus tradition.

However, although we cannot rule out a later influence in the other direction, it is clear that the account of the crossing of the sea and that of the crossing of the Jordan both go back to original and independent traditions. A comparison of the terminology in Ex. 14; 15 with that of Josh. 3; 4 must certainly lead to this conclusion.[63] Of course the account of the crossing of the sea eventually overshadowed that of the crossing of the Jordan in the tradition.

3.6 *Dating*

The question of the dating of the sojourn in Egypt and the exodus is an extremely difficult one. There has been a good deal of writing and discussion on it. Of course it is impossible and unnecessary here to give even a summary of the discussion.[64] I shall content myself with noting just the most important points.

3.6.1 *Some numbers in the Old Testament*

Some of these numbers have already been mentioned in connection with the dating of the patriarchs: cf. Gen. 15.13, 16; Ex. 12.40; I Kings 6.1; Gal. 3.17. It was evident there that these texts do not give us any closer information about that dating. On the basis of the arguments which were advanced in the previous chapter, the same can also be said of the dating of the sojourn in Egypt and the exodus.[65] In connection with I Kings 6.1 I would again draw attention to the divergent figures which are given in the different traditions in connection with the exodus. In I Kings 6.1, LXX does not have the 480 of MT, but 440 years, and Josephus mentions 592 and 612 years in this context.[66]

The same kind of remarks can be made about the texts which give figures for the length of the stay in Egypt. In Gen. 15.16 it is said that the fourth generation after Abraham will return from Egypt. However, Ex. 6.15ff. makes this the seventh generation. Gen. 15.13 gives the duration of the sojourn in Egypt as 400 years, but Ex. 12.40 gives it as 430 years.

Now Gen. 15.13, 16 is always assigned to E and Ex. 6.15ff.; 12.40 to P. So we see that in one tradition four generations cover a period of four hundred years, and in the other, seven generations cover a period of four hundred and thirty years. We therefore see that the various traditions here do not present a homogeneous picture.[67] This should warn us to take the utmost care when dealing with these chronological data in the Old Testament. Clearly we cannot and may not take these indications as exact information about the duration of the stay in Egypt.

In addition to the texts mentioned above, Judg. 11.26 might finally be mentioned in this connection. Here the time between the capture of Heshbon and Jephthah is put at three hundred years. However, the figure three hundred here is in dispute,[68] as is also the context of this passage in the story of Jephthah.[69]

3.6.2 *Pithom and Raamses*

In 3.2.2 I mentioned several arguments which were thought to indicate the possibility that Ramses II (*c*. 1290–1224) can be regarded as the Pharaoh of the oppression.[70] Another important argument may perhaps be added to them. In the book of Exodus there is just one mention of a change of ruler during the time of the oppression: that is in Ex. 2.23. This might suggest a Pharaoh who was in power for a very long time. Such a qualification can really apply only to one figure, Ramses II. If that is the case, then in all probability the exodus must have taken place under his successor Merneptah.[71]

Quite apart from the question whether the Pharaohs just mentioned were in fact the Pharaohs of the oppression and the exodus, a dating of the exodus in the thirteenth century BC seems very likely. At all events, in many respects this century was a very turbulent period for the Egyptians, above all because of the rise of the 'Sea Peoples'.[72] Conditions of this kind could certainly have favoured a flight or an expulsion from Egypt. It seems very natural that oppressed slaves would have exploited such a situation.[73]

3.6.3 *The so-called Israel stele*

This memorial stone contains a victory song[74] from the fifth year of Merneptah. It can be dated about 1220 BC and includes mention of a victory by

Pharaoh over the inhabitants of Canaan. It is said of Israel that it is devastated and that its descendants are no more.

The interpretation of the text raises great problems. What is meant by Israel here?[75] Given the geographical information presented in the text we might think of a group in northern or central Canaan, but that is by no means certain. The only fact that we can infer from the text is that about 1220 BC, somewhere in Canaan, there was a group which bore the name Israel. If this group were identical with the people who came out of Egypt, that would be evidence for the date of the exodus. However, we are completely in the dark as far as the identity of the group is concerned. Consequently the memorial cannot be used as evidence over the question of dating.

3.6.4 *The Hyksos*

In section 3.6.2 it seemed that the most probable dating for the exodus was the thirteenth century BC. We have much less supporting evidence in the case of the duration of the sojourn in Egypt. Figures relating to it in the Old Testament range from 430 years to about 160 (four generations). There is also little or no extra-biblical evidence on the question.

Of course some scholars try to resolve this problem by pointing to a connection between the Joseph stories and the Hyksos,[76] who for a time held power in Egypt. The goodwill shown by the Pharaoh to Joseph (Gen. 41) and the permission given to his kinsfolk at a later date to settle in Egypt (Gen. 47) is thought to accord with the policy of the Hyksos, who could have seen these groups as kindred tribes.[77]

It is generally recognized that Hyksos rule was not the result of a sudden invasion but of a gradual infiltration extending over a fairly long period.[78] Hyksos rule must have lasted for about a century.[79] It must therefore have begun round about 1720 BC.[80] In that case the rise of Joseph and the arrival of his kinsfolk in Egypt must have happened, roughly speaking, in the seventeenth century BC.

However, it is far from certain whether these events can be dated in the time of the Hyksos. The arguments against this view are rather more than those which support it. Thus the information in Gen. 41.45 that Joseph took as wife a daughter of the priest of On does not seem to fit in with the period of the Hyksos, who promoted the worship of Seth.[81]

3.6.5 *Akhenaten*

Another suggestion is that the rise of Joseph and the arrival of his kinsfolk in Egypt should be connected with the rule of Akhenaten (Amenophis IV) and his monotheism.[82] He reigned from about 1364 to 1347 BC, which would mean that the arrival of Joseph and his kinsfolk in Egypt would have taken place in the so-called Amarna period. However, a dating in this period is highly problematical and there is no concrete evidence at all for it. The same is also true of the view that Moses was brought up in the Egyptian court at this time and that this factor influenced Moses' monotheism and his idea of God.[83]

3.6.6 *Conclusion*

The results of an investigation into the dating of the exodus and the sojourn in Egypt must inevitably be extremely sparse. We can be reasonably sure of talking about the exodus in terms of the thirteenth century BC, but of course it is questionable whether we can speak of *the* exodus. It seems more probable that what we have here are several groups, each of which was driven out of Egypt or took flight in a different way (see 3.4.1).

It is much harder to date the sojourn in Egypt. There is no extra-biblical evidence for it, and the indications and figures in the Old Testament present a varied picture (3.6.1). If these are not simply based on a particular theological structure and an artificial chronological system, they could be an indication that we should see the arrival and stay in Egypt as involving different groups at different periods.

Chapter 4

The Wilderness Period

4.1 *The connection with the exodus*

In their present context in the Old Testament, there seems to be a clear relationship between the events at the exodus and those which took place during the stay at Sinai and in Kadesh. However, according to Noth[1] and von Rad[2] in particular, this picture does not correspond to historical reality. They claim that here we have different traditions which originally had independent existences as the particular traditions of different groups. These traditions will have been brought together as a unity only at a later stage, after the settlement in Canaan.

With a number of qualifications, this theory has found some support,[3] but there are also others who challenge it fiercely.[4] Above all, the position of Moses plays an important part in criticism of the views of Noth and von Rad. One important argument is that both the exodus and the events at Sinai and in Kadesh call for a great personality. No figure can be assigned this role other than the one indicated by the tradition, Moses.[5]

This last argument[6] sounds the most convincing, though we need to remember that even it cannot be demonstrated with absolute certainty.

However, on the basis of the evidence at our disposal it seems most probable that the same group or groups were involved both in the exodus and in the events around Sinai and in Kadesh. But that does not imply the identity of this group or groups with *all* the ancestors of those who later formed the population of the kingdoms of Israel and Judah. That is out of the question, as will emerge increasingly clearly in subsequent chapters of this book.[7]

4.2 *The events associated with Sinai*

After a few comments on the location of Sinai, in this section I shall be concerned with the information in the earliest collections of tradition associated with the events at Sinai. After that we shall look at the making of the covenant and the giving of the law. Cultic institutions like the ark, the tabernacle and so on will be discussed in one of the following sections of this chapter.

4.2.1 *The location of Sinai*

There is great uncertainty over the location of Sinai. The Old Testament gives us only vague indications. Thus in this connection there are allusions to the mountains of Seir and Paran (Deut. 1.2; Judg. 5.4–5; Hab. 3.3) and to a distance of eleven days' journey from Kadesh (Deut. 1.2) or forty days south from Beersheba (I Kings 19.8). Furthermore there is even disagreement in the Old Testament tradition about the name of this mountain. Sometimes it is called Sinai (in J and P), sometimes Horeb (in E), and even 'mountain of God',[8] or just 'the mountain'.[9] Although various attempts have been made to determine the exact location of Sinai,[10] hitherto these seem to have produced no tangible results.

4.2.2 *The earliest collections of tradition*

We find the nucleus of the earliest traditions which deal with the events at Sinai in Ex. 19–24.[11] This section also forms the nucleus of the book of Exodus and already demonstrates the way in which this book of the Bible has been carefully and thoughtfully composed: Ex. 19–24 forms the centre of the book and at the same time also contains its central theme, the making of the covenant on Sinai. That this is based on a later theological conception needs no demonstration, but it does not follow that there can be no early material here.

We probably have the earliest tradition in Ex. 24.9–11.[12] At all events, this passage speaks of a theophany in which Moses has less of a prominent position than, for example, in that described in Ex. 19.9–20.

The question now is whether we can speak of a covenant-making as well as a theophany in Ex. 24.9–11. Verse 11 says that 'they ate and drank'. According to McCarthy,[13] this points to a meal to confirm a covenant. Although it seems impossible to be certain of a conclusion based only on these few words, without the appearance of the word *berīt* ('covenant'), the possibility indicated here is a very real one.[14] It is hard to avoid the impression that on Sinai there came to be a close relationship between Yahweh and those who had come out of Egypt. And there is no reason why the meal mentioned in Ex. 24.11 could not be the endorsement of this relationship.

4.2.3 *Covenant-making and lawgiving*

Sinai unmistakably occupies an important place in the religion and tradition of Israel; Yahweh is called Lord of Sinai not only in the earliest collections of tradition in Ex. 19–24 but also in other ancient reports.[15] This means that arguments can certainly be adduced to show that a covenant-making on Sinai falls within the sphere of historical possibility. For example, the fact that an ancient song like Judg. 5[16] can already celebrate Yahweh as the Lord (v. 4) of Sinai can confidently be derived from the experience of a particular group in the past. If we suppose that the time between this song and the events at Sinai was about two hundred years, a period of this length is not too long for the oral tradition of whatever took place at Sinai. That is certainly a possibility for a time when memory had a much greater function than it does in modern society.

The role of Moses is also important in this complex. He is not only the leader of the exodus, but also a central figure closely involved in the events which take place around Sinai.[17] It is almost inconceivable that in all these functions Moses should be a creation of a later tradition. Such decisive events call for a great figure to match them. Moses was the one who brought the group from Egypt into a relationship with Yahweh at Sinai.

The whole of the law-giving contained in the books from Exodus to Deuteronomy is connected with Moses and the events on Sinai. The dating of these laws raises a number of problems.[18] It is clear that in many instances they show similarities not only in form but also in content with those of peoples who were Israel's historical neighbours. It is also clear that these laws can be said to have been extended or adapted to a specific situation at a later period.[19]

One characteristic example of this is in fact the Decalogue.[20] The last four prohibitions strongly suggest that the first six commandments were originally formulated in a similar short form. There is little reason to doubt that the Decalogue – at least in a short form – could derive from the time of Moses.[21] Some prohibitions, like those against murder and theft, could be even older. Furthermore, the use of prohibitions in the Decalogue, along with the two commands which appear in it, could also be indications of considerable antiquity.[22]

Thus to associate the events at Sinai with the Decalogue is by no means impossible, though there is no proof of any kind. However, it does seem certain that we cannot describe this Decalogue as an act of covenant formed on the model of old Hittite vassal treaties from the thirteenth and fourteenth centuries BC.[23]

The view that the worship of Yahweh as the Lord of Sinai was taken over by Moses from the Midianites[24] is, to say the least, extremely dubious. At all events, the Old Testament texts provide no evidence whatsoever for such a view. Granted, there are clear indications that there were contacts with the Midianites during the wilderness period. Leaving aside Moses' stay in Midian and his contacts there, one might refer to the appearance of Jethro mentioned in Ex. 18. This last chapter may well contain an ancient historical nucleus indicating that the earliest Israelite popular legislation may be borrowed from the Midianites.[25]

Texts like Judg. 1.16; I Sam. 15.6 also point to close relations with the Midianites or Kenites. Doubtless a number of these people were also incorporated into what later became Israel.

Although much must remain unclear, on the basis of what has been said above it can be affirmed that there is enough material to show that the events at Sinai created a relationship with Yahweh which cannot be eliminated from Israelite history. This relationship formed the basis for the existence of Israel as Yahweh's people.

4.3 The time in Kadesh-barnea

According to Deut. 1.2, Kadesh was eleven days' journey from Sinai. We must envisage Kadesh as a large oasis in the south of the Negeb. The various traditions in the Old Testament are unanimous in their understanding that there was a long stay at Kadesh. In this connection the author of Num. 14.34 (probably P) talks of a period of forty years, though in all probability we should not take this as an exact figure.[26] Deut. 1.46 talks in terms of 'a long time' and 'many days'.

The many events which are mentioned in connection with a stay at Kadesh would suggest that a long time was spent there. Miriam was buried in Kadesh (Num. 20.1), and perhaps Mount Hor, where Aaron died (Num. 20.22–29), should also be sought in this area. According to Num. 13 it was also from Kadesh that the spies were sent out, and it was from there too that the attack on Hormah,[27] mentioned in Num. 14.40–45, was launched, only to end in failure.[28]

These are only some examples of events connected in the Old Testament with a stay in Kadesh; however, they should be enough to show that this area could have served as a base for a long time during the journey through the wilderness. All of which has led some scholars to argue that the groups which came out of Egypt went directly to Kadesh.[29] They are thought then to have spent almost the whole of the wilderness period in this area and to have undertaken a pilgrimage to Sinai from there. Starting from his notion of two different traditions of the exodus, de Vaux[30] considers the possibility that a different group from the one which went to Sinai under the leadership of Moses went directly to Kadesh without going by Sinai.[31]

A pilgrimage from Kadesh to Sinai probably means that there was not too great a distance between these places. And there are in fact some indications that Sinai lay in the vicinity of Kadesh.[32] However, we cannot be at all sure in this respect (3.2.1).

This view of de Vaux's finds support in the fact that in the account of the settlement in Canaan there is mention of operations both from the south (cf. Num. 21.1–3) and from Transjordan. However, this last point need not of itself mean that during the wilderness period we are dealing with groups which always remain strictly separate. Although groups travelling around in the wilderness will probably have tended to keep at some distance from one another, that need not rule out contacts, certainly at a religious ceremony like that of Sinai.

Still, one thing is certain. We have to reconcile ourselves to the fact that we are in no position to arrive at an exact historical reconstruction of the wilderness period. That is not only because we have no extra-biblical evidence whatsoever which might cast some light on the issue, but above all because the picture of this period presented by the Old Testament derives from a variety of times and traditions. And these traditions are much more concerned with theological reflection on the wilderness period than with a geographical and historical reconstruction of facts and events.

4.4 *Conflicts*

In this section I shall first discuss the internal conflicts which are constantly mentioned in the Old Testament tradition as having happened during the journey through the wilderness, and then the battle with the Amalekites.

4.4.1 *Internal conflicts*

The period spent by Israel in the wilderness is characterized by countless conflicts which took place at this time. These are mostly disputes with Moses, but they are regularly interpreted as rebellion against Yahweh.

We find the relevant stories chiefly in Exodus and Numbers.[33] We also find references to similar events during the wilderness period elsewhere in the Old Testament.[34] Such mention of 'revolt' or 'rebellion' represents an important and often-recurring theme in the tradition of Israel in the wilderness and probably finds its most characteristic expression in Deut. 9.7, where it is said: 'From the day you came out of the land of Egypt, until you came to this place, you have been rebellious against the Lord.'

One important element here is the opposition to Moses' leadership. We often hear that this opposition comes from the 'whole people', but sometimes it is a rebellion of a few individuals, like that of Miriam and Aaron in Num. 12. In other instances, as in the rebellion of Korah, Dathan and Abiram in Num. 16, it is clear that only one group is involved.

It is obvious that in this matter of 'rebellion' in the wilderness we are dealing with different traditions.[35] According to Coats, this theme of 'rebellion' in the wilderness arose from Jewish polemic directed against the cult in the northern kingdom, as installed by Jeroboam I.[36] Carroll sees the stories in which this theme comes to the fore as containing elements which reflect different social situations in the history of Israel.[37]

The latter view seems more acceptable. However, as Carroll himself rightly points out,[38] this does not mean that the accounts could not go back to real situations in the wilderness period. Thus it seems reasonable to suppose that the difficulties of living in the wilderness may often have been the occasion for conflict, and it almost goes without saying that in such circumstances the conflict would be expressed in terms of rebellion against the leadership. For that very reason, the theme of 'rebellion' in the wilderness may well go back to an ancient historical tradition.[39] However, in their present form the stories about the rebellions are creations of a later period which served a homiletic purpose and were constructed and interpreted above all with an eye to the specific problems of the later time in which they were written. Emphasis must be placed on the fact that the problem of leadership in both Israel and Judah always assumed considerable importance.

Alongside the theme of the 'rebellion', considerable importance is also attached in the later history of Israel to the theme of the faithfulness which Yahweh showed to the people in the wilderness. Thus the Qumran community later went into the wilderness 'to await the beginning of the time of salvation there'.[40]

4.4.2 *The battle with Amalek*

During the wilderness period we hear not only of internal conflicts but also of a battle with another people, the Amalekites. We find the story which describes the battle with them in Ex. 17.8–16.[41]

According to Gen. 14.7, the Amalekites lived in the area of Kadesh.[42] Their abode is said to have been the Negeb in Num. 13.29; 14.43–45; I Sam. 15.7; 27.8. Thus all this information, which is derived from different traditions, is probably in agreement over the Amalekite territory. We have no extra-biblical information about the Amalekites, so that here again we are thrown back on information from the Old Testament. However, we should probably look for their territory somewhere in the region of Kadesh.[43]

Now it is very probable that the constant hostility between Israel and Amalek which existed at a later period influenced the final form of the account in Ex. 17.8–16. However, there is no reason to doubt that the nucleus of this report goes back to something which really happened at the time of the wanderings in the wilderness.[44] It commonly happens that such groups have disputes over the possession of pasturage and sources of water. In fact, we might well be surprised that there is only one account of this kind in the tradition about the wilderness period.

4.5 *Religious institutions*

To end this chapter, I propose to consider some religious institutions which according to the Old Testament became established permanently during the wilderness period.

4.5.1 *The ark*

It is obvious that the ark functioned in a later period, in the Jerusalem temple, as a symbol of Yahweh's presence among the people. We are told in Ex. 25.10–22; 37.1–9 that this ark was made in the wilderness, at Yahweh's command.

In their present form, these accounts derive from the Priestly tradition. Although the tradition is from a later period and is certainly stamped with the theological presuppositions of that period, good arguments can be adduced to show that the ark was already used in the wilderness.[45] That seems all the more likely, given that at an early period other wandering groups already had a portable sanctuary.[46]

One important question concerning the ark is that of its significance and function as a cultic object. The answer is far from easy because in the course of time this significance continually changed. Thus we can see that the ark was used, for example, as a store place for the stone tablets (Deut. 10.1–5), as a palladium in war (I Sam. 4), as a divine throne (Num. 7.89), as God's footstool (Ps. 132.7f.), and as a symbol of God's presence (Num. 10.33–36; II Sam. 7.6–7).

The Hebrew word for ark probably had the original meaning of 'chest' (cf. Gen. 50.26; II Kings 12.10). If that is correct, the earliest function of the ark may have been as a store place for one or more cultic objects. In that case the tradition (Deut. 10.1–5) that the ark fulfilled this function could also be the earliest.

4.5.2 *The tabernacle*

Christians have become accustomed to talk of the 'tabernacle', under the influence of the Vulgate. However, the Hebrew text of the Old Testament talks of a 'tent', describing it as the 'tent of assembly or meeting'.

We find the legislation about the tabernacle in Ex. 25ff.[47] It is clear that this legislation is of Priestly origin. When we read the chapters in the Old Testament which relate to the tabernacle, it is striking that sometimes it is described as a tent and that at others the description suggests a temple building. This gives us the impression that the legislation about the tabernacle is based on at least two different traditions. Without doubt the one which sees the tabernacle as a tent is the earlier of the two,[48] and may well go back to ancient memories of a time when a portable sanctuary was still necessary. These particular features make it likely that a sanctuary of this kind originated in the wilderness period.[49]

In a later period the tabernacle was then replaced with a permanent sanctuary. It is possible that this had already happened in Shiloh. At any rate, we get this impression from I Sam. 1.9; 3.3. On the other hand, there is express mention of a tent in Shiloh in Josh. 18.1; 19.51. But even archaeological investigations have not yet been able to answer the question whether there was in fact a temple in Shiloh.

Excursus II

The Tribes of Israel

In an important study,[1] Noth has shown that the Old Testament contains two systems relating to the twelve tribes of Israel. He finds evidence for the first in Gen. 49.3–27, and according to him it is the earlier.[2] The passage gives these tribes in the following order: Reuben, Simeon, Levi, Judah, Zebulun, Issachar, Dan, Gad, Asher, Naphtali, Joseph and Benjamin. The second system, of which we have the earliest account in Num. 26.5–51,[3] which has a marked geographical character, gives the following list: Reuben, Simeon, Gad, Judah, Issachar, Zebulun, Manasseh, Ephraim, Benjamin, Dan, Asher and Naphtali.

Apart from the order, the most important difference between these two systems is the absence of the names of Levi and Joseph from the second list. We can see that Levi and Joseph have disappeared and that the number twelve has been made up by the incorporation of Manasseh and Ephraim.

H. Weippert[4] has found a variant to the second, geographical system in five passages in the Old Testament.[5] A special characteristic of this last series is that this list of tribes begins with Judah and ends with Asher and Naphtali.[6]

Noth thinks that both these systems come from the time of the judges, the first from a rather earlier period than the second.[7] It might also have been at this time, he thinks, that the twelve tribes of Israel were organized into a unity. And from this Noth goes on to arrive at his theory[8] of the existence of an early Israelite amphictyony. This he supposed to be a sacral alliance between twelve tribes whose religious focus was a central sanctuary. According to Noth, this amphictyony was brought into being at the assembly in Shechem reported in Josh. 24.[9] The tribal alliance can thus be described primarily as a religious community.

Although to begin with Noth's theory found much support, especially in Germany, it has meanwhile been rejected by the majority of scholars on the basis of good arguments.[10]

An important point here is that we should not take the number twelve in the lists mentioned earlier as a real figure. It cannot be a coincidence that the number twelve is very often used in the Old Testament simply in connection with descendants. We are told of Nahor (Gen. 22.20–24), Ishmael (Gen. 25.13–16) and also of Esau (Gen. 36.10–14) that they each had twelve offspring. This strongly suggests that the figure in the texts is not exact but must rather be seen as symbolic. Furthermore, there is much to be said for the view that here the number twelve is meant to express a totality.[11] Thus lists of twelve tribes are usually a theoretical scheme, representing all Israel.

However, this scheme is not just theoretical; it is an idealized picture or, rather, a theological construction from a later period. In fact we continually come across different tribes and groups of tribes in the Old Testament. We are able to see this in the systems mentioned right at the beginning of this excursus, and as we progress further we shall notice that other tribes are mentioned in addition to those which we have already encountered.

Be that as it may, it is clear that the systems mentioned by Noth and H. Weippert are not the earliest combinations of tribes of which we have evidence. The oldest and most authentic relevant text we possess is the Song of Deborah (Judg. 5.14–18).[12] It mentions the following ten tribes: Ephraim, Benjamin, Machir, Zebulun, Issachar, Reuben, Gilead, Dan, Asher and Naphtali. If we compare this with the two schemes identified by Noth, we find that the names of Judah, Simeon and Gad seem to be missing. Furthermore, we also lack the names of Levi and Joseph, which appear in Noth's first system, and that of Manasseh, which is a feature of Noth's second system. Finally, in Judg. 5.14–18 we find two names which are completely absent from Noth's systems, Machir and Gilead.

Hoftijzer[13] gives two possibilities for the absence of the names of Judah and Simeon in Judg. 5.14–18: at that time they were still not part of Israel, or the kingdom of Jebus hindered contacts between these two tribes and those in the north.

Those seem to be real possibilities. At all events, we have no information which would seem to support another alternative. In the case of Simeon, it is perhaps conceivable that at the time the tribe had already ceased to exist.[14]

The absence of the name of Gad is harder to explain. It has been suggested that Gilead in Judg. 5.17 could in fact mean Gad,[15] above all because in the Deuteronomistic literature Gad is always mentioned after Reuben, as Gilead is here. However, it seems most likely that Gad did not yet exist at this time.[16]

In connection with the absence of the names of Levi and Joseph in Judg. 5.14–18 it must be observed that the Old Testament does not really give us sufficient indication that there ever was a secular tribe of Levi,[17] and the same is probably the case with the existence of a tribe of Joseph.[18] It seems certain that the expression 'house of Joseph' was coined only in the time of the early monarchy as a counterpart to Judah or 'the house of Judah'.[19]

The names of Machir and Gilead in the song of Deborah are striking. In various places in the Old Testament Machir is said to be a son of Manasseh[20] and the father of Gilead.[21] In other places, however, it seems that Machir conquered the territory of Gilead (Num. 32.39) and took it over (Josh. 13.31; 17.1). Furthermore, in the texts mentioned above, both Machir and Gilead are regarded as sub-divisions of Manasseh. So clearly in Judg. 5.14–18, Machir and Gilead are two tribes or groups who in later Old Testament tradition together, or with others, formed the tribe of Manasseh.[22]

The tribes or groups mentioned in the song of Deborah inhabited territory which, after the death of Solomon, roughly speaking comprised the kingdom of Israel.

For the situation prior to the Song of Deborah we should certainly envisage the existence of yet other groups or 'clans'. Among other things, there was probably a 'clan' which already bore the name Israel.[23] It is equally possible that the Song of Deborah is far from giving a complete list of names from this period.[24]

In addition to these names, which primarily relate to central and northern Canaan and Transjordan, we also find in the Old Testament a number of names of groups and tribes which can be located in the south. In this connection, in addition to Judah and Simeon one might mention the Calebites, with Hebron as a centre (Josh. 15.13); the Jerahmeelites (I Sam. 27.10); the Othnielites, with Debir as a centre (Josh. 15.15–19); and the Kenites (Judg. 1.17) – also Jeshurun.[25] It is only in the time of David that Judah came fully to the foreground in the history of Israel. Until then it must have led a very isolated existence in the south (cf. also Gen. 38). This is also a period about which we have little certain knowledge. However, ancient tribal sayings like Gen. 49.9 suggest that the situation was not without its particular problems.[26] It seems most likely that Judah was made up later from a combination of the survivors of the tribe of Simeon, which had virtually disappeared in the time of the judges, and the Calebites,[27] Jerahmeelites, Othnielites and Kenites.[28]

According to Seebass,[29] before the time of David there was already a tribal alliance in the south which consisted of the four groups or clans just mentioned, along with Judah and Simeon, with Hebron as its centre. In that case Jeshurun in Deut. 33.5 is the designation for the four non-Israelite groups (see above) living in alliance with Judah, and then takes the place of Simeon, which at that time no longer existed. The designation Jeshurun was probably used in the early period of Solomon's reign.[30]

It seems evident from the survey given here that there was never a real alliance of twelve tribes in the history of Israel. It also emerges that in the course of this history two groups increasingly make themselves felt, which later were to form the two states of Israel and Judah.

Chapter 5

The Settlement in Canaan

5.1 *The political and socio-economic situation in Canaan* c. *1300 BC*

5.1.1 *The international situation*

The main feature of the last two centuries of the second millennium BC was the weakening of Egyptian power over Canaan. This situation had really already begun to develop in the fourteenth century BC, during the reign of Amenophis IV (Akhenaten), who attached more importance to his domestic religious reform[1] than to Egyptian foreign policy. The chief reason for this decline in Egyptian influence, however, was probably the confrontation with other peoples, who at this time were coming increasingly to the fore.

First of all, then, in this connection we need to consider the Hittite empire (see Map 1) which at that time was established in Asia Minor. This kingdom and that of Egypt can be regarded as the two great powers of the time; as always in history, they were also rivals. An important battle took place between the armies of these two countries early in the thirteenth century BC at Kadesh (on the Orontes). This battle – the last between the two powers – was indecisive. It turned out worse for Egypt, who probably under the leadership of Ramses II had made a supreme effort in this war to win back the dominant position it held in the fifteenth century BC. From now on the Egyptians had to concede that Northern Syria and adjoining regions fell under the sphere of Hittite influence.[2]

However, with this, difficulties for Egypt were by no means over. New dangers now threatened from the west. During the reign of Merneptah (*c.* 1224–1204), an invasion took place from this direction: the Libyans, who had long posed a threat to the frontiers of Egypt, now penetrated as far as the Nile delta. The Egyptians managed to defeat the Libyans and the allies who had joined them, but this too did no good to Egyptian supremacy.[3]

The greatest threat of all posed to the Egyptians came from the so-called Sea Peoples. These peoples, very probably of Aegean origin, penetrated primarily the coastal areas of Asia Minor, Syria and Egypt during the late Bronze Age. Their invasion was in fact part of a great population movement. The Philistines (designated *plst* in Egyptian texts) also belonged to these peoples, but they make an appearance only at a very late stage of this development.

In the first instance, these immigrants still seem to have been quite peaceful. Some of them evidently served as mercenaries among the Egyptian, Hittite and even Libyan forces. At a later stage they became hostile to Egypt.

A well known inscription relevant to the Sea Peoples is that of Medinet Habu,[4] which gives an account of a battle between them and Ramses III (*c.* 1184–1153). Ramses evidently managed to defeat them on both land and sea, so that they did not succeed in invading Egypt. However, this victory did not achieve more than that, because the appearance of the Sea Peoples again represented a considerable weakening of Egyptian supremacy in the territory around.[5]

It was logical that others should exploit this weakness in the Egyptian position. We should probably see the foundation of independent kingdoms like those of Ammon, Edom and Moab during the transition from the Bronze Age to the Iron Age in this light.[6] We shall see later that all these events also left their mark on Canaan.

5.1.2 *The political situation in Canaan*

We get most of our information about the situation in Canaan in this period from the Amarna letters and a number of texts from the fifteenth century BC found in Taanach. At this time Canaan seems to have been divided into a number of city states. In the Amarna letters we find mention of e.g. Hazor,[7] Megiddo,[8] Shechem,[9] Gezer,[10] Jerusalem[11] and Lachish.[12] Most of the city states lay in the territory between the hill country and the great plains.[13]

A few firm conclusions may be drawn from the information given in the Amarna letters. First of all, there seems to have been a very large number of city states in Canaan. This picture also seems to correspond well with the information in the book of Joshua, which constantly talks about the kings of cities. In the Amarna letters, however, these rulers are seldom referred to as kings.[14]

A second conclusion is that Egyptian authority in Canaan at this time was very weak. This is evident, for example, from the rise of Labaya of Shechem, who clearly saw an opportunity to extend his territory considerably.[15] Milkilu of Gezer also seems to have functioned for a long period as an independent ruler.[16] Evidently such city states grew steadily stronger, the more Egyptian power became weaker.

The letters from Taanach,[17] addressed to the ruler of Taanach, with instructions to send troops and material to Megiddo and Gaza, give us the impression that Egyptian rule in Canaan was certainly not stable.

A third conclusion which really already follows from what has been said so far is that by this time some city states had evidently already developed into a larger concentration. In addition to Shechem (see above), perhaps Hazor[18] can also be mentioned in this connection. The growing independence of the city states and the weakness of the Egyptian regime is also clear from the appearance of the 'Apiru. Various letters speak of unrest which they cause.[19] However, these 'Apiru more than once are supported by Pharaoh's vassals agaist their lord.[20]

The picture which this information from Canaan gives us is of a land going through a turbulent period in which local rulers probably had most of the power in their own hands and Egypt could exercise little or no authority.

This will have been the case even more after the battle at Kadesh and at a time when Egypt suffered more than ever from attacks launched by the Sea Peoples (see 5.1.1). We may probably assume that the Philistines and perhaps kindred groups had already settled on the coastal plain in the twelfth and eleventh centuries BC.[21]

5.1.3 *The social and economic situation in Canaan*

As we have seen, the Amarna letters often speak of the 'Apiru. According to Mendenhall,[22] the 'Apiru belonged to the indigenous population of Canaan.[23] However, they were not city-dwellers, but lived in the country. There was sharp conflict between these two groups.

Those who lived in the country were oppressed by the city states and subjected to various kinds of forced labour. According to Mendenhall, when the Amarna letters report the rebellion of 'Apiru, they are in fact talking about a revolt of those living in the country against the city states.

Now it seems clear that about 1300 BC important changes had taken place in both the social and the economic spheres, first of all at a technical level. Peoples and groups, like the Philistines at a later stage, who were the first to make use of the new material, iron, certainly gained great advantages from it.

We can also observe another important shift in the matter of population settlement. Alt[24] already pointed out that various towns grew up in the hill country for the first time at the beginning of the Iron Age, which were clearly founded there by the Israelites. This has later been confirmed by various excavations.[25] These settlements were helped on by the fact that from about 1200 BC onwards people learned how to manufacture and use iron implements. This enabled them to deforest the slopes of the hills and make them fit for agricultural use. Furthermore, iron tools could be used to construct terraces on these slopes[26] and provide means of irrigation.[27] All this led to the rise of a new class of peasant farmers. The iron which began to be made in this period was easier to use and more readily available than the bronze of the earlier period.[28]

However, this last point also indicates a difficulty in the views of Mendenhall which I have sketched out above. It is clear that the structure of the population of Canaan at the beginning of the Iron Age was more complex than Mendenhall suggests. It was not just a matter of the city states on one hand and the members of the 'Apiru[29] on the other. Indeed, the texts themselves seem to tell against a contrast between the country population (the 'Apiru) and the city states as envisaged by Mendenhall. I have already noted that the Amarna letters more than once talk of collaboration between the 'Apiru and the city states.

5.2 *The character of the settlement*

A reconstruction of the way in which Israel settled in Canaan presents numerous problems. We can already see this in the variety of names which have been used in connection with this process or event. People talk about the 'conquest',[30] the 'conquest and settlement',[31] the 'settlement',[32] 'the occupation of the land',[33] and the 'penetration'.[34] These few examples already illustrate clearly the different approaches to the matter.[35]

The Old Testament tradition itself offers a very complicated picture of the affair. At all events, we can deduce from it that the settlement was a very long-drawn-out process and that whatever else, it was in no way the consequence of a large-scale conquest.[36] The accounts in Joshua 1–11 do, though, give the impression that we are dealing with a large, rapid and massive operation which took place under the leadership of Joshua.

However, if we read these chapters carefully, it is evident that in fact they deal only with events which take place in the tiny territory of Benjamin. Only in two passages is there mention of a campaign in the south (10.16–42) and in the north (11.1–15). By contrast, Judg. 1 makes quite a different impression. Here we do not even find mention of the name of Joshua in this connection, and we hear of operations carried out by tribes either separately or sometimes in small alliances. Furthermore, in Josh. 13.1–7 and in Judg. 1.27–36 we are told explicitly that large areas and many cities were not occupied, 'because the Canaanites persisted in dwelling in that land'.[37] This is an important piece of information. As we shall see when we come to discuss the period in question, it is evident that these Canaanites were gradually incorporated into the population of Israel and Judah, above all from the time of David and Solomon.

This implies that we may suppose that the same thing happened with other groups as well, like the 'Apiru.

We may add to that the conclusion that the people who in the Old Testament tradition are later called Israel and Judah, or just Israel, need not originally have come from elsewhere. In other words, a large proportion of the people may have been native to Canaan. Of course certain groups came from elsewhere. This is especially true of those who came from Egypt and through the wilderness to Canaan. They probably arrived from two directions, one group from Kadesh-barnea into southern Canaan, and one through Transjordan to the centre and north of Canaan.

Neither Old Testament[38] nor archaeological[39] evidence supports the view that there was a mass invasion or a violent invasion of the country by large groups.

Of course this does not mean that there was no fighting, or that there were never conflicts between groups which wanted to settle in a particular area and the people already living there. In the next section we shall subject all this to a closer investigation.

5.3 *The settlement in Transjordan*

5.3.1 *Descriptions of routes*

We find two different traditions in the Old Testament about the route followed from Kadesh to Transjordan. One describes how the Israelites left Kadesh after the death of Aaron on Mount Hor, travelled via Edom and Moab direct to 'the fields of Moab', and there camped by the Jordan opposite Jericho. We find the clearest account of this in the Priestly tradition of Num. 33 (vv. 37–49).[40] There seems to be a parallel to this in the report in Deut. 2.29, where it is said that Edom and Moab had given permission for the passage through their lands. However, another and probably earlier tradition (Num. 20.14–21; 21.4; Deut. 2.1; Judg. 11.17f.) says that the Israelites travelled from Kadesh along the 'reed sea',[41] round Moab and Edom, because these two countries had refused to allow them to pass through. In this way they then arrived in the territory of Sihon, the king of Heshbon (Num. 21.21ff.; Deut. 2.26ff.).

5.3.2 *The appearance of Balaam*

In neither of the two traditions just mentioned is there any mention of fighting with Edom and Moab. This must mean that the stories about Balaam in Num. 22–24 and also the account of the apostasy in Baal-peor[42] in Num. 25.1–5 do not fit easily into this framework. At all events, the fact that Moab feels threatened by Israel, as is indicated in Num. 22–24, is hard to reconcile with Deut. 2.9, where it is explicitly said that no violence may be used against Moab. The strong position which Moab must have occupied in about 1200 BC[43] also seems best to fit in with this latest piece of information.

Although the name of the prophet Balaam in Num. 22–24 may go back to an ancient tradition,[44] and the sayings there could be very old, this section presumably had no connection at all in the first place with the settlement in Transjordan. The same is true of the account of the apostasy of Israel with Baal-peor in Num. 25.1–5, of which according to Num. 31.16 Balaam was the instigator. Numbers 25.1–5, too, certainly contains an ancient tradition, since it is already mentioned in Hos. 9.10. However, we must probably follow de Vaux[45] in presupposing that this account, like that of Num. 22–24, originally related to a historical situation in the period between the settlement and the reign of David.

5.3.3 *Sihon and Og*

Taking account of all that has emerged above, we can see that it is most probable that the group under the leadership of Moses went round Edom and Moab until they arrived at the frontier of the kingdom of Sihon. This does not exclude the possibility that one tradition recalls a group which went through Edom and Moab along the so-called Royal Road.

Like Edom and Moab, Sihon too refused to allow the Israelites to pass through, whereupon according to Num. 21.21–31 there was a battle, as a result of which this territory was conquered. We do not know how large Sihon's kingdom was. The majority of scholars tend to see it as a small Canaanite kingdom to the north of the Arnon, with Hehbon as its centre and capital.[46]

The song that we find in 21.27b–30 is important for the interpretation of this pericope.[47] It seems most probable that in its present form this song celebrates the Israelite victory and recalls an earlier victory of Sihon over Moab.[48]

It is striking that the name of Moses is not mentioned in Num. 21.21–31, but this need not mean that he had no role here.[49] There is much to suggest that this account has in fact preserved an ancient tradition from the time of the settlement in Transjordan. In support of this is, for example, the fact that the battle against Sihon took place near a certain Jahas (v. 23), which is probably to be located to the south of Heshbon.[50] This could indicate that here Sihon was confronted with a group which invaded his land from the south and thus from the wilderness.

In that case it is also very possible that Num. 21.21–31 contains earlier traditions about a conquest in Transjordan.[51] These could certainly go back to a period of settlement in about the thirteenth century BC.[52] That is not the case with the narrative about Og king of Bashan in Num. 21.33–35, which is usually regarded as a derivative of the almost literal parallel in Deut. 3.1–3.

The area spoken of here is the region in which the half-tribe of Manasseh settled. However, this must have happened in a later stage of the period of the judges.[53] The purpose of this account is therefore to stress the later claims of Manasseh to this area. Further support for this can be found in the fact that in Deut. 3.11 Og is called 'the last of the Rephaim', and is evidently regarded as a legendary figure.[54] Of course, the name Og does not appear elsewhere as a personal name.

5.3.4 *Reuben and Gad*

We find important information about the settlement in Transjordan in Num. 32.[55] The whole chapter is presumably to be ascribed to the Priestly Writing, though that does not mean that it could not contain earlier traditions. According to Wüst[56] that is certainly true of vv. 1, 16a, where it is said that the tribes of Reuben and Gad wanted to settle in Jasher and Gilead.

Now it is almost certain that the tribe of Reuben no longer existed in the time of the judges. However, it must once have been important.[57] There is an indication of its decline in Gen. 49.3f.; Deut. 33.6. Reuben might once have had a major role in connection with a settlement in Transjordan, in which it would have been involved at a very early stage. The tribe of Gad must also have settled in Transjordan early on. This can be deduced from a clause on the so-called Moabite stone (*c.*840 BC), which states that 'the people of Gad had long dwelt in the land of Ataroth'.[58] De Geus thinks here in terms of the beginning of the tenth century BC.[59] In the long run Reuben was probably incorporated completely into Gad, and so vanished from the scene.[60]

I should stress that in Num. 32 there is no mention of any dispute or conquest in connection with Reuben or Gad. The peaceful aspect of these groups is also stressed by the information in Josh. 1–11 and Judg. 1. There is no sign there that Reuben and Gad engaged in any fighting to occupy the land west of the Jordan. Furthermore, there is some reason to assume that these tribes originally settled independently of those coming into Transjordan from west of the Jordan, or had already lived there for a long time.[61] It is, of course, possible that, like for example Machir, other groups from west of the Jordan also settled in Transjordan.[62]

It is impossible to be certain about any of this. At best the material at our disposal enables us only to make a very fragmentary reconstruction of the settlement in Transjordan.

To sum up, it can be said that apart from the battle against Sihon, this must largely have followed a peaceful course and have extended over a long period.

5.4 *The settlement in the south*

5.4.1 *The battle at Hormah*

In Num. 21.1–3 (= J or JE) the Israelites are said to have captured Hormah and
some other cities in the region of Arad and put them to the ban. The account
in which this event is narrated must clearly be seen in the framework of the
wilderness tradition.[63] In Judg. 1.17, however, the same event is attributed to a
joint expedition made by Judah and Simeon, which therefore took place after
the death of Joshua.

Numbers 21.1–3 must certainly be regarded as the earlier of these two
traditions. A tradition can be detected in the Old Testament which knows of a
group entering Canaan from the south. The story of the spies can be
connected with this: in Num. 13.17b–20, 22, great emphasis is placed on the
reconnaisance from the south (the Negeb). Like Num. 21.1–3, these verses too
probably come from a Yahwistic tradition.

However, this notion of an invasion from the south differs completely from
the version of the invasion of the country which we find in the book of Joshua
(see 5.4.2). This strongly suggests that in Num. 21.1–3 the Yahwist took up an
ancient and independent tradition.[64]

It is impossible to discover with any certainty when this battle at Hormah
might have taken place. Aharoni[65] thinks in terms of a period long before the
thirteenth century BC. At all events, the explanation of the name Hormah in
Num. 21.3 (cf. Judg. 1.17) clearly has an aetiological character.

5.4.2 *The information in Joshua and Judges 1*

Apart from the passages discussed so far, we find the most important material
for the subject under consideration in Joshua and Judg. 1. Both give us an
independent version of the way in which the land came to be occupied.

In the book of Joshua the whole event is described as a process involving all
Israel, under the leadership of Joshua, in a great campaign. By contrast, in
Judg. 1 this event is imagined as an action performed by various groups
independently of one another.

It is clear that in their present form, both these accounts of the events in
question rest on a later literary and above all theological reconstruction.
However, this need not mean that they have not incorporated earlier
traditions. Of the two, Judg. 1 is usually regarded as the more authentic and
reliable tradition.[66] De Geus regards Judg. 1.1—2.5 as a later Deuteronomistic

insertion.[67] But even if his position is adopted, it does not imply that this pericope does not in some respects present a picture of a historical reality from a distant past. This is especially true of the different arrivals and actions of the various groups as they are described in Judg. 1. The report in Judg. 1.27–36 (and Josh. 13.1–7) that a large number of cities remained in the possession of the Canaanites must also go back to an early and reliable tradition. This is supported by the fact, first that they were only captured or annexed at a later period, largely by David; and secondly, only from the beginning of the Iron Age onwards do we have Israelite settlements, and then only in the hill country. That is true not just of the settlement in the south, but also of the settlement in the centre and north of the country.[68]

5.4.3 *Hebron and Debir*

Hebron plays a very important role in the tradition about Caleb and the Calebites in the Old Testament.[69] According to Josh. 15.14, this city was conquered by Caleb. Judges 1.10 says that it was conquered by Judah, and Josh. 10.36 says that it was conquered by Joshua. All these mentions, though, agree in one thing, that Hebron was the abode of the Calebites. We must therefore presuppose *a priori* that any conquest of Hebron must be attributed to them.

In fact we know nothing of the origin of the Calebites. So it is even possible that they had always lived in the Negeb, around Hebron. The role of Caleb in the story of the spies (Num. 13–14) and the texts about the conquest of Hebron which I have just mentioned could therefore have been intended to explain the incorporation of Caleb into Judah. However, the Calebites clearly regarded themselves as an independent group in Judah for a long time, right down to the fifth century BC. Happenings in their city of Hebron also suggest this. It was here that David began his kingship (directed against the dynasty of Saul), and here too that Absalom began his rebellion.

There is also mention of a conquest of Debir or Kiriath-sepher, as there is of a conquest of Hebron.[70] According to Josh. 10.38, Kiriath-sepher or Debir was conquered by Joshua, but according to Josh. 15.16ff.; Judg. 1.12ff., it was conquered by Othniel.

These accounts of the conquest of Debir seem virtually identical to those of the occupation of Hebron. In all probability we should see the Calebites and Othnielites as kindred groups.[71]

5.4.4 *The battle against the five kings*

In Josh. 10 there is mention of a battle with the kings of Jerusalem, Hebron,

Yarmuth, Lachish and Eglon. According to Josh. 10.28–39, Israel, under the leadership of Joshua, is able to come from the south, defeat these kings and occupy a large number of cities in southern Canaan.

However, these reports relate to cities which for the most part were conquered only at a much later date by the Israelites.[72] Thus according to Josh. 10 the king of Jerusalem was one who met an overwhelming defeat, whereas David was the first person to be able to capture Jerusalem (Jebus). The report in Judg. 1.21 that the Benjaminites were not able to drive out the inhabitants of Jerusalem also fits into this context. It is also certain that Gezer, mentioned in Josh. 10.33, was occupied only in the time of Solomon (I Kings 9.16). As to the expedition in Josh. 10, one can therefore only agree with de Vaux's conclusion[73] that it is impossible to ascribe this campaign in the south to Joshua and to Israel.

Finally, it must also be said here that all the information mentioned in this section about the settlement in the south gives no indication of conquests on a large scale. These occur only at a later period. We shall come across them in subsequent chapters.

5.5 *The settlement in the centre of the country*

5.5.1 *The figure of Joshua*

In fact we find information about the settlement in central Canaan only in the book of Joshua. Judges 1.22–26 simply contains a short note that the house of Joseph succeeded in taking possession of Bethel by a stratagem.[74] Furthermore, an account like Gen. 34 could indicate that at an early stage Simeon and Levi already made attempts to settle in Shechem and its environs. However, that is by no means certain.[75] So for the history of the settlement in this part of Canaan we are primarily dependent on the book of Joshua.

First of all we must consider the figure of Joshua, who plays a major role in the book. In this connection it is quite remarkable that Joshua is hardly ever mentioned later in the Old Testament.[76] Furthermore, there is reason to assume that Joshua is chiefly an important figure in the traditions of the tribes in central Canaan and thus in the later kingdom of Israel, i.e. the northern kingdom.[77] These traditions were increasingly suppressed as time went on by those from Judah.

This seems equally evident from the fact that the events related in the book of Joshua take place primarily in the region to the north of Jerusalem. Thus we can see that the accounts in Josh. 2–9 are almost always[78] connected with incidents which take place in the territory of Benjamin.[79] This must mean that there we have specifically Benjaminite traditions. Gilgal, in the territory of

Benjamin, is regarded as the place from which they originated.[80] However, at the earliest this cannot have been until the Iron Age, since archaeological investigations have not produced any trace of a sanctuary in the Late Bronze Age.[81]

Given the fact that Joshua came from the tribe of Ephraim,[82] traditions from this tribe could also play a part in the tradition about his person. However, it is impossible to provide an exact reconstruction. Apart from that, there are no reasons whatsoever why Joshua should not be a historical figure in the tradition of Josh. 2–9.

5.5.2 *The invasion*

In Joshua 2–9 it seems possible to make a clear reconstruction of a route followed by the group under Joshua's leadership in their invasion of central Canaan: Jordan–Jericho–Ai–Gibeon. The crossing of the Jordan need not have presented any great problems, especially for a sizeable group. Many armies have crossed the Jordan in the course of history.[83] However, in Israel this crossing of the Jordan was always seen as a miracle brought about by Yahweh. In the history of Israel all the stress is placed on this aspect.[84] Obviously the account of the crossing in its present form is very complex in construction. Investigation of it is still far from arriving at any unanimous result.[85] However, one can well imagine that such a decisive event – above all from a theological perspective – was handed down in many circles in different ways.

5.5.3 *Jericho and Ai*

Archaeological investigations have not provided any evidence that could point to a conquest of Jericho in the thirteenth century under the leadership of Joshua. As will be understood, these investigations were carried out above all on the walls of the city. It has emerged that this oldest city in the world has been destroyed on numerous occasions, but no trace whatsoever has been found of a devastation or collapse of walls in connection with the events mentioned in Josh. 6.[86]

However, there is another tradition about Jericho and the invasion apart from the account in Josh. 6. In Josh. 24.11 we hear that the inhabitants of Jericho fought against the Israelites after the crossing of the Jordan and were then defeated by them. This could point to a capture of Jericho; on the basis of archaeological evidence we can assume that in the time of Joshua this city was only lightly fortified, if it was fortified at all.

The account in Josh. 6 which describes how the walls fell down without

Israel doing anything about it must in that case be seen as later theological reflection, that Yahweh kept his promise about the gift of the land without human intervention at the time of the Israelite entry.

As to Ai, it is striking that wherever this place-name appears in the Old Testament, with the exception of Jer. 49.3, it always occurs with the article, so that in translation it literally means 'the heap of ruins'. This designation accords with the results of archaeological investigation, from which it emerges that as early as about 2000 BC the place was completely devastated; it only became a small, unfortified settlement in about 1200.[87]

Albright's attempt to make the account of the conquest of Ai in Josh. 7–8 acceptable by explaining that this was really a military outpost (*et-tell*) of Bethel,[88] must be rejected. A 'solution' of this kind strongly suggests a desperate attempt to make the Old Testament into a historical account of events.

It seems most probable that this is an aetiological tradition[89] which seeks to give an explanation of the origin of 'the heap of ruins'. Furthermore, from a theological point of view, in many respects this account suggests that of Josh. 6.

5.5.4 *The alliance with the Gibeonites*

We find a characteristic example of the way in which the settlement in Canaan was not implemented only by force in Josh. 9, where there is mention of a treaty between Israel and Gibeon.[90] It is certain that Gibeon (*el-Jib*) had already existed for a long time in the period of Joshua.[91] According to Josh. 9.7; 11.19, the inhabitants of Gibeon were Hivites. There were three other cities in their territory as well as Gibeon (see Josh. 9.17).

We know virtually nothing about these Hivites. Joshua 9.11 suggests that they did not have the same organization as the Canaanite city states and that they were governed by elders instead of by a king. A treaty between Gibeon and Israel at an early stage is certainly within the realm of possibility. In support of this is perhaps the fact that the special position of the Gibeonites within Israel is constantly stressed in the Old Testament. Thus, for example, it is expressly said in II Sam. 21.2, in connection with the time of David, that they did not belong to Israel, and at this time such a remark is never made in connection with other peoples and groups like, say, the Jebusites.[92] They were clearly regarded at a later stage as having been integrated into Judah and Israel. In this connection it is significant that prominent Jebusites like Uriah the Hittite performed important functions at the time of David.[93] The infringement of the treaty with the Gibeonites by Saul referred to in II Sam. 21.1–14 could well indicate the existence of a similar treaty at an early period.

5.5.5 *The territory of the tribes of Machir and Dan*

Central Canaan is in the first instance the area occupied by Benjamin, Ephraim, Machir/Manasseh and Dan. We are given the boundaries of these tribes in Josh. 16–17; 18.11–26; 19.40–48. These sections are part of the lists in chs. 13–19 which, among other information, give the boundaries of the tribes. As Alt has convincingly demonstrated,[94] the descriptions of the boundaries in these chapters must go back to the time before the founding of the monarchy.

In this context, the change of territory of the tribes of Machir and Dan is remarkable. It is clear that the tribe of Machir was still settled west of the Jordan at the time of the Song of Deborah (Judg. 5). In this song, Machir (v. 14) is mentioned after Ephraim and Benjamin and before Zebulun, Issachar and Naphtali, and we may assume that this listing follows a geographical pattern. Later, however, there is mention only of Machir in Transjordan, as is evident, say, from Num. 32.39–40; Josh. 17.1.

According to Josh. 19.40–46; Judg. 1.34f.; Judg. 13—14 (Samson), the tribe of Dan is settled in central Canaan. However, in Judg. 18 we are told that the tribe of Dan is still in search of territory and then finds it in the north.[95] Probably Dan was driven out of central Canaan at a certain moment, as is indicated by Judg. 1.35 and possibly also Josh. 19.47–48. So the settlement in the north must have taken place at a later stage.[96] Furthermore, Dan had virtually no significance in the history of Israel. Presumably the tribe is a very ancient group.[97]

These facts about Machir and Dan indicate that the settlement in Canaan was not only a long-drawn-out but also a very complicated process.

5.6 *The settlement in the north*

The tribes of Issachar, Asher, Zebulun and Naphtali lived in the north.[98] We find only scanty information in the Old Testament about the time and manner in which they arrived there.

In Josh. 11.1–15 we hear of an expedition into this region under the leadership of Joshua, against a coalition which was led by Jabin king of Hazor. The result of this expedition was that Jabin and his allies were defeated and killed and that Hazor was devastated by Joshua. However, it is remarkable that in Judg. 4 we are told that in the time of Deborah and Barak the land was under the rule of Jabin, 'the king of Canaan, who ruled over Hazor' (v. 2). Here too there is mention of the annihilation of Jabin (v. 24). However, the scene of the battle varies. In Josh. 11.1–15 it is the hill-country of Galilee, and in Judg. 4 it is the plain of Jezreel. Furthermore, in Josh. 11.1–15 there is mention of 'all Israel' taking part in this battle and in Judg. 4 of Naphtali and Benjamin, whereas in

Judg. 5.14–18 Ephraim, Benjamin, Machir and Issachar are mentioned in this connection.

The question now is whether in Josh. 11; Judg. 4—5 we have two different versions of the same event or two accounts each describing a different event. Both views have their supporters and their critics.[99]

The fact that in Josh. 11 and Judg. 4 we have two totally different settings and that in fact the opponent in Judg. 4–5 is Sisera is the strongest argument for two different events.[100]

As to the destruction of Hazor, excavations seem in fact to have shown that the city was devastated in the Late Bronze Age.[101] However, that does not mean that it was done by the Israelites. It is just as possible that it happened as a result of the Sea Peoples, who destroyed many important cities in this period, including Alalakh and Ugarit.[102] But all this need not mean that in Josh. 11.1–15 there are no historical reminiscences which are connected with the whole question of the settlement in the north of Canaan.

For example, in Josh. 11.9 we hear that Joshua hamstrung the horses and burned the chariots with fire. This indicates that people clearly did not know what to do with them. Since horses were used in Israel only from the time of David, this could be an indication of an old tradition. Verse 10 could be a second important piece of information, with its comment, 'Hazor was formerly the head of all those kingdoms'. This fact corresponds with the Amarna letters, in which the king of Hazor is one of the Canaanite rulers actually to be called 'king'.[103] It indicates that the king of Hazor had an important position in the fourteenth century BC.

This could suggest that the nucleus of an old tradition has been preserved in Josh. 11.1–15, which speaks of a dispute between certain Israelite groups and Canaanites.

Obviously in this connection we should think especially of the northern tribes. Of these, Naphtali was closest to the territory of Hazor. Therefore it is not inconceivable that there is a reference in Josh. 11.1–15 to a conflict which flared up when Naphtali and other groups tried to leave the hill-country and move into more fertile areas.[104] This may have happened in a period when the power of the Canaanites in this region had been weakened by the rise of the Sea Peoples and Hazor was devastated. As to that last event, we are given no evidence in the only source we have, Josh. 11.1–15: it provides us with no further information in this connection.

5.7 *Dating*

There is no need to spend much time on the dating of the events which were discussed in the previous sections. We are almost completely in the dark about it, so I shall limit myself to just a few comments.

Certainly archaeological research has not given any indication that round about the thirteenth century BC a large-scale invasion of a new group of population was launched throughout Canaan.[105] What seems most likely is that small groups entered Canaan by their own routes and at different times. These will have included those groups who had been oppressed for a long period in Egypt. They were joined by other, perhaps kindred groups, which were probably entirely or partly indigenous to Canaan. In the time of David and Solomon there then came into being what later went down in the history of Israel as the kingdoms of Israel and Judah. All the original inhabitants of the country were incorporated into these groups. The origin of the two different kingdoms must be sought in geographical factors. Up to the time of David, the existence of the Jebusite kingdom made contacts between the southern and northern tribes extremely difficult.

We have three pieces of information about the time when the first Israelite groups settled in Canaan. The first is connected with a point which has already been made, namely that from the beginning of the thirteenth century BC there is evidence of Israelite towns in the hill country.[106] Secondly, we may reasonably conclude from the Merneptah stele that there was a group in Canaan round about 1200 BC which bore the name Israel.[107] We find a third piece of information in the Song of Deborah (Judg. 5). If this song is to be dated in about 1100 BC, as is generally accepted, it means that about this time a number of groups or tribes were more or less settled in Canaan.[108]

These three pieces of information show that already at the beginning of the Iron Age, various tribes who later came to make up Israel were already settled in the country. It seems certain that we must see the settlement in Canaan as being connected with the emergence of particular groups and tribes or of small combinations of tribes and groups.

5.8 The asssembly at Shechem

5.8.1 Shechem

Shechem was an extremely ancient Canaanite city. Its name is mentioned as early as texts from the nineteenth century BC[109] and already appears in the Amarna letters.[110]

From the time of the patriarchs down to the Samaritans, Shechem always had a significant role in the history of Israel. In the Old Testament it is first mentioned in connection with Abraham (Gen. 12.6–7) and later with Jacob. In the traditions of both these patriarchs there is mention of a sacred 'tree' at Shechem.[111]

Shechem lay in central Canaan, about thirty miles north of Jerusalem. In the Old Testament it is sometimes situated in the territory of Manasseh (Num. 26.31=P) and sometimes in the territory of Ephraim (Josh. 17.7; I Chron. 7.28). Probably the best explanation of the different locations is that Shechem lay on the frontier between these two tribes. Neither in the book of Joshua nor in Judg. 1 is Shechem mentioned among the cities conquered, nor does it appear in the list of cities in Josh. 13.1–7; Judg. 1.27–36 which the Israelites could not capture. This is presumably a strong indication that Shechem was inhabited by a group which had friendly relationships with the Israelites.[112]

5.8.2 *The information in Josh. 24*

So far, research into the origin and dating of Josh. 24 has not led to any unanimous result.[113] It is, however, clear that this chapter has undergone Deuteronomistic revision, as is already evident in the first verse, which mentions 'all the tribes of Israel'.

Apart from this, there is general agreement that this chapter may contain early traditions. This is particularly true of vv. 25–27.[114] These verses mention the making of a covenant,[115] legislation which was established in this connection, and a stone which was set up under the 'tree' in the holy place.

There is much to suggest that these traditions go back to a real historical reminiscence from the time of Joshua. One important factor is Schmitt's comment that the significance of Shechem declines during the period of the judges in favour of Shiloh.[116]

5.8.3 *The making of the covenant in Shechem*

It is even more difficult to discover how this covenant was made and precisely what it implied. Opinions on the question differ. According to Rowley,[117] Josh. 24 reproduces an ancient tradition which describes an agreement between the ancestors of the Israelites and the Canaanites; what he has in mind here is above all the agreement reported in Gen. 34. Noth sees this event as being the origin of the amphictyony of the twelve tribes,[118] and de Vaux sees it as an agreement between the group to which Joshua belonged and the tribes from the north, which at all events included Zebulon and Issachar. According to de Vaux, the northern tribes had not been in Egypt and did not know Yahweh. Hence the summons in vv. 14–15, which also reproduces an old tradition, to put away alien gods and serve Yahweh.[119] Finally, Fohrer thinks in terms of an event in which the 'Joseph tribe' (with or without Benjamin) promised to serve Yahweh.[120]

This difference of opinion illustrates how little can be assumed with any certainty. It is clear that there can be no question of an agreement in which all the Israelite tribes throughout Canaan were involved (see 5.8.2 above). Because of their geographical dispersion, an undertaking of this kind would certainly have been impossible in a relatively early period.

It seems most likely that among the groups who assembled at Shechem there were some who did not know Yahweh and who served strange gods. If we consider all this, there is perhaps most to be said for the view of de Vaux, though its hypothetical character cannot be denied. In that case a meeting of this kind, of course involving only a limited group and the making of a covenant at Shechem, could have taken place at the end of the thirteenth century BC.[121] Given the fact that at a somewhat later period (*c.* 1100 BC) there is already mention in the Song of Deborah (Judg. 5) of a kind of tribal community, particularly involving tribes from central and northern Canaan, this dating is to be preferred.

It is clear that whatever happened at Shechem occupied a considerable period and was not just one special day. Furthermore, in view of what has been said, it is also evident that the assembly at Shechem did not take place on the basis of an *a priori* religious conviction shared by the whole group. In the first instance, the primary reasons for the assembly must have been social, political and economic interests. These were the factors which over the course of history constantly brought the tribes closer together and compelled them to collaborate. This is evident above all in the later development of the history of Israel. The fact that religion played an important role here, particularly among groups which came out of Egypt, is especially relevant.

Chapter 6

The Period of the Judges

6.1 *The political and economic situation*

This question need not take up much of our time. The developments outlined in the first section of the previous chapter also influenced the political and economic situation in the time of the judges. Thus for example it appears from the account of the travels of Wen-Amun about 1076 BC[1] that the weakening of Egyptian power and influence in Syria and Canaan also continued in the period between about 1200 and 1050 BC.

When we consider all this, we should not be surprised that in the book of Judges,[2] the period of the judges is described as an extremely turbulent one. That suggests that although the book was subjected at least to a later Deuteronomistic revision and thus was given a specific theological framework, it may well provide authentic information about the period.

It seems certain that at the beginning of the period of the judges,[3] only a small part of Canaan was settled by Israelite tribes or groups, and that in terms of culture, politics and society, for a long time the Canaanites were still the most important population group in the region.[4]

In the time of the judges the various Israelite tribes and groups settled in Canaan still seem to have lacked any kind of mutual bond. As we saw in the previous chapter, only now and then can there have been some kind of common enterprise by a number of tribes.

At a later time the mutual bond between the tribes seems primarily to have been furthered by the struggle against common enemies. Among these, the Philistines, who had settled particularly in the coastal plain, came increasingly to the fore.[5] It was they above all who in the long run forced the Israelite tribes towards centralization, a process in which first of all the northern tribes and later the tribe of Judah came to occupy an increasingly dominant position.[6]

In the first instance, however, the conflicts mentioned in the book of Judges primarily took place locally, in a geographically limited area. In the older traditions the judges are above all saviours who rid their group or tribe of oppressors.[7]

It seems highly improbable that the relationship between the Israelites and the Canaanites in the time of the judges was such that the Israelites did not want to, or were not allowed to, have any association with their neighbours.[8] Rather, we must assume that both Israelites and Canaanites, who were each increasingly dependent on the Philistines in economic and military matters,[9] usually maintained very good relations at this time. This may have come about above all because the power of the city states, which was at one time considerable, was gradually diminishing. The chief reason for this development was probably that agriculture in the hill country was taking on increasing importance.[10] That meant that the Israelite settlements (cities) in this area began to play a steadily more important role which produced a kind of political equilibrium, particularly in the time of the judges. Only in the time of David and Solomon do the Canaanites seem increasingly to have been forced into a minority position. In this period, conflicts between these two groups in the population seem to have been heightened.

All in all, the time of the judges seems to have been a tumultuous and dynamic period. This aspect clearly emerges from the book of Judges. In view of what has been said above, it is hardly conceivable that this view of the period in question is to be attributed to the Deuteronomistic revision of the book. The Deuteronomist simply put what material he had from this period in a particular framework, and this gave the book of Judges, among other things, a marked pro-monarchical colouring. This comes out above all at the end (Judg. 21.25), with the saying, 'In those days there was no king in Israel: every man did what was good in his own eyes.'

However, it is difficult to avoid the impression that the book also gives quite a realistic picture of the political and social situation in Canaan in the time before the rise of the monarchy.[11]

6.2 *The judges*

6.2.1 *The so-called 'minor judges'*

There has been a good deal of discussion over a long period about the judges whose stories are told in Judg. 3.7 – ch. 16. An important position in this discussion is occupied by M. Noth. Noth developed the thesis that we must make a distinction between the 'minor' and the 'major' judges. According to him, only the former, the minor judges, were judges in the strict sense of the word: i.e., only they gave judgements. On the basis of Micah 4.14, Noth then concludes that this office of judge already existed before the time of David in the context of the amphictyony, and that it still continued to exist even in the period of the monarchy.[12]

A number of doubts have been raised about this theory of Noth's. Thus in languages related to Hebrew the verb *špt*, with which the word *šopēt*, judge, is connected, does not so much have the specific meaning of 'give judgment'; it means, rather, 'rule', 'exercise lordship'.[13] Now it is clear that these things also go together in the Old Testament.[14] The one who rules or emerges as leader also gives judgment, as is the case, say, with the figure of the king[15] and the elders of Israel. Therefore one cannot argue for a specific office of judge in the strictly juridical sense simply from the use of the word judge.

We find information about the minor judges in the Old Testament only in Judg. 10.1–5; 12.8–15. There we find successive mention of the judges Tola (10.1–2), Jair (10.3–5), Ibzan (12.8–10), Elon (12.11–12) and Abdon (12.13–15). It is already evident from this list that very little was handed down about these so-called minor judges.[16] All that is said of them is that they 'judged Israel'; otherwise, we are told only of their families and the places where they were buried.

One can assume that four of these judges must have been very well-to-do. Except in the case of Elon, we are told that they had many children. This implies that they also must have had several wives – a sign of prosperity in this period.

The territory within which they emerged as judges seems usually limited to their home or a slightly wider region. If we assume that the birthplace of Ibzan is meant to be Bethlehem in Zebulun, all these minor judges come from the territory which comprised the state of Israel after the death of Solomon. This is not surprising, given the fact that Judah began to play a significant role in the history of Israel and in the Old Testament only with the rise of David.

As to the precise function of these judges, the information in the Old Testament does not get us any further. At best we can say that in all probability they were influential figures in their immediate surroundings.

6.2.2 *The so-called 'major judges'*

More can be said about the figures referred to as the major judges. Here the question is who we must include. The following come under consideration in Judges: Othniel, Ehud, Deborah, Barak, Gideon, Jephthah and Samson. In addition, however, we might also mention Samuel and, very probably, Eli.[17]

Attempts to combine these figures with the so-called minor judges and Shamgar to form a group of twelve do not seem very fruitful, particularly bearing in mind the completely different conclusions to which people come as a result.[18] One can arrive at this number only by keeping to the judges who are mentioned in the framework of the book of Judges.[19] Here, however, we would do well to remember that in this respect we have a theological construction on the part of the Deuteronomist. That also goes for the fact that the actions of the judges have not been put in chronological order, and for the chronological notes which are given in connection with the judges. The use of the period of forty years (or divisions or multiples of it) is also characteristic here.[20]

These judges mostly exercised their functions in their immediate neighbourhood. However, in some cases, as with Deborah (Barak), Gideon, Eli and Samuel, their sphere of activity seems to extend further than that of their own tribe. So what was in fact the function of the great judges?

We have already seen that the verb *špt* primarily points in the direction of 'giving leadership'. A meaning of this kind can, however, have different aspects. We can also see this in the case of the judges who are mentioned, in so far as the Old Testament actually gives us information about them. With some, the military aspect comes to the fore, and with others (Eli and Samuel) this feature is completely absent. Many are also involved in the cult (Deborah, Gideon, Jephthah, Eli and Samuel). However, the most important aspect is that of political leadership,[21] and this doubtless (see 6.2.1) also implies the giving of judgments. This last aspect is particularly stressed in all the more recent studies of the judges.[22]

It is possible that the judges emerged from among the elders of the city in which they lived.[23] As we know, for a long time these elders had an important role, in the period before the rise of the monarchy and then still at least during its early days. This democratic institution seems to have continued still longer, above all in Israel (the later northern kingdom).[24]

6.3 *Relations with the Canaanites*

Two accounts call for our attention here. The first is that of the battle against Sisera narrated in Judg. 4–5, and the second concerns the events narrated in Judg. 9.

6.3.1 *The battle against Sisera*

We have already seen in the previous chapter (5.6) that the real opponent in Judg. 4; 5 is not Jabin of Hazor, but Sisera. Now is this Sisera to be regarded as a Canaanite? On this point opinions differ. Both Alt[25] and Albright[26] think that the name Sisera indicates that the person concerned is a leader of the Sea Peoples. However, this is by no means certain. The investigation by Gröndahl[27] into the name Sisera has proved completely inconclusive, and de

Vaux[28] rightly points out that there is no reference whatsoever to the Sea Peoples in Judg. 4. It seems most likely that in Judg. 4; 5 we have a small-scale, local confrontation with Canaanites.[29]

It is difficult for us to form an exact picture of what actually happened. As well as the Song of Deborah in Judg. 5 we also have the prose account in Judg. 4. The latter mentions only Naphtali and Zebulun (Judg. 4.6, 10) as the tribes which take part in the battle against Sisera. In Judg. 5, on the other hand, Ephraim, Benjamin, Machir and Issachar are mentioned in this connection. Some scholars have put forward the view that the Song of Deborah is a festal liturgy celebrating the victory of Naphtali and Zebulun mentioned in Judg. 5.18. In that case the mention of the tribes in Judg. 5.14–17 has no connection with the battle against Sisera, but relates solely to whether or not these tribes took part in this festal liturgy.[30] This interpretation does not seem very convincing.[31] We have no evidence whatsoever for the existence of such a feast. It certainly seems likely that Naphtali and Zebulun played a principal role in the battle against Sisera and that the other tribes mentioned in Judg. 5.14–17 played a very incidental role in the matter.

It is extremely difficult to establish in which of the two traditions, Judg. 4 or 5, the earliest traditions about the event have been preserved. In any case, here we have two independent traditions. Both talk of a confrontation with the Canaanites in the plain of Jezreel. In all probability this took place in the period between about 1200 and 1100 BC.[32]

6.3.2 *The rise of Abimelech*

Judges 9 describes how Abimelech was called to be king in Shechem. He was a son of Jerubbaal (Gideon) and a woman from Shechem. The fact that he could become king in his mother's city might indicate that Gideon's wife came from the leading circles of Shechem.

Abimelech, we are told, killed all seventy sons of Jerubbaal with the exception of the youngest, Jotham, who was able to hide.[33] Abimelech was able to maintain his rule in Shechem for about three years, albeit with difficulty, since he came up against constant opposition there. When he went on to try to take over the city of Tebes, about ten miles north-east of Shechem, he met with his death.[34]

It is clear that this account, too, shows traces of a later, primarily theological redaction. Thus Crüsemann[35] has rightly shown that two figures are contrasted in the link between Judg. 6–8 and 9, one who does not want to be king and saves his people with the help of Yahweh (Gideon), and the other who seeks the kingship and brings his subjects death and destruction (Abimelech). In a later period this picture must have been presented to the people as two alternatives. However, that does not mean that old information has not been preserved in this account.

It is inconceivable, for example, that at a later period people would speak in such a matter-of-fact way about a 'marriage' between Gideon and a Shechemite woman. Furthermore, archaeological data suggest that Shechem was destroyed in the course of the twelfth century BC.[36] This devastation could be connected with the attack by Abimelech mentioned in Judg. 9.45. Again, the fact that Judg. 9 suggests that not all the inhabitants of Shechem wanted too close a link with the Israelites seems a likely pointer to the time of the judges. So the opposition to Abimelech, who was of mixed Israelite and Canaanite descent, led by Gaal, could very well go back to an ancient tradition.

6.4 *Conflicts with other peoples*

It is striking that the accounts of the actions of the judges mentioned in the previous section have been put in a particular theological framework deriving from the Deuteronomist. Each story begins with a mention of Israel's apostasy[37] and ends with the report that the land now had rest for a number of years.[38] We shall now consider the judges in connection with their various opponents.

6.4.1 *Cushan-rishathaim*

The judge who came to the fore against Cushan-rishathaim, a king of Mesopotamia, is Othniel (Judg. 3.7–11). Here Othniel is called a kinsman of Caleb (v. 9). At the same time this is the only occasion on which we probably have mention of a judge from Judah! However, the account in Judg. 3.7–11, which has strong Deuteronomistic colouring, gives us no information about the time and the circumstances in which the events narrated here took place.[39] Furthermore, the figures of both Othniel and his opponent remain completely in the shadows.

6.4.2 *Moabites*

Ehud, a judge from Benjamin, fights against Moabites, Ammonites and Amalekites (Judg. 3.12–30) who had conquered the 'city of palms' (v. 13).[40] The two last-mentioned people are mentioned only in this verse, so that we must assume that the actual opponents were the Moabites and their king Eglon. It is not clear what precisely is meant by the 'city of palms'. This may be another name for Jericho. According to the Old Testament, this city remained devastated between the time of Joshua and that of Ahab. Furthermore, archaeological evidence seems to show that Jericho was not inhabited again before the seventh century BC, although a tomb has been found there dating from the tenth century BC.[41] Apart from this, however, it seems possible that in Judg. 3.13 there is an allusion to an occupation of the oasis of Jericho. That is perhaps why there is a mention here of the 'city of palms' rather than Jericho.

The information in this pericope also suggests that the Moabites occupied only this region. Furthermore, it seems probable that only Benjamin was involved in the action mentioned in Judg. 3.12–30. If that is the case, this rise of Moab must have taken place at a very early period – the beginning of the twelfth century BC,[42] at a time when Benjamin was still a powerful tribe.

6.4.3 *Midianites*

As well as mention of the Midianites, in Judg. 6–8 there are also several mentions of Amalekites and 'the tribes from the East'. However, the real oppressors in this account seem always to be the Midianites. The fact that these Midianites could make their plundering forays into Canaan indicates that at that time not only the Egyptian power but also that of the Canaanite city states had been weakened. This could mean that these forays took place at a later period than the events narrated in Judg. 4 and 5. In connection with this, Bright[43] also points to the devastation of Shechem by Abimelech. In that case the battle against the Midianites would have taken place in a much later period.

These Midianites were finally defeated by a judge who is sometimes called Gideon and sometimes Jerubbaal. It is possible that both these names are given to the same person.[44] Gideon's victory seems to be firmly rooted in the tradition, as is evident e.g. in Isa. 9.4; 10.26; Ps. 83.10. Evidently this confrontation remained a vivid memory as an important and decisive event from the time of the judges.

The first encounter between Gideon and the Midianites took place by the brook Harod, i.e. close to the entrance to the plain of Jezreel and perhaps not far from Gideon's home in Ophrah.[45] After this, we are then told in Judg. 8.4–21, Gideon pursued the Midianites into Transjordan, and that evidently signified the end of the period of oppression by the Midianites.[46]

It is possible that in Judg. 6.33—7.25 and 8.4–21 we have two independent traditions about the victory over Midian.[47] This would suggest all the more that here we do in fact have a historical event.

6.4.4 *Ammonites*

The fight against the Ammonites was led by the judge Jephthah, who came from Gilead. Because he was not a son of his father's wife (i.e. his chief wife), he was cast out by his brothers (Judg. 11.2). After that Jephthah became the leader of a group of people who led a wandering life, as did David and his followers later, in the hill country of Judah, when they were sought by Saul. At the request of the elders of Gilead Jephthah later undertook a campaign against the Ammonites (Judg. 11.5-33). According to de Vaux,[48] this conflict with the Ammonites took place early in the period of the judges. Bright[49] thinks rather in terms of the end of this period.[50]

6.4.5 *Philistines*

The main opponents of the Israelites in the period of the judges and long afterwards were without doubt the Philistines.[51] These Philistines had settled in the coastal plain and had formed a coalition of five cities in the south of it.[52]. There were increasing conflicts in the twelfth and eleventh centuries BC between the Philistines and the groups or tribes which later came to form Israel.

The Philistines had the initial advantage in this confrontation. We know that they were one of the first peoples to learn how to use the materials provided by the new period (the Iron Age). They quickly made use of iron objects for both military and technical purposes, and also of horses, which were only introduced into Israel on a large scale at the time of Solomon.[53] It was above all thanks to the use of iron that they were able to extend their territory significantly in the twelfth and eleventh centuries BC. This expansion extended both to the north and to the east. It was probably as a result of it that the tribe of Dan also had to leave its original territory and move northwards (see also 5.5.5).[54]

If we leave Shamgar out of account,[55] we find no less than three judges mentioned in the Old Testament in connection with the Philistines: Samson (Judg. 13—16), Eli (I Sam. 4) and Samuel (I Sam. 7). The story of Samson, from the tribe of Dan, has still maintained the marked character of a popular tale in its Old Testament context. It is possible that the background to these accounts of individual actions by Samson was formed by events which took place before the rise of the monarchy, in the border territory between the Philistines and the Israelite tribes.[56] The account in Judg. 15.15-17 to some degree resembles that of Shamgar in Judg. 3.31 and of Shammah in II Sam. 23.11f. Only in the time of Eli and Samuel does there seem really to be mention of a larger-scale confrontation between Israelites and Philistines.

In I Sam. 4 we learn how the Philistines managed to defeat the Israelites at Aphek. The suggestion that on this occasion the sanctuary of Shiloh was also destroyed by the Philistines[57] has not in any event been confirmed by the results of archaeological research.[58] Nor do we find any pointer in this direction in I Sam. 4. It seems likely, though, that this was a decisive victory which for a long time put the Philistines in a position of domination over the Israelite tribes. According to the Old Testament tradition, however, this did not represent a definitive establishment of Philistine rule throughout Canaan. At least Transjordan and the north (Galilee) fell outside the Philistine sphere of influence.

We also hear in I Sam. 4 that the ark was taken into battle against the Philistines. This is very striking, seeing that it does not have any role elsewhere in the Old Testament tradition in connection with the period of the judges. It must be very seriously doubted whether the account in I Sam. 4 does in fact rest on a historical tradition. Only in the time of David does the ark seem to begin to occupy an important part in worship.

The defeat at Aphek is generally dated to about 1050 BC.[59] A number of years after the defeat at Aphek, the Israelite tribes were again able to record a successful action against the Philistines (I Sam. 7). According to the tradition this took place at Mizpah. Mizpah fell within the territory of Benjamin and seems to have been occupied again for the first time after a long period during the eleventh century BC.[60] Thus it is quite possible that I Sam. 7 preserves an old tradition. According to it, Samuel was the central inspiration in all these events.

We may conclude from this information that resistance against the Philistines continued. The result of this resistance was that at a later stage Israelite tribes increasingly began to form a unity.

6.5   Religion

6.5.1   The ark

From the Old Testament tradition we get the impression that in fact the ark had no significant role in the period of the judges. This seems a plausible assumption. At any rate, it is difficult to conceive that a later tradition would keep silent about the significance of the ark before this period, given its significance in the time of David.

The only mention of the ark in the book of Judges is the report that it stood in Bethel and that the Israelites took counsel of the Lord there (Judg. 20.27). In I Sam. 3 and 4, the ark seems to be located in Shiloh. We are not told where it stood in Bethel, but on the basis of I Sam. 1.9—3.3 we may assume that the ark was set up in a permanent sanctuary in Shiloh.[61] This sanctuary is also mentioned in Judg. 18.31. We should perhaps conclude from this that the ark which according to Josh. 4.16–19 first stood in Gilgal was later placed in Bethel and finally in Shiloh. It is uncertain whether the ark was also put in Shechem, as might seem indicated by Josh. 8.33.[62] However, it is certain that in the period of the judges there was still no centralization of the cult.[63] That is equally true of the time of Samuel and Saul.[64] This centralization of the cult only starts, as so often in history, after political unification, which begins to be implemented in the time of David and Solomon.

6.5.2 *Holy places and sanctuaries*

A large number of holy places are mentioned in connection with the time of the judges, as they are, for example, in connection with the patriarchs. We have the 'sacred tree' under which Deborah sat (Judg. 4.5), the 'terebinth at Ophrah' where Gideon was called (Judg. 6.11), the 'terebinth of the pillar' at Shechem where Abimelech was called to be 'king' (Judg. 9.6), Beth-shemesh where the ark was put after its return from the land of the Philistines (I Sam. 6.12–15),[65] and the high place at Ramah (I Sam. 9).[66]

Particular sanctuaries, as well as holy places, are also mentioned in connection with this period. Thus we hear in Judg. 17—18[67] about the founding of two sanctuaries, first that of Micah the Ephraimite (Judg. 17.1ff.) and then the sanctuary at Dan (Judg. 18.30–31).[68]

All these examples show that people felt quite free to talk about all kinds of holy places and sanctuaries in connection with Israelite worship in the Old Testament literature which describes the period before the kings. This strongly suggests that this information has not been worked over by the Deuteronomist and that it goes back to old traditions. We also see that important events took place at these sanctuaries. For example, sacrificial meals were held there (see e.g. I Sam. 1.4ff.), important political decisions were taken, and a king was chosen (I Sam. 10.17–24).

Shiloh also seems to have been an important sanctuary in the period of the judges. Here the 'house of Eli' principally comes to the fore. After the death of Eli, the role of Shiloh seems to have come to an end. At all events, it is striking that Samuel who, according to the information in I Sam. 1–3, seems in all respects to be nominated the successor of Eli, exercised his function as judge after Eli's death in Bethel, Gilgal, Mizpah and above all in Ramah (I Sam. 7.15–17). By contrast, as late as the time of Solomon (I Kings 11.29–39), the prophet Ahijah from Shiloh comes strongly to the fore in the appointment of Jeroboam I as king over the ten tribes of Israel.[69]

The information about Shiloh is probably tradition from the northern kingdom which hardly took precedence in the final redaction of the literature of this period (which was made in Judah). This is presumably in turn connected with the fact that in Shiloh there was evidently a strongly hostile feeling about the Jerusalem cultic traditions. It seems no coincidence, moreover, that in the later stories about Samuel there is no further mention about his past association with Shiloh.[70] Samuel is primarily the figure connected with the rise of the monarchy and then above all with the rise of David, who came from Judah.[71]

Thus we find a very varied picture of worship in the time of the judges. It emerges from all this that there can be no question of a unity here.

The picture of worship in this period can be said to be not only varied but also vague. Thus we still find traces of the existence of a Nazirate (Samson and Samuel) and perhaps of seers (cf. I Sam. 9.9). However, these traces do not take us any further, and the vague information about these groups in the period described does not help us to discover their origins. In this respect, too, the time of the judges remains an obscure one.

Chapter 7

The Rise of the Monarchy

7.1 *The request for a king*

In I Sam. 8.5 the elders approach Samuel with a request for him to appoint a king over them. We read at the beginning of the chapter that the occasion for this request is the corruption of Samuel's sons, who function as judges in Beersheba. This seems unmistakably to be an early, pre-Deuteronomistic tradition,[1] and suggests that although we cannot go into the origins in any detail, there were already groups during the time of the judges who wanted a king.

It was probably above all the Philistines who had furthered this request. Philistine pressure and the many conflicts with them could have increased the need for a more central authority. At the same time, the result of all this was that relations between kindred (Israelite) tribes and with the Canaanites steadily improved,[2] since the latter suffered just as much under the dominant position of the Philistines. In a later period there is even increasing mention of a coming together of these two groups. This last development begins to take place especially in the time of David and Solomon.

In the meantime there was no lack of opponents of the monarchy. We find one indication of this in Judg. 8.22–23, where 'men of Israel' offer Gideon the hereditary monarchy. In many respects Gideon's refusal corresponds with the attitude of Samuel in I Sam. 8.[3] For this reason it is assumed that this so-called Gideon saying comes from the time of Samuel.[4]

At all events, the purpose of the composition of Judg. 8.22–23 is to make Gideon produce some disclaimers to Abimelech's kingship (Judg. 9). An extremely important role is also played in this connection by the whole context of Judg. 8 and 9, and above all by Jotham's fable (Judg. 9.8–15). Crüsemann rightly points out that the words of and about the thorn (Judg. 9.15b) are of decisive importance in this context. The point of this saying is that the monarchy is unproductive and provides neither shadow nor fruit.[5]

The opposition to kingship certainly has old roots, and is not least associated with a change in the ancient structures which went with it. In the long run, the kingship primarily meant an increase of scale, and this implied that smaller communities like family and tribe would increasingly lose their significance. It also implied that the old forms of social organization based primarily on solidarity and collective responsibility gradually faded into the background.[6]

All this is very probably also the background to the sayings about the rights of the king which are expressed in I Sam. 8.10–18 (cf. also Deut. 17.14–20). These sayings, which presumably recall the measures taken by Solomon,[7] have a very negative tone. It is clearly meant here that the king will appropriate to himself the rights that are mentioned.[8] Such a course of action would naturally come into opposition to the principles on which the old structures were based.

The immediate juxtaposition of different views for and against the monarchy in the Deuteronomistic history work strongly suggests that this work incorporates different ancient Israelite traditions.[9] Here one can at least point to the historical fact that in the time before the monarchy there was a growing sense that central leadership and organization was necessary to cope with various problems. Here political considerations played the principal role. Only when political unification was complete, under David, did centralization of the cult also come into consideration.

7.2 *The choice of Saul*

We have three reports of the way in which Saul became king. In the first (I Sam. 9.1–10.16) we are told that Samuel anointed Saul secretly, at Ramah; in the second (I Sam. 10.17–27) Saul was called to be king in Mizpah; and in the third (I Sam. 11) this happened at Gilgal.[10] Thus in the tradition we have three different accounts of the beginning of Saul's kingship. This must certainly mean that some old traditions have been included in the composition of the books of Samuel as we now have them. Here we must take into account that all these accounts are coloured by later views of the kingship and theological reflections on it. All this makes it extremely difficult for us to form a real picture of precisely what happened.

One great problem is how Saul succeeded in wresting the city of Jabesh in Gilead from the Ammonites (I Sam. 11). To do this he must have travelled through territory occupied by the Philistines. The messengers from Jabesh even came to Saul in Gibeah, where we know that there was a Philistine garrison.[11] It is possible that for one reason or another the Philistines connived at Saul's operation.[12] However, we have no certain information. Nevertheless, perhaps I Sam. 11 provides one point of contact which might give us some insight into the way in which Saul became king.

Saul is clearly regarded as a transitional figure. The way in which he takes initiatives and goes to fight against the Ammonites in I Sam. 11 strongly suggests the figure of a judge.[13] This might indicate that in I Sam. 11.1–11.15 we possibly have not only the earliest but also a very trustworthy tradition about the beginning of the reign of Saul.[14]

Now according to I Sam. 11.15 the place where Saul was made king was Gilgal. This place was in an area which was not under the direct control of the Philistines.

It is striking that in I Sam. 9.16 and 10.1 it is emphatically said that Saul was anointed *nagīd* (and not king). There is still dispute over the meaning of this word *nagīd*. Recent studies seem to suggest that the original meaning of the word was that the person so described had been designated 'heir' or 'crown prince'[15] by the reigning king. The earliest text in which it appears in this sense is I Kings 1.35.[16] In I Sam. 9.16; 10.1 we presumably have a more theological use of the term which comes from a later period, in which the main stress is on the divine appointment of the future king.[17]

One important question concerns the region over which Saul becomes king. It was certainly very limited. In the first place, most of Canaan was occupied by the Philistines. Furthermore, in none of the stories about the choice of Saul is there a single word about Judah and the other southern tribes, far less about those from the north.

Perhaps the three separate accounts of the choice of Saul give us some information here.[18] Thus I Sam. 10.17–27 might indicate that at any rate Saul's own tribe of Benjamin formed part of Saul's territory. The same is probably the case with Ephraim. Saul was anointed *nagīd* in the territory of Ephraim (I Sam. 9.1—10.16). As well as Benjamin and Ephraim, Gilead may also have belonged to Saul's territory, given the fact that Saul liberated Jabesh in Gilead (I Sam. 11).

A kingdom embracing these territories would also correspond, roughly speaking, with the list in II Sam. 2.9 which, with the exception of the conclusion of that verse, could belong to an old tradition.[19] Perhaps Gibeah was the capital of this kingdom. At any rate, archaeological investigations seem to indicate that Saul had a fortress here.[20] However, there are also indications that Saul attempted to make Gibeon his capital.[21] In this connection reference is made to II Sam. 21.1–14, in which we are told that David handed over seven descendants of Saul to the Gibeonites so that they could avenge themselves of Saul. Some scholars[22] think that this refers to an attempt by Saul to take control of Gibeon, causing a great blood-bath. However, that is far from certain. There is perhaps more reason to suppose that here David was seeking an occasion to rid himself of Saul's descendants, so that they could not pose any threat to his throne.[23]

This event bears witness to the sharp conflict between Saul and David. According to the Old Testament tradition, Saul was involved in this very soon after he had been chosen king. In this context Saul primarily plays the role of David's adversary.[24] It all makes Saul a tragic figure in the Old Testament. However, we should do well to bear in mind that the story of Saul's kingship and above all his conflict with David arose in circles which were very favourably disposed towards David.

We shall come back to this problem in one of the later sections. First, however, we must consider the relationship between Samuel and Saul.

7.3 *Samuel and Saul*

Samuel is portrayed for us in the Old Testament tradition as a many-sided figure.[25] He is called prophet (e.g. I Sam. 3.20), man of God (e.g. I Sam. 9.6), seer (I Sam. 9.11) and judge (e.g. I Sam. 7.15). The word priest is never used in connection with him.

We find an account of Samuel's attitude to the monarchy and to Saul in I Sam. 7–15.[26] Broadly speaking, this attitude can be said to be critical. Here Samuel has a position which we constantly come up against in the history of Israel in connection with the figure of the prophet. In it we repeatedly see the prophet functioning as critic of the king.[27] Of itself, that need not mean that in the case of Samuel we have a back-projection of the situation of a later period. Rather, we must reckon with the possibility that from the beginning critical voices had been raised in prophetic circles against the institution of the monarchy. So this cannot be characterized as a product of Deuteronomistic theology, but is rather a reflection of the differences in social structure in the periods before and after the rise of the monarchy.[28]

Throughout the complex of stories in I Sam. 7–15 we find on Samuel's part a reserved, if not negative, attitude towards the institution of the monarchy. This also seems the best explanation of the total break which develops between Saul and Samuel. We might identify two possible causes for this clash between the two men. First of all, Samuel may have been concerned with a new political institution, given also the position of the Canaanite city kings. It is conceivable that Samuel was afraid that in the long term Saul would exercise too much power. Secondly, we cannot exclude the possibility of personal rivalry between them.[29]

We should probably also consider I Sam. 13.4b—15, where Saul offers a sacrifice, in this light. Such an account, in which a king is rebuked for offering a sacrifice, can hardly be attributed to the Deuteronomist, seeing that later kings, like Solomon (I Kings 8), often perform functions which in later times were reserved for priests, without the Deuteronomist uttering a word of criticism.[30] So it is very possible that in I Sam. 13.4–15 we have elements of an old tradition[31] which preserved the recollection of an ancient dispute over the competence of the king in the sphere of worship. This is a conflict which may have arisen, for example, at the beginning of the monarchy.

On the other hand, we should not lose sight of the fact that the later redaction, favourably disposed towards David, has given the conflict between Samuel and Saul a brighter colouring than it originally possessed. At all events, it is striking that to the end of his reign Saul clearly had the support of virtually all his people.

7.4 *Saul and David*

The cycle of stories in the Old Testament which is largely concerned with the confrontation between Saul and David is generally referred to as the 'History of the Rise of David' (roughly speaking I Sam. 16.14–II Sam. 5.25). However, not everyone is convinced that this is an independent complex of stories.[32] And there is a lack of agreement among those who hold this view as to the exact extent of this cycle.

We cannot go more deeply into these questions,[33] but must begin from the general consensus that the stories have some degree of originality and were handed down not too long after the events described in them. However, there is not the least doubt that above all their final redaction took place in circles which were well disposed towards David – not so much David the man as the idealized figure of David. Still, there are also parts which bear witness to a sympathetic attitude towards Saul, like I Sam. 31. Such passages show that other voices can be heard behind the text in its present form.

Saul's jealousy is given as the most important reason for the dissension between Saul and David (cf. e.g. I Sam. 18.6–9); also the fact that Saul was mentally sick (see e.g. I Sam. 16.14–16; 19.9).

It is difficult to suppose that Saul's jealousy was of decisive significance. It emerges clearly from the tradition in the books of Samuel that Saul was far from being unpopular with the people and he evidently had considerable influence. At all events, the fugitive David finds little support, and must finally even seek refuge with the Philistines, because he cannot survive in the hill country of Judah.

It is also difficult to reconcile Saul's popularity and influence with his supposed fluctuations of mood. Rather, we may suppose that the 'History of the Rise of David' is a kind of apologetic, theological writing.[34] It is particularly striking how favourably the picture of David is drawn over against that of Saul.[35] David is the only one who can bring Saul peace; he is a great warrior, a hero, and extremely clever (see I Sam. 16.18ff.). By contrast, Saul is possessed by an evil spirit (I Sam. 16.14).

In this connection it is striking that in I Sam. 17 David is portrayed as the victor over Goliath and is celebrated as a great hero, whereas this same tradition in II Sam. 21.19 is ascribed to Elhanan, who comes from Bethlehem.[36]

These few examples already show the apologetic character of these stories. Their clear aim is to justify David's kingship and to indicate that he did not wrest it from Saul illegally. We must also see in this light the texts which stress that David always regarded Saul as the lawful king (see e.g. I Sam. 24.7; 26.9–11). I Samuel 24.12 deserves special attention in this respect. Here David addresses Saul as 'my father', and Saul in turn addresses David as 'my son' (I Sam. 24.17).[37] Scholars have wanted to see this as an ancient Near Eastern formula of adoption.[38] If that is the case, it would mean that Saul regarded David as his adopted son. This could then imply that David could be seen as a legitimate successor to Saul. However, an adoption in this sense never occurs in the Old Testament.[39] We do, though, find a clear example in the Hittite texts, in which there is mention of the adoption of a crown prince,[40] so it is not impossible that the relevant texts in I Sam. 24 (and 26) must be regarded as an attempt to designate David Saul's lawful successor. This is not improbable, also given the fact that David clearly thought it important to marry into Saul's family. This is quite evident from David's request to Abner, above all to bring him back Michal, Saul's daughter (II Sam. 3.13).[41] At a later period, when his authority was definitively established, this concern evidently (see e.g. II Sam. 6) faded right into the background.

One of the groups supporting David in his confrontation with Saul was evidently the priestly group at Nob. This context might also explain the murder of the priests in Nob narrated in I Sam. 22.6–23. This story, in which above all the priest Abiathar (who also comes clearly to the fore at a later date) plays an important part, may certainly contain early material.[42]

We shall study in more detail in the next chapter the way in which David finally succeeded in taking the place of Saul and his lawful successors.

7.5 *The end of Saul*

During his reign, which probably lasted longer than two years,[43] Saul was confronted with a series of problems. In the previous section we have already considered his conflicts with Samuel and David. However, the Old Testament does not give the impression that these conflicts were of decisive significance for Saul. Two other factors affected him more: problems of organization and fighting with the Philistines.

7.5.1 *Problems of organization*

We find nothing in the Old Testament tradition which in any way seems to indicate that Saul had much feeling for organization or diplomacy. Yet these were the two characteristics with which his opponent and successor David was extremely well endowed.[44] David is the cool and calculating figure who knows how to bide his time. By contrast, Saul has with some justification been called the 'peasant king', and is to be seen more as a charismatic leader. Compared with David, the organizer, Saul appears as more of an impulsive leader. This is indicated, for example, by his reaction to the news brought by the messengers from Jabesh (I Sam. 11) and to David's actions reported in I Sam. 24 and 26. So it is not surprising that we hear nothing of the institution of an effective government by Saul.[45] He did not have a palace, but perhaps just a kind of fortress in Gibeah.[46]

We also hear little or nothing about any form of organization of his army.

In contrast to David, who later has a mercenary army, as we shall see, Saul's army seems very much to be an improvised one.

All these factors greatly increased the difficulties with which Saul had to contend, not least in his fight with the Philistines. In this conflict Saul probably had at his disposal only the manpower which the tribes were prepared to allow him.[47] It was here that the fact that there was no question of a central authority in the time of Saul took its toll.

7.5.2 *Saul's struggle with the Philistines*

Without any doubt there is a clear historical background to the accounts of Saul's struggle with the Philistines.[48] To begin with, Saul was able to defeat the Philistines on various occasions, but these were presumably just skirmishes with small groups on a limited scale. One of the most important of them seems to have been the battle at Michmash (I Sam. 13.2—14.46). The figure of Jonathan above all comes into the foreground in the present context of this story.[49]

It is likely that after these skirmishes the Philistines took steps to put an end to things. All this ultimately led to the heavy defeat at Gilboa, where both Saul and Jonathan met their deaths. This battle was a lost cause for Saul from the start, since the Philistines were far superior in both organization and weapons.[50] The mustering of their troops at Aphek, mentioned in I Sam. 29.1–2, gives the impression of efficient organization and preparedness.

The opposite seems to have been the case with Saul, who had assembled his army at the foot of Mount Gilboa.[51] Saul probably had only a small army there.

On the basis of I Sam. 31.7 it can perhaps be assumed that neither the tribes from Transjordan nor those from the north took part in this battle.[52]

After the defeat the Philistines were even able to capture the important city of Beth-shean (I Sam. 31.10).[53] The corpses of Saul and his sons were exposed there. But this is not the last we hear about Saul in I Samuel. A story has been handed down about how the inhabitants of Jabesh in Gilead travelled through the night to bring away the bodies of Saul and his sons and to bury them in Jabesh. A good indication of the popularity of Saul with the inhabitants of the city!

And here ends the story of Saul's reign. It is a story which was written – and this fact needs to be emphasized yet again – in circles and at a time in which the figure of David was assuming increasing theological importance. It goes without saying that this fact coloured the story in a special way. Despite this, it will not escape the objective reader of the books of Samuel that as a king Saul comes over more sympathetically than his rival and successor David. At the same time that is an indication that the ancient traditions about Saul have been coloured by their author (or authors), but not completely blurred.

Chapter 8

David

8.1 *The rise of David*

8.1.1 *The anointing by Samuel*

The first story about David in the Old Testament is that of his anointing by Samuel in Bethlehem (I Sam. 16.1–13). Elsewhere there are two further mentions of an anointing of David, in II Sam. 2.4; 5.3. However, these are anointings of quite another kind and we shall consider them further in the next section.

In many respects the anointing mentioned in I Sam. 16.1–13 recalls those of Saul (I Sam. 9f.) and of Solomon (I Kings 1). The people play no role whatsoever in these three anointings. In every instance it is a 'divine anointing', carried out by a figure closely bound up with the cult. In the case of Saul and David this is Samuel, and in the case of Solomon it is Zadok (see ch. 9). The agreements between the anointing of David and that of Solomon are particularly striking. In both cases it is the younger son. The verbal agreements between I Sam. 16.13a and I Kings 1.39a are also very striking. There is therefore something to be said for the view that the anointing of David in I Sam. 16.1–13 may have served as a kind of aetiology for that of Solomon in I Kings 1.[1]

The agreements between the anointing of Saul and that of David are also important in this respect. The comment in I Sam. 16.13 that the spirit of Yahweh fell upon David directly recalls a similar remark in connection with Saul in I Sam. 10.10. The search in I Sam. 16.6–10 in which the sons of Jesse are presented to Samuel one by one recalls the events described in I Sam. 10.20–21. Both Saul (I Sam. 10.21–22) and David (I Sam. 16.11) are absent at the decisive moment. Further, Eliab's description (his appearance and stature) in I Sam. 16.7 directly suggests the figure of Saul as this is described in I Sam. 10.23–24. All these agreements suggest a relationship between these different traditions. It seems certain that I Sam. 10.17–27 contains an earlier tradition than I Sam. 16.1–13[2], and that is probably also true of I Sam. 9.1–10.16.[3]

The question whether I Sam. 16.1–13 is part of the work known as 'The History of the Rise of David' has been answered both positively[4] and negatively.[5] The former seems to be the more likely. Thus we find the apologetic theological tendency which is clearly evident in the subsequent account also in I Sam. 16.1–13.[6] These stories, which generally speaking comprise I Sam. 15 up to and including II Sam. 8,[7] are in any case characterized by a markedly pro-Davidic attitude. This is certainly true in respect of the final redaction of this complex, although here too there are traces which indicate that there are also traditions with a more critical attitude behind some of the stories.[8]

8.1.2 *David in the wilderness of Judah*

In the stories which follow his anointing by Samuel, David is constantly referred to as a mighty warrior and an able general.[9] Regardless of whether these accounts go back to an earlier or a later tradition, such characterizations seem to correspond to historical reality. For example, when it is said in I Sam. 22.1–2 that at Adullam David was the leader of a group of 400 men, there is much to suggest that this can be regarded as the beginning of the mercenary army with which David later achieved such great successes.[10]

With this group David waged a kind of guerrilla war against Saul in the wilderness of Judah. Evidently he did not engage in a direct confrontation with Saul. We even gain the impression that David wanted to avoid this at any price. This must mean that Saul was much stronger than David, and again illustrates that Saul still found much support and enjoyed much trust (see 7.4 above).

It is clear from this that David used this period above all to strengthen his position and establish his power, first of all in Judah. The story of David and Abigail is a characteristic example of this (I Sam. 25).[11] Here David emerges as the protector of peasant communities. His marriages to Abigail and Ahinoam (I Sam. 25.42–43) must also be seen in this light. In this way he was able to develop close associations with Calebite families from the south of Judah.[12]

David's success in this connection is shown by the fact that he was able to become king over Judah very soon after the death of Saul. Here, too, David shows how skilfully he could exploit a given situation. While Saul and the Philistines were preoccupied with one another elsewhere in the country, he was able to develop a strong position in the south. In all probability, David's time in the wilderness of Judah is to be seen as a decisive turning point in the history of Israel. From this moment on, Judah, which hitherto had remained completely in the background, began to play an increasingly important role in this history. And that continued until (round about the Persian period) all the other Israelite groups had virtually disappeared from the scene.[13]

8.1.3 *David among the Philistines*

Despite everything, David evidently could not remain in the wilderness of Judah. Even the wilderness and the inaccessible region of En-gedi[14] could not offer him complete security in the end. There is an indication that in these circumstances David sought refuge in Moab. In the account which mentions this (I Sam. 22.3–5), we probably have an independent and historical tradition which has, however, been handed down in very fragmentary form.[15]

In any event, David succeeded in coming to an agreement with the Philistines (I Sam. 27).[16] This account is generally regarded as a reliable historical tradition. There is something to be said for the view that Achish arrived at this treaty with David as a result of David's appearance in Keilah (I Sam. 23.1–13).[17] The Philistines, or at least Achish, will have hoped to have won an important ally to their side in the person of this opponent of Saul. On the basis of the agreement David now became a vassal of the Philistines and was assigned the city of Ziklag[18] as his abode.

With this transaction David certainly not only found himself in a difficult position, but also began to play an extremely dangerous double role. Without any doubt this illustrates once again how strong Saul's position and popularity were at this time.[19] It is hard to think of any other explanation for this last recourse of David's. It was certainly quite contradictory to his acute insight into political affairs and diplomatic arrangements to take such a dangerous step, except in a case of extreme need. In that case he will have realized the precarious situation he found himself in.

This would also explain the harsh and merciless treatment by David of those whom he defeated in his campaigns from Ziklag. They were all killed, both men and women, on the pretext, 'Lest they should tell about us' (I Sam. 27.11). This refers to the fact that David launched campaigns from Ziklag which, contrary to Achish's intentions, were beneficial to Judah.

This double role almost proved fatal to David when Achish summoned him to fight with the Philistines against his own people (I Sam. 28.1–2). In the end the mistrust of the other Philistines saved him from this catastrophe (I Sam. 29.2–5).

8.2 *David becomes king over Judah and Israel*

8.2.1 *David is anointed king of Judah*

In the Old Testament we hear little or nothing of the direct consequences of the defeat at Gilboa. Above all after the deaths of Saul and Jonathan, a confused situation must inevitably have resulted. Remarkably enough, we hear of no further activities after this on the part of the Philistines. It is possible that they thought that with this victory they had dealt adequately with their opponents. It may also be that they were preoccupied elsewhere and so were not in a position to profit from the victory. Be this as it may, we have no information on this question.

We are informed about David's activities after the battle of Gilboa in a short report in II Sam. 2.1–4. Here we are told that David had taken counsel of Yahweh[20] and then gone with his wives and followers to Hebron. This journey was obviously carefully prepared. He had already made many friends in Judah during his stay in the wilderness there (8.1.3). He did the same thing later from Ziklag by sending presents (from his plunder) to friends and elders in Judah (I Sam. 30.26–31). David's wives Ahinoam and Abigail, who went with him to Hebron (II Sam. 2.2), also play an important role in all this, as we have already seen.

How the Philistines reacted to David's move to Hebron is not known. Presumably it happened with their approval, as David was their vassal. The report that David also took with him to Hebron 'his men who were with him' (II Sam. 2.3)[21] implies that his mercenary army entered the city (which at that time was probably fairly small). This implies that from that moment on, power in Hebron and its surroundings was entirely in David's hands. In such a situation, it is not surprising to hear in II Sam. 2.4 that the 'men of Judah' anointed David king in Hebron. However, this is clearly a different anointing from that mentioned in I Sam. 16.1–13.

There is no question that the anointing by the 'men of Judah' was a sacral action. Bright's view that this anointing took place at the ancient sanctuary of Hebron finds no support in the text as it has come down to us.[22] Evidently the civic anointing mentioned in II Sam. 2.4 (and in II Sam. 5.3) represents an earlier literary tradition from the sacral anointing mentioned, for example, in I Sam. 16.1–13. In this earliest phase the king is anointed in the name of the people, and a treaty is made between the king and the people.[23] Such an anointing had the significance of a contract both in Israel and elsewhere in the ancient Near East. Its historical origin is uncertain. One might well think here of a derivation from the pre-monarchical anointing of a man to be *nagīd*.[24] It is also possible that this action was influenced by the Egyptian custom of anointing officials and vassals;[25] or perhaps there is Hittite influence here.[26]

It is not clear from the brief account in II Sam. 2.4 how far the people of Judah were in fact affected by this choice of David as king. Evidently they remained passive. Presumably the troops which David had at his disposal here will not have left open many other possibilities.[27] On the other hand, such a demonstration of strength may also have given the people of Judah a sense of security, so that a king like David could have seemed attractive in the confused situation of that time.

8.2.2 David's anointing as king over Israel

Very soon after his anointing at Hebron, David sent messengers to Jabesh in Gilead (II Sam. 2.5–7). The inhabitants of this city, who were mostly faithful supporters of Saul, were praised by David because they had buried the corpse of Saul after the battle at Gilboa. However, this is clearly not the most important message that David has for the inhabitants of Jabesh. The stress falls unmistakably on the conclusion of this message in v. 7: 'The house of Judah has anointed me king over them.' At this point Herrmann[28] rightly observes: 'between the lines there is dynamite!' David's words contain a veiled warning to recognize his authority.

After the death of Saul, one of his sons, Ishbosheth,[29] became king. He was little more than a puppet of Saul's commander-in-chief, Abner. The actual power rested with the general. We do not know precisely when Ishbosheth became king, but it cannot have been long after the death of Saul.[30]

Ishbosheth ruled for only two years. Disagreements with Abner (II Sam. 3.6–11) in fact meant his downfall,[31] after which Abner began negotiations with David (II Sam. 3.12–21). The words with which Abner suggests to David that they should begin negotiations (v. 12) give the impression that Abner was well aware that there was little point in opposing David's claims. The strength of David's position in these negotiations is clear from the fact that as a prior condition he demands that Abner should first restore to him Michal, Saul's daughter. It is remarkable that according to II Sam. 3.15–16 Ishbosheth collaborates with Abner in this transaction.

As I remarked earlier (7.4), the reason why David asked for the return of Michal is obvious.[32] A marriage to a daughter from the house of Saul would considerably strengthen his claims as a pretender to the throne. This is also the reason why at a later stage he takes over Saul's harem (II Sam. 12.8).[33]

Before Abner came to Hebron, he first negotiated with the elders of Israel, and had separate negotiations with those of Benjamin (II Sam. 3.17–19). The latter were the most zealous supporters of Saul. Clearly negotiations with them were by far the most difficult. After all this, Abner brought news of the negotiations to David at Hebron. Although we do not have any more information about their content, it is clear that they were concerned with making David king of Israel as well.

On his journey from Hebron, Abner was murdered by Joab as an act of revenge (see II Sam. 3.22–23, 27). Ishbosheth, too, was assassinated (II Sam. 4.5–6). It is uncertain who was behind this murder – was it political? At least it is striking that David does everything possible to prevent the feeling that he himself was behind it. He personally ordered the death of Ishbosheth's killers (II Sam. 4.12).

After these events David was now also anointed king over Israel by the elders of Israel (II Sam. 5.1–3).[34] It is evident from this fact alone that Judah and Israel formed two different entities. David's kingship over Israel and Judah, like that of Solomon at a later stage, had the character of a personal union.[35] This last anointing was preceded by a covenant between the elders, who represented the people of Israel, and David.[36] There was no question of a covenant when he was anointed king over Judah (see 8.2.1). The covenant between the elders of Israel and David was obviously prepared by Abner (see above). This indicates that Israel had to be given more of a say than Judah in the elevation of David to be king. Evidently there was more of a democratic tendency here than in Judah. This fact was also to play a significant role, especially after the death of Solomon.

8.3 *The capture of Jerusalem*

8.3.1 *Jerusalem in the period before David*

The two kingdoms over which David now ruled, Israel and Judah, were divided from each other by the territory of the Jebusites. The city of Jerusalem is already mentioned in Egyptian execration texts of the nineteenth and eighteenth centuries BC and in the Amarna letters from the fourteenth century BC.[37]

In the Old Testament we have two mentions of Jerusalem in which we are told that either the men of Judah (Josh. 15.63) or the Benjaminites (Judg. 1.21) did not succeed in capturing the city of Jerusalem. Both reports also say that the Jebusites continued to live among the men of Judah/Benjamin 'to the present day'. The fact that the city was evidently hard to capture is also clear from the later history of Israel.

In both the texts mentioned above and in II Sam. 5.6, the Jebusites are said to have been the inhabitants of Jerusalem. The fact that the Jebusites lived in

Jerusalem does not, however, of itself mean that Jerusalem can be identified with Jebus.[38]

8.3.2 *The occupation of Jerusalem*

We do not know how David captured Jerusalem, since the Old Testament hardly gives us any information on the subject. II Samuel 5.8 mentions a 'water shaft' in this connection. However, there is some dispute over the meaning of this word in the Hebrew text,[39] and it does not appear at all in II Chron. 11. It does, though, seem certain that the city was not captured by Israelite or Judaean troops but by David's own mercenary army ('the king and his men').[40] This could also mean that Jerusalem became the personal possession of David and his dynasty,[41] and could not be regarded as the possession of either Israel or Judah. Such a view is also supported by the fact that here David had himself surrounded by a group of functionaries and mercenary soldiers who had little or no connections with Israel and Judah. In this context it is worth remembering figures like Uriah the Hittite; Ahithophel and Zadok; and the Cherethites and Pelethites, who formed a considerable part of David's mercenary army.[42] The purchase of the threshing-floor of Araunah mentioned in II Sam. 24.18–25 also points in this direction. It is possible that this Araunah was the last ruler of the Jebusites in Jerusalem.[43]

It is certain that the conquest of Jerusalem was of far-reaching importance in both political and religious terms. It lay outside the territory of Israel and Judah, and moreover was extremely suitable because of its central position to serve as a religious and political centre. Furthermore, the capture of a Canaanite city state which lay precisely between the two kingdoms meant that the communications between Israel and Judah fell into David's hands; at the same time, a hindrance had been removed which hitherto had made contacts between the two territories extremely difficult, if not impossible. So from this moment on Jerusalem increasingly became the political and religious centre of the history of Israel. This was a development which was considerably furthered, above all, by David and Solomon.[44]

All these facts again confirm that David was a clever and skilful politician. Furthermore, Alt rightly sees the conquest of Jerusalem not primarily as an important military act but rather as a political action of the first order in the context of the foundation of the Davidic kingdom.[45] It is very likely that there was no fighting in connection with the occupation of Jerusalem. Presumably this was more a matter of diplomatic activity and of a peaceful integration of the Jebusites. The texts from Joshua and Judges cited above also point in this direction: here it is said that the Jebusites lived among the Judaeans and the Benjaminites 'until the present day'. A further striking point in connection with the occupation of Jerusalem is that stress is laid on the occupation of the 'stronghold of Zion' (II Sam. 5.7; I Chron. 11.5). Afterwards this stronghold acquired a new name, the 'city of David'.[46] We often find throughout the ancient East that the fact that a city is given a new name indicates that it has passed over into the possession of another master.[47]

8.4 *The expansion of the kingdom of David*

8.4.1 *The subjection of the Philistines*

In all probability, for a long time the Philistines still regarded David as a loyal vassal and a faithful ally. Otherwise it is difficult to explain their neutral attitude towards him over quite a long period. According to the Old Testament this attitude changed once David also became king over Israel (II Sam. 5.17). It is not clear whether this happened before or after the capture of Jerusalem. That also depends on what we have to understand by the 'fortress' mentioned in II Sam. 5.17.[48]

Be this as it may, in II Sam. 5.17–25 (I Chron. 14.8–17) we are told that the Philistines now launched a campaign against David. However, in fact here we have not just one, but two campaigns,[49] and both times David comes out on top. This put paid to the key position which the Philistines had occupied in this area for some time.[50] From now on this position was taken over by David. One important factor in this shift of power was doubtless the fact that David had control of his own well-trained army. Furthermore, we might also imagine that David had made good use of his time with the Philistines and had learnt a great deal about weapons and their manufacture.

Another important fact which favoured this change in power was the weakening of the power of the old city states. At any rate, it is clear that from the time of David they no longer have any significant role to play in Canaan. This is clearly connected with changes in the economic sphere. Whereas earlier the economic focus was to be found principally in the coastal plain, there was an increasing shift eastwards, towards the hill country.[51] At the same time this meant that political and military power also shifted in this direction.

8.4.2 *Other conquests*

After his victories over the Philistines, David had a completely independent domestic and foreign policy. The main aim of this policy was clearly to establish a great and well organized kingdom. The former goal was achieved by a series of campaigns in Transjordan and against the Aramaeans.[52] Megiddo, a place of considerable strategic and economic importance, also came into David's hands. However, this probably did not happen through a conquest.[53]

The expeditions against the Philistines, especially in the first instance, could be described as defensive wars. This could not, however, be said of the campaigns just mentioned. These were wars which aimed at expanding David's territory and power. Economic reasons were also involved, like the possession of the ore and copper mines of Edom.[54] Through these conquests David was able to build up a powerful kingdom. This stretched, for example, as far as Sidon in the north.[55]

However, such territorial expansion had its own consequences; for example, it meant that other groups were now incorporated into the population of Israel. As well as the inhabitants of Jerusalem and other Canaanite cities, we should also think of Philistines and other ethnic groups in this connection.[56] This mixture of various groups, and especially the incorporation of Canaanite cities into the kingdom of David, had far reaching consequences not only for religious but also for social and economic affairs.[57]

The most important reason why David was able to expand his territory in this way is surely that at this time the great powers of the ancient Near East, Egypt and Mesopotamia, were clearly weakened and could exercise little or no influence in and around Canaan. Perhaps that is also the reason why there is no mention whatsoever of David and Solomon and their kingdom in the literature of the ancient Near East.

8.5 *David's political and religious policy*

8.5.1 *The bringing of the ark to Jerusalem*

In the previous section it has already emerged to some degree that David wanted to make Jerusalem the capital of the two kingdoms of Israel and Judah. To achieve this end, one of his first initiatives was to bring the ark from Kiriath-jearim to Jerusalem (II Sam. 6; I Chron. 13). It was probably precisely this decision which also gave Jerusalem its great significance over the course of the centuries.[58]

This action by David again shows his acute political insight. He probably understood all too well that Jerusalem could only function properly as a political centre if it also attained the status of a religious centre in his kingdom. It is obvious that here he was thinking especially of Israel, which in this respect at any rate – in contrast to Judah– could look back on a much greater tradition. In this connection it is important to note that virtually all the places of worship mentioned in Joshua, Judges and the earlier chapters of Samuel almost certainly lay in Israel. It was presumably also for this reason that David had the ark brought from Kiriath-jearim.

The striking thing is that the Old Testament gives the impression that after (according to I Sam. 4) it had been captured by the Philistines, the ark ceased to play any significant role and really seems to have been forgotten.[59] However, for David this ark was clearly of great significance, presumably above all because it had played a major role in the tribes of Benjamin (Saul's tribe!) and Ephraim. In this context it says a great deal that the last resting place of the ark had been Kiriath-jearim, an ancient Benjaminite city. By contrast, we have no certain knowledge of any function the ark may possibly have had in Judah at an earlier stage.

8.5.2 *The religious significance of Jerusalem*

The result of bringing the ark to Jerusalem was that the city increasingly became the focal point of the cult. According to II Sam. 6.17, on this occasion the ark was placed in a tent which David had erected in Jerusalem. It is possible that we might connect this place with the threshing floor which David bought from Araunah the Jebusite (II Sam. 24.21–24). Given that the threshing floor often also has a cultic function in the Old Testament, it is possible that the account implies that on this occasion David took over the Jebusite sanctuary of Jerusalem.[60]

David nominated Abiathar, who came from the priests of Shiloh,[61] and Zadok, about whose origins we have no certain information,[62] to be priests in the sanctuary at Jerusalem.

It is clear that all these activities had a political aim, i.e. to establish the Davidic dynasty. To achieve this end the ancient traditions of Israel were connected with Jerusalem. Thus for example we see that in II Chron. 3.1 it is said that Solomon had the temple built on Mount Moriah. In the parallel account of the building of the temple in I Kings 6, however, there is no mention of Moriah. So clearly we have here a later tradition of the Chronicler which makes a connection with Gen. 22.2, where Abraham is asked to offer a sacrifice on one of the mountains in the land of Moriah. The designation 'mountain of the Lord' in Gen. 22.14b also seems to be a clear reference to the temple mount.

Furthermore, the clear aim of Ps. 110.4 is to connect the monarchy and Jerusalem priesthood with the tradition about Abraham which we find in Gen. 14.18–20: Abraham's encounter with Melchizedek, the priest-king of Salem.[63] The view that is still widespread, that all this was primarily aimed at urging the Israelites to accept a synthesis of Yahweh worship and the Jebusite cult of El Elyon,[64] at least requires us to be sure that El Elyon was worshipped as the chief god in Jerusalem before the time of David. However, this must be seriously doubted. Rather, it must be assumed that the designation El Elyon contains an epithet of El, the chief God of the Ugaritic pantheon, that this epithet was later transferred to Yahweh, and that it is used as such in the Old Testament.[65]

Of course all this does not mean that there can be no suggestion of assimilation or syncretism – also given David's policy of friendship towards the Canaanite and other cities incorporated into his kingdom.[66] Rather, we may reasonably suppose that people accepted the conqueror's form of worship rather than vice versa.[67] All these developments imply that there was increasing centralization of the various religious traditions and that religion gradually took on a more nationalistic character. This was particularly significant from a political point of view. It strengthened the position of Jerusalem and that of the Davidic dynasty. We can see this especially in the rise of two traditions of election: Yahweh's choice of Zion and that of the 'house of David'. The stability of the Davidic dynasty was based on this choice.[68]

Of course it is only natural that all these developments should have taken place gradually and were still in their very early stages in the time of David.

8.5.3 *The development and organization of the kingdom*

Other ethnic groups were incorporated in the Davidic kingdom as well as more or less kindred Israelite groups. Chief place among the former must be accorded to the Canaanites, who in one sense were accorded equal rights as citizens in the Davidic state. Along with them it is very probable that a number of Philistines and other groups were also integrated. It goes without saying that all this created problems, particularly in the long run, and at the same time brought about various changes. The most important cause of these changes and the conflicts to which they gave rise must be seen in the fact that the cities – many of which were still entirely Canaanite – increasingly became the centres of political and economic life. Social context gradually became more important than ties of affinity.[69] One of the consequences of this was that the economy of the countryside increasingly declined. Along with this there also developed a sharp opposition between town and country.[70]

A first reaction to this can probably be seen in the attitude of the Rechabites, who aimed at a more nomadic ideal (Jer. 35). Later, we can see another reaction against the increasingly prominent position of city culture in the preaching of the eighth-century prophets, in which we can detect a concern for a synthesis.[71] At the time of David, however, it is clear that all these groups simply lived together in one kingdom, thanks to the powerful personality and the great organizational capacities of David. Here David clearly was able to lay the foundations of a form of government after an Egyptian or Canaanite model.[72]

Later developments, however, show that Israel and Judah remained two distinct entities which even had different characteristics. These found marked expression especially after the death of Solomon. This also emerges from the boundary changes made during and after Solomon's reign in connection with other population groups which lived on the periphery of David's kingdom.

One thing is certain, that David's political and religious policies not only had far-reaching consequences for the future, but were also decisive in establishing the Davidic dynasty.

8.6 *Nathan's prophecy*

In II Sam. 5.11; 7.1 we hear that David had a palace built for himself in Jerusalem. Obviously David also planned to build a temple there, as is evident from, say, II Sam. 7.2. It is even possible that he had already made preparations for it. At least the purchase of the threshing floor of Araunah[73] (II Sam. 24.21–24; I Chron. 21.21–25) could point in this direction.[74]

At all events, during the time of David there seems to have been serious opposition to such a plan. This is expressed particularly in what is known as 'Nathan's prophecy', which we find in II Sam. 7.1–17; I Chron 17.1–15. A good deal has been written and said about this pericope.[75] It seems most probable that it is a literary composition made up of various elements deriving from various periods; as a whole it perhaps comes from the time shortly after Solomon.[76] The numerous quotations of, and allusions to,[77] the 'prophecy of Nathan' in the Old Testament could suggest this, though the question remains where we should put the original recension of this 'prophecy'. Some scholars think they can find it in Ps. 89,[78] while others think of II Sam. 7 in this connection.[79]

Opposition to the building of the temple is expressed in II Sam. 7.4–7. Along with vv. 2, 3, this part is probably the earliest section of the 'prophecy of Nathan' and should be regarded as an originally independent tradition.[80] Nothing can be said with any certainty about the background of the opposition to the building of the temple expressed here. However, it is clear that the prophet Nathan played an important role in this respect.

In that connection it is striking that in the Old Testament Nathan is mentioned only in connection with Solomon's succession to the throne. It is therefore quite possible that Nathan belonged to the non-Israelite party at the court,[81] which may also have included figures like Benaiah, Zadok and Bathsheba. At all events, this was the very group which later supported

Solomon in his claim to the throne. In that case, this would be the party which later, in the time of Solomon, clearly no longer had any doubts about the building of the temple. That might suggest that Nathan's opposition to the building of a temple in the time of David was connected with particular factors which were then dominant. Here one might perhaps think above all of the rivalry between the priests Abiathar and Zadok. Furthermore, it is possible that Nathan was afraid that Abiathar might come to occupy too prominent a position in a new temple in comparison with his 'protégé' Zadok.[82] After the accession of Solomon, Abiathar's role had come to an end (I Kings 2.26–27), and this barrier to building the temple was removed. We can have no certainty here, but it is difficult to find any other explanation for the fact that all the obstacles in the way of building the temple were removed in such a relatively short space of time.

'Nathan's prophecy' is also of great significance in another respect, apart from the rejection of David's plans for building a temple. Here we find the divine legitimation of the Davidic dynasty.[83] David will not make a house (temple) for God, but God will build him a house (dynasty). The clear pointers towards the figure of Solomon in these verses show that in any case 'Nathan's prophecy' was subjected to reinterpretation during the time of Solomon or afterwards.[84]

The way in which this prophecy speaks about the relationship between God and king is also of great significance. This relationship is seen as one between father and son (II Sam. 7.14).[85] The formula used here suggests a formula of adoption common in the ancient Near East. However, this adoption does not imply that the king is the divine son of God; rather, it must be seen as a form of dependent relationship on the part of the king towards God.[86] It indicates that the relationship between God and the 'house of David' is the same as that between God and the people, i.e. a covenant relationship.[87] This covenant with David in various respects suggests that between God and Abraham mentioned in Gen. 15.[88] In this connection it is also striking that the frontiers of the land promised to Abraham in the making of the covenant in Gen. 15.18–21 largely coincide with those of the Davidic kingdom.

8.7 *Rebellions during David's reign*

8.7.1 *The succession narrative*

The rebellions during David's reign which will be discussed in this section are recorded in that part of II Samuel and the beginning of I Kings which is known to Old Testament scholars as the 'succession narrative'. Since a study by Rost,[89] this series of narratives has been generally[90] regarded as the work of a contemporary author. Roughly speaking, the complex of narratives comprises II Sam. 9–20 and I Kings 1–2.[91]

On investigation, the content of the narratives shows certain features which make it difficult to accept the assumption that the author is a contemporary who would then certainly have to come from court circles. Above all, the description of the way in which Solomon dealt with his rivals in I Kings 2 seems hard to ascribe to someone from his time or his immediate entourage. Rather, we must assume that here we have a later theological apologia.

Of course, all this does not mean that these accounts do not incorporate old and authentic material. The way in which Solomon comes to power in I Kings 2 and the opposition, especially from Israel, to David's rule which emerges from the accounts of rebellions against him narrated in II Samuel, seem authentic. It is evident that later theological revisions were not able to suppress such critical comments.

8.7.2 *Absalom's revolt*

In previous sections we have continually been able to note that David evidently carried out an extremely effective policy as regards both diplomacy and organization. However, in one respect he clearly failed completely, namely in the attitude which he adopted towards his sons. The rape of Tamar by her half-brother Amnon (II Sam. 13.1–22);[92] the murder of Amnon by Absalom (II Sam. 13.23–39),[93] that of Adonijah by Solomon (I Kings 2.13–25), and Absalom's revolt are a clear indication of this. One important factor here was doubtless that David was evidently not in a position to control his followers, or that for one reason or another he could not and would not do this.

That is one of the chief causes of the troubles during David's reign, but it is not the only one. There still seem to have been numerous supporters of Saul in Israel who, to put it mildly, clearly mistrusted David. With some justification, they suspected David of having had a hand in the murder of Saul's descendants by the Gibeonites (II Sam. 21.1–14): this is clear from the words of Shimei in II Sam. 16.5–8. And quite apart from this, there was clearly discontent in other respects, as we can see for example in II Sam. 15.1–6, where the Israelites (from what later became the northern kingdom) were evidently extremely discontented with David's government. An account like that of the census of the people in II Sam. 24 also points rather in the same direction.[94]

One of the most dangerous revolts with which David had to deal was that of Absalom, mentioned in II Sam. 13–19. After the murder of his half-brother Amnon, Absalom was forced to spend three years in Geshur, the home of his mother. Thanks to the mediation of Joab he was then able to return home, but it was another two years before David became reconciled to him again.[95] Absalom was then preoccupied for four years (II Sam. 15.7) with preparations for a rebellion against David. Here he tried above all, evidently not without success, to gain the trust of the inhabitants of Israel, as is clear from II Sam. 15.1–6. Obviously David's position was weaker in Israel than in Judah. There charismatic and democratic leadership evidently had a much stronger background than in the south.

However, Absalom was able to assemble around him others apart from Israelites who were discontented with David's rule. So we hear of people from David's immediate entourage who chose to support Absalom. Mention should be made here of Ahithophel (II Sam. 15.12), an important adviser of David's, and Amasa, commander-in-chief, who was related both to David and to Joab (II Sam. 17.25; II Chron. 2.15–17). It is clear that Saul's supporters were at the least sympathetic towards Absalom's rebellion.

It is not always plain precisely what were the motives of those who followed Absalom. It is possible that David's imperialistic policy and his behaviour in the matter of Bathsheba and Uriah had provoked much disapproval in certain circles,[96] but this is by no means certain. The signal for the uprising was given in Hebron (II Sam. 15.10–12). This is remarkable, seeing that the account of this rebellion in the Old Testament suggests that Judah remained neutral.[97] Only some individuals from Judah, like Ahithophel, seem to have taken part in the revolt.

There is therefore much to suggest that Absalom's aim was to make a personal approach to Jerusalem from Hebron with a number of followers, while the Israelites did the same thing from the north.[98] This view also provides the best explanation of David's extremely rapid flight from Jerusalem. As a skilful general he saw in time the danger of a complete encirclement. He took adequate precautions in advance, for example by leaving behind one of his able advisers, Hushai, in Jerusalem. David rightly sensed that here there was a need for someone to oppose Ahithophel. Subsequent developments show how right his view was (II Sam. 17). In fact this decision sealed Absalom's fate.

After his departure from Jerusalem, above all on the urging of Hushai (II Sam. 17.16), David went to Transjordan, where he prepared his army for battle against Absalom. The decisive fight took place on Ephraimite territory, and there Absalom was defeated and killed.[99]

It is clear that David owed this victory to his own personal troops. The conflict between David and Absalom is continually described in II Sam. 18 (vv. 6, 7, 9, 17) as a battle between the 'servants of David' and 'all Israel'. This last reference again seems a strong indication of the neutral attitude of Judah in this conflict. So David had one state (Israel) against him, while the other

(Judah) remained aloof. David could only save his throne with foreign troops.

Furthermore, the death of Absalom did not yet mean the final end of the rebellion. Israel was still seething, but people were obviously puzzled about what to do. The defeat and death of Absalom represented a considerable loss to the rebels, and people sensed all too well that David was again much stronger. Further, they were probably all too aware of David's skills and potentials in the military sphere. So there was now dissension as to what attitude should be adopted towards him (II Sam. 19.9). On David's advice or at his command (II Sam. 19.11), the elders of Judah had already come to meet him at the Jordan to welcome him again as king. It is possible that in connection with this, one concession which David granted Judah was freedom from taxation.[100] The absence of Judah from the list of Solomon's districts, organized with a view to taxation, in I Kings 4.7–19 could point in this direction.[101] David's favouring of Judah is also expressed in the heightened rivalry between Israelites and Judaeans (II Sam. 19.41–43). David must, of course, have foreseen this danger, but he clearly had no other choice.

According to II Sam. 19.40, half Israel, as well as Judah, came to meet David at the Jordan. These were obviously men of Israel who had first taken Absalom's side or had waited to see what would happen (II Sam. 19.15ff.). How precarious the situation remained despite all this is evident from the measures which David took against his earlier opponents. They were given a complete amnesty and Amasa, the leader of Absalom's army (II Sam. 17.25), was himself appointed in Joab's place by David (II Sam. 19.13).

8.7.3 *Sheba's revolt*

However, all these measures did not prevent the outbreak of a new revolt even before David had returned to Jerusalem. This was led by Sheba, a Benjaminite and a kinsman and follower of the 'house of Saul' (II Sam. 20.1–2, 4–22). Unlike Absalom's revolt, this one was not directed against David's person but against his dynasty, and was therefore even more dangerous. It is clear that David also recognized this from his words in II Sam. 20.6: 'Now Sheba will do us more harm than Absalom.' However, David was able to remain master of the situation, once again thanks to his personal army: 'the Cherethites and Pelethites and all the mighty men' (II Sam. 7). With these troops in particular, Joab was able to drive Sheba steadily further north until he managed to lay siege to him in the city of Abel-beth-maacah in the extreme north. By means of a 'wise woman', we are told in II Sam. 20.16ff., Sheba was killed and thus this rebellion too became a thing of the past.

It seems that this rebellion, given Sheba's origin and kinsfolk, began in

Benjamin and secured the support of many people in Israel. The words with which Sheba's revolt is introduced in II Sam. 20.1b are striking:

> 'We have no portion in David,
> and we have no inheritance in the son of Jesse;
> every man to his tents, O Israel!'

We find similar words later in the popular assembly at Shechem, when Israel rejected Rehoboam as king (I Kings 12.16). Presumably this was the Israelite battle-cry, which indicated their refusal to surrender their personal and democratic rights to the absolute and central authority of the Davidic dynasty. After the rebellion of Sheba, Israel, which did not dare to rebel against David yet again, was in fact little more than a vassal.[102] The personal union between Israel and Judah was now little more than a fiction. So it could only be maintained under the absolute monarchy of the time of David and Solomon. However, the final break between these two kingdoms after the death of Solomon already had its roots in the rebellions during David's rule. Above all, Sheba's revolt is to be seen as a prelude to this break.

8.7.4 *The accession of Solomon*

One last rebellion took place at the end of David's reign, but only in Jerusalem and above all in court circles. David's succession was still not settled. Two parties now formed at the court (see also 8.6), one round Adonijah, the oldest of David's sons still living and, according to the principle that was almost always followed in Judah and in the 'house of David',[103] the lawful successor to the throne, and a second group, which wanted Solomon as David's successor. Both parties had important supporters. Members of Adonijah's party were Joab, the commander-in-chief, and the priest Abiathar; Solomon was supported by Nathan the prophet, Zadok the priest and Benaiah, the commander of the Cherethites and Pelethites (II Sam. 20.23). It is evident from this list of names which we find in I Kings 1.7–8 that the dividing lines between these parties can also be seen among the priests and in the army.

It is clear that it was an unequal struggle. As often, the position of the army proved decisive. In this case it was inevitable that from the start, Joab with his ordinary soldiers should be at a disadvantage against the mercenaries under the leadership of Benaiah. David was in fact no longer capable of ruling (I Kings 1.1–4). He was persuaded by Nathan through Bathsheba to choose Solomon, who was then immediately anointed king by Zadok at the brook Gihon. Thus once again David's personal army, the Cherethites and Pelethites (see I Kings 1.38), had played a decisive role in the history of the Davidic dynasty.

All this now means that Solomon already became king over Israel and Judah during David's lifetime. Here we have a so-called co-regency; i.e., the successor to the throne already took over while the previous king was still alive, but was no longer capable of ruling because of old age – as here – or for some other reason. It is possible that this co-regency was based on an Egyptian model.[104] The purpose of such an institution was to avoid the trouble and political chaos which often went with a change of ruler in the ancient Near East.

One point deserves special consideration in connection with this transfer of the throne to Solomon. There is no question of any influence being exercised by the people. Whereas the choice of Saul involved a popular assembly, and both the elders of Judah and of Israel had a role in that of David,[105] the choice of Solomon by-passed the people completely. Only some leading figures, escorted by the Cherethites and Pelethites, come to the fore.

The result of this 'undemocratic' approach was that the personal union between Israel and Judah remained, but at the same time it meant the establishment of an even more absolute monarchy than that in the time of David. Although I Kings 1, which describes the transfer of power to Solomon, shows marked traces of a later revision,[106] this chapter too must in many respects go back to ancient historical material. The many critical comments which are continually made in this account of the transfer of the throne to Solomon can hardly be ascribed only to a later period, which was so easily led to idealize the past, and above all the time of David and Solomon.

Chapter 9

Solomon

9.1 *The beginning of Solomon's reign*

At the end of the 'succession narrative' (in I Kings 2), we hear of the way in which Solomon dealt with his former opponents: Adonijah, Joab and Shimei were killed, and Abiathar the priest was exiled to his estate at Anathoth. The harsh measures taken against Joab and Abiathar, who had served David faithfully all their lives, seem particularly cruel to us. However, the fact that Solomon's methods are described so openly here suggests that the events narrated may well go back to a reliable tradition. Otherwise we would expect a less critical account of Solomon's career.[1]

After the 'succession narrative', which ends in I Kings 2, for a reconstruction of later events we are thrown back on accounts which usually show signs of a much more marked theological revision by the Deuteronomist or the Chronicler. In this chapter, therefore, we shall be more concerned with the question which original data have been preserved in these theological reconstructions of events.[2]

The first narrative which raises this question is that of I Kings 3.4–15. Here we are told that Solomon offered a sacrifice at the high place[3] of Gibeon[4] and that in a dream God appeared to him and asked him, 'What shall I give you?' (I Kings 3.5b; cf. Ps. 2.8). As we know well, Solomon thereupon asked for wisdom.

The interpretation of this account offers great scope. In antiquity it was quite usual for people to sleep in a sanctuary in the hope that they would have a vision of the deity in a dream.[5] In particular, someone who had just become king – like Solomon here – did this often. Furthermore, we find stories in the literature of the ancient Near East which can be seen more or less as parallels to I Kings 3.4–15.[6] At all events, there are different statements and expressions here which seem to derive from extra-biblical parallels.[7]

It is striking that in I Kings 3.4 we hear quite naturally that Solomon offers a sacrifice in the 'high place' of Gibeon, while according to v. 15 this was also possible in Jerusalem. This information in v. 4 must go back to an old tradition, since such an action would no longer be tolerated at a later date. Moreover, we see that an explanation for it is given in a later tradition in II Chron. 1.3. There we read that the 'tent of meeting' was in Gibeon at the time, a piece of information that we are given nowhere else, even in I Kings 3. It is impossible to establish the exact historical background to this account in I Kings 3.4–15 with any certainty. The most important purpose of the narrative seems to be to show that the kingship of Solomon was endorsed with a divine legitimation.[8] It is further stressed that Solomon's wisdom is a gift of God.

We shall be occupied with this last theme in the next section.

9.2 *Solomon's wisdom*

In addition to his legendary riches, Solomon has gone down in history above all as the king who was extremely gifted with the possession of wisdom. The account of Solomon's wise judgment in I Kings 3.16–28 is still the most vivid illustration of this.[9] Furthermore, in the Old Testament the titles of various collections of wisdom literature (Prov. 1.1; 10.1; 25.1; Eccl. 1.1) also ascribe wisdom to him. In I Kings 4.32 we hear of 3000 proverbs which Solomon uttered (not that he composed himself!), and in I Kings 4.29–34 of the international reputation which he gained for himself with this wisdom.

Now we need to remember that in making such statements the Old Testament does not mean that this wisdom should be seen as limited to the king. The aim is to show that wisdom flourished greatly at the time of Solomon and was characteristic of many circles. And this brings us in particular to consider Solomon's immediate entourage.

The most important cause of the rise and eventual flourishing of wisdom at the time of Solomon can be seen as an increase in international contacts in this period. At all events, it is clear that Israelite wisdom was influenced by that of Egypt and Mesopotamia.[10] Solomon's reign created a particularly favourable climate for all this. In contrast to the reign of David, his was a reign of peace. This will have furthered international contacts considerably; they were clearly established, above all in the direction of Egypt. It is striking that the Egyptian princess – a daughter of Pharaoh and mentioned as one of Solomon's many wives – is given very special treatment. She is singled out on no less than five occasions, and is mentioned regularly in another connection.[11] We find important comparative material of Egyptian origin in, for example, the famous Onomasticon of Amenemope.[12] This is an example of so-called 'knowledge by lists': the Onomasticon contains a list of things and beings in heaven, on earth and in the water. It might well be described as a kind of scientific encyclopaedia of antiquity.

It seems from I Kings 4.33 that Solomon (or circles close to him) was occupied with this kind of science. Psalm 148 and Job 38 strongly suggest this 'knowledge by lists'. So it is probably no coincidence that in I Kings 4.30 Solomon's wisdom is compared with that of other people, and above all with that of Egypt. This suggests that people were familiar with wisdom coming from abroad. The same also applies in connection with the wise men Ethan, Heman, Calcol and Darda, who according to I Kings 4.31, were inferior to Solomon in wisdom. The names of these four men show that there may have been Canaanite influence on Israelite wisdom. At least it is evident that these figures have specifically Canaanite names.[13]

Although we cannot be completely certain in any respect, the time of Solomon clearly offered possibilities which could have favoured the rise of wisdom and led to its hey-day. The fact that the tradition in the Old Testament is almost unanimous in pointing to Solomon in connection with wisdom is further support in this direction.

9.3 *The building of the temple in Jerusalem*

Alongside his wisdom, Solomon is also famous for building a temple in Jerusalem. We find the account of this in I Kings 5.1—9.9; II Chron. 2.1—7.22. These accounts broadly agree. According to the Chronicler, David made the preparations for building the temple, even down to details (see especially I Chron. 22; 28), a fact which does not emerge from the book of Kings. There is another difference, for example, over the place where the temple is built. In II Chron. 3.1 the site is said to be the mountain of Moriah, the place where Abraham was to offer his son (Gen. 22.2), while in Kings there is no mention of this place.[14] Furthermore, there are differences in the accounts of the building of the temple and the objects placed in it between I Kings 6; 7.13–51 and II Chron. 3.1—5.1.[15] Roughly speaking, one can say that the Chronicler mainly stresses the fact that Solomon is the temple-builder chosen by God.[16]

According to Rupprecht, this temple is not a new buiding, but a conversion of the Jebusite sanctuary in Jerusalem. This was renovated and extended by Solomon.[17] Busink's thorough study, by contrast, arrives at quite a different result. He regards this temple as specifically Israelite, and a creation of Solomon's.[18] We can gain only a rough idea of precisely where the temple was and what it must have looked like. Its location must be envisaged in the area of the present-day Dome of the Rock. It is more difficult to arrive at a reconstruction of this temple. Different attempts have hitherto failed to achieve a unanimous result.[19] However, by our standards Solomon's temple was evidently not very big, though this need not mean that was simply a kind of court chapel.[20]

It is striking that Solomon can implement this project with no problems. We do not hear of a single word of protest, as according to II Sam. 7 was the case in the time of David. In 8.6 I already pointed out that at that time the opposition between, for example, Abiathar and Zadok was an important reason for Nathan's protest against David's plan to build a temple. Of course that does not mean that there was no such opposition at the time of Solomon. The difference from the earlier period is that Solomon was far more of an absolute ruler than David. This already emerged at the end of the previous chapter in the way in which he became king and came to power without the people having any say. That could very well mean that at this time there was no opportunity to express opposition to, or criticism of, the building of the temple. Furthermore, Solomon could probably rely completely on the support of important religious leaders like Nathan the prophet and Zadok the priest.

The building of the temple also implies that Jerusalem increased in importance as the central city and capital. From now on it developed politically, and also increasingly as a religious centre. However, that does not mean that from the time of Solomon the other, older sanctuaries ceased to exist. Solomon's temple was primarily the cultic centre for Jerusalem, but of course it had the potential in the long run to overshadow all the rest.[21] This happened later, above all after Josiah's reformation. A characteristic example here is offered by the remains of a temple in Arad discovered by Aharoni.[22] This temple must have been built in the reign of Solomon. Its structure and orientation seem to correspond completely with those of the Jerusalem temple.[23] The temple in Arad continued to serve as a legitimate sanctuary of Yahweh down to the time of Josiah's reformation, i.e. almost four hundred years after the building of Solomon's temple.

The most that can be said for the Israelites in the north is that they recognized Solomon's temple as a sanctuary during his reign. Presumably, apart from individual exceptions, they never used it, but had their own sanctuaries (cf. Amos 7.13). However, we have little concrete information about any sanctuaries in the north. This is probably because the writings of the Old Testament, including those which contained Israelite traditions, were all revised in Judah, and specifically in Jerusalem.

9.4 *Other building works during the time of Solomon*

The temple in Jerusalem was about seven years in the building. However, in I Kings 7.1 – and we can sense the criticism in these words – we are told that Solomon took thirteen years to build his palace. It is striking that this critical note is missing from the later tradition in Chronicles. There we are simply told that the building of the temple and the palace together took twenty years (II Chron. 8.1). According to the accounts in I Kings the palace eclipsed the temple in size and splendour.[24] In Chronicles no comment is made about this. That is typical of the Chronicler who, in contrast to what we find in the books of Samuel and Kings, keeps quiet about Solomon's and David's weak points.[25]

There is therefore much to support the view that in Kings we have the earliest and (in the historical sense) most reliable tradition about these events. In later literature, the figures of these kings were described in increasingly idealistic terms.[26] Then, however, people were thinking not so much of the persons bearing the names but of the messianic notions embodied in these names. In addition to his palace,[27] Solomon had a separate house built for Pharaoh's daughter (I Kings 7.8; cf. II Chron. 8.11).

Through all these building activities Solomon made Jerusalem a great and important city for its time. In comparison with the time of David the city had probably grown to a considerable extent. New walls were evidently built round this extended city (I Kings 9.15).[28] According to I Kings 9.15, however, Solomon's building work was not limited to Jerusalem, but also went on in Hazor, Gezer and Megiddo. Archaeological investigations seem to confirm this report. At any rate, traces seem to have been found which point to building activity in these places in the time of Solomon.[29] In all probability these were defensive works, aimed at strengthening the cities in question. The same is also true of the three places mentioned in I Kings 9.18–19, namely Beth-horon the lower, Baalath and Tamar. Furthermore, on the basis of archaeological excavations Aharoni has come to the conclusion that in the time of Solomon a chain of fortresses was established aimed at protecting the caravan routes through the Negeb as far as Ezion-geber.[30]

Obviously all these enterprises cost a great deal of money. In the last sections of this chapter we shall see what measures Solomon took to raise it and the result that they had. Before that, however, we shall first pay some attention to Solomon's skill in foreign policy.

9.5 *Solomon's foreign policy*

I have already pointed out that in contrast to the time of David, Solomon's reign can be described in the Bible as a period of peace. In this connection it is striking that the name Solomon is connected with the Hebrew word for peace and prosperity, *shālōm*.[31] However, presumably this was not his original name, but the name which he later took as king. At any rate, in II Sam. 12.25 we hear that at birth he was given the name Jedidiah (friend or beloved of Yahweh), a name which clearly remained completely in the background and is not mentioned at all in the later tradition in Chronicles.

Evidently Solomon's reign did not pass without any military problems at all. Developments were taking place on the frontiers of his kingdom which ushered in the break-up of the great Davidic empire. In the south, Hadad, a prince of Edom who had fled to Egypt in the time of David, evidently succeeded in recapturing some of Edom from Solomon and began to reign there again. In this account, fragments of which have come down to us in I Kings 11.14–22, there is nothing to suggest that Solomon took any action against Hadad.[32]

There were also problems in the north. There a certain Rezon, who came from Zobah, became king in Damascus (I Kings 11.23–25). This kingdom became an increasingly dangerous opponent, later above all of the kingdom of Israel. Here, too, we do not learn of any measures taken by Solomon. However, Solomon not only had fortresses built (see 9.4), but also strengthened his army.

We may assume that at the beginning of his reign Solomon took over David's mercenary army. We also hear that he equipped his army with chariots.[33] The cities mentioned in the previous section evidently served as garrison cities (I Kings 10.26) for these chariots drawn by horses. Under Solomon the ordinary troops drawn from the people increasingly faded into the background. His was above all a mercenary army, troops of foreign origin who were used to protect the frontiers and trade routes.

Solomon managed to enlarge his frontiers to a limited extent, taking over the ancient Canaanite city of Gezer, which was the last to hold out. This city was in fact seized by a Pharaoh of Egypt and then given to Solomon as a dowry for his daughter (I Kings 9.16). Who this Pharaoh is and why he gave this strategically important city to Solomon is uncertain.[34]

However, Solomon's most important activities in the sphere of foreign policy involved his diplomatic contacts. His concern was evidently to build up as many friendly relationships as possible, above all with neighbouring countries, among which Egypt in particular held an important place. We find one indication of this in a report in I Kings 11.1 where we are told that 'as well as Pharaoh's daughter'[35] Solomon 'loved many foreign women: Moabite, Ammonite,[36] Edomite, Sidonian and Hittite women'. These are women from the countries surrounding Solomon's kingdom. This seems thoroughly characteristic of Solomon's foreign policy.

The contacts which he maintained with Hiram king of Tyre are particularly important.[37] In addition to help for building the temple and other works, Solomon also had help from Tyre in the manning and equipping of his trading fleet. It seems from I Kings 9.11 that Hiram only gave this in return for a *quid pro quo*,[38] since according to this verse Solomon ceded him twenty cities in Galilee. That was a large amount of territory for that time, though according to I Kings 9.12–14[39] Hiram still does not seem to have been satisfied with it.

It is remarkable in all this that despite all his activities abroad, like David, Solomon is not mentioned once in the literature of the ancient Near East. Thus in this respect we are thrown back on the information given us in the Old Testament traditions which are later and have undergone theological revision. That there may be a historical background to them is a real possibility, though in this respect we have virtually no certain evidence.

9.6 *Trade and economic affairs*

9.6.1 *Trade and industry*

Closely connected with Solomon's foreign policy are the activities in which he became involved in the sphere of trade and economic affairs. In trade, Solomon skilfully exploited the position occupied by his country in relation to the important trade routes between the north and the south. Here he succeeded in bringing trade relations to a height which had hitherto been unknown in Israel and Judah. The most important development in this connection was the trading fleet which Solomon had built. Because there were clearly few people in his own country with knowledge and experience of sea-faring, Solomon – as I remarked earlier – had to invoke the help of the Phoenicians in building and manning this fleet.[40] As we hear in I Kings 9.26–28; 10.11, it was used for trade with Ophir. The home port for these ships was Ezion-geber, a city situated near Elath on the Gulf of Akaba. The location of Ophir is uncertain. Most scholars are inclined to put it in Arabia.[41]

The noteworthy visit of the queen of Sheba should perhaps also be seen in the context of these trade contacts (I Kings 10.13). The historical background to the story might possibly be sought in Solomon's trade relations with Arabia, above all because the exchange of goods plays a considerable role in it. This is by no means certain, because it has yet to be shown convincingly that this queen in fact came from Arabia. However, there are strong indications in this direction. Thus the kingdom of Saba is known to have existed in antiquity in south-west Arabia, and its most important source of income lay in the handling of trade.[42] Archaeological excavations, too, seem to indicate that in about 1000 BC there was a flourishing trade in this area.[43]

Another remarkable kind of trading is mentioned in I Kings 10.28–29. This mentions the purchase of horses from 'Misraim and Kue',[44] which are then to be sold to the Hittites and Aramaeans.

Ezion-geber had an economic significance over and above that of being a port (see above). There were mines in the region, which Glueck originally saw as enterprises from the time of Solomon. Later, however, it emerged that these mines were already disused in the twelfth century BC.[45]

9.6.2 *Social and economic developments*

The gold and other materials resulting from this trade clearly did not benefit the whole population of Israel and Judah. The lists of Solomon's riches are very colourful and sometimes exaggerated, like other descriptions in I Kings 10.14ff., but they suggest that this wealth served simply to enrich the king and his immediate entourage. Deuteronomy 17.16–18 points in a similar direction. At all events, it is clear that these later, critical notes envisage what we are told about Solomon. Matters like the possession of many horses, many women and much silver and gold, which according to Deut. 17.16–18 are prohibited to the king, are particularly relevant to Solomon's possessions. Therefore we would probably be right in supposing that especially in the time of Solomon a process had begun in which the rich grew steadily richer and the poor grew steadily poorer.

To a considerable degree the development of trade favoured the prosperity and expansion of the cities. This is not surprising. Given the fact that in the Old Testament 'Canaanite' is often a designation for merchant, we may reasonably suppose that the inhabitants of the former Canaanite city states had an important role in the expansion of trade. In this way the cities increasingly became the centres of political and economic life,[46] and there gradually came into being an upper class of city-dwelling landowners and a large group of Israelites who had no land at all.

However, all the riches which Solomon was able to assemble through all his trading seem to have been far from adequate to provide for the enormous needs of the king and his entourage. In the next section we shall see the measures which Solomon took to remedy this deficit.

9.7 *The fiscal divisions of the kingdom*

9.7.1 *Solomon's tax districts*

As I remarked in the previous paragraph, Solomon's trading produced substantial riches. In addition, his time is characterized by a great cultural development (wisdom), the expansion of cities and the beginnings of great building projects. All these developments have led to Solomon's era being seen later as a golden age. However, this is a very one-sided assessment of the period. The Old Testament shows us another side, the colouring of which has a much darker hue. As so often in history, the greatest riches went hand in hand with the utmost poverty. In order to be able to sustain the exalted life-style thought necessary for the king and his immediate entourage and to implement the great projects which he undertook, Solomon organized a system of districts. This was aimed principally at raising taxes in a systematic way. We have information about this in particular from a list of the tax districts into which Israel (not Judah, see 8.7.2) was divided. The list is given in I Kings 4.7–19. Various studies have shown how the list is of great historical significance.[47]

It emerges from this document that under Solomon Israel was divided into twelve tax districts. Each of these districts – supervised by a chief official[48] – had to support the court (and perhaps also the temple) for one month in each year. To achieve this, heavy taxation was imposed through the system in the form of natural produce and forced labour.

We have reason to suppose that in one way or another this system derives from an Egyptian model. In particular, a study by Redford,[49] which demonstrates the specific parallels between I Kings 4.7–19 and a similar account on an inscription from the time of Pharaoh Shoshenk I,[50] a younger contemporary of Solomon, argues strongly in this direction.

9.7.2 *Forced labour*

The system of forced labour was directly connected with the institution of tax districts. The Old Testament tradition differs over the question who was involved in this forced labour. I Kings 5.13 mentions 'all Israel', and I Kings 11.28 the house of Joseph, whereas in this context I Kings 9.20–22 speaks of 'non-Israelites'. It is striking that the parallel text to I Kings 5.13, II Chron. 17–18, does not speak of 'all Israel', but of foreigners.

It is possible that these differences derive from the fact that there were several types of forced labour.[51] However, it is certain that the system mentioned in I Kings 5.13 aroused the greatest opposition in Israel. This kind of forced labour was also one of the foremost grievances mentioned by the Israelites who did not want Rehoboam to be king after Solomon's death (I Kings 12). On this occasion the director of forced labour, Adoniram, was stoned by 'all Israel'.

It appears from all this that the principle of forced labour and taxation under Solomon must have represented an extremely difficult operation in the economic situation of that time. The forced labour can, moreover, rightly be seen as exploitation, and was clearly hated bitterly by the people.

The Old Testament also gives the impression that such forced labour was never imposed at a later date to the degree that it was in the time of Solomon.

Thus after Adoniram (see above) we never hear of a director of forced labour.

In all probability this continued as a major enterprise and a regular institution only in the time of Solomon. Later, it only appears incidentally, as in the case of Jehoiakim, who sought to build a palace for himself (Jer. 22.13).

If we take account of all this, the time of Solomon was certainly no golden age. On the contrary, in that respect this period can be seen only as a time of profound apostasy, which left its deep marks on the later history of Israel and Judah. Solomon's forced labour, more than anything else, led to the break between these two states and thus also laid the foundations for centuries of conflict between the people of Judah and those who were later to become the Samaritans.[52]

9.8 *Opposition to Solomon*

We can understand how Solomon's measures over taxation and forced labour, in particular, led to opposition. In view of all that has already been said in the previous section (8.7.2), it is clear that this opposition came principally from Israel, seeing that Judah was probably exempt from obligations (see 9.7.2).

The mouthpiece for this opposition was Jeroboam, who came from Ephraim, one of the most important tribes in Israel (I Kings 11.26). This Jeroboam was designated king over the kingdom of Israel by Ahijah the prophet, who came from Shiloh. It might be inferred from the emergence of this prophet that the religious group in Shiloh backed the revolt against Solomon. Such a view is strengthened if we follow Caquot in assuming[53] that in religious terms there was rivalry between Shiloh and Jerusalem. In the account in I Kings 11.29–39,[54] in which Ahijah of Shiloh designated Jeroboam king over Israel, only religious motives are mentioned for the division of Solomon's kingdom. However, according to I Kings 12.1–20, the heavy taxation and the forced labour played an equally imporant part.

The conspiracy between Ahijah and Jeroboam was dicovered and the latter fled to Egypt (I Kings 11.40). This clearly laid the foundation for a break in the personal union between Israel and Judah. At any rate, it became a fact immediately after the death of Solomon.

In addition, there are a number of critical comments on Solomon's reign in the book of Kings. Thus Solomon's idolatry and his great harem are clearly criticized in I Kings 11.1–13. There seems no doubt that this information – apart from the high figure of a thousand wives given in I Kings 11.3 – goes back to a historical reality. This is the more likely because the later tradition increasingly shows a tendency to keep quiet about Solomon's negative side. In a later period Solomon's wisdom becomes more prominent, along with his fame as builder of the temple and his international reputation. Furthermore, we see that both the information in I Kings 11.29–39 (see above) and that in I Kings 11.1–13 are absent from the books of Chronicles.[55] Moreover, the division of the kingdom is not seen in Chronicles (II Chron. 11.13–17) as a consequence of Solomon's lack of faith in Yahweh, as it is in Kings, but rather as the consequence of Israel's apostasy from the true form of worship practised in Jerusalem.

Chronology of the Kings of Israel and Judah

We know that different systems were used in the ancient Near East for denoting time. In the earliest period, both in Egypt and in Babylon, each year had a special name, usually relating to an important or a recent event which had taken place in the previous year. These names were then written down in lists and preserved.[1] In Assyria in the earliest period the names were called after a so-called eponymus. This eponymus was a king or another important person from his entourage. In Assyria, too, these names were written in lists.[2] In this way both the sequence and the names of the years were preserved. In a later period the years were named after the years of the kings' rule.

We also find this last system in the Old Testament, i.e. in the time of the kings. What happened in an earlier period is almost completely unknown. On some occasions this connection there is a reference to an important event, as for example in Num. 9.1 'in the second year of their exodus from the land of Egypt', and in Amos 1.1 we have 'two years before the earthquake'.

We find the first example of dating in accordance with the years of a king's reign in I Kings 6.1 (II Chron. 3.2): 'in the fourth year of Solomon's reign'. In the period of separate kingdoms of Israel and Judah this became a firm rule. Separate mention should be made of the method used by Ezekiel. He gives the years from the time when Jehoiachin was led into exile. Thus, for example, in Ezek. 1.2 we read, 'the fifth year of the captivity of king Jehoiachin'.[3] The fact that years were reckoned in accordance with the years of a king's reign raises a number of problems. For example, how did people reckon the year in which a king came to power? There are two possibilities. Either the first year of the new king was calculated from the New Year preceding his accession, or this first year was made to begin with the New Year festival following his accession. The former practice is referred to as ante-dating and the latter as post-dating. It is clear that in the first case a year is counted twice, namely in the reign of the previous king and then again in that of his successor. There is a further possibility that the years of a king's reign are made to begin on the day of his accession. In this case there was no question that a king's regnal year would coincide with a 'civic' year.[4]

Another problem is when the New Year began. This could be either in the spring or in the autumn. Both systems seem to have been used in the time of the kings. In the earliest period the beginning of a year was in the autumn, and in the later period it was in the spring. We are not absolutely certain when the change between the two took place.[5]

Furthermore, in the Old Testament we find indications of the duration of the reigns of the kings of Israel and Judah.[6] Thus for example in I Kings 14.21; II Chron. 12.13 we read that Rehoboam reigned for seventeen years. Quite apart from the question whether in all these instances we have ante-dating or post-dating, we do not know whether these indications also include the years in which a king acted as co-regent.

Furthermore, in the Old Testament we find numerous synchronisms.[7] Here it is particularly important that the beginning of the reign of a king in Israel or Judah is always indicated by the year of the reign of the king who was in power at that time in the other of the two kingdoms.[8] However, these synchronisms do not always by any means correspond with the indications of the durations of reigns.[9] The synchronisms also often differ from one another in the figures that they give.[10] And all this becomes even more problematical when we also take into account the information in the Septuagint.[11] Furthermore, the synchronisms with the Assyrian and Babylonian kings also play a prominent role.[12]

It is understandable that a good deal has been written about these problems.[13] In what follows I shall try to give some details of important studies in this field. They include those by Albright,[14] Andersen,[15] Begrich,[16] Jepsen,[17] Maxwell Miller,[18] Pavlovsky and Vogt,[19] Thiele[20] and Wifall.[21]

Albright's starting point is that the figures concerning the kings of Judah and Israel in the Old Testament were originally authentic and that the contradictions which appear in them must be explained by the use of different calendars, systems of calculation, etc. This is one of the reasons, according to him, why the datings in the Old Testament contain contradictions and are only approximately correct. A number of them are correct to within two years, but in most instances we must allow a margin of five years. Begrich begins by assuming that with a few exceptions the synchronisms in the Old Testament must be regarded as being more authentic than the indications of the durations of reigns.[22] As to the calendar year, Begrich thinks that in the earliest period in Israel and Judah it began in the autumn, and later, somewhere around 620 BC, began in the spring. Originally, too, ante-dating was used, but after Tiglath-pileser III (744–727)[23] had conquered Israel and

Judah, they went over to post-dating.[24] Begrich was not so much concerned with the question precisely when changes took place in connection with the calendar year and the method of dating. This was investigated above all by Jepsen, who followed the main lines of Begrich's investigation. He came to the conclusion that this must have happened in Israel with the accession of Pekahiah, and in Judah with that of Hezekiah,[25] seeing that these were the first kings who were already vassals of Assyria at the time of their accession.

Andersen comes to the conclusion that as long as Israel and Judah led separate existences, they used ante-dating and the calendar began in the autumn. Further, co-regencies and periods of a rival king were not included in the official years of a king's reign.[26] Thiele made an attempt to make all chronological indications agree together. He succeeded in doing this, one or two synchronisms apart. However, the result must be seen as something of a Pyrrhic victory. He was only able to achieve his aim with the help of a large number of hypotheses.[27] The starting point of the work of Pavlovsky and Vogt is that with few exceptions, post-dating was practised in Judah and ante-dating in Israel.[28]

According to Wifall, post-dating was used in both kingdoms from the death of Solomon to the end of Israel. Some modifications are introduced in his chronology. An editor tried at a later stage to produce the original text of the books of Kings and to restore the chronology by means of ante-dating.[29] Finally, Maxwell Miller claims that the Lucianic synchronisms connected with the period of Omri may have more claim to authenticity than those of the Massoretic text and that the first surrender of Jerusalem to Babylon must be dated in 597 BC.[30]

Despite the vast amount of literature which has been produced on these chronological problems, the last word on the question has certainly not yet been said. In the present book we shall largely follow the chronology given by Andersen.[31] In my view his is the most consistent and the least hypothetical in character. In giving his datings, unless otherwise stated, I am always taking them to be approximate.

At the end of the book, however, I have included a table with a survey of the most important chronological systems which ahve been put forward. The reader can judge them and compare them.

Chapter 10

The First Fifty Years after Solomon

10.1 *The end of the personal union*

I Kings 12.1–20 and II Chronicles 10 describe the break in the personal union between Israel and Judah. These accounts differ from one another in just a few points.[1] One problem is the report in I Kings 12.2–3 (cf. II Chron. 10.2–3) and I Kings 12.20 about Jeroboam's return from Egypt. Verse 20 gives the impression that Jeroboam only returned when the schism was a fact,[2] while vv. 2–3 suggest that he came back before it. The reading in v. 20 seems more original,[3] since for reasons of security Jeroboam probably could not come back before then.

Directly after the death of Solomon, we hear in I Kings 11.43; II Chron. 9.31, Rehoboam succeeded him as king. Clearly there was no longer any question as to who the appointed successor of Solomon would be, as there was in the succession to David. The Old Testament reports give us the impression that at least in Judah, Rehoboam automatically ascended his father's throne. In Israel, however, the situation was clearly rather different. I have already pointed out that attitudes here were much more democratic than in Judah. That now emerges.

Rehoboam went to Shechem, there to have himself proclaimed king over Israel. There is nothing to show that in the first instance Israel was opposed to this. As happened earlier, except with Solomon, this proclamation as king was made on the basis of an agreement. Both Saul and David became king of Israel by virtue of an agreement with the people.[4]

The conditions put by Israel to Rehoboam in Shechem required him to make a considerable reduction in taxation and in demands for forced labour. Rehoboam did not answer this request directly, but sought time for further consultation. He then asked advice from two groups, who in I Kings 12 and II Chron. 10 are described as 'old' and 'young' men. It is not clear from the relevant texts what precisely is meant by these two groups. Some want to see the expressions as indicating simply the relative ages of the advisers;[5] others suppose that the 'old' are elders,[6] or a royal council,[7] and that the 'young men' are the princes at court[8] or young friends of Rehoboam.[9] We cannot be at all certain here, but the additional explanation that the 'old men' had already served Solomon (I Kings 12.6; II Chron. 10.6) and that the 'young men' had grown up with Rehoboam seems most likely to indicate that these terms point to a difference in generation. Be this as it may, Rehoboam rejects the advice of the elders to accede to the people's requests, and accepts the advice of the young men to do precisely the opposite.

It emerges from all this that the advice is in no way binding on the king. Thus these advisers do not represent any kind of democratic institution.

The decisive encounter[10] between king and people takes place in Shechem on the third day. The result of Rehoboam's harsh answer is that Israel rejects him as king. That now meant the definitive end of the personal union between Israel and Judah. Thus it had only managed to survive for a relatively short space of time, during the reigns of two kings, one of whom (David) had more or less absolute command and the other (Solomon) had absolute command. The schism, moreover, implies that in fact the situation returned to what it was before the time of David.

As to the dynastic principle, further developments in the two kingdoms led in different directions. Judah remained faithful to the dynasty of David to the end. In Israel, there was no stability in this respect. There people to some degree went back to a charismatic leadership such as that which already existed in the time before David. Furthermore, there we have different dynasties, only one of which was able to sustain itself for any length of time.

Something of all this is already expressed in the choice of Jeroboam. This Jeroboam was clearly a skilful man[11] and an inspired leader. At any rate, after the division of the kingdoms he seemed to be the obvious figure to ascend the throne of Israel.[12]

10.2 *Relations between Israel and Judah*

10.2.1 *The general political situation*

The break in the personal union at the same time meant the end of the great kingdom which had existed in the time of David and Solomon. We have already seen in the previous chapter (9.5) that this kingdom was already showing signs of collapse and decay. Furthermore, the fact that after the death of Solomon Israel succeeded in breaking loose from the personal union and the dynasty of David is evidence enough in this direction. However, what was left of the great kingdom after the division was two miniature states, which in the future were almost incapable of exerting any influence. There is reason to suppose that these developments were closely connected with the influence of Egypt, whose power was rising again. Obviously it was increasingly successful in getting a grip on events in Canaan. This is also indicated by the campaign against Jerusalem undertaken by Pharaoh Shishak, according to I Kings 14.25–26; II Chron. 12.2–9, in the fifth year of Rehoboam.

The account in I Kings 14 is very succinct and tells us only that Shishak attacked Jerusalem and plundered the treasures of the temple and the palace. It is possible that here we have an extract from ancient temple annals which simply related the consequence of this campaign for the temple in Jerusalem.[13] In the rather longer account in II Chron. 12, we are told that during this campaign Shishak also succeeded in capturing various fortresses in Judah.

The report of a campaign by Shishak contained in the Old Testament seems to be confirmed by an Egyptian source. A so-called 'city list' has been found on the wall of a temple of Amon in Karnak with the mention of cities which Shishak conquered on this campaign in Canaan.[14] This list also includes the names of various places in Israel which are not mentioned at all in the Old Testament. This, however, must be ascribed to the fact that the Deuteronomist and even more the Chronicler primarily concentrated on events in Judah. Israel appears only rarely, and then above all in a polemical context. It is striking that Jerusalem does not appear on the list at all. Presumably it felt seriously threatened and Rehoboam paid over the temple and palace treasures to Shishak.[15] At all events, these reports show that after the death of Solomon Canaan again came very much under Egyptian influence.

10.2.2 *Mutual conflicts*

In I Kings 12.21–24 (II Chron. 11.4) we hear that Rehoboam had a plan to impose the personal union on Israel by force of arms, but Shemaiah, a man of God, is said to have prevented this. Another account in I Kings 14.30; II Chron. 12.15, however, records that there was constant war between Jeroboam and Rehoboam. We should presumably see this as the more authentic tradition in this respect. The former account is probably a later addition of Judaean origin, which seeks to explain how the legitimate ruler in Jerusalem let go of Israel.[16] It is evident, however, from I Kings 15.16–22 (see below) that, on the contrary, Judah constantly had its back to the wall in a confrontation with Israel. The view that I Kings 12.21–24 should be seen as a later addition is also supported by the fact that v. 21 states that Benjamin, too, took the side of Rehoboam. However, in the context of the pericope, only Judah is mentioned. I Kings 15.20–22 simply reports that Judah later, with foreign help, succeeded in occupying the northern part of Benjamin.[17]

In this connection we must now return to the encounter between Jeroboam

and Ahijah, already mentioned earlier (9.8); it is described in I Kings 11.29–39.
In this story ten tribes are promised to Jeroboam, while the dynasty of David
will have one tribe left to it.[18] The motivation behind this last saying is
indicated in the words, 'that David my servant may always have a lamp before
me in Jerusalem' (v. 36).[19] The question is, who is meant by this one tribe? On
this point opinions are divided. Some suppose it to be Benjamin.[20] However,
given what has gone before, it seems highly probable that we should take it to
be Judah.[21]

The greatest conflict between Israel and Judah in the first decades after the
division is narrated in I Kings 15.16–22 (II Chron. 16.1–6). In this account we
hear of a war between Baasha of Israel and Asa of Judah. It is clear that in this
battle Judah very soon came off worst. Baasha evidently soon managed to
occupy the city of Ramah, about five miles north of Jerusalem. He fortified this
city with the aim of thus isolating Jerusalem from the north. This produced a
dangerous situation for Jerusalem. Asa was able to avert the danger by calling
in the help of Benhadad, king of Aram, who resided in Damascus.
Benhadad[22] now broke his treaty with Israel and came to the help of Asa.
However, in the long run this military support had to be paid for. According to
I Kings 15.18; II Chron. 16.2, Asa had to give all the silver and gold that were
still in the temple and the palace. The Hebrew word used for this gift by Asa to
Benhadad in Kings 15.19 can often denote a purchase price. This last meaning
seems very appropriate here.

Through the intervention of Benhadad, Baasha was now compelled to
evacuate Ramah, whereupon Asa immediately took measures to prevent the
repetition of such an event in the future. With the material intended for the
fortification of Ramah, which Baasha had to leave behind in his over-hasty
retreat, he now strengthened the cities of Geba and Mizpah. In this way he
moved the frontier of Judah further north, making Jerusalem less vulnerable
to a possible attack by Israel.

That is the end of the account in I Kings 15, but there is a sequel in II Chron.
16.7–10. There we hear that Hanani the seer rebuked Asa[23] for this alliance
with Aram and that as a result the seer was imprisoned by Asa. Presumably this
addition in Chronicles is closely connected with the theological views of the
Chronicler, who judges the kings primarily in the light of their fidelity to
Yahweh and to the cult in Jerusalem. The striking thing is that this theological
conception of the Chronicler's is primarily expressed in those parts of
Chronicles to which there are no parallels in the books of Kings.[24]

10.3 *Judah in the time of Rehoboam, Abijah and Asa*

10.3.1 *Rehoboam (932/31 – 916/15)*

As I have already pointed out, Rehoboam was king over a kingdom which was no more than a rump state in comparison with that of his predecessors.[25] Internationally, too, it was of minimal significance. Doubtless this last fact contributed to Judah's success in continuing to exist as a more or less independent state for 135 years longer than Israel.

Apart from the invasion of Pharaoh Shishak mentioned in the previous section (10.2.1), the relevant texts from Kings and Chronicles give us the impression that the reign of Rehoboam was a relatively peaceful period. The Old Testament provides hardly any information about the time during which he reigned as king over Judah. Only in II Chron. 11.5–12 do we find a further important piece of information, namely that Rehoboam fortified various cities in the south. We do not know whether he did this before or after the invasion of Shishak. However, archaeological evidence does in fact seem to confirm that Rehoboam was occupied with the building of fortifications in the south.[26] After a reign of seventeen years, Rehoboam died and was succeeded by his son Abijam (I Kings 14.31; II Chron. 12.16).

10.3.2 *Abijam (916/15 – 914/13)*

We are told almost nothing about Abijam in the book of Kings.[27] In fact it contains only two brief notes about him. There is one in I Kings 15.7b, where we are told that 'there was war between Abijam and Jeroboam', and a remark in I Kings 15.1–5 that Abijam was not wholly devoted to God.[28] This last detail is omitted in Chronicles, which in contrast gives extensive details (II Chron. 13.2–20) of a war (cf. I Kings 15.7b) between Abijam and Jeroboam which was decided completely in favour of the former. In fact, however, this last account is concerned not so much with this war as with the discourse in II Chron. 13.5–12, which is typical of the preaching of the Chronicler.[29] We have no further information about the cause and nature of this dispute between Abijam and Jeroboam. Abijam reigned for only three years. After him his son Asa became king of Judah.

10.3.3 *Asa (914/13 – 874/73)*

Apart from mentioning Asa's war with Baasha of Israel, which we have already discussed (10.2.2), the book of Kings refers only to his attitude to alien cultic practices. In this part (I Kings 15.11–15), which is typical of the theological conceptions of the Deuteronomist, we hear that Asa strove to remove all pagan accretions from the worship of Yahweh. According to I Kings 15.14, he was not completely successful in this, since the high places continued to exist.

In addition, in Chronicles (II Chron. 14.9–15) we are told that Asa fought against Zerah the Cushite. The Chronicler does not give us any exact information about the circumstances and course of this conflict. Bright thinks it possible that Zerah was a garrison commander left behind in Gerar by Shishak.[30] However, we have no evidence for this at all.

It is clear that both Kings and Chronicles provide us only with sparse information about the roughly forty years during which Asa was king over Judah. Presumably this information will have been contained in the 'Book of the Chronicles of the kings of Judah' mentioned in I Kings 15.23 and the 'Book of the kings of Judah and Israel' mentioned in II Chron. 16.11.

10.4 *Jeroboam's religious policy*

Jeroboam is probably best known in the Old Testament for the fact that he set up statues of golden 'calves' in the sanctuaries at Bethel and Dan (I Kings 12.28–29). The Deuteronomistic expression 'walk in the sin of Jeroboam, the son of Nebat' became a classical expression in the Old Testament for describing a king's breach of faith towards Yahweh. Furthermore, this is a typical Deuteronomistic expression. In fact Jeroboam's action amounted to raising the status of the old sanctuaries in Dan and Bethel, lying respectively in the north and south of Israel, to that of national sanctuaries.[31]

Although the passage (I Kings 12.26–32) in which the erection of statues in Bethel and Dan is reported (v. 29) was worked over later in Judah and has a marked polemical character, the report as such can certainly be said to be reliable historically.[32] At the time of Amos (7.13), at any rate, the national sanctuary in Bethel seems to have become an established institution. The statues of bulls clearly served here as symbols of Yahweh. At all events, there are indications that such images had already had this function in Israel in earlier times.[33] Although there still does not seem to be convincing proof, we should also remember that for a long time the image of a bull had served as a symbol for a deity in Canaan (Ugarit). It is thus quite possible that such a usage had already been taken over formally in Israel before the time of Jeroboam.[34] For that reason alone it is wrong to accuse Jeroboam I of anti-Yahwism, or to claim him as the founder of a new kind of worship. Brongers[35] rightly observes that Jeroboam wanted to worship Yahweh just as much as did his rival in Judah, and that the measures he took were primarily of political significance.

Furthermore, the customs at the sanctuaries in Bethel and Dan, which very probably go back to an ancient, typically Israelite tradition,[36] will certainly not have been regarded as unlawful in his time. In this connection it is clear that the remark in I Kings 12.27–28 about the temple in Jerusalem must be ascribed to a later revision in Judah or Jerusalem. The story of the man of God in I Kings 12.33—13.34 is also from a later period.[37] All this is evident, for example, from the fact that the centralization of the cult in Jerusalem took place only very gradually and was achieved more or less successfully only in the time of Josiah. We can also see how insignificant the Jerusalem temple was at an early period from the attitude of specifically northern Israelite prophets like Elijah and Hosea, who fiercely attack the worship of Baal, but never mention the temple in Jerusalem.

It is therefore most improbable that Jeroboam wanted to develop the sanctuaries in Bethel and Dan because he was afraid that many people in his own country would seek to make Jerusalem the centre of their worship. We must assume, rather, that Jeroboam wanted to achieve some kind of centralization of worship in his kingdom, as David and Solomon had tried to do earlier in connection with Jerusalem.

Furthermore, the problems with which Jeroboam had to contend during his reign were not connected so much with his religious policy, as with the heterogeneous composition of Israel. In this connection the choice of Bethel and Dan may have led to rivalry among different tribes or groups who perhaps thought that other sanctuaries near them could make more of a claim.

10.5 *Israel from Jeroboam to Omri*

10.5.1 *Jeroboam I (932/31–911/10)*

Jeroboam moved his capital three times during his reign, successively to Shechem, Penuel and Tirzah. According to I Kings 12.25, the first two of these cities were fortified by him at that time. Given its previous history and its strategic situation, the choice of Shechem seems very logical, so it is all the more surprising that Jeroboam later moved his residence to Penuel in Transjordan. We are completely in the dark as to the reasons for this. Herrmann[38] has conjectured that it might be connected with the campaign of Pharaoh Shishak, mentioned earlier. However, this is by no means certain. The same can also be said of Allan's view[39] that the presence of many Levites in Shechem who were regarded as Jerusalem agents might be behind Jeroboam's move away from there. Anyway, Jeroboam did not remain in Penuel, but chose as his next residence the city of Tirzah, which was about six miles north-east of Shechem (cf. I Kings 14.17).

The conflict with the prophet Ahijah of Shiloh described in I Kings 14.1–18 also falls during Jeroboam's stay in this last city. This is the very prophet who once designated him as king over Israel (I Kings 11.37). Although this account in I Kings 14.1–18 may well contain old material, in the present context it has been subjected to a marked Deuteronomistic redaction.[40] That is also the reason why it is extremely difficult to establish the original cause of this conflict.[41] It is also characteristic here that in the present state of the text we are not told in detail what precisely the 'sin' of Jeroboam was.

This conflict also seems to be a sign of the instability which can constantly be noted in the state of Israel. Here the scanty information which we get from the Old Testament through the Deuteronomist says a great deal. At all events, the numerous conflicts with prophets and the many changes of dynasty point in this direction. Presumably the heterogeneous make-up of the people played a very important part here. Alt thought that the principal cause for the frequent changes of dynasty in Israel lay in the fact that these dynasties were to a considerable degree based on charismatic leadership.[42] This view of Alt's has been widely shared.[43] One important factor which must certainly be mentioned alongside it is the constant rivalry between various groups and tribes in Israel. In this particular respect, Israel was very different from Judah, where the population was much more homogeneous than it was in Israel.

10.5.2 *From Nadab to Omri*

After ruling for about twenty-two years, Jeroboam was succeeded by his son Nadab (911/10 – 910/09). However, the latter only reigned for about two years (I Kings 15.25–28). He was killed by Baasha, of the tribe of Issachar, who then himself became king over Israel and reigned for about twenty-four years (910/09 – 887/86). This is the first time that a usurper seized the throne in Israel by force and displaced the reigning dynasty. In the two centuries of its existence, from the death of Solomon to the captivity in Assyria, Israel experienced such usurpers no less than nine times!

Of this king, apart from his war with Asa of Judah (10.3.2), we hear only that a prophet Jehu son of Hanani – of whom we know nothing but the name[44] – was opposed to him. The word of God handed down in I Kings 16.2–4 in connection with this is in every respect strongly reminiscent of the words of Ahijah to Jeroboam in I Kings 14.7–11, and does not seem to be particularly original.

Baasha, too, was unable to establish a lasting dynasty in Israel. Scarcely had his son Elah become king (887/86 – 886/85) than he was murdered by his minister Zimri (I Kings 16.9–10). But Zimri reigned for only seven days and was then killed in the palace which he himself had set on fire at the approach of the new pretender to the throne, Omri (I Kings 16.15–19). Omri, an army commander, was made king over Israel after the death of Elah, by the army (I Kings 16.15–16). However, before he definitively acceded to the throne, he had to deal with another rival, Tibni (I Kings 16.21–22). Evidently this did not take him long.[45]

The terse account of these events, which in fact does not provide any further facts or details, was perhaps taken from the lost 'book of the chronicles of the kings of Israel'.[46]

Chapter II

The Dynasty of Omri

In contrast to the previous period, in the time of the dynasty of Omri there is no mention of conflicts between Israel and Judah. The Old Testament itself mentions an alliance with Judah which Ahab made during his reign (I Kings 22; II Chron. 18). This confederacy was obviously endorsed by wedding between Joram,[1] the son of Jehoshaphat of Judah, and Athaliah, Ahab's daughter or sister.[2]

The friendly relationship between the two states was doubtless also governed by the dominant position which Israel had over Judah. Otherwise, the foreign policy of Omri's dynasty was strongly influenced by relations with Moab and the rise of Aram and Assyria. We shall consider these aspects in the next sections.

II.I.I *The subjection of Moab*

In II Kings 1.1 there is a brief note to the effect that after the death of Ahab, Moab rebelled against Israel, and in II Kings 3 we hear that Jehoram son of Ahab made an unsuccessful attempt to reestablish Israelite authority over Moab.

Now it is remarkable that there is not a word in the Old Testament about a conquest of Moab by Israel. Thanks to the information on the so-called Moabite Stone, we now know that this territory was in fact conquered by Omri.[3] This inscription, which dates from about 840 BC, tells how, after a long period of subjection to the house of Omri, Moab rebelled against Israel during the reign of Jehoram.

The fact that the Old Testament says nothing about this conquest must certainly be ascribed to the theological presuppositions of the Deuteronomists. They determined the facts and the material which were included in the Deuteronomistic history work and worked over there. In the foreground of the

Deuteronomistic history we have the temple in Jerusalem as the only legitimate place of worship, something which was simply taken for granted in the time of the Deuteronomist, after the exile, and the kings of Israel and Judah are judged and discussed in the light of this.

It is clear that the kings of Israel come off very badly in this respect. Omri and Ahab, in particular, are subjected to extremely fierce criticism. That also explains why there is no mention of the conquest of Moab by Omri. Granted, as we saw, II Kings 3 recounts in some detail a clearly unsuccessful campaign by Jehoram against Moab, but here the focal point is rather the prophet Elisha and his criticism of the house of Omri. Nevertheless, it is clear from the scanty evidence in the Old Testament and above all from the content of the Mesha inscription that by the period of the dynasty of Omri, Moab had long belonged within the Israelite sphere of influence.

It is already clear from what has been said that in the time of the Omrids Israel played a significant role. This impression is strengthened by the fact that in the Assyrian royal inscriptions Israel is often referred to as the 'house of Omri' or the 'land of Omri'.[4] The name Omri was used by the Assyrians even after his dynasty was exterminated. Thus Jehu is called a 'king of Omri(land)' in Assyrian inscriptions.[5]

11.1.2 *Relations with Aram and Assyria*

At this time another power came to the fore in Syria–Palestine in addition to Israel. This was the Aramaean kingdom of Damascus, which had won its independence in the time of Solomon and had gradually grown stronger and more important. It seems clear that at this period Israel and Aram were the predominant powers in this region. We may also legitimately suppose that there was a degree of rivalry between these two states in various spheres. Doubtless economic motives were also involved here.

One important indication of this last factor is the marriage which Ahab made with Jezebel, the daughter of the Phoenician king Ethbaal. This marriage was in all probability arranged by Omri.[6] Because such a marriage never happened without ulterior motives, and the Phoenicians were well-known in antiquity as merchants and seafarers, we may assume that primarily economic factors were involved. All this strengthened the position of the Omrids.

According to I Kings 20.34, Aram too had to allow Israel certain trade facilities.[7] However, it is not certain that this happened during the time of the Omrids. The context (I Kings 20) of this report raises a number of problems. In this account there is a mention of a war against Benhadad of Damascus. However, this happened much later than Ahab, whose contemporary was not

Benhadad II but Hadadezer. Furthermore, in I Kings 20 the name of Ahab is mentioned only twice (vv. 2, 13); elsewhere we find simply 'the king of Israel'. Consequently there is reason to suppose that the name Ahab is secondary in this account. That is further suggested by the sympathetic attitude adopted by the unknown prophet to the king here. Ahab is hardly likely to have been regarded so favourably. Albright's conjecture[8] that Benhadad was the throne-name of Hadad seems an unrealistic solution. The only thing which seems to fit the time of the Omrids well in this story is the granting of trade facilities mentioned above (I Kings 20.34).

What has been said above can also, broadly speaking, be applied to the war between Ahab of Israel and Jehoshaphat of Judah on the one hand, and Aram on the other, mentioned in I Kings 22 (and in II Chron. 18). Here the name of Ahab appears only once (I Kings 22.20).[9] In this passage, too, the names of Ahab and Jehoshaphat seem to be secondary.[10] At all events, it is clear that in I Kings 22; II Chron. 18 there is more stress on the opposition between the true prophet (Micaiah ben Imlah) and the false prophets than on a war with Aram. Furthermore, this account has a markedly prophetic character. So we do not know for sure whether there were military conflicts between Israel and Aram in the time of Omri and Ahab. We may be certain that there was an alliance between Ahab and the king of Aram. Both belonged to a great coalition which was formed to resist the growing threat from Assyria. The Old Testament says nothing about this event, but the Assyrian annals of Shalmaneser III (858–824) record that this king of Assyria undertook an expedition to Syria–Palestine which ended in a battle at Karkar against a coalition which, according to the account, included Ahab of Israel.[11] Although the annals as usual make no mention of a defeat, they give the impression that things did not turn out too favourably for Assyria. Clearly this expedition did not achieve its purpose, and the danger from Assyria was repelled by the confederate kings – at least for the moment.[12] On this occasion Ahab is said to have committed no less than 2,000 chariots and 10,000 foot-soldiers to the battle.[13]

11.2 Domestic policy

11.2.1 The political and economic situation in the kingdom

One of the most important initiatives taken by Omri during his twelve-year reign (886/5–875/4) was the purchase of the mount of Samaria (I Kings 16.24). On this mountain Omri established a new capital for his kingdom. In his enterprise Omri presumably had the same aim as David in the capture of Jebus (see 8.3.2), namely of creating a capital which was outside the territory of the mutually competing tribes. For this reason alone it seems improbable that the foundation of Samaria also had the aim of shifting the focal point of the kingdom to the tribal territory of Issachar.[14] The purchase and founding of Samaria at the same time made this city the private possession of the king of Israel. It is clear, especially from the ostraca from *c.* 795 and 776 BC found at Samaria, that in the course of time this possession (the crown property) of the kings of Israel offered numerous advantages.[15] Archaeological investigations have shown that here Omri in fact built an entire new city.[16] The strategic position of Samaria as a capital was particularly favourable. The city lay on a hill which could easily be defended and could well withstand a long siege.

One complication is that the Omrids are known to have had a second residence, in Jezreel. According to Alt,[17] Samaria was primarily the centre of the Canaanite part of the population in the state of Israel, whereas Jezreel was more the centre for the Israelite part; however, this view has been challenged by de Vaux.[18] At all events, it seems certain that until the rise of Jehu, Samaria was an important centre for the worship of Baal. At least, the information in II Kings 10 points in this direction. However, that was probably not the main purpose of Omri's choice of Samaria. Were that so we might well ask why he did not prefer a specifically Canaanite city like Shechem as the capital for the Canaanite part of the population.

After Omri, Ahab was also involved in building in the city of Samaria.[19] We know of the palace or palace-complex, which shows signs of work from the time of Ahab and Jeroboam II as well as from that of Omri. The so-called 'ivory house'[20] was particularly famous. The building work of Ahab was not limited to Samaria. There are also remains of buildings, 'Ahab's stables', in Megiddo from the time of Ahab.[21] Furthermore, texts like I Kings 16.34; 22.39 could be an indication that the building works in the time of Ahab were not limited to the places named above.

At the same time, all these activities show that in the period of the Omrids, Israel must have enjoyed a time of considerable material prosperity. In many respects this must have recalled that of Solomon during the personal union with Judah. Israel now reached the point attained by Judah in the time of Solomon. However, despite this prosperity and the powerful position occupied by Israel during the dynasty of Omri, we get a strong impression that the peasant population in particular had a hard time of it. Just as in the time of Solomon, poverty seemed to be on the increase, especially in the country. We find an indication of this in the stories of the prophets Elijah and Elisha. One example is the report in II Kings 4.1 about a creditor who threatens to seize a widow's two sons as slaves. It is also striking that these prophets evidently found a following mainly in the country, and above all among the peasant farmers.

In this context the story of the purchase of Naboth's vineyard in I Kings 21 is also interesting. Here we have an attempt by Ahab to extend his estates in the capital by the purchase of this vineyard. However, he came up against great difficulties because Naboth refused to allow the purchase of his ancestral property. Ahab, however, was able to achieve his purpose by doing away with Naboth.[22] II Kings 9.25–26 suggests that this action was held against Ahab at the time of Jehu's rebellion.

As Welten[23] has shown, this conflict between the royal house in Jezreel and Naboth rests on a historical event. Although we have no direct evidence, we can assume that this is not just one chance happening. The words of Amos, about a century later, seem to suggest that there was an increase in the size of land-holdings in the previous period. Something of this kind could come about only at the expense of many other people.

11.2.2 The religious policy of the Omrids

In the previous sections I have already alluded in passing to one of the greatest domestic problems with which the Omrids were confronted. This was the question of the two different population groups who lived in Israel. Many Canaanites were established here as well as Israelites. This created religious as well as sociological and economic problems, and it is almost impossible to separate one from the other in considering the course of history. In Israel, the Canaanites were chiefly supporters of the cult of Baal.

Like Solomon earlier,[24] the Omrids opted for a policy of apartheid for these different groups.[25] Although they allowed the followers of Baal to practise their religion, we may not presuppose that they themselves were fervent supporters of it. The names of Ahab's sons in fact suggest the opposite. At all events, Ahaziah and Jehoram are theophoric names in which we can clearly recognize the divine name Yahweh. It is probable that in addition to the various factors mentioned in 11.2.1, above all the tolerance towards the cult of Baal and the religious policy of Jezebel were the factors which aroused fierce opposition to the Omrids among many people, especially the prophets of Yahweh.

The fact, mentioned in I Kings 16.32, that after his marriage with Jezebel Ahab erected an altar for Baal in his temple in Samaria doubtless played an important part here. Solomon, too, had established separate sanctuaries for his pagan wives, but Ahab obviously went further. Evidently the sanctuary in Samaria was not only meant for his wife and her retinue from Tyre but also served as the official sanctuary for the Canaanite part of the population. In fact this amounted to an official recognition of the religion of Baal in the state of

Israel.[26] This was something which many people could not or would not tolerate. In the situation of conflict which arose as a result, the prophets of Yahweh came to the fore.

11.3 *Confrontation with the prophets*

11.3.1 *The figure of the prophet*

There has already been occasional mention of the rise of a prophet in the previous chapters. Here above all the figure of Nathan came to the fore. He could best be described as a prophet in the service of the court and the temple – a kind of court prophet – and in any case someone who could be called more or less a functionary of an institution.

We can say little with any certainty about the origin of prophetism. As we find it in the Old Testament, prophetism is in a particular phase of development. This is clear, for example, in the well-known statement in I Sam. 9.9, where we are told: 'He who is now called a prophet was formerly called a seer'. However, seeing that the two words seer and prophet are used as virtual synonyms in the Old Testament, a statement of this kind is of little help to us in answering the question of the rise of prophetism in Israel. Nor do we get much further with the generally accepted view that prophecy in the Old Testament goes back to seers (as found among the nomads) and ecstatic prophecy as known in the ancient Near East.

It emerges from this last comment that prophecy and the figure of the prophet were not a typically Israelite phenomenon. People were familiar with particular forms of prophecy outside Israel as well.[27] One important difference between this prophecy and that in Israel is probably the critical attitude often adopted by the Old Testament prophets to temple, king and people.

In the Old Testament we can also distinguish different types of prophets, such as court prophets, cultic prophets and individual or free prophets. In addition, we can also see a difference between true and false prophets.[28] As to the latter, we need to remember that this dividing line need not coincide with that between a prophet associated with an institution and a free prophet. A court prophet need not be a false prophet, and conversely the free or individual prophet is not by definition a true prophet.

This brief survey already shows that there were considerable and rich distinctions in the Old Testament within both prophetism and prophecy.[29] Thus the prophets who emerge in the time of the Omrids in Israel are clearly of a different type from the prophet Nathan mentioned earlier. There is also mention here of 'schools of prophets' and 'sons of prophets' which have not

appeared hitherto, though we can probably also envisage such a group in
I Sam. 10.10 (on the return of Saul from Ramah).

This will emerge further in the next section.

11.3.2 *The rise of the prophets*

At first sight we get the impression that a good deal of attention is paid to the
time of the Omrids in I and II Kings. This period takes up the account from
I Kings 16.15 to II Kings 10.27; more, for example, than the space devoted to
Solomon. On closer inspection, however, it is evident that the greater part of
the account is devoted to the prophets Elijah[30] and Elisha.[31] There is also
mention of a certain Micaiah ben Imlah (I Kings 22.8–28) who announces
Ahab's downfall in the battle with Aram, and some unnamed prophets or
groups of prophets. Thus an unknown prophet (I Kings 20.13–15) and a 'man
of God' (I Kings 20.28) say that Ahab will gain a victory over the Aramaeans,
and another anonymous prophet (I Kings 20.35–42) rebukes Ahab for his
indulgent attitude towards Benhadad.[32]

Apart from these figures, we also hear of prophets emerging in public (see
above) or living together in groups. There were evidently such groups, for
example, in Bethel (II Kings 2.3), Jericho (II Kings 2.15–18) and Gilgal (II
Kings 4.38). It is possible that these prophets and groups of prophets (who are
not identified further) were attached to particular sanctuaries. The mention of
places like Bethel and Gilgal could point in this direction. On the other hand,
they might also be 'lay prophets'.[33] According to the information in the books
of Kings, the prophets Elijah and Elisha had very close contacts with these
figures and groups.

In all probability, in these books we have collections of stories about
prophets which had already been made independently. The incorporation and
extensive reproduction of these stories in the Deuteronomistic history work is
perhaps connected with the fact that it was written at a time when preaching of
and about the prophets was a central point of interest. In these stories, Elijah
and Elisha occupy pride of place. Moreover, it is striking that with the sole
exception of a mention of Elijah in II Chron. 21.12, neither of these prophets
appears at all in Chronicles.

It is also clear that the stories about Elijah and Elisha in each case have a
character of their own. We must assume that tales of these prophets were first
handed down orally in the circles of their respective disciples or followers.
Later, with various additions, they will have been collected together as a
whole. This collection is characterized by a particular theological conception.
Above all the stories of Elijah have the stamp of fierce polemic against Baal
worship. Of course such polemic – and this applies to the whole of the Old

Testament – gives us only a vague and one-sided picture of the precise content of this cult.[34] However, a text like I Kings 18.27 gives the impression that Elijah will have been very well acquainted with this Baal worship.[35]

I have already remarked in the previous section (II.2.2) that Ahab founded a place of worship for Baal in Samaria. It can be inferred from I Kings 18.19–40, which may go back to a historical background from the time of Ahab,[36] that there was also such a place of sacrifice on Carmel. Doubtless this, too, was connected with the religious policy carried out by the Omrids and especially by Ahab. However, the story of the prophets of Baal in I Kings 18 can be a clear indication that Jezebel strongly encouraged the worship of the Baal of Tyre.[37] That Elijah played a prominent part in confrontation with these prophets seems unmistakable. In I Kings 19, which describes Elijah's flight to Horeb, there are many elements which suggest the figure of Moses. For example, there is the note in v. 8 that this journey took forty days and forty nights.[38] The purpose of the story seems to be to characterize Elijah quite clearly as a second Moses. A remarkable feature in it is the command to anoint three different people: Jehu as king over Israel, Hazael as king over Aram and Elisha as prophet (I Kings 19.15–16). We hear nothing of these commands being carried out. On the contrary, Jehu is later anointed by a disciple of Elisha (II Kings 9.1–10), and in II Kings 8.7–15 a connection is made between the beginning of Hazael's rule and Elisha.[39]

The polemic of Elijah against the worship of Baal was also indirectly aimed at the figure of the king. This is clearly indicated in the accounts I have just mentioned. I noted earlier (II.2.1) the influence of political and economic factors, and they clearly also play a prominent part here. The stories about the prophet Elisha have a different character. Here polemic against Baal worship fades right into the background.[40] He had much closer contact than Elijah with the groups of 'sons of the prophets' already mentioned earlier. Politically speaking, above all he seems to have had a hand in the overthrow of the dynasty of the Omrids (II Kings 9.1–15).

II.4 *Judah at the time of the dynasty of Omri*

II.4.1 *The period from Jehoshaphat to Ahaziah*

The words in I Kings 22.44, 'Jehoshaphat also made peace with the king of Israel', are characteristic of the relationship between Israel and Judah in the time of the Omrids. The fierce confrontations and skirmishes of the period before the Omrids came to power had disappeared. Furthermore, we have seen that now there is even often mention of an alliance between Israel and Judah (I Kings 22; II Kings 3.4–27). This development was certainly not least influenced by the strong position which Israel occupied during the time of the dynasty of Omri. Throughout this whole period it is clear that Israel played a much more important role than Judah.

At a later date, however, people were not entirely happy about Judah's policy of peace towards Israel. Whereas there is no detectable criticism in the books of Kings of Jehoshaphat's alliance with Ahab, he is sharply criticized for this alliance by the Chronicler (II Chron. 19.1–3).

Despite this, the Chronicler also describes Jehoshaphat as a good and righteous king. Furthermore, in the books of Chronicles, in contrast to the books of Kings, considerable attention is paid to the reign of Jehoshaphat (874/73–850/49). In Kings, apart from the treaty with Ahab in I Kings 22, mentioned above, all that we are in fact told is that Jehoshaphat made attempts to restore the trade with Ophir which previously existed at the time of Solomon (I Kings 22.48–50). According to I Kings 22.50, Jehoshaphat refused to accept help from Ahaziah, son of Ahab, in this respect. However, II Chron. 20.35–37 says that Jehoshaphat did in fact accept this help and that for this reason Yahweh destroyed the ships built at Ezion-geber. The one thing that is certain in this disputed affair is that trade with Ophir came to nothing.

Jehoshaphat seems to have had rather more success in his domestic policy,[41] though we have little specific information. Some archaeological discoveries[42] perhaps confirm the information given briefly in II Chron. 17.13 that Jehoshaphat built fortresses and store-cities.

We have little certain information about the reign of Jehoshaphat's son Joram (850/49–843/42), apart from what was said earlier (11.1). In both Kings (II Kings 8.18) and Chronicles (II Chron. 21.6) he is fiercely criticized for his marriage with Athaliah. It seems that Edom rebelled during his reign (II Kings 8.20–22; II Chron. 21.8–10). In the time of Jehoshaphat Edom was still under the control of a governor (I Kings 22.48) who is probably also to be seen as a vassal of Judah. Jehoshaphat's attempt, mentioned above, to restore trade with Ophir via the south seems also to correspond with this. An enterprise of this kind would be impossible in practice without some control over Edom. The report that Judah was supported by Edom in the campaign mentioned in II Kings 3–4 may also indicate that Edom was in a dependent position. At all events, after Joram we hear no more of Edom as a state dependent on Judah.

Joram's successor Ahaziah reigned for only a year (843/42–842/41). He died in Megiddo, having been wounded seriously, according to II Kings 9.27, by followers of Jehu in the neighbourhood of Jezreel. However, the Chronicler gives a completely different account of Ahaziah's death. In II Chron. 22.9 it is reported that Ahaziah was put to death by Jehu in Samaria. We can no longer discover which of these two accounts is the correct interpretation of this event.

11.4.2 *Athaliah*

After the death of Ahaziah, the dynasty of David was out of power in Judah for about five years. In this period the throne of Judah was occupied by one of the Omrids, Athaliah (842/41–837/36).

After Jehu's revolution in Israel, in which all the dynasty of Omri[43] and also Ahaziah of Judah were killed, the position of this woman had become particularly precarious. A brief account in II Kings 11.1–3 and II Chron. 22.10–12 records that, after the death of Ahaziah, Athaliah succeeded in seizing power in Judah through harsh and merciless action. All the male descendants of David were killed in this palace revolution. Only Joash, the one-year-old son of Ahaziah, was saved by Jehosheba, one of Ahaziah's sisters, and kept hidden from Athaliah. During her reign he stayed in the temple, where he was entrusted to the care of the priest Jehoiada. We can understand that as a result Jehoiada gained great influence over this last descendant of David. About 837/36, Jehoiada succeeded in liquidating Athaliah and having Joash (836/35–797/96) proclaimed king over Judah.[44]

The temple guard came particularly to the fore in this revolution. However, the priests from the Jerusalem temple played a special role in the *coup d'état*. These were evidently supported by a group which in II Kings 11.18, 20 is referred to as the 'people of the land'. II Kings 11.20, which we find in almost the same words in II Chron. 23.21, is especially instructive in helping us to understand the events described here. In this verse we hear that 'the people of the land' rejoiced over the revolution and that 'the city remained quiet'. This last piece of information strongly suggests that the population of Jerusalem was not particularly happy with the change of rule, but could be kept under restraint. Things were different with the 'people of the land', who were clearly in full agreement with this action. The question now is who precisely these people were. The term obviously does not have the same meaning everywhere in the Old Testament, and it has undergone an evident change of meaning.[45] Many people think that in II Kings 11.18, 20 it refers to the country people of Judah.[46] This interpretation seems to do full justice to the events in II Kings 11.

The fall of Athaliah once again emphasizes how strongly the position of the Davidic dynasty was rooted in Judah. That very factor was of decisive significance in this revolution in Jerusalem. Political reasons, above all, must have brought it about. The result of all this was that the influence and power of the priests in the Jerusalem temple increased considerably. The information in both II Kings 11 and II Chron. 23 at least points us firmly in this direction.

Chapter 12

The Dynasty of Jehu

12.1 *Jehu's revolution*

12.1.1 *The Old Testament evidence*

As with the Omrids, the Old Testament provides us with little information about the period during which the dynasty of Jehu was in power in Israel. The most detailed account is that of Jehu and his revolution, reported in II Kings 9—10 and II Chron. 22.1–9.

The considerable attention paid to Jehu's revolution in II Kings 9–10 is typical of the theological views of the Deuteronomist, who usually has little interest in the state of Israel. This is sharply expressed, for example, in his account of the reign of Jeroboam II. This king ruled Israel for about thirty years at a time when the country enjoyed a period of great prosperity. However, the Deuteronomist does not think that this is worth more than about six verses (II Kings 14.23–29).

Jehu's revolution was aimed primarily against the Canaanites and the supporters of Baal worship. We have already seen that the Deuteronomist has a great interest in this theme. Furthermore, the account of these events in II Kings 9–10 reflects clear sympathy for Jehu's rise.

The Chronicler is even less interested than the Deuteronomist in events in Israel. This also goes for Jehu's revolution. All we are told in II Chron. 22.1–9 is that Ahaziah, king of Judah, who was on a visit to Joram in Jezreel, was also killed in it.[1]

In addition to the information in the Deuteronomist and the Chronicler, Hos. 1.4 also has a late recollection of the events which took place at the time of Jehu's revolution. Here we can see a completely different view of events. It is evident that Jehu's bloodbath in Jezreel had etched itself deep into memories even a century later. But whereas for the author of II Kings 9, Jehu's action was evidence of his faithfulness towards Yahweh, Hosea describes it as blood-guilt which Jehu's dynasty brought on itself and which led to its downfall.

12.1.2 *Jehu's revolt*

The account in II Kings 9 begins with the report that a disciple of the prophet Elisha anointed Jehu king over Israel. This anointing took place at Ramoth in Gilead, where Jehu was stationed at the head of his troops. Thus once again, as with Omri, we have a general seizing power and establishing a dynasty. The army immediately supported Jehu, whereupon he set out for Jezreel, where Joram was seeking to recover from the wound he had received in the battle against Aram (II Kings 9.15). Joram was murdered by Jehu when they met at Naboth's vineyard, and his corpse was then left there. The two verses in II Kings 9 (vv. 25–26) which mention this very probably go back to an ancient tradition[2] and show that the conflict between Ahab and Naboth (I Kings 21) was blamed largely on Ahab, and not on Jezebel.[3]

Jehu then set off for the palace at Jezreel. At his command some courtiers threw Jezebel out of the palace window. Her end is described in gruesome detail. However, Jehu's bloodbath did not end in Jezreel. At that time the most important bastion of the Omrids, Samaria, was not yet in his hands. The account in II Kings 10 suggests that he was able to capture it without much difficulty.

As soon as this city was in Jehu's possession, the sons of Ahab living there (II Kings 10.1–7), seventy in number,[4] and all the other members of Ahab's family (II Kings 10.17), were put to death. In II Kings 10.18ff. we are then told that Jehu had everyone put to death who was involved in Baal worship, and had everything in Samaria connected with this cult destroyed. This would include the temple of Baal established in the city. However, this description is somewhat exaggerated. The report in II Kings 13.6 that the 'sacred tree' remained in Samaria indicates that the destruction mentioned above was not absolute. Furthermore, II Kings 10 gives the impression that the action was only local.

This means that Jehu's revolution certainly did not do away with all the worship of Baal. The ongoing polemic against Baal worship uttered by the prophet Hosea a century later also points in this direction.[5] Jehonadab ben Rechab is said to have been one of Jehu's collaborators in this revolt (II Kings 10.15–16, 23). In the Old Testament Rechab was regarded as the tribal ancestor of the Rechabites. The latter were a group who rejected the benefits of agricultural civilizations like living in cities, tilling the land, and so on. Evidently they strove for a kind of nomadic ideal, and except in emergencies

(Jer. 35.11) lived outside the cities in tents. The adherents of this group were known to be faithful followers of Yahweh. However, their rejection of the generally accepted life style must be seen more as a sociological than a religious matter.[6]

According to Stolz,[7] the conservative ideals of the Rechabites were one of the most important reasons for their support of Jehu's revolution. Their opposition was directed above all against city culture, which became increasingly influential as Canaanite cities were incorporated into Israel. Jehu's attack on a city like Samaria, with marked Canaanite influence, could not but arouse their sympathy. At all events, it is striking that according to II Kings 10 Jehonadab ben Rechab supported Jehu in the attack on this city in particular.

12.2 *The international situation*

12.2.1 *The rise of Assyria*

I have already pointed out at the beginning of this chapter that, leaving aside Jehu's revolution, the Old Testament does not give us much information about Israel. However, on the basis of this scanty information and that provided by the literature of the ancient Near East, we can see that in the next period events in Canaan and further afield were strongly influenced by the rise of Assyria.

After the battle of Karkar in 853 BC (11.1.2), Shalmaneser III of Assyria remained in the background for some time. However, according to an Assyrian inscription, in the eighteenth year of his reign, i.e. in 841 BC, he undertook an expedition against Damascus.[8] The same inscription states that at this time Jehu also had to pay tribute to Shalmaneser III. This subjection of Jehu is also expressed vividly on the so-called Black Obelisk.[9]

That must already have happened at the beginning of Jehu's reign (842/41–815/14). One explanation of his subjection could be that in this way Jehu sought support from Assyria against opposition to his seizure of power, either at home or abroad. Such opposition was by no means inconceivable.[10] However, the Old Testament does not tell us anything at all about this tribute paid by Jehu to Assyria. After the death of Jehu, Israel was confronted with new Assyrian campaigns. These took place in the time of the Assyrian king Adad-nirari III (810–783). An inscription found at Tell al-Rima in Iraq in 1967 is particularly important in this connection.[11] It mentions a campaign by Adad-nirari in Syria-Palestine, one of the consequences of which was that 'Ia'asu the Samarian' had to pay tribute to the king of Assyria. One problem with the inscription is that it is not clear whether the 'Ia'asu' here refers to

Jehoahaz (815/14–799/98) the son of Jehu or his grandson Jehoash (799/98–784/83). It seems most probable, however, that we should suppose it to be the latter.[12]

The Old Testament does not mention this tribute paid by Jehoash any more than it mentions that paid by Jehu. However, the extra-biblical evidence[13] suggests that Assyrian influence on Israel and the surrounding region increased from the time of Jehu.

12.2.2 *Israel's relations with neighbouring countries*

One of the reasons for the increase in Assyrian power is doubtless that the coalition which was still able to hold back Assyria at Karkar in 853 BC had meanwhile begun to fall apart. Not only do we cease to hear of contacts with Tyre from the time of Jehu on, but good relations with Judah had since ceased. Even earlier, good relations with Aram, Ahab's ally at the time of the battle of Karkar, had been destroyed. This is evident from the fact that just before seizing power, Jehu was with the army at Ramoth in Gilead where, according to II Kings 9.14–15 (II Chron. 22.6), Joram had been wounded in the battle against Aram shortly beforehand.[14] It is possible that Joram wanted to take advantage of a confrontation between Aram and Assyria at that time to seize Ramoth from Aram (see 12.2.1). Things did not turn out successfully, though, since according to II Kings 10.32–33 Jehu lost a good deal of territory in Transjordan to Hazael the king of Aram.

There is also mention of conflict with Aram at the time of Jehoahaz (II Kings 13.3–5, 7, 22), in which Israel fared badly. However, we do not have further details of this confrontation.[15] Hazael and his son Benhadad are said to have been the kings of Aram at the time.

In this connection there is a remarkable note in II Kings 13.5 that Yahweh gave Israel a saviour so that it was saved from the power of Aram. We are not told how this happened, nor do we have any further information about the person of this saviour. Be this as it may, at a later period Jehoash and Jeroboam II succeeded in winning back from Aram the lost territory (II Kings 13.25; 14.25). According to II Kings 14.28, Jeroboam II (784/83–753/52) even succeeded in expanding his territory at the expense of Aram.[16]

This could come about because at that time Aram was at war with the kingdom of Hamath, lying to the north of Damascus,[17] and later had its hands full resisting a new Assyrian threat. About 773 BC, Shalmaneser IV (782–773) launched a campaign against Damascus, and this fight against Aram was continued by his successor Ashur-dan III (772–755).[18]

Worsening relations with Judah, already indicated earlier, were expressed in a conflict between Jehoash and Amaziah of Judah. According to II Kings

14.8–15 (II Chron. 25.17–24), there was an encounter between these two kingdoms in which Judah came off worst. On this occasion Jerusalem itself was plundered and occupied by the troops of Israel. This is the only time – so far as we know – that Jerusalem was captured by Israel. Since the temple is also mentioned in this report (v. 14), it may come from the temple annals of Judah. In that case there can be little doubt about the authenticity of the report.

All these conflicts between Aram, Israel and Judah give a clear picture of the divisions in this area. As a result the lands became a much easier prey for Assyria, whose power was steadily growing stronger.

12.3 *Domestic problems*

The Deuteronomist tells us little more about the domestic policy of the kings of Jehu's dynasty than that 'they did evil in the sight of the Lord and followed the sins of Jeroboam the son of Nebat, which he made Israel to sin'.[19] However, thanks above all to the information in the book of Amos, we know something more about the domestic situation in the time of king Jeroboam II.

From the information there we may infer that in many respects this period can be seen as a time of prosperity and economic progress. As so often in history, however, the advantages which this produced were of principal benefit to a small group, the upper stratum of the population. We find one indication of this in the prophet Amos. Justice and right are nowhere to be found; the rich live in luxurious houses and the poor are oppressed (Amos 5.10–11; 8.4–6).[20] According to Amos (5.21–24), in such a situation all religion is rotten and the songs of praise which are sung are no more than empty sounds.

Of course the criticisms made by Amos here were not heeded at all in a society where such practices were current, not even by those who were regarded as being the specific defenders of religion. Thus Amaziah the priest himself takes the initiative in having Amos banned from speaking in the sanctuary in Bethel (Amos 7.10–17). We also find allusions in Hosea to the great prosperity in the time of Jeroboam II. In this connection Hosea speaks of an abundance of corn, wine and olives (Hos. 2.4, 7–8). The building of 'palaces' mentioned in Hos. 8.14 probably fits into the framework of this time.[21]

The archaeological excavations made at Tirzah under the direction of R. de Vaux in the period between 1946 and 1960 are instructive in this respect. The way in which houses were built shows that above all in the eighth century BC there was a great contrast between rich and poor.[22] Furthermore, the ostraca found in Samaria in 1910,[23] which date from the time of Jehoash and Jeroboam II, give us a picture of the situation in Israel in the time of these kings. These ostraca contain a list of the taxation in kind which was raised from the royal domains at the request of the court. Furthermore they also mention, for example, the places from which this produce came and the official responsible for the particular consignment.

The proper names on these ostraca indicate that the population around Samaria at that time had a very heterogenous character. We find names of Egyptian, Israelite and also Canaanite origin.[24] Furthermore, the place names show us something of the administrative organization of at least a certain part of the state of Israel.[25]

In the meanwhile, Jehu's dynasty does not seem to have lasted. After the death of Jeroboam II, his son Zechariah (753/52–752/51) seems to have reigned for only six months (II Kings 15.8). A certain Shallum, described as the 'son of Jabesh', then organized a conspiracy against Zechariah and did away with him. This led once again to a time of great trouble and disorder in Israel which was to last for twenty years and finally end with the downfall of Israel in 722/21.

12.4 *Amos and Hosea*

12.4.1 *Amos*

According to the title of the book of Amos (1.1, which comes from a later date), the prophet's preaching took place in the time of Jeroboam II. This seems broadly in line with the content of the book.

We know nothing more about the date of his birth or the time of his death, but Amos evidently began his prophetic activity about 750 BC. He came from Tekoa in Judah (1.1). According to Amos 7.14 he had cattle and was a grower of mulberry trees. This might indicate that he was a farmer by occupation.[26]

The activity of Amos is characterized by a great social concern and a very critical attitude towards the power structures of his time. In this respect it is also not surprising that the word 'righteousness' plays a very important part in his preaching.[27] His criticism is primarily directed against the exploitation of the poor by the rich.[28] The background to this prophetic preaching must be sought above all in the social change, prosperity and increase in the size of property holdings which went along with it. Another important factor here was the growth in trade. All this developed above all in the time of Jeroboam II, a period of political stability and economic prosperity.[29]

In this situation, the country people in particular were forced to foot the bill. Their position became more and more difficult, and they were increasingly made dependent upon the cities. The development was not limited to Israel and Judah, but seems to have been taking place throughout the ancient Near East.[30] In Israel, the opposition between the various population groups was also a factor. About half the population were Canaanites, and they lived principally in the cities.[31]

The critical attitude of the prophets of the eighth century BC, like Amos, must be seen especially in this context. Hitherto the prophets had directed themselves almost exclusively against particular persons and events.[32] According to Koch, this changed with the rise of Amos. The eighth-century prophets attacked the whole social structure of their time.[33] However, this does not imply of itself that these prophets, including Amos, at the same time had an entirely new economic structure in mind.[34]

No matter how revolutionary the preaching of Amos may sound, in essence it remains conservative. It envisages no revolutionary changes.[35] Rather, the prophet's gaze is directed more towards a society like that expressed in the Old Testament laws, which envisage especially an agrarian structure.[36] However, it would be utterly wrong to suppose that Amos' preaching was directed towards the past in a purely negative way. His visions, for example, bear witness to a vision of the future and a concern for it. In the time of Jeroboam II, characterized by great prosperity and peace, he was already turning his attention towards the approaching end. Obviously his preaching, with its announcement of a coming annihilation and downfall, met with little response. However, as so often in history, the future showed to what extent the words of this prophet became reality.

12.4.2 *Hosea*

Like Amos, Hosea was active in the time of Jeroboam II (Hos. 1.1). We know still less about the personal circumstances of this prophet than we do about Amos. His great knowledge of the land of Israel and its places of worship and political situation, along with his use of language,[37] do however suggest quite strongly that he came from Israel.[38] Hosea was also evidently a younger contemporary of Amos and came to the fore in a rather later period.

Whereas in Amos' preaching the word 'righteousness' played an important part, with Hosea the word 'love'[39] or faithfulness chiefly comes to the fore. These words already play a prominent part in the first chapters about Hosea's marriage.[40]

His preaching is especially characterized by a fierce polemic against Baal worship as practised in Israel in his time. Specifically this often meant that although people served Yahweh with their lips, they in fact worshipped Baal, with all that that implied. Such behaviour is fiercely attacked by Hosea.[41] Even priests and prophets (Hos. 4.4–6; 9.7–8) are evidently guilty of it.

Now of course it is conceivable that the prophecies of Hosea, which were collected in Judah at a later date, paint the situation in rather too lurid colours. Against this, however, we should note that the writings from Elephantine, dating from the fifth century BC and deriving from the descendants of Hosea's Israelite fellow-citizens, also show clear signs of a similar syncretism.[42]

In addition to all this, the prophet is also concerned with social and economic problems. This emerges, for example, from Hos. 12.8–9, where he attacks the corrupt attitudes of merchants out to exploit their fellow men. The word 'Canaan' is used in this connection. The Canaanites were originally those who traded in Canaan. Only later did the Israelites increasingly engage in this occupation. In the course of time the name 'Canaanite' even became the designation for 'merchant' or 'trader'.

Another characteristic of Hosea is his critical attitude[43] towards the patriarch Jacob (ch. 12),[44] and the great influence which he exercised, for example, on the thought of the prophet Jeremiah.[45] Despite everything, Hosea continued to trust in a final restoration of Israel, as we find it described in Hos. 2.13–14. During a transitional period Israel will again be led out into the 'wilderness' in order to make a new beginning there. This last thought in particular made a deep impression and exercised an influence on later history. We can see it, for example, in Jeremiah (31.2), Deutero-Isaiah (40.3–4) and John the Baptist (Mark 1.2–4). The Essenes, too, expected the beginning of a new time of salvation in the wilderness.[46]

Hosea's confidence in a new beginning for Israel is also expressed in the way in which he changes the names of his children (Hos. 1.6–11; 1.12) and in the prophecy of salvation that we find in 14.5–9.

12.5 *Judah at the time of Jehu*

During the period when the dynasty of Jehu was in power in Israel, the rulers in Judah – leaving aside Athaliah (see 11.4.2) – were the kings Joash, Amaziah and Azariah.

12.5.1 *Joash (836/35–797/96)*

The books both of Kings (II Kings 11.21—12.2) and Chronicles (II Chron. 24) devote their attention almost exclusively to the policy carried out by Joash towards the cult. Evidently Joash was very much under the influence of the priest Jehoiada, especially at the beginning of his reign. One comment seems significant in this respect: 'And Joash did what was right in the eyes of the Lord all his days, because Jehoiada the priest instructed him' (II Kings 12.2). However, in II Chron. 24.2 the term used in this context is not 'instructed' but 'lived'.[48] We cannot establish which of these two readings is the right one, though one might suppose that the older he got, the more Joash emerged from

Jehoiada's influence. At any rate, it is certain that the Chronicler is much more critical about Joash than the Deuteronomist in II Kings 12.[49]

Both reviews of the reign of Joash pay considerable attention to the measures which were taken to restore the temple in Jerusalem. The restoration may have been connected with a strengthening of the position of this temple in his time. This could be a natural consequence of the fact that the influence of the priests in Jerusalem increased considerably with his accession (see 11.4.2). The report in II Kings 12.17–18, in which it is said that when Hazael the king of Aram advanced against Jerusalem, Joash took the gold from the temple to buy off Hazael's attack, is interesting in this connection. We may suppose that the priests in Jerusalem did not always get off so lightly. Chronicles also mentions this expedition (II Chron. 24.23–24), but does not say anything about the treasure I have just mentioned; it records only the penal measures which were taken against Joash. It is possible that Hazael's campaign here referred to is connected with that in Transjordan recorded in II Kings 13.3–7.

The accounts of Joash in Kings and Chronicles end with the note that he was killed by two of his servants. The Old Testament does not give us any indication of the reason for this murder. Presumably no *coup d'état* was intended. At all events, Joash was succeeded by his son Amaziah.

12.5.2 *Amaziah (797/96–769/68)*

We hear very little about Amaziah: only about his religious policy (of which it is said that Amaziah did not do any more than his father Joash to abolish the high places), his conflict with Jehoash of Israel (12.2.2), his fight with the Edomites and the conspiracy against him in Jerusalem. In II Kings only one verse (14.7) is devoted to the fight with Edom. However, the Chronicler spends much more time on this material (II Chron. 25.11–16). Nevertheless, the only concrete information in both accounts is that the Edomites were defeated. It is conceivable that here Amaziah made an attempt to recapture the trade route to the Red Sea which had been lost at the time of Joram (*c.* 850 BC). In II Chron. 25.5–10 we also hear how Amaziah mustered his army, which included Israelite mercenary troops. It is not clear whether this happened also with an eye to the battle against Edom. However, a man of God commanded Amaziah to send away the 'Ephraimites'.

Amaziah's life came to an untimely end, like that of his father. Following a conspiracy he fled to Lachish, where he was killed by his pursuers (II Kings 14.19–20; II Chron. 25.27–28). However, we are completely in the dark about the why and wherefore of this conspiracy.

12.5.3 *Azariah (769/68–741/40)*

As we are explicitly told in II Kings 14.31 and II Chron. 26.1, Amaziah's son was 'taken by the whole people of Judah and made king'. Probably this statement combines two facts: the emergence of Azariah as co-regent and his acclamation as king by the people.[50] His name is interesting: apart from II Kings 15.32 it always appears as Azariah in the books of Kings, but in other places in the Old Testament he is always called Uzziah.[51]

The Old Testament gives us little information about Azariah, despite the length of his reign, which according to II Kings 15.2; II Chron. 26.3 covered a period of fifty-two years. Both in II Kings 14.22 and II Chron. 26.2 we are told that Azariah fortified the city of Elath. This fact seems certain, seeing that a kind of signet ring was found there bearing the name of Jotham, the son of Azariah. This ring may have belonged to someone governing in Elath in the name of Jotham.[52]

Apart from this fortification of Elath and Azariah's attitude towards worship in the high places, which he did not abolish, all that we hear in II Kings is that Azariah was a leper (15.5). In II Chron. 26.6–8, however, we are also told of victories over the Philistines, Arabians and Meunites, while according to this account the Ammonites were forced to pay tribute to him.[53] The Chronicler also goes into some detail about Azariah's leprosy (II Chron. 26.16–21), ascribed to the fact that he wanted to perform priestly service in the temple. However, this is a later interpretation, seeing that not only is there no mention of it in II Kings 15.1–7 but such an action seems to have been quite legitimate in an early period, as for example in the cases of David (II Sam. 6.17–18; I Chron. 16.1) and Solomon (I Kings 8; II Chron. 6–7).

Because Azariah was a leper, according to II Kings 15.5; II Chron. 26.21, his son Jotham acted as co-regent. According to Isa. 6.1, Isaiah's call took place in the year in which Azariah died.[54]

Chapter 13

The Confrontation with Assyria

13.1 *The international situation*

After the death of Jeroboam II, the time of prosperity and peace which had been the principal characteristic of his reign rapidly came to an end. The reason for this must be sought in the changes which took place in the international sphere. The three kings succeeding Adad-nirari III in Assyria (see 12.2.1) could pay little attention to the lands lying to the west of their kingdom. This was because of domestic problems, and also because of a conflict with Urartu, with whom Assyria was at war at this time.[1] However, this situation changed entirely once Tiglath-pileser III (744–727) had become king of Assyria.[2]

Tiglath-pileser III is regarded as one of the greatest conquerors among the kings of Assyria. Not only did he have great successes in Syria and Canaan, but he was also able to conquer Babylon.[3] In this way he succeeded in making Assyria a great world power. There are a number of things that we must remember when we consider how all this could come about. First of all there was the political situation. At that time other great powers, like Egypt and Urartu, were clearly too weak to put up adequate opposition. Furthermore, the other states had too many differences among themselves to form a common front against Assyria. The Syro-Ephraimite war[4] is a characteristic example of this.

In addition, three other factors played an important role: the efficient organization of the Assyrian government and army, the fearful cruelties and 'punishments' which the Assyrians inflicted on the peoples they conquered, and the large-scale deportations which they practised.[5]

The main characteristic of their mode of government was strict control and efficient communications.[6] The army was organized in such a way that troops were always available at very short notice, and its equipment and weapons were modern for its time.[7] The main aim of the cruelty and punishments which it practised was to produce fear and terror.[8] The deportations especially affected the upper class of conquered peoples and were practised in order to break their power and to neutralize all possible opposition from the start.

The Assyrian royal inscriptions give us considerable information about the conquests of Tiglath-pileser III. One of the first countries he dealt with was the kingdom of Urartu, to the north of Assyria,[9] inhabited by a Hurrian population. His conquests also extended westwards, to include Syria and Canaan. He made many expeditions in this direction.[10]

As we shall see in subsequent sections, the rise to power of this king and his successors was of decisive importance for further developments in Israel and Judah in the roughly 150 years during which Assyrian supremacy lasted.

13.2 *The Syro-Ephraimite war*

13.2.1 *The prelude*

Shallum (752/51–751/50), who killed Zechariah king of Israel after a *coup d'état* (12.3), only ruled for a month. He was then killed in his turn by Menahem (II Kings 15.13–14). On becoming king Menahem clearly carried out a pro-Assyrian policy. At any rate, we are told in II Kings 15.19 that Menahem gave Pul (Tiglath-pileser III) 'a thousand talents of silver, that he might help him to confirm his hold of the royal power'. This report seems to be confirmed by the information in a so-called 'tribute list' of Tiglath-pileser III, which says, among other things, that 'Menahem of Samaria' paid him tribute.[11]

This tribute must then have been raised and paid about the end of Menahem's rule (751/50–742/41), seeing that Tiglath-pileser came to power in Assyria round about 744 BC.[12] In that case it must have happened on this king's first campaign to the west in about 743–738 BC, when a number of Syrian provinces and important cities in northern Phoenicia were annexed.[13] According to II Kings 15.20, Menahem in turn exacted this tribute 'from Israel, that is, from all the wealthy men', whereupon the king of Assyria withdrew.

By acting in this way Menahem clearly succeeded in gaining a considerable degree of independence. However, this policy evidently did not find undivided approval in Israel. Presumably the heavy taxation brought about by the payment of tribute to Assyria was very significant here. Probably many people preferred to take up arms rather than bear this burden. That is evident from the fact that Pekahiah, the son of Menahem, remained in power for only two years (742/41–741/40). A new *coup d'état*, led by Pekah, clearly aimed at implementing a different policy, then put an end to Pekahiah's rule and his life.[14]

13.2.2 *The war*

Pekah (741/40–730/29), the new king of Israel, must be seen as one of the instigators of the so-called Syro-Ephraimite war. In the books of Kings (II Kings 15.29–30, 37; 16.5–6) and Chronicles (II Chron. 28.5ff.) this war is mentioned very much in passing. In addition, however, we find information about it in the prophets Isaiah and Hosea.[15] The inscriptions of Tiglath-pileser III also give us some information about its course.[16]

We may infer from the Old Testament evidence that the war was a conflict between Ahaz of Judah on the one hand and Pekah of Israel and Rezin of Damascus on the other. The cause of the war is taken to be the fact that Rezin and Pekah wanted to conclude an alliance against Assyria, in which Ahaz refused to be involved. It is possible that the first two kings mentioned then tried to compel Ahaz by force to join them,[17] but that cannot be read directly from the relevant texts. Perhaps the course of the war can be reconstructed, broadly speaking, as follows.[18]

Pekah and Rezin attacked Ahaz and according to II Kings 16.5 laid siege to Jerusalem. There is no mention of a siege of Jerusalem in II Chron. 28.5ff., but there is mention of the great losses suffered by Judah. At all events, it seems certain that Ahaz was put in a precarious position. The aim of the confederate kings was to establish 'the son of Tabeel' (Isa. 7.6) as king of Judah in place of Ahaz. However, this attack failed because Ahaz enlisted the help of Tiglath-pileser III (II Kings 16.7; II Chron. 28.16). Thus Ahaz did what Asa had done at an earlier period, in summoning Benhadad of Aram to his aid when he was attacked by Baasha of Israel (see 10.2.2). Ahaz probably resorted to this action because he saw it as the only possibility of securing some form of independence for Judah. That meant that he now became a voluntary vassal of Assyria. In all this he acted against the pressing advice of the prophet Isaiah (Isa. 7.3–9).

Tiglath-pileser evidently reacted quickly to Ahaz's request. This is clear not only from the Old Testament evidence (II Kings 16.9) but also from the inscriptions of Tiglath-pileser himself.[19] The latter state that the inhabitants of Israel were deported to Assyria and that Tiglath-pileser appointed Hoshea king over Israel in place of Pekah. This information corresponds with what we are told in II Kings 15.29–30. There, however, we are not told that Hoshea was appointed king by Tiglath-pileser.

It is also evident from the inscriptions of Tiglath-pileser already mentioned and from II Kings 15.29 that the territory of Israel was at that time cut down by Assyria, so that only a rump state remained. Thus on this occasion Galilee, for example, was lost to Israel.[20]

Tigleth-pileser also dealt with Damascus. The city was occupied and some of the population of the region was deported. Rezin king of Aram was put to death (II Kings 16.9).

13.2.3 *Consequences*

These events betokened the end of the Syro-Ephraimite war, a war which had far-reaching consequences above all for Israel. Since the reign of Menaham, Israel so far had escaped paying tribute to Assyria.[21] Now there was little left of Israel's independence.

The war also had serious consequences for Judah. The help given by Tiglath-pileser had to be paid for. In one of the inscriptions of Tiglath-pileser III, Ahaz of Judah is mentioned alongside, for example, the kings of Edom and Moab as one of those who had to pay tribute to Assyria.[22] This is further confirmed by the letters which were found in about 1950 in the excavations at Nimrod, the residence of Tiglath-pileser III.[23] II Kings 16.8 reports that Ahaz sent the silver and gold from the temple as a 'present' to the king of Assyria (cf. also II Chron. 28.21). But here the word 'present' must be understood as 'tribute'. In this context the words 'I am your servant and your son' addressed, according to II Kings 16.7, by Ahaz to Tiglath-pileser III, are highly significant. They made him an Assyrian vassal.

However, most attention is paid in the Old Testament to the fact that Ahaz had an altar of Assyrian type placed in the temple in Jerusalem (II Kings 16.10–18), while in II Chron. 28.22–25 it is even said that he put a complete end to the worship of Yahweh. The Old Testament does not tell us that as a vassal Ahaz was also obliged to take over Assyrian worship. However, this is quite probable, seeing that in Assyrian worship the king played an important role.[24] It is possible that this king also wanted to exercise similar influence over the peoples he conquered. At all events, it is most unlikely that Ahaz resorted to such an action of his own free will.[25]

13.3 *The end of the kingdom of Israel*

Thus after the death of Pekah, Hoshea (730/29–722/21) became king over Israel. We can understand that in contrast to his predecessor he again adopted a more pro-Assyrian policy. He also paid tribute to Shalmaneser V (726–722), the successor of Tiglath-pileser III (II Kings 17.3). However, Hoshea made another attempt to throw off the Assyrian yoke. In II Kings 17.4 we hear that he sent messengers to So king of Egypt and that payment of tribute to Assyria again ceased. From a political point of view, Hoshea clearly made a serious error here. No help came from Egypt, and Hoshea was imprisoned by the king of Assyria. Samaria was besieged and captured after a siege of about three years (722/721). A number of Israelites were again deported.

Assyrian sources[26] ascribe the conquest of Samaria to Sargon II (721–705), while in the so-called 'Babylonian Chronicle'[27] Shalmaneser V is mentioned in this connection. At all events, the extra-biblical evidence confirms what we are told in II Kings 17.5–6 about the conquest of Samaria.

This, then, put a final end to the existence of the state of Israel. However, that does not mean that this country and Samaria did not play a further role in the later history of the Israelite people. Obviously not all Israel was deported by the Assyrians. The number 27,290 mentioned in this connection (*ANET*, 285) is probably on the high side, but that apart, at that time the inhabitants of Israel totalled more than this. So while Israel may have ceased to exist as a political entity, in other spheres, including that of religion, it still played an important part in later history. In this connection it is interesting to look for a moment at II Kings 17.24–41. Those deported from Israel were in part replaced (II Kings 17.24) by the inhabitants of Babylon, Hamath and Cuthah. We read in II Kings 17.27 that the king of Assyria then acceded to a request to send back one of the deported priests to Israel to teach these people 'the true worship of the God of the land'. According to II Kings 17.28 this priest then settled in Bethel. The relevant part of II Kings 17 clearly shows that this worship of Yahweh had a marked syncretistic character, though at the same time we need to remember that the information may have been added by a later redaction in Judah. However, the word 'Samaritan' in II Kings 17.29 certainly does not denote the later religious group known as the Samaritans. It simply refers to the population of Samaria.

People were slow to give up the hope of a restoration of the state of Israel. This hope certainly continued for a century after the fall of Samaria. We find a clear indication of it, for example, in Nahum 2.2 and Jer. 31.20. In Ezekiel (37.15ff.), it is modified into the expectation of a purified future kingdom under the dynasty of David.[28]

13.4 *Isaiah, Micah and Nahum*

It seems right here to pause to consider the prophets Isaiah, Micah and Nahum, who came to the fore in the period discussed in this chapter.

13.4.1 *Isaiah*

In speaking of Isaiah here I am referring to the prophet mentioned in Isaiah 1–39. This prophet must have lived about 730 BC. Just as Jeremiah seems to have been influenced by Hosea, so Isaiah seems to have been influenced by Amos.[29]

According to Isa. 6.1, the activity of Isaiah began in the year in which Uzziah (Azariah) died.[30] He was prominent as a prophet above all during the time when Ahaz and Hezekiah were kings of Judah. As with most prophets, we know little of his origins and personal life. In Isa. 1.1 he is called son of Amoz. According to Isa. 8.3, his wife was a prophetess.[31] Two of his children bore symbolic names: Shear-jashub, 'a remnant will return' (Isa. 7.3), and Maher-shalal-hash-baz, 'hasty prey, speedy spoil' (Isa. 8.3). These two names, like the prophet's own name Isaiah, 'Yahweh is help', are characteristic of his preaching. We do not know whether Isaiah had other children in addition to the two just mentioned. Nor do we know when he died, any more than we know when he was born. The report that he was sawn asunder by a wood saw in the time of Manasseh[32] is hardly trustworthy.

It is possible that Isaiah's call (Isa. 6) took place in the temple in Jerusalem.[33] For this reason, and because of his close contacts with the palace, it has been thought that Isaiah was officially connected as a prophet with the temple or the court.[34] The arguments adduced in support of this seem quite convincing, though it is clear that Isaiah constantly adopts a very critical attitude towards the king. One characteristic of his preaching is his stress on Yahweh as the 'Holy One of Israel',[35] and the notion of a remnant which will be preserved. This last idea is expressed, for example, in the name which he gives to one of his sons (see above).

Isaiah also launches a fierce attack on social injustice[36] and is strongly opposed to political alliances made by kings of Judah with powerful foreign rulers. Thus he opposes Ahaz when the king invokes the aid of Assyria in the 'Syro-Ephraimite war' (see 13.2 above) and calls upon him to trust solely in God. Isaiah's words in Isa. 7.9, 'If you do not believe, you will not be established', are significant in this connection. When Ahaz refused to listen, Isaiah evidently withdrew for some time from public life (see Isa. 8.16ff.).

After the death of Ahaz (Isa. 14.28) Isaiah clearly comes very much to the fore again. In the time of Hezekiah, for example, he opposed a confederacy with Egypt directed against Assyria (Isa. 30.1–5; 31.1–3). Isaiah was more in favour of a policy of neutrality. We also know how Isaiah supported Hezekiah in the difficult period when Sennacherib laid siege to Jerusalem (II Kings 18.13–19.37; Isa. 36–37).

13.4.2 *Micah*

This prophet[37] emerged in the period about 720–700, as we may probably infer from Jer. 26.18 and Micah 1.1. Micah presumably came from Moresheth-gath, a place in the south-west of Judah, about twenty miles from Jerusalem and not far from the important fortified city of Lachish. We can be sure that Micah also exercised his prophetic activity in Jerusalem, but in addition he was also active in the countryside of Judah. This last must be inferred from Jer. 26.17–18, where about a century later 'elders of the land' still refer to Micah's preaching. This preaching shows affinity not only with Amos and Hosea, but also with Isaiah.[38]

Micah was the first prophet to announce openly the destruction of Jerusalem and the temple (3.12). Like Amos, he protests chiefly against injustice and exploitation. For example, in his preaching he attacks the exploitation of the country people of Judah by a certain élite who live in the cities, and also attacks the corruption practised by judges, officials, prophets and priests.[39] Most prominent in Micah 6–7[40] is a fierce polemic against Canaanite worship. Micah 6.16 mentions 'the statutes of Omri' and the 'works of the house of Ahab' in this connection. His criticism is also directed against sacrifice (Micah 6.6–7). Some of the prophet's most impressive words are to be found in Micah 6.8: 'He has showed you, O man, what is good; and what does the Lord require of you but to do justice, and to love kindness?'

13.4.3 *Nahum*

According to the title of this book (Nahum 1.1), the words of the prophet handed down in it must be dated to a time when the city of Nineveh was still standing. Since Nineveh was destroyed in 612 BC, the words must therefore come from before that year. Nahum 3.8 seems to presuppose the destruction of the Egyptian city of No-Amon (Thebes) by the Assyrians. This must have taken place in about 663 BC.

The evidence thus points to a dating of the prophet Nahum in the period between 663 and 612 BC. It seems most likely that Nahum should be regarded as a contemporary of Manasseh (697/96–642/41). His prophetic activity would then have taken place in the second half of Manasseh's reign.[41]

On the basis, for example, of a large number of loan-words in this book, van der Woude[42] argues that Nahum was one of the deportees who were taken from North Israel to Assyria, and that his prophecy was proclaimed in Judah in the form of a letter sent to particular people there through merchants. Be this as it may, it is clear that these deported exiles are well to the fore in this book of the Bible, as we can see for instance in Nahum 2.1–3.

13.5 *Judah at the time of Hezekiah*

13.5.1 *Hezekiah as an Assyrian vassal*

Judah was one of the few states in Canaan and Syria which was not completely subdued by Assyria. One important reason for this was doubtless the fact that politically and geographically it was of little significance. This was the reason why Judah could continue to exist as a state about 150 years longer than Israel, though for most of that time it was a vassal state.

We have already seen that as a result of the Syro-Ephraimite war (13.2.3) Ahaz had to pay tribute to Assyria. The end of Israel and the fall of Samaria made the situation even more difficult. Judah was now on the very frontier of the Assyrian empire, since Israel had become an Assyrian province. The dependence of Judah on Assyria thus became all the greater.

These were the circumstances in which Hezekiah (715/14–697/96) ascended the throne of Judah.[43] They were far from ideal. Judah now not only was a vassal of Assyria,[44] but also had less territory than ever. It had had to surrender a good deal in the Syro-Ephraimite war, including Edom and the important port of Ezion-geber, which never returned to the possession of Judah.[45] From an economic point of view that was a serious blow, because it meant the loss of a very important trade route.

We can understand that in such a situation people were anxious to regain at least some of the old power and glory. We can see how important this was to Hezekiah and those around him from the reactions to such an idea from the prophet Isaiah.[46] He vigorously opposed this kind of thinking. The visions of peace in Isa. 2.2–5 (and Micah 4.1–4) probably also belong in this context.

It is clear that Isaiah championed a policy of neutrality. His comment in Isa. 30.15 is characteristic: 'In quietness and trust shall be your strength.'[47] These words are obviously a serious warning to his fellow-citizens not to become involved in an anti-Assyrian adventure.

As often, the words of the prophet clearly made little impression on the people of his own time. Hezekiah and his supporters rebelled against Assyria (II Kings 18.7).

13.5.2 *The rebellion and its consequences*

According to II Kings 18 this revolution was coupled with a religious reformation. Hezekiah removed all kinds of cultic symbols (v. 4), while II Chron. 29–31 talks in some detail about a restoration of temple worship and a celebration of the passover.[48] The connection between this rebellion and the reformation of the cult is not immediately obvious. Naturally, it will have affected Assyrian cult symbols (see 13.2.3). However, the names of the symbols given in II Kings 18.4 suggest Canaanite rather than Assyrian features.

Furthermore, this reformation of the cult must be seen in connection with the political aspirations which Hezekiah obviously cherished. In II Kings 18.8 we also hear that he defeated the Philistines. All these things were possible because of changes at that time on an international level. In the first place, the position of Egypt clearly became rather stronger again at this time. At all events, Hezekiah sought contact with Egypt then. There seems to be a reflection of this in Isa. 18.1–6.[49] It is clear from the reaction of this prophet that Isaiah was fiercely opposed to a confederacy with Egypt (cf. also Isa. 30.1–5; 31.1–8). Hezekiah sought friendly relations with Babylon as well as with Egypt (II Kings 20.12–19; Isa. 39); Isaiah also opposed links with Egypt and argued for a position of neutrality.

In addition to these developments in the international sphere, reference can also be made to difficulties in connection with a change of ruler in Assyria. About 705 BC, Sargon II was succeeded as king by Sennacherib. Only in about 701 BC was Sennacherib in a position to undertake a campaign[50] in the west.[51] Sennacherib's advance in Syria and Canaan went particularly well. He conquered Ashkelon and Ashdod and defeated the Egyptians at Eltekeh.[52] Then he moved on Judah and Jerusalem. According to Sennacherib's own account, forty-six cities of Judah were occupied at that time.[53] According to II Kings 18.17, these included the city of Lachish. In addition, excavations seem to show that Beersheba was also devastated during this campaign.[54] Isaiah 10.28–32 might be another source of information about the conquest of various cities of Judah by Sennacherib were it not that there are problems about the dating of this section.[55]

In the Old Testament, however, most stress seems to be laid on the siege of Jerusalem in accounts of this campaign. Probably Hezekiah had reckoned with the possibility of such a siege in his preparations. Some indication of this is the construction of a tunnel to ensure water supplies in time of siege. There is an account of the making of such a tunnel in II Kings 20.20. This was confirmed in 1882 when an inscription was discovered indicating its existence.[56]

However, it is also possible that this tunnel was made because of the considerable increase in the population of Jerusalem in *c.* 700 BC. This might have happened as the result of the arrival of a great many refugees from the northern kingdom.[57]

Sennacherib himself records in connection with the siege that his army had shut up Hezekiah in Jerusalem 'like a bird in a cage'.[58] We can also see how critical this period was for Hezekiah from II Kings 18.13—19.34; II Chron. 32.1–23; Isa. 37—38. According to Sennacherib the campaign ended with a complete victory for Assyria. The Old Testament records that Hezekiah paid very heavy tribute to Sennacherib (II Kings 18.14–16), but it says nothing of a definitive victory by Sennacherib or of an occupation of Jerusalem. Presumably Sennacherib's victory was rather less absolute than he himself suggested. This conjecture is supported by the fact that neither the Old Testament nor Assyrian records suggest that Hezekiah was deposed as king, which would certainly have been the case had things been as the Assyrians indicated. Such a course of action had been adopted by the Assyrians at an earlier date over the king of Israel (13.2.1) and, for example, over the king of Sidon on the expedition in question.[59]

Nevertheless, this rebellion caused Hezekiah heavy losses. He lost large areas of his territory. Lachish continued to be occupied by the enemy under an Assyrian governor, and as a vassal he himself had to pay substantial tribute to Assyria.[60] We also find a remarkable account in II Kings 19.35–36 (=Isa. 37.36–37) and II Chron. 32.21 which tells how a messenger of Yahweh slew 185,000 Assyrians in one night. Because of this, Sennacherib is said to have abandoned the siege of Jerusalem and to have returned to Nineveh.

Now it is striking that Herodotus has given us a similar account from Egypt. Here we are told that in a dream Pharaoh Sethos was promised the help of a deity against Sennacherib. During the night, a whole army of field-mice then destroyed the equipment of the Assyrians, so that they had to flee without their weapons.[61]

It is extremely difficult to interpret the kind of report that we find in II Kings 19.35–36. However, it seems probable that Sennacherib had to abandon the siege of Jerusalem prematurely. This was perhaps because of an epidemic or because other problems called for his presence elsewhere.

13.6 *Manasseh and Amon*

The combined reigns of Manasseh (697/96–642/41) and Amon (642/41–640/39) amounted to almost sixty years. However, in the books of Kings and Chronicles only one chapter (II Kings 21; II Chron. 33) is devoted to this period. In II Kings 21.1–18, attention is focused almost exclusively on the abuses Manasseh is said to have committed in the sphere of religion and worship. Thus we hear that he rebuilt the high places, erected altars for Baal and even 'made his son pass through the fire' (II Kings 21.6). II Chronicles 33.6 actually makes the sons plural in this connection. Furthermore, Manasseh is also accused of having shed innocent blood (II Kings 21.16).

Although II Kings 21 has strong Deuteronomistic colouring, we cannot escape the impression that at this period Judah was going through a period of considerable decline in the religious sphere. II Kings 23 and Jer. 2 also point in this direction.[62] We can probably identify a number of reasons for this. The political situation seems to be one of the most important. The greater part of Judah was occupied by the Assyrians. This, and their great successes, doubtless made a deep impression and encouraged syncretism. The kind of allusions to worship of sidereal deities on Assyrian lines[63] that we find, for example, in II Kings 21.3; 23.5; Zeph. 1.4–5, also seem to confirm this impression.

Another remarkable feature is an account that we find only in II Chron. 33.11–13. Here we are told that at one time Manasseh was taken as a prisoner to Babylon by the Assyrians. There he is said to have been converted,[64] whereupon he returned to Jerusalem as king.[65] Perhaps this account is connected with the fact that Manasseh was once summoned by Esarhaddon and his successor Assurbanipal.[66] However, we have no certain information in this connection.

The information in the Old Testament about Amon is as scanty as that about Manasseh. Apart from the fact that he carried on the same religious policy as his father (II Kings 21.19–22; II Chron. 33.22–23), all that we hear is that Amon's life and brief reign came to an end as the result of a conspiracy (II Kings 21.23; II Chron. 33.24). We are completely in the dark as to the exact circumstances, but it is striking that 'the people of the land'[67] again intervened in favour of the Davidic dynasty. They killed the conspirators and made Amon's eight-year-old son Josiah king in his place.

Despite the relative silence about the period of Manasseh and Amon in the Old Testament, on an international level it was primarily a time of change. At this stage Assyria was at the zenith of its power,[68] and Egypt was clearly doomed to impotence. The Assyrians were even able, for example, to conquer the Egyptian city of Thebes.[69] It is clear that these events exercised considerable influence on the situation in Judah. During the reigns of Manasseh and Amon the country was completely dependent on Assyria, so that the kings had no choice but to pursue a completely pro-Assyrian policy. Pro-Egyptian or nationalist groups would therefore have had little chance of making themselves felt.

This long period of dependence on Assyria left its mark in many spheres in Judah, not only on its worship (see above) but also on its literature.[70]

Chapter 14

Judah in the Period of Transition between Assyrian and Babylonian Rule

14.1 *The fall of Assyria*

At the time when Josiah (640/39–609/08) became king of Judah, Assyrian power in the ancient Near East was already on the decline. As so often in history, the Assyrian empire gradually succumbed to its own size. In Babylon there were constant revolts which proved increasingly difficult to put down. Another important factor was the gradual restoration of Assyria's old rival, Egypt. There the Twenty-Sixth Dynasty was founded by Psammetichus[1] in 660 BC.

After this, the position of Egypt *vis-à-vis* Assyria gradually changed from that of vassal to ally on the same level. Round about 650 BC the Assyrian troops seem to have evacuated Egypt, whereupon the country again succeeded in extending its influence eastwards. In about 630 BC, Egypt must again have managed to gain some foothold in the old Philistine territory.[2] This probably happened at the time when the Assyrians had their hands full with a Scythian invasion of Syria (*c.* 630–625).

At about the same period (*c.* 626 BC) there was another revolt in Babylonia, which Assyria – weakened by the above-mentioned invasion and by internal conflicts – was unable to repress. The Chaldaean Nabopolassar then came to power in Babylon and made an alliance with the Medes; together, these two powers were able to overthrow Nineveh in 612 BC. However, this did not mean the final end of Assyria. Assur-uballit II, a high priest of Haran, was proclaimed king over Assyria there, and was able to maintain himself as such until 610–609 BC.

Egypt remained an ally of Assyria until the end. Assur-uballit II sought support there after the fall of Haran in about 610 BC.[3] He received it from Pharaoh Necho, who raised an army – probably consisting largely of foreign mercenaries. Along with the rest of the troops which Assur-uballit still had, he made an attempt to conquer Haran, but this failed. In *c.* 608 Necho set out on a new campaign. Josiah, who sought to oppose him, was killed at Megiddo on this occasion.

However, this expedition was not launched to help Assyria, which in fact no longer existed at that time; doubtless Necho wanted to have his share of plunder from the fallen empire. In the first instance he seems to have been at least partially successful.[4]

14.2 *Josiah's reform*

The events which took place during Josiah's reign in Judah cannot be separated from the international situation outlined in 14.1. In this connection the time of Josiah is best described as one of transition between Babylonian and Assyrian rule. During it Judah was virtually free from foreign domination.

14.2.1 *The reformation of the cult*

The most important expression of all this can be seen in the Old Testament in a far-reaching reform of the cult[5] and a quite considerable expansion of power (14.3) which in Judah may have recalled the time of David and Solomon. The reformation of the cult (II Kings 22.3; II Chron. 34.8) began in the eighteenth year of Josiah's reign. According to II Kings 22[6] and II Chron. 34, the occasion for it was the discovery of a law book in the temple by the high priest Hilkiah.[7] When the king had read this law book, he took counsel of the prophetess Huldah.[8] She told him that it contained the only true Torah of God. That showed that hitherto people had not been observing the Torah.

It has been generally assumed that the book of the Torah referred to in II Kings 22 and II Chron. 34 broadly corresponded with the book we know as Deuteronomy. The fact that many of the measures taken by Josiah after the discovery of this book strongly suggest its contents is the chief support for this view.[9] It has further been argued that the book above all contains traditions from the northern kingdom which were written down after the fall of Samaria and brought to Jerusalem by refugees.[10] In that case it is remarkable that it was not found in Jerusalem until about a century later.

We find an account of the measures taken by Josiah in II Kings 23.1ff.;[11] II Chron. 34.29ff. First of all an assembly was called of the elders from Judah and Jerusalem. There a covenant was concluded before the face of Yahweh (II Kings 23.3; II Chron. 34.32). Then all the cultic symbols which had any connection with Assyrian supremacy or came into being as a result of it were removed from the land. Without any question these reforms were stimulated by the fact that people wanted again to be independent of Assyria.

It therefore makes sense to distinguish these reforms from the concern to centralize the cult which comes to the fore at about the same time. The latter must be seen as the real reformation. Among other things, it meant that the places where sacrifice was offered, including Bethel (II Kings 23.15),[12] were destroyed or desecrated. The temple of Arad, which had been in quite legitimate use since the time of Solomon, was also razed to the ground in the same period (see 9.3).

The aim of this centralization of the cult was that from then on the temple in Jerusalem should function as the one legitimate place of worship. This concern comes to the fore especially in Deuteronomy (see Deut. 12) and the Deuteronomistic history work.

14.2.2 *Consequences and effect*

This centralization of the cult had important consequences for the priests who served at the high places. They were not to serve in the central sanctuary, the temple in Jerusalem. However, they did receive a portion of the income of this temple (II Kings 23.9). The priests of these local sanctuaries are referred to in the Deuteronomistic literature as 'Levites' or as 'Levitical priests' (Deut. 18.6–8). So here they were regarded as priests, with the same rights as the priests in the central sanctuary.

Changes took place here from the time of Josiah. The priests who served and had served in the local sanctuaries were from now on regarded as a lower class of cult personnel. From now on their specific title was that of Levite, and the name 'priest' was reserved for those who were connected as priests with the Jerusalem temple, and for their descendants.[13] Broadly speaking, all this presumably applied only to the priests of the local sanctuaries in Judah. In Israel, Josiah was probably more rigorous in this connection. At least, in II Kings 23.15–20 it is said that the priests in Bethel were killed and that the graves in the temple there were defiled. This last piece of evidence shows that Josiah was pursuing political as well as religious ends in his reformation.[14]

Furthermore, the destruction of the high places obviously did not command general assent. This is evident from the fact that the local places of worship quickly came back into use, as can be inferred, for instance, from Ezek. 6.1–6. It is striking that we hear virtually nothing more about this reformation under Josiah's successors. That must lead us to conclude that in the religious sphere – and along with that, in all its political and social consequences – in the long run, the reformation did not bring any substantial renewal. There seem to be two reasons for this.

In the first place, the reformation was imposed too much from above. The king especially was behind it, probably prompted above all by the priests in Jerusalem. Secondly, the political situation was against it. This already changed towards the end of Josiah's reign. His successors again had to cope with a new overlord, and to adapt themselves in every respect.

There is one further reason which was perhaps the main cause of the failure. The Old Testament accounts certainly do not give us the impression that this was a real 'religious revival and renewal'. On the contrary, they show that there was an attempt in both the court and the temple in Jerusalem to use the reform to gain more power and influence. The words of Jeremiah about the temple (Jer. 7.7–15; 26) and about the king's conduct (Jer. 22.13–19), which were of course spoken very soon after the beginning of the reformation, give us a clear message in this respect.

14.3 *Territorial expansion under Josiah*

I have already pointed out in the previous section that the centralization of the cult in Jerusalem was closely connected with political aspirations. At the same time it also represented a strengthening of the central political authority in Jerusalem over the provinces. Attempts to extend this reformation far beyond the bounds of Judah must also be seen in this connection. This happened in areas which at that time were still in fact Assyrian provinces, where the population partly consisted of people who had been brought there by the Assyrians (see 13.3).

This affected Bethel and Samaria (II Kings 23.4ff.) and, according to Chronicles, other parts of former Israel (II Chron. 34.6–7). The defeat at Megiddo could also indicate (see 14.4) that Josiah's power and influence extended still further north.[15] How far this was in fact the case is difficult to establish. Probably the information in Kings is not too far from the truth. It is supported by archaeological evidence from this period, which gives us information about government administration during Josiah's reign. This comes largely from Judah,[16] though the north is certainly also represented. Thus an ostracon from Jabneh, about nine miles north-east of Ashdod, shows that there was a Judaean fortification there at the time of Josiah.[17] So it seems that in this period Judah spread both towards the coastal plain and towards the north. However, we must leave open the question of the exact extent of these boundaries. At all events, the kingdom of Judah had more territory to the north than since the death of Solomon.

At the same time, the ostracon from Jabneh mentioned above gives us some idea of developments in peasant farming, of the contacts between different social groupings and the organization of justice in this part of the country. In this ostracon, a letter to a man who as military commandant was presumably also responsible for justice there, a reaper complains of having been wrongfully dispossessed of an article of clothing.[18] He asserts his innocence and calls on the official to undo the wrong committed against him.

14.4 *The end of Josiah*

14.4.1 *The battle at Megiddo*

In the year following the fall of Haran, Necho launched a new attack from Egypt towards the Euphrates (14.1). In it he followed the old caravan route through Canaan. This route took him through the plain of Megiddo. In II Kings 23.29; II Chron 35.20 we hear that Josiah met Necho there to join battle with him. According to Malamat,[19] at that time Megiddo must have been an Egyptian base. The fact that Josiah nevertheless chose to meet Necho here[20] may be connected with a recognition that from a military point of view such an undertaking was completely impossible on the coastal plain. Furthermore, Megiddo can be seen as the most important strategic place on the Via Maris. There have been numerous battles there over the course of history.

The Old Testament does not tell us in detail about Josiah's motives for intercepting Pharaoh Necho. However, the only explanation for his action is that he was pursuing a pro-Babylonian policy. At any rate, an Egyptian conquest of Babylon would doubtless have had political consequences for the independence of Judah. This recognition, and the knowledge that a previous Egyptian expedition to the region of the Euphrates had not been particularly successful, obviously persuaded Josiah to join in the fight.

In II Chron. 35.21–22 there is a report that Necho had earlier sent messengers to Josiah telling him that the expedition was not against him but against another power. We find no trace of such a report in II Kings 23. Be this as it may, Josiah joined battle with Necho at Megiddo. In this battle Judah came off worst and king Josiah was killed. The Old Testament tradition is not unanimous about the circumstances of his death. According to II Kings 23.29 Josiah was killed in Megiddo, while in II Chron. 35.23–24 there is a report that he was seriously wounded at Megiddo and died of his wounds after being brought back to Jerusalem. It seem impossible to decide which description is the correct one.

Another question is whether there was actually a battle at Megiddo. That does not seem to be clearly stated in either Kings or Chronicles. According to Brongers,[21] the expression 'as soon as he saw him' in II Kings 23.29 would mean 'as soon as battle was joined'. We could be quite certain about this if on the basis of archaeological evidence it could be demonstrated that Megiddo was in fact destroyed in this period. However, that has not been established with certainty.[22] Josephus, a later source, suggests that the battle began when Josiah was wounded.[23]

14.4.2 *The consequences of Josiah's defeat*

The death of Josiah brought an end to the brief period of Judah's independence. However one interprets the events at Megiddo mentioned above, it is certain that Necho got the better of Josiah.

Thus Judah fell out of the hands of one world power into those of the other. After a short interval, Assyrian domination was replaced by that of Egypt. That evidently did not come about immediately. After the events at Megiddo, Necho hastened to continue his campaign and advanced to Carchemish, an important centre in the north of Syria. But that only meant a stay of execution for Judah. The Judaeans were soon enough to discover that Pharaoh Necho would take Judah completely in hand. We shall see what that means in the next chapter.

14.5 *The prophets Habakkuk and Zephaniah*

In this section we shall consider two prophets whom in all probability we can associate with the period of Josiah's reign over Judah. The same perhaps also applies to some degree to the prophet Jeremiah, but we shall discuss him in the next chapter.

14.5.1 *Habakkuk*

In view of Humbert's study,[24] it is almost certain that this prophet lived at the end of the seventh century BC. In all probability he was one of the temple prophets who were active in the temple at Jerusalem.[25] We know nothing more of the circumstances in which he lived.

At the beginning of his work, the prophet turns to the Chasdim (Hab. 1.6), a term which is generally held to denote the Babylonians. The last (third) chapter is a song in which the prophet expresses his expectation of the salvation which Yahweh will bring. It does not appear in the manuscript 1 QpHab found at Qumran. Habakkuk sees the Chasdim (Babylonians) as the coming world power. However, he does not expect any improvement in conditions under the new rulers: there will still be violence and injustice. This is the context in which Habakkuk utters the well-known words, 'The righteous shall live through his faith' (2.4).[26]

In Hab. 2.5–20 the prophet then launches a fierce attack on those who enrich themselves at the expense of others, make illegal profits, shed innocent blood, dishonour their neighbours and bow down to idols. He very probably had Babylon in mind as the oppressor who would do all this and bring it about. However, the words that Habakkuk speaks here are very apt in the historical context of any period. Those who act in such a way cannot begin from the God of the Bible and seek refuge in the image of a God which they have made up for themselves.

14.5.2 *Zephaniah*

The title of this prophetic book (1.1) expressly states that Zephaniah worked in the time of Josiah. This seems to accord with the content of his work. He was active in an earlier period than that of Habakkuk. We may probably infer from Zeph. 2.13–15 that Assyria was still in existence in his time and that the city of Nineveh had not yet been destroyed, though these verses give the impression that its fall was not far off. On the other hand, Zeph. 1.4–5, 8–9 seem to suggest that Josiah's reform (*c.* 622 BC) had not yet begun. These last remarks may then have been made not long before this reform of the cult.

The book of Zephaniah puts great emphasis on the announcement of the 'Day of the Lord',[27] of which we find the earliest mention in Amos 5.18–20. Views differ over the origin and interpretation of this phrase.[28]

Zephaniah was probably active for the most part in Jerusalem. His fierce polemic against abuses in the city at any rate suggests that in many respects he was well aware of the situation there.

Chapter 15

The Babylonian Advance

15.1 *Judah as a vassal of Egypt and the beginning of Babylonian rule*

15.1.1 *Vassal of Egypt*

Accounts of Necho's campaign in the direction of the Euphrates suggest that for the moment the struggle for power between Egypt and Babylon remained indecisive.[1] Necho did not succeed in recapturing Haran for the Assyrians. Since then Assyrian power had been in a state of collapse.

After that, at least for the moment, Necho seems to have gained a firm footing in Syria and Canaan. For example, Herodotus records[2] that Necho occupied Cadytes (Kadesh), and an Egyptian inscription seems to point to Egyptian rule over Phoenicia in this period.[3] The measures Necho took in connection with Judah seem to accord completely with this. After the death of Josiah, Jehoahaz[4] was anointed king over Judah by 'the people of the land' (II Kings 23.30; II Chron. 36.1). This Jehoahaz was not Josiah's oldest son. Presumably he was chosen because he was expected to pursue his father's anti-Egyptian policy. At all events, Jehoahaz reigned only three months (609/08), since Necho, immediately after his campaign in the east, summoned him to Riblah and deposed him.

Necho then appointed another son of Josiah king over Judah in his place. He was called Eliakim, but Necho changed his name to Jehoiakim (II Kings 23.31–34; II Chron. 36.1–4). This action by Necho is strongly reminiscent of the action of the Egyptian Pharaohs towards Canaanite city-rulers in the Amarna period, when these rulers could be seen as Egyptian vassals. We can see a reaction to these events in Judah in Jer. 22.10–12, where this prophet announces that Shallum (= Jehoahaz) will not return to Judah again.

Jehoiakim ruled for eleven years (609/08–598/97) in Judah. He had to impose very heavy taxation on the people in order to pay to Egypt the tribute due to it from a vassal state (II Kings 23.35; II Chron. 36.3). Such action will certainly not have increased his popularity. For a good deal of his reign

Jehoiakim pursued a pro-Egyptian policy – probably compelled to by circumstances. The presence of two Cushites at the court of Jerusalem in the time of Jeremiah is another probable indication of considerable Egyptian influence in Judah.[5] However, this policy had catastrophic consequences for the kingdom of Judah. Like Hoshea of Israel before him (see 13.3), Jehoiakim and his entourage had totally underestimated the new power relationships in the ancient Near East. They did not pay sufficient attention to Babylon's increasingly powerful position over against Egypt, or perhaps did not take note of it at all.

15.1.2 *Judah's subjection to Babylon*

The year 605 BC was decisive in the struggle for power between Egypt and Babylon. In that year Nebuchadnezzar, crown prince of Babylon, succeeded in inflicting a decisive defeat on the Egyptians at Carchemish.[6] This gave the Babylonians the upper hand in Syria and Canaan. As a vassal of Nebuchadnezzar II, who had become king of Babylon in the meantime, Jehoiakim of Judah had to submit to him and pay him tribute (II Kings 24.1). This Jehoiakim did for three years. Then a campaign of Nebuchadnezzar's against Egypt seemed to fail,[7] and Jehoiakim returned to his early pro-Egyptian policy by refusing to pay further tribute to Babylon.

Nebuchadnezzar II probably reacted to this revolt in the first place by sending troops from the provinces bordering on Judah to Jerusalem. At least this impression is given by II Kings 24.2, which speaks of bands of Chaldaeans, Aram, Moab and the Ammonites, advancing on Judah. At all events, it is evident from Babylonian accounts that Nebuchadnezzar needed time to reorganize his army. 'In the fifth year the king of Akkad remained in his land and gathered together his chariots and horses in large numbers.'[8] This was done in connection with a campaign in 'the land of the Hatti', which Nebuchadnezzar had held earlier and which he occupied again in the following year.

Only in the seventh year of his reign,[9] i.e. in 598/97, did Nebuchadnezzar himself return to Judah and bring the siege of Jerusalem to an end. However, Jehoiakim had died before his arrival, though it is also possible that he was killed during the siege. The latter possibility may perhaps be inferred from Jer. 22.19; 36.30. Be this as it may, it is certain that Jehoiakim's son Jehoiachin was now faced with the impossible task of confronting the Babylonians. He did the best he could in the circumstances, and surrendered unconditionally to Nebuchadnezzar. In so doing he avoided a pointless massacre and for the moment saved Judah from downfall.

15.2 *The prophet Jeremiah*

15.2.1 *The circumstances of Jeremiah's life*

Jeremiah is a prophet about whose personal circumstances and historical background we know more than we do in the case of any other prophet. It is evident from the title (1.1–3) of the book which bears his name that his prophetic activity took place at the time of the kings Josiah, Jehoiakim and Zedekiah. The names of Jehoahaz and Jehoiachin are missing from the list of kings of Judah given here, but they only reigned for three months. However, the activity of Jeremiah did not end with the fall of Zedekiah, the last king of Judah; at any rate, that seems to be clear from, for example, Jer. 42.1—43.13.

Jeremiah came from a family of priests who lived in Anathoth in the territory of Benjamin. There is uncertainty as to the time when he began his prophetic activity. It is usually assumed that this must have been in about 627 BC,[10] but a later date does not seem to be impossible.[11] After the death of Gedaliah (see 16.2.1), Jeremiah was taken to Egypt, where he possibly uttered further prophecies (Jer. 43.8—44.3).

Jeremiah also had a scribe. He was called Baruch, and we are told quite plainly (Jer. 36.2) that he wrote down various of the prophet's utterances. At the same time Baruch was one of Jeremiah's few friends and supporters during his lifetime. More than any other prophet, in his prophetic activity Jeremiah had to fight against fierce criticism and bitter hostility. His political attitudes made him countless enemies and his life was threatened on several occasions. The clearest indication of the hostility towards him can be seen in the fate of the prophet Uriah, probably a disciple and in any case one of his supporters. After his flight to Egypt he was handed over and then killed on the orders of Jehoiakim and the most important members of his government (Jer. 26.20–23). Jeremiah himself narrowly escaped this fate on several occasions. This was not least thanks to the protection which he was given by Ahikam (Jer. 26.24), a man who occupied an important position at the Jerusalem court.

15.2.2 *Jeremiah's activity*

I have already indicated that Jeremiah's political attitude was the reason for the great hostility against him. Like Isaiah before him, Jeremiah was in favour of a policy of neutrality. He himself argued for submitting to Babylon (Jer. 27) because at all costs he wanted to avoid a military adventure with all its catastrophic consequences. A characteristic expression of his thought in this respect is his well-known letter to the exiles in Babylon (Jer. 29.4–14), in which he urges them to seek peace for themselves and the city in which they live.

This attitude will certainly not have done Jeremiah any good. He was thought to be pro-Babylonian and a traitor. Because of his views he had the king and the majority of the political leaders against him. Even the inhabitants of his own town turned against him (Jer. 11.21–23). As so often in history, people in any case preferred to listen at that time to prophets who reflected popular opinion and adopted a different viewpoint from Jeremiah, talking in the name of the Lord about casting off the yoke of Babylon.[12] One well-known instance of this is the appearance of the prophet Hananiah (Jer. 28), who proclaimed liberation from Babylon while Jeremiah was forecasting the downfall of the city and the land.

In addition to all this, Jeremiah also adopted a sharply critical attitude to the king and other leaders. His criticism of the monarchy is probably expressed most fiercely in Jer. 22.13–22, in which he shows up the injustice of Jehoiakim. Instead of giving the poor and unprivileged their rights, as is his duty (compare Ps. 72.4), this king thinks only of his own advantage: 'But you have eyes and heart only for dishonest gain, for shedding innocent blood and for practising oppression and violence' (Jer. 22.17). It is striking in this connection that excavations have shown that in the time of Jehoiakim a splendid palace must have been built mid-way between Bethlehem and Jerusalem.[13] This happened at a time in which the economic situation of the people certainly cannot be said to have been rose-coloured.[14]

Finally in this connection mention should be made of Jeremiah's attitude towards the cult and the temple.[15] In very fierce language, Jeremiah attacks all those who think that the presence of the temple is a divine guarantee of the invulnerability of city and temple and that this implicitly means that everything that happens in the temple is beyond criticism (Jer. 7.1–15). Jeremiah also explicitly announces the downfall of this temple (Jer. 26.1–19). For this reason it is above all the priests and prophets (26.11) who want to kill him because of what he says. Criticism of an institution like a temple clearly always arouses the fiercest opposition. We can see the same sort of thing later, when Jesus, too, attacks the temple (see Mark 11.15ff.; Luke 19.45ff.).

Thus the whole of Jeremiah's activity was characterized by misunderstanding, hate and hostility. With Jeremiah, more than with any other prophet, we see that a prophet is without honour not only in his own country but also in his own time.[16]

15.3 *The first deportation to Babylon*

Judah seems to have offered hardly any resistance when Nebuchadnezzar II appeared before the gates of Jerusalem in 598/97.[17] At that time, of course, Jehoiachin virtually put himself straight into Nebuchadnezzar's hands

(15.1.2). He was thereupon immediately deposed as king and deported to Babylon as a prisoner. So he was king of Judah for only about three months (598/97). Nebuchadnezzar then appointed his own king over Judah, as Necho had done in the past. He was again a son of Josiah and thus an uncle of Jehoiachin. The name of this new king was Mattaniah, but Nebuchadnezzar changed his name to Zedekiah (II Kings 24.17). Zedekiah was king of Judah for eleven years (598/97–587/86).

We find confirmation of all this in the Babylonian chronicles, where it is said that Nebuchadnezzar appointed a new king over Judah,[18] though the name of this new king is not mentioned. The name of Jehoiachin also occurs in an administrative text found in Babylon which mentions provisions for prisoners and others who belonged to the royal household in the time of Nebuchadnezzar II.[19] This confirms that Jehoiachin did in fact remain in Babylon as a prisoner. In II Kings 25.27–30 (Jer. 52.31–34) we further hear that after being imprisoned for thirty-seven years, Jehoiachin was pardoned by Evil-Merodach, the successor of Nebuchadnezzar II (561-60).

Jehoiachin's surrender had meanwhile saved Jerusalem from disaster, but the country was desperately hard-hit. Nebuchadnezzar took all the treasure from the temple and the royal palace to Babylon (II Kings 24.13).[20] The removal of the temple vessels made a particularly deep impression. This emerges, for example, in the confrontation between the prophets Jeremiah and Hananiah (15.2.2). There the prophet Hananiah announces that everything will be brought back quickly. This stands in contrast to the words of Jeremiah (Jer. 28.6ff.).

Others were taken into captivity as well as Jehoiachin and members of the royal family. They included leading figures, soldiers, craftsmen, smiths, elders, prophets and priests.[21] These last included the priest Ezekiel (Ezek. 1.1–3), who functioned as a prophet in Babylon. It is impossible to determine the total number of the deportees. The figures given for them in the Old Testament are contradictory. A number of 3023 is given in Jer. 52.28; II Kings 24.14 mentions 10,000 able-bodied men plus craftsmen and smiths, and II Kings 24.16 a total of 8000 exiles. It is, however, certain that an important proportion of the leading figures from Judah were among these captives. In this way Nebuchadnezzar probably hoped to have nipped in the bud any new form of oppression. The future, however, would show that this hope was vain.

15.4 *The end of the state of Judah*

15.4.1 *Zedekiah's government*

Zedekiah means 'the Lord is righteousness'. We find an allusion to this name in Jer. 23.6. From the passage in Jeremiah in which it occurs (23.5–8), we get the impression that Jeremiah had high expectations of the king at the beginning of his reign. However, he was deeply disappointed in these expectations, as appears especially in the image of the bad figs (Jer. 24.8). It is evident from the book of Jeremiah that the prophet was often opposed to this king. Still, on other occasions Zedekiah again asked the advice of Jeremiah, even if he almost always took no notice of it. It is evident from this that Zedekiah was not a powerful personality.

He allowed his political policy to be directed largely by groups and advisers who had strongly nationalistic and anti-Babylonian feelings. They found it very difficult to reconcile themselves to the fact that Judah had now – like Israel, earlier, in the last phase of its existence – been reduced to a small, insignificant rump state.[22] Clearly this group could count on a large following among the people for all kinds of reasons. By contrast the prophet Jeremiah, who urged the people to accept the existing situation as a *fait accompli*, found little hearing.

In these circumstances it is obvious that reckless attempts would be made to throw off the yoke of Babylon. A first attempt perhaps took place as early as 594 BC. At least, in Ezek. 17.15 we hear that there were contacts with Egypt. It is possible that they relate to this period.[23] At any rate, there were certainly negotiations at the time with Edom, Ammon, Moab, Tyre and Sidon (Jer. 27.3). For one reason or another none of the discussions produced more than talk: no action was taken. At all events, we hear nothing about the outbreak of a revolt. It is possible that it was already smothered at birth. Be this as it may, Zedekiah evidently saw a chance to convince Nebuchadnezzar of his loyalty. This probably happened when Zedekiah paid a visit to Babylon in the fourth year of his reign (see Jer. 51.59).

15.4.2 *The rebellion*

This rebellion took place in *c.* 588 BC. However, reports in the Old Testament are extremely reticent about the struggle which now began. In II Kings 25.1ff.; II Chron. 36.13ff., most attention is paid to the capture of Jerusalem and the devastation of palace and temple. From, for example, Jer. 37.5–11; Ezek. 29–31, it could be inferred that Egypt had promised support for the rebellion in one form or another and did to some degree provide it. That also seems to follow from the facts provided by the Lachish ostraca (which come from the archives of the city commander of the time).[24] It is already evident from them that Judah was not alone in the revolt. According to Josephus, Tyre joined in as well.[25] This account refers to the siege of Tyre by the Babylonians, which lasted from 585 to 572 B C.[26] Furthermore, Ezek. 21.20 contains an indication that Ammon, too, was affected in some way by this rebellion against Babylon.

Nevertheless, Zedekiah's rebellion was doomed from the start. Judah was too small to accomplish anything by itself (see above). Evidently the leaders of the army, supported by many prophets (see Jer. 28–29), were the ones principally behind this military adventure. Presumably all hopes were pinned on Egypt. The prophet Jeremiah was one of the few who opposed the rebellion with all his might. However, no one listened to him.

Nebuchadnezzar, at the height of his power, reacted very quickly to this revolt in Judah. He immediately advanced on Judah with an army, appeared before Jerusalem and laid siege to the city. Evidently only Jerusalem and two other cities succeeded in holding out against the Babylonians. We know this from Jer. 34.7, where the prophet mentions the places Jerusalem, Lachish and Azekah in this connection. We find his account confirmed in the Lachish ostraca, mentioned above. Ostracon 4 states that contacts between Lachish and Jerusalem are maintained by messengers and those between Lachish and Azekah by signals. In lines 12–13, we read, 'We cannot see the signals from Azekah'.[27] Perhaps this means that Azekah had by then fallen into the hands of the Babylonians.[28]

15.4.3 *The fall of Jerusalem*

Zedekiah was not able to hold out for long against the great supremacy of Nebuchadnezzar. He was captured by the Babylonians while attempting to escape from the city, and taken to Nebuchadnezzar at Riblah. There his sons were killed before his eyes and Zedekiah himself was blinded and led captive to Babylon (II Kings 25.4–7; Jer. 52.7–11). That decided the fate of Jerusalem. The city was taken, its walls were destroyed and the palace and temple razed to the ground (II Kings 25.8–17). Again some of the population were taken in exile to Babylon. According to Jer. 52.29 – probably the most authentic tradition – the number of people deported totalled 832. II Kings 25.11 mentions in this connection 'the rest of the people who were left in the city'. It is evident from all this not only that the Babylonians had military control but also that they were very well informed about the situation in Judah. Thus Jeremiah was released from prison on the orders of Nebuchadnezzar and protected by the Babylonians (Jer. 39.11–14). By mistake he was later included in the group of captives on their way to Babylon (Jer. 40.1ff.), but when the mistake was discovered he was given the choice of either going to Babylon as a free man or of remaining in Judah. He chose the latter. Thus the Babylonians evidently knew what Jeremiah's attitude had been towards the rebellion against Babylon.

There is still disagreement as to precisely when Jerusalem fell into the hands of the Babylonians. Views vary between the summer of 587 BC[29] and the summer of 586.[30] In fact uncertainty over the chronological system then in use in Judah for marking the kings' reigns makes it impossible to arrive at an exact date. So we do not know whether during this period the year in Judah – as in Babylon – was reckoned from Nisan to Nisan[31] (from spring to spring) or from Tishri to Tishri (from autumn to autumn). Another problem is presented by the different systems of dating which are applied to this period in the Old Testament.[32] For example, Jeremiah and Ezekiel date some events in connection with the captivity of Jehoiachin (e.g. Ezek. 33.21) and others in connection with the reigns of the Babylonian kings (e.g. II Kings 25.8; Jer. 52.12).

Chapter 16

The Captivity in Babylon

6.1 *The consequences of the fall of Jerusalem*

It is difficult to understimate the consequences for later history of the fall of Jerusalem and the end of the kingdom of Judah. First of all it meant that in Judah the dynasty of David, which had continued to rule there for about 400 years, now came to an end. Although this dynasty never returned to power, thoughts of it were firmly rooted in the thinking of later times. The dynasty, and above all the figure of David, increasingly became the symbol of a coming time of salvation and was associated with it.[1]

The loss of independence also meant that from now on stress was increasingly laid on the religious aspect of the people's existence. A special factor in this connection was the way in which the Babylonian practice of deportation differed from that of the Assyrians. The Babylonians did not introduce other ethnic groups into Judah to replace those who were deported. This meant that the danger of syncretism in religion was less acute. Furthermore, the Babylonians again differed from the Assyrians in that evidently they settled most of the deported Jews in the same area in Babylon. It is clear that this was a considerable help in maintaining mutual links and contacts.

In the course of time this group of exiles in particular made an important contribution towards the formation and development of later Judaism. Although many of the exiles in Babylon were given permission to return home to Judah in 539 BC, very few of them took advantage of it. Later, and above all in the Roman period, this group was further strengthened by the arrival of new immigrants from Judah. In the course of time, works like the Babylonian Talmud[2] and some of the Targums[3] were produced here in Babylon.

Thanks, among other things, to the preaching of the prophets, the realization later dawned that the decline of Judah and the fall of Jerusalem had to be seen as a divine judgment. Once this had been realized, people again began to reflect on a future in which conditions would be completely changed.

Thus the period from 598/97 to 539/38 was extremely important for Judah in many respects.

It should be emphasised particularly in this context that Judah[4] had survived the catastrophe of 587/86 as the representative of Israel. While other people who, like Judah, had lost their political independence and were also deported, at least partially, disappeared from history completely, this Israel was able to preserve its own identity.

Apart from the work of, for example, the prophets Ezekiel and Deutero-Isaiah, an important part was played in this development by the theological reflection and the literary activity which now began. Furthermore, the time of this exile can rightly be seen as a turning point in the history and religion of Israel (Judah).

16.2 *The situation in Judah after 587/86 BC*

16.2 *Gedaliah's government*

Despite everything that had happened, after 587/86 Nebuchadnezzar still adopted a very tolerant attitude towards Judah. The reason for this must have been the presence in Jerusalem of a party which, if it was not pro-Babylonian, had certainly been against the rebellion.

After the fall of Jerusalem, the government of Judah was entrusted to Gedaliah (II Kings 25.22; Jer. 40.5). He was a son of Ahikam, who can be regarded as Jeremiah's protector (15.2.1). It is evident from the Old Testament that Gedaliah wanted to implement a careful and wise policy, which at least in its main outlines corresponded with the policy envisaged by the prophet Jeremiah (see Jer. 40.7ff.). Gedaliah settled in Mizpah[5] and planned to govern the country from there. We may assume that the territory under his control was smaller than the kingdom of Judah in the days of Zedekiah.[6] Edom in particular seems to have profited from the difficult position in Judah in 598/97 and/or 587/86 BC.[7] The bitterness about this is evident in Jer. 49.7ff. and in Obadiah 1ff. Directly after assuming power, Gedaliah took steps to put things in order. Everything goes to show that he sought to avoid any new confrontation with the Babylonians, and above all wanted to restore peace and tranquility to the country. So he urged the countryfolk to bring in the harvest. This was probably aimed above all at producing a rapid economic recovery.

Unfortunately, however, this period of wise government lasted for only a short time. Although he had been warned of the danger beforehand, Gedaliah was assassinated (Jer. 40.13–16). A certain Ishmael, a member of the royal family, killed him and many people who were with him or who had come to

him (Jer. 41.1–9). Johanan, an army commander, was later able to liberate the
people of Mizpah, whom Ishmael wanted to lead to Ammon (Jer. 41.10–15).
However, neither Johanan nor the population of Mizpah could remain in
Judah any longer. They were afraid that the wrath of Nebuchadnezzar would
fall upon them because of Gedaliah's murder (Jer. 41.16–18). They asked the
prophet Jeremiah for advice. He counselled them not to flee, but they took no
notice, and the whole group went off to Egypt. Despite his protests, they took
Jeremiah with them (Jer. 42.1–43.7).

We do not know whether this group or part of it later returned to Judah.
Jeremiah 44.13–14 seems to exclude such a return.[8] According to Josephus,[9]
after Nebuchadnezzar had conquered Egypt, this group too was deported to
Babylon. However, everything is uncertain in this connection.

16.2.2 *The population of Judah after 587/86 BC*

Although after the fall of Jerusalem, as in 598/97, only a relatively small
number of people were taken to Babylon, and the number of those who fled to
Egypt after the murder of Gedaliah would not amount to much, it all led to a
change in the make-up of the population. Those deported to Babylon must
have included the leading groups in Judah. That means that now others could
come to the fore there. Mention is made in this connection of the 'poor of the
land'. On the basis of Jer. 39.10; 52.16 (II Kings 25.12) this must be taken to
mean those without possessions who were now made farmers and workers in
the vineyards. They were probably land-owners or tenants under Babylonian
control.[10] Gedaliah had been entrusted with the oversight of these 'poor of the
land' (Jer. 40.7).

Although we cannot exclude the possibility that the designation 'poor of the
land'[11] in the long run increasingly took on a theological as well as a social
significance, and came to mean the 'pious', it is evident that at the time of
Gedaliah the social significance was to the fore.

As to the general situation in the country, it is clear that many cities had
been destroyed by the Babylonians in their last campaign.[12] After a short
interval, these were probably inhabited again, at least in part.[13] However, the
destruction of the temple does not seem to have put an end to worship in
Jerusalem. At all events, in Jer. 41.5 we hear that a group of eighty people from
Shechem, Shiloh and Samaria came to 'the house of the Lord' to offer a
sacrifice there. Although we are not told so explicitly, it seems reasonable to
suppose that they wanted to do this in Jerusalem. Probably an altar was
soon reconstructed on the site of the temple.[14] It is difficult to conceive that
there was no activity at all in the sphere of worship, religion and so on in
Judah during the time of the exile,[15] and it is clear that Jerusalem and the place

where the temple had stood would have played an important role. For this reason too we should not overestimate the activities of the relatively small group of exiles in Babylon and underestimate that of those who were left behind in Judah.[16]

Although we have no precise information here, it seems certain that, among other things, there were various kinds of literary activity in Judah as well. We shall discuss this further in one of the later sections of this chapter.

16.3 The situation in Babylon

16.3.1 The position of the exiles

We do not know when the first Judaeans came to Babylon. Presumably Judaeans had already settled in Babylon (and elsewhere) on a voluntary basis before the arrival of the first people to be deported.[17] According to Larsson,[18] it can be demonstrated on the basis of Babylonian texts that there were already Judaean prisoners in Babylon in 605 BC. It is certain that any group of Judaeans which may have been in Babylon was substantially increased by the deportations in 598/97 and 587/86 BC.

The Old Testament gives us some information about the places in which the exiles in Babylon lived. The river Chebar and Tel-Abib are mentioned in this connection in Ezek. 1.3; 3.15, and Tel-melah, Tel-harsa, Cherub, Addan and Immer in Ezra 2.59 and Neh. 7.61. Information from Babylon itself confirms the presence of Judaeans there. That presence can be established, for example, from the appearance of Judaean and Yahwistic names in Babylon then and in subsequent periods.[19] However, we have little detailed information about the feelings among the exiles. We might conclude from Ezek. 40—48 (the vision of the new temple) and Ps. 137.5, with the well-known saying, 'If I forget you, O Jerusalem, let my right hand wither', that there was a deep longing to return among at least some of the exiles, but it is obvious that by no means everyone felt the same way. It is evident from Deutero-Isaiah that a large number of the exiles did not want to return to Judah, because they prospered in Babylon and regarded it as their second homeland.

Information of Babylonian origin confirms that many Judaeans there had good positions. In an archive found at Nippur which comes from some kind of trading house, we find the names of many Judaeans at this period who were making important transactions in Babylon.[20] One thing seems certain, however: many exiles, both among those who remained in Babylon and those who later returned to Judah, held on tightly to their religious identity. In all probability, institutions like the sabbath and the command to honour parents were emphasized very strongly in this period. Thus the formulation of the relevant commandments in Lev. 19.3 could well mean that in this situation the elders were seen above all as the ones who handed on the old traditions.[21]

Nevertheless, it must be said that we have no clear picture of religious life during the Babylonian captivity. In contrast to Elephantine in Egypt, where colonists of Judaean and Israelite origin had a temple for Yahweh (see 18.4), we know nothing of the existence of any temple in Babylon.[22] Furthermore, there is no definitive proof that we should put the beginning of synagogue worship in this period.[23]

16.3.2 *The influence of Babylonian culture*

One important development for the exiles was that in Babylon they were sharply brought face to face with another religion and culture. Its influence seems to have been quite considerable, particularly in the cultural sphere. Here, above all, people came in contact with the literature of the ancient Near East. We might recall the various creation and flood stories which were in circulation. Thus, for example, in the biblical creation narrative in Gen.1.1–2.4a we can obviously see fierce polemic against other creation stories – current – at the time.[24]

Of course that does not mean that there is no question of such influence at an early period. This will have been furthered by other trade contacts and the long vassal relationship of Judah to Assyria and Babylon. However, this period made the influence very much stronger on those who had been deported to Babylon. Here I should make special mention of the influence of Aramaic. This language was used increasingly after the exile in Babylon. In the Old Testament, we find it in books like Ezra and Daniel, which were written partly in Hebrew and partly in Aramaic.

Finally, in this context, mention should be made of the names of the Jewish leaders in the period shortly after the exile. There is clear Babylonian influence in the case of some of them, like Zerubbabel (Ezra 2.2) and Sheshbazzar (Ezra 1.8).

16.4 *Ezekiel*

16.4.1 *The person of the prophet*

Ezekiel's call to be a prophet (Ezek. 1.1–3.15) took place at Tel-Abib by the river Chebar and therefore in Babylon. Ezekiel was a priest[25] and was one of the exiles who were taken into captivity in 598/97 along with king Jehoiachin. According to Ezek. 1.2,[26] this call took place in the fifth year of his captivity, which must therefore have been 593/92. Ezekiel was active as a prophet in Babylon for at least twenty years.[27]

As with most of the prophets, we know very little about his personal circumstances. We know from what he tells us himself (Ezek. 24.18) that he was married and that his father was called Buzi (Ezek. 1.3). His great interest in the temple and his knowledge of cultic matters indicates a close connection with priestly circles. It is striking that in the visions, of which there are a great many in his book, Ezekiel is often to the fore and plays a very active part. This indicates one of his characteristic features. We can see not only that the visionary element plays an important role with Ezekiel but also that his whole being was caught up in the message that he brought: he ate a scroll (Ezek. 3.2–3), cut off his hair and used it to present a picture of the fate of the inhabitants of Jerusalem (Ezek. 5.1–5). All this is in full agreement with the fact that Ezekiel's person is itself often said to be a sign.[28] Here his own personal feelings only rarely come to the fore. This happens occasionally in the form of a lament, as for example in Ezek. 4.14; 9.8; 21.5.

16.4.2 *Ezekiel's prophecies: audience and content*

Apart from his prophecies against foreign nations in Ezek. 25–32 and 35, Ezekiel addresses himself primarily towards the leaders in Jerusalem (Ezek. 8), Zedekiah (Ezek. 17), prophets and prophetesses (Ezek. 13), representatives of the exiles (Ezek. 8.1; 14.1; 20.1) and also to those who have been left behind in Judah (Ezek. 11.15; 33.23–29).

It is striking that Ezekiel often refers to the people as 'house of Israel'. Baltzer rightly observes that this is a term for an entity which no longer has a political existence[29] So here in Ezekiel it has more of a religious or theological significance. Ezekiel also uses the title 'watchman over the house of Israel'.[30] This designation is probably connected with the law.[31] The degree to which Ezekiel was preoccupied with this is clearly expressed, for example, in Ezek. 18; 33. His task is to disclose injustice; that is the prophet's responsibilty. If he does not perform his task of warning the people in this connection, the guilt of the godless will fall upon him personally.

As a result, in Ezekiel in particular there is great stress on personal responsibility. Precisely in order to emphasize this, the prophet probably wanted to warn his people against pessimistic fatalism and summoned them to face reality as responsible individuals.

There is a clear turning point in Ezekiel's prophecy after the fall of Jerusalem in 587/86. The proclamation of judgment fades into the background and from now on salvation and encouragement come more to the fore in his preaching. We find a fine illustration of this turning point in Ezek. 37.1–14. The imagery of the dry bones shows that God will raise his people as though from the dead.

16.4.3 *Ezekiel's influence on later developments*

The vision of the new temple and the account of the tasks of the various functionaries of it contained in Ezek. 40–48 is important for Ezekiel's vision of the future.[32] A typical statement here is that in Ezek. 43.7 where God says, 'This is the place . . . where I will dwell in the midst of the people of Israel for ever.' This is at the same time an indication of the extremely important place that Zion and Jerusalem occupy in the book of Ezekiel.[33] It should be emphasized that in Ezekiel's vision the temple is seen as being entirely God's work. Human hands are not involved in it. That seems to indicate a clear difference from the earlier temple, which in fact could be called a royal temple. If we bear this in mind, we might be inclined to conclude that in this connection Ezekiel made an important contribution to the reorganization of the religion of Israel. However, his plan for a new temple and all that goes with it was not put into practice in the building of the second temple. Although this temple was no longer a royal temple, it was nevertheless more a symbol of power than what Ezekiel had envisaged in his visions.

Ezekiel was also seen as the founder of later Judaism. This is probably putting it too strongly. However, it seems certain that elements came to the fore in Ezekiel's preaching which were influential in this direction. They include the great stress which he placed on keeping the sabbath (Ezek. 20.12–24; 44.24),[34] something completely new in comparison with the earlier prophets. Ezekiel also seems to have been a pioneer in quite a different respect. That is in connection with apocalyptic. Apocalyptic flourished above all in the period round about the beginning of the Christian era. It is focused not least on the unveiling of divine secrets about the last days. Angels also play a great part in it, here and in the world to come. Apocalyptic is also full of colourful descriptions. It is to be found above all in intertestamental literature.[35] We also find some shorter passages in both the Old and the New Testaments which can be said to be apocalyptic.[36] However, these passages have a more moderate tone than those in apocalyptic literature outside the Bible, and are quite closely related to prophecy.

Ezekiel 38 and 39, which are about Gog and Magog, played a particularly important role in later apocalyptic.[37] In Ezekiel Gog was the designation of the evil power which threatened Jerusalem from the north (Magog). This threat was turned away by Yahweh, after which Israel was completely restored.

To sum up, one can say that Ezekiel prevented his people during the exile from deviating into syncretism, and in some respects prepared for developments which took place after the exile.

16.5 *Deutero-Isaiah*

This name is used to denote the prophet to whom, broadly speaking, Isa. 40–55 is ascribed. It is generally assumed that Deutero-Isaiah was active during the exile. Isaiah 40-48 may be connected with events from before the fall of Babylon, while Isa. 49–55 is perhaps connected more with events after the fall of that city.[38] We are as ignorant about the person of the prophet as we are about his name. The best-known part of his book is the so-called Servant Songs.[39] Interpretations of these songs differ markedly,[40] and there is even argument as to whether the servant in them is to be seen as an individual or as a collective. It seems most reasonable to apply both interpretations here.

The people whom Deutero-Isaiah addresses in his prophecies are very probably those who are exiles in Babylon.[41] The political background to his emergence seems to be determined primarily by the rise of Cyrus and the gradual decline of the Babylonian empire. Clearly all the events connected with this had a great influence on the preaching of Deutero-Isaiah. He even calls Cyrus the Lord's anointed (45.1). The great theme in Deutero-Isaiah's preaching is the announcement that the people's time of suffering is over and that God will again dwell in the midst of his people on Zion. We can already see this from the first words of the prophet in Isa. 40.1–11.

He bases his confidence in the return of the people from exile on his conviction that Yahweh is the Lord of history and the Lord of the nations. In this connection, he lays great stress on the creative activity of Yahweh.[42] His remarks about the exodus must be seen in the same light.[43]

It is almost certain that the words of Deutero-Isaiah announcing liberation and a return from Babylon found very little echo in his own time and among his own contemporaries. Remarks like those in Isa. 42.18–20; 49.14 and 50.2 show that his words had little effect. The fact that only a small number of exiles later seized the possibility of returning home also seems to justify this conclusion. So this prophet too, like his predecessors and successors at a later period, remained all too clearly a voice in the wilderness during the time of his activity.

16.6 *Literary activities*

The period of the exile in all probability had considerable influence on the literature of ancient Israel. Closer contacts with Babylonian culture (16.3.2) and the dispersion certainly meant that people began to collect together oral traditions and set them down in writing. In this section I shall be looking at two important works in this connection: the Deuteronomistic history work and the Priestly Writing.

16.6.1 *The Deuteronomistic history work*

According to Noth,[44] we have in the Old Testament a history work which begins with Deut. 1.1 and ends with the account of Jehoiachin's pardon in II Kings 25.27–30. This last piece of information also indicates the earliest date at which the work can have appeared, i.e. after 561 BC when Jehoiachin was pardoned by Evil-merodach of Babylon (561–560).[45] The work has been called the Deuteronomistic history work. It makes no mention of the rebuilding of the temple and the Persian empire, which suggests that it must have been completed not long after 561 BC and in any case before about 520 BC. All this does not of course exclude the possibility that it contains old material, much less that it may have worked over a number of traditions coming from different periods. Thus Dietrich[46] distinguishes within it a Dtr G, in which history has a central role, a Dtr N, in which an important place is occupied by the Deuteronomic law, and a Dtr P, in which prophecy comes to the fore.

One important question is where the work was written. Most people seem to place it in Canaan,[47] but we cannot be certain about this, so that other possibilities remain open.[48] However, it is clear that in his account of earlier history the Deuteronomist is attempting to give an explanation of the divine judgment in 587/86 BC. This earlier history is written in the light of that and is intended above all to judge the actions of the kings of Israel and Judah. The work is thus a particular interpretation of history which describes how the people of God have reacted to God's election and his liberation.

16.6.2 *The Priestly Writing*

It is now generally accepted that the specifically Priestly parts of the first books of the Old Testament were collected at the time of the exile in Babylon and probably to a large degree written down there.[49] We have no precise information, but part of it had perhaps already been completed in this period, Similarly, there is virtual unanimity that the origin of the work should be sought among the Judaeans in Babylon rather than among those in Judah. Furthermore, there seems to be a clear relationship between the sending of Ezra (18.2) and this priestly lawgiving, which evidently came to Jerusalem through Ezra.[50] The affinity with Ezekiel which can be observed in the Priestly Writing and above all in the Holiness Code (Lev. 17–26) also indicates that the work was composed in the exile,[51] though it is also quite possible that the Priestly Writing contains early material which Ezekiel already knew beforehand as a priest.

Presumably we should look for this old material in the first place in the various cultic laws and rituals, though other passages may also be ancient. It can be demonstrated on the basis of, for example, Lev. 19, which in its present context must be attributed to the Holiness Code and thus to the Priestly Writing, that ancient regulations of different origin were given a new context.[52] Furthermore, it hardly seems conceivable that different rituals, like those in the sacrificial laws of Lev. 1–7 and the like, had not been in use earlier in one form or another in Solomon's temple or in other temples at an earlier period. However, it does seem that the catastrophe of 587/86 proved a stimulus to collect together and put down in writing a great deal of material that was around. This provided the best guarantee that it would be available for posterity. The main aim of the revisions and reinterpretations which took place here was to express the function of this work and these traditions.

16.7 *The fall of Babylon*

16.7.1 *The dismantling of the neo-Babylonian empire*

Nebuchadnezzar II's great empire did not last for very long. The dismantling of it began to gather momentum soon after his death.

Nebuchadnezzar was succeeded by his son Awil-Marduk, who is called Evil-merodach in the Old Testament. He ruled only from 561 to 560 BC. A revolution led by Neriglissar, son-in-law of Nebuchadnezzar, then put an end to his rule and his life. Neriglissar now became king of Babylon himself. At that time he must already have been quite old, since he is mentioned in Jer. 39.3, 13 as one of the generals involved in the capture of Jerusalem in 587/86 BC. In c. 557 this king seems to have had some successes in the military sphere. At least, that is recorded in the Babylonian Chronicles.[53] He, too, reigned for only a short time, and was then succeeded by his son Labashi-Marduk.

The latter had scarcely ascended the throne when a new revolution broke out, so that Labashi-Marduk reigned only three months as king. This revolution also put an end to the existing dynasty. The new king was Nabonidus. His name has also been preserved in the so-called 'Prayer of Nabonidus', one of the Dead Sea Scrolls.[54] Nabonidus ruled from 555 to the end of the neo-Babylonian empire in 539 BC. His mother was presumably a priestess of the moon god Sin in the temple of Haran. This background would also seem to explain the fact that Nabonidus encouraged the worship of this moon god in his empire. Presumably this attitude was also the driving force behind Nabonidus' revolution, since later the city of Babylon and the priests of Marduk could be counted among its most important opponents.[55] At all events, it is clear that his powerful group of priests never could nor would tolerate such a privileged position for the moon god, not only because this put Marduk, the chief god of Babylon, in second place, but above all because their own position was affected.[56] It was presumably also because of this opposition that Nabonidus spent more time in his residence in Tema, in Arabia, than in Babylon.[57] He was more a scholar than a ruler, and left matters of state to his son Belshazzar.[58]

16.7.2 *The fall of Babylon*

All these events indicate that the domestic situation within the neo-Babylonian empire was far from favourable. However, confrontation with foreign powers was even more critical. A new power was rising, the Persian empire under the leadership of Cyrus. There seem to be clear allusions to this, for example, in Isa 44.28; 45.1. The Persians gradually succeeded in taking over the whole of the neo-Babylonian empire. This empire, too, collapsed because of its size (cf. 14.1). Tensions within it played a very large part in its fall.

The final end came in 539 BC, when the Persian army occupied the city of Babylon. It is unlikely that the Persians encountered any significant resistance.[59] Presumably the priests of Marduk did not see Cyrus as a conqueror but rather welcomed him as a liberator. That could also be inferred from the contents of the so-called 'Cyrus cylinder'.[60] Here it is said that Nabonidus had to be imprisoned by Cyrus because of the godless measures which he had undertaken in the religious and social sphere. We can see a remarkable agreement between Deutero-Isaiah and the priests of Marduk in Babylon. Like the latter, Deutero-Isaiah, too, saw Cyrus as a liberator (Isa. 45.1ff.).

The downfall of the neo-Babylonian empire in 539 BC also put an end to the Babylonian rule over Judah. From now on Judah was under the domination of the Persian empire. This did not mean a return of its own independence, but it did bring great changes.

Chapter 17

The Return and the Rebuilding of the Temple

17.1 *The policy of the Persian rulers*

The transition from Babylonian to Persian rule brought great changes in various areas, so it can rightly be regarded as an important turning point in the history of this time. Compared with the period of Babylonian domination, that of Persia lasted for a long period. As we can see, it extended from the fall of the city of Babylon in 539 BC to the battle of Issus in 333 BC, in which Alexander the Great inflicted a final defeat on the Persians.

After the fall of Babylon, Cyrus left the administrative organization of the Babylonian empire intact. This was closely connected with his policy of treating the people he conquered as though he was their native ruler.[1] Part of this policy was the very tolerant attitude which Cyrus and his successors adopted towards the peoples they conquered in many respects, including the spheres of worship and religion. Thus Cyrus had all the divine images which had been brought by Nabonidus to Babylon restored to their original sanctuaries.[2] It was presumably for precisely this reason that on capturing Babylon in 539 BC Cyrus entered the city not as a conqueror but as its liberator (see 16.7.2).

Cyrus probably also allowed the temple vessels which Nabonidus' predecessors had brought from conquered lands like Judah to be returned to their place of origin. At any rate this seems likely in view of Cyrus' actions in Babylon (see above) and the so-called 'Edict of Cyrus' (see 17.2.1). One important difference in the religious policy introduced by the Persian rulers was presumably that in the Persian period the temples were obliged to make substantial contribution in kind to the king (the state).[3] The opposite had been the case in earlier times.

A report from an extra-biblical source indicates that those who had been deported were also sent back to their former country or place of origin. At least, in this report it is said, 'I (Cyrus) also gathered together all earlier inhabitants and let them return to their dwelling places.'[4] Thus the Persian rulers tried as far as possible to encourage individual practices among the different peoples in their realm in the spheres of law, religion and worship. It is perhaps also primarily because of this policy that the Persian empire lasted so long and in addition enjoyed considerable stability.

17.2 *The edict of Cyrus and its consequences*

17.2.1 *'The edict of Cyrus'*

Cyrus' policy of toleration towards the conquered peoples also had consequences for Judah. His decree about the return of the exiles to their original dwelling places and the restoration of indigenous worship also clearly affected Judah, though that country is not mentioned specially.[5] We find indications of this in II Chron. 36.22–23, which is almost identical with Ezra 1.1–3a.[6] In addition, in Ezra 6.3–5 we find a document written in Aramaic, which has come to be known as the 'Edict of Cyrus'.[7] There seems to be a clear relationship between these two reports in connection with the rebuilding of the Jerusalem temple. We have no reason to doubt the authenticity of the 'Edict of Cyrus',[8] though perhaps only part of it has been handed down in Ezra 6.3–5.

The rebuilding of the temple occupies a central position in these passages. According to Ezra 1.3, it is to this end that the Judaeans in Babylon are encouraged to return to Jerusalem. In Ezra 1.4 it is even said in this connection that Cyrus commanded the people living in those places from which people were returning to Judah to provide them with silver, gold and appropriate materials, and also to send gifts for the temple. According to Ezra 1.7–11, Cyrus did yet more. He also allowed the temple vessels which Nebuchadnezzar II had brought to Babylon to be taken back to Jerusalem. A certain Sheshbazzar (Ezra 1.8) was responsible for transporting them. It is not clear what function he had. Possibly he was a special Persian government commissar for Judah,[9] or someone with special responsibility for temple matters.[10]

There are a number of problems about the background to the edict of Cyrus. In particular, Ezra 1 describes a completely different course of events from Ezra 6.3–5.[11] This second passage shows that the rebuilding of the temple did not happen immediately after Cyrus took over power, though something of the kind is clearly suggested in Ezra 1. Another question is how it is possible that the king of an empire like this could pay so much attention to a relatively small and insignificant area like Judah and to the worship in the temple at Jerusalem, which will have seemed so unattractive at the time. However, this is less impossible than it seems. Given the attitude of Deutero-Isaiah towards Cyrus (16.5), it seems reasonable to suppose that even before the fall of

Babylon Cyrus had supporters among the Judaeans in Babylon, as he had among the Babylonians themselves (17.7.2), some of whom could have drawn Cyrus' attention to this temple.[12] In these circumstances, though, it remains quite remarkable that the temple was not rebuilt immediately on the return from Babylon.

17.2.2 *The return*

All these considerations have suggested to some scholars that no Judaeans had yet returned to their own land in the time of Cyrus (538–530). This is thought to be the case above all because Haggai and Zechariah make no mention of a return at the time of Cyrus.

However, such a hypothesis seems highly improbable, because it is clear that Cyrus offered this possibility (17.1), and it would be strange if some Judaeans had not taken advantage of it.[13] On the other hand, that need not of itself mean that many exiles returned to Judah on the basis of the permission. Rather, we should assume quite the contrary. If we begin from the fact that the last group had been deported to Babylon in 587/86 BC, it follows that in c. 539 BC most of these exiles will have already died. We can well imagine that the new generation, who had no personal recollections of Judah, will not have been particularly enthusiastic to return there. Another fact which indicates that there can have been no large-scale return is that from this time on there always seems to have been a large Jewish community in Babylon. Furthermore, many Jews seem to have established good positions (16.3.1).

It seems most probable that after 538 BC, small groups steadily returned to Jerusalem and Judah, presumably each with different leaders, like Sheshbazzar in the earliest phase. We have two parallel lists of the number of those who returned, in Ezra 2.1–67 and in Neh. 7.6–63.[14] It is impossible to establish with certainty the date of these lists. Some people think that they comprise a revised census list from about the time of Nehemiah.[15] Others think that the list is of those who returned about 538 BC.[16] It amounts to about 50,000 names, which is quite a respectable figure. The greater part of the return is likely to have taken place over an extended period. Since these lists also mention large numbers of descendants, we can assume, that they come from a later period. In that case they contain not only the names of those who returned but also those of people who had never been in Babylon. If that is correct, then it would be most appropriate to say that they do indeed form 'a revised census list' (see above).

Be this as it may, with Persian rule a new period dawned for Judah as well, and doutbless those who returned from Babylon played their part in it.

17.3 *The situation in the home country*

17.3.1 *Government administration*

I have already pointed out in the previous section (17.2.1) that Sheshbazzar was made responsible for the restoration of the temple vessels. As we have seen, it is uncertain in which capacity he did this. One major factor in this uncertainty is that the Aramaic title given to Sheshbazzar in Ezra 5.14 is rather difficult to interpret. If the title implies that Sheshbazzar was governor, that would mean that Judah was a separate province of the Persian empire. Against this view it has been argued that during this period Judah is regarded, rather, as part of a province of Samaria;[17] it became an independent province only in the time of Nehemiah.

Now we know that the administration of the Persian empire underwent a number of changes in the course of time. Thus Herodotus[18] reports that Darius I (521–486) again divided the territory into twenty satrapies. Each satrapy was further sub-divided into a number of districts. So it is quite possible that in the long run there was also a difference in administration between Judah and Samaria. On the other hand, archaeological evidence[19] seems to suggest that Judah was already an independent province or district before the time of Nehemiah and had no administrative ties with Samaria. Furthermore, many people are inclined to regard Judah as having been a separate administrative unit right from the beginning of the Persian period.[20]

One important task for the governors of satrapies and districts was to collect taxes on behalf of the Persian king. In this connection it is interesting to note that a new means of payment came into use under Persian rule, in the form of coins. In the next chapter (18.3.2), we shall see what important consequences this had.

17.3.2 *The general situation*

It is certain that the temple was not rebuilt at once. About twenty years were to go by before this could happen. Granted, Ezra 5.16 says that Sheshbazzar had already laid the foundations of this temple, but Haggai (1.4) reports that in his time the temple still 'lay desolate'. This seems most likely to have been the real situation. The Old Testament does not in fact give us any information about why the temple was not rebuilt until later. In Hag. 1.2 this is ascribed to the prevailing opinion that the time was not yet ripe. It is left unclear precisely what this means, but presumably the inference is that economic conditions were bad. At any rate, both Haggai (2.16–20) and Zechariah (8.10) speak in this connection of crop failure and insecurity.

In addition, there is mention in Ezra 4.4–5 of opposition to the building of the temple from 'the people of the land'.[21] It is uncertain who these are in this context. Perhaps they are the same group as those who often come to the fore in the time before the exile (see 11.4.2).[22] If this group is meant to be the same as that mentioned in Ezra 4.1–2, then the 'people of the land' mentioned here must be meant to be the inhabitants of what was once Israel, who had been brought there by the Assyrians in about 722 BC (Ezra 4.2).[23]

At all events, the delay in rebuilding the temple indicates that the situation in Judah in the period immediately after the exile was in many respects far from being a favourable one. This should hardly surprise us. One can hardly expect differently at a time when one world power is overcome by another. Furthermore, we may assume that difficult problems will have arisen in Judah between the exiles who returned and those who had remained there all along. There will certainly have been such problems in the economic and social spheres, in view of the measures taken here by the Babylonians in 587/86 BC (16.2.2).

So we may be certain that the time between the edict of Cyrus in *c.* 538 BC and the start of the rebuilding of the temple in *c.* 520 BC was rather more turbulent than the information given in Ezra and Nehemiah might suggest.[24]

17.4 *The rebuilding of the temple*

17.4.1 *The political and economic situation*

The rebuilding of the temple, then, was seriously taken in hand only in about 520 BC. It is difficult to establish how it came about that people suddenly made an energetic start on this project. We know too little about the situation in Judah at this period to construct an accurate picture.

It has been conjectured that the return of a large group of exiles from Babylon under the leadership of Zerubbabel encouraged this initiative.[25] According to others, however, Zerubbabel returned from Babylon much earlier.[26] He was a grandson of Jehoiachin and thus one of the descendants of the Davidic dynasty. This doubtless aroused certain expectations connected with his arrival and his person.[27] Other circumstances, too, seem to have aroused such expectation. The Persian empire was in a difficult situation at this time. Darius I, who ascended the Persian throne in 521 BC, seems to have had some difficulty in establishing his authority – as often happened at that time with a change of ruler. At the end of the reign of Darius' predecessor Cambyses, a certain Gaumata had led a rebellion. Supported by his army, Darius was soon able to defeat this Gaumata in Media,[28] but at this time there were several further rebellions in his empire, including one in Babylon.[29]

We can understand that in such circumstances considerable impetus was given to the hope, still alive in some circles, of a restoration of the Davidic dynasty. It seems possible to detect an echo of this in, for example, Haggai 2.22f.[30] Naturally this expectation was concentrated on the figure of Zerubbabel and, alongside him, on the high priest Joshua. This is probably the background against which we should seek to explain the great efforts now made to rebuild the temple. Both the political and the economic situation encouraged this undertaking. The rise of the prophets Haggai and Zechariah was certainly also a major factor.[31]

Haggai seems primarily to have expressed political aspirations, while Zechariah laid more stress on economic problems hindering the building of the temple and the organization of the community in Jerusalem. That there were problems in connection with this organization and that there was some rivalry between Zerubbabel and Joshua seems to be clearly reflected in the first chapters of Zechariah.[32] The words of warning against Zerubbabel in Zech. 4.6 are characteristic in this respect: 'Not by might, nor by power, but by my Spirit, says the Lord.' It is also striking that after about 519 BC Zerubbabel disappears completely from the scene. Given the strong position which the priests increasingly developed in the community of the Jerusalem temple, it is possible that Joshua more or less came out on top in this rivalry.

17.4.2 *The new temple*

Despite all the problems,[33] the temple was now finished in a very short space of time. From 515 BC Jerusalem had a temple once again. According to Ezra 5.16ff., it was solemnly consecrated with the offering of many sacrifices. These sacrifices, like the building of the temple itself, were paid for by the state (Ezra 6.4, 8–9). The reason given in Ezra 6.10 for this is that prayers are to be offered in this temple 'for the life of the king and his sons'. So although the temple cannot directly be called a royal sanctuary, as it was before the exile, it seems to have enjoyed a considerable degree of state support. Furthermore, this was evidently accepted without any protest. It is also evident that this temple was very different from the new temple which Ezekiel had seen in his visions (Ezek. 40—48), not only in structure but also in purpose.

We have no exact information about its dimensions and arrangement. We can only suppose that in comparison to the temple of Herod,[34] known from the New Testament period, it was much closer to that of Solomon. In many respects the building of this second temple was extremely significant. For a long time it formed the connecting link between the Jews in the home country and those in the dispersion. We should also note the increasing influence exercised by the priestly class as a result. In this connection it is certainly no coincidence that there is convincing evidence for the anointing of priests only in the post-exilic literature. In many respects the high priest now took over the same function in connection with the temple and with other matters as that performed earlier by the kings. In this context it is also interesting to note that Zech. 6.9–15 speaks of a royal throne for the high priest Joshua.

17.5 Haggai and Zechariah

17.5.1 Haggai

Like Zechariah, Ezra and Nehemiah, Haggai uses a system of dating following the reigns of the Persian kings. His prophecies are all dated in the second year of Darius I (Haggai 1.1; 2.11), i.e. in 520 BC. Their content relates principally to the building of the temple in Jerusalem. Only Haggai 2.11–15 is concerned with the impurity which threatens the temple and its cult, while 2.21–23 is concerned with the election of Zerubbabel.

Remarkably, all his prophecies are written in the third person. That means that the book of Haggai must be seen as a historical work about this prophet.

We know nothing for certain about Haggai as a person. There are some indications that he was one of the Judaeans who did not go into exile.[35] Apart from his method of dating, Haggai, like Zechariah, completely ignores the Persian rulers and their empire. It is also striking that neither of these prophets mentions the important role played by both Cyrus and Darius in the rebuilding of the temple. We are completely in the dark as to the background of this. It is possible that the role played by these kings was suppressed in a later redaction or that the prophets themselves attached no importance at all to such state support and therefore left it completely out of account. This latter alternative is more probable, since later redaction might also have altered other writings in which the involvement of the Persian government is mentioned.

It is clear that Haggai does not see the rebuilding of the Temple as an isolated affair. He is concerned above all with the purpose that can be achieved by it, namely, making an appropriate place for the service of God. This notion comes to the fore in various passages of his book.[36] Furthermore, Haggai sees the new time which is dawning as a period during which the temple is the focal point of interest. The words of Haggai to Zerubbabel, in which he says that God will make Zerubbabel a signet ring (Haggai 2.23), should probably also be seen in this context. Presumably this signet ring is regarded as a sign that Zerubbabel is appearing as head of the people and acting as God's representative.[37]

17.5.2 *Zechariah*

In speaking of Zechariah, I have in mind the prophet whose words are contained in Zech. 1–8. The other chapters of this book are written in a completely different style and come from a later period. These passages are usually referred to as Deutero-Zechariah (9–11; and Trito-Zechariah (12–14).[38]

So here we are looking at the prophet who was active at the same time as Haggai and is also mentioned alongside him in Ezra 5.1; 6.14. The first six chapters of Zechariah are dated in the same year as the prophecies of Haggai, i.e. in the second year of Darius (520 BC). Chapter 7 is dated in the fourth year of Darius. We know no more about Zechariah than we do about Haggai. In Zech. 1.1, 7 he is said to be grandson of Iddo and in Ezra 5.1; 6.14 to be son of Iddo. According to Neh. 12.4, 16, this Iddo came from a priestly family.

Whereas Haggai's main interest was in the temple and its rebuilding, in Zechariah great emphasis is placed above all on Jerusalem as the city of God and the centre of the world. This is also expressed in the eight visions which we find in Zech. 1–6.[39] The major role assigned to the high priest Joshua in Zech. 3; 6.9–15 is also extremely significant in this context. Therefore it is probably not a coincidence that from now on the figures of the king and the prophet increasingly fade into the background. The high priest is increasingly seen as the one who represents spiritual and secular authority in Judah. In the Hasmonaean period he even exercised the role of king.[40]

Another difference between Zechariah and Haggai is the former's greater concern for the world as a whole. This is particularly evident in Zech. 1–6 alongside his concern for the future community of Jerusalem. Like Haggai, Zechariah sees the rebuilding of the temple as the beginning of a new community and a new age.[41] According to Zechariah, the priestly class will have a prominent role here.[42] All peoples will finally recognize and accept the salvation that this new age will bring. Its climax will be reached when the people say to Judah, 'Let us go with you, for we have heard that God is with you' (Zech. 8.23).

Chapter 18

The Period of the Second Temple
up to *c.* 330 B C

18.1 *Chronological problems*

We have virtually no definite information about events after 515 BC, the year in which the second temple was completed, especially when it comes to chronology. Thus for example it is unclear whether the prophet Malachi[1] exercised his prophetic activity before, during or after the appearance of Ezra and Nehemiah. However, the greatest problem in this period is the dating of the period and the sequence in which Ezra and Nehemiah carried on their activities in Jerusalem.

According to Ezra 7.7–8, Ezra arrived in Jerusalem in the seventh year of Artaxerxes, king of Persia, and Nehemiah in the twentieth year of Artaxerxes (Neh. 2.1). If the reference in both cases is to king Artaxerxes I Longimanus (464–424), the dates would be 458 BC and 445 BC respectively. That would mean that Ezra worked in Jerusalem before Nehemiah.[2] Now in the case of Nehemiah, it seems certain that the king mentioned in Neh. 2.1 is indeed Artaxerxes I Longimanus. We know from the Elephantine papyri that in 408 BC a certain Johanan was high priest in Jerusalem.[3] He is mentioned in Neh. 12.22 as the grandson of the high priest Eliashib (cf. Neh. 3.1). On the basis of this information we may assume that the dating of Nehemiah's arrival in Jerusalem mentioned above does refer to Artaxerxes I Longimanus.

The dating of Ezra's arrival is a different matter. The king mentioned in Ezra 7.1 could also have been Artaxerxes II Mnemon (404–359). In that case Ezra would have come to Jerusalem in 398 BC. That would imply that his activity there took place after that of Nehemiah. This view has also found a good deal of support.[4] In addition, there has also been support for the view that Ezra was in Jerusalem twice, once with Nehemiah and again by himself.[5] There is not enough evidence for us to be sure that any of these positions is the right one. We simply do not have the facts for arriving at an adequate conclusion. However, the tradition which puts Ezra before Nehemiah seems to be the strongest one.[6]

As a result of this, I find it impossible to make a definitive statement on the problem. So the sequence in which I shall go on to treat the appearance of Ezra and Nehemiah in Jerusalem, first Ezra and then Nehemiah, simply indicates a slight preference for the first of the possibilities mentioned. It goes without saying that this is not without consequences for the discussion of this period.

18.2 *Ezra's mission*

18.2.1 *Ezra's task*

Ezra was one of the exiles who had not returned home after the edict of Cyrus. According to Ezra 7.1–5, 7, he was a priest of the family of Aaron. As well as being a priest, in the same chapter Ezra is also said to have been a 'scholar (literally scribe) in the law of the God of heaven' (Ezra 7.12, 21). This title suggests that he came as an adviser to the Persian government on matters of Jewish religion.

The fact that men from Judah sometimes performed important functions for the Persian authorities can also be seen in the case of Nehemiah (see 18.3).[7] Furthermore, there is much to be said for the view that the word 'scholar' or 'scribe' in Ezra 7.12, 21 derives from the Babylonian word *šapirum*, which denotes an administrative function. So it is not surprising in this connection that Ezra was sent to Jerusalem by the Persian king in order to put things in order there.

This commission is contained in a letter from Artaxerxes, an Aramaic version of which we find in Ezra 7.12–26. This letter says that Ezra, with other priests and levites from the Persian empire who wish to accompany him, is to go to Jerusalem. On arrival there he is to make an investigation into the legal situation in Judah and Jerusalem, with special concern for the observance of laws. In addition, the Persian government made money available for the worship and the economy of Judah. Ezra was also to appoint judges and officials in Jerusalem and Judah.[8]

It goes without saying that this document is extremely important for understanding Ezra's mission in Jerusalem and Judah, assuming, of course, that we can take it to be historically authentic. Many scholars feel that this is indeed the case.[9] Arguments in its favour are the appearance of a variety of Persian loan words, the possibility that men of Judah could hold important positions in the Persian government, and the fact that a rebellion had broken out in Egypt in about 460 BC.[10] The last point in particular seems to be an important argument. At all events, it would mean that the Persians were particularly concerned at this time to put things in order in Judah and to have loyal subjects there.[11] The document in Ezra 7.12–26 would fit such a situation admirably.

18.2.2 *Ezra's arrival*

There is an account of Ezra's activities in Ezra 9–10 and Neh. 8–10.[12] According to the information here, one of his first measures was the prohibition and dissolution of mixed marriages. Such a measure must have caused some hostility, seeing that hitherto such a course of action had been completely acceptable.[13] King David himself was a descendent of a mixed marriage (Ruth 4.18–22). Deuteronomy 7.1–4 prohibits marriages with Canaanite women, but this is a regulation which dates from the seventh century BC at the earliest. Furthermore, there are strong indications that Ezra's prohibition also, and perhaps primarily, concerned marriages with women from the former state of Israel. That might be suggested by the fact that this question was discussed only with 'all the men of Judah and Benjamin' (Ezra 10.9).

We hear nothing of other measures mentioned in Ezra 7.12–26, like the appointment of judges and officials. By far the most important event we do hear of in connection with Ezra's stay in Jerusalem is the reading of the law. This event, described in Neh. 8–10,[14] took place on the first day of the seventh month (Neh. 8.3), up to and including the day of the feast of Tabernacles (Neh. 8.19).

It is not clear from the texts in the Old Testament precisely what is meant by the 'law' which Ezra read here. Therefore scholars differ widely in their views. It has been thought to be virtually identical with the Deuteronomic law,[15] the Pentateuch,[16] the Priestly Writing,[17] or a collection of laws from the Pentateuch.[18] We do not have sufficient proof for any of these four hypotheses. However, in view of the fact that the whole of this law book was read out and expounded (Neh. 8.9), in all probability we should not think of such a large work as the Pentateuch.

After this event, we hear nothing more about the person of Ezra in the Old Testament. We do not know whether his mission to Jerusalem was a success or failure. At all events, the evidence in the Old Testament indicates that his arrival provoked opposition, especially over his attitude towards mixed marriages (Ezra 10.15–16). This is clear, for example, from the sanctions threatened against anyone not coming to Jerusalem for a discussion of this question. It is obvious that Ezra's work considerably furthered a religious division between the people of Israel and the people of Judah, even if it did not make such a division complete. So Ezra's mission was also of great influence on the development of later Judaism. (It is also worth mentioning in this connection that in the time before Ezra the people are customarily called 'Israel' and 'Judah', and the name Jews is used only for the period after him.)

18.3 *The work of Nehemiah*

18.3.1 *Nehemiah and the rebuilding of the walls of Jerusalem*

With the exception of Neh. 8–9 and some lists in Neh. 3; 7.6–72 (=Ezra 2) and 10–12, the book of Nehemiah is almost entirely written in the first person. This part is known as 'Nehemiah's memoirs'. There is a widespread view that these memoirs were originally an independent work and that they are an important source of information for this period.[19] However, we should remember that the work gives only one particular picture of the events of its time, and is far from being a record of all contemporary events.

The occasion for Nehemiah's journey to Jerusalem was the appearance of reports of the precarious situation there which he received from his brother Hanani and some other men of Judah (Neh. 1.1–3). These described in particular the desolate state into which the walls and gates of Jerusalem had fallen.[20] At that time Nehemiah was cup-bearer at the court of Artaxerxes. When he appeared before the king to offer him wine with a sorrowful face, because of the impact of these reports, the king asked why he was so sad. Nehemiah gained the king's ear and thereupon was sent to Jerusalem with extensive powers (Neh. 2.1–9).[21] He arrived there in 445 BC.

This event is rightly seen as a turning point in political developments in the community during the period of the second temple.[22] The most important work carried out by Nehemiah in this connection was the rebuilding of the walls of Jerusalem. This does not seem to have been considered at an earlier date. Some scholars have conjectured that Zerubbabel already had similar plans.[23] However, it should be said that while Cyrus agreed to the rebuilding of the temple, he did not give permission for the city walls to be rebuilt. Probably for good reasons Nehemiah first of all kept secret the purpose of his coming to Jerusalem. This must be seen in the light of the circumstances of the rebuilding of the walls. Opposition to it came above all from Sanballat I,[24] the governor of Samaria, Tobias the Ammonite, Geshem the Arabian and the Ashdodites (Neh. 2.19; 4.7). The Ashdodites are not mentioned in the Septuagint. Tobias was probably governor of Ammon[25] and Geshem perhaps king of an Arabian kingdom of Kedar.[26] Nehemiah was even accused before the supreme council (Neh. 5.6–9). Doubtless his chief opponent was Sanballat of Samaria, who was also supported by people in Jerusalem. These included a grandson of the high priest Eliashib who was deported from Jerusalem by Nehemiah (13.28). We do not know the precise reason for this opposition. However, it is presumably to be attributed, among other things, to the attitude of Nehemiah and his followers, who were concerned to segregate themselves completely from other groups, including the former Israelites. At any rate, this must have seemed to be the clear purport of Nehemiah's words to Sanballat and his followers in Neh. 2.20: 'But you have no portion or right or memorial in Jerusalem.'

All this is clearly the result of a policy of isolation which was implemented by force, both by Ezra and by Nehemiah.

The walls of the city were completed with great speed, in fifty-two days (Neh. 6.15). However, that is evidently not a record, since according to Thucydides[27] the walls of Athens were built even more quickly in 479/78 BC. After the walls of Jerusalem had been completed, according to Neh. 12.27–43 they were dedicated at a solemn ceremony. The Levites played a considerable role in it.

18.3.2 *Social and economic problems*

According to Neh. 5.1–13, Nehemiah also took various measures in the social and economic spheres. From what we are told in Neh. 5, we get the impression that there was great poverty at this time. Some were starving, others had to pledge their fields and vineyards or resort to loans (Neh. 5.1–4). These bad economic conditions could have come about as a result of the taxes which had to be raised for the rebuilding of the walls of Jerusalem. This would doubtless make the difficult position of the poor considerably worse. However, it cannot have been the main source of their problems. That must be sought in the great changes in the financial sphere brought about by the Persian government. We have already seen in the previous chapter (17.3.1) that the government introduced a new form of currency, in the form of coins.[28]

The introduction of money meant the development of a new economic structure and furthered the rise of capitalism. For example, there now arose a kind of banking system in which the temple and the palace played major roles. The high priest seems to have been given the right to mint coinage by the Persian government, not only in Judah but also in other countries.[29] This new structure put especially the small farmers in Judah in a difficult and often critical position. Perhaps we can see a reflection of this in Neh. 5.1–13.

Nehemiah forced the nobles and leaders to restore to the poor the houses, fields and vineyards which they had gained possession of through their profiteering. In addition, he also took steps to improve the social position of the priests, Levites and other temple servants. In Neh. 12.44–47[30] we hear that he also introduced a special system for the collection of offerings.

After a period of about twenty years (see Neh. 5.14; 13.6), in 433 BC

Nehemiah was recalled to Persia. However, he returned to Jerusalem again; according to Kellermann,[31] though, in a private capacity. That is possible, since even Josephus knows nothing of a second period in which Nehemiah returned to Jerusalem as governor.[32] When this was is not clear from the information in Neh. 13.6. All we hear is that Nehemiah again removed his enemy Tobias from the temple, where he had been given a room by Eliashib, restored the contributions to the Levites (Neh. 13.10–13) and took forceful measures for maintaining observance of the sabbath (Neh. 13.15–22).

The Old Testament says nothing further about Nehemiah's career. Without doubt the measures which he took during his stay in Jerusalem over religious, political and social matters[33] were as important for the further development and consolidation of later Judaism as those of Ezra. In the case of Ezra, religious factors came to the fore, while with Nehemiah political factors were most important. In the first place this also led to a heightening of the conflict with the Samaritans (see 18.5).

18.4 *The Jewish colony in Elephantine*

This colony has already been mentioned several times in previous chapters. In this section I shall consider more closely some matters relating to it.

We owe our knowledge of the colony to the discovery of a number of papyri and ostraca made in 1890 and after.[34] Elephantine was a small island in the Nile on which a Jewish military garrison was based, responsible for protecting the southern frontier of Egypt. We have no idea when this garrison was first established and when the Jewish settlement arose. The earliest documents we have from the settlement are from about the end of the fifth century BC. Of course this does not mean that the colony cannot have been established in Elephantine at a much earlier date.[35]

It is evident from all this that there was a temple on Elephantine dedicated to Yahu. This name suggests the divine name Yahweh (Lord) which occurs often in the Old Testament. However, on Elephantine not only was Yahu worshipped but also, for example, the god Bethel and the goddess Anath. This seems to indicate that the group came from the northern state of Israel. As the names of the deities worshipped on Elephantine suggest, worship here had a marked syncretistic character and the existence of a temple shows that the inhabitants had not been affected by Josiah's centralization of the cult in Jerusalem.[36]

The people of Elephantine evidently had close contacts with Samaria as well as with Jerusalem. This is clear from a letter which was sent to Jerusalem in about 407 BC. This states that the Jews in Elephantine have also sent a letter to Delaiah and Shelemiah, the sons of Sanballat the governor of Samaria.[37] In this letter we read that the temple of Elephantine was destroyed in the fourteenth year of Darius II (423–405), i.e. in 410 BC, probably at the instigation of Egyptian priests. This happened when the Persian satrap of Egypt had gone to Babylon and Susa for a short time. Widengren[38] sees principally political and not religious motives behind this destruction, given that the Jews were soldiers in the service of the Persians, and thus represented the forces of occupation. This is also evident from the fact that immediately after this event the inhabitants of Elephantine called on the help of the Persians.[39]

The letter mentioned above, addressed to Bagoas the Persian governor of Judah, the high priest Johanan and the priests in Jerusalem, contained a repeated request to be allowed to rebuild the temple in Elephantine. We do not know whether this request was ever granted. Given developments in Judah at the time that seems highly improbable. However, the colony in Elephantine continued to exist for a long time, even when the Persians had left Egypt.[40]

18.5 *The conflict with the Samaritans*

18.5.1 *Political and religious tensions*

The refusal of Israel to accept a successor from the dynasty of David after the death of Solomon represented, politically, a break between the kingdoms of Israel and Judah. At some periods, especially during the Omri dynasty, there were good relations between the two kingdoms, but there was never again a political union. In Judah – and here one might think above all of the time of Josiah (14.3) – further attempts were made to regain control of Israel. However, there were never such aspirations for national revival in Israel itself.[41] In a later period it is clear that the people of Judah gradually accepted the *status quo*, though hope of a restoration of the personal union or of a union of the two kingdoms under the dynasty of David would flicker again now and then. However, after the time of Zerubbabel this ideal seems more or less to have been abandoned.[42]

From that time on relations between Israel and Judah became steadily worse. Finally these conflicts ended in a definitive break between Jews and Samaritans in the religious sphere.[43] According to later Samaritan evidence the basis for this break had already been laid in the time of Eli. The Deuteronomist sees this division as having taken place in the eight century BC, when a mixing of exiles, brought by the Assyrians from elsewhere to Israel, with the established population led to a syncretistic form of religion (II Kings 17). By contrast the Chronicler stresses the illegality of the priests functioning in Samaria because they were not of the line of Aaron (II Chron. 13.9).

However, there is still no trace in the Old Testament of a final break between the communities in Judah and Samaria.

It seems most likely that the break between Jews and Samaritans came about gradually[44] and that the process of segregation accelerated in the time of Ezra and Nehemiah. Perhaps political factors especially were involved in the time of Nehemiah. That will certainly have been the case when Judah became an independent province. Precisely for this reason Nehemiah's work may have been fiercely opposed in Samaria. However, later traditions stress the religious aspect of the conflict. This can be seen above all from the fact that the Samaritan tradition associates the break between Judah and Samaria far more with Ezra than with Nehemiah.[45]

18.5.2 *The break*

The conflicts described here finally led to a schism between the communities of Judah and Samaria and thus to the building of a temple on Mount Gerizim, by the ancient city of Shechem. The choice of this place shows that the Samaritans were deliberately concerned to continue an ancient tradition in Israel. Shechem had long been an extremely important place of worship. It was here, for example, that Abraham had built the first altar to the Lord in the new land (Gen. 12.7), and here that according to Josh. 24 an important assembly took place to renew the covenant between God and people.

We do not know precisely when this temple was built.[46] According to Josephus,[47] it happened when Alexander the Great had conquered Canaan. It is not impossible that there is a grain of truth in this report in so far as the temple had not been built in the time of Persian rule. At any rate, we may rightly follow Widengren[48] in concluding that the Persians favoured the temple in Jerusalem above the Samaritan places of worship.

There is mention of rivalry between the sanctuaries in Samaria and Jerusalem in later Jewish traditions like the Apocrypha, Pseudepigrapha and Josephus.[49] This might indicate that the Samaritan temple was at least in existence in the second century BC. From this perspective the Hellenistic period seems the most likely time for the building of the temple in Samaria.

The canon of the Pentateuch must have been virtually complete at the time of the break between the Jewish community and the Samaritans. We must infer this from the fact that there are minimal differences between the Massoretic text of the Pentateuch and that of the Samaritan Pentateuch.[50] Unfortunately, however, again we cannot be sure precisely when the canon came into being. All we know is that this must already have happened by the time of Jesus Sirach in about 1900 BC.[51] It is also generally assumed that the

Pentateuch was already translated into Greek in the third century BC.[52] This too points to the Hellenistic period for the origin of the Samaritan community.

18.6 *The literature of the Persian period*

The Chronicler's history is regarded as one of the most important works from this period. Here again, as in the case of the Deuteronomistic history work (16.6.1), Martin Noth[53] is the scholar who has tried to demonstrate its existence. He believes that the Chronicler's history included Ezra and Nehemiah as well as the books of Chronicles, and his view is shared by the majority of scholars.

However, in quite a recent study Williamson[54] had challenged this view, producing arguments which certainly need to be taken seriously. For example, he points out that in Chronicles, unlike Ezra and Nehemiah, no difficulties are expressed over mixed marriages and that great emphasis is laid on the covenant with David, whereas in Ezra and Nehemiah the community of Judah is seen as a continuation of the community from the time of the exodus, in which the covenant with David plays no part. Apart from this, however, it is clear that both the Chronicler's history work and Chronicles on the one side and Ezra/Nehemiah on the other could have arisen as a literary entity at the earliest in the fourth century BC.

At any rate, the last accounts from Ezra and Nehemiah relate to the period of *c.* 430 BC and even later. I Chronicles 3.19–24 mentions five generations after Zerubbabel and Neh. 12.10–11 mentions five after Joshua the high priest. This means that these books could have been completed roughly speaking a century after these two figures, who lived about 515 BC. A further argument is that in many respects they reflect ideas current in the community of Judah after the exile. The events which they relate are described and interpreted in this spirit, though it is clear that a good deal of old material has been incorporated and revised, especially in Chronicles.[55] Here the interpretation of the name Israel is particularly important. In Chronicles it is still connected with all the tribes, whereas in Ezra and Nehemiah Israel is used only of the Jewish community (Judah and Benjamin) after the exile.[56]

The books of Joel, Trito-Isaiah, Ruth, Esther, part of Daniel (1—6) and certain Psalms, like Pss. 126; 137, might also be included in the literature of the Persian period.[57]

Although incomplete, this survey shows that broadly speaking the Persian period produced important literary works. In addition, it should also be emphasized that at this time the process of canonization was probably well developed. That is particularly true of the Pentateuch and presumably also of the prophets. However, this subject is specifically the concern of Old Testament introduction, and we cannot go further into it here.

18.7 *The end of Persian rule*

18.7.1 *The end of the Persian empire*

When Darius III (335–331) ascended the Persian throne, the empire was already on the verge of decline. The Persian empire of that time was nothing like the empire of Cyrus and Darius I. Years of fighting the Greeks for supremacy had gradually exhausted it. To begin with, the Persians easily gained the upper hand, but gradually the Greeks proved more than a match for them.[58] During the period of transition Egypt succeeded for a while in extricating itself from Persian rule, and from about 400 BC it was able to lead an independent existence for around sixty years.[59] Artaxerxes III managed to reconquer it in about 340 BC.

After that things went rapidly downhill for the Persians. This was not least because of the personality and rule of Philip II of Macedon (who ruled from 359–336). Thanks to an efficiently organized army and a great many bribes,[60] he succeeded in uniting the Greeks under his rule. In this way he also made it possible for his son Alexander to conquer the Persians.

However, the conflict between the Persians and the Greeks must not be seen purely as a military struggle for power. One important factor which also led to this situation of conflict was economic. For centuries, Greek merchants had been active in Persia and its neighbouring lands. Because of this it was extremely important for the Greeks to have key Phoenician trading cities like Tyre in their hands. It is also vital to note that the period in which these conflicts between Persians and Greeks developed (*c.* 500–300 BC) can be described as a time of great social and economic change.[61] At that time we can see a great increase in the circulation of money, growing urbanization and concentrations of political and economic power.

It is clear that eventually the Greeks proved the stronger as far as these last factors were concerned, and their military successes must also be regarded in this perspective. Alexander's victory over the last Persian king Darius III in 333 BC, in Issus in north-west Syria, in fact meant the final end of the Persian empire. After it the whole of Syria and Palestine lay open to Alexander. Only the important port of Tyre opposed him. After a siege of about seven months Alexander also took control of Tyre, and then went on to attack Egypt.[62]

18.7.2 *Consequences in and for Judah*

After the rise of Ezra and Nehemiah, the Old Testament gives us no information about events in Judah and Samaria during the last century of Persian rule. The name of the last high priest to be mentioned in the Old

Testament is Jaddua, son of Johanan (Neh. 12.22). We know nothing of the first successors of this Jaddua.

Nor do we know anything about what happened in Samaria and Judah while the Persian empire was gradually declining.[63] However, this cannot but have affected life in the region – as so often happens in such situations.

There is perhaps one allusion to Alexander the Great. We might suppose that the he-goat mentioned in Dan. 8.5, 21 refers to this Macedonian king.[64] We might also associate Zech. 9.1–8 with him,[65] but that is by no means certain. The name of Alexander is probably mentioned explicitly for the first time in the literature of ancient Israel in I Macc. 1.1–8; 6.2.

According to Josephus, Alexander paid a personal visit to Jerusalem shortly after the capture of Tyre.[66] However, this account has a marked legendary character and is not confirmed in any other source either outside the Old Testament or in it.

Thus in many respects this period remains an obscure one. That is all the more regrettable because it was an important time of transition. Persia was the last world power from the ancient Near East to have control of the region. Now another power had taken over. After the conquests of Alexander the Great in the East, this area came completely and utterly under Greek influence, a development which had been in the making for a long time. With the arrival of Alexander the Great there dawned in Syria and Palestine what has gone down in history as the Hellenistic period.[67]

For centuries Israel and Judah had been subject to powers from the East. Now these were replaced by powers from the West. So the fall of the Persian empire did not usher in a period of independence and peace but simply amounted to a change of rule. The region first fell into the hands of the Greeks, Ptolemies and Seleucids, and then into the hands of the Romans. Only a brief period in the time of the Maccabees[68] (*c.* 164–63 BC) brought a short spell of freedom and self-government.[69]

NOTES

Chapter 1 Introduction

1. G. van Leeuwen, *Om mens te zijn*, Antwerp-Amsterdam nd, 17, 21.
2. For the value of all these sources and the results of archaeological research see 1.2.
3. See 1.3.
4. R. de Vaux, *EHI*, x.
5. See F. R. Kraus, 'Mesopotamische archäische kleitabletten als archeologische voorwerpen', *Akkadica* 4, 1977, 3f.
6. Cf. II Sam. 24.1, where Yahweh is given as the instigator of David's census, as opposed to Satan in I Chron. 21.1.
7. However, there are different variations on this position. See C. van Leeuwen, 'Het huidige onderzoek in enkele takken van de oudtestamentische wetenschap (1965–1971)', *NTT* 26, 1972, 232.
8. On this see e.g. R. Rendtorff, 'The "Yahwist" as Theologian? The Dilemma of Pentateuchal Criticism', *JSOT* 3, 1977, 2–10 (the whole issue is devoted to a thorough discussion of the problem) id., *Das überlieferungsgeschichtliche Problem des Pentateuch*, BZAW 147, 1977; H. H. Schmid, *Der sogennante Jahwist. Beobachtungen und Fragen zur Pentateuchforschung*, Zurich 1976.
9. J. van Seters, *Abraham in History and Tradition*, New Haven and London 1975, 310.
10. Schmid, op. cit., 167.
11. Rendtorff, *Das überlieferungsgeschichtliche Problem des Pentateuch*, 167ff.
12. Rendtorff, 'The "Yahwist" as Theologian?', 5–10; cf. also *Das überlieferungsgeschichtliche Problem des Pentateuch*, 65ff.
13. Schmid, op. cit., 168–70.
14. The argument for the existence of these two historical works has been put forward by M. Noth, *Überlieferungsgeschichtliche Studien. Die sammelnden und bearbeitenden Geschichtswerke im Alten Testament*, Darmstadt ³1967. There is a partial translation, *The Deuteronomistic History*, JSOT Supplement Series 15, 1981, covering pp. 1–110 of the original.
15. However, there are other views. On this see the surveys by van Leeuwen, op. cit., 234–6, and A. N. Radjawane, 'Das deuteronomistische Geschichtswerk. Ein Forschungsbericht', *ThR* 38, 1974, 177–216.
16. W. Dietrich, *Prophetie und Geschichte. Eine redaktionsgeschichtliche Untersuchung zum deuteronomistische Geschichtswerk*, FRLANT 108, 1972. This view is very widely held.
17. For this history work see the survey and the literature mentioned by van Leeuwen, op. cit., 236–8, and also P. Welten, *Geschichte und Geschichtsdarstellung in den Chronikbüchern*, WMANT 42, 1973.
18. Jer. 36 is a classic instance of this.
19. P. Matthiae, 'Tell Mardikh (Syria). Excavations of 1967 and 1968', *Archaeology* 24,

1971, 60f.; G. Pettinato, *MAIS, Rapporto preliminare delle campagne 1967–1968*, Rome 1972, p. 37.

20. For the discoveries in Ebla and the problems connected with them see K. R. Veenhof, 'Tell Mardich-Ebla', *NTT* 32, 1978, 1–11, and the literature mentioned on p. 11; A. R. Millard, 'Les découvertes d'Ebla et l'Ancien Testament', *Hokhma* 1977, 55–61; P. Matthiae, 'Le Palais Royal et les Archives d'Etat d'Ebla protosyrienne', *Akkadica* 2, 1977, 2–19; G. Pettinato, 'Relations entre les Royaumes d'Ebla et de Mari au troisième millénaire, d'après les Archives Royales de Tell Mardikh-Ebla', *Akkadica* 2, 1977, 20–28.

21. See *ANET*, 18–22.

22. Cf. W. Helck, *Die Beziehungen Ägyptens zu Vorderasien im 3. und 2. Jahrtausend v. Chr.*, Wiesbaden ²1971, 40f.

23. However, there is some dispute over the dating of these texts. See e.g. Helck, op. cit., 44–67.

24. For the texts see K. Sethe, *Die Ächtung feindlicher Fürsten, Völker und Dinge auf altägyptischen Tongefässcherbendes Mittleren Reiches*, APAW Phil. hist. Kl. No. 5, Berlin 1926; and G. Posner, *Princes et pays d'Asie et du Nubie. Textes hiératiques sur des figurines d'envoûtement du Moyen Empire*, Brussels 1940. There is a partial translation of these texts in *ANET*, 328f.

25. See e.g. N. H. Ridderbos, 'Israëls profetie en "profetie" buiten Israel', *Exegetica* 2, 1, The Hague 1955, 14–25; F. Ellermeier, *Prophetie in Mari und Israel*, Herzberg 1968, and E. Noort, *Untersuchungen zum Gottesbescheid in Mari. Die "Mari prophetie" in der alttestamentlichen Forschung*, AOAT 202, 1977.

26. Texts and translations can be found in *ARM*.

27. For a translation of some of the most important texts in this connection see *ANET*, 219f.

28. An edition of the texts and a translation has been produced by J. A. Knudtzon, *Die El-Amarna-Tafeln*, Aalen ²1964. This is supplemented by A. F. Rainy, *El Amarna Tablets 359–79: Supplement to J. A. Knudtzon, Die El-Amarna-Tafeln*, AOAT 8, ²1978.

29. There is an edition of the texts produced by M. Dietrich, O. Loretz and J. Sanmartin, *Die keilalphabetischen Texte aus Ugarit*, AOAT 24, 1, 1976. There is a translation of a large number of the fragments belonging to the Baal cycle with an extended commentary in J. C. de Moor, *The Seasonal Pattern in the Ugaritic Myth of Ba'lu*, AOAT 16, 1971. Translations of other texts can be found in *PRU* II–VI; G. R. Driver, *Canaanite Myths and Legends*, Edinburgh 1956.

30. On this see J. Simons, *Handbook for the Study of Egyptian Topographical Lists Relating to Western Asia*, Leiden 1937.

31. It is called the Israel stele because the name Israel is mentioned here for the first time in a non-biblical text.

32. See W. F. Edgerton and J. A. Wilson, *Historical Records of Ramses III*, Studies in Ancient Oriental Civilization 12, Chicago 1936.

33. There is a translation of this material in D. D. Luckenbill, *Ancient Records of Assyria and Babylonia*, 2 vols., Chicago ²1968, cf. also D. J. Wiseman, *Chronicles of Chaldaean Kings (626–556 BC) in the British Museum*, London ²1961, and A. K. Grayson, *Assyrian Royal Inscriptions*, Vol. 1, 2, Wiesbaden 1972 and 1976.

34. There is an edition of these texts with a translation and notes: A. Cowley, *Aramaic Papyri of the Fifth Century BC*, Oxford 1923.

35. Selections of translations of most of the texts which are relevant to the history of Israel are available in *ANET, AOT, KAI* and *TGI*, and also in A. Jepsen, *Von Sinuhe bis*

Nebukadnezar. Dokumente aus der Umwelt des Alten Testaments, Stuttgart–Munich ²1976.
   36. On this see H. A. Brongers, *Oud-Oosters en Bijbels recht*, Nijkerk 1960.
   37. In this connection see the admonitory remarks by H. J. Franken in C. A. Franken-Battershill, *A Primer of Old Testament Archaeology*, Leiden 1963, 19–33; J. Maxwell Miller, *The Old Testament and the Historian*, Philadelphia 1976, 46–8.
   38. There is an exhaustive summary of material relating to biblical archaeology in, e.g. H. Bardtke, *Bibel Spaten und Geschichte*, Göttingen ²1971, and H. Donner, *Einführung in die biblische Landes- und Altertumskunde*, Darmstadt 1976, 51–62; see above all *EAEHL, AOTS*.
   39. For text and translation see *KAI* no. 181; *DOTT*, 195–8.
   40. *KAI* no. 189; *DOTT*, 209–11.
   41. For these texts see now J. Hoftijzer and G. van der Kooij, *Aramaic Texts from Deir 'Alla*, Leiden 1976.
   42. These have been collected together, with an exhaustive commentary, in *IH*.
   43. See P. Welten, *Die Königs-stempel*, Wiesbaden 1969.
   44. For a survey of the writings found there see *LOI*, 367–80; bibliography *LOI*, 429–33.
   45. See W. Whiston, *Josephus. Complete Works*, Grand Rapids ⁸1970.
   46. See E. Schürer, *The History of the Jewish People in the Age of Jesus Christ (175 BC–AD 135), Vol. 1, A new English version revised and edited by G. Vermes and F. Millar*, Edinburgh 1973, 43–63, and the bibliography given there.
   47. For the text and translation see S. Smith, *The Statue of Idrimi*, London 1949.
   48. See e.g. A. van Selms, 'The Canaanites in the Book of Genesis', *OTS* XII, Leiden 1958, 182f., and Y. Aharoni, *The Land of the Bible. A Historical Geography*, London ³1974, 62ff.
   49. Gen. 9.18, 22; 10.6; I Chron. 1.8.
   50. Ps. 78.51; 105.23, 27; 106.22.
   51. Gen. 10.6; I Chron 1.8.
   52. See e.g. Num. 13.2; Deut. 32.49.
   53. Herodotus, *Histories* I, 105; III, 5,91; VII, 89.
   54. On this see *KBL*, 422; *THAT*, col. 782, and further M. Noth, *Die israelitischen Personennamen*, Hildesheim 1966 (= Stuttgart 1928), 207–9; C. H. J. de Geus, *The Tribes of Israel*, Assen 1976, 187–92, and the literature mentioned there.
   55. At least according to G. Pettinato, 'The Royal Archives of Tell Mardikh-Ebla', *BA* 39, 1976, 48. We also find a name *yšr-il* in Ugarit (*PRU* V, 69 line 3). However, it has long been disputed whether or not this name is to be seen as a parallel to 'Israel'. Of course the occurrence of the name in these texts does not mean that the reference is to the Israel which is mentioned in one form or another in the Old Testament.
   56. It is no longer possible to say with any certainty what was the extent of the territory in which this group settled.
   57. There is a detailed discussion of all this in e.g. A. R. Hulst, *Wat betekent de naam Israël in het Oude Testament?*, Miniaturen No. 1, The Hague 1962.
   58. See n.57 and e.g. A. R. Hulst, 'Der Name "Israel" im Deuteronomium', *OTS* IX, 1951, 65–106.

Excursus I   'Apiru and Hebrews

   1. For discussion of the correct way of writing these last two words see the lexica *AHW* and *CAD*.

2. The names of the countries here are related to the language in which the relevant texts are written.

3. On this see J. Bottéro, *Le Problème des Habiru à la 4e Rencontre Assyriologique Internationale*, Paris 1954; M. Greenberg, *The Hab/piru*, New Haven 1955, and R. de Vaux, 'Le Problème des Hapiru après quinze années', *JNES* 27, 1968, 221–8. Also, e.g., N. A. van Uchelen, *Abraham de Hebreeër*, Assen 1964, pp. 71–105; M. Weippert, *The Settlement of the Israelite Tribes in Palestine*, SBT II 21, 1971, 63–102, and G. E. Mendenhall, 'The 'Apîru Movements in the Late Bronze Age', *The Tenth Generation*, Baltimore ²1976, pp. 122–41.

4. For a discussion of these problems see de Vaux, *EHI*, 105f.

5. Thus e.g. by R. de Langhe, *Les Textes de Ras Shamra-Ugarit et leurs Rapports avec le milieu de l'Ancien Testament*, II, Paris 1945, 465; R. Borger, 'Das Problem der 'Apîru (Ḥabiru)', *ZDPV* LXXIV, 1958, 121–32, and W. F. Albright, *Yahweh and the Gods of Canaan*, London 1968, 64–79, all of whom think in this connection of some meaning such as 'dust'.

6. See e.g. van Uchelen, op. cit., 73; Weippert, op. cit., 65–75; id., 'Abraham der Hebräer? Bemerkungen zu Albrights Deutung der Väter Israels', *Biblica* 52, 1971, 412ff.; J. Bright, *HI*, 93f., and J. R. Kupper in *CAH* II, 1,27.

7. *EHI*, 112.

8. J. van Seters, *Abraham in History and Tradition*, New Haven and London 1975, 57, raises the possibility that the word 'Apiru was perhaps originally an ethnological nomenclature which later took on the connotation of a social grouping. Of course, there is no certain proof here.

9. B 6 and 8.

10. B 5.

11. B 9–16.

12. B 18–34.

13. B 36.

14. B 72.

15. B 38–44.

16. B 67–69.

17. B 49–66.

18. Perhaps to be compared with the position of the Hebrew slave in Ex. 21.2–11. Cf. Deut. 15.2–17; Jer. 34.9, 14.

19. B 49, 50, 56 and 63.

20. See e.g. *ANET*, 485–90.

21. See also G 101–18, which here gives a survey of the Amarna letters which come from Canaan.

22. B 187, 188.

23. B 154–63.

24. B 157.

25. G 137.

26. For the different functions which they can have here see H. Cazelles, 'The Hebrews', *POTT*, 9.

27. Gen. 39.17; 40.15; 41.12; 43.32; Ex. 1.15, 16, 19, 22; 2.6,7, 11, 13; 3.18; 5.3; 7.16; 9.1, 13.

28. In one sense Gen. 14.13 and Jonah 1.9 could also be counted in this category. In both instances, here too the word 'Hebrew' is used in connection with non-Israelites.

29. Namely Joseph in Gen. 39.17; 40.15; 41.12.

30. Only in Gen. 43.32 (a general statement) are neither of these two categories applicable.

31. I Sam. 4.6, 9; 13.3, 7, 19; 14.11, 21; 29.3.

32. This is also true of Gen. 14.13.

33. E.g. Borger, op. cit., 121–32; Greenberg, op. cit., 91,96.

34. E.g. Cazelles, op. cit., 23, and Mendenhall, op. cit., esp. 137.

35. For this see e.g. Weippert, *The Settlement of the Israelite Tribes*, 76–84, and *EHI*, 209ff.

36. See also Num. 24.24.

37. See Gen. 10.25–30; 11.16ff. See also van Uchelen, op.cit., 5f.

38. See n.18.

Chapter 2   The Patriarchs

1. Gen. 11.28 (J); 11.31 (P); 15.7 (J?); Neh. 9.7.

2. See W. F. Albright, *The Biblical Period from Abraham to Ezra*, New York ⁴1963, 97 n.1.

3. Literally Kaldu (in the OT *kasdîm*). The name is probably derived from Chesed (cf. Gen. 22.22). For all this see e.g. W. F. Leemans, 'Marduk-Apal-Iddina II, zijn tijd en zijn geslacht', *JEOL* 10, 1945–1948, esp. 435–7.

4. Thus e.g. A. van Selms, *Genesis* I, POT, 1967, 175; C. J. Gadd, *AOTS*, London 1969, 94; *EHI*, 187f.

5. For these texts see e.g. F. R. Kraus, 'Mesopotamische archäische kleittabletten als archeologische voorwerpen', *Akkadica* 4, 1977, esp. 9, 20f. See also K. H. Bernhardt, *Die Umwelt des Alten Testaments* I, Berlin 1967, 153ff.

6. See inter alia C. L. Woolley, *Excavations at Ur*, London ⁴1963.

7. See C. H. Gordon, 'Abraham of Ur', in *Hebrew and Semetic Studies*, Festschrift for G. R. Driver, Oxford 1963, 83, and the literature mentioned there.

8. Gordon, op. cit., 79ff.

9. *PRU* IV, 34, line 6 (= RS 17, 130).

10. See also the critical comments made in *EHI*, 186ff.

11. For the meaning of this expression see now J. P. U. Lilley, 'By the River-side', *VT* XXVIII, 1978, 165–75.

12. According to J. A. Soggin, *Joshua*, OTL, 1972, 14, Josh. 24 is 'certainly a pre-Deuteronomic narrative'. Cf. also H. Cazelles (ed.), *Introduction critique à l'Ancien Testament*, Paris 1973, 252ff.; *EHI*, 667ff.

13. Note too that the Targ. Jon. speaks of these places as being not 'over the River', but 'over the Euphrates', and that in the Vulgate we find Mesopotamia at Josh. 24.3,14,15, instead of 'on the other side of the River'.

14. In connection with this see T. C. Vriezen, 'Bemerkungen zu Genesis 12.1–7', *Symbolae Biblicae et Mesopotamicae*, Festschrift F. M. T. de Liagre Böhl, Leiden 1973, 389–92.

15. It is uncertain whether Gen. 24.10; 27.43 belong to J, E or JE.

16. So whereas in Gen. 27.43 (see n.15) Jacob is to flee to Haran, in this context P has Paddan-Aram.

17. Literally 'Aram of the two rivers'. It is not entirely clear that these two rivers are meant to be the Euphrates and the Tigris.

18. Thus e.g. E. Dhorme, 'Abraham dans le cadre de l'Histoire', *RB* 37, 1928, 487,

and R. T. O'Callaghan, *Aram Naharaim. A Contribution to the History of Upper Mesopotamia in the Second Millenium*, Rome ²1961, 96.

19. Thus e.g. W. F. Albright, *From the Stone Age to Christianity*, New York ²1957, 237; *EHI*, 195. See also Hos. 12.13.

20. The place Haran is mentioned in *ARM(T)* V 75, 8; VII,112, 3; 176, 3; Nahor in *ARM(T)* I, 107, 8; II, 62, 5; V, 51, 12. See also *EHI*, 195f.

21. For the problems in translating this passage see M. A. Beek, 'Das Problem des aramäischen Stammvaters', *OTS* VIII, 1950, 193ff.

22. On this see G. von Rad, 'The Problem of the Hexateuch', in *The Problem of the Hexateuch and Other Essays*, Edinburgh 1966, 3ff., 41ff.; *EHI*, 200.

23. Thus Beek, op. cit., 211, and H. Seebas, *Der Erzvater Israel*, BZAW 98, 1966, 9f.

24. It is the name in Gen. 10.22f.; I Chron. 1.17 of one of Shem's sons; in Gen. 22.21 of a grandson of Nahor, brother of Abraham; and in I Chron. 7.34 of one of the descendants of Asher.

25. This tradition would then have been transferred at a later stage to Haran in North Mesopotamia. In connection with this see T. L. Thompson, *The Historicity of the Patriarchal Narratives*, BZAW 133, 1974, 301, and the literature cited there.

26. See *ANET*, 275. Some scholars, including A. Dupont-Sommer, 'Sur les débuts de l'histoire araméenne', SVT 1, 1953, 42, think that this designation can already be found in a text from the twenty-third century BC. However, so far it can hardly be said that there is agreement on this question. There is also doubt about the meaning of *bn 'armi* in *PRU* II, 46,7 and 9, and 64, 10.

27. See J. R. Kupper, *Les Nomades en Mesopotamie au temps des rois de Mari*, Paris 1957, 114.

28. See M. Birot, 'Textes Économiques de Mari (III)', *RA* 49, 1955, 21. A. Parrot, *Abraham et son temps*, Paris 1962, 49, differs.

29. See e.g. M. Noth, 'Die Ursprünge des alten Israel im Lichte neuer Quellen' (1961), *Aufsätze* II, Neukirchen 1971, 262ff.

30. Noth, op. cit., 263; see also nn. 59, 60.

31. See R. de Vaux, 'The Hebrew Patriarchs and History', in *The Bible and the Ancient Near East*, London 1972, 118.

32. See also the criticism by D. O. Edzard, 'Mari und Aramäer?', *ZA* 22, 1964, 142–9; A. Malamat, 'The Aramaeans', *POTT*, 140, and Thompson, op. cit., 76ff.

33. See C. van Gelderen, *Het boek Amos*, Kampen 1933, 20; cf. also W. H. Gispen, *Genesis* I, COT, 1974, 355.

34. Thirty-two times in all.

35. The book by N. A. van Uchelen, *Abraham de Hebreeër*, Assen 1964, which I have already mentioned, is entirely devoted to this subject.

36. See J. P. Lettinga, *Grammatica van het Bijbels Hebreeuws*, Leiden ⁸1976, par.22 j 3.

37. For an extended survey see Thompson, op. cit., 22–51.

38. J, E, D, P and Dtr and the Chronicler.

39. Though at present more emphasis is laid on the existence of peaceful contacts. See e.g. M. B. Rowton, 'The Physical Environment and the Problem of the Nomads', *RAI*, XV, 1967, 109–21; J. Henninger, *Uber Lebensraum und Lebensformen der Frühsemiten*, AFLNW 151, 1968.

40. See n.39 and also, among others, J. R. Kupper, *Les Nomades en Mésopotamie au temps des rois de Mari*, Paris 1957; R. Giveon, *Les bédouins Shosou des documents égyptiens*, Leiden 1971; and M. Weippert, 'Nomaden des 2. Jahrtausends', *Biblica* 55, 1974, 265–280, 427–443.

41. See e.g. K. Dittmer, *Algemene Volkenkunde*, Utrecht-Antwerp 1962, esp. 219–95.

42. See e.g. W. Nagel, *Frühe Tierwelt im Werden im Orient. Ein archäologischer Beitrag zur Zoologie*, Wittenberg 1965, 54–7.

43. Gen. 12.16; 24.10–64.

44. Gen. 30.43; 31.17, 34; 32.7, 15.

45. It is also interesting that there is no mention of a camel in the Septuagint at Gen. 12.16; 30.43; 32.7.

46. W. F. Albright, 'Abram the Hebrew, A New Archaeological Interpretation', *BASOR* 163, 1961, 36–54.

47. J. Van Seters, *Abraham in History and Tradition*, New Haven–London 1975, 13f.

48. M. Weippert, 'Abraham der Hebräer? Bemerkungen zu W. F. Albrights Deutung der Väter Israels', *Biblica* 52, 1971, 419, therefore calls them 'marginal nomads'.

49. See e.g. G. Dossin, 'Les bédouins dans les textes de Mari', in *L'Antica Società Beduina*, ed. F. Gabriella, Rome 1959, 35–52; Kupper, op. cit.; A. Malamat, 'Mari and the Bible. Some Patterns of Tribal Organization and Institutions', *JAOS* 82, 1962, 143–50; id., 'Aspects of Tribal Societies in Mari and Israel', *RAI* XV, 1967, 129–38.

50. See *AHW* II, 771.

51. See Dossin, op. cit., 51 n.36; Kupper, op. cit., 14f.

52. See e.g. Kupper op. cit., 13, 56; D. O. Edzard, 'Altbabylonisch *nawûm*', *ZA* 53, 1959, 170f.; Noth, op. cit., 252f.; M. Weippert, *The Settlement of the Israelite Tribes in Palestine*, 117f.

53. B. Zuber, *Vier Studien zu den Ursprüngen Israels*, Göttingen 1976, 104f.

54. Van Seters, op. cit., 17.

55. See *ANET*, 288.

56. See e.g. W. F. Albright, 'Abram the Hebrew. A New Archaeological Interpretation', *BASOR* 1963 (1961), 36–54, and id., *The Biblical Period* (n.2 above), 5–9.

57. C. H. Gordon, 'Abraham and the Merchants of Ura', *JNES* 17, 1958, 28–31.

58. Gen. 34.10, 31; 42.34; cf. also Gen. 23.16.

59. Among others, S. Yeivin, 'The Age of the Patriarchs', *RSO* 38, 1963, 277–302.

60. M. Weippert, 'Abraham der Hebräer? Bemerkungen zu W. F. Albrights Deutung der Väter Israels', *Biblica* 52, 1971, 407–32.

61. Thompson, op. cit., 172–86.

62. So also *EHI*, 229–33; cf. Herrmann, *HIOTT*, 47.

63. This identification has been defended e.g. by C. H. Gordon, 'Biblical Customs and the Nuzi Tablets', *BA* 3, 1940, 1–12; W. F. Albright, *From the Stone Age to Christianity*, New York ³1957, 237; C. J. Mullo Weir, 'Nuzi', *AOTS*, 1967, 73–86, and R. Martin-Achard, *Actualité d'Abraham*, Neuchâtel 1969, 27–32; Bright, *HI*, 78.

64. See e.g. Gordon, op. cit., 5–6; Mullo Weir, op. cit., 73f., amd further e.g. E. A. Speiser, *Genesis*, AB, ²1964, 112.

65. See L. A. Snijders, 'Genesis XV. The Covenant with Abram', *OTS* XII, 1958, 269–71.

66. Thompson, op. cit., 203–30; van Seters, op. cit., 86ff., and now also e.g. *EHI*, 242f.

67. See e.g. Gordon, op. cit., 5–6; Mullo Weir, op. cit., 74; *HI*, 78.

68. See e.g. Thompson, op. cit., 269–80; van Seters, op. cit., 78–85; C. Westermann, *Genesis*, BKAT I, 12, 1977, 84.

69. There is a selection of the relevant Nuzu texts in *ANET*, 219f.

70. For the etymology of this word see C. L. Labuschagne, 'Teraphim – A New Proposal for its Etymology', *VT* XVI, 1966, 115–17.

71. So, among others, Gordon, op. cit., 5–6; Speiser, op. cit., 250; S. M. Paul and W. G. Dever, *Biblical Archaeology*, Jerusalem 1973, 268.

72. In connection with this see above all the criticism of the above views by M. Greenberg, 'Another Look at Rachel's Theft of the Teraphim', *JBL* 81, 1962, 239–48.

73. E. A. Speiser, 'The Wife-Sister Motif in the Patriarchal Narratives', in *Studies and Texts, Vol. 1, Biblical and Other Studies*, ed. A. Altmann, Cambridge 1963, 15–28. See also his commentary, mentioned above, 91–94, 184f.

74. For the relevant texts and criticism of this view see above all Thompson, op. cit., 234–48, and van Seters, op. cit., 71ff.

75. Though we must regard at least the name Bethuel in Gen. 24.50 as a gloss. On this see e.g. A. van Selms, *Genesis* II, POT, 1967, 44.

76. See e.g. van Seters, op. cit., 74.

77. Thus e.g. Speiser, op. cit., 26f., and his commentary, 184f., 226f. See also M. Burrows, 'The Complaint of Laban's Daughters', *JAOS* 57, 1937, 259–76, and C. H. Gordon, 'The Story of Jacob and Laban in the Light of the Nuzi Tablets', *BASOR* 66, 1937, 25–27.

78. E. A. Speiser, 'Ethnic Movements in the Near East in the Second Millennium', *AASOR* 13, 1933, 44, and his commentary on Genesis cited above, 120f., 250f.

79. Thus e.g. Mullo Weir, op. cit., 75; F. C. Fensham, 'The Son of a Handmaid in Northwest Semitic', *VT* XIX, 1969, 312–21; *HI*, 78.

80. See esp. Thompson, op. cit., 253ff.; van Seters, op. cit., 68ff.

81. See Gen. 21.10; 25.5 (Isaac); 25.23 (Jacob); 48.18–19 (Ephraim); 49.8 (Judah).

82. *CH*, par. 24.

83. On the question whether in e.g. *ARM(T)* VIII, 1, 24 one can read 'two-thirds' instead of 'double', see Noth, op. cit., 255.

84. For the texts see esp. van Seters, op. cit., 89ff.

85. For example, Isaac gets all Abraham's possessions (Gen. 25.5)!

86. Among others, with *CH*, 261–7.

87. Van Seters, op. cit., 95–98, esp. 98.

88. *EHI*, 254.

89. Thus, among others, by E. A. Speiser, *Genesis*, AB, ²1964, 172; van Selms, op. cit., 31; *EHI*, 255. Parrot, op. cit., 112 n.l., is among those who differ.

90. M. R. Lehman, 'Abraham's Purchase of Machpelah and Hittite Law', *BASOR* 129, 1953, 15–18.

91. H. A. Hoffner, 'Some Contributions of Hittitology to OT Study', *Tyndale Bulletin* 20, 1969, 27–55. See also H. Petschow, 'Die neubabylonische Zwiegesprächsurkunde und Gen. 23', *JCS* 23, 1965, 103–20; G. M. Tucker, 'The Legal Background of Genesis 23', *JBL* 85, 1966, 77–84; Thompson, op. cit., 295f.; van Seters, op. cit., 98–100.

92. On this see above all van Seters, op. cit., 99–100.

93. For a survey see e.g. H. Weidmann, *Die Patriarchen und ihre Religion*, Göttingen 1968; J. Scharbert, 'Patriarchentradition und Patriarchenreligion. Ein Forschungs- und Literaturbericht', *VuF* 2, 1974, 2–22; C. Westermann, *Genesis 12–50*, Darmstadt 1975, 94–123; B. Diebner, 'Die Götter der Väter. Eine Kritik der "Vätergötter"- Hypothese', *Dielheimer Blätter zum Alten Testament* 9, 1975, 21–51, and E. Ruprecht, 'Die Religion der Väter. Hauptlinien der Forschungsgeschichte', *Dielheimer Blätter zum Alten Testament* 11, 1976, 2–29.

94. Included in A. Alt, *Essays on Old Testament History and Religion*, Oxford 1966, 3–77.

95. The translation of the last two names is the one in common use. However, the meaning of these names is by no means established. See e.g. Ruprecht, op. cit., 11ff.

96. Alt, op. cit., 8f.

97. See M. Noth, *History of Israel*, London ²1960, 122ff.

98. B. Gemser, *Vragen rondom de patriarchenreligie*, Groningen 1958, 19f.

99. For a detailed account of both the success and the criticism of Alt's views see the literature mentioned in n.93 above.

100. J. Hoftijzer, *Die Verheissungen an die Erzväter*, Leiden 1956, 84ff. Cf. also his criticism of the use of the Nabataean and Palmyrene inscriptions, which Alt adduces as the foundation for his hypothesis (67ff.). In this connection see also F. M. Cross, *CMHE*, 6ff.

101. For this see M. H. Pope, *El in the Ugaritic Texts*, SVT II, 1955, and J. C. de Moor, 'The Semitic Pantheon of Ugarit', *UF* 2, 1970, 187ff.

102. In English translations (e.g. Gen. 14.18; 17.1; 21.33) these are usually rendered 'God Most High', 'God Almighty', and 'Everlasting God' respectively. All these translations are extremely dubious. For them and other epithets of El, see e.g. M. J. Mulder, 'Kanaänitische goden in het Oude Testament', *Exegetica* 4,4 and 5, The Hague 1965, 14ff., and *CMHE*, 46–60.

103. O. Eissfeldt, 'El and Jahweh', *JSS* 1, 1956, 27–37. This is developed still further at a later stage in 'Jakobs Begegnung mit El und Moses Begegnung mit JHWH', *OLZ* 58, 1963, 325–31.

104. *CMHE*, 3–75.

105. C. Westermann, *Genesis*, BKAT I, 12, 1977, 118.

106. The name Baal for a deity, which plays a great role in Ugarit, is absent from the patriarchal narratives. For criticism of the view expressed by R. Rendtorff, 'El, Ba'al und Jahwe, Erwägungen zum Verhältnis von kanaanäischer und israelitischer Religion', *ZAW* 78, 1966, 282, that Elyon is an epithet of Baal, see H. Gese, in H. Gese, M. Höfner and K. Rudolph, *Die Religionen Altsyriens, Altarabiens und der Mandäer*, Stuttgart, Berlin, Cologne and Mainz 1970, 16f.

107. In this connection see also J. Blommendaal, *El als fundament en als exponent van het Oud-Testamentisch universalisme*, Utrecht 1972, 13, 147.

108. For views on Gen. 14.18–20 see J. A. Emerton, 'The Riddle of Genesis XIV', *VT* XXI, 1971, 407ff.

109. Evidently 'laymen' could still do this in the early period of the monarchy, cf. e.g. I Kings 8.64 (Solomon).

110. See e.g. Gen. 12.7f.; 13.18; 26.25; and H. A. Brongers, 'Die Wendung *bešem yhwh* im Alten Testament', *ZAW* 72, 1965, 12f.

111. See R. de Vaux, *Ancient Israel*, London 1961, 406.

112. The translation of this word still presents some problems. We should, however, probably think of some kind of tree, of the kind that had a special role, e.g., also in Ugaritic worship. See now M. Liverani, 'La Chêne de Sherdanu', *VT* XXVII, 1977, 212–16.

113. See A. S. van der Woude, *Micha*, POT, 1976, 186f.

114. For a detailed discussion see de Vaux, *Ancient Israel*, 46f., and also E. Isaac, 'Circumcision as a Covenant Rite', *Anthropos* 59, 1964, 444–56.

115. For a survey see Scharbert, op. cit., 8ff.; Westermann, *Genesis*, 73–90.

116. Thompson, op. cit., esp. 224–6.

117. Thompson predominantly uses traditio-historical criticism, whereas van Seters makes more use of form criticism.

118. Van Seters, op. cit., 120ff.

119. In the relevant texts there is mention of MAR-TU (= Sumerian) and Ammurrú (= Akkadian). The designation 'Westerners' must be seen from a Mesopotamian perspective.

120. See Albright, *The Biblical Period*, 3.

121. See the literature mentioned in n.115.

122. On this see K. M. Kenyon, *Amorities and Canaanites*, London 1966, and *CAH* I, 2, 567–94. Also, among others, R. Amiran, 'The Pottery of the Middle Bronze Age I in Palestine', *IEJ* 10, 1960, 204–25.

123. See S. Yeivin, 'The Age of the Patriarchs', *RSO* 38, 1963, 277–302; C. H. J. de Geus, 'The Amorites in the Archaeology of Palestine', *UF* 3, 1971, 44ff.; Thompson, op. cit., 144–71; van Seters, op. cit., 104–12.

124. Gen. 15.13 gives a period of four hundred years for the stay in Egypt. Gen. 15.16 gives four generations and Gal. 3.17 speaks of an interval of 430 years between Abraham and Moses.

125. Theologically speaking, the figures twelve and forty play a substantial role in the Old Testament. In this context, the number twelve will certainly suggest the twelve tribes of Israel. For the figure forty see e.g. H. Jagersma, '. . . Veertig dagen en veertig nachten . . .', *NTT* 28, 1974, 1–15.

126. On this see A. van den Born, *Koningen*, BOT IV 2, Roermond-Maaseik 1958, 44f., and J. Gray, *I & II Kings*, OTL, London ²1970, 159f.

127. Thus among others de Vaux, *EHI*, 191f., 195–200, 264: Bright, *HI*, 77f. Herrmann, *HIOTT*, 49, differs.

128. See C. H. Gordon, *The World of the Old Testament*, New York 1958, 115f.

129. Op. cit., 87ff.

130. G. Fohrer, *Geschichte Israels*, Heidelberg 1977, 34f. See also the same author's *History of Israelite Religion*, London 1973, 32 n.15.

131. See Gen. 10.10–32; 22.20–24; 25.1–4; 25.13–16; 36.10–14.

132. See *HIOTT*, 45.

133. For a detailed discussion, with bibliography, see J. H. Kroeze, *Genesis Veertien*, Hilversum 1937; J. A. Emerton, 'Some False Clues in the Study of Genesis XIV', *VT* XXI, 1971, 24–47, and 'The Riddle of Genesis XIV', *VT* XXI, 1971, 403–39.

134. See also vv. 2, 7, 8, 17. It is remarkable that 'that is Jerusalem' has not been added to Salem in v. 18. This could be a point against the generally accepted identification of Salem with Jerusalem.

135. See e.g. Deut. 2.10–12, 20; Josh. 17.15; Isa. 17.5.

136. See e.g. the account in *BA* 40, 1977, 4.

137. In this connection see also the comment by M. Noth, 'Der Beitrag der Archäologie zur Geschichte Israels', SVT VII, 1960, 270f. 'Thus very little light is shed directly on the Old Testament patriarchs by extra-biblical evidence. Of course this light illuminates their background, but it is not sufficient for dating them.' See now the more cautious reaction on the part of R. de Vaux to a relationship between legal customs in Nuzu and those among the patriarchs, *EHI*, 255f.; this differs from his more optimistic views in earlier works like *Die Patriarchenerzählungen und die Geschichte*, SBS 3, ²1968, 34f.

138. See esp. 2.5.3.

139. See 2.4.2; 2.4.3.

140. See e.g. J. C de Moor, 'Studies in the New Alphabetic Texts from Ras Shamra', *UF* I, 1969, 168; Gese, op. cit., 120.

Chapter 3   The Sojourn in Egypt and the Exodus

1. For all these questions see G. von Rad, 'The Joseph Narrative and Ancient Wisdom', in *The Problem of the Hexateuch*, Edinburgh 1966, 292–300; M. Noth, *A History of Pentateuchal Traditions*, Englewood Cliffs, NJ 1972, 208–13; R. N. Whybray, 'The Joseph Story and Pentateuchal Criticism', *VT* XVIII, 1968, 522–8; G. W. Coats, *From Canaan to Egypt. Structural and Theological Context for the Joseph Story*, Washington 1976; and H. Donner, *Die literarische Gestalt der alttestamentlichen Josephsgeschichte*, Heidelberg 1976.

2. On this see J. M. A. Janssen, 'Egyptological Remarks on the Story of Joseph in Genesis', *JEOL* 14, 1955–56, 63–72; J. Vergote, *Joseph en Egypte*, OBL III, 1959; D. B. Redford, *The Study of the Biblical Story of Joseph*, SVT XX, 1970.

3. See n.2.

4. So e.g. S. Morenz, 'Joseph in Ägypten', *TLZ* 84, 1959, 401–16, and Redford, op. cit., 189.

5. C. Westermann, *Genesis 12–50, Erträge der Forschung*, Darmstadt 1975, 59. Cf. also S. Herrmann, 'Joseph in Ägypten. Ein Wort zu J. Vergotes Buch *Joseph en Égypte*', *TLZ* 85, 1960, 827–30; Redford, op. cit., 191ff.

6. Vergote, op. cit., 209f. Cf. also the criticism of Vergote's book by H. Donner, *BiOr* XVIII, 1961, 45f.

7. Redford, op. cit., 242.

8. See also *EHI*, 313ff.

9. Gen. 37.25, 27.

10. Gen. 37.28.

11. On this see *EHI*, 311.

12. Thus also *EHI*, 312f.

13. See W. Helck, *Die Beziehungen Ägyptens zu Vorderasien im 3. und 2. Jahrtausend v.Chr.*, Wiesbaden ²1971, 81.

14. Furthermore we have only very sparse information about this period. See e.g. Helck, op. cit., 89–106.

15. See Janssen, op. cit., 66f., and Helck, op. cit., 369.

16. As Gen. 46.1ff. expressly indicates, these come from Beersheba, and thus from the south!

17. For this see P. Montet, *Egypte et la Bible*, Paris; S. Hermann, *Israel in Egypt*, SBT II 27, 1973, 8ff.

18. See *ANET*, 259. According to R. Giveon, *Les Bédouins Shosou des Documents Égyptiens*, Leiden 1971, 232, the name Shasu seems to be a general designation for those tending herds of livestock in a later period.

19. For a more detailed analysis of this pericope and of other passages from Exodus which are to be discussed later in this chapter see e.g. G. Fohrer, *Ueberlieferung und Geschichte des Exodus*, BZAW 91, 1964; P. Weimar and E. Zenger, *Exodus. Geschichten und Geschichte der Befreiung Israels*, SBS 75, 1975, 22–99.

20. See *ANET*, 553.

21. See e.g. *WUS* no. 2246.

22. *EHI*, 324.

23. For the location of these two cities see e.g. E. P. Uphill, 'Pithom and Raamses. Their Location and Significance', *JNES* 17, 1968, 291–316; 18, 1969, 15–39; F. C. Fensham, *Exodus*, POT, 1970, 16f., and esp. n.7; T. L. Thompson, in *IJH*, 153f.

24. Thompson, op. cit., 153. D. B. Redford, 'Exodus I 11', *VT* XIII, 1963, 401–413, represents a different view.

25. See B 187 and Excursus I.

26. See B 189 and 190.

27. See *EHI*, 325.

28. Thus e.g. Bright, *HI*, 119. However, W. H. Schmidt, *Exodus*, BKAT II, 1, 1974, 66f., and others differ.

29. H. H. Rowley, *From Joseph to Joshua. Biblical Traditions in the Light of Archaeology*, London 1948, 122ff., mentions Joseph, Judah, part of the Levites and perhaps Simeon in this connection. It is supposed that the last two groups could have arrived in Egypt after the debacle at Shechem (Gen. 34). In this connection, O. Eissfeldt, *CAH* II, 2, 220, 223, thinks only in terms of the 'house of Joseph' or part of it, and some members of the tribe of Levi.

30. The literature of the ancient Near East contains a number of stories about the birth and deliverance of important figures which show some signs of similarity with this account. See e.g. the birth narrative of Sargon of Akkad in *ANET*, 119. See also J. G. Frazer, *Folk-lore in the Old Testament* II, London 1919, 437–55.

31. See the literature mentioned in n.19 and also H. Schmid, *Mose Ueberlieferung und Geschichte*, BZAW 110, 1968; *LOI*, 174ff.

32. J. Pedersen, 'Passahfest und Passahlegende', *ZAW* NF 11, 1934, 160–75; id., *Israel. Its Life and Culture*, III–IV, Copenhagen and London 1947, 728ff.

33. See. e.g. Num. 25.6–9; Judg. 6–8.

34. So also e.g. Fohrer, op. cit., 27; H. Seebass, *Der Erzvater Israel*, BZAW 98, 1966, 86f.; R. Smend, *Yahweh War and Tribal Confederation*, Nashville 1970, *EHI*, 330; *HIOTT*, 61f. Moses' flight to Midian recalls the flight of Sinuhe (*ANET*, 18–22), who escaped pursuit and arrest in the same way.

35. For literature discussing this question see Rowley, op. cit., 149ff., who even thinks that this Kenite hypothesis is acceptable (see esp. 154). Cf. C. Brekelmans, 'Exodus XVIII and the Origins of Yahwism in Israel', *OTS* X, 1954, 215–24, esp. 222.

36. See e.g. *EHI*, 338ff., and F. Michaeli, *Le Livre de l'Exode*, CAT II, 1974, 57.

37. So also *HIOTT*, 61f.

38. According to F. Cornelius, 'Mose urkundlich', *ZAW* 78, 1966, 75–78, an Egyptian text from the thirteenth century BC mentions a Moses who occupies an important political position in Egypt. This is thought to be a strong suggestion of the figure of Moses in Exodus.

39. For a detailed account on this see R. de Vaux, *Ancient Israel*, London 1961, 484ff., and J. Henninger, *Les fêtes de printemps chez les sémites et la pâque israélite*, Études Bibliques, Paris 1975. The passover and the feast of unleavened bread were originally unconnected, cf. Ex. 34.18, 25.

40. Thus also e.g. *EHI*, 370f., and Michaeli, op. cit., 118.

41. See e.g. B. S. Childs, *Exodus*, OTL 1974, 184ff.

42. On this see e.g. A. Malamat, in Fischer, *Weltgeschichte* 3, Frankfurt am Main 1966, 205f.; H. D. Preuss, *Jahweglaube und Zukunftserwartung*, BWANT 7, 1968, 9–39; J. Kühlewein, *Geschichte in den Psalmen*, Stuttgart 1973, 136–8, 144f., and 154–8; E. W. Nicholson, *Exodus and Sinai in History and Tradition*, Oxford 1973.

43. This is Ex. 6.1 in the MT.

44. A passage which in one sense recalls Gen. 12.20.

45. See *EHI*, 370, and esp. 375, 380.

46. E. Auerbach, *Moses*, Amsterdam 1953, esp. 114ff., has defended the theory that the Levites had settled in Kadesh as an independent tribe even in the time before Moses. The tribe is thought to have preserved very old traditions which were later taken up by Moses, whose parents are both said by Ex. 2.1 to have been Levites. This theory, which has not gained much acceptance, has been rightly rejected e.g. by M. A. Beek, *SHI*, 34–36.

47. *EHI*, 375f.

48. Thus *HIOTT*, 70f.

49. Thus B. Mazar, *The World History of the Jewish People*, Vol. III, *Judges*, 1971, p.70; *HI*, 130, 136; Weimar and Zenger, op. cit., 114; A. H. J. Gunneweg, *Geschichte Israels bis Bar Kochba*, Stuttgart ²1976, 26. See also K. Koch, 'Die Hebräer vom Auszug aus Ägypten bis zum Grossreich Davids', *VT* XIX, 1969, esp. 50ff.

50. In this connection see O. Eissfeldt, 'Israels Führer in der Zeit vom Auszug aus Ägypten bis zur Landnahme', *Studia Biblica et Semitica*, Festschrift for T. C. Vriezen, Wageningen 1966, 62–5.

51. See *ANET*, 243, 259, 485.

52. O. Eissfeldt, *Baal Zaphon, Zeus Kasios und der Durchzug der Israeliten durchs Meer*, Halle 1932.

53. On this question see also Mazar, op. cit., 73f.

54. M. Noth, 'Der Schauplatz des Meereswunders', *Festschrift für Otto Eissfeldt*, Halle 1947 = *Aufsätze* 1, Neukirchen-Vluyn 1971, 105f.

55. See e.g. Jer. 41.16ff.

56. On this see Fohrer, op. cit., 98ff.; G. te Stroete, *Exodus*, BOT I/II, 1966, 99f.; Childs, *Exodus*, 218ff.

57. Cf., however, A. R. Hulst, 'Der Jordan in den alttestamentlichen Ueberlieferungen', *OTS* XIV, 1965, 179 n.1.

58. O. Kaiser, *Die mythische Bedeutung des Meeres in Ägypten, Ugarit und Israel*, BZAW 78, 1959, 133.

59. Cross, *CMHE*, 124. Cf. also P. C. Craigie, 'An Egyptian Expression in the Song of the Sea (Exodus XV 4)', *VT* XX, 1970, esp. p.83 n.4.

60. For this see Fohrer, op. cit., 111.

61. See e.g. Deut. 11.4; Josh. 24.6f.; Ps. 78.13; 106.9; 136.12–15; Neh. 9.9. Cf. also Weimar and Zenger, op. cit., 139–66; S. I. L. Norin, *Er spaltete das Meer. Die Auszugsüberlieferung in Psalmen und Kult des alten Israel*, Lund 1977.

62. Thus e.g. by G. W. Coats, 'The Traditio-Historical Character of the Reed Sea Motif', *VT* XVII, 1967, 253ff.; Childs, op. cit., 223.

63. On this see Hulst, op. cit., 179ff.; *EHI*, 386.

64. This has been done in great detail by Rowley, op. cit., and J. J. Bimson, *Redating the Exodus and Conquest*, JSOT Supplementary Series 5, 1978, 18ff.

65. See 2.5.1 and nn.124, 125.

66. *Antt.* VIII, 3, 1; XX, 10, 1.

67. In connection with Gal. 3.17 it should be observed that here Paul clearly follows the reading of the Samaritan Pentateuch and LXX in Ex. 12.40, where the time of the patriarchs and that of the stay in Egypt are added up to make 430 years.

68. See W. Richter, 'Die Ueberlieferungen um Jephtah, Ri 10, 17—12, 6', *Biblica* 47, 1966, 523 n.1.

69. Richter, op. cit., 522–47, and M. Wüst, 'Die Einschaltung in die Jiftachgeschichte Ri 11, 13—26', *Biblica* 56, 1975, 464–79.

70. So W. F. Albright, *From the Stone Age to Christianity*, New York ²1957, 255ff. For the building activities of Ramses II see also especially A. Alt, 'Die Deltaresidenz der Ramessiden', Berlin 1954=*KS* III, 176–85.

71. De Vaux, *EHI*, 390f., differs, as do Bright, *HI*, 122, and Mazar, op. cit., p.72; they regard Ramses II as the Pharaoh of the exodus. See also *HIOTT*, 62.

72. For this see esp. A. Ströbel, *Der spätbronzezeitliche Seevölkersturm*, BZAW 145, 1976, esp. 265ff.

73. However, Bimson, op. cit., has argued for dating the exodus in the fifteenth century BC, above all on the basis of archaeological data. This thorough study is still open to the question whether the archaeological data are convincing in this respect.

74. *ANET*, 376–8.

75. In this text Israel is expressly designated a 'people'. However, the designation could rest on a mistake in the orthography. See *ANET*, 378 n.18.

76. For the Hyksos see J. Vercoutter in Fischer, *Weltgeschichte* 2, Frankfurt am Main 1965, 350ff., and W. C. Hayes in *CAH* II, 1, 1973, 54ff. Also J. Leibowitch, 'Le problème des Hyksos et celui de l'Exode', *IEJ* 3, 1953, 90–112; J. van Seters, *The Hyksos. A New Investigation*, New Haven–London 1966; B. Couroyer, 'Les Aamou-Hyksos', *RB* 81, 1974, 321–54, 481–523, and W. A. Ward, 'Some Personal Names of the Hyksos Period Rulers and Notes on the Epigraphy of their Scarabs', *UF* 8, 1977, 353–65.

77. There is a continuing controversy over the origin of the Hyksos. See A. Alt, 'Die Herkunft der Hyksos in neuer Sicht', Berlin 1964 = *KS* III, 72–98. The majority think that they were probably Semites. Cf. Vercoutter, op. cit., 351; Hayes, op. cit., 54.

78. See Vercoutter, op. cit., 351; Hayes, op. cit., 54.

79. See Vercoutter, op. cit., 351ff.

80. A dating which is based on the 'Stele of the year 400', see *ANET* 252–3. Redford, op. cit., 188, differs in thinking in terms of 1650 BC.

81. For other arguments against a link with the Hyksos see Herrmann, *Israel in Egypt*, 21f.

82. Thus Rowley, op. cit., 116ff., and (at least in part) J. Scheckenhofer *Von Abraham bis David II: Israel in Ägypten, Moses*, Regensburg 1967. For the monotheism of Akhenaten see now R. North, 'Akhenaten secularized', *Biblica* 58, 1977, 246–58; but see Herrmann, op. cit., 14.

83. Thus H. Cazelles et al., *Moïse, l'homme de l'alliance*, Paris 1955, 17. Herrmann, op. cit. 22, differs.

Chapter 4   The Wilderness Period

1. M. Noth, *A History of Pentateuchal Traditions*, Englewood Cliffs NJ 1972, 42–62; cf. also id., *History of Israel*, London ²1960, 133f.

2. G. von Rad, 'The Problem of the Hexateuch', in *The Problem of the Hexateuch and Other Essays*, Edinburgh 1966, 1–78.

3. Thus H. Gese, 'Bemerkungen zur Sinaitradition', *ZAW* 79, 1967, 137–54; A. H. J. Gunneweg, *Geschichte Israels bis Bar Kochba*, Stuttgart ²1976, 23ff.

4. Thus by A. S. van der Woude, *Uittocht en Sinaï*, Nijkerk 1960; W. Beyerlin, *The Origins and History of the Oldest Sinaitic Traditions*, Philadelphia and Oxford 1965, 151ff., and E. W. Nicholson, *Exodus and Sinai in History and Tradition*, Oxford 1973.

5. See van der Woude, op. cit., 13; Schmid, *Mose Ueberlieferung*, 113, and *HI*, 124.

6. For other arguments see also van der Woude, op. cit., 10ff.; Brekelmans, op. cit.

7. See also Excursus II.

8. See e.g. Ex. 3.1; 18.5.

9. Above all in Deuteronomy.

10. See F. C. Fensham, *Exodus*, POT, 1970, 23 n.4; J. Koenig, *Le site de al-Jaw dans l'ancien pays de Madian*, Paris 1971; in connection with this last see the criticism by J. Pirenne, 'Le site préislamique de al-Jaw, la Bible, le Coran et le Midrache', *RB* 82, 1975, 34–69. See also B. Zuber, *Vier Studien zu den Ursprüngen Israels*. Göttingen 1976, 15–49.

11. For an extensive analysis and discussion of these earliest collections of traditions see O. Eissfeldt, 'Die älteste Erzählung vom Sinaibund', *ZAW* 73, 1961, 137–46; Beyerlin, op. cit., and Nicholson, op. cit., 33–84.

12. Thus also Beyerlin, op. cit., 34, and Nicholson, op. cit., 79ff. Nicholson holds that in its original form Ex. 24.9–11 originated in the period before the exodus (p.83). For a detailed study of Ex. 24.9–11 see T. C. Vriezen, 'The Exegesis of Exodus XXIV 9–11', *OTS* XVII, 1972, 100–33.

13. D. J. McCarthy, *Old Testament Covenant. A Survey of Current Opinions*, Oxford 1972, 30. Cf. also T. Gaster, *Thespis*, New York ²1961, 372–5.

14. See also Vriezen, op. cit., 117. L. Perlitt, *Bundestheologie im Alten Testament*, WMANT 36, 1969, 186ff., and Nicholson, op. cit., 80, are among those who differ.

15. E.g. in Judg. 5.4; Ps. 68.9.

16. Judges 5 is without doubt one of the earliest passages in the Old Testament and probably dates from about 1100 BC. For the whole question see M. Buber, *The Prophetic Faith*, New York 1949, 8–12; G. Gerleman, 'The Song of Deborah in the Light of Stylistics', *VT* 1, 1951, 168–80, and *LOI*, 36ff.

17. Cf. also the account of his calling in Ex. 3 and on this M. A. Beek, 'Der Dornbusch als Wohnsitz Gottes (Deut. XXXIII)', *OTS* XIV, 1965, 155–62.

18. For the dating, etc., of these laws see e.g. *LOI*, 182–95, and for a survey of the discussion of this material, W. Schottroff, 'Zum alttestamentlichen Recht', *VuF Heft Altes Testament*, 1977, 3–29.

19. One example of this last is the decalogue in Lev. 19.3–4, 11–18, and the prescription in 19.23–25, which clearly presuppose the situation of the exile. For this see H. Jagersma, *Leviticus 19. Identiteit-Bevrijding-Gemeenschap*, Assen 1972, 74ff., 119f., 123f.

20. Ex. 20.1–17; Deut. 5.6–21.

21. On this see J. J. Stamm, 'Dreissig Jahre Dekalogforschung', *ThR NF* 27, 1961, 226ff., and id., *The Ten Commandments in Recent Research*, SBT II 2, 1967, 25ff.

22. On this see Jagersma, op. cit., 45–50, 55–58, and the literature mentioned there.

23. Thus G. E. Mendenhall, *Law and Covenant in Israel and the Ancient Near East*, Pittsburgh 1955. For a critical discussion of this material see McCarthy, op. cit., and Jagersma, op. cit., 45ff.

24. Thus e.g. B. D. Eerdmans in his *Godsdienst van Israel* I, Huis ter Heide 1930, 35–39, and A. H. J. Gunneweg, *Geschichte Israels bis Bar Kochba*, Stuttgart ²1976, 27f.; it is rejected, however, by *EHI*, 338; *HIOTT*, 75.

25. On this see also C. H. W. Brekelmans, 'Exodus XVIII and the Origins of Yahwism', *OTS* X, 1954, esp. 223f.

26. For the significance of the phrase 'forty years' see J. Jagersma, '. . . Veertig dagen en veertig nachten . . .', *NTT* 28, 1974, 13f.

27. Hormah probably lay between Beersheba and Arad. See Y. Aharoni, *The Land of the Bible. A Historical Geography*, London 1967, 184.
28. Cf. also Num. 21.1–3; Judg. 1.17, and on it e.g. O. Eissfeldt, *CAH* II 2, 328.
29. Thus E. Auerbach, *Moses*, Amsterdam 1953, 74ff.; Beyerlin, op. cit., 151, and S. Mowinckel, *Israels opphav og eldste historie*, Oslo 1967, 45ff.
30. See 3.4.1.
31. *EHI*, 380f.
32. Van der Woude, op. cit., II, produces a number of possible arguments.
33. For a survey see now R. P. Carroll, 'Rebellion and Dissent in Ancient Israelite Society', *ZAW* 89, 1977, 182f. For an analysis and extensive discussion of the relevant stories see also e.g. Schmid, op. cit., 81–97; G. W. Coats, *The Murmuring Motif in the Wilderness Traditions of the Old Testament – Rebellion in the Wilderness*, Nashville–New York 1968; and V. Fritz, *Israel in der Wüste. Traditionsgeschichtliche Untersuchung der Wüstenüberlieferung des Jahwisten*, Marburg 1970, esp. 4–96.
34. See e.g. Deut. 1.20–46; 9.7; 11.2–7; Ezek. 20.8; Pss. 78.17ff.; 95.8–11; 106.23; Neh. 9.16–21.
35. See B. S. Childs, *Exodus*, OTL, 1974, 259ff.
36. Coats, op. cit., esp. 221–4. S. J. de Vries, 'The Origin of the Murmuring Tradition', *JBL* 87, 1968, 51–8, and others differ.
37. Carroll, op. cit., 191–203.
38. Ibid., 191.
39. So also C. Barth, 'Zur Bedeutung dert Wüstentradition', SVT XV, 1966, 14–23.
40. A. S. van der Woude, *Die messianischen Vorstellungen der Gemeinde von Qumran*, Assen 1957, 236f. Cf. also e.g. Hos. 2.13–14, where there is no longer mention of a 'rebellion'.
41. For a detailed analysis of this story see e.g. J. H. Grønbaek, 'Juda und Amalek. Ueberlieferungsgeschichtliche Erwägungen zu Ex. 17, 8–16', *StTh* 18, 1964, 26–45; Schmid, op. cit., 62–64; Fritz, op. cit., 10–13, 55–63; G. W. Coats, 'Moses versus Amalek: aetiology and legend in Exodus XVII 8–16', SVT XXVIII, 1975, 29–41.
42. Called En-mishpat in Gen. 14.7.
43. Thus Grønbaek, op. cit., 37; Schmid, op. cit., 62; *EHI*, 527. Fritz, op. cit., 56, and others differ.
44. So also Grønbaek, op. cit., 26–45, and G. te Stroete, *Exodus*, BOT I/II, 1966, 126.
45. For these arguments see R. Schmitt, *Zelt und Lade*, Gütersloh 1972, 65ff. A different view is put forward by von Rad, 'The Tent and the Ark', in *The Problem of the Hexateuch*, 103–24; on other grounds he argues that it originated in Canaan. The suggestion has also been made that the ark derives from the Midianites. But against this see Schmitt, op. cit., 78ff.
46. On this see J. Morgenstern, 'The Ark, the Ephod and the Tent of Meeting', *HUCA* XVII, 1942–43, 153ff. and XVIII, 1943/1944, 1ff.
47. For a detailed analysis of these chapters see K. Koch, *Die Priesterschrift von Exodus 25 bis Leviticus 26. Eine überlieferungsgeschichtliche und literarkritische Untersuchung*, Göttingen 1959; te Stroete, op. cit., 187f.; and Childs, *Exodus*, 512ff.
48. It does not seem necessary here to go into the possible background of these traditions in detail. See the literature mentioned in n. 47 and also M. Görg, *Das Zelt der Begegnung. Untersuchung zur Gestalt der sakrale Zelttraditionen Altisraels*, BBB 27, 1967;

J. G. Vink, 'The Date and Origin of the Priestly Code in the Old Testaments', *OTS* XV, 1969, 99ff.; Schmitt, op. cit., 175ff.

49. Thus also R. de Vaux, 'Ark of the Covenant and Test of Reunion', in *The Bible and the Ancient Near East*, London 1972, 136–51; *EHI*, 468; *HI*, 161.

Excursus II   The Tribes of Israel

1. M. Noth, *Das System der Zwölf Stämme Israels*, Darmstadt 1966 (1930), 3–28.
2. See also Gen. 29.31—30.24; 35.23–26; 46.8–25; Ex. 1.2–4; Deut, 27.12–14; Ezek. 48.31–35; I Chron. 2.2 (lists of Jacob's sons).
3. See also Num. 1.5–15, 20–43; 2.3–31 (cf. 10.14–28); 7.12–83; 13.4–15; Josh. 13—19; Ezek. 48.1–29.
4. H. Weippert, 'Das geographische System der Stämme Israels', *VT* XXIII, 1973, 76–89. De Vaux, EHI, 6f, 9, points to yet a third system in Josh. 13–19. But see C. H. J. de Geus, *The Tribes of Israel*, Assen 1976, 71 n. 6a.
5. Num. 24.19–29; Josh. 21.4–8, 9–42; Judg. 1.1–35; I Chron. 6.49–66.
6. Weippert, op. cit., 78 n. 1.
7. De Geus, op. cit., 111, differs – to my mind rightly.
8. Noth, op. cit., 59.
9. Noth, op. cit., 66ff.
10. Thus by G. Fohrer, 'Altes Testament – "Amphiktyonie" und "Bund"?', *TLZ* 91, 1966, 801–16, 893–904; R. de Vaux, 'La Thèse de l' "Amphictyonie Israélite"', *HTR* 64, 1971, 415–36=*EHI*, 695–715; A. D. H. Mayes, 'Israel in the pre-monarchy Period', *VT* XXIII, 1973, 151–70; id., *Israel in the Period of the Judges*, SBT II 29, London 1974, 15–83; E. Otto, 'Jakob in Bethel. Ein Beitrag zur Geschichte der Jakobüberlieferung', *ZAW* 88, 1976, 165–90; de Geus, op. cit., see esp. 193ff. Support for the amphictyony hypothesis, albeit with qualifications, can be found in K. D. Schunck, *Benjamin*, BZAW 86, Berlin 1963; H. J. Zobel, *Stammesspruch und Geschichte*, BZAW 95, Berlin 1965; A. H. J. Gunneweg, *Geschichte Israels bis Bar Kochba*, Stuttgart ²1976, 41–47.
11. Thus de Geus, op. cit., 117.
12. Noth, op. cit., 5f., does not, however, want to regard Judg. 5.14–18 as an earlier stage of the twelve-tribe system. This is principally because he wants to begin *a priori* from the twelve-tribe system.
13. J. Hoftijzer, 'Enige opmerkingen rond het Israelitische 12-stammen-systeem', *NTT* XIV, 1959–60, 253f. Thus also e.g. *EHI*, 549; cf. also Weippert, op. cit., 87f.
14. Cf. also Deut.33, which comes from a somewhat later time. For this see C. J. Labuschagne, 'The Tribes in the Blessing of Moses', *OTS* XIX, 1974, 97–112, esp. 105, 109f.
15. Thus J. Simons, *The Geographical and Topographical Texts of the Old Testament*, Leiden 1959, p. 290, and already C. Steuernagel, *Die Einwanderung der israelitischen Stämme in Kanaan*, Berlin 1901, 20f.
16. Thus Hoftijzer, op. cit., 254; de Geus, op. cit., 108–11. Cf. also Zobel, op. cit., 98–101.
17. de Geus, op. cit., 102. Cf. again Zobel, op. cit., 98–101.
18. See A. H. J. Gunneweg, *Leviten und Priester*, FRLANT 89, 1965, 60, and de Geus, op. cit., 95.
19. Thus E. Täubler, *Biblische Studien. Die Epoche der Richter* (ed. H. J. Zobel), Tübingen 1958, 199; de Geus, op. cit., 95.
20. E.g. Gen. 50.23; Num. 32.39f.; Josh. 17.1.

21. E.g. Num. 26.29; 27.1; Josh. 17.1; I Chron. 2.21.

22. See Noth, op. cit., 36; Hoftijzer, op. cit., 243; and cf. also Zobel, op. cit., 112; also J. Ottoson, *Gilead, Tradition and History*, Lund 1969, 136ff.

23. See A. Lemaire, 'Asriel, *šr'l*, Israel et l'origine de la confédération Israelite', *VT* XXIII, 1973, 239–43, and cf. also the Israel stele from about 1220 BC in *ANET*, 276–8.

24. Of course the figure ten can serve just as well as the figure twelve to indicate a totality. See H. A. Brongers, 'Die Zehnzahl in der Bibel und in ihrer Umwelt', *Studia Biblica et Semitica*, Festschrift for T. C. Vriezen, Wageningen 1966, 34ff. Cf. also Schunck, op. cit., 53 n. 32.

25. Mentioned only in Deut. 32.15; 33.5, 26; Isa. 44.2; Sirach 37.25.

26. See further Zobel, op. cit., 72–80.

27. For Caleb and the Calebites see now the detailed study by W. Beltz, *Die Kaleb-traditionen im Alten Testament*, BWANT 98, 1974.

28. On this see above all *EHI*, 523–50.

29. H. Seebass, 'Die Stämmeliste von Dtn XXXIII', *VT* XXVII, 1977, 158–69, esp. 161.

30. According to Seebass, op. cit., 168, Deut. 33.5, 26 is to be dated to the early period of Solomon. Labuschagne, op. cit., 101, and others differ in putting it at the beginning of the Davidic period.

Chapter 5   The Settlement in Canaan

1. See also 3.6.3.

2. For a detailed account of the whole question see W. Helck, *Die Beziehungen Agyptens zu Vorderasien im 3. und 2. Jahrtausend V. Chr.*, Wiesbaden ²1971, 168ff.; R. O. Faulkner, *CAH* II, 2, 217ff.; J. Černý and J. Yoyotte, *Fischer Weltgeschichte 3. Die Altorientalischen Reiche II. Das Ende des 2. Jahrtausend*, Frankfurt am Main 1976, 222ff.

3. For a detailed account of these events see Faulkner, op. cit., 232ff.; Černý and Yoyotte, op. cit., 274ff.

4. See *ANET*, 262ff., and W. F. Edgerton and J. A. Wilson, *Historical Records of Ramses III*, Studies in Ancient Oriental Civilization 12, Chicago 1936.

5. For details about the Sea Peoples see G. E. Mendenhall, 'The "Sea-Peoples" in Palestine', *The Tenth Generation*, Baltimore-London 1974, 142–73, and A. Ströbel, *Der Spät-bronzezeitliche Seevölkersturm*, BZAW 145, 1976.

6. For these peoples see further J. R. Bartlett, 'The Moabites and Edomites', *POTT*, 229–58, and the literature mentioned there. Also A. N. van Zyl, *The Moabites*, Leiden 1960.

7. E.g. in *EA* 148, 227, 228.

8. E.g. in *EA* 244, 245 (*ANET*, 485).

9. E.g. in *EA* 289 (*ANET*, 489).

10. E.g. in *EA*, 254, 287 (*ANET*, 486, 488).

11. E.g. in *EA* 289, 290 (*ANET*, 489).

12. E.g. in *EA* 328, 329.

13. For a survey of the division of territory between the city states in Canaan in this period see A. Alt, 'The Settlement of the Israelites in Palestine', in *EOTHR*, 145ff.

14. *EA* 148 is one exception.

15. See *EA* 252–4 and M. Reviv, 'Regarding the History of the Territory of Shechem in the El Amarna Period', *Tarbiz* 33, 1963, 1–7.

16. See *EA* 289, 290 and J. F. Ross, 'Gezer in the Tell el-Amarna Letters', *BA* 30, 1967, 62–70.

17. A. Albright gives a detailed study of these letters in 'A Prince of Taanach in the Fifteenth Century BC', *BASOR* 94, 1944, 12–27.

18. Thus e.g. Y. Yadin, *The Head of All Those Kingdoms*, Schweich Lectures 1970. London 1972.

19. See e.g. *EA* 271, 290.

20. Thus e.g. by Labaya of Shechem (*EA* 287, 289).

21. See K. A. Kitchen, 'The Philistines', *POTT*, 60; Strobel, op. cit., 87.

22. G. E. Mendenhall, 'The Hebrew Conquest of Palestine', *BA* 25, 1962, 66–87.

23. According to Mendenhall, this is also true of the Israelites. In his view the terms Israelites, Hebrews and 'Apiru are virtual synonyms. However, this view is rightly rejected by M. Weippert, *The Settlement of the Israelite Tribes in Palestine*, SBT II 21, 1971, 63–102.

24. Alt, op. cit., 135–69; id., *Erwägungen über die Landnahme der Israeliten in Palästina*, Berlin 1939=*KS* I, 126f., 144f.

25. Cf. e.g. Josh. 17.14–18 and see further M. Kochavi, ed., *Judaea, Samaria and the Golan. Archaeological Survey 1967–1968*, Jerusalem 1972, and Y. Aharoni, *The Land of the Bible. A Historical Geography*, London 1974.

26. See Z. Ron, 'Agricultural Terraces in the Judaean Mountains', *IEJ* 16, 1966, 33–49, 111–122; C. H. J. de Geus, 'The Importance of Archaeological Research into the Palestinian Agricultural Terraces, with an Excursus on the Hebrew word *gbi*', *PEQ* 105, 1975, 65–76.

27. See Aharoni, op. cit., 219f.

28. Cf. G. Childe, *What Happened in History*, Harmondsworth 1976, esp. p. 191.

29. Cf. also n. 23.

30. Inter alia, *SHI*, 34–6; W. F. Albright, *The Biblical Period from Abraham to Ezra*, New York 1963, 24–29.

31. E.g. Aharoni, op. cit., 174ff.

32. *EHI*, 523ff.

33. Above all in Germany, and taken over by A. Alt.

34. *HIOTT*, 86ff.

35. It is not difficult to deduce the supporters of the various 'schools' from this nomenclature; Albright always talks about 'conquest' and Alt-Noth always about 'settlement'.

36. See also the following paragraphs.

37. Judg. 1.34ff. mentions Amorites in this connection. In the OT this designation is to be taken to be virtually synonymous with Canaanites. For this problem see C. H. J. de Geus, 'The Amorites in the Archaeology of Palestine', *UF* 3, 1971, 41–60.

38. See the two works by Alt mentioned in n. 24, and also Weippert, op. cit., esp. 18ff.; Aharoni, op. cit., 188.

39. See above all C. H. J. de Geus, *The Tribes of Israel*, Assen 1976, 166ff.

40. Num. 33 contains a list of all the stages of the journey through the wilderness. See G. W. Coats, 'The Wilderness Itinerary', *CBQ* 34, 1972, 135–52, and also M. Noth, 'Der Wallfahrtsweg zum Sinai (Nu. 33)' (1940)=*Aufsätze* I, 55–74, and e.g. H. Schmid, *Mose, Ueberlieferung und Geschichte*, BZAW 110, 1968, 17ff.

41. For this nomenclature see 3.5.1.

42. Peor is probably the name of a mountain (top). See M. J. Mulder, *Ba'al in het Oude Testament*, The Hague 1962, 120f.

43. See 5.1.1.

44. Cf. also J. Hoftijzer and G. van der Kooij, *Aramaic Texts from Deir 'Alla*, Leiden 1976, 271; J. Hoftijzer, 'De Arameese teksten uit Deir 'Alla', *Phoenix* 22, 1977, 87.

45. *EHI*, 568, 591. Cf. also M. Noth, 'Israelitische Stämme zwischen Ammon und Moab', *ZAW* 60, 1944=*Aufsätze* I, 402ff., and G. W. Coats, 'Balaam: Sinner or Saint?', *BR* 18, 1973, 21–29. W. H. Gispen, *Numeri* II, COT, 1964, 71f., differs. There is an extensive discussion of Num. 22–24 by W. Gross in *Bileam. Literatur- und formkritische Untersuchung der Prosa in Num. 22–24*, Munich 1974.

46. Thus *EHI*, 565, and rather more reluctantly J. R. Bartlett, *VT* XX, 1970, 258f.

47. For the various possible interpretations of this song see *EHI*, 565.

48. Cf. also M. Noth, 'Nu 21 als Glied der "Hexateuch"-Erzählung', *ZAW* 58, 1940/41=*Aufsätze* I, 79ff.; N. H. Snaith, *Leviticus and Numbers*, CB 1967, 284; *EHI*, 565.

49. In Num. 21.21 (cf. Judg. 11.19) LXX has 'Moses' (cf. Num. 20.14) in place of 'Israel'. In my view, the LXX tradition is probably the earliest, given the fact that later theological reflection on all these events had a tendency to attribute the whole settlement in Canaan simply to 'Israel'.

50. See F. M. Abel, *Géographie de la Palestine* II, Paris 1967, 354.

51. Thus e.g. O. Eissfeldt, *CAH* II, 2, 330; *EHI*, 565; van Zyl, op. cit., 9. A different view is put forward e.g. by J. van Seters, 'The Conquest of Sihon's Kingdom: A Literary Examination', *JBL* 91, 1972, 182–97 (but see D. M. Gunn, 'The "Battle Report": Oral or Scribal Convention?', *JBL* 93, 1974, 513–18), and J. Maxwell Miller in *IJH*, 227.

52. Thus e.g. Aharoni, op. cit., 188.

53. See Excursus II.

54. See e.g. Deut. 2.11, 20; II Sam. 5.18, 22. In Deut. 3.11 Og has a bed fourteen feet long!

55. For different views of Num. 32 cf. M. Ottosson, *Gilead. Tradition and History*, Lund 1969.

56. M. Wüst, *Untersuchungen zu den siedlungsgeographischen Texten des Alten Testaments I. Ostjordanland*, Wiesbaden 1975, 95.

57. In this connection, de Vaux, *EHI*, 577, points to the fact that Reuben is regularly called Jacob's oldest son and is always mentioned first in the genealogies.

58. *KAI* 181, 10 (*ANET*, 320).

59. De Geus, op. cit., 110.

60. Note that in Num. 32.34–38 the territory of Reuben is almost entirely surrounded by the cities of the Gadites. For this see also Ottosson, op. cit., 80. J. B. Curtis, 'Some Suggestions concerning the History of the Tribe of Reuben', *JBR* 35, 1965, 247–50, differs. For the origin of the tribe of Gad see also Excursus II.

61. The view of N. Glueck, 'Transjordan', *AOTS*, 443, that Transjordan was largely emptied of civilized settlement about five hundred years before the Iron Age has been refuted by S. Mittmann, *Beiträge zur Siedlungs- und Territorialgeschichte des nördlichen Ostjordanlandes*, ADPV, 1970.

62. According to *HIOTT*, 101f., this whole process of settlement in Transjordan took place from the west.

63. Cf. e.g. G. W. Coats, 'Conquest Traditions in the Wilderness Theme', *JBL* 95, 1976, 177–90, and also Fritz, op. cit., 90. Cf. also Num. 14.45. Here the name Hormah should perhaps be taken as secondary, see Fritz, op. cit., 92.

64. Thus e.g. Fritz, op. cit., 90.

65. Y. Aharoni, 'Nothing Early and Nothing Late', *BA* 39, 1976, 55–76. Cf. also B.

Mazar, 'The Sanctuary of Arad and the Family of Hobab the Kenite', *JNES* 24, 1965, 297–303.

66. See G. von Rad, *Der Heilige Krieg im alten Israel*, Göttingen 1965, 15; Y. Aharoni, *The Land of the Bible*, London 1974, 197 n.62; G. W. Anderson, *The History and Religion of Israel*, Oxford ²1976, 30.

67. C. H. J. de Geus, 'Richteren 1:1–2:5', *VoxTh* XXXVI, 1966, 32–54, esp. 51, and id., op. cit., 181 n.233.

68. For this question see 5.1.3.

69. See Num. 13.22; 14.24; Josh. 14.12–14; 15.13–14; Judg. 1.20.

70. For problems connected with the location of Debir see M. Weippert, op. cit., 30 n.84. Probably Debir lay south-west of Hebron.

71. According to Josh. 15.16ff.; Judg. 1.12ff., Othniel was a son-in-law of Caleb.

72. See M. Noth, 'Die fünf Könige in der Höhle von Makkeda', *PJB* 33, 1937=*Aufsätze* I, 281–93, see esp. 288. Cf. also Weippert, op. cit., 29ff., and the literature mentioned there. See also 5.4.3.

73. *EHI*, 545.

74. W. F. Albright, 'The Kyle Memorial Excavation at Bethel,' *BASOR* 56, 1934, 2–15, and id., *The Biblical Period*, 29, is of the opinion that we can almost certainly identify Bethel with Ai, mentioned in Josh. 7–8. Others, e.g. Beek, *SHI*, 42–44, and de Vaux, *EHI*, 615f., differ. In any case the designation 'house of Joseph' is current only in the time of the early monarchy; see de Geus, op. cit., 95.

75. For this group of problems see A. de Pury, 'Genèse XXXIV et l'histoire', *RB* 76, 1969, 5–49; W.T. In der Smitten, 'Gen 34', *BiOr* 30, 1973, 7–9; F. C. Fensham, 'Gen. XXXIV and Mari', *JNSL* 4, 1975, 87–90.

76. Again only in Judg. 1.1; 2.6–8, 21–23; I Kings 16.34; Neh. 8.17; I Chron. 7.27. This fact already tells against the view of J. Dus, 'Moses or Joshua? On the Problem of the Founder of the Israelite Religion', *Radical Religion* 2, 2/3, 1975, 26–41, who would see Joshua rather than Moses as the founder of Israelite religion.

77. There is no dispute over the fact that Joshua comes into the foreground primarily in the Deuteronomistic literature, given that Deuteronomy uses northern traditions. For Deuteronomy see now C. L. Labuschagne, 'Redactie en theologie van het boek Deuteronomium', *VoxTh* 43, 1973, 171–84.

78. With the exception of Josh. 8.30–35. For this narrative see A. Alt, 'Die Wallfahrt von Sichem nach Bethel', Riga 1938=*KS* I, 79–88; J. A. Soggin, 'Zwei umstrittene Stellen aus dem Ueberlieferungskreis um Shechem', *ZAW* 73, 1961, 82ff.; J. G. Vink, 'The Date and Origin of the Priestly Code in the Old Testament', *OTS* XV, 1969, 77–80.

79. For the boundaries of this tribe see Aharoni, op. cit., 235, and for the history of Benjamin, K. D. Schunck, *Benjamin. Untersuchungen zur Entstehung und Geschichte eines israelitischen Stammes*, BZAW 86, 1963.

80. See J. A. Soggin, 'Gilal, Passah und Landnahme. Eine Untersuchung des kultischen Zusammenhangs der Kap. III–VI des Josuabuches', SVT XV, 1966, 263–78; F. Langlamet, *Gilgal et les recits de la traversée du Jourdain (Jos. III–IV)*, Cahiers de la Revue Biblique XI, Paris 1969; E. Otto, *Das Mazzotfest in Gilgal*, BWANT 7, 1975, esp. 306ff.

81. See H. J. Franken, 'Tell es-Sultan and Old Testament Jericho', *OTS* XIV, 1965, 200f. Cf. also Otto, op. cit., 12ff., and Hos. 12.11.

82. See Josh. 19.49f.; 24.30; Judg. 2.8f.

83. See M. Noth, 'Der Jordan in der alten Geschichte Palästinas', *ZDPV* 72, 1956, 123–48. Cf. also II Sam. 10.17; 17.22, 24 (the armies of David and Absalom).

84. In addition to Josh. 3–4, cf. e.g. Ps. 66.6; 114.3.

85. See e.g. A. R. Hulst, 'Der Jordan in den alttestamentliche Ueberlieferungen', *OTS* XIV, 1965, 168ff.; Otto, op. cit., 26ff., 118ff.

86. See e.g. Franken, op. cit., 163–89; K. M. Kenyon, 'Jericho', *AOTS*, 264–75, esp. 273, and now above all H. and M. Weippert, 'Jericho in der Eisenzeit', *ZDPV* 92, 1976, 105–48; J. A. Soggin, 'Anatomie d'une conquête', *RHPR* 57, 1977, 1ff.

87. For all this see e.g. J. Callaway, 'Excavating Ai (et Tell): 1964–1972', *BA* 39, 1976, 18–30.

88. See n.74. This view is taken over by e.g. J. Bright, *HI*, 128.

89. Thus already A. Alt, *Joshua*, BZAW 61, 1936=*KS* I, 182f.

90. For this see e.g. F. C. Fensham, 'The Treaty between Israel and the Gibeonites', *BA* 27, 1964, 76–100; J. Blenkinsopp, 'Are There Traces of the Gibeonite Covenant in Deuteronomy?' *CBQ* 28, 1966, 96–100; B. Holpern, 'Gibeon: Israelite Diplomacy in the Conquest Era', *CBQ* 37, 1975, 303–16.

91. See e.g. W. L. Reed, 'Gibeon', *AOTS*, 237ff.

92. For the history of the Gibeonites, etc., see J. Blenkinsopp, *Gibeon and Israel. The Role of Gibeon and the Gibeonites in the Political and Religious History of Early Israel*, London 1972; cf. also the partly critical review by M. Weinfeld in *IEJ* 26, 1976, 60–64.

93. See S. Yeivin, 'Social, Religious and Cultural Trends in Jerusalem under the Davidic Dynasty', *VT* III, 1953, 149–66; B. Mazar, 'The Scribe of King David and the Problems of the High Officials in the Monarchy of Israel', in *Canaan and Israel. Historical Essays*, Jerusalem 1974, 208–21 (in Hebrew).

94. A. Alt, 'Das System der Stammesgrenzen im Buche Joshua', *Sellin Festschrift*, Leipzig 1927=*KS* I, 193–202.

95. For Josh. 19.40–48 see e.g. J. Strange, 'The Inheritance of Dan', *Studia Theologica* XX, 1966, 120–39, and for Judg. 18, A. Malamat, 'The Danite Migration and the Pan-Israelite Exodus-Conquest. A Biblical Narrative pattern', *Biblica* 51, 1970, 1–16.

96. For problems of dating see e.g. H. J. Zobel, *Stammesspruch und Geschichte*, BZAW 95, 1965, 88–96.

97. See e.g. Y. Yadin, 'And Dan, why did he remain in ships? (Judges V 17)', *AJBA* I, 1, 1968, 9–23.

98. And later Dan, see 5.5.5.

99. The first view is supported by e.g. O. Eissfeldt, *CAH* II, 2, 546, and A. H. J. Gunneweg, *Geschichte Israels bis Bar Kochba*, Stuttgart ²1976, and the second by e.g. F. Maass, 'Hazor und das Problem der Landnahme', *Von Ugarit nach Qumran*, Festschrift for O. Eissfeldt, BZAW 77, ²1961, 111; J. H. Kroeze, *Josua*, COT, 1968, 142; *HI*, 173 n.82.

100. Jabin is probably secondary in Judg. 4.2. Note also that he is not mentioned at all in Judg. 5. We shall return to Judg. 4–5 in the next chapter.

101. See Y. A. Yadin, *Hazor*, London 1972.

102. Thus V. Fritz, 'Das Ende der spätbronzezeitlichen Stadt Hazor Stratum XIII und die biblische Ueberlieferung in Joshua II und Richter 4', *UF* 5, 1973, 123–41. A different view is taken by P. W. Lapp, 'The Conquest of Palestine in the Light of Archaeology', *CTM* XXXVIII, 1967, 283–300, and Yadin, op. cit.

103. See *EA* 148 and also A. Malamat, 'Hazor "The Head of All Those Kingdoms"', *JBL* 79, 1960, 12–19, esp. 19, and F. M. Tocci, 'Hazor nell'età del medio e tardo bronzo', *RSO* 37, 1962, 59–64.

104. Thus *EHI*, 665f. For the history of Naphtali see also W. Herrmann, 'Issakar', *FuF*, 21–26.

105. In this connection see e.g. M. Ottoson, 'Josuansk erövering och salomonisk konsolidering i Israels arkeologi', *Religion och Bibel* 30, 1971, 29–35; de Geus, op. cit., 164ff., and the literature mentioned there.

106. See 5.1.3.

107. See 3.6.3.

108. See Excursus II.

109. See *ANET* 230, 329 n.8.

110. See e.g. *EA* 289.

111. See 2.4.3.

112. In this connection see e.g. also H. Reviv, 'The Government of Shechem in the El Amarna Period and in the Days of Abimelech', *IEJ* 16, 1966, 252–8. Cf. also Gen. 34; Judg. 8–9.

113. See G. Schmitt, *Der Landtag von Sichem*, Stuttgart 1964, 8–32, and K. Jaroš, *Eine archäologische und religionsgeschichtliche Studie mit besonderer Berücksichtigung von Jos 24*, Göttingen 1976, 129–253.

114. Thus e.g. Schmitt, op. cit., 81; *EHI*, 669; J. A. Soggin, *Joshua*, OTL, 1972, 240; Jaroš, op. cit., 148. E.g. L. Perlitt, *Bundestheologie im Alten Testament*, WMANT 36, 1969, 267, however, differs.

115. There is a good deal of literature on this question. See G. E. Mendenhall, *Law and Covenant in Israel and the Ancient Near East*.; K. Baltzer, *The Covenant Formulary*, Philadelphia and Oxford 1971, 19ff.; Schmitt, op. cit., 58ff.; V. Maag, 'Sichembund und Vätergötter', SVT XVI, 1967, 205–18; Perlitt, op. cit., 239ff.; D. J. McCarthy, *Old Testament Covenant. A Survey of Current Opinions*, Oxford 1972, passim.

116. Schmitt, op. cit., 82. Cf. also the fact that LXX has Shiloh instead of Shechem in Josh. 24.1.

117. H. H. Rowley, *From Joseph to Joshua. Biblical Traditions in the Light of Archaeology*, London 1964, 127f.

118. See Excursus II.

119. *EHI*, 668f. We also have a call in the mouth of Jacob to put away strange gods in Gen. 35.2–4. Cf. J. A. Soggin, 'Zwei umstrittene Stellen aus dem Ueberlieferungskreis um Sichem', *ZAW*, 1961, 78ff.

120. G. Fohrer, *Geschichte Israels*, Heidelberg 1977, 68.

121. So also Jaroš, op. cit., 152.

Chapter 6   The Period of the Judges

1. See *ANET*, 25–9.

2. For a literary analysis, etc., of the book of Judges see e.g. W. Richter, *Traditionsgeschichtliche Untersuchungen zum Richterbuch*, BBB 18, 1963; id., *Die Bearbeitungen des 'Retterbuches' in der deuteronomistischen Epoche*, BBB 21, 1964, and now also R. G. Boling, *Judges. A New Translation with Introduction and Commentary*, AB, 1975. Cf. also the detailed discussion of this last book in *JSOT* 1, 1976, 30–52.

3. Cf. e.g. Judg. 1.21, 27–36.

4. Thus excavations have shown that Canaanite culture still persisted long after 1200 BC, e.g. in the plain of Jezreel. See M. Dothan, 'The Excavation at 'Afula', *'Atiqot* 1, 1955, 19–70.

5. See A.Alt, 'The Formation of the Israelite State in Palestine', *EOTHR*, 171–237; id., 'Ägyptische Tempel in Palästina und die Landnahme der Philister', *ZDPV* 67, 1944 = *KS* I, 226ff.

6. See S. Herrmann, 'Das Werden Israels', *TLZ* 87, 1962, 561–74.

7. For this see M. Weinfeld, 'The Period of the Conquest and of the Judges as seen by the Earlier and the Later Sources', *VT* XVII, 1967, 93–114.

8. G. Schmitt, *Du sollst keinen Frieden schliessen mit den Bewohner des Landes. Die Weisungen gegen die Kanaanäer in Israels Geschichte und Geschichtsschreibung*. BWANT 91, 1970, differs. But see M. Weber, *Ancient Judaism*, New York and London 1967, esp. 236.

9. See N. A. van Uchelen, 'De Filistijnen in het Oude Testament. Beeld en werkelijkheid', *NTT* 20, 1966, 341.

10. See 5.1.3.

11. For developments in this period see now also W. Thiel, *Die soziale Entwicklung Israels in vorstaatlicher Zeit*, Berlin 1976.

12. M. Noth, 'Das Amt des "Richters Israels"', *Festschrift Alfred Bertholet*, Tübingen 1950 = *GS* II, 71–85.

13. See e.g. J. Dus, 'Die "Sufeten Israels"', *ArOr* 31, 1963, 444–69; W. Richter, 'Zu den "Richtern Israels"', *ZAW* 78, 1965, 40–72; I. L. Seeligmann, 'Zur Terminologie für des Gerichtsverfahren im Wortschatz des biblischen Hebräisch', SVT XVI, 1967, 273; T. Ishida, 'The Leaders of the Tribal League "Israel" in the pre-Monarchic Period', *RB* 80, 1973, 317ff.

14. See the literature mentioned in n.13 and K. D. Schunck, 'Die Richter Israels und ihr Amt', SVT XV, 1966, 252–62.

15. Thus the words 'king' and 'judge' in e.g. Micah 4.14 are to be taken as synonyms. See A. S. van der Woude, *Micha*, POT, 1976, 164f.

16. The same is true for Shamgar, mentioned in Judg. 3.31. Of him we are told only that he is a son of Anath and smote the Philistines. The question is whether we can regard Shamgar as a judge and an Israelite. On this see A. van Selms, 'Judge Shamgar', *VT* XIV, 1964, 294–309, and P. C. Craigie, 'A Reconsideration of Shamgar ben Anath (Judges 3.31; 5.6)', *JBL* 91, 1972, 239–40.

17. Independently of whether we see I Sam. 4.18b as a redactional addition or not. Most scholars, like R. de Vaux, *EHI*, 752f., seem to think that it is. Among those who differ are C. H. J. de Geus, 'De Richteren van Israel', *NTT* 20, 1965, 92; Ishida, op. cit., 528. The reasons adduced by the two last-mentioned seem to be strong ones.

18. Cf. de Geus, op. cit., 96;. Schunck, op. cit., 255.

19. Thus S. Hermann, *HIOTT*, 115. However, it would then be better to substitute the name of Barak for Shamgar (see n.16).

20. On this see de Geus, op. cit., 96ff.

21. Little of this is evident in the case of Samson.

22. See de Geus, op. cit., 99; Richter, op. cit., 71; Schunck, op. cit., 529.

23. Thus de Geus, op. cit., 99; Richter, op. cit., 71. This seems less probable in the case of Jephthah and of Samson. However, they could perhaps be characterized more as folk heroes. Note too that the story of Samson markedly has the character of a popular tale and shows few traces of later revision. For the function of elders in Israel see J. Dus, 'Die Ältesten Israels', *Communio viatorum* 3, 1960, 232–42, and also above all H. Klengel, *Zwischen Zelt und Palast. Die Begegnung von Nomaden und Sesshaften im alten Vorderasien*, Leipzig 1971, 126ff.

24. Cf. II Sam. 17.4, 15; II Kings 10.1.

25. A. Alt, 'Megiddo im Uebergang vom kanaanäischen zum israelitischen Zeitalter', *ZAW*, NF 19,1944 = *KS* I, 266 n.3.

26. W. F. Albright, in *The Biblical Period from Abraham to Ezra*, New York 1963, 39. Thus e.g. also *HI*, 172.

27. F. Gröndahl, *Die Personennamen der Texte aus Ugarit*, Rome 1967, 306.

28. *EHI*, 792.

29. So also *EHI*, 792; G. Fohrer, *Geschichte Israels*, Heidelberg 1977, 68f. Cf. also e.g. Judg. 4.13; 5.19.

30. A Weiser, '"Das Deboralied"', *ZAW* 71, 1959, 67–97.

31. See also the criticism by A. D. H. Mayes, *Israel in the Period of the Judges*, SBT II 29, 1974, 85ff.

32. This lone of thinking is also followed by Bright, *HI*, 172 (*c.* 1125 BC); Herrmann, *HIOTT*, 118 (*c.* 1200 BC); de Vaux, *EHI*, 794f. (*c.* 1150 BC); and Fohrer, op. cit., 69 (*c.* 1150 BC).

33. The figure seventy is often used in the Old Testament and ancient Near Eastern literature. However, it by no means denotes an exact number. See now F. C. Fensham, 'The Numeral Seventy in the Old Testament and the Family of Jerubbaal, Ahab, Panammuwa and Athirat', *PEQ* 109, 1977, 113–15.

34. For a thorough discussion of Judg. 9 see above all W. Richter, *Traditionsgeschichtliche Untersuchungen zum Richterbuch*, BBB 18, 1963, 142–71; K. Jaroš, *Sichem. Eine archäologische und religionsgeschichtliche Studie mit besonderer Berücksichtigung von Jos. 24*, Göttingen 1976, 76–83.

35. F. Crüsemann, *Der Widerstand gegen das Königtum. Die antikönigliche Texte des Alten Testaments und der Kampf um den frühen israelitischen Staat*, WMANT 49, 1978, 42.

36. See now G. E. Wright, 'Shechem', *AOTS*, 364.

37. This is indirectly expressed in the stories about Eli and Samuel.

38. Except in the stories of Samson, Eli and Samuel.

39. De Geus rightly therefore raises the possibility, op. cit., 93, that Judg. 3.7–11 is part of the Deuteronomistic introduction to the book of Judges.

40. For a description of the details of this story see now H. N. Rösel, 'Zur Ehud-Erzählung', *ZAW* 89, 1977, 270–2.

41. See K. M. Kenyon, *Excavations at Jericho* II, London 1965, 482–9; id., 'Jericho', *AOTS*, 274.

42. So too *HI*, 172; *EHI*, 812.

43. *HI*, 173 n.83.

44. For these problems see now J. A. Emerton, 'Gideon and Jerubbaal', *JTS*, NS 27, 1976, 289–312.

45. However, the location of Ophrah is uncertain.

46. For the topographical details of Gideon's campaign see H. N. Rösel, 'Studien zur Topografie der Kriege in den Büchern Josua und Richter', *ZDPV* 92, 1976, 10ff.

47. So *EHI*, 815f.

48. *EHI*, 821.

49. *HI*, 173.

50. For a detailed discussion of Judg. 10.17—12.6 see W. Richter, 'Die Ueberlieferung um Jephtah, Ri. 10, 17–12, 6', *Biblica* 47, 1966, 485–556.

51. For the Philistines see also 5.1.1, 5.1.2, 5.1.3 and the literature already mentioned there.

52. See T. C. Mitchell, 'Philistia', *AOTS*, 413.

53. For the first appearance of horses in the ancient Near East see Klengel, op. cit., 155ff.

54. Thus *HI*, 174; A. H. J. Gunneweg, *Geschichte Israels bis Bar Kochba*, Stuttgart 1972, 35; F. A. Spina, 'The Dan Story Historically Reconsidered', *JSOT* 4, 1977, 60–71.

55. See n.16. The mention of Shamgar in Judg. 3.31 (cf. 5.6) is probably an allusion to the Canaanite revolt against the Philistines. Thus e.g. also van Uchelen, op. cit., 340; *EHI*, 822.

56. For this story see e.g. A. G. van Daalen, *Simson*, Assen 1966, esp. 39ff.; J. L. Crenshaw, 'The Samson Saga: Filial Devotion or Erotic Attachment?', *ZAW* 86, 1974, 470–503.

57. Thus B. Mazar, *The World History of the Jewish People, Vol. III: Judges*, London 1971, 176; *HI*, 181; *HIOTT*, 141 n.1.

58. See M. L. Buhl and S. Holm-Nielsen, *Shiloh. The Danish Excavation at Tall Sailun, Palestine, in 1926, 1929, 1932 and 1963. The pre-Hellenistic Remains*, Copenhagen 1969; J. van Rossum, 'Wanneer is Silo verwoest?', *NTT* 24, 1970, 321–32.

59. See Mazar, op. cit., 174; *HI*, 181; Eissfeldt, *CAH* II, 2, 571. Mayes, op. cit., 94, thinks in terms of the end of the eleventh century BC.

60. For this see D. Diringer, 'Mizpah', *AOTS*, 312; *EAEHL*, 914.

61. Archaeological excavations have still not shown the existence of a temple in Shiloh. See Buhl and Holm-Nielsen, op. cit.

62. For the stay of the ark in these places see H. Irwin, 'Le sanctuaire central avant l'établissement de la monarchie', *RB* 72, 1965, 161–85.

63. See A. Besters, 'Le sanctuaire central dans Jud. XIX–XXI', *ETL* XVI, 1965, 20–42.

64. In connection with this period see also J. Blenkinsopp, 'Kiriath-Jearim and the Ark', *JBL* LXXXVIII, 1969, 143–56.

65. But see in connection with this J. A. Emerton, 'Beth-Shemesh', *AOTS*, 197ff., esp. 202 n.14.

66. According to J. M. Grintz, 'Some Observations on the "High Places" in the History of Israel', *VT* XXVII, 1977, 111–13, the view that worship in the high places was a practice taken over from the Canaanites must be revised

67. For the backgrond to these chapters see e.g. M. Noth, 'The Background of Judges 17–18', in *Israel's Prophetic Heritage, Essays in Honor of James Muilenburg*, London 1962, 68–85.; T. Veijola, *Das Königtum in der Beurteilung der deuteronomistischen Historiographie*, Helsinki 1977, 15–20.

68. In Judg. 18.30 the origin of the Levitical priesthood and thus of the priests of Dan is derived from Moses. For this see now F. M. Cross, *CMHE*, 197f.

69. In this connection see M. A. Cohen, 'The Role of the Shilonite Priesthood in the United Monarchy in Ancient Israel', *HUCA* 36, 1965, 59–98.

70. J. T. Willis, 'An anti-Elide Narrative Tradition from a Prophetic Circle at the Ramah Sanctuary', *JBL* XC, 1971, 288–308, sees the background of I Sam. 7 in circles of prophetic disciples centred on Samuel in the sanctuary at Ramah. For the figure of Eli and Samuel in Shiloh see now also N. R. M. Poulssen, 'De stoel van Heli. Het wel en wee van een priesterlijke bediening volgens het eerste Samuelboek', *Tussentijds*, Tilburg 1974, 168–88.

71. For a discussion of the chapters in I Sam. 1ff. which deal with Samuel see e.g. H. J. Stoebe, *Das Erste Buch Samuelis*, KAT VIII, 1, 1973, esp. 84–8. Cf. also M. Noth, 'Samuel and Silo', *VT* XIII, 1963 = *Aufsätze* I, 148–56.

Chapter 7 The Rise of the Monarchy

1. Cf. also Hos. 13.10. See further J. A. Soggin, *Das Königtum in Israel, Ursprünge, Spannungen, Entwicklung,* BZAW 104, 1967, 32 n.9, and the literature mentioned there. For I Sam. 8 and the problems connected with this chapter see Soggin, op. cit., 31ff.; H. J. Boecker, *Die Beurteilung der Anfänge des Königtums in den deuteronomistischen Abschnitten des I. Samuelbuches,* WMANT 31, 1969, 10ff.; B. C. Birch, *The Rise of the Israelite Monarchy. The Growth and Development of I Samuel 7–15,* Missoula 1976, 21ff.; F. Crüsemann, *Der Widerstand gegen das Königtum,* Neukirchen-Vluyn 1978, 54ff.

2. See e.g. I Sam. 7.14. Amorites are mentioned here. What are meant, however, are the non-Israelite inhabitants of Canaan, the Canaanites. See ch. 5 n.37.

3. According to J. Dishon, 'Gideon and the beginnings of Monarchy in Israel', *Tarbiz* 41, 1972, 255–68, Gideon in fact accepts the kingship. A. Weiser, 'Samuel und die Vorgeschichte des israelitischen Königtums', *ZTK* 57, 1960, 141–61, does not see Samuel's opposition in I Sam. 8 as being directed against the kingdom as such; Samuel wanted a different kind of monarchy, i.e. one in which the rule of Yahweh was expressed. For Judg. 8.22–23 see Boecker, op. cit., 20–23; Crüsemann, op. cit., 42ff.

4. So T. Ishida, *The Royal Dynasties in Ancient Israel,* BZAW 142, 1977, 185. Crüsemann, op. cit., 45ff. differs; he thinks of the time of Solomon (52).

5. Crüsemann, op. cit., 29; for Judg. 8; 9, see also 6.3.2.

6. For all this see A. Causse, *Du groupe ethnique à la Communauté religieuse. Le problème sociologique de la religion d'Israel,* Paris 1937, esp. 15–57; H. Klengel, *Zwischen Zelt und Palast. Die Begegnung von Nomaden und Sesshaften im alten Vorderasien,* Leipzig 1972; F. Stolz, 'Aspekte religiöser und sozialer Ordnung im alten Israel', *ZEE* 17, 1973, 145–59. However, Causse's book is still based on the old conception of nomadism.

7. See R. E. Clements, 'The Deuteronomistic Interpretation of the Founding of the Monarchy in I Sam. VIII', *VT* XXIV, 1974, 398–410; Crüsemann, op. cit., 70, and the literature mentioned in n.20 there.

8. Cf. also Boecker, op. cit., 16ff., and above all P.A.H. de Boer, 'I Sam. 8, v.16B', in *Travels in the World of the Old Testament. Studies presented to Prof. M. A. Beek on the occasion of his 65th Birthday,* Assen 1974, 29.

9. In this connection see e.g. Boecker, op. cit., and the review of his book by P. A. H. de Boer in *VT* XX, 1970, esp. 380f. Also H. Weippert, 'Die "deuteronomistischen" Beurteilungen der Könige von Israel und Juda und das Problem der Redaktion der Königsbücher', *Biblica* 53, 1972, 301–39.

10. See Soggin, op. cit., 31ff.; Boecker, op. cit., 12ff., 35ff.; Birch, op. cit., 29ff.; T. N. D. Mettinger, *King and Messiah,* Lund 1976, 64ff.; T. Veijola, *Das Königtum in der Beurteilung der deuteronomistischen Historiographie,* Helsinki 1977, 39ff.; K. A. D. Smelik, *Saul, de vorstelling van Israëls eerste koning in de Masoretische tekst van het oude Testament,* Amsterdam 1977, 101–15. The last-mentioned does not see these accounts as duplicates, but rather as complementary (101f.).

11. Cf. L. A. Sinclair, 'An Archaeological Study of Gibeah', *BA* 27, 1964, 52–64.

12. Thus e.g. *SHI,* 63. A different view is held by A. H. J. Gunneweg, *Geschichte Israels bis Bar Kochba,* ²1976, 56, who puts the liberation of Jabesh in Saul's youth.

13. See also R. Hallevy, 'Charismatic kingship in Israel', *Tarbiz* 30, 1960/61, 314–40, and Soggin, op. cit., 45. Cf., however, W. Beyerlin, 'Das Königscharisma bei Saul', *ZAW* 73, 1961, 186–201, who emphasizes the differences.

14. See also e.g. Soggin, op. cit., 41ff.; Mettinger, op. cit., 87, 96. According to

H. Seebass, 'Die Vorgeschichte der Königserhebung Sauls', *ZAW* 79, 1967, 155, Saul's victory over the Ammonites was the occasion of the anointing of Saul mentioned in I Sam. 9.16—10.1.

15. Thus E. Lipiński, 'Nagid, der Kronprinz', *VT* XXIV, 1974, 497–9. See also Mettinger, op. cit., 152ff., and passim. Other views are those of W. Richter, 'Die *nagid*-Formel. Ein Beitrag zur Erhellung des *nagid*-Problems', *BZ*, NF 9, 1965, 81f.: the *nagid* is the 'saviour'; L. Schmidt, *Menschlicher Erfolg und Jahwes Initiative, Studien zu Tradition, Interpretation und Historie in den Ueberlieferungen von Gideon, Saul und David*, WMANT 38, 1970, 141–171: the *nagid* is the leader of the tribal militia from the time before the monarchy. There is an outstanding survey of the use and significance of this title in the Old Testament by T. Ishida, '*Nagid*. Term for the Legitimation of the Kingship', *AJBI* III, 1977, 35–51.

16. See Lipiński, op. cit., and Mettinger, op. cit., 158.

17. See now Smelik, op. cit., 187ff.

18. See also G. Wallis, 'Die Anfange des Königtums in Israel', *WZMLUHW* 12, 1963, 239–47.

19. See e.g. Veijola, op. cit., 91.

20. Thus e.g. Sinclair, op. cit., 52ff.

21. According to J. Blenkinsopp, 'Did Saul Make Gibeon his Capital?', *VT* XXIV, 1974, 1–7, he was even successful for a while.

22. E.g. K. D. Schunck, *Benjamin. Untersuchungen zur Enststehung und Geschichte eines israelitischen Stammes*, BZAW 86, 1963, 131f., and Blenkinsopp, op. cit., 1–7.

23. So also Ishida, *The Royal Dynasties in Ancient Israel*, 77.

24. The book by K. A. D. Smelik (see n.10 above) gives a good picture of this.

25. For the figure of Samuel in the Old Testament see e.g. A. Weiser, '*Samuel'. Seine geschichtliche Aufxgabe und religiöse Bedeutung*, FRLANT 81, 1962; J. L. McKenzie, 'The Four Samuels', *BR* 7, 1963, 3–18; H. Bardtke, 'Samuel und Saul. Gedanken zur Entstehung des Königtums in Israel', *BiOr* XXV, 1968, 289–302.

26. For these chapters see Soggin, op. cit., 29ff.; Boecker, op. cit.; Birch, op. cit.; Veijola, op. cit., 30ff.; Smelik, op. cit., 100ff. Crüsemann, op. cit., 54ff.

27. The last to be mentioned in this respect might be John the Baptist. See Matt. 14.3–5 par.

28. Cf. e.g. I Sam. 8.11–17, and see 7.1.

29. *HI*, 187.

30. Soggin, op. cit., 55.

31. See Soggin, op. cit., 65f., and H. J. Stoebe, *Das erste Buch Samuelis*, KAT VIII 1, 1973, 240.

32. This view has been rejected e.g. by O. Eissfeldt, *The Old Testament. An Introduction*, Oxford 1965, 137ff., 271ff. Vriezen regards I Sam. 11—14; 16.14–I Kings 2 as a unity. See LOI, 210.

33. See the surveys in Mettinger, op. cit., 33–47; Ishida, op. cit., 55f.; and W. Dietrich, 'David in Ueberlieferung und Geschichte', *VuF* 22/1, 1977, 49ff., and also esp. J. H. Grønbaek, *Die Geschichte vom Aufstieg Davids (I Sam. 15 — II Sam. 5). Tradition und Komposition*, Copenhagen 1971; F. Schiklberger, 'Die Daviden und das Nordreich. Beobachtungen zur sogenannte Geschichte vom Aufstieg Davids', *BZ* NF 18, 1974, 255–63; W. Thiel, 'Die David-Geschichten im Alten Testament', *ZdZ* 31, 1977, 161ff.

34. Soggin, op. cit., 58.

35. Perhaps in this context Jonathan too should be seen as standing in contrast to

Saul. See D. Jobling, 'Saul's Fall and Jonathan's Rise. Tradition and Redaction in
I Sam. 14.1–46', *JBL* 95, 1976, 367–76. Cf. also I Sam. 19–20.

36. Cf. also the attempt at harmonization in I Chron. 20.5.

37. See also I Sam. 26.17, 21, 25.

38. So also M. David, *Die Adoption im altbabylonischen Recht*, Leipzig 1927, 78f.;
Ishida, op. cit., 61. Cf. e.g. also Ps. 2.7.

39. On this see R. de Vaux, *Ancient Israel*, London 1961, 51f.

40. See O. R. Gurney, *The Hittites*, Harmondsworth ³1961, 171.

41. Michal, who in the meantime had been married again, was then separated from
her husband with great force. See II Sam. 3.15–16.

42. See Stoebe, op. cit., 411.

43. As is supposed by M. Noth, *History of Israel*, London ²1960, 176f., on the basis of
I Sam. 13.1. Stoebe, op. cit., 246, has strong arguments to the contrary.

44. In this connection see e.g. the good psychological character sketch given of
David by J. Pedersen, *Israel. Its Life and Culture*, I, II, Copenhagen 1926, 188ff.

45. Y. Aharoni, *The Land of the Bible*, London 1974, 255–7, raises the possibility that
II Sam. 2.8–9 speaks of five administrative districts instituted by Saul.

46. See above, 7.2, and also P. W. Lapp, 'Tell el-Fûl', *BA* 28, 1965, 2–10.

47. Including perhaps the 'Apiru. See Excursus I and J. Weingreen, 'Saul and the
Habiru', FWCJS, Papers, Vol.I, Jerusalem 1967, 63–66.

48. See now Smelik, op. cit., 211ff.

49. We find other accounts which deal with fights of this kind in I Sam. 17; 18.6–7;
23.1–5. However, this is not so much a question of Saul as of David.

50. See 6.4.5.

51. The uncertainty of Saul is illustrated by the Deuteronomistic redaction with the
story of Saul's visit to the witch of Endor (I Sam. 28.3–25). For this see now W. A. M.
Beuken, 'I Samuel 28: The Prophet as "Hammer of Witches"', *JSOT* 6, 1976, 3–17.

52. According to T. Koizumi, 'On the Battle of Gilboa', *AJBI* 2, 1976, 61–78, Saul was
killed by the Philistines, who came to the support of Canaanites to the north of the plain
of Jezreel whom Saul was attempting to subject.

53. For the importance of this city see A. Alt, 'Zur Geschichte von Beth-Sean
1500–1000 v. Chr.', *PJB* 22, 1926 = *KS* I, 246–255, and G. M. Fitzgerald, 'Beth-shean',
AOTS, 185–96.

Chapter 8 David

1. Thus T. N. D. Mettinger, *King and Messiah. The Civil and Sacral Legitimation of the
Israelite Kings*, Lund 1976, 207. Cf. also the detailed discussion of these problems in
Mettinger, op. cit., 123ff., 174ff., 208ff.

2. Thus Mettinger, op. cit., 177.

3. Thus J. H. Grønbaek, *Die Geschichte vom Aufstieg Davids (I. Sam 15—
2.Sam.5).Tradition und Komposition*, Copenhagen 1971, 71ff., and T. Ishida, *The Royal
Dynasties in Ancient Israel*, Berlin–New York 1977, 77. Mettinger, op. cit., 177ff., differs.

4. Thus A. Weiser, 'Die Legitimation des Königs David', *VT* XVI, 1966, 325–54;
Grønbaek, op. cit., 16ff.; Mettinger, op. cit., 35.

5. Thus already A. Alt, 'The Formation of the Israelite State in Palestine',
EOTHR, 186 n.34; *HIOTT*, 149f.; G. Fohrer, *Geschichte Israels*, Heidelberg 1977, 92.

6. J. Conrad, 'Zum geschichtlichen Hintergrund der Darstellung von Davids
Aufsteig', *TLZ* 97, 1972, 321–32, sees 'the history of the rise of David' as a 'consciously

shaped' account directed against the later usurpers of the northern kingdom.

7. For other views about the end of the complex see the surveys in Mettinger, op. cit., 33ff., and Ishida, op. cit., 55f.

8. Like e.g. I Sam. 21.2–9; I Sam. 31. See further also Ishida, op. cit., 59 n.20.

9. See also 7.4.

10. For David's standing army see also A. van Selms, 'The Armed Forces under Saul and David. Studies on the Books of Samuel', *OTWSA* 3, 1960, esp. 60ff.

11. This account is certainly based on an old tradition and records a historical situation. See H. J. Stoebe, *Das Erste Buch Samuelis*, KAT VIII, 1, 1973, 452f.

12. For the origins of these wives see the account in Ishida, op. cit., 64 and n.40.

13. See ch.18.

14. For En-gedi see B. Mazar, 'En-gedi', *AOTS*, esp. 223.

15. See Stoebe, op. cit., 406f.

16. There also seems to be mention of an attempt in this direction in I Sam. 21.10–15 (which came to nothing). See J. A. Soggin, *Das Königtum in Israel. Ursprünge, Spannungen, Entwicklung*, BZAW 104, 1967, 62 n.7.

17. Thus also Soggin, op. cit., 62 n.7, and Stoebe, op. cit., 475.

18. The location of this place is unknown. Cf. *HIOTT*, 169n. 18.

19. Cf. also the statement in I Sam. 23.12 that the inhabitants of Keilah would certainly hand him over to Saul.

20. For this action see B. O. Long, 'The Effect of Divination upon Israelite Literature', *JBL* 92, 1974, 489–97. Perhaps this inquiry indicates that the move to Hebron represented a critical stage. Thus at least Soggin, op. cit., 64.

21. I Chron. 12.23ff. gives a list of the men who were with David in Hebron. For the numbers given here see K. Roubos, *I Kronieken*, POT, 1969, 198.

22. *HI*, 191.

23. For this development see Mettinger, op. cit., 185ff.

24. Thus W. Richter, *Traditionsgeschichtliche Untersuchungen zum Richterbuch*, BBB 18, 1963, 289ff., and id., 'Die *nagid*-Formel', *BZ* 9, 1965, 76 and 83.

25. Thus R. de Vaux 'The King of Israel, Vassal of Yahweh', in *The Bible and the Ancient Near East*, London 1972, 152–80.

26. Thus E. Kutsch, *Salbung als Rechtsakt im Alten Testament und alten Orient*, BZAW 87, 1963, 56.

27. At any event, the text of II Sam. 2 does not state explicitly that there is an alliance between the men of Judah and David (thus Alt, *EOTHR*, 217).

28. *HIOTT*, 153.

29. Called Ishbaal in e.g. I Chron. 8.33.

30. J. A. Soggin, 'The Reign of 'Esba'al, Son of Saul', *Old Testament and Oriental Studies*, BiOp 29, 1975, 40.

31. In II Sam. 2.12–32 we also have a remarkable account of a mock-battle between the young men of Abner and Joab. See F. C. Fensham, 'The Battle between the Men of Joab as a possible Ordeal by Battle', *VT* XX, 1970, 356–8, who refers to some extra-biblical parallels.

32. H. J. Stoebe, 'David und Mikal, Ueberlieferungen zur Jugendgeschichte Davids', *Von Ugarit nach Qumran*, Festschrift für O. Eissfeldt, BZAW 77, 1961, 224–243, doubts whether one can speak of an earlier marriage between David and Michal, see also id., op. cit., 352f.

33. This was quite a common occurrence in the ancient Near East. For it, and for parallels, see now Ishida, op. cit., 74.

34. See also I Chron. 11.1–3. Chronicles does not mention the anointing by the men of Judah.

35. Thus already *EOTHR*, 217, and also e.g. *HIOTT*, 159, Fohrer, op. cit., 95. C. J. Goslinga, 'Het koningschap van David over de twaalf stammen Israels', *Exegetica* 4, 1, The Hague 1963, 8ff., fiercely challenges this.

36. Here we have the usual pattern: 1. appointment by Yahweh; 2. confirmation by the assembly of the people; 3. anointing. For this see e.g. Soggin, op. cit., 69, and also 8.1.1 and the literature mentioned there.

37. See *ANET*, 329 and *EA* 287, 289, 290 respectively. For Jerusalem in this period see also B. Mazar (Maissler), 'Das vordavidische Jerusalem', *JPOS* X, 1930, 181–91; D. R. Ap-Thomas, 'Jerusalem', *AOTS*, 1969, 277ff.; K. D. Schunck, 'Juda und Jerusalem in vor- und frühisraelitischer Zeit', *Schalom, Festschrift für A. Jepsen*, Berlin 1971, 50ff., and *EAEHL*, 579f. For the question of the census in II Sam. 5.6 see also W. G. E. Watson, 'David ousts the City Ruler of Jebus', *VT* XXX, 1970, 501f.

38. So e.g. J. Maxwell Miller, 'Jebus and Jerusalem: A Case of Mistaken Identity', *ZDPV* 90, 1974, 115–27. A different view is taken by G. Buccellati, *Cities and Nations of Ancient Syria. An Essay on Political Institutions with Special Reference to the Israelite Kingdoms*, Rome 1967, 237; T. A. Busink, *Der Tempel von Jerusalem. Von Salomo bis Herodes* I, Leiden 1970, 98.

39. See e.g. H. J. Stoebe, 'Die Einnahme Jerusalems und der Sinnôr', *ZDVP* 73, 1957, 73–99. On associated problems see further K. M. Kenyon, 'Excavations in Jerusalem', *BA* 27, 1964, 34–52.

40. II Sam. 5.6. In I Chron. 11.4 there is mention of 'all Israel' in this connection. However, this is a later tradition.

41. But see Ishida, op. cit., 129f.

42. For David's officials and the development of his administration along Egyptian and Canaanite lines see e.g. R. de Vaux, *Ancient Israel*, 127ff., and T. N. D. Mettinger, *Solomonic State Officials. A Study of the Civil Government Officials of the Israelite Monarchy*, Lund 1971. For the Cherethites and Pelethites see further e.g. L. M. Muntingh, 'The Cherethites and the Pelethites. A Historical and Sociological Discussion', *OTWSA* 3, 1960, 43–53. Herrmann, *HIOTT* 171 n.46, points in particular to the international character of these troops.

43. For discussion of this point see Ishida, op. cit., 129 n.76.

44. See above all A. Alt, 'Jerusalems Aufstieg', *ZDMG* 79, 1925 = *KS* III, 243–57.

45. Alt, op. cit., 253.

46. For the archaeological evidence relating to the city of David, see K. M. Kenyon, 'Excavations at Jerusalem', *PEQ* 98, 1966, 77ff.; Ap-Thomas, op. cit., 285ff.; *EAEHL*, 587ff.

47. See e.g. Num. 21.26 (Heshbon becomes the 'city of Sihon') and Judg. 18.29 (Laish becomes Dan). For other, non-biblical parallels, see now Ishida, op. cit., 122ff.

48. According to C. E. Hauer, 'Jerusalem, the stronghold and Rephaim', *CBQ* 32, 1970, 571–8.

49. Cf. II Sam. 17, 22 and see also Hauer, op. cit.

50. Cf. also II Sam. 8.1; I Chron. 18.1.

51. See 5.1.3.

52. See II Sam. 8.1–14 (I Chron. 18.2–13); II Sam. 10 (I Chron. 19); II Sam. 12.26–31 (I Chron. 20.1–3) and A. Malamat, 'Aspects of the Foreign Policies of David and Solomon', *JNES* 22, 1963, 1–17; M.Bič, 'Davids Kriegsführung und Salomos

Notes to pages 103–105

243

Bautätigkeit', *Travels in the World of the Old Testament*, Festschrift for M. A. Beek, Assen 1974, 1–12.

53. See A. Alt, 'Megiddo im Uebergang vom Kanaanäischen zum Israelitischen Zeitalter', *ZAW* 19 (1944) = *KS* 1, 271f.

54. See e.g. J. C. Craviotti, 'Estrategia de David al servicio de la economia', *Rivista Biblica* 22, 1960, 65–71.

55. They probably did not include the city of Tyre, cf. II Sam. 5.11; I Kings 5.1. In this connection see also K. Elliger, 'Die Nordgrenze des Reiches Davids', *PJB* XXXII, 1936, 34–73, and for other boundaries, O. Eissfeldt, 'Israelitisch-philistäische Grenz-verschiebungen von David bis auf die Assyrerzeit', *ZDVP* 66, 1943=*KS* II, 453–63.

56. See F. Stolz, 'Aspekte religiöser und sozialer Ordnung im alten Israel', *ZEE* 17, 1973, 145–59.

57. See also 8.5.2.

58. See M. Noth, 'Jerusalem and the Israelite Tradition', *The Laws in the Pentateuch and Other Studies*, Edinburgh 1966, 132–44 and O. Eissfeldt, 'Silo und Jerusalem', SVT IV, 1957, 138–48.

59. Cf., however, J. Dus, 'Die Länge der Gefangenschaft der Lade in Philisterland', *NTT* 18, 1963–64, 440–52, and P. R. Davies, 'The History of the Ark in the Books of Samuel', *JNSL* 5, 1977, 9–18.

60. See H. Ringgren, *Israelite Religion*, London 1969, 60.

61. Cf. I Sam. 14.3; 22.20.

62. Many people are of the opinion that he belonged to the Jebusite priesthood in Jerusalem. See e.g. H. H. Rowley, *Men of God, Studies in Old Testament History and Prophecy*, London and Edinburgh 1963, 264 n.3. F. M. Cross, *CMHE*, 208, regards Zadok as an Aaronite priest from Hebron. For other views of Zadok's origins see A. Cody, *A History of the Old Testament Priesthood*, Rome 1969, 88–93.

63. The interpretation of Gen. 14.18–20 presents great problems. See now especially J. A. Emerton, 'Some False Clues in the Study of Genesis XIV', *VT* XXI, 1971, 24–47, and id., 'The Riddle of Genesis XIV', *VT* XXI, 1971, 403–39, esp. 407–26. These verses are usually dated in the time of David or shortly afterwards (Emerton, 426). However, we cannot be sufficiently certain about this.

64. Thus Emerton, op. cit., 437.

65. See e.g. M. J. Mulder, 'Kanaänitische goden in het Oude Testament', *Exegetica* 4/4, 5, The Hague 1965, 16, 18 and Ishida, op. cit., 137f.

66. See e.g. J. A. Soggin, 'Der offiziell geförderte Synkretismus in Israel während des 10. Jahrhunderts', *ZAW* 78, 1966, 179–204.

67. Ishida, op. cit., 139.

68. See Ishida, op. cit., 179. These traditions come to the fore particularly in the Psalms. See e.g. J. Kühlewein, *Geschichte in den Psalmen*, Stuttgart 1973, 141–3, 145f.

69. H. Klengel, *Zwischen Zelt und Palast. Die Begegnung von Nomaden und Sesshaften im alten Vorderasien*, Leipzig 1972, 138.

70. For these developments and the conflicts connected with them see e.g. Stolz, op. cit., 145–59. Also A. Alt, 'Das Anteil des Königtums an der sozialen Entwicklung in den Reichen Israel und Juda', *KS* III, 348–72, who regards the introduction of the monarchy as the main cause of these changes.

71. Thus at least Stolz, op. cit., 151ff. A different view is taken, however, by e.g. A. Causse, *Du groupe ethnique à la Communauté religieuse. Le problème sociologique de la religion d'Israel*, Paris 1937, 62, who sees the programme of these prophets as a 'return to

the past'. Cf. also M. Weber, *Ancient Judaism*, New York and London 1967, 123.

72. See also 8.4.2 and the literature mentioned in n.42 there. Perhaps the title 'king's friend' also betrays Egyptian influence; it is given to both Hushai (II Sam 15.37) and Zabud (I Kings 4.5). See H. Donner, 'Der "Freund des Konigs"', *ZAW* 73, 1961, 269–77.

73. For this purchase and the problems connected with it see now the extensive study by K. Rupprecht, *Der Tempel von Jerusalem. Gründung Salomos oder jebusitisches Erbe?*, BZAW 144, 1976.

74. A different view is taken by N. R. M. Poulssen, *König und Tempel im Glaubenszeugnis des Alten Testaments*, Stuttgart 1967, 175. See also 9.3 below.

75. For a survey of this material see C. J. Goslinga, *II Samuël*, COT, 1962, 132ff.; Ishida, op. cit., 81ff.

76. For this see Mettinger, op. cit., 48–63; Ishida, op. cit., 81ff., and esp. 98.

77. For a survey see Ishida, op. cit., 81 n.1.

78. Thus E. Lipiński, *Le poème royal du Psaume LXXXIX, 1–5, 20–38*, Paris 1967, 91.

79. Thus E. S. Mulder, 'The Prophecy of Nathan in II Sam. 7', *Studies on the Books of Samuel*, OTWSA 3, 1960, 36; Ishida, op. cit., 82.

80. So also Cross, op. cit., 254; Mettinger, op. cit., 61.

81. H. Gese, 'Der Davidsbund und die Zionserwählung', *ZTK*, NF 61, 1964, 20.

82. Cf. also G. W. Ahlström, 'Der Prophet Nathan und der Tempelbau', *VT* XI, 1961, 113–27.

83. II Sam. 7.8–16. For the literary problems in this pericope see T. Veijola, *Die ewige Dynastie. David und die Enstehung seiner Dynastie nach der deuteronomistischen Darstellung*. Helsinki 1976, 68ff.; Mettinger, op. cit., 52ff.; Ishida, op. cit., 97f.

84. The authenticity of v.13 (the reference to Solomon building the temple) plays an important role in the discussion. Some scholars defend it, including C. J. Labuschagne, 'Some Remarks on the Prayer of David in II Sam. 7', OTWSA 3, 1960, 32, and Gese, op. cit., 23. According to Mettinger, op. cit., 57, v.13a serves to stress that Solomon is the particular son of David whose kingship is established by God (v.12a). Poulssen, op. cit., 44ff., sees v.13 as the connecting link between various traditions.

85. In this connection see e.g. also Ex. 4.22; Ps. 2.7; 89.27–28.

86. The vassal treaties from the ancient Near East are instructive in this respect. See D. J. McCarthy, *Old Testament Covenant*, Oxford 1972, 66. Cf. also G. Cooke, 'The Israelite King as Son of God', *ZAW* 73, 1961, 210–18.

87. See also Cooke, op. cit., 225.

88. See above all R. E. Clements, *Abraham and David. Genesis 15 and its Meaning for Israelite Tradition*, SBT II 5, 1967.

89. L. Rost, *Die Ueberlieferung von der Thronnachfolge Davids*, BWANT III, 6, 1926.

90. Some scholars, e.g. R. A. Carlson, *David the Chosen King. A Traditio-Historical Approach to the Second Book of Samuel*, Uppsala 1964, 131ff.; K. A. D. Smelik, *Saul, de voorstelling van Israels eerste koning in de Masoretische text van het Oude Testament*, Amsterdam 1977, 76ff., hold different views.

91. For the literary-critical problems and the extent of this series of stories see now D. M. Gunn, 'Narrative Patterns and Oral Tradition in Judges and Samuel', *VT* XXIV, 1974, 286ff.; id., 'Traditional Composition in the "Successive Narrative"', *VT* XXVI, 1976, 214ff., and J. van Seters, 'Problems in the Literary Analysis of the Court History of David', *JSOT* 1, 1976, 22ff. In addition to Rost (see n.89), see also J. W. Flanagan, 'Court History or Succession Document? A Study of 2. Sam. 9–20 and I Kings 1–2',

JBL 91, 1972, and E. Würthwein, *Die Erzählung von der Thronnachfolge Davids – theologische oder politische Geschichtsschreibung?*, Zurich 1974, who puts particular stress on the critical attitude to David in these stories. Cf. also R. N. Whybray, *The Succession Narrative: A Study of II Samuel 9—20 and I Kings 1 and 2*, SBT II 9, 1968, who points, for example, to borrowing from Wisdom circles.

92. For this story see now J. Hoftijzer, 'Absalom and Tamar: A Case of Fratriarchy?', *Schrift en Uitleg*, Festschrift for W. H. Gispen, Kampen 1970, 55–61.

93. In II Sam. 14.1–24 a reconciliation takes place between David and Absalom, who had fled after the murder of Amnon to Geshur, where his mother came from. See J. Hoftijzer, 'David and the Tekoite Woman', *VT* XX, 1970, 419–44.

94. We also get some impression from this story of the boundaries of David's kingdom. See P. W. Skean, 'Joab's Census: How far North? (II Sam. 24.6)', *CBQ* XXXI, 1969, 42–9.

95. See above, esp. nn.92, 93.

96. So J. Weingreen, 'The Rebellion of Absalom', *VT* XIX, 1969, 263–6. Ahithophel was probably Bathsheba's grandfather! (cf. II Sam. 23.34; 11.3).

97. Thus e.g. *HIOTT*, 164. Cf. also H. Bardtke, 'Erwägungen zur Rolle Judas im Aufstand des Absalom', *Wort und Geschichte*, Festschrift for K. Elliger, AOAT 18, 1973, 1–8.

98. *HIOTT*, 164.

99. In II Sam. 18.18 there is mention of a monument to Absalom. In connection with this see now the ostracon of Ophel, where lines 2 and 3 mention 'the valley of the monument'. On this see *IH*, 239–43.

100. Thus e.g. Ishida, op. cit., 70f. R. de Vaux, *Ancient Israel*, 140, differs.

101. According to *SHI*, 86, the absence of the name Judah from these lists can also mean that Judah had its own system for collecting taxes.

102. Thus e.g. also *HIOTT*, 177.

103. See Ishida, op. cit., 152.

104. See E. Ball, 'The Co-regency of David and Solomon (I Kings 1)', *VT* XXVII, 1977, 268–80.

105. See above, e.g. 7.2; 8.2.

106. For this see also Veijola, op. cit., 16ff., and F. Langlemet, 'Pour ou contre Salomon? La rédaction prosalomonienne de I Rois I-II', *RB* 83, 1976, 321–79, 481–528.

Chapter 9 Solomon

1. See especially the study by F. Langlamet, cited in ch. 8 n.106.

2. For the sources of the Deuteronomist in the books of Kings see e.g. A. Jepsen, *Die Quellen des Königsbuches*, Halle ²1956; *LOI*, 215ff.; J. Gray, *I & II Kings*, OTL, ²1970, 6ff. For Chronicles see e.g. W. Rudolph, *Chronikbücher*, HAT 21, 1955, X–XIII, and *LOI*, 305f. For this material see also below, 16.6 and 18.6.

3. For these high places see e.g. R. de Vaux, *Ancient Israel*, 284–8.

4. = el-Jib, about six miles north-west of Jerusalem.

5. See e.g. A. L. Oppenheim, *The Interpretation of Dreams in the Ancient Near East*, Philadelphia 1956.

6. See *ANET*, 448ff. Cf. also S. Herrmann, 'Die Königsnovelle in Ägypten und in Israel', *WZUL* 3, 1953/54, 51–62; M. Görg, *Gott-König-Reden in Israel und Aegypten*, BWANT VI, 5, 1975, 16–115, who see a connection with Egyptian texts, and e.g. A. S.

Kapelrud, 'Temple Building a Task for Gods and Kings', *Orient* 32, 1963, 56–62, who affirms the same thing on the basis of Akkadian texts.

7. See H. A. Brongers, *I. Koningen*, POT, 1967, 51ff., and Gray, op. cit., 133ff.

8. So too J. A. Soggin in *IJH*, 366.

9. Different versions of this story also occur in the literature of Jainism. See J. G. Frazer, *Folklore in the Old Testament* II, London 1919, 570f.

10. For this see M. Noth and D. Winton Thomas, eds., *Wisdom in Israel and in the Ancient Near East. Presented to H. H. Rowley in celebration of his 65th birthday*, SVT III, 1955, and H. H. Schmid, *Wesen und Geschichte der Weisheit. Eine Untersuchung zur Altorientalischen und Israelitischen Weisheitsliteratur*, BZAW 101, 1966.

11. I Kings 3.1; 7.8; 9.16; 9.24; 11.1.

12. The text, along with a detailed commentary, may be found in A. H. Gardiner, *Ancient Egyptian Onomastica*, I–III, London 1947.

13. Thus W. F. Albright, *Yahweh and the Gods of Canaan*, New York and London 1968, 217–19.

14. See also 8.5.2.

15. See K. Roubos, *I Kronieken*, POT, 1969, 30–58.

16. Thus especially R. Braun, 'Solomon, the Chosen Temple Builder: The Significance of I Chronicles 22.28 and 29 for the Theology of Chronicles', *JBL* 95, 1976, 581–90.

17. K. Rupprecht, *Der Tempel von Jerusalem. Gründung Salomos oder jebusitischen Erbe?*, BZAW 144, 1976, 5ff., 105ff.; id., 'Die Zuverlässigkeit der Ueberlieferung von Salomos Tempelgründung', ZAW 89, 1977, 205–14.

18. T. A. Busink, *Der Tempel von Jerusalem von Salomo bis Herodes. Eine archäologisch-historische Studie unter Berücksichtigung des Westsemitischen Tempelbaus. I. Der Tempel Salomos*, Leiden 1970, esp. 617ff. H. Ringgren, *Israelite Religion*, London 1966, 61, differs.

19. For a detailed comment on this whole question see Busink, op. cit., 1–76.

20. Thus Alt, *EOTHR*, 218, and Brongers, op. cit., 76. A different view is taken by T. Ishida, *The Royal Dynasties in Ancient Israel*, BZAW 142, 1977, 144. Cf. also Busink, op. cit., 618ff.

21. T. C. Vriezen, *The Religion of Ancient Israel*, London 1967, 183.

22. See Y. Aharoni, 'The Negeb', *AOTS*, 395–7.

23. This differed, therefore, from Canaanite temples, the orientation of which was to the east or the north.

24. See e.g. I Kings 6.2; 7.2.

25. According to Vriezen, there are two possibilities here: either the author concentrated on the building of the temple, or he preferred to keep quiet about the sins of these kings. See *LOI*, 305.

26. See e.g. M. Bič, 'Davids Kriegsführung und Salomos Bautätigkeit', *Travels in the World of the Old Testament*, Festschrift for M. A. Beek, Assen 1974, 1–11.

27. The designation 'house: wood of Lebanon' in I Kings 7.2 is a strange one. See Brongers, op. cit., 83, and M. J. Mulder, 'Einige Bemerkungen zur Beschreibung des Libanonwaldhaus in I Reg 7, 2f'., *ZAW* 88, 1976, 99–105.

28. For this see K. R. Veenhof, 'De muren van Jerusalem', *Phoenix* XI, 1965, 214–21, and now also *EAEHL* II, 584 (map), 587ff.

29. See now *EAEHL* II, 485, 441; III, 853ff. In other places, too, archaeological investigations have brought to light the remains of building work from the time of

Solomon. E.g. there are the remains of a citadel in Arad. See J. Campbell, 'The Renascence of the Iron Age of Arad', *BA* 40, 1977, 34–37.

30. Y. Aharoni, 'Forerunners of the *Limes*: Iron Age Fortresses in the Negev', *IEJ* 17, 1967, 1–17.

31. See also Ps. 72, a psalm which is attributed to Solomon and in which the word 'peace' has an important role.

32. For this account see now e.g. J. R. Bartlett, 'An Adversary against Solomon, Hadad the Edomite', *ZAW* 88, 1975, 205–26.

33. See I Kings 9.19; 10.26.

34. For these problems see Gray, op. cit., 118ff., and also S. H. Horn, 'Who was Solomon's Egyptian Father-in-Law?', *BR* 12, 1967, 3–17.

35. These words are generally regarded as a gloss.

36. Naamah, the mother of Rehoboam, was an Ammonite woman (I Kings 14.21).

37. See H. J. Katzenstein, *The History of Tyre*, Jerusalem 1973, 96ff., and S. Moscati, *The World of the Phoenicians*, London 1973, esp. 31ff.

38. See also F. C. Fensham, 'The Treaty between the Israelites and the Tyrians', *SVT* XVII, 1969, 71–87.

39. M. Noth, *Könige*, BKAT IX, 1, 1968, 210, however, regards these two verses as a later addition.

40. See Fensham, op. cit., 78.

41. Thus C. van Gelderen, *De boeken der Koningen* II, KV, 1956, 193f.; Noth, op. cit., 215; Gray, op. cit., 256. Bright, *HI*, 210 differs; he thinks in terms of Somalia.

42. For this see e.g. D. S. Attema, 'Arabië en de Bijbel', *Exegetica* 3/4, The Hague 1961, 41–43.

43. See Attema, op. cit., 25–27.

44. For these problematical names see e.g. H. Tadmor, 'Que and Musri', *IEJ* 11, 1961, 143–50.

45. See N. Glueck, 'Ezion-Geber', *BA* 28, 1965, 70–87. Cf. here above all B. Rothenberg, 'Ancient Copper Industries in the Western Arabah', *PEQ* 94, 1962, 5–71; id., *Timna: Valley of the Biblical Copper Mines*, London 1972.

46. See also 8.5.3 and E. Neufeld, 'The Emergence of a Royal-Urban Society in Ancient Israel', *HUCA* 31, 1960, 31–53.

47. Thus e.g. A. Alt, *Israels Gaue unter Salomo*, Leipzig 1913=*KS II*, 76–89; W. F. Albright, 'The Administrative Divisions of Israel and Judah', *JPOS* V, 1925, 17–54, and G. E. Wright, 'The Provinces of Solomon', *EI* VIII, 1967, 58–68.

48. For Solomon's officials see now e.g. T. N. D. Mettinger, *Solomonic State Officials. A Study of the Civil Government Officials of the Israelite Monarchy*, Lund 1971.

49. D. B. Redford, 'Studies in Relations between Palestine and Egypt during the First Millennium BC: I The Taxation System of Solomon', in J. W. Wevers and D. B. Redford (eds.), *Studies on the Ancient World presented to Professor F. V. Winnett on the Occasion of his Retirement*, TSTS 2, Toronto 1972, 141–56.

50. In the OT this is Shishak (see I Kings 14.25).

51. See A. F. Rainey, 'Compulsory Labour Gangs in Ancient Israel', *IEJ* 20, 1970, 191–202. For this material see also J. Schifman, 'Royal Service Obligation in Palestine in the First Half of the First Millennium BC, according to Biblical Tradition', *VDI* 1967.1, 38–48 (Russian with English summary).

52. See e.g. in the NT John 4.9.

53. A. Caquot, 'Ahiyya de Silo et Jéroboam Ier', *Semitica* XI, 1961, 17–28. According

to M. A. Cohen, 'The Role of the Shilonite Priesthood in the United Monarchy of Ancient Israel', *HUCA* 36, 1965, 59–98, the priests of Shiloh played a prominent role in the political changes between Saul and David and Solomon and Jeroboam.

54. According to A. van der Born, *Koningen*, BOT, 1958, 76, I Kings 11.29–31, 36f. is a Deuteronomistic composition. Noth, op. cit., 246f., differs.

55. For a discussion of the dating of Chronicles see e.g. the excursus in P. Welten, *Geschichte und Geschichtsdarstellung in den Chronikbuchern*, WMANT 42, 1973, 199–200, and now H. G. M. Williamson, *Israel in the Books of Chronicles*, Cambridge 1977, 83–86. The latter thinks in terms of the fourth century BC, the former of the third century BC.

Excursus III   Chronology of the Kings of Israel and Judah

1. For Babylon, see e.g. *ANET*, 271.

2. See e.g. *ANET*, 274.

3. See also Ezek. 33.21; 40.1: 'in the twelfth (twenty-fifth) year of our captivity'. Ezekiel was among the captives taken into exile at the same time as Jehoiachin.

4. This last method was often used in Egypt. See J. Finegan, *Handbook of Biblical Chronology*, Princeton 1964, 77–82.

5. According to M. Weippert, *BRL*, 165ff., the evidence of the Gezer calendar from about 925 BC shows that in this area the year still began in the autumn. E. R. Thiele, *The Mysterious Numbers of the Hebrew Kings*, Chicago ²1965, however, stresses that in Israel the year began in the spring from the time of Jeroboam I. As to Judah, A. Malamat, 'The Last Kings of Judah and the Fall of Jerusalem', *IEJ* 18, 1968, 137–56, thinks that until the fall of Jerusalem people there still counted the years of the kings' reigns from New Year's Day in the spring. A different view, however, is held by E. Kutsch, 'Das Jahr der Katastrophe, 587 v. Chr., Kritische Erwägungen zu neueren chronologischen Versuchen', *Biblica* 55, 1974, 520–45.

6. In Chronicles only in respect of the kings of Judah.

7. For this see e.g. C. Schedl, 'Textkritische Bemerkungen zu den Synchronismen der Könige von Israel und Juda', *VT* XII, 1962, 88–119.

8. See e.g. I Kings 15.1.

9. Cf. e.g. II Kings 13.1 with 13.10.

10. Cf. e.g. II Kings 8.25 with II Kings 9.29.

11. See J. D. Shenkel, *Chronology and Recensional Development in the Greek Text of Kings*, Cambridge, Mass. 1968.

12. See e.g. J. Maxwell Miller, *The Old Testament and the Historian*, Philadelphia 1976, 85f.

13. In addition to the works mentioned in this section see also J. Gray, *I & II Kings*, OTL, ²1970, 55–75; G. Larsson, *The Secret System. A Study in the Chronology of the Old Testament*, Leiden 1973.

14. W. F. Albright, 'The Chronology of the Divided Monarchy of Israel', *BASOR* 100, 1945, 16–22, and id., 'Prolegomenon', in C. F. Burney, *The Book of Judges with Introduction and notes on the Hebrew Text of the Books of Kings*, New York 1970, 1–38.

15. K. T. Andersen, *Die Chronologie der Könige von Israel und Juda*, ST 23, 1969, 69–114.

16. J. Begrich, *Die Chronologie der Könige von Israel und Juda*, Tübingen 1929.

17. A. Jepsen and R. Hanhart, *Untersuchungen zur israelitisch-jüdischen Chronologie*, BZAW 88, 1964, 1–48; A. Jepsen, 'Noch einmal zur israelitisch-jüdischen Chronologie', *VT* XVIII, 1968, 31–46.

18. J. Maxwell Miller, 'Another Look at the Chronology of the Early Divided Monarchy', *JBL* 86, 1967, 276–88.

19. V. Pavlovsky and E. Vogt, 'Die Jahre der Könige von Juda und Israel', *Biblica* 45, 1964, 321–47.

20. Thiele, op. cit., and id., 'Coregencies and Overlapping Reigns among the Hebrew Kings', *JBL* 93, 1974, 174–200.

21. R. Wifall, 'The Chronology of the Divided Monarchy of Israel', *ZAW* 80, 1968, 319–37.

22. Begrich, op. cit., 10, 114.

23. The reigns of the kings of the ancient Near East will be given on the basis of J. A. Brinkman, 'Mesopotamian Chronology of the Historical Period', in A. L. Oppenheim, *Ancient Mesopotamia, Portrait of a Dead Civilization*, Chicago-London 1977, 335–48. For the later period see also R. Parker and W. H. Dubberstein, *Babylonian Chronology 626 BC–AD 75*, Providence ⁴1971.

24. Begrich, op. cit., 66–94.

25. Jepsen and Hanhart, op. cit., 28.

26. Andersen, op. cit., see esp. 73.

27. E.g. the assumption of different calendars and dating systems in the two kingdoms. See also E. R. Thiele, *The Mysterious Numbers of the Hebrew Kings*, Chicago ²1965, 14ff.

28. Pavlovsky and Vogt, op. cit., esp. 323.

29. Wifall, op. cit., see esp. the survey on pp. 335f.

30. Maxwell Miller, op. cit.

31. Any discrepancies will be discussed as they appear.

Chapter 10   The First Fifty Years after Solomon

1. See e.g. K. Roubos, *2 Kronieken*, POT, 1972, 117–21. For a further analysis of I Kings 12.1–20 see also e.g. H. A. Brongers, *I Koningen*, POT, 1967, 129ff.; M. Noth, *Könige I*, BKAT IX/1, 1968, 270ff.

2. This information is missing in II Chron. 10.

3. So also e.g. Brongers, op. cit., 129; Noth, op. cit., 273. Note too that the name Jeroboam is missing in I Kings 12.12 LXX.

4. See I Sam. 10.24; II Sam. 5.3.

5. Thus e.g. D. G. Evans, 'Rehoboam's Advisers at Shechem and Political Institutions in Israel and Sumer', *JNES* 25, 1966, 273–79.

6. Thus e.g. A. Malamat, 'Organs of State-Craft in the Israelite Monarchy', *BA* 28, 1965, 34–65.

7. Thus e.g. A. Aruyyah, 'Rehoboam at Shechem (I Reg. 12.6–16)', *Bet Miqrá* 11, 1965/66, Issue 3(27), 156–8 (in Hebrew).

8. Malamat, op. cit., 34–65.

9. Aruyyah, op. cit., 156–8.

10. It is striking that the expression 'on the third day' or 'the third day' almost always has the meaning, in both Old and New Testaments, of a day on which an event happens which is decisive for the history and religion of Israel. See H. Jagersma, '. . . *Ten Derden Dage* . . . ', Kampen 1976, esp. 17ff.

11. According to I Kings 11.28, Solomon had already noted this.

12. On this see e.g. D. W. Gooding, 'The Septuagint's Rival Versions of Jeroboam's

Rise to Power', *VT* XVII, 1967, 173–89; H. Seebass, 'Zur Königserhebung Jerobeams', *VT* XVII, 1967, 325–33.

13. So e.g. *HIOTT*, 196.

14. *ANET*, 242f. This list has been closely investigated e.g. by M. Noth, 'Die Schoschenkliste', *ZDPV* 61, 1938, 277–304, and Y. Aharoni, *The Land of the Bible. A Historical Geography*, London ⁴1974, 283–90. Traces of this campaign have also been found in Megiddo. See J. N. Schofield, 'Megiddo', *AOTS*, 323.

15. So also *HIOTT*, 196.

16. See e.g. J. Debus, *Die Sünde Jerobeams. Studien zur Darstellung Jerobeams und der Geschichte des Nordreichs in der deuteronomistischen Geschichtsschreibung*, FRLANT 93, 1967, 34.

17. For the problems relating to the boundaries between Israel and Judah see A. Alt, 'Zur Geschichte der Grenze zwischen Judäa und Samaria', *PJ* XXXI, 1935, 94-III; Y. Aharoni, 'The Northern Boundary of Judah', *PEQ* XC, 1958, 27–31.

18. Ahijah divided the mantle into twelve pieces, but 10+1=11! For these problems and the discussions of them see M. Noth, *Könige I*, BKAT, IX/1, 1968, 259f.

19. See A. van der Kooij, 'David, "het licht van Israel"', *Vrchten van de Uithof*, Festschrift for H. A. Brongers, Utrecht 1974, esp. 52ff.

20. Thus e.g. K. D. Schunck, *Benjamin, Untersuchungen zur Entstehung und Geschichte eines israelitischen Stammes*, BZAW 86, 1963, 141; *HIOTT*, 198.

21. So also Noth, op. cit., 259.

22. For this name, etc., see now *KAI* 201.

23. Cf. also Isa. 7.9, where Isaiah rebukes king Ahaz for a similar kind of action.

24. See W. I. Chang, *The Tendency of the Chronicler*, Hartford 1973.

25. See F. M. Cross and G. E. Wright, 'The Boundary and Province Lists of the Kingdom of Judah', *JBL* 80, 1956, 202–26, and Y. Yadin, 'The Fourfold Division of Judah', *BASOR* 163, 1961, 6–12.

26. See G. Beyer, 'Das Festungssystem Rechabeams', *ZDPV* 54, 1931, 113–34; O. Tufnell, 'Lachish', *AOTS*, 304.

27. Called Abijah in Chronicles.

28. Noth, op. cit., 332ff., sees this section as typically Deuteronomistic material.

29. G. von Rad, *Old Testament Theology* I, London 1975, 353, calls this discourse 'a brief compendium of the Chronicler's theology'.

30. *HI*, 231. For these problems see further A. van den Born, *Kronieken*, BOT, 1962, 166, and Roubos, op. cit., 151.

31. The view that during his reign Jeroboam also erected a temple in Dor, put forward by N. Avigad, 'The Priest of Dor?', *IEJ* 25, 1975, 101–5, is challenged by M. Haran, 'A Temple at Dor?', *IEJ* 27, 1977, 12–15.

32. For this, in addition to the commentaries see now Debus, op. cit., 35ff.

33. See Vriezen, *The Religion of Ancient Israel*, 187f.; cf. also O. Eissfeldt, 'Lade und Stierbild', *ZAW* 58, 1940/41, 190–215; M. Weippert, 'Gott und Stier', *ZDPV* 77, 1961, 93–117, and J. Dus, 'Ein richterzeitliches Stierbildheiligtum zu Bethel? Die Aufeinanderfolge der frühisraelitischen Zentralkultstatten', *ZAW* 77, 1965, 268–86, who in this connection refers to Ex. 32 (272ff.). For this passage see also M. Auerbach and L. Smolar, 'Aaron, Jeroboam and the Golden Calves', *JBL* 86, 1967, 129–41.

34. Just as, for example, many divine names, like Elyon, were used for Yahweh.

35. Brongers, op. cit., 136.

36. See e.g. Gen. 28.10–22; Judg. 17–18.

37. According to Noth, op. cit., 295, it derived from prophetic circles in northern Israel.
38. *HIOTT*, 194. So also Noth, op. cit., 281.
39. N. Allan, 'Jerobeam and Shechem', *VT* XXIV, 1974, 353–7.
40. See e.g. Debus, op. cit., 49ff.; Noth, op. cit., 312. Cf. also LXX B in 1 Kings 14. 12, 24g-n.
41. According to H. Seebass, 'Die Verwerfung Jerobeams I und Salomos durch die Prophetie des Ahia von Silo', *WO* IV, 1967/68, 163–82, Jeroboam was rejected for the same reasons as Solomon had been.
42. *EOTHR*, 245, 250, 256ff.; cf. also id., 'Das Königtum in den Reichen Israel und Juda', *VT* 1, 1951=*KS* II, 116ff.
43. Thus e.g. by J. A. Soggin, *Das Königtum in Israel. Ursprünge, Spannungen, Entwicklung*, BZAW 104, 1967, 98f.; *HI*, 234; *HIOTT*, 200. A different view is held e.g. by G. Buccellati, *Cities and Nations of Ancient Syria. An Essay on Political Institutions with Special Reference to the Israelite Kingdoms*, Rome 1967, 200ff.; Ishida, op. cit., 151ff.
44. Cf. also II Chron. 19.2–3; 20.34.
45. For this short description see J. M. Miller, 'So Tibni Died (I Kings XVI 22), *VT* XVIII, 1968, 392–4; J. A. Soggin, 'Tibni King of Israel in the First Half of the Ninth Century BC', *RSO* 47, 1972, 171–6.
46. So Soggin, op. cit., 173.

Chapter 11 The Dynasty of Omri

1. According to J. Strange, 'Joram, King of Israel and Judah', *VT* XXV, 1975, 191–201, this Joram of Judah and Ahab's son Jehoram would be one and the same person.
2. According to II Kings 8.18; II Chron. 21.6, a 'daughter of Ahab', and according to II Kings 8.26; II Chron. 22.2, a 'daughter of Omri', and thus a sister of Ahab.
3. See *KAI*, 181, and *ANET*, 320f.
4. See *ANET*, 281, 284, 285.
5. And not 'son of Omri' as e.g. in *ANET*, 280. Cf. H. Tadmor, 'The Historical Inscription of Adad-Nirari III', *Iraq* 35, 1973, 149.
6. So also G. W. Anderson, *The History and Religion of Israel*, Oxford [6]1976, 90. But cf. H. J. Katzenstein, *The History of Tyre*, Jerusalem 1973, 144, and for trade with Tyre, 146ff.
7. For the problems over the translation of this verse see e.g. A. S. van der Woude, 'I Reg. 20, 34', *ZAW* 76, 1964, 188–91, and also G. R. Driver, 'Forgotten Hebrew Idioms', *ZAW* 78, 1966, 1–4.
8. W. F. Albright, 'A Votive Stele erected by Ben-Hadad I of Damascus to the God Melcarth', *BASOR* 87, 1942, 28.
9. The name Ahab is mentioned quite often in II Chron. 18. For a comparison of this chapter with I Kings 22 see K. Roubos, *II Kronieken*, POT, 1972, 178ff.
10. So also *HIOTT*, 215, and H. Donner in *IJH*, 400. Bright, *HI*, 239 n.47, differs.
11. See *ANET*, 278.
12. According to M. Elat, 'The Campaigns of Shalmanezer III against Aram and Israel', *IEJ* 25, 1975, 25–35, the success of this coalition was primarily the consequence of their supremacy in chariots.
13. See *ANET*, 279.
14. Thus A. M. Gazov-Ginzberg, 'Bor'b etničeskich grupp ("kolen") za vlast' v Israil'skom Carstve', *Palestinskij sbornik* II(74), 1964, 25–38.
15. The texts of these ostraca, along with an extensive commentary, may be found in

IH, 25–81. Cf. also *KAI*, 183–8. See further M. Noth, 'Das Krongut der israelitischen Könige und seine Verwaltung', *ZDPV* 50, 1927, = *Aufsätze I*, 159–82, esp. 164ff.

16. See A. Parrot, *Samaria*, London 1958, 15–83; P. R. Ackroyd, 'Samaria', *AOTS*, 343f., and above all J. Maxwell Miller, *The Old Testament and the Historian*, Philadelphia 1976, 40–8.

17. A. Alt, *Der Stadtstaat Samaria*, Berlin 1954 = *KS* III, 258–402. So also Donner, op. cit., 401.

18. R. de Vaux, *RB* 62, 1955, 101–6, in a review of the study by Alt mentioned in previous note.

19. See the literature mentioned in n.16.

20. See I Kings 22.39; Amos 3.15; Ps. 45.8. Cf. also Ackroyd, op. cit., 345.

21. See J. N. Schofield, 'Megiddo', *AOTS*, 1969, 323.

22. For this account see above all F. I. Andersen, 'The Socio-juridical Background of the Naboth Incident', *JBL* 85, 1966, 46–58.

23. P. Welten, 'Naboths Weinberg (I Könige 21)', *EvTh* 33, 1973, 30f., who regards I Kings 21.1–20a as a unity in both form and content (26f.). A different view is taken by O. H. Steck, *Überlieferung und Zeitgeschichte in den Elia-Erzählungen*, WMANT 26, 1968, 32–77. Note, however, that the account of the murder of Naboth's sons in II Kings 9.25f. is missing in I Kings 21. See now G. Hentschel, *Die Eliaerzählungen*, Leipzig 1977, 293.

24. According to I Kings 4.7–20, he put the Israelites and Canaanites in different districts.

25. For this group of problems see now e.g. Donner, op. cit., 401.

26. Thus *HIOTT*, 209.

27. See the studies by Ridderbos, Ellermeier and Noort mentioned in ch. 1 n.25. Further M. Stol. 'Profetie in Mari', *Phoenix* 15, 1969, 205–9.

28. See C. L. Labuschagne, 'De valse profetie in Israël, *Rondom het Woord* XI, 1969, 142–9, and A. S. van der Woude, 'Ware en valse profetie in het Oude Testament', *Rondom het Woord* XIV, 1972, 7–14.

29. See the following studies and the extensive bibliographies which they contain: C. van Leeuwen, 'De oudtestamentische profeten in het onderzoek van de laatste tien jaar', *NTT* 27, 1973, 289–317; id., 'De "Kleine Profeten" in het onderzoek van der laatste tien jaar', *NTT* 28, 1974, 113–29; R. E. Clements, *Prophecy and Tradition*, Oxford 1975.

30. For Elijah see L. Bronner, *The Stories of Elijah and Elisha as Polemic against Baal Worship*, Leiden 1968; G. Fohrer, *Elia*, Zurich ²1968; Steck, op. cit.; R. Smend, 'Der biblische und historische Elia', SVT XXVIII, 1975, 167–84; Hentschel, op. cit.

31. For Elisha see J. Maxwell Miller, 'The Elisha Cycle and the Accounts of the Omride Wars', *JBL* 85, 1966, 441–55; H. C. Schmitt, *Elisa. Traditionsgeschichtliche Untersuchungen zur vorklassischen nordisraelitischen Prophetie*, Gütersloh 1972.

32. See II.1.2.

33. This last type also occurs in Mari. See *ARM (T)* XIII, 112–14. The agreement with Mari is primarily formal.

34. The texts from Ugarit give more information in this connection. See e.g. *KTU* 1.1—1.6 (the so-called Baal epic).

35. See H. Jagersma, '*jsn* in 1. Könige XVIII 27', *VT* XXV, 1975, 674–6.

36. See Fohrer, op. cit., 42; Hentschel, op. cit., 280ff.

37. For these prophets and the events on Carmel see A. Alt, *Das Gottesurteil auf dem Karmel*, Stuttgart 1935 = *KS* II, 135–49; R. de Vaux, 'Les prophètes de Baal sur le mont Carmel', *BMB* V, 1941, 7–20.

38. See H. Jagersma, '. . .Veertig dagen en veertig nachten. . .' *NTT* 28, 1974, 9ff.
39. For these problems see K. Seybold, 'Elia am Gottesberg. Vorstellungen prophetischen Wirkens nach I. Könige 19', *EvTh* 33, 1973, 3–18, and also E. Ruprecht, 'Entstehung und zeitgeschichtlicher Bezug der Erzählung von der Designation Hasaels durch Elisa (2. Kon. XIII 7–15)', *VT* XXVIII, 1978, 73–82.
40. Bronner, op. cit., differs.
41. Thus at least S. Yeivin, 'King Jehoshaphat', *Eretz-Israel* VII, 1964, 6–17.
42. See the account of the excavations in Kuntilat 'Ajrud, *IEJ* 27, 1977, 52f.
43. See the next chapter.
44. The account in II Kings 11.1–20 in which all this is narrated probably goes back to two different traditions. See H. A. Brongers, *II Koningen*, POT, 1970, 109; J. Gray, *I & II Kings*, OTL, ²1970, 566f.
45. For discussion and further literature on this question see now T. Ishida, *The Royal Dynasties in Ancient Israel*, BZAW 142, 1977, 160–8.
46. So E. Würthwein, *Der 'amm ha' arez im Alten Testament*, BWANT 4, 17, 1936, 25; A. van der Born, *Koningen*, BOT, 1958, 169; Ishida, op. cit., 162. G. Buccellati, *Cities and Nations of Ancient Syria*, Rome 1967, 224ff., differs.

Chapter 12 The Dynasty of Jehu

1. See also 11.4.1.
2. See O. H. Steck, *Überlieferung und Zeitgeschichte in den Elia-Erzählungen*, WMANT 26, 1968, 33.
3. See P. Welten, 'Naboths Weinberg (I Könige 21)', *EvTh* 33, 1973, 27f., and the literature mentioned there.
4. Cf. Judg. 9.5, and for this figure see now F. C. Fensham, 'The Numeral Seventy in the Old Testament and the Family of Jerubbaal, Ahab, Panammuwa and Athirat', *PEQ* 109, 1977, esp. 114f.
5. See Hos. 2.7, 12, 16; 11.2; 13.1. For a thorough discussion of these texts see M. J. Mulder, *Ba'al in het Oude Testament*, The Hague 1962, 17–112; C. van Leeuwen, *Hosea*, POT, 1968, 60, 64, 73f., 222–4, 255f.
6. See F. S. Frick, 'The Rechabites Reconsidered', *JBL* 90, 1971, 279–87; A. van Selms, *Jeremia II*, POT, 1974, 128–31 (an excursus on the Rechabites).
7. F. Stolz, 'Aspekte religiöser und sozialer Ordnung im alten Israel', *ZEE* 17, 1973, esp. pp. 151, 158.
8. See *ANET*, 280f.
9. See *ANET*, 122.
10. However, according to P. K. McCarter, 'Yaw, Son of "Omri": A Philological Note on Israelite Chronology', *BASOR* 216, 1974, 5–7, Joram and not Jehu is meant on this inscription. That seems improbable. See M. Weippert, '*Jau(a) mār Ḥumri* – Joram oder Jehu von Israel?', *VT* XXVIII, 1978, 113ff. An intermediate position is more or less occupied by E. R. Thiele, 'Chronological Note on Yaw, Son of 'Omri', *BASOR* 222, 1976, 19–23.
11. For a translation see A. Jepsen, ed., *Von Sinuhe bis Nebukadnezar. Dokumente aus der Umwelt des Alten Testaments*, Stuttgart-Munich ²1976, 158f.
12. So S. Page, 'A Stela of Adad-Nirari III and Nergal-Eres from Tell al Rimah', *Iraq* 30, 1968, 139–53; A. Cody, 'A New Inscription from Tell al-Rimah and King Jehoash of Israel', *CBQ* 32, 1970, 325–40; Jepsen, op. cit., 159.
13. See also *ANET*, 281f.

14. According to M. C. Astour, '841 BC: The First Assyrian Invasion of Israel', *JAOS* 91, 1971, 383–9, however, Joram was not wounded in a battle against Aram, but in a battle against Assyria. In support he refers to e.g. Hos. 10.14. However, the interpretation of this text presents a number of problems. See van Leeuwsen, op. cit., 219.

15. According to J. Maxwell Miller, 'The Rest of the Acts of Jehoahaz (I Kings 20; 22.1–38)', *ZAW* 80, 1968, 337–42, the battles with Aram mentioned in I Kings 20 and 22.1–38 relate to the time of Jehoahaz.

16. On this see also M. Haran, 'The Rise and Fall of the Empire of Jeroboam II', *Zion* 31, 1966/67, 18ff., and id., 'Problems in Biblical History', *Tarbiz* 38, 1968/69, 1ff.

17. For this see also *KAI* 202 (the so-called ZKR inscription).

18. See A. Malamat, 'The Aramaeans', *POTT*, 146, and S. A. Cooke, *CAH* III, 377.

19. II Kings 10.29, 31 (Jehu); 13.2 (Jehoahaz); 13.11 (Jehoash); 14.24 (Jeroboam II); 15.9 (Zechariah).

20. Cf. also Hos. 4.2.

21. Thus also van Leeuwen, op. cit., 180. H. W. Wolff, *Hosea*, Hermeneia, Philadelphia 1974, 146, differs.

22. See R. de Vaux, 'Tirzah', *AOTS*, esp. 378f.

23. For these ostraca see e.g. P. R. Ackroyd, 'Samaria', *AOTS*, esp. 346f., and above all *IH*, 23–81. Cf. also *KAI*, nos. 183–8.

24. See *IH*, 47–55.

25. See *IH*, 55–64.

26. According to H. W. Wolff, *Amos the Prophet. The Man and his Background*, Philadelphia 1973, the background to Amos' preaching must not be sought in a cultic milieu but in the oral traditions of old-Israelite wisdom which still flourished in semi-nomadic circles. For this see now C. van Leeuwen, 'De "Kleine Profeten" in het onderzoek van de laatste tien jaar', *NTT* 28, 1974, 119.

27. See M. Buber, *The Prophetic Faith*, New York 1945, 96–110.

28. See e.g. Amos 4.1; 5.10–11; 8.4–6.

29. Cf. also 12.3 above and for more details M. Fendler, 'Zur Sozialkritik des Amos. Versuch einer Wirtschafts- und sozialgeschichtlichen Interpretation alttes-tamentlicher Texte', *EvTh* 33, 1973, 32–53, and the literature mentioned there.

30. See e.g. H. Bobek, *Die Hauptstufen der Gesellschafts- und Wirtschaftsentfaltung in geographischer Sicht*, and E. Wirth, *Wirtschaftsgeographie*, Darmstadt 1969, 462–73.

31. See Fendler, op. cit., 35, and also 12.3 (on the Samaria ostraca).

32. Cf. e.g. Nathan to David over Bathsheba and Elijah to Ahab over Jezebel.

33. K. Koch, 'Die Enstehung der sozialen Kritik bei den Propheten,' *Probleme biblischer Theologie*, Festschrift for G. von Rad, Munich 1971, esp. 238.

34. See also O. Loretz, 'Die prophetische Kritik des Rentenkapitalismus, Grund-lagen-Probleme der Prophetenforschung,' *UF* 7, 1975, 273.

35. Fendler, op. cit., 53, also comes to this conclusion. See also G. Wanke, 'Zu Grundlagen und Absicht prophetischer Sozialkritik', *KuD* 18, 1972, 11.

36. Cf. e.g. Amos 2.8 with Ex. 22. 25f.; Deut. 24. 12f.

37. According to H. S. Nyberg, *Studien zum Hoseabuch. Zugleich ein Beitrag zur Klärung des Problems der alttestatmentlichen Textkritik*, Uppsala 1935, 12, this should be seen as a northern dialect of Hebrew.

38. H. W. Wolff, 'Hoseas geistige Heimat', *TLZ* 81, 1956, 83–94, sees a close connection between the emergence of Hosea and that of the levitical prophetic circles in northern Israel who were opposed to the official cultic institutions.

39. See Buber, op. cit., 110–26.
40. For the problems connected with Hosea's marriage see now especially C. van Leeuwen, *Hosea*, POT, 1968, 29ff., and the literature mentioned there.
41. See e.g. Hos. 1–3; 4.11–14.
42. See 18.4.
43. P. R. Ackroyd, 'Hosea and Jacob', *VT* XIII, 1963, 245–59 differs.
44. For this chapter see also T. C. Vriezen, 'La Tradition de Jacob dans Osée XII', *OTS* I, 1942, 64–78; E. M. Good, 'Hosea and the Jacob Tradition', *VT* XVI, 1966, 137–51; Ackroyd, op. cit; L. Ruppert, 'Herkunft und Bedeutung der Jakob-Tradition bei Hosea', *Biblica* 52, 1971, 488–504.
45. Cf. e.g. Hos. 2; Jer. 2.2f. See further K. Gross, 'Der Einfluss des Hosea auf Jeremias Anschauungen', *NKZ* 42, 1931, 241ff., 327ff.
46. The expression 'door of hope' in IQM XI, 9 (War Scroll) recalls Hos. 2.15. Cf. also 1 QM I, 2–3; 4Qp Ps. 37, III, 1.
47. In II Chron. 26; Isa. 1.1; 6.1; 7.1; Hos. 1.1; Amos 1.1, this king is called Uzziah.
48. The death of Jehoiada is also mentioned in II Chron. 24.15–16. No mention is made of this in II Kings.
49. See II Chron. 24.17–22.
50. Thus H. A. Brongers, *II Koningen*, POT, 1970, 136; J. Gray, *I & II Kings*, OTL, ²1970, 555. That would also then be true of II Chron. 26.1.
51. See n.47.
52. See N. Glueck, 'Transjordan', *AOTS*, 441.
53. Azariah is probably also mentioned in a text from the annals of Tiglath-pileser III (*ANET*, 282). However, this text is too fragmentary for us to be able to come to any conclusions.
54. See also A. Zeron, 'Die Anmassung des Königs Usia im Lichte von Jesajas Berufung. Zu 2. Chr. 26, 16–22 und Jes. 6, 1ff.', *TZ* 33, 1977, 65–68.

Chapter 13   The Confrontation with Assyria

1. There is a succinct survey of this period in e.g. W. W. Hallo and W. K. Simpson, *The Ancient Near East. A History*, New York 1971, 131f.
2. This king is sometimes called Pul in the OT (see e.g. II Kings 15.19). The name Pulu also occurs in a Babylonian king-list. See *ANET*, 272.
3. See A. Jepsen, *Von Sinuhe bis Nebukadnezar. Dokumente aus der Umwelt des Alten Testaments*, Stuttgart-Munich ²1976, 164f.
4. See the following section.
5. See H. Donner, *Israel unter den Völkern. Die Stellung der klassischen Propheten des 8. Jahrhunderts v. Chr. zur Aussenpolitik der Könige von Israel und Juda*, SVT XI, 1964, 1–3.
6. See E. Forrer, *Die Provinzeinteilung des Assyrischen Reiches*, Leipzig 1920.
7. See H. W. F. Saggs, 'Assyrian Warfare in the Sargonid Period', *Iraq* 25, 1963, 145–54.
8. See W. von Soden, 'Die Assyrier und der Krieg', *Iraq* 25, 1963, 131–44.
9. Called Ararat in the OT. See e.g. Gen. 8.4; II Kings 19.37; Jer. 51.27.
10. See *TGI*, 56ff., and *ANET*, 283. Cf. also H. Tadmor, 'Philistia under Assyrian Rule', *BA* 29, 1966, 86–102; B. Oded, 'The Phoenician Cities and the Assyrian Empire in the time of Tiglath-pilezer III', *ZDPV* 90, 1974, 38–49.
11. *ANET*, 283. For the text, translation, etc., of this inscription see also M.

Weippert, 'Menahem von Israel und seine Zeitgenossen in einer Steleninschrift des assyrischen Königs Tiglathpileser III. aus dem Iran', *ZDPV* 89, 1973, 26–53.

12. Weippert, op. cit., dates the inscription mentioned in n.11 in about 737 BC.

13. See Hallo and Simpson, op. cit., and above all Oded, op. cit.

14. According to H. J. Cook, 'Pekah', *VT* XIV, 1964, 121–35, from 752 to 740 BC Israel will have been a divided kingdom. Menahem and Pekahiah were then ruling in Samaria, while Pekah governed part of Transjordan and Galilee. Then in 740 BC Pekah succeeded in gaining control of all Israel.

15. See e.g. Isa. 7.1–17; 8.1–15; Hos. 5.8—6.6. For a discussion of all the relevant texts see Donner, op. cit., 7–59. However, for Hos. 5.8—6.6 see E. M. Good, 'Hosea 5.8—6.6: An alternative to Alt', *JBL* 85, 1966, 273–86.

16. See *ANET*, 282–4.

17. So *SHI*, III, and G. Fohrer, *Geschichte Israels*, Heidelberg 1977, 151. A different view is held by B. Oded, 'The Historical Background of the War between Rezin and Pekah against Achaz', *Tarbiz* 38, 1968/69, 205–24, and id., 'The Historical Background of the Syro-Ephraimite War Reconsidered', *CBQ* 34, 1972, 153–65.

18. J. Begrich, 'Der Syrisch-Ephraimitische Krieg und seine weltpolitische Zusammenhänge', *ZDMG* 83, 1929, 213–37, is still an important study of this conflict.

19. See *ANET*, 284.

20. See A. Alt, *Jesaja 8.23—9.6. Befreiungsnacht und Krönungstag*, Tübingen 1950= *KS* II, 209ff.

21. See *ANET*, 283.

22. See *ANET*, 283: here called Jauhazi – Jehoahaz.

23. See M. E. L. Mallowan, 'Nimrud', *AOTS*, 65.

24. See G. van Driel, *The Cult of Aššur*, Assen 1969, 170ff.

25. So M. Cogan, *Imperialism and Religion: Assyria, Judah and Israel in the Eighth and Seventh Centuries BC*, Pennsylvania 1971.

26. See *ANET*, 284f.

27. See *TGI*, 60.

28. For this material see further D. C. Greenwood, 'On the Jewish Hope for Restored Northern Kingdom', *ZAW* 88, 1976, 376–85, and cf. also N. Lohfink, 'Die Einheit von Israel und Juda', *Una Sancta* 26, 1971, 154–64.

29. See R. Fey, *Amos und Jesaja. Abhängigkeit und Eigenständigkeit des Jesaja*, WMANT 12, 1963.

30. According to E. Jenni, 'Jesajas Berufung in der neueren Forschung', *TZ* 15, 1959, 320, Ahaz would also be meant in Isa. 14.28. For Isa. 6.1 see also L. A. Snijders, *Jesaja deel I*, POT, 1969, 82f.

31. There is often mention of prophetesses in the OT. See Snijders, op. cit., 108 n.75.

32. *Martyrdom of Isaiah* 3.11. Cf. also Heb. 11.37.

33. For the agreements between Isa. 6.1–4 and I Kings 22.19–20 (the vision of Micaiah ben Imlah) see A. Alt, 'Gedanken über das Königtum Jahwes', *KS* I, 351f., and Snijders, op. cit., 83.

34. See W. Dietrich, *Jesaja und die Politik*, Munich 1976, 200, and now also A. Schoors, 'Isaiah, the Minister of Royal Anointment', *OTS* XX, 1977, 85–107, and esp. 107: 'Isaiah appears to be a court prophet, a late successor of Nathan'.

35. See e.g. Isa. 1.4; 5.19; 30.11–12; 31.1.

36. See e.g. Isa. 1.21–23; 5.8–23; 10.1–4. Cf. Dietrich, op. cit., 37–55.

37. According to A. S. van der Woude, *Micha*, POT, 1976, 195–9, in Micah 6–7 we

have a prophet from northern Israel (Deutero-Micah) who emerged at the time of the fall of Samaria.

38. See e.g. Isa. 2.2–4; Micah 4.1–3. Cf., however, van der Woude, op. cit., 131f., who regards Micah 4.1–3 as words of Micah's opponents.

39. See e.g. Micah 2.1–5; 3.9–11.

40. Cf. n.37.

41. For these problems see now e.g. A. S. van der Woude, *Jona-Nahum*, POT, 1978, 67ff.; B. Becking, 'Is het boek Nahum een literaire eenheid?', *NTT* 32, 1978, 124. A different view is taken by e.g. Vriezen in *LOI*, 252f.

42. Op. cit., 70ff. See also id., 'The Book of Nahum: A Letter written in Exile', *OTS* XX, 1977, 108–26.

43. For the synchronisms between Hezekiah and Hoshea in II Kings 18.1, 9–10 see K. T. Anderson, *Die Chronologie der Könige von Israel und Juda*, ST 23, 1969, 103–5. Perhaps this is connected with a co-regency of Hezekiah's. So at least S. H. Horn, 'The Chronology of King Hezekiah's Reign', *AUSS* 2, 1964, 40–52.

44. See *ANET*, 301.

45. The king of Edom is mentioned in the inscriptions of Tiglath-pileser III, Sargon II, Esarhaddon and Assurbanpal as one of those who paid tribute to Assyria. See *ANET*, 282, 287, 291, 294.

46. For the relationship between Hezekiah and Isaiah, in addition to Dietrich, op. cit., 100ff., see also W. Zimmerli, 'Jesaja und Hiskia', *AOT* 18, 1973 = *GS* II, 88–113.

47. Thus e.g. also *SHI*, 114f. Cf. also Dietrich, op. cit., 223, 275.

48. However, II Chron. 29–31 is hardly to be seen as historical information from the time of Hezekiah. See P. Welten, *Die Königs-Stempel. Ein Beitrag zur Militär-politik Judas unter Hiskia und Josia*, Wiesbaden 1969, 159.

49. So Donner, op. cit., 121–6; Dietrich, op. cit., 128ff.

50. See *ANET*, 287ff.

51. Some scholars think that two campaigns are involved here. So C. van Leeuwen, 'Sanherib devant Jérusalem', *OTS* XIV, Leiden 1965, 245–72; *HI*, 396–8. This is not the view of W. W. Hallo, 'From Qarqar to Carchemish', *BA* 23, 1960, 34–61; K. A. Kitchen, 'Late Egyptian Chronology and the Hebrew Monarchy', *JANES* 5, 1973, 225–33.

52. See *ANET*, 287.

53. See *ANET*, 288.

54. See Y. Aharoni, 'Excavations at Tell Beer-sheba', *BA* 35, 1972, 111–27.

55. See Donner, op. cit., 30–38, and H. Wildberger, *Jesaja 1–12*, BKAT X, 1, 1972, 423–35.

56. For this inscription see *KAI* no. 189; *DOTT*, 209–11; and also N. Shaheen, 'The Siloam End of Hezekiah's Tunnel', *PEQ* 101, 1977, 107–12.

57. See e.g. M. Broshi, 'The Expansion of Jerusalem in the Reigns of Hezekiah and Manasseh', *IEJ* 24, 1974, 21ff.

58. See *ANET*, 288.

59. See *ANET*, 288.

60. See e.g. M. Elat, 'On the Political Status of Judah after Sennacherib's Conquest of Lachish', *Yediot* 31, 1966/67, 140ff.; id., 'The Political Status of the Kingdom of Judah within the 7th century BCE', in Y. Aharoni (ed.), *Investigations at Lachish. The Sanctuary and the Residency (Lachish V)*, Tel Aviv 1975, 61–70.

61. See Herodotus II, 141.

62. According to E. Nielsen, 'Politiske forhold og kulturelle strømminger i Israël og

Juda under Manasse', *DDT* 29, 1966, 1–10, Manasseh's cultic measures aroused resistance both among the Jerusalem priests and among the Levites in the countryside of Judah. The opposition of the latter would then be expressed in Lev. 18–23.
63. See also e.g. M. Weinfeld, 'The Worship of Molech and of the Queen of Heaven and its Background', *UF* 4, 1972, 133–54.
64. Cf. also the apocryphal writing 'The Prayer of Manasseh'.
65. According to K. Roubos, *II Kronieken*, POT, 1972, 281, there is no reason to doubt the historicity of this report.
66. See *ANET*, 291, 294 respectively.
67. See the section on the 'people of the land', 11.4.2.
68. See *ANET*, 291ff.
69. See *ANET*, 294, cf. also 13.4.3.
70. Cf. e.g. the book of Nahum (13.4.3 above) and Ezekiel. For the latter see R. Frankena, *Kanttekeningen van een Assyrioloog bij Ezechiël*, Leiden 1965.

Chapter 14 Judah in the Period of Transition between Assyrian and Babylonian Rule

1. This name is perhaps of Libyan origin. See H. R. Hall, *CAH* III, 291. For the period of this Pharaoh's reign see also Herodotus II, 151. Trade played a prominent role in the coming to power of Psammetichus and the increase of Egyptian might.
2. For the siege of Ashdod see e.g. Hall, op. cit., 95 and K. A. Kitchen, 'The Philistines', *POTT*, 65.
3. For all these events see D. J. Wiseman, *Chronicles of Chaldaean Kings (526–556 BC) in the British Museum*, London 1974, 61ff.
4. See *ANET*, 303–5, and also Hall, op. cit., 294ff.
5. For the earlier history of this see e.g. L. Rost, 'Zur Vorgeschichte der Kultusreform des Josia', *VT* XIX, 1969, 113–20.
6. See now the careful analysis of II Kings 22–23 by E. Würthwein, 'Die Josianische Reform und das Deuteronomium', *ZTK* 73, 1976, 395–423.
7. For this lawbook see now also W. Dietrich, 'Josia und das Gesetzbuch (2. Reg. XXII)', *VT* XXVII, 1977, 13–25.
8. For this see M. Rose, 'Bemerkungen zum historischen Fundament des Josia-Bildes in II Reg. 22f.', *ZAW* 89, 1977, 50–63.
9. See H. H. Schmid, 'Das Verständnis der Geschichte im Deuteronomium', *ZTK* 64, 1967, 1–15; R. Abba, 'Priests and Levites in Deuteronomy', *VT* XXVII, 1977, 257–67, and id., 'Priests and Levites in Ezekiel', *VT* XXVIII, 1978, 4f.
10. For all this see C. J. Labuschagne, 'Redactie en Theologie van het boek Deuteronomium', *VoxT*, 1973, 171–84.
11. In addition to the works mentioned in nn. 6, 7, 8, see now also H. Hollenstein, 'Literarkritische Erwägungen zum Bericht über die Reformmassnahmen Josias 2 Kön. XXIII 4ff.', *VT* XXVII, 1977, 321–36.
12. According to H. W. Wolff, 'Das Ende des Heiligtums in Bethel', *Archäologie und Altes Testament*, Festschrift for K. Galling, Tübingen, 1970, 287–98, this devastation probably took place between 628 and 622.
13. For a detailed discussion of these developments see e.g. A. H. J. Gunneweg, *Leviten und Priester. Hauptlinien der Traditionsbildung und Geschichte des israelitisch-*

jüdischen Kultpersonals, FRLANT 89, 1965, 118ff. See also T. Booij, *Godswoorden in de Psalmen, hun funktie en achtergronden*, Amsterdam 1978, 68.

14. For this see the following section.

15. According to Bright, *HI*, 321, this probably included the provinces of Samaria, Megiddo and also Gilead. Cf. also A. Alt, 'Judas Gaue unter Josia', *PJB* 21, 1925, 100–16; Josh. 15–19.

16. See e.g. P. Welten, *Die Königs-Stempel. Ein Beitrag zur Militärpolitik Judas unter Hiskia und Josia*, Wiesbaden 1969, 167ff.; D. Diringer, 'Mizpah', *AOTS*, 337; N. Avigad, 'The Governor of the City', *IEJ* 26, 1976, 178–82, where there is mention of a governor of Jerusalem.

17. *KAI* no. 200. For this see e.g. J. Naveh, 'A Hebrew Letter from the Seventh Century BC', *IEJ* 10, 1960, 129–39; *IH*, 259–68.

18. Probably as a pledge. Cf. Ex. 22.25–26; Deut. 24.12–13.

19. A. Malamat, 'Josiah's Bid for Armageddon. The Background of the Judaean-Egyptian Encounter in 609 BC', *JANES* 5, 1973, 267–79, and id., 'Megiddo, 609 BC. The Conflict Re-examined', *AAASH* 22, 1974, 445–9.

20. According to Y. Yadin, 'The Historical Significance of Inscription 88 from Arad: A Suggestion', *IEJ* 26, 1976, 9–14, the Arad inscription no. 88 is also connected with this campaign by Necho. Y. Aharoni, *Arad Inscriptions*, Jerusalem 1975, 103f. (Hebrew) differs.

21. H. A. Brongers, *II Koningen*, POT, 1970, 224.

22. A different view is taken by G. E. Wright, *Biblical Archaeology*, London ²1962, 202, and with some hesitation also by J. N. Schofield, 'Megiddo', *AOTS*, 1969, 326.

23. *Antiquities* X, 5, 1.

24. P. Humbert, *Problèmes du livre d'Habacuc*, Neuchâtel 1944.

25. D. E. Gowan, 'Habakkuk and Wisdom', *Perspective* 9, 1968, 157–66, differs in connecting Habakkuk more with wisdom.

26. Cf. Rom. 1.17; Gal. 3.11.

27. See e.g. Zeph. 1.7, 14, 18; 2.2.

28. See C. van Leeuwen, 'De oudtestamentische profeten in het onderzoek van de laatste tien jaar,' *NTT* 27, 1973, 301f., and the literature mentioned there.

Chapter 15   The Babylonian Advance

1. See *ANET*, 305.

2. *Hist.* II, 159. Cf. also Jer. 47.1.

3. See F. K. Kienitz in Fischer, *Weltgeschichte. Die Altorientalischen Reiche III. Die erste Hälfte des I. Jahrtausends*, Frankfurt am Main 1973, 267, and also II Kings 24.7.

4. Also called Shallum: see I Chron. 3.15.

5. Viz. Jehudi for Jehoiakim (Jer. 36.14, 2, 23) and Ebed-melek for Zedekiah (Jer. 38.7, 8, 10–12; 39.16). On this see G. Rice, 'Two Black Contemporaries of Jeremiah', *JRT* 32, 1975, 95–109, who gives as probable reasons for their presence in Jerusalem the link with Egypt, which was then ruled by a Cushite dynasty.

6. See D. J. Wiseman, *Chronicles of Chaldaean Kings (626–556 BC) in the British Museum*, London 1974, 66–68. See also Jer. 46.2.

7. See *ANET*, 563, and cf. also E. Lipiński, 'The Egyptian-Babylonian War of the Winter 601–600 BC', *AION*, NS 32, 1972, 235–41, and A. Malamat, 'The Twilight of Judah in the Egyptian-Babylonian Maelstrom', *SVT* XXVIII, 1975, 131f.

8. See Wiseman, op. cit., 71.

9. See Wiseman, op. cit., 72.

10. Thus *LOI*, 229; K. Baltzer, *Die Biographie der Propheten*, Neukirchen-Vluyn 1975, 114.

11. Cf. e.g. J. P. Hyatt, 'The Beginning of Jeremiah's Prophecy', *ZAW* 78, 1966, 204–14 (in 605 BC), and C. F. Whitley, 'Carchemish and Jeremiah', *ZAW* 80, 1968, 38ff. (in 605 BC).

12. For Jeremiah's relationship to this type of prophet see now e.g. I. Meyer, *Jeremia und die falschen Propheten*, Fribourg 1977.

13. See Y. Aharoni, 'Beth-haccherem', *AOTS*, 1969, 171, 181f.

14. For Jeremiah's attitude towards the king see also e.g. Jer. 21.11—22.9.

15. See e.g. Jer. 7.21–28; 18.18–23; 23.9–40. For Jeremiah's attitude to sacrifice see now also J. Milgrom, 'Concerning Jeremiah's Repudiation of Sacrifice', *ZAW* 89, 1977, 273–5.

16. M. Buber, *The Prophetic Faith*, 158–183, has an attractive and still very instructive discussion of Jeremiah.

17. See M. Noth, 'Die Einnahme von Jerusalem im Jahre 597 v. Chr.', *ZDPV* 74, 1958, 133–57. According to A. F. Johns, 'The Military Attacks on the Jews', *VT* XIII, 1963, 482–6, the days on which Jerusalem was attacked in both 598/7 and 587/6 were sabbath days.

18. See Wiseman, op. cit., 73.

19. See *ANET*, 308.

20. According to II Chron. 36.7, however, this was only a part of the vessels from the temple.

21. See e.g. II Kings 24.14–16; Jer. 24.1; 27.29; 29.1–2.

22. For the extent of Judah at this time see Jer. 13.19; Ezek. 17.14.

23. Or a somewhat later period. See below and cf. also W. Zimmerli, *Ezekiel* I, Hermeneia, Philadelphia 1979, 365.

24. See ostracon no. 3 in *KAI*, no. 193 or *ANET*, 322.

25. *Contra Apionem* I.21.

26. See E. Unger, 'Nebukadnezar II, und sein Sandabakku (Oberkommissar) in Tyrus', *ZAW* 44, 1926, 314–17.

27. See *KAI* no. 194 or *ANET*, 322.

28. But see *IH*, 117.

29. So *HI*, 329; E. Kutsch, 'Das Jahr der Katastrophe: 587 v. Chr. Kritische Erwägungen zu neuere chronologische Versuchen', *Biblica* 55, 1974, 520–45.

30. So C. Schedl, 'Nochmals das Jahr der Zerstörung Jerusalems, 587 oder 586 v. Chr.', *ZAW* 74, 1962, 209–13; *HIOTT*, 283.

31. Thus D. J. A. Clines, 'Regnal Year Reckoning in the Last Years of the Kingdom of Judah', *ABR* 2, 1, 1972, 9–34.

32. For these problems see J. Maxwell Miller, *The Old Testament and the Historian*, Philadelphia 1976, 81f. See also Excursus III.

Chapter 16 The Captivity in Babylon

1. In this connection see e.g. K. Baltzer, 'Das Ende des Staates Juda und die Messias-Frage', *Studien zur Theologie der alttestamentliche Überlieferungen*, Festschrift for G. von Rad, Neukirchen 1961, 33–43.

2. See e.g. R. C. Musaph-Andriesse, *From Torah to Kabbalah*, London 1981, 39ff.

3. The Targum Onkelos and the Targum Jonathan, at least in their final redaction. See Musaph-Andriesse, op. cit. IIf.

4. Note, too, that the later word Jew is derived from Judah, Judaean.

5. Inscriptions have been found in Mizpah which could be connected with the rise of Gedaliah. At least D. Diringer, 'Mizpah', *AOTS*, 1969, 336, connects the name Jaaezaniah, which occurs on some of these inscriptions, with the person of the same name mentioned in II Kings 24.33; Jer. 40.8. But see *EAEHL*, 916.

6. On this see H. P. Müller, 'Phoenizien und Juda in exilisch-nachexilischer Zeit', WO 6, 1970–71, 189ff.

7. According to C. A. Keller in E. Jacob, C. A. Keller and S. Amsler, *Osée, Joël, Amos, Abdias, Jonas*, CAT XIa, 1965, 251, and Y. Kaufmann, *History of the Religion of Israel. From the Babylonian Captivity to the End of Prophecy*, Vol. IV, New York and Jerusalem 1977, 431ff., in 587/86 BC. See also Arad ostracon no. 24 in *IH*, 188.

8. See also W. Rudolph, *Jeremia*, HAT 12, ³1968, 260, 262.

9. *Jewish Antiquities* X, 9, 7.

10. Cf. Ezek. 33.24.

11. *dallat hāʾāreṣ*.

12. See K. M. Kenyon, *Archaeology in the Holy Land*, London ⁴1979, 299ff.

13. Thus e.g. also P. R. Ackroyd, *Exile and Restoration*, London 1968, 25, and G. Fohrer, *Geschichte Israels*, Heidelberg 1977, 188.

14. For the discussion of this point see Ackroyd, op. cit., 25–9, and the literature mentioned there.

15. See F. I. Andersen, 'Who Built the Second Temple?', *ABR* 6, 1958, 1–35.

16. D. W. Thomas, 'The Sixth Century BC: A Creative Epoch in the History of Israel', *JSS* 6, 1961, 33–66, points more or less in this direction.

17. On this see F. C. B. MacLaurin, 'The Beginning of the Israelite Diaspora', *AJBA* 1, 4, 1971, 82–95.

18. G. Larsson, 'When did the Babylonian Capitivity Begin?', *JTS*, NS 18, 1967, 417–23.

19. See M. D. Coogan, 'Patterns in Jewish Personal Names in the Babylonian Diaspora', *JSJ* 4, 1973, 183–191; id., 'Life in the Diaspora. Jews at Nippur in the Fifth Century BC', *BA* 37, 1974, 6–12; R. Zadok, *The Jews in Babylonia in the Chaldean and Achaemenian Period in the Light of the Babylonian Sources*, Tel Aviv 1976.

20. See *ANET*, 221–2.

21. For this see H. Jagersma, *Leviticus 19. Identiteit-Bevrijding-Gemeenschap*, Assen 1972, 74ff.; A. Cholewiński, *Heiligkeitsgesetz und Deuteronomium. Eine vergleichende Studie*, Rome 1976, 261f.

22. According to Ackroyd, op. cit., 34, Ezek. 11.16 might represent the mention of a sanctuary. But cf. e.g. W. Zimmerli, *Ezekiel* I, Hermeneia, Philadelphia 1979, 115f.

23. For the discussion of this point see Ackroyd, op. cit., 32–35, and the literature mentioned there.

24. For a survey of the content of these various creation stories see e.g. C. Westermann, *Genesis 1–11*, BKAT I, 1, 1974, 26ff.

25. For Ezekiel as priest see B. J. Oosterhof, 'De priester Ezechiël', *Bulletin der theologische radiocolleges* 1, 4, 1959, 28–30.

26. Zimmerli, *Ezekiel* I, 100f., regards Ezek. 1.1–3a as secondary. However, a different view is taken by K. Baltzer, *Die Biographie der Propheten*, Neukirchen-Vluyn 1975, 129, n. 438.

27. See Ezek. 1.2; 40.1.

28. See e.g. Ezek. 12.6; 24.24.

29. Baltzer, op. cit., 131.

30. See e.g. Ezek. 3.17; 33.7–9. Cf. also Jer. 6.17; Hab. 2.1 and also Graf Reventlow, *Wächter über Israel. Ezechiël und seine Tradition*, BZAW 82, 1962.

31. So also Baltzer, op. cit., 133.

32. According to Zimmerli, *Ezechiel* II, BKAT XIII, 11, Neukirchen-Vluyn 1969, 993f., 1240ff., Ezek. 40–48 derives from a later writing of Ezekiel. See further on this material M. Schmidt, *Prophet und Tempel*, Zurich 1948, 129–71; R. de Vaux, 'Le Temple de Jerusalem', *BeO*, 1967, 309f.; Ackroyd, op. cit., 111ff.

33. For the development of the significance of Jerusalem in a theological sense from the captivity onwards see N. W. Porteous, 'Jerusalem-Zion: The Growth of a Symbol', *Living the Mystery: Collected Essays*, Oxford 1968, 93–111.

34. For Ezek. 20 see J. Lust, *Traditie, redactie en kerygma bij Ezechiël (20.1–26)*, Brussels 1969; W. A. M. Beuken, 'Ezechiël 20', *Bijdragen* 33, 1972, 39–64.

35. See M. A. Beek, *Inleiding in de Joodse Apocalyptiek van het Oud- en Nieuw-Testamentisch tijdvak*, Theologia VI, Haarlem 1950, 40ff.; D. S. Russell, *Between the Testaments*, London ²1963, esp. 93ff., and J. M. Schmidt, *Die Jüdische Apokalyptik*, Neukirchen-Vluyn ²1976, 11ff., 64ff.

36. See Beek, op. cit., 5ff.; Russell, op. cit., esp. 95ff.; Schmidt, op. cit., 35ff., 87ff.

37. See e.g. Enoch 56.5–8; Rev. 20.7–9.

38. For all these problems see e.g. A. Schoors, *Jesaja II*, BOT IXB, 1973, 229ff.; Ackroyd, op. cit., 118ff.; Kaufmann, op. cit., 51ff.

39. Isa. 42.1–9, 49.1–6; 50.4–9; 52.13—53.12.

40. See P. A. H. de Boer, 'Second Isaiah's Message', *OTS* XI, 1956, 102–17; Baltzer, op. cit., 171–7, and the literature mentioned there.

41. In this connection see now esp. J. L. Koole, 'De beeldenstorm van Deutero-jesaja', *Loven en Geloven*, Festschrift for N. H. Ridderbos, Amsterdam 1975, 77–93.

42. De Boer, op. cit., 84f., refers especially to Isa. 40 in this connection.

43. See e.g. Isa. 40.3–5; 42.13–16; 51.9–10. Deutero-Isaiah shares this stress on Exodus with other prophets, thus de Boer, op. cit., 86.

44. M. Noth, *The Deuteronomistic History*, JSOT Supplement Series 15, 1981.

45. See *ANET*, 308, and above all E. F. Weidner, 'Jojachin, König von Juda in babylonischen Keilschrifttexten', *Mélanges syriens offerts à Monsieur René Dussaud* II, Paris 1939, 923–35.

46. W. Dietrich, *Prophetie und Geschichte. Eine redaktionsgeschichtliche Untersuchung zum deuteronomistischen Geschichtswerk*, FRLANT 108, Göttingen 1972.

47. Noth, op. cit., 99, 142n. 10, and E. Janssen, *Juda in der Exilszeit, Ein Beitrag zur Frage der Entstehung des Judentums*, FRLANT 69, 1956, 16ff.

48. Cf. Ackroyd, op. cit., 67.

49. Here see especially J. G. Vink, 'The Date and Origin of the Priestly Code in the Old Testament', *OTS* XV, 1969, 1–144, esp. 12ff.

50. For all this see e.g. Vink, op. cit., 18ff.

51. G. Fohrer, *Die Hauptprobleme des Buches Ezechiel*, BZAW 72, 1952; L. E. Elliott-Binns, 'Some Problems of the Holiness Code', *ZAW* 67, 1955, 26–40; K. Elliger, *Leviticus*, HAT, 1966, 14ff.; B. Maarsingh, *Leviticus*, POT, 1974, 9f.

52. See Jagersma, *Leviticus 19*, esp. 119–25.

53. See D. J. Wiseman, *Chronicles of Chaldaean Kings (626–556 BC) in the British Museum*, London 1974, 75f.

54. 4Q or Nab. On this see e.g. D. S. Attema, 'Het gebed van Nabonidus', *Schrift en*

Uitleg, Festschrift for W. H. Gispen, Kampen 1970, 7–20, and A. S. van der Woude, 'Bemerkungen zum Gebet des Nabonides (4Q or Nab)', in M. Delcor, *Qumrán. Sa Piété, sa théologie et son milieu*, BETL XLVI, 1978, 121–9.

55. See e.g. K. Galling, *Studien zur Geschichte Israels im persischen Zeitalter*, Tübingen 1964, 6ff.

56. See *ANET*, 312ff.

57. See *TGI*, 79f.

58. This historical situation is perhaps also the background to Dan. 5.1—6.1. But here Belshazzar is called king of Babylon.

59. See *ANET*, 306.

60. See *ANET*, 315f.

Chapter 17   The Return and the Rebuilding of the Temple

1. On this see G. Widengren, 'The Persians', *POTT*, 318.

2. For all this see *ANET*, 316.

3. Ibid.

4. See 17.1, and nn.2, 3.

5. For all this material see R. Mayer, 'Das achämenidische Weltreich und seine Bedeutung in der politischen und religiösen Geschichte des antiken Orients', *BZ*, NF 12, 1968, 1–16.

6. For the relationship between these pericopes see H. H. Grosheide, *Ezra-Nehemia* I, COT, 1963, 12f., and K. Galling, *Studien zur Geschichte Israels im persischen Zeitalter*, Tübingen 1964, 61–77.

7. For this see the details in Galling, op. cit., 78–88.

8. Thus also e.g. Galling, op. cit., 41, and *HIOTT*, 300.

9. Thus *HIOTT*, 299.

10. Thus Galling, op. cit., 133.

11. According to Y. Kaufmann, *History of the Religion of Israel from the Babylonian Captivity to the End of Prophecy*, Vol. IV, New York and Jerusalem 1977, 190f., Ezra 1.1–4 is based on an original Aramaic source. The details in Ezra 1 and 6.3–5 are not contradictory, but supplementary.

12. *HIOTT*, 300.

13. Galling, op. cit., 40f., 127ff., thinks in this connection of a small number. Grosheide, op. cit., 73f., and Widengren, op. cit., 319, think of a large number.

14. For a detailed discussion of these lists see e.g. H. L. Alrik, 'The Lists of Zerubbabel (Nehemiah 7 and Ezra 2) and the Hebrew Numeral Notation', *BASOR* 136, 1954, 21–27, and Galling, op. cit., 89–108.

15. Thus Alrik, op. cit., and *HI*, 378.

16. Thus Grosheide, op. cit., 109f., and G. Fohrer, *Geschichte Israels*, Heidelberg 1977, 199.

17. So A. Alt, 'Die Rolle Samarias bei der Entstehung des Judentums', *Festschrift O. Procksch*, Leipzig 1934 = *KS* II, 333f., and Galling, op. cit., 135. Cf. also P. R. Ackroyd, *Exile and Restoration*, London 1976, 144 n.27.

18. III 89. See also G. B. Gray and M. Cary, *CAH* IV, 194ff.

19. See e.g. N. Avigad, *Bullae and Seals from a Post-Exilic Judean Archive*, Jerusalem 1976.

20. Fohrer, op. cit., 199f.; Kaufmann, op. cit., 204.

21. According to K. Koch, 'Haggais unreines Volk', *ZAW* 79, 1967, 64f., Ezra 4.1–5 is an insertion by the Chronicler to explain the delay in rebuilding the temple.

22. So R. J. Coggins, 'The Interpretation of Ezra IV 4', *JTS* 16, 1965, 126.

23. However, this information could relate to the time of Ezra and Nehemiah. Cf. J. de Fraine, *Esdras en Nehemias*, BOT, 1961, 37.

24. See W. T. In der Smitten, 'Historische Probleme zum Kyrosedikt und Jerusalemer Tempelbau von 515', *Persica* 6, 1972–74, 167–78.

25. Thus Galling, op. cit., 56–9.

26. Thus J. Schoneveld in S. P. Dee and J. Schoenveld, *Bijbelse Encyclopedie met Handboek en Concordante*, Deel I, Baarn 1963, 302; Grosheide, op. cit., 85; Kaufmann, op. cit., 223.

27. For details see K. M. Beyse, *Serubbabel und die Königserwartungen des Propheten Haggai und Sacharja*, Stuttgart 1972.

28. Cf. Herodotus III, 61ff., and Widengren, op. cit., 321f.

29. On this see F. M. T. de Liagre Bohl, 'Die babylonischen Prätendenten zur Anfangszeit des Darius (Dareios)', *BiOr* 25, 1968, 150–3.

30. So *SHI*, 142.

31. See also G. Sauer, 'Serubbabel in der Sicht Haggais und Sacharjas', *Das ferne und nahe Wort*, Festschrift for L. Rost, BZAW 105, 1967, 199–207.

32. In this connection see also the expression 'the two anointed' in Zech 4.14. According to A. S. van der Woude, 'Die beiden Söhne des Öls (Sach. 4.14), messianische Gestalten?', *Travels in the World of the Old Testament*, Festschrift for M. A. Beek, Assen 1974, 262–8, here Zerubbabel and Joshua are presented as 'saviour figures'.

33. See also 17.3.2.

34. See A. Parrot, *The Temple of Jerusalem*, London 1957, 68ff.

35. So W. A. M. Beuken, *Haggai-Sacharja 1–8. Studien zur Überlieferungsgeschichte der frühnachexilischen Prophetie*, Assen 1967, 221. A different view is taken by e.g. K. Elliger in A. Weiser and K. Elliger, *Das Buch der zwölf kleinen Propheten* II, ATD 24, ⁶1976, 84.

36. See also Ackroyd, op. cit., 156ff.

37. Cf. Jer. 22.24 and see also Ackroyd, op. cit., 164.

38. For these chapters see B. Otzen, *Studien über Deuterosacharja*, Copenhagen 1964, and M. Saebø, *Sacharja 9–14*, WMANT 34, 1969.

39. See e.g. Zech. 1.17; 2.4–5; 2.13; 3.2; 8.3, 15.

40. On this see E. Schürer, *The History of the Jewish People in the Age of Jesus Christ (175 BC–AD 135)*, Vol.1, ed. G. Vermes and F. Millar, Edinburgh 1973, 193ff.

41. For more detail see Ackroyd, op. cit., 175–200.

42. On this see also Beuken, op. cit., 275–82, 303–17.

Chapter 18 The Period of the Second Temple to *c.* 330 BC

1. It is also possible that the name Malachi is not a proper name but is taken from the words 'my messenger' (*mal'āki*) in Mal. 3.1.

2. *SHI*, 149. J. Schoneveld, in S. P. Dee and J. Schoneveld, *Bijbelse Encyclopedie met Handboek en Concordantie*, Deel I, Baarn 1963, 303; H. H. Grosheide, *Ezra-Nehemiah*, COT, 1963, 47; U. Kellermann, 'Erwägungen zum Problem der Esra-datierung', *ZAW* 80, 1968, 55–87.

3. See Pap. Eleph. 30.18; 31.17. Cf. *ANET*, 492.

4. K. Galling, *Studien zur Geschichte Israels im perzischen Zeitalter*, Tübingen 1964, 149ff., and J. A. Emerton, 'Did Ezra go to Jerusalem in 428 BC?', *JTS*, NS 17, 1966, 1–19.

5. Thus e.g. A. van Hoonacker, 'La succession chronologique Néhemie-Esdras', *RB* 32, 1923, 481–94, and *RB* 33, 1924, 33–64. For further details of the chronological problems connected with Ezra and Nehemiah see J. de Fraine, *Esdras en Nehemias*, BOT, 1961, 13f., and Grosheide, op. cit., pp. 35ff.

6. See Josephus, *Jewish Antiquities* XI, 5, 1–7, and also the order Ezra I and Ezra II (= Nehemiah) in the canon of LXX and the Vulgate.

7. Cf. also Esther, 8.2; 10.3.

8. See B. Meissner, *Babylonien und Assyrien* I, Heidelberg 1920, 121. Cf. also Galling, op. cit., 166f. Grosheide, op. cit., 195ff., differs.

9. Thus E. Meyer, *Die Enstehung des Judentums*, Halle 1896, 60–71; de Fraine, op. cit., 54; Grosheide, op. cit., 204–17; G. Widengren in *IJH*, 498. A. S. Kapelrud, *The Question of Authorship in the Ezra Narrative: A Lexical Investigation*, SNVAO, 1944, 27–42, differs.

10. Thus E. Bresciani in *Fischer Weltgeschichte 5, Griechen und Perser. Die Mittelmeerwelt im Altertum I*, Frankfurt am Main 1965, 317, and cf. also Herodotus III, 12, 15; VII, 7.

11. This could also be an indication that Ezra's arrival in Jerusalem is to be dated in 458 BC.

12. According to W. T. In der Smitten, *Esra, Quellen, Überlieferungen und Geschichte*, Assen 1973, these chapters for the most part derive from the Chronicler, though they certainly contain material which goes back to an earlier oral or written tradition. In contrast, Y. Kaufmann, *History of the Religion of Israel from the Babylonian Captivity to the End of Prophecy*, Vol. IV, New York and Jerusalem 1977, 638–49, argues that e.g. in Neh. 8–10 we have original material.

13. See e.g. Gen. 16 (Abram and Hagar); Gen. 38 (Judah and Tamar); Ex. 2 (Moses and Zipporah) and also the foreign wives of the kings of Judah.

14. For these chapters, in addition to the commentaries see e.g. also U. Kellermann, 'Erwägungen zum Ezragesetz', *ZAW* 80, 1968, 373–85.

15. Kellermann, op. cit., 383.

16. S. Mowinckel, *Studien zu dem Buche Ezra-Nehemia, III: Die Ezrageschichte und das Gesetz Moses*, SNVAO, 1965, 124ff., and with some qualifications also Grosheide, op. cit., 197f.

17. Meyer, op. cit., 206–16; E. Auerbach, *Wüste und Gelobtes Land* II, Berlin 1936, 252–4.

18. R. Kittel, *Geschichte des Volkes Israel*, 3, 2, Stuttgart 1929, 652f.; G. von Rad, *Old Testament Theology* 1, London 1975, 89.

19. See Widengren, op. cit., 491. For this work see also G. von Rad, 'Die Nehemia-Denkschrift', *ZAW* 76, 1964, 176–84; S. Mowinckel, *Studien zu dem Buche Ezra-Nehemia II: Die Nehemia Denkschrift*, SNVAO, 1965.

20. For a detailed account of the situation in Jerusalem about the middle of the fifth century BC see J. Simons, *Jerusalem in the Old Testament*, Leiden 1952, 437ff., and H. H. Grosheide, *Deernis met haar puin*, Kamper Cahiers no. 27, Kampen nd.

21. See e.g. also H. H. Rowley, 'Nehemiah's Mission and its Background', *BJRL*, 87, 1954/55, 528–61.

22. Thus e.g. W. T. In den Smitten, *Gottesherrschaft und Gemeinde. Beobachtungen an Frühformen eines jüdischen Nationalismus in der Spätzeit des Alten Testaments*, Bern 1974.

23. Thus Kittel, op. cit., 458. However, Galling, op. cit., 116, 140f., differs.

24. In a later period there was probably another governor in Samaria who also had the name Sanballat. See K. Galling, op. cit., 209f.

25. Thus B. Mazar, 'The Tobiads', *IEJ* 7, 1957, 137–45, 229–38. U. Kellermann, *Nehemia. Quellen, Ueberlieferung und Geschichte*, BZAW 102, 1967, 167ff., differs.

26. See I. Rabinowitz, 'Aramaic Inscriptions of the Fifth Century B.C. from a North-Arab Shrine in Egypt', *JNES* XV, 1956, 1–9.

27. Thucydides I, 93.

28. In Judah this came into use above all in the fifth century BC. See Ezra 2.69; 8.27; Neh. 7.69–71.

29. See H. Bardtke, *Bibel, Spaten und Geschichte*, Göttingen ²1971, 309. We should conclude from II Macc. 3.11 that this brought the high priest considerable prosperity.

30. The note 'in the days of Zerubbabel and in the days of Nehemiah' in Neh. 12.47, however, points to a later revision, according to Kellermann, op. cit., 47.

31. Op. cit., 50.

32. *Jewish Antiquities* XI, 5, 6.

33. According to M. Smith, *Palestinian Parties and Politics that Shaped the Old Testament*, New York, 1971, 141–4, this was in almost a dictatorial way.

34. These texts have been edited with a translation by A. Cowley, *Aramaic Papyri of the Fifth Century B.C.*, London 1923.

35. E. G. Kraeling, *The Brooklyn Museum Aramaic Papyri*, New Haven 1953, 41–48, thinks in terms of at least a century earlier.

36. For details of the worship of this community see A. Vincent, *La Religion des judéo-araméens d'Eléphantine*, Paris 1937.

37. For this letter see *ANET*, 492.

38. Widengren, op. cit., 533.

39. See Pap. Eleph. 27, lines 1–2, 24.

40. Kraeling, op. cit., 283–90.

41. On this see Kaufmann, op. cit., 619–28. A similar view is also of importance in the interpretation of Ezra 4.

42. See e.g. D. C. Greenwood, 'On the Jewish Hope for a Restored Northern Kingdom', *ZAW* 88, 1976, 376–85.

43. However, according to M. Delcor, 'Hinweise auf des samaritanische Schisma in Alten Testament', *ZAW* 74, 1962, 281–91, the political aspect is still fully present in Deutero-Zechariah.

44. So also Smith, op. cit., 148–92, and R. J. Coggins, *Samaritans and Jews. The Origins of Samaritanism Reconsidered*, Oxford 1975, 164.

45. H. H. Rowley, 'Sanballat and the Samaritan Temple', *Men of God*, London 1963, (246–76) 270f.

46. Cf. also the different views in this area. Thus F. M. Cross, 'Aspects of Samaritan and Jewish History in Late Persian and Hellenistic Times', *HTR* 59, 1966, 201–11, in 100 BC, and I. H. Eybers, 'Relations between Jews and Samaritans in the Persian Period', *Biblical Essays* 1966, 72–89, in 400–360 BC.

47. *Jewish Antiquities*, XI 8, 4.

48. Op. cit., 513f.

49. See R. J. Coggins, op. cit., 82–100, and cf. also John 4.20.

50. On this see W. Bloemendaal, *De tekst van het Oude Testament*, Baarn 1966, 47ff., and E. Würthwein, *The Text of the Old Testament*, London ²1979, 42ff.

51. See Sirach 44–45.

52. See R. Hanhart, *BHW* V, col. 12.
53. M. Noth, *Uberlieferungsgeschichtliche Studien. Die sammelnden und bearbeitenden Geschichtswerke im Alten Testament*, Darmstadt ³1967, 110ff.
54. H. G. M. Williamson, *Israel in the Books of Chronicles*, Cambridge 1976, 5ff.
55. Cf. also P. Welten, *Geschichte und Geschichtsdarstellung in den Chronikbüchern*, WMANT 42, 1973.
56. Cf. also Williamson, op. cit., 87ff.
57. For details see the relevant commentaries and the introductions to the Old Testament.
58. See G. B. Gray and M. Cary, *CAH* IV, 214ff.; J. A. R. Munro, *CAH* IV, 229ff., 268ff.
59. See F. K. Kienitz, *Die politische Geschichte Ägyptens vom 7. bis zum 4. Jahrhundert vor der Zeitwende*, Berlin 1953, 76ff.
60. See H. Bengtson in *Fischer Weltgeschichte, Griechen und Perser. Die Mittelmeerwelt im Altertum* I, Frankfurt am Main 1965. 162ff.
61. See P. Weinberg, 'Bemerkungen zum Problem "Der Vorhellenismus im Vorderen Orient"', *KLIO* 58, 1, 1976, 5–20.
62. See Bengtson, op. cit., 292f.
63. According to J. Morgenstern, 'Further Light from the Book of Isaiah upon the Catastrophe of 485 B.C.', *HUCA* 37, 1966, 1–28, there was a change of ruler in Persia in 485 BC which led to a revolt against the Persians in Judah and elsewhere.
64. So e.g. O. Plöger, *Das Buch Daniel*, KAT XVIII, 1965, 124f., and M. Delcor, *Le Livre de Daniel*, Paris 1971, 171, 180. A different view is taken e.g. by G. C. Aalders, *Daniel*, COT, 1962, 188, who sees an indication of a kingdom here.
65. Thus M. Delcor, 'Allusions à Alexandre le Grand dans Zach. IX 1–8', *VT* I, 1951, 110–24. B. Otzen, *Studien über Deuterosacharja*, Copenhagen 1964, 116f., differs.
66. *Jewish Antiquities* XI, 8, 5.
67. See M. Hengel, *Jews, Greeks and Barbarians*, London and Philadelphia 1980, 49–126.
68. For this period see E. Schürer, *The History of the Jewish People in the Age of Jesus Christ (175 BC – AD 135)*, Vol. I, ed. G. Vermes and F. Millar, Edinburgh 1973, pp. 125–242.
69. For the period after Persian rule which falls outside the scope of this book see the literature mentioned in nn. 67, 68, and for the Samaritans see esp. H. G. Kippenberg, *Garizim und Synagoge. Traditionsgeschichtliche Untersuchungen zur samaritanischen Religion der aramäischen Periode*, RGVV XXX, Berlin and New York 1971, 33ff. Brief descriptions of this later period can be found in *SHI*, 153.; Schoneveld, op. cit., 304ff.; and in A. J. Bronkhorst, *De Geschiedenis van Israel van Alexander de Grote tot Bar Kochba*, Baarn 1964, 22ff.

Chronology of the kings of Israel and Judah according to:

	Albright	Andersen	Begrich-Jepson	Miller	Pavlovsky-Vogt	Thiele
Israel						
Jeroboam I	922–901	932/31–911/10	927/26–907	925/23–905/03	931–910/09	931/30–910/09
Nadab	901–900	911/10–910/09	907–906	905/03–904/08	910/09–909/08	910/09–909/08
Baasha	900–877	910/09–887/86	906–883	904/02–887/85	909/08–886/85	909/08–886/5
Elah	877–876	887/86–886/85	883–882	887/85–886/84	886/85–885/84	886/85–885/84
Zimri	876	886/85	882	886/84	885/84	885/84
Tibni	876	886/85	882/878	886/84	885/84–881/80	885/84
Omri	876–869	886/85–875/74	882–871	886/84–875/73	885/84–874/73	885/84–874/73
Ahab	869–850	875/74–854/53	871–852	875/73–853/51	874/73–853	874/73–853
Ahaziah	850/49	854/53–853/52	852–851	853/51–851/49	853–852	853–852
Jehoram	849–842	853/52–842/41	851–845	851/49–844/42	852–841	852–841
Jehu	842–815	842/41–815/14	845–818	844/42	841–813	841–814/13
Jehoahaz	815–801	815/14–799/98	818–802		813–797	814/13–798
Jehoash	801–786	799/98–784/83	802–787		797–782/81	798–782/81
Jeroboam II	786–746	784/83–753/52	787–747		782/81–753	782/81–753
Zechariah	746–745	753/52–752/51	747		753–753/52	753–752
Shallum	745	752/51–751/50	747		752/52	752
Menahem	745–738	751/50–742/41	747–738		753/52–742/41	752–742/41
Pekahiah	738–737	742/41–741/40	737–736		742/41–740/39	742/41–740/39
Pekah	737–732	741/40–730/29	735–732		740/39–731	752–732/31
Hoshea	732–724	730/29–722/21	731–723		731–722	732/31–723/22

Judah

	Albright	Andersen	Begrich-Jepsen	Miller	Pavlovsky-Vogt	Thiele
Rehoboam	922–915	932/31–916/15	926–910	925/23–908/07	931–914	931/30–913
Abijam	915–913	916/15–914/13	910–908	908/07–906/04	914–912/11	913–911/10
Asa	913–873	914/13–874/73	908–868	906/04–876/74	912/11–871/70	911/10–870/69
Jehoshaphat	873–849	874/73–850/49	868–847	876/74–852/50	871/70–848	870/69–848
Joram	849–842	850/49–843/42	847–845	852/50–844/42	848–841	848–841
Ahaziah	842	843/42–842/41	845	844/42	841–841/40	841
Athaliah	842–837	842/41–837/36	845–840	844/42	841/40–835	841–835
Joash	837–800	836/35–797/96	840–801		835–796	835–796
Amaziah	800–783	797/96–769/68	801–773		796–767	796–767
Azariah/Uzziah	783–742	769/68–741/40	773–736		767–739	767–740/39
Jotham	742–735	741/40–734/33			739–734/33	740/39–732/31
Ahaz	735–715	734/33–715/14	736–729(736–726)		734/33–728/27	732/31–716/15
Hezekiah	715–687	715/14–697/96	728–700(725–697)		728/27–699	716/15–687/86
Manasseh	687–642	697/96–642/41	696–642		699–643/42	687/86–643/42
Amon	642–640	642/41–640/39	641–640		643/42–641/40	643/42–641/40
Josiah	640–609	640/39–609/08	639–609		641/40–609	641/40–609
Jehoahaz	609	609/08	609		609	609
Jehoiakim	609–598	609/08–598/97	609–598		609–598/97	609–598
Jehoiachin	598	598/97	598		598/97–597	598–597
Zedekiah	598–587	598/97–587/86	598–587		597–586	597–586

Chronological tables

1. Some important events from the time before c. 1200 BC

	Egypt	Canaan	Hittite kingdom	Syria	Mesopotamia
				c. 2250	
2000				Ebla destroyed	
	Sinuhe				End of Ur III
1900					
		Patriarchal period			
1800					
				Mari destroyed	
1700					
1600					
					Nuzu
1500					
1400		Amarna period			
	Akhenaten				
1300	Rameses II				
	Exodus	Entry and invasion		Ugarit destroyed	
	Merneptah	of Philistines			
1200	Sea Peoples defeated		End of Hittite empire		

2. c. 1200–900 BC

	Egypt	Canaan	Assyria
1200		Period of the judges (c. 1200–1030)	
	Ramses III Sea Peoples defeated		
1150		Deborah	
1100			
1050		Samuel Philistine domination	
	Weakening of	Saul	Assyria insignificant
1000	Egyptian power and influence	David	
950		Solomon	
	Pharaoh Shisha.. (c. 935)	Break-up of the personal union (c. 932/31)	Rise of Assyria (c. 935–900)

3. *c.* 900–600 BC

	Egypt	Judah	Israel	Syria	Assyria
	Shiskak	Rehoboam	Jeroboam		
		Abijam			
900		Asa			
			Nadab		
			Baasha		
			Elah		
			Zimri/Tibni		
			Omri		
		Jehoshaphat	Ahab	Hadadezer	Shalmaneser III
850			(Elijah)	853 Battle of	
			Ahaziah	Karkar	
			Joram		
		Ahaziah			
		Athaliah	Jehu	Hazael	
		Joash			
			Jehoahaz		
				Ben-hadad	Adad-nirari III
800		Amaziah	Joash		
			Jeroboam II		
		Azariah	(Amos		
			Hosea)		
			Zechariah		
			Shallum		
750			Menahem		Tiglath-pileser III
		Jotham	Pekahiah	Rezin	
		Ahaz	Syro-Ephraimite		
			war		
		(Isaiah	Hoshea		Shalmaneser V
		Micah)	Fall of Samaria		
			(722/21)		
		Hezekiah			Sargon II
					Sennacherib
700		Manasseh			
					Esarhaddon
					(Nahum?)
	Psammetichus				
650		Amon			
		Josiah			
		(Jeremiah)			

Egypt	Judah	Israel	Syria	Assyria
	(Zephaniah)			
	(Habakkuk)			Fall of Nineveh 612
Necho II				Asshuruballit II
600				

4. *c.* 600–300 BC

	Egypt	Judah	Babylon	Media
	Necho II	Jehoahaz (Jeremiah) Jehoiakim		
600		Jehoiachin First deportation Zedekiah Fall of Jerusalem and second deportation Gedaliah	Nebuchadnezzar II (Ezekiel)	
550			Evil-merodach (Deutero-Isaiah) Nabonidus	Cyrus II
		Return of small groups	Fall of Babylon	Edict of Cyrus (538)
	Cambyses conquers Egypt	Zerubbabel Rebuilding of the temple		Cambyses II Darius I
500		(Haggai, Zechariah)		
				Xerxes I
		Ezra 458?		Artaxerxes I
450		Nehemiah		
	Temple of Elephantine destroyed	Bagoas		Artaxerxes II
400	Egypt independent again			
				Artaxerxes III
350	Egypt conquered again			Darius III Battle of Issus (333) Fall of Persian empire
	Alexander the Great and the beginning of Greek rule			
300				

INDEX OF MODERN SCHOLARS

INDEX OF BIBLICAL REFERENCES

2. New Testament

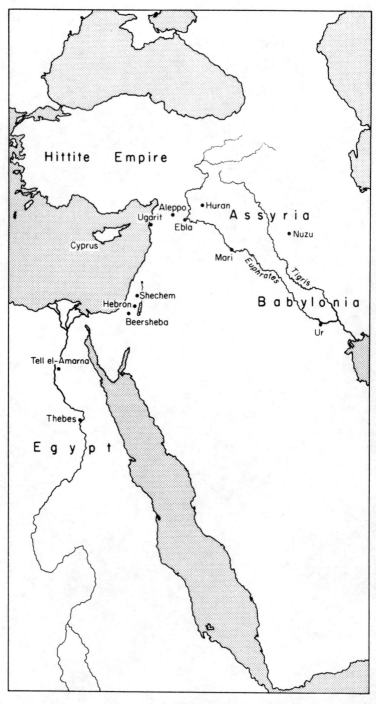

1. The Ancient Near East

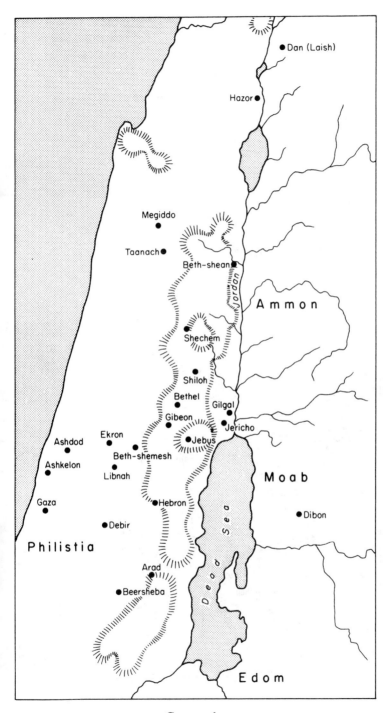

2. Canaan about 1200 BC

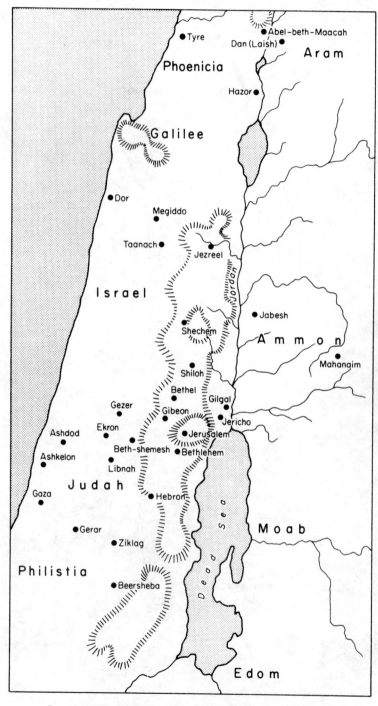

3. Israel and Judah in the Time of David and Solomon

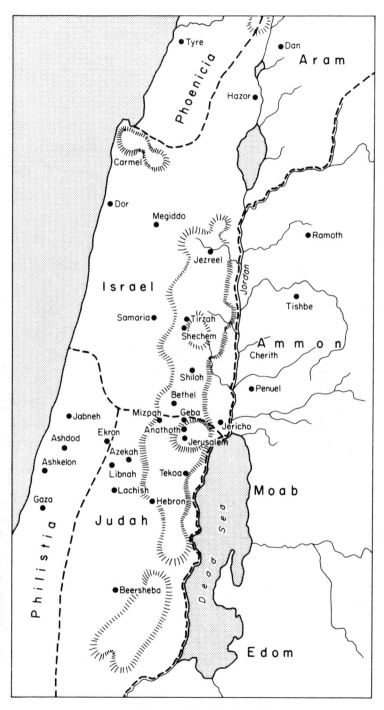

4. Israel and Judah after Solomon

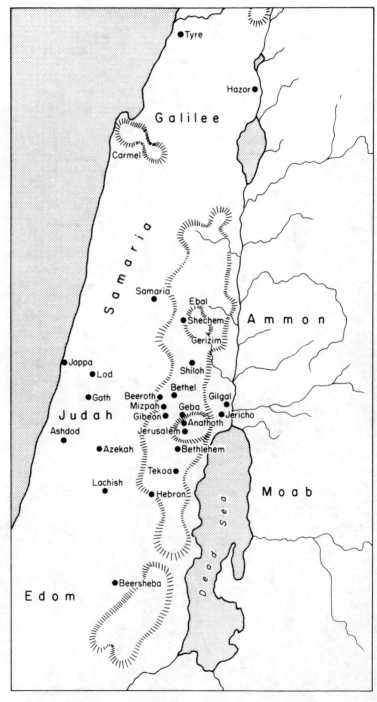

5. Judah and Surrounding Countries in the Persian Period

Part II

From Alexander the Great
to Bar Kochba

CONTENTS

ABBREVIATIONS

AASOR	Annual of the American Schools of Oriental Research
AB	The Anchor Bible
ABLA	M.Noth, *Aufsätze zur biblischen Landes- und Altertumskunde 1 and 2*, Neukirchen-Vluyn 1971
AGAJU	Arbeiten zur Geschichte des Antiken Judentums und des Urchristentums
AJBI	*Annual of the Japanese Biblical Institute*
AJSR	*Association for Jewish Studies Review*
ALGHJ	Arbeiten zur Literatur und Geschichte des Hellenistischen Judentums
ANRW	*Aufstieg und Niedergang der Römischen Welt*
AJ	Josephus, *Antiquitates Judaicae*
AOTS	*Archaeology and Old Testament Study*, ed. D.Winton Thomas, Oxford 1969
ARNa	Aboth de Rabbi Nathan, version A
ARNb	Aboth de Rabbi Nathan, version B
ASTI	*Annual of the Swedish Theological Institute*
b	Babylonian Talmud
BA	*Biblical Archaeologist*
BAR	*The Biblical Archaeologist Reader*
BA Rev	*The Biblical Archaeologist Review*
BB	Tractate Baba Bathra
BeO	R.de Vaux, *Bible et Orient*, Paris 1967
Ber	Tractate Berakoth
BH	*Bijbels Handboek*
Bikk	Tractate Bikkurim
BJ	Josephus, *Bellum Judaicum*
BKAT	Biblischer Kommentar Altes Testament
BM	Tractate Baba Metzia
BOT	De Boeken van het Oude Testament
BWAT	Beiträge zur Wissenschaft vom Alten Testament
BZ	*Biblische Zeitschrift*

BZAW	Beihefte zur Zeitschrift für die Alttestamentliche Wissenschaft
CAH	The Cambridge Ancient History
CAT	Commentaire de l'Ancien Testament
CBC	The Cambridge Bible Commentary
CBQ	*Catholic Biblical Quarterly*
CD	Damascus Document
CPJ	*Corpus Papyrorum Judaicarum* I-III, ed. V.A.Tcherikover, A.Fuks and M.Stern, 1957-1964
CRINT	*Compendium Rerum Iudaicarum ad Novum Testamentum* I 1,2, ed. S.Safrai and M.Stern, 1974-1976
Dio Cassius	Dio Cassius, *Historia Romana*
Diodorus Siculus	Diodorus Siculus, *Bibliotheca Historica*
DJD	*Discoveries in the Judean Desert*, 1955ff.
EAEHL	*Encyclopedia of Archaeological Excavations in the Holy Land*, I-IV, ed. M.Avi-Yona and M.Stern (1975-1978)
EdF	Erträge der Forschung
ETL	*Ephemerides Theologicae Lovanienses*
FS	*Festschrift*
FWG	*Fischer Weltgeschichte* 5-8, 1965-1966
GCS	Die griechischen christlichen Schriftsteller der ersten Jahrhunderte
Gitt	Tractate Gittin
GLAJJ	M.Stern, *Greek and Latin Authors on Jews and Judaism* I,II, Jerusalem 1974-1980
GS	*Gesammelte Studien*
HA	*Historia Augusta*
HTR	*Harvard Theological Review*
HUCA	*Hebrew Union College Annual*
IEJ	*Israel Exploration Journal*
IJH	*Israelite and Judaean History*, ed. J.H.Hayes and J.Maxwell Miller, London and Philadelphia 1977
j	Jerusalem Talmud
JAOS	*Journal of the American Oriental Society*
JBL	*Journal of Biblical Literature*
JEOL	*Jaarbericht Ex Oriente Lux*
JJS	*Journal of Jewish Studies*
JNES	*Journal of Near Eastern Studies*
JQR	*Jewish Quarterly Review*

JRS	*Journal of Roman Studies*
JSHRZ	Jüdische Schriften aus hellenistisch-römischer Zeit
JSJ	*Journal for the Study of Judaism in the Persian, Hellenistic and Roman Period*
JSOT	*Journal for the Study of the Old Testament*
JSS	*Journal of Semitic Studies*
JTS	*Journal of Theological Studies*
KAT	Kommentar zum Alten Testament
KS	*Kleine Schriften*
m	Mishnah
Meg Ta'an	Megillat Ta'anit (Fast scroll)
Mur	*Documents from Murabba'at*, ed. J.T. Milik
Ned	Tractate Nedarim
NF (NS)	Neue Folge (New Series)
NT	*Novum Testamentum*
NTT	*Nederlands Theologisch Tijdschrift*
NTS	*New Testament Studies*
OBO	Orbis Biblicus et Orientalis
OLZ	*Orientalische Literaturzeitung*
OTS	*Oudtestamentische Studiën*
p	Pesher (commentary)
par.	parallels
PEQ	*Palestine Exploration Quarterly*
PNT	De prediking van het Nieuw Testament
Polybius	Polybius, *Histories*
PsSol	Psalms of Solomon
Q	Qumran
1Q, 2Q, etc.	First, second, etc. Qumran cave
1QpHab	Habakkuk Commentary
4QpNah	Nahum Commentary
RB	*Revue Biblique*
RBPH	*Revue Belge de Philologie et d'Histoire*
RGG	*Die Religion in Geschichte und Gegenwart*
RHR	*Revue de l'histoire des religions*
RivBib	*Rivista Biblica*
RQ	*Revue de Qumrân*
Sanh	Tractate Sanhedrin
SB	Sources Bibliques
SBS	Stuttgarter Bibelstudien
Schürer	E. Schürer, *The History of the Jewish People in the Age of Jesus Christ (175 BC – AD 135)*, I,II, revised and

	edited by G.Vermes, F.Millar and M.Black, I 1973, II 1979
SJLA	*Studies in Judaism in Late Antiquity*
SPB	Studia Post-Biblica
Strabo	Strabo, *Geographica*
SVT	Supplements to *Vetus Testamentum*
Ta'an	Tractate Ta'anith
TLZ	*Theologische Literaturzeitung*
TR	*Theologische Rundschau*
VT	*Vetus Testamentum*
WdF	Wege der Forschung
WMANT	Wissenschaftliche Monographien zum Alten und Neuen Testament
WUNT	Wissenschaftliche Untersuchungen zum Neuen Testament
ZAW	*Zeitschrift für die alttestamentliche Wissenschaft*
ZDPV	*Zeitschrift des Deutschen Palästina-Vereins*
ZNW	*Zeitschrift für die neutestamentliche Wissenschaft*

Chapter 1

Introduction

1.1 *An explanation*

This book attempts to reconstruct the history of Israel[1] between *c.*330 BC and AD 135. The choice of this period is determined on the one hand by the fact that the book is intended as a sequel to an earlier work[2] which covered the history of Israel up to about 330 BC. On the other hand, it is logical to choose the year AD 135 as the end of this history because in that year Israel ceased to exist as a state.

In reconstructing this period of the history of Israel we have often to struggle with a great many uncertainties and hypotheses. The most important reason for this is that the sources at our disposal often do not set out to write history in our sense of the word or – in other cases – certainly cannot be said to be objective historiography (see 1.2). Moreover, more than once we are confronted with the fact that for a particular period we have few sources or none at all, and no other data at our disposal. The result of all this is that on many points there is virtually no agreed opinion in academic discussion of this period in the history of Israel. The aim of this book is to indicate the various diverging views within reasonable limits. The way in which I shall do this is to indicate as far as possible divergent and alternative perspectives and make regular use of words like 'perhaps' and 'probably' in connection with subjects on which there is uncertainty. Such an account is much preferable to the so-called 'consecutive narrative' in which the reader often wrongly gets the impression that everything happened 'just like that'.

However, what I have just said certainly does not mean that the sources I have mentioned are of no help at all in a reconstruction of the history of Israel between 330 BC and AD 135. These sources are often written against a historical background or contain allusions to particular historical events. Our task is therefore to deal carefully and critically with the sources and thus try to establish what in fact happened. Here we must not limit ourselves to political history, but pay just as much attention to religious life, the various trends in this period, cultural and literary aspects, and social questions. Especial attention needs to be paid to the economic background. As so often, this background in particular is of decisive significance for the course of history and the most important events which took place in it.[3] Before we move on to that, I want to make some comments on the area and the people with which the book deals. The question of terminology must also be given special attention in this particular connection. First of all, however, I shall give a brief account of the most important sources that we shall be using.

1.2 *Sources*

1.2.1 *The Old Testament*

Only a few parts of the Old Testament are related to the period of the history of Israel which is to be described here. The most important of them is without doubt the book of Daniel. This book, which is usually dated to about 165 BC,[4] has an apocalyptic part (7-12) as well as a series of narratives (Dan.1-6). It is written in order to glorify God and to encourage those who continue to trust in this God – in very difficult circumstances – by announcing the coming of the kingdom of God. As will emerge in due course, this does not mean that we must *a priori* deny the book any historical character. Historical accuracy is not, however, the main concern here. The accuracy improves the nearer we come to the time in which the book must have been written (see also 7.6.1).[5]

In addition to the book of Daniel, the book of Koheleth (Ecclesiastes, *c.* 250 BC) can also be consulted for our period. Koheleth seems above all to provide some information about the social and economic situation of its time (see also 4.4).[6]

1.2.2 *Apocrypha and pseudepigrapha*

The historical value of most of these works must be assumed to be very small. Of course they often give us some insight into the religious developments and situation at the time when they were written.[7] One notable exception to this lack of historical value is I and II Maccabees. The final redaction of these two books took place in *c.* 100 BC.

I Maccabees describes the period from about 175 to 135 BC. The book gives the impression of having been written along the lines of books like I and II Samuel and I and II Kings, aiming to demonstrate the legitimacy of the Hasmonaean dynasty. As such, it has a polemical character.[8] Its historical value must also be judged in that light.

The author of II Maccabees, who probably came from Alexandria in Egypt, calls his book a summary of a five-volume work by a certain Jason of Cyrene (see II Macc. 2.23). There are no good reasons why such a book should not have existed. The central features of II Maccabees are divine protection, the important role of the temple and the cult, and trust in the Torah. Despite the fact that Judas occupies a prominent place in his work, the author of II Maccabees is much more critical of the Maccabees than that of I Maccabees.[9] II Maccabees deals with the same events as I Maccabees with the difference that the prehistory in II Maccabees (= II Macc.3-5) is much more detailed than in I Maccabbees (= I Macc.1.1-9). When there are differences, I Maccabees is usually regarded as the more trustworthy tradition.[10] I shall discuss this problem in more detail when we come to the period in question. I shall also discuss later the authenticity of the many documents which have been preserved in I and II Maccabees and of the specific historical events that can be inferred from the rest of the apocrypha and pseudepigrapha.

1.2.3 *Philo of Alexandria*

Philo (*c.*20 BC – AD 50) was a member of the Jewish community in Alexandria. It emerges from his works that he had a very broad and good Greek education and he can be regarded as the most important Jewish philosopher of classical antiquity.

In about AD 40, Philo was entrusted with the leadership of a delegation from Alexandria to plead the interests of the Jewish community there with Caligula (the emperor Caius Julius Caesar Germanicus, AD 37-41) in Rome. He described his experiences on this occasion in a book entitled *Legatio ad Gaium*. In this work we also find much information about Agrippa I, who was tetrarch of Galilee and Batanaea from AD 37 and king of Judaea from AD 41-44. In the rest of his work we only find sporadic information which is relevant to our purpose.

1.2.4 *Flavius Josephus*

The works of Josephus are without doubt the most important source for our knowledge of the history of Israel in the years between 330 BC and AD 135. At the beginning of the First Jewish War, this Jewish historian, who lived from about AD 37-100, was a commander in Galilee, where in 67 he went over to Vespasian. He wrote *De bello judaico* ('On the Jewish War'), in which, after discussing the prior history from 175 BC to AD 66 (Books I and II), he gives an account of this struggle with Rome, above all from his own experience (Books III-VII). He also wrote *Antiquitates Judaicae* ('Jewish Antiquities'), a history of the Jewish people from creation to about AD 66. In addition he wrote *Contra Apionem* (Against Apion), an apology for Judaism, which is also called 'On the Antiquity of the Jewish people', and a *Vita* (The Life of Josephus), along with another apologia, this time directed against Justus of Tiberias, who criticized Josephus' attitude at the time of the Jewish war.[11] The two first-mentioned works are most important for our purpose.

Like the books of Maccabees, the works of Josephus have been written with a considerable bias. *The Jewish War* betrays considerable sympathy for Vespasian and Titus. For this reason Josephus is rightly regarded as a kind of court historian of the Flavians.[12] At the same time it emerges from his works that his view is also clearly governed by his Pharisaic background and a desire to justify his own conduct during the Jewish War.[13]

In his *Jewish Antiquities* Josephus seems to feel himself under pressure above all to make the Jewish religion accessible to his non-Jewish readers. This may perhaps explain why he tries to describe Judaism as a 'philosophy',[14] and describes groups like the Sadducees, Pharisees, Essenes and Zealots as 'philosophical trends'.

In composing his works Josephus had both written sources and oral information at his disposal. The first category included not only the Old Testament but I Maccabees, a 'World History' (now lost) in 144 volumes by Nicolaus of Damascus, the secretary of Herod the Great, the works of Polybius and Strabo, and many others. He did not always use his sources very carefully, particularly the non-biblical ones.[15] Moreover, his use of them was governed by his motivation for writing his works,[16] which has already been mentioned. Josephus must have had help from Greek assistants in completing his work.[17] However, he was not so modest as always to make this clear.[18]

1.2.5 *Greek and Latin authors*

In general it can be said that these writers paid relatively little attention to what happened in Palestine. The country was only the object of their concern when their own land was affected. However, in this connection their information can often be useful to us.[19] The most important of these authors are as follows.

Polybius (*c.*203-120 BC) wrote a world history in forty volumes (some of which has come down to us), covering the years from 220 to 146 BC. Convinced of the inevitability of Roman rule over the world, he tried to analyse events in order to explain the rise of Rome and the decline of the Hellenistic kingdoms.

Diodorus Siculus (first century BC) wrote a historical survey (part of which has been preserved), the value of which is markedly dependent on the sources which he used (some of which are unknown to us).

The works of Strabo (*c.* 64 BC to AD 21), some of which are lost, seem above all to have been written for leaders and statesmen. They include descriptions of various areas including Palestine.

Livy (*c.* 59 BC – AD 17) is particularly concerned with the foreign policy and the growth of Rome. Palestine is mentioned twice in his *Periochae* (brief summaries of the history of the last century BC).

Plutarch (c.AD 46-120) gives a number of biographies of figures including Gracchus, Marius, Sulla, Pompey and Caesar. Here he stresses character and pays little attention to political circumstances.

Tacitus (born *c.*AD 55) is a supporter of the republic and has little sympathy for the emperors. In his *Annals* he covers the period from the death of Augustus (AD 14) to that of Nero (AD 68). Of his *Histories*, only the books about the year of the four emperors (AD 69) and the year AD 70 have been preserved. In V, 1-13 Tacitus gives a survey of Jewish history up to the First Jewish War.[20] The book breaks off in the middle of the account of the siege of Jerusalem by Titus.

Suetonius (AD 69-140) wrote a number of biographies including lives of the Roman emperors from Augustus to Domitian (AD 81-96). In these works the stress lies on the personal lives of the emperors concerned.

All the works of Appian (second century AD) which deal with the period between *c.* 133 and 27 BC have been preserved. Although his work is not always historically reliable, it must be taken into account because of the overall picture he gives of the first century BC.

That part of the history of Rome by Dio Cassius (*c.* AD 155-235) which deals with the period from 69 BC to AD 46 has been preserved. His expertise in the historical sphere must not be rated too highly. His work is valuable simply as a supplement to other sources.

1.2.6 *The Dead Sea Scrolls*

Since 1947, a large number of scrolls, fragments, papyri and ostraca with writing on them have been found by the Dead Sea, dating from the last centuries before the beginning of the Christian era to AD 135. What is unique about them is that they give us information about a group through documents actually produced by the group.[21] In addition, they give us insights into the religion of Israel, above all when the Hasmonaeans were in power. Although none of the writings discovered can be regarded as a historical document in the strict sense of the term, they certainly contain allusions to historical and political events.[22] However, they should be used with great care.

1.2.7 *The New Testament*

The writings of the New Testament were not composed to serve as historical documents, but to bear witness that Jesus is the Christ (cf. John 20.30f.). So the evangelists described the life and message of Jesus in this light. Such an aim does not, however, meant that they give us no historical information. But it is particularly valuable that there are four evangelists, each of whom gives a selection of stories about Jesus. In particular, the differences between the three Synoptic Gospels and that of John are striking. One good example of this is the difference over the length of Jesus' ministry. In the Synoptic Gospels this period seems to cover one year, but in John it covers two or three. The fact that there are differences of this kind is an indication that where the Gospels agree about historical circumstances they may well go back to a real event. Thus both Matthew and Luke give Bethlehem as the place where Jesus was born and according to all four evangelists the crucifixion took place in the time of Pontius Pilate. These and other instances give us a basis for reconstructing the history of Israel in this period.

The Acts of the Apostles and the other writings in the New Testament give us less information in this respect, not least because these books are not as concerned with events in Palestine as are the Gospels.[23]

1.2.8 *The rabbinic literature*

The rabbinic literature came into being after AD 70. Here I shall only mention what is most relevant for us. It consists of extensive collections which in their present form have come down to us after a process which sometimes lasted for several centuries. The term is used to cover the Mishnah, the Tosephta, the Talmuds, the Midrashim and the Targums.[24]

The Mishnah (final redaction about AD 200) contains a collection of laws, regulations and casuistry derived from the Old Testament. According to rabbinic tradition it goes back to Moses through oral tradition. The whole work consists of six parts, sub-divided into tractates which are arranged by themes.

The Tosephta (final redaction about AD 500) has the same division as the Mishnah and contains sayings by rabbis from the time of the Tannaim, which were not incorporated into the Mishnah. The Tosephta (= Supplement) can therefore be regarded more or less as a supplement to the Mishnah.

After the period of the Tannaim (*c.* AD 200) there begins that of the Amoraim, learned men who were primarily concerned with the interpretation and exposition of the Mishnah. Their written works are known as the Gemara. It came into being in two collections, one in Palestine and one in Babylon. The combination of Mishnah and Gemara is known as the Talmud; the two collections are known respectively as the Jerusalem or Palestinian Talmud (final redaction about AD 500) and the Babylonian Talmud (final redaction about AD 700). The latter is regarded as the more important.

The Midrashim are ancient rabbinic commentaries on the Old Testament which presumably derive from readings and addresses in the synagogue. The earliest form of the oldest, Mekilta, Sifre and Sifra, which contain commentaries on parts of Exodus, Leviticus and Numbers-Deuteronomy respectively, probably comes from the time of the Tannaim.

The Targums are translations (often paraphrases) of the Old Testament into Aramaic. The existence of such Targums may go back to the inter-testamental period, as is evident from the discoveries by the Dead Sea.[25]

Too much importance should not be attached to the historical value of this rabbinic literature for a reconstruction of the history of Israel in our period. Although it may contain early material, for the most part it is based on later interpretations and traditions. But when there are allusions to historical events, they need to be taken seriously. However, we must remember that this literature has a very strong and one-sided Pharisaic stamp. The Pharisees were the only important group left in Judaism after the fall of Jerusalem, and they were the ones who gave new stimulus to Judaism so that it could surmount the catastrophe.

Finally, mention should be made of the Megillat Ta'anit (the Fast Scroll),[26] which has some importance as a historical source. This scroll, which probably can be dated to the first century AD, contains a summary of memorial days on which fasting is forbidden. These commemorations recall joyful events from the time of the Maccabees.

1.2.9 *The evidence of archaeology*

Through archaeology we can get some insight into the pattern of settlement, living conditions, the structure of cities and buildings, cultural developments, and so on, in particular periods.[27] In addition to excavations, ostraca, inscriptions and finds of coins[28] are very important for the period with which we shall be dealing. Discoveries of documents are also very important indeed. I shall now mention some of the most significant ones.

Wadi ed-Daliyeh lies about nine miles north of Jericho. Samaritan papyri were found here from the time between about 375 and 335 BC. These papyri belonged to people who had fled into a cave in the wadi before the destruction of Samaria in the time of Alexander the Great and were discovered there later by the Macedonians and killed. These papyri tell us about the governors in power in Samaria in the fourth century BC.[29]

The Zeno papyri were found in 1915, in Fayyum, an oasis in Egypt. They represent the archives of a certain Zeno, who had made a tour of inspection through 'Syria and Phoenicia' on behalf of Apollonius, a kind of minister of Ptolemy II Philadelphus (284-246 BC) of Egypt, between 260 and 258 BC. Among other places he also visited Transjordan. These papyri give us some insight into the administrative and economic situation in Palestine during the third century BC.[30]

Material discovered in Masada, the rock fortress built by Alexander Jannaeus (103-76 BC) and extended by Herod the Great (37-4 BC), gives us information about the history of Masada under the rule of Herod and at the time of the First Jewish War, when this fortress was occupied and lived in by the Zealots.[31]

The letters of Bar Kochba were found in the caves of Murabba'at and at Nahal Hever, i.e. in the region of the Dead Sea (cf. 1.2.6). The letters and the coins also found there have extended our knowledge about the period of the Bar Kochba revolt in AD 132-135 (see also ch.18).[32]

1.3 *The land and the people*

1.3.1 *The land*

It almost goes without saying that in any study of the history of Israel between Alexander the Great and Bar Kochba, most of the emphasis lies on Judaea and Jerusalem. Not only do the most important events take place in this area – as far as we know – but we also have most information about it in this period. Alongside that, however, other areas are also relevant. Foremost among these are Samaria and Galilee, then the territories on the other side of the Jordan, like Gaulanitis, the Decapolis and Peraea, and finally to a lesser extent Ituraea and Idumaea. Broadly speaking, this whole area corresponds to the kingdom which came under the rule of the Hasmoneans in the time of John Hyrcanus I.

I shall use the name Palestine as a general designation of this territory. This name seems already to have been known to Herodotus,[33] but it came to the fore when it became the name of the Roman province in this area after AD 135. However, the name is already used widely in scholarly literature for the period we are dealing with here.[34]

1.3.2 *The people*

Without any doubt, many Judaeans also lived in the area outside Judaea. However, Samaria and certainly also part of Galilee and the territory on the other side of the Jordan were mainly populated by, among others, descendants of the former kingdom of Israel, and the inhabitants of Ituraea and Idumaea were made up of quite different population groups.[35]

In addition to this population, in both the Hellenistic and the Roman period other groups also settled in the land. Foreign rulers left behind garrisons in various places, and they and their families formed military colonies. Alongside these, Graeco-Macedonian and later also Roman colonies grew up over the course of time in various places, made up largely of citizens drawn from the Hellenistic kingdoms. This eventually led to cities which were inhabited almost entirely by Greeks or Greek speakers. One well-known example of this is the Decapolis. As we shall see later, this was also wholly or partially the case with other cities, including Samaria. Even Jerusalem was not spared in this respect. In both the Hellenistic and the Roman period it constantly had to put up with military colonists of foreign origin.

Chapter 2

The Beginning of the Hellenistic Period

2.1 *Hellenism*

The conquest of the ancient Near East by Alexander the Great (333-323 BC) is regarded as the beginning of a new period, referred to as the Hellenistic period. Hellenism is a term used in connection with the cultural movement after Alexander as a result of which Greek language and civilization came to occupy a dominant position in the then known world,[1] and especially among leading groups in the cities.[2] Even in Palestine we have the phenomenon of the so-called Hellenistic cities. In such cities there was usually an ephebate, a training period for young men in citizenship (Greek citizenship), often lasting for a year, and a gymnasium, a public place for sport where instruction was also given. As well as furthering the Greek language, the main aim of both institutions was to cultivate the Greek way of life and Greek customs.[3]

This does not mean that with the arrival of Alexander in the Near East Hellenism suddenly descended out of thin air. In the coastal areas along the Mediterranean in this part of Asia there were cities which had regarded themselves as Greek colonies long before the coming of Alexander. Greek culture had already exercised its influence to some degree from such places. This process now began to accelerate. Soldiers settled as occupying forces in conquered territory and merchants who, with their caravans, now penetrated it increasingly deeply, largely furthered the breakthrough of Hellenism.

The conquests of Alexander the Great also meant an upsurge of Hellenism in the Greek homeland and especially in Macedonia. The expedition against the Persians was felt there to be a second Trojan war in which Alexander was seen more or less as a new Achilles.[4] All this was a stimulus to many Greeks to reflect again on the sources of their own culture.

2.2 *The general political and economic situation*

2.2.1 *The expansion of Alexander's empire*

After the battle of Issus in 333 BC, Alexander first directed his attention to the coastal cities in Syria and Palestine. He succeeded in capturing them very quickly, with the exception of Tyre, which only capitulated after a siege lasting about seven months.[5] At this same time Alexander must also have conquered Judaea and Samaria (see 3.2). After the fall of Tyre, he moved southwards. There Gaza, an important post and trading centre, offered vigorous opposition which was only broken after a two months' siege (332 BC). After that he hastened to Egypt, which he was able to conquer without too much difficulty. There in 331 BC he founded Alexandria, a city which in a later period was well-known, among other things, for its large and active Jewish population.

Soon afterwards a last and decisive power struggle took place between Alexander and Darius III, the last king of the Persians. In 331 BC Darius was killed at Gaugamela, which lay in the plain of Arbela east of the Tigris. The following year Darius was killed by one of his satraps. His kingdom and all his possessions now fell into the hands of Alexander, as soon did the rest of the Persian empire.

However, there was still no end to Alexander's campaigns. These extended as far as India (327-325 BC). But when the Macedonian soldiers got that far they refused to go any further, so Alexander was forced to withdraw. This did not mean that Alexander now planned to end his campaigns of conquest. In Babylon, which he intended to make the capital of his empire, he began to prepare an expedition to Arabia. Moreover he wanted to create a great port there with the aim of establishing a link with Egypt from the mouth of the Euphrates via the sea.[6] The implementation of Alexander's plans was thwarted by his death, from malaria, in Babylon in 323 BC.

2.2.2 *Alexander's political administration*

The cornerstone of Alexander's policy was undoubtedly his attempt to unite Macedonians and Persians in one kingdom and to make them one people. The great wedding he organized in Susa, in which he himself, his chief generals, and presumably at least ten thousand other Macedonians married Persian wives, also fits into this context.[7] Other ways in which he planned to achieve his goal were by transforming the army into a battle force consisting of Persians and Macedonians, and appointing both Macedonians and native aristocrats to administrative posts in the conquered territories.

Despite all his efforts, however, Alexander did not succeed in making the

Persians and the Macedonians one people. The difference in historical traditions and cultural development between the two people was too great for it to be possible to forge a unity.

By way of administration, Alexander took over the Persian system of a division into satrapies. During his campaigns he also founded Graeco-Macedonian *poleis* (cities) in many places, the best-known of which was Alexandria in Egypt. As garrison cities, these settlements had primarily a strategic purpose.

Like the Persian kings who had gone before him, Alexander also followed a policy of religious tolerance. The change of ruling power which followed his arrival therefore led to hardly any change in the religious community in Jerusalem.

2.2.3 *Economic conditions*

The Greeks will have been well aware of economic circumstances in the new territory because their merchants had already been engaged in trade activities there since the seventh century BC. As so often in history, the merchants were now followed by the soldiers. It is therefore no coincidence that Alexander's first aim in his campaign against the Persians was to secure important ports and trading cities like Tyre and Gaza. By conquering these places he not only robbed the Persian fleet of its bases but at the same time did away with competition for the Greek merchants.

One of the most far-reaching consequences of the Hellenistic period for economics[8] was the way in which the hoards of precious metals gathered by the Persian kings were turned into coinage. This measure, coupled with an adaptation to the Attic monetary standard, represented great progress in economic matters. With coins as a means of payment trade could be much more flexible.

There were also a great many important resources in the conquered territories. Moreover, the people there had long been accustomed to living under an absolute monarchy, so they were easy to govern. This was the area into which the Macedonians now came, with their spirit of enterprise, their trading methods and their banks. The combination of these factors was a powerful stimulus for the economy. Above all, the city economy in the many *poleis* which the Greeks and Macedonians founded in the conquered territories (cf. 2.2.2), and which they later extended to other cities, played an important role here.

2.3 *Palestine in 333 – 323* BC

2.3.1 *Judaea*

In speaking about Judaea, at this period we are talking of an area limited to Jerusalem and its immediate surroudings and governed by a high priest. We have little more than very fragmentary information about what happened there in the time of Alexander the Great.

The Old Testament is virtually silent about the rise of Alexander. Only one allusion, in Dan.8.5 ('A he-goat from the west'), may relate to this king's campaign in the East. Whether Zech. 9.1-8 also refers to Alexander cannot be established with any certainty.[9] The scanty allusions to Alexander in I Macc.1.1-7 also say nothing about Judaea and even less about Palestine in this period.

The reason for this silence may be that at this point in time nothing serious happened in connection with Judaea, because the war did not affect it. Moreover, it may well have been that the transfer of power did not bring any significant changes for the community in Jerusalem except that from then on the taxes had to be paid to a new ruler. Moreover, Alexander's 'religious tolerance' probably meant that the introverted community in Jerusalem could simply let things pass over their heads. The consequences of the advent of the Hellenistic ruler would only be felt in the country much later.

We find accounts of contacts of Alexander the Great with Judaea in Josephus and the Babylonian Talmud. According to Josephus,[10] after the conquest of Gaza in 332 BC, Alexander visited Jerusalem and there had a meeting with the high priest Jaddua. The whole account is markedly legendary in character. Alexander's visit to the temple in Jerusalem may well have a historical nucleus, in the light of his later action in Egypt, but it is equally conceivable that by analogy with this event Josephus created a similar story about Jerusalem. The Talmud[11] mentions a meeting between the high priest and Alexander at Kefar Saba (later Antipatris) in the coastal plain. In favour of the historicity of this account it seems plausible that a ruler should have invited the governor of a small subject country to meet him. However, the problem here is that the high priest is given as Simon the Just, who lived about a century later.

2.3.2 *Samaria*

In his *Jewish Antiquities*[12] Josephus reports that a certain Sanballat of Samaria came to the aid of Alexander at the siege of Tyre with a force of eight thousand men. Soon after this Sanballat died. Now on the basis of papyrus finds in the Wadi ed-Daliyeh it is certainly possible that at the time of Alexander there

was a governor in Samaria with the name Sanballat.[13] This must have been
Sanballat III. Furthermore, the defection of a local leader to a conquering
general was also a regular phenomenon at that time. The report about Sanballat
by Josephus therefore sounds very plausible.

Another credible account appears in the biography of Alexander by Curtius
Rufus.[14] According to this, while Alexander was in Egypt the inhabitants of
Samaria rebelled and burned alive Andromachus, the Macedonian governor
of Coele-Syria (i.e. the whole of Phoenicia and Palestine). Alexander thereupon
undertook a punitive expedition against the city in which the rebels were put
to death. Supplementary information about this event is given by a chronicle
of Eusebius.[15] After suppressing this rebellion Alexander is said to have taken
a number of inhabitants of Samaria into captivity and then settled a group of
Macedonians there. All these reports seem to be confirmed by the information
provided by the papyri discoveries in Wadi ed-Daliyeh mentioned earlier. In
addition to papyri, about three hundred skeletons were found there. It is now
supposed that these are the skeletons of inhabitants of Samaria who attempted
to escape the punitive expedition made by Alexander's troops against this city
in 331 BC by fleeing to a cave in the Wadi ed-Daliyeh north of Jericho and
were later discovered there by the Macedonians and killed.[16]

All this information is connected with a rebuilding of Shechem at this time
by inhabitants of Samaria. The old city of Shechem is said to have been
uninhabited between about 480 and 330 BC. Archaeological evidence would
seem to indicate that there are again traces of habitation after 330 BC.[17]
However, there is considerable uncertainty about this. On the basis of the
same archaeological material it is also argued that Shechem had already been
inhabited again before the coming of Alexander the Great.[18] The former view
seems to me to be most convincing.

2.3.3 *The Samaritan temple*

The question of the rebuilding of Shechem also raises the question of the
building of the 'Samaritan'[19] temple on Gerizim. It is usually thought to have
been in the Hellenistic period,[20] but the date still needs to be made more
precise.

In the section of Flavius Josephus' *Jewish Antiquities* mentioned in the
previous paragraph, Josephus reports that when Sanballat declared himself
subject to Alexander, at the same time he received permission from Alexander
to build a temple on Gerizim. However, it is remarkable that in Josephus'
description of a later event during Alexander's stay in Palestine, this temple
seems already to have been built.[21] The temple certainly could not have been
built during the short time that Alexander stayed in the area, so it seems likely

that we should not attach too much importance to the report of Alexander's concern with the building of a temple on Gerizim.[22] It is better to assume that the temple came into being about the same time as the rebuilding of Shechem in about 330 BC and the years following, and in conjunction with it. Specialist studies of this area[23] also suggest that the building of the temple on Gerizim must have taken place about the end of the fourth century BC.

The building of this temple need not of itself imply that there was a schism with temple worship in Jerusalem. Despite all the accounts which seem to tell against this, it is clear that until the Hellenistic period several temples quite legitimately existed alongside that of Jerusalem, including one in Leontopolis in Egypt and probably one in ʿAraq-el-Emir in Transjordan.[24] A breach between Jews and 'Samaritans' in which worship on Gerizim began to have more or less a life of its own alongside that in Jerusalem only came about gradually. This process developed in the period from the third century BC to the second century BC[25] or the beginning of the Christian era.[26]

The building of the temple on Gerizim meant in the first place that Shechem – the city which was also so significant from a religious point of view in the Old Testament period[27] - became the centre of the cult of the 'Samaritans'. Here the term 'Samaritans' should not be associated with the city of Samaria. That place, which can rightly be called the first Hellenistic city in Palestine,[28] belongs in quite a different context. Similarly, mention of 'Samaritans' in a later period should suggest the environs of Shechem and the province of Samaria rather than the city of Samaria.

Chapter 3

The Period of the Diadochi
(*c.* 323-301 BC)

3.1 *The general situation after the death of Alexander*

When Alexander died in 323 BC, there was in fact no successor capable of taking his place. Neither the child who was born after his death nor his weak half-brother Philip Arrideus were in a position to take over power. The real power came into the hands of the so-called Diadochi ('successors'). The term Diadochi denotes the generals who after the death of Alexander took over rule of the Macedonian-Persian world empire, which had only been founded in 330, and later divided it among themselves. This happened when in the course of time they had murdered all the legal heirs of Alexander (see above). The three most important kingdoms of the Didadochi, which eventually survived after many internecine wars, were those of the Ptolemies in Egypt, the Seleucids in Syria-Palestine and the Antigonids in the European part of Alexander's former empire.

In these wars among the Diadochi, Palestine, too, was the scene of a long and bitter struggle, first particularly between the Antigonids and the Ptolemies and later between the Ptolemies and the Seleucids.

3.2 *The struggle for the possession of Palestine*

In 322 BC Ptolemy arrived in Egypt. Once there he set himself up as Alexander's successor and ruler of an independent territory. This is the perspective from which we must view the fact that one of his first actions was to bring the body of Alexander the Great with great pomp and splendour to Egypt.[1]

Like the Pharaohs before him, Ptolemy understood that Coele-Syria (like 'Syria and Palestine', a term used to denote the whole of Palestine and Phoenicia) was a very good base for an attack on Egypt. For this reason alone he was concerned to gain control over the area. In 320 BC he was able to achieve his aim through military means. For the moment, Ptolemy held Palestine for only a very short time. Among other things, he first had to reckon with Antigonus Monophthalmus ('the one-eyed'), a powerful opponent, who also had aspirations to appropriate Alexander's legacy.

After the death of Alexander, Antigonus had become governor over Asia Minor. In about 317 BC he was able to drive out Seleucus, who had been appointed satrap of Babylon. Seleucus thereupon fled to Egypt, where he sought and obtained sanctuary with Ptolemy. Meanwhile Antigonus advanced further towards Syria and Palestine, capturing Tyre, Joppa, Gaza and other places in the process. Ptolemy could do little about this since his hands were tied elsewhere. However, Antigonus, too, had to retreat to Asia Minor because of difficulties there. He handed over government of the conquered areas of Coele-Syria and command of the troops there to his son Demetrius. Demetrius was killed in battle in Gaza in 312 by Alexander's experienced former generals, Ptolemy and Seleucus. After this victory Ptolemy was able to establish his rule over Palestine once again within a short time.

After the battle at Gaza, Seleucus advanced with an army to Babylon and captured the city. This happened on 1 October 312 BC. This date forms the beginning of the so-called Seleucid chronology.

However, the victory at Gaza had not brought Ptolemy long-term success. Barely six months later, Demetrius was able to surprise an army of his and defeat it.[2] When after that Antigonus himself invaded Syria with an army and occupied the cities of Acco, Joppa, Samaria and Gaza, all Ptolemy could do was to retreat back to Egypt.[3]

This situation continued until Seleucus and his allies[4] inflicted a decisive defeat on Antigonus in 301 at the battle of Ipsus (in Phrygia). After this victory a new division of Alexander's empire was made, in which among other things Seleucus was assigned Syria and Palestine. However, Ptolemy, who was not affected either by the battle of Ipsus or the division which followed it, succeeded in making himself master of Palestine. He did this while his allies were still entangled in the struggle with Antigonus, and after the battle of Ipsus he refused to give up the area again.

It goes without saying that this course of action caused his former friend and ally Seleucus, who after Ipsus again laid claim to the area, to be very angry. Throughout the whole of the third century BC Palestine was a cause of dispute between the Ptolemies and the Seleucids. We can find a reflection of this in Dan.11.5-6.[5] As far as Palestine was concerned, matters were provisionally settled in favour of the Ptolemies. From 201-198 BC they were able to retain possession of the land.

3.3 *Consequences for the land and the people*

3.3.1 *The period from 323-311* BC

In this period, land and people suffered appallingly from the struggle that was waged in the area. The constant changes of controlling power and the battles that went with them will certainly have left deep scars. Above all the coastal cities, and especially Gaza (see above), must have suffered heavily.

We can certainly infer this much, even though we have virtually no information at all about Palestine at this time. This need not cause us any surprise. In this period Judaea and Jerusalem in particular were politically and economically so insignificant that Greek writers had no need to pay much attention to them.[6] Jewish sources are also almost silent about this period. In I Macc.1.9 it is simply said that the Diadochi 'caused many evils on the earth', though that statement in itself is evocative enough of the suffering in which the land was involved at that time.

It is also worth noting a report in Josephus[7] taken from a work of Hecataeus of Abdera from the fourth century BC. This reports how after the battle at Gaza in 312 BC many inhabitants of 'Syria' (i.e. Palestine) followed Ptolemy to Egypt because of his 'friendly and humane atittude'. They are said to have included the sixty-six year old Hezekiah, an important priest from this time, with a number of supporters. It is impossible to say how reliable this report is. The attitude of Ptolemy as described here seems difficult to reconcile with his later activity (see 3.3.2). On the other hand, however, we cannot exclude the possibility that on the advance of Antigonus, supporters of Ptolemy took the road to Egypt. These could well have included priests.[8]

The above-named Hezekiah is probably the figure referred to by the name *Yehizqiyyo* on an old coin which comes from the late Persian period.[9] However, there is no certainty about this.

3.3.2 *The period from 311 to 301* BC

By contrast the next period, at least to begin with, was one of considerable peace and quiet. This was because during it Antigonus had virtually consolidated his position and had obtained a firm footing in Coele-Syria.

Antigonus seems to have had most problems in the first instance during this period with the Nabataeans.[10] The Nabataeans occupied a key position in connection with the important caravan route from Syria to the Persian Gulf. In 312 BC Antigonus sent his general Athenaeus with an army to conquer their territory. This expedition failed.[11] An attempt soon afterwards by Demetrius to take the 'rock', later Petra, by surprise, also achieved no results.[12]

We may, however, suppose that Antigonus will have established military settlements in the area east of the Jordan in order to be able to have some control over the caravan route. At all events there are indications that he was responsible for the foundation or extension of a city like Pella.[13]

Apart from this, the sources are silent about events in Palestine during the time that it was under the control of Antigonus. This changes after the battle of Ipsus (see 3.2), when Ptolemy was again able to get a footing in the land. According to Josephus, who is here quoting from a lost work of Agatharcides of Cnidus,[14] at this period Ptolemy occupied Jerusalem on a sabbath, because the inhabitants of the city refused to take up arms on that day. On this occasion Ptolemy is also said to have taken prisoner many from Jerusalem and its environs, the hill-country of Judaea, Samaria and Gerizim, and brought them to Egypt.[15] This report by Josephus seems to be confirmed by a report in the Letter of Aristeas,[16] which relates that Ptolemy I had about 100,000 inhabitants of Judaea deported to Egypt. This number may be on the high side, but the deportation may well be a historical fact given the different sources which mention it and the large number of Jews who later lived in Egypt.

Although some[17] scholars think that the capture of Jerusalem mentioned here took place directly after the battle near Gaza in 312 BC, it seems more likely that we should put it in 301 BC. After the battle near Gaza Ptolemy returned directly to Phoenicia.[18]

This conquest of Jerusalem in 301 BC and the harsh treatment by Ptolemy of the inhabitants strongly suggests that there were those among the people and especially among the leaders in Jerusalem who had associated closely with the régime of Antigonus. However, we have no more detailed information.

3.4 *The administrative situation*

3.4.1 *The overall division*

In all probability Antigonus Monophthalmus to some degree developed the system of dividing Palestine into toparchies which was later used by the Ptolemies.[19] A toparchy usually consisted of a city, where the seat of government was established, and the territory of a number of neighbouring villages. A toparchy of this kind was the smallest administrative unit and authority which collected taxes. Taken together, a number of toparchies formed the next largest unit, the hyparchy. This administrative unit presumably corresponded roughly with what in Ptolemaic Egypt was known as the *nomos*. The name of these hyparchies have perhaps been preserved in place names ending with -itis, like Gaulanitis and Galaaditis, and in the (Greek) names ending in

-ia, like Iudaia, Idumaia, Samareia and Galilaia.[20] As the smallest adminis-trative unit and authority for raising taxes the toparchy seems to have existed down to the time of Herod the Great.

The most important administrative positions in both the hyparchies and the toparchies were usually occupied by Greeks in the Hellenistic period.

3.4.2 *The administration in Jerusalem and Judaea*

It is almost certain that the government of Judaea and Jerusalem in this period had rather a different structure from that in the rest of the country. As early as the Persian period,[21] this area must have been governed by a council which had its seat in Jerusalem. In rabbinic literature, which in any case sees the assembly of the seventy elders in Num.11.16 as the Sanhedrin of this time, this council is designated the Great Assembly.[22] The term Josephus[23] uses for the period around 200 BC is *gerousia*, 'the assembly of the elders'. Only in Roman times was this institution given the name Sanhedrin ('court of judgment'), which is also known from the New Testament.

The new authorities evidently left unchanged this administrative situation in Jerusalem dating from the Persian period. Of course it is clear that the council only had limited authority primarily relating to legal and executive powers in domestic matters.

The members of this council were prominent priests and 'elders', presum-ably a reference to the heads of well-to-do families. The whole council was led by the high priest, who thus had a very important position in the administration of the country.[24] As a rule the high priesthood was handed down from father to son, though there were already exceptions to this regular practice in the early Hellenistic period.[25]

The last high priest to be mentioned in the Old Testament is Jaddua (Neh.12.22), a contemporary of Darius III and Alexander the Great (see also 2.3.1). According to Josephus he was succeeded by his son Onias I.[26] Onias was therefore high priest in the period between 323 and 301 BC. In I Macc.12.22-23 (cf. *AJ* XII, 226-7) there is mention of a letter which Onias is said to have received from Arius I, king of Sparta (309-265 BC). This Arius was an important opponent of Antigonus. The presupposition is that the aim of this letter was to prompt him to rebel against Antigonus.[27] However, the authenticity of the letter is difficult to defend.[28] It seems most likely that the letter is based on a later fiction deriving from circles which at a later date wanted to demonstrate that from of old there had been links with Greece.

Nothing is known about the attitude adopted by Onias I in the dispute between Antigonus and Ptolemy, or about his activity as high priest. The only thing we know with certainty is that he was succeeded by his son Simon I, whom Josephus calls 'the Just'.[29] However, this must be a slip or the result of false information. The Simon who bore this epithet must be Simon II, who lived about 200 BC. That would also fit in better with what is said in Sirach 50 and several traditions preserved in rabbinic literature.[30]

When Simon I took over the office of high priest from his father, a new period had already dawned for the land, that of Ptolemaic rule. We know just as little about the activities of Simon I as we do about those of his father. However, it is certain that the high-priestly family of the Oniads was to go on to play a very important role in the further course of history.

3.4.3 *Administration in the rest of the country*

We have even less information about the administration of the rest of Palestine in this period than we do about that of Judaea. In all probability the region of Samaria formed a more or less independent administrative unity (hyparchy).[31] Whether this also applied to an area like Galilee is unknown. We get the impression from *AJ* XII, 154 and I Macc.10.30 that under Seleucid rule Galilee was part of the administrative unit of Samaria, but it is far from certain whether that was already the case in an earlier period.[32]

In Transjordan there were still tribes with native sheikhs who continued to have a large degree of independence. Moreover, an increasing number of Greek cities came into being there (cf.2.2.2) which later formed the Decapolis.[33] Decapolis must of course be regarded purely as a geographical term.[34] Like the large coastal cities and other Greek settlements in the land, those of what was later the Decapolis should be regarded as independent Greek cities.[35] This means that the inhabitants of these cities could regulate their own internal affairs, but in military terms were completely dependent on the Hellenic authorities, to whom they were also obliged to pay taxes. The administration of such a city lay in the hands of a council, which could consist of several hundred members. Thus according to Josephus,[36] that of Gaza numbered five hundred people.

Chapter 4

The First Half-Century of Ptolemaic Rule
(301-246 BC)

4.1 *The position of the Ptolemaic king*

The reign of the Ptolemaic kings in Egypt can be seen as a continuation of that of the former Pharaohs. Like the latter, the Ptolemies could rely on a strong central authority and their position as kings was almost unassailable. The divine worship which the Pharaohs allowed to be offered to them in former times was also largely offered to the Ptolemaic kings. The efforts of especially the first Ptolemaic kings were in fact directed towards creating a form of state which went back to old Egyptian institutions, adapted to Greek insights about the state as an institution.[1]

Above all from a social and economic point of view, the power and influence of the Ptolemaic king was particularly great. As with the Pharaohs, all land was in principle regarded as the property of the king.[2] Part of this land was leased out to the temple. Greek mercenaries could also buy land which they then sub-let to the Egyptians. Moreover, a good deal of land was worked by peasants under the strict supervision of royal officials. All this implies that the king had substantial income from this so-called 'royal land'.

Another source of income was provided by the royal monopoly in the most important forms of trade.[3] In fact all means of production and all barter were in the hands of the state, in other words, in the possession of the king.[4] In addition to all this the king also controlled the collection of the various taxes and tolls.

All this income which the Ptolemies were able to acquire made them the richest and consequently the most powerful rulers in the ancient Near East during the third century BC. The reverse side of the coin is, as so often in history, that a large proportion of the population in their kingdom, in this case especially the native Egyptians, suffered harsh poverty. Only the king and his immediate entourage profited to any degree from these riches. Among the latter were the senior Macedonian and Greek soldiers who served in the army of the Ptolemies.[5]

4.2 *Political developments in c. 301-246* BC

4.2.1 *The time of Ptolemy I Soter (323-283* BC)

Ptolemy I, surnamed Soter, 'saviour', 'deliverer', can be regarded as the founder of the Hellenistic state of Egypt which existed until 30 BC. In 305 BC Ptolemy had taken the crown for himself, although in fact from 323 BC he already had power over the greater part of the kingdom. The capital of this kingdom was the city of Alexandria, founded by Alexander the Great.

The province of 'Syria and Phoenicia', which also included Palestine, was still not completely in the hands of Ptolemy I after the battle of Ipsus (see 3.2). Apart from the claims to this area by Seleucus I, though these were apparently ineffective in the third century BC, Demetrius – the son of Antigonus – still had possession of the cities of Tyre and Sidon. According to Eusebius,[6] in 296 BC Demetrius again devastated the city of Samaria in an attack on Palestine. However, there is considerable uncertainty about the trustworthiness of this account. It is certain, though, that Tyre and Sidon were in the possession of the Ptolemies at the latest in 286 BC. That meant that the whole of the province of Syria and Phoenicia was in their power.

In particular, their rule over Palestine meant that the Ptolemies could continue the policy of the former Pharaohs. Anyone who occupied Palestine controlled the trade and caravan routes like those from Mesopotamia to Egypt and from Syria and Mesopotamia to the Gulf of Akaba.[7] Economically this area was therefore extremely important for Egypt. In military terms, too, Palestine was very important for the Ptolemies. Strategically it formed a frontier post for the defence of Egypt. The whole policy of Ptolemy I was directed towards strengthening and consolidating his position in Palestine as a military and economic base. It could be said that in fact he had achieved this goal by the end of his reign.

4.2.2 *The period of Ptolemy II Philadelphus (283-246* BC)

During the reign of Ptolemy II the Ptolemies were at the zenith of their power. Both in the First (274-271 BC) and the Second Syrian War (260-253 BC), he succeeded in defending his position in 'Syria and Phoenicia' against the claims of the Seleucids.

After the Second Syrian War it even seemed that the dispute over this area between the Ptolemies and the Seleucids was finally going to come to an end because a marriage had been arranged between Berenice, the daughter of Ptolemy II, and Antiochus II, the Seleucid king. On this occasion Ptolemy II gave his daughter a large dowry on condition that Antiochus II divorced his first wife, but after the death of Ptolemy II Antiochus II sought to be reconciled with the latter. She, however, managed to have Antiochus II, Berenice and their child killed (cf. Dan.11.6). This became one of the causes of the Third Syrian War (see 5.1.1).

About 278 BC, Ptolemy II also defeated the Nabataeans; the result was that the trade route from Petra to the northern part of Syria was cut off. From then on trade with southern Arabia ran through Gaza. In order to keep the Nabataeans further in check, the southern and eastern frontiers of Palestine were fortified.

To strengthen his position Ptolemy had several cities built (or rebuilt) and fortified in Palestine. They probably included Acco, which was now called Ptolemais;[8] Beth-shean, which in the time of the Ptolemies was called Scythopolis and in the time of the Seleucids Nyssa;[9] Philoteria, which can perhaps be identified with the original Beth-jerach;[10] and Rabbah, the old capital of Ammon, which was later called Philadelphia.[11]

All the developments outlined here had consequences for Palestine. On the basis of the information which we have about this period, which is fragmentary and scarce, we get the impression that in political and military terms little happened. The two Syrian wars seem to have left the greater part of the land unscathed. The greatest changes took place in the social and economic spheres.

4.3 *Social and economic consequences in Palestine*

4.3.1 *Social consequences*

The fact that the Ptolemies built new cities or had old and abandoned ones rebuilt had obvious consequences for the population structure of Palestine. Hitherto it had consisted primarily of Judaeans in Judah, and for the most part of descendants of the former Israel in Samaria and Galilee. Alongside that the process which had already begun under Alexander the Great, as a result of which large groups of Macedonians and Greeks came to live in the land, developed to an increasing degree (cf.1.3.2). These groups settled mainly in the cities along the coast and in Transjordan. These particular locations should not come as any surprise to us. They were the areas which were of great signifiance in both military and economic terms, because the most important trade and caravan routes ran through them. The majority of the new inhabitants were soldiers and merchants with their families and following.

All this helps us to understand how Hellenism could be most easily established in these particular cities. For the most part the better off among the indigenous population were the ones who gradually adopted the new (Hellenistic) life-style.[12] In the country, the villages and cities were able to maintain their original character, even in a later period. One exception to this was the city of Samaria, which already had a Macedonian population in the time of Alexander the Great (see 2.3.2). Above all in Judaea and there particularly in Jerusalem, the process of Hellenization developed very slowly among the leading groups. Here we can only demonstrate it with some certainty in the period after Ptolemy II Philadelphus. In all probability in the first instance economic factors were paramount.

In general it can be said that the period of Ptolemy I and Ptolemy II was a time of peace and quiet in Palestine. That makes a report by Polybius[13] that the inhabitants of Coele-Syria were well-disposed to the Ptolemies seem very plausible. And in the circumstances we can well see how Jewish units could at this time make up part of the Ptolemaic army.[14]

4.3.2 *Economic consequences*

Ptolemaic rule had primarily economic consequences. The position of the Ptolemaic king outlined in 4.1 could not fail to have an effect here in Palestine as well.

It is clear that the state became very strong in the economic sphere during the Ptolemaic period.[15] The authorities in Alexandria (i.e. the king) were concerned to exploit all land as far as possible to their own advantage. The introduction of the Greek system of state leasing served this end.[16] Given that the Ptolemies wanted to make their income as high as possible,[17] they had to levy high taxes. Above all the small farmers were the victims of this. Then came the well-to-do farmers, who were able to occupy a quite independent position over against the king.[18]

So-called 'tax farmers' were entrusted with the collection of this state taxation and other taxes. These people were usually members of the population of the city or region where the taxes were raised; however, the income from the taxes did not benefit the city or region concerned, but the central authority in Alexandria.[19] The position of 'tax farmer' was held by the most well-to-do. A good deal of money was needed for it. Moreover, large 'presents' were often given to the king and above all to officials to exclude rivals.

The income which the king received from these taxes from 'Syria and Phoenicia' seems to have been enormous.[20] When we remember that the 'tax farmers' made their own profit out of them as well, it is clear that the population were oppressed by a heavy burden. On the other hand it should also be pointed out that Ptolemy II Philadelphus took steps against an uncontrolled slave trade in 'Syria and Phoenicia'.[21] Even free farmers who could not pay their debts could be sold as slaves.

We get important information about the economic situation in Palestine during this period from the so-called Zeno papyri.[22] These mention a certain Zeno who, on behalf of Apollonius, as it were a finance minister to Ptolemy II, made a tour of inspection to Palestine in about 261-258 BC. Two of these papyri[23] mention a certain Tobias who lived in a kind of fortress in Ammanitis (Transjordan). The papyri detail gifts which Tobias sent to Ptolemy and Apollonius. Such gifts are an indication of the close relations which Tobias must have had with the court in Alexandria. It is not certain whether this Tobias is a descendant of the Tobiah mentioned in Neh.6.17-19 and 13.4-9, but it is clear, as we shall see in the next chapter, that the descendants of the Tobias mentioned in the Zeno papyri played a major role at the time of Ptolemaic rule in Palestine.

One of the aims of Zeno's journey was to introduce as efficient political and above all economic control in Palestine as there was in the mother country, Egypt. There is no doubt that here figures like Tobias in particular had given a helping hand.

We need to pay special attention in this respect to Judaea and Jerusalem. Judaea, i.e. Jerusalem and its immediate environs, can be regarded as a kind of temple state,[24] governed by a high priest with the support of a kind of council (see 3.4.2). It certainly had no political independence. The high priest paid a tax to the Ptolemies in the name of the people, as his predecessors had done earlier to the Persian rulers. This tax was raised from the populace by a special tax on land.[25] It is not clear whether in this capacity the high priest should also be regarded as a kind of tax farmer. That does not seem completely impossible, although it is more probable that the foreign rulers appointed a Judaean temple official alongside the high priest to be specially responsible for financial matters in Judaea and in the temple.[26]

Without any doubt it can be said that the existence of such officials and of tax farmers did a good deal to further collaboration with the Ptolemies in higher circles. However, at the same time this produced much greater alienation between particular aristocratic circles and the rest of the population.[27] Koheleth (Ecclesiastes) in particular seems illuminating in this respect. For that reason we must pay some attention to its content.

4.4 *Koheleth (Ecclesiastes)*

It is almost universally assumed that Koheleth was written in the third century BC.[28] Its place of origin is generally taken to be Jerusalem.

The use of the name Koheleth, usually translated 'preacher', to denote the author, indicates that he was an important official in Judaean society. Furthermore he is also called a 'wise man' (Koh.12.9; cf. also 2.15). These designations typify him as a member of the higher circles which could be found above all in Jerusalem.[29] We get the impression that in many respects Koheleth also expressed the views of this group. Seen in this light it is not surprising that Koheleth constantly calls on people to accept the existing situation – primarily the social and economic situation. All opposition to it is useless (cf. 8.2-4). Criticism of the king and his system is rejected out of hand (cf. 8.2-4). Everything is essentially unchangeable, and therefore according to Koheleth changes are clearly also impossible (1.15; cf. 7.13). And since everything will be as it must be, his advice is to 'enjoy life' (cf. 9.7ff.). However, it should be remembered that this enjoyment is in fact only possible for the well-to-do with the means for it. For the oppressed, death is a way out (cf.4.1-2).[30]

All this does not alter the fact that Koheleth is also critical of the attitude and life-style of those who are involved only in the aimless pursuit of amassing riches (cf.2.4-8; 5.9-10).

These brief comments from Koheleth indicate the background to an opposition between the aristocracy in Judaea (or at least part of them) on the one hand and the ordinary people on the other, which steadily increased over the course of time. This opposition was finally to lead, among other things, to armed conflict in the time of the Maccabees.[31]

Chapter 5

The Second Half-Century of Ptolemaic Rule
(246-198 BC)

5.1 *The Third Syrian War (246-241 BC)*

5.1.1 *The course of the war*

This war broke out when Ptolemy III Euergetes (246-221 BC) had only just come to the throne. It arose directly out of the intrigues around Berenice, the sister of Ptolemy III and the second wife of the Seleucid prince Antiochus II (see 4.2.2). Essentially, of course, it was another expression of the old conflict between Ptolemies and Seleucids over rule in this part of the world. It is also clear that the war was an attempt on the part of Ptolemy III to prevent Seleucus II, the successor to Antiochus II, from setting foot in Asia Minor.[1]

At first the campaign against Seleucus II begun by Ptolemy III went particularly well for Ptolemy. Among other things he succeeded in occupying the major part of Syria and advancing as far as the Euphrates. In 245 BC, however, he seems suddenly to be back in Alexandria again. We cannot tell with any certainty what the reason was. It is possible that a rebellion in Egypt compelled Ptolemy to make a personal appearance there.[2] Another factor may have been the defeat at sea which Antigonus, king of Macedon, inflicted on the Ptolemies in 245 BC.[3] Be this as it may, Seleucus seems to have been stronger at a later stage than the beginning of the war might have suggested. So he succeeded in regaining possession of virtually all of his father's kingdom. Despite all this, Ptolemy succeeded in concluding a peace treaty in his own favour in 241 BC. This left him in possession of the enclave of Seleucia, the port of Antioch and important areas in the south of Asia Minor.[4] The reason why Seleucus accepted a treaty at the end of the Third Syrian War which was so unsatisfactory for him was that he had to deal with his brother Antiochus Hierax, who wanted to be independent ruler of part of the Seleucid kingdom.

The course of the Third Syrian War seems to have been followed with interest in Jerusalem and its environs. We find a reflection of this in Dan.11.6-9. This interest is also expressed by the advent of Onias II in the course of this war.

5.1.2 *The situation in Jerusalem during the Third Syrian War*

Towards the end of the Third Syrian War the then high priest Onias II refused to go on paying tribute to the Ptolemies. We find this report in Josephus,[5] but he puts the event wrongly in the time of Ptolemy V Epiphanes, who ruled from 204 to 180 BC.[6] According to Josephus, this action of Onias was prompted by his limited spiritual capacity and great greed. However, we must assume that Onias II embarked on his course of action on the assumption that Seleucus II would come out best from the Third Syrian War. In all probability he reckoned that the war might mean the end of Ptolemaic rule. One might conclude from this that there were people in Jerusalem who more or less welcomed the prospect of the end of this rule. At any rate, it is inconceivable that Onias will have been alone in his opposition to the Ptolemies. One important factor that prompted hostility to the Ptolemies was that the people were heavily taxed by them. The high priest handed over the tax, but the people had to provide it.

Josephus also reports that Ptolemy III now sent a delegation to Jerusalem to put pressure on Onias. If the country persisted in its refusal to pay tribute, it would be put under military rule.[7] Not everyone was happy with this course of events. The most important representative of the opposition was Joseph, the son of Tobias (cf.5.2). Joseph was clearly the leader, or at any rate the spokesman, of a group in Jerusalem which, if not Hellenistic, was at least pro-Ptolemaic. Presumably this was a group which accepted Ptolemaic rule, above all from economic considerations.

Joseph saw an opportunity to bring the conflict between Onias II and Ptolemy III to an end. One result of this was that the *de facto* political, social and economic power in Jerusalem now fell into his hands. Onias II remained high priest, but in future he had little or no influence.

Another report, also from Josephus,[8] tells of a visit which Ptolemy III is said to have made to Jerusalem during the course of the Third Syrian War. On this occasion Ptolemy is said to have sacrificed to God in the Jerusalem temple, rather than to the gods of Egypt, to give thanks for the favourable outcome of the war. This report has a markedly legendary character. Josephus has foreign leaders visiting the temple of Jerusalem on many occasions (cf.2.3.1), clearly with the aim of convincing his non-Jewish readers of the exceptional character

of Israel's religion. There may be a historical nucleus in his report in that
Ptolemy may indeed have been in Jerusalem at that time, but it will have been
to settle things in connection with the advent of Onias II.

5.2 *Oniads and Tobiads*

In the previous section we have seen how Onias II and Josephus, the son of
Tobias, can be seen as representatives of a particular group. Behind each was
a particular family; the families are designated the Oniads and Tobiads. We
must now look more closely at them, since they play a prominent role in the
history of Israel over the next decades.

The designation Oniads is derived from the high priests who were called
Onias. The first to bear this name was Onias I, who held office as high priest
in Jerusalem between *c.*323 and 300 BC. In particular, the high priests from
this family come into the foreground with the Oniads. Here, in addition to
Onias II, as we shall see, Simon II the Just, Onias III and Onias IV were the
main figures. It will subsequently become clear that these high priests and
their followers, i.e. the Oniads, certainly cannot be said to be specifically
inclined towards Hellenism. At the same time this means that in the leading
circles in Jerusalem we can occasionally see two groups, one of which can be
described as favourable towards Hellenism and the other not. The Tobiads
make up the former group.

We know nothing about their origins. It has been assumed that there was a
link between the Tobiads from the Hellenistic period and the 'son of Tabeel'
mentioned in Isa.7.6,[9] but no convincing proof of this can be given (see also
4.3.2). We find most information about the Tobiads in Josephus, in the so-
called Tobiad romance,[10] though the information there must be read with a
very critical eye. Josephus puts the events he describes in quite the wrong
context, in 198 BC; moreover, this story gives the strong impression that its
main concern is to make Joseph and his son Hyrcanus the great figures of the
Tobiads.[11]

It is certain that this Joseph is a son of the Tobias mentioned in the Zeno
papyri.[12] We may infer from them that the Tobiads had both land and a
residence (fortress) in Transjordan.[13] This fortress was in Ammanitis
(cf.4.3.2), and must have been in the neigbourhood of ʿAraq el-Emir.[14] Clearly
the Tobiads had an important position there. Later they also seem to have had
considerable influence in Jerusalem and Samaria, as is particularly evident
from the rise of Joseph.

5.3 *The rise of Joseph the Tobiad*

The controversy between Onias II and Joseph described in 5.1.2 is the first clash we know of between the Oniads and the Tobiads. It emerges from this that Joseph had shifted the activities of the Tobiads to Jerusalem, where he doubtless belonged to the city aristocracy. In 5.1.2 we noted that he considerably strengthened his position through his opposition to the high priest Onias II, whose authority he was largely able to take over.

After these events Joseph also seems to have been appointed as 'tax farmer' for Palestine and perhaps even for the whole of 'Syria and Phoenicia'.[15] This function he performed for twenty-two years, probably between 239 and 217 BC,[16] and he did so with a harshness and cruelty which spared nothing and no one. In cities like Ashkelon and Scythopolis he had the chief citizens killed for the slightest protest against the high taxes and confiscated their properties.[17]

Now for the first time in history Jerusalem, too, becomes an important international city. The rise of Joseph also signified a great economic boom. Hengel[18] rightly points out that from now on Jerusalem also becomes important for classical authors and is no longer seen as a small and insignificant state round a temple.

The example of Joseph shows that the rich began to settle in the city, contrary to what had happened earlier. Thus Jerusalem increasingly became a financial and economic centre. In fact Joseph and his family can be regarded as the first great bankers there. Moreover, they had a patron in Alexandria,[19] something which presumably owes a good deal to the large number of Jews who gradually settled there.

A pro-Hellenistic attitude clearly comes to the fore in the life-style of Joseph and the Tobiads. This affinity emerges from their contacts with Samaria,[20] the payment of bribes to the king and his immediate entourage,[21] and the scant respect they seem to have had for Jewish legislation.[22] Thus Joseph can be regarded as an important forerunner to a Hellenistic trend among the aristocracy in Jerusalem and its environs. This trend becomes increasingly strong, and because the Tobiads, apart from Hyrcanus, chose the Seleucid side in about 200 BC, their influence on the course of events in Jerusalem continued to be great and often decisive, even after the end of Ptolemaic rule.

5.4 *The Fourth Syrian War (221-217 BC)*

5.4.1 *The prelude*

After many internal conflicts[23] Antiochus III became king over the Seleucid empire in 223 BC at the age of twenty. Although he was inexperienced, he was soon able to put things in order. He restored the unity of his kingdom by eliminating some of his rivals. After that he prepared for a campaign against Egypt with the aim of conquering the old disputed area of 'Syria and Phoenicia'.

In the meantime, Ptolemy III Euergetes (246-221 BC) had died in Egypt; he was succeeded by his son Ptolemy IV Philopator (221-204 BC). This king was also very young (seventeen years old) when he occupied the throne. His position was far from enviable. After the Third Syrian War his father had completely neglected the Egyptian army. Moreover the young king in fact had no influence. Everything was in the hands of his vizier Sosibius. Sosibius was principally concerned to establish peace in the land and to avoid or eliminate conspiracies. Ptolemy IV also seems to have been all too ready to delegate such matters to others. He preferred to occupy himself with art and religious problems.[24]

Given all this, circumstances seemed particularly favourable for Antiochus finally to wrest from the Ptolemies this territory which for so long had been in dispute.

5.4.2 *The course of the war*

To begin with, success was wholly on the side of Antiochus III. First of all he captured Seleucia,[25] the port of Antioch, which had remained in the possession of Ptolemy III after the Third Syrian War. Then he moved southwards, where he captured the cities of Tyre and Acco (Ptolemais), virtually without striking a blow. These cities also brought him substantial provisions and about forty ships.[26] After that he spent an unnecessarily long time capturing various small cities in Phoenicia and Palestine and on a long-drawn-out siege of the fortress of Dor, a port on the Mediterranean coast south of Carmel. Had Antiochus III continued his advance, he would certainly have succeeded in inflicting a final defeat on Ptolemy, given the deplorable state of the Egyptian army.

By delaying, he played completely into the hands of Sosibius, who was concerned to gain time. Here he succeeded completely, by persuading Antiochus III to accept a four-month cease fire. After this, fortunes were reversed, because Sosibius used the pause to raise a new army. This army included soldiers from the military settlements and, for the first time in the history of the Ptolemies, native Egyptians.

In 217 BC there was a battle at Raphia, which ended with the defeat of Antiochus III. The Seleucid king then had no alternative but to make peace with Ptolemy IV; here the political situation was restored to what it had been before the outbreak of the Fourth Syrian War. Daniel 11.10b-12 gives a summary of the war.

However, the Ptolemies did not exploit their victory. They allowed Antiochus III to withdraw in peace. This tactical error would soon demand its price.

5.4.3 *Palestine in and after the Fourth Syrian War*

In contrast to the three previous Syrian wars, Palestine suffered a great deal from action during the fourth war.

Polybius[27] reports that Antiochus III conquered Philadelphia – which he gives its old name, Rabbath-ammon – in the territory of Samaria. According to some scholars,[28] Samaria also included the territory of Judah. Be this as it may, it is at any rate certain that Antiochus III directed his main attention to the coastal cities and Transjordan. The fact that he fought in Palestine for more than two years is itself an indication that the sufferings in the area were great.

After the battle of Raphia in 217 BC, Ptolemy III stayed in the country with his sister Arsinoe. They visited various cities and sanctuaries at this time. Inscriptions in Joppa and Marisa (on the border between Judaea and Idumaea) bear witness to these visits.[29]

We do not know whether they went to Jerusalem then. The non-canonical III Macc. 1.7ff. suggests something of the kind.[30] According to III Macc.2.25ff., after his return to Egypt Ptolemy IV persecuted the Jews in Alexandria. Both passages suggest that there were bad relations between this king and Judaea, but we have no further details. Neither Josephus nor other sources give us any information on these points. However, it does not seem improbable that relations between Ptolemy and Judaea were not at their best at this time, given the sympathy shown for Antiochus III in Judaea and Jerusalem during the Fifth Syrian War, as we shall soon see. For want of enough evidence, however, we cannot do more than guess. Hengel's view that on the visit to Palestine mentioned above Ptolemy carried out an administrative reform which also put paid to Joseph the Tobiad's twenty-two-year activity as 'tax farmer' over 'Syria and Phoenicia' is also no more than a hypothesis.[31]

5.5 *The expulsion of the Ptolemies from Palestine*

5.5.1 *The political situation after the Fourth Syrian War*

Despite the fact that the Ptolemies had finally proved victorious in the Fourth Syrian War, the days of their rule over Palestine were numbered.

The victory at Raphia on the one hand meant a great personal triumph for Sosibius, but on the other it also led to a major revival among the native population of Egypt. Thanks to their contribution, the advance of Antiochus

III had been brought to a standstill and the Seleucid army had been forced to retreat. No wonder, then, that this native population made itself felt after the war. It was clear that the Greek overlords had lost their reputation. And now it also emerged that there had never really been a genuine unification of Greeks and Egyptians.[32]

In addition to all this, moreover, the government of Ptolemy IV can be said to have been extremely weak both in domestic and in foreign policy (cf. 5.4.1). This situation did not improve in the slightest when after the death of Ptolemy IV in 204 BC the five-year-old Ptolemy V ascended the throne., Circumstances were quite different for his opponent who had been defeated in 217 BC.

Antiochus III had spent the first years after the defeat at Raphia in putting the eastern frontiers of his empire in order. He was able to extend his empire and influence there and restore the frontiers of his territory to their at the time of Seleucus I (312-281 BC). He also made a secret treaty with Philip V of Macedon, in which agreements were made over a division of the foreign possessions of the Ptolemaic empire.

5.5.2 *The Fifth Syrian War (202-198 BC)*

In 201 BC, Antiochus III – who had taken the title 'the Great' because of his successes – invaded 'Syria and Phoenicia' at the head of a large Seleucid army. He succeeded in occupying virtually the whole territory in a very short time. Evidently the Ptolemies offered him hardly any resistance. The opposition to Antiochus must have come mainly from the military garrisons in this area, but there was not much of it. One exception was the city of Gaza, which put up fierce resistance for a long time. We need not be surprised that Gaza should have been the city to do this. It was the terminus of Arab trade with Egypt. So the city was economically of vital importance and for this reason was also the strongest in military terms.

We have a report of the battle for Gaza from the historian Polybius,[33] in which he reports the fierce opposition of the city.

In the spring of that year (201 BC), Palestine was virtually completely in the hands of Antiochus III. After establishing garrisons and occupying forces throughout the region, he again left the country.

The Ptolemaic general Scopas took advantage of these conditions to launch a counter-attack. In the winter of 201-200 BC he in fact succeeded in conquering a large number of provinces of the territory he had lost. However, this success was only of short duration. In 200 BC Antiochus inflicted a decisive defeat on Scopas at Panium (Caesarea Philippi, well known from the New Testament), at the sources of the Jordan. Two years later 'Syria and Phoenicia' was under Seleucid rule as far as the frontier with Egypt.

5.5.3 *Palestine at the time of the Fifth Syrian War*

Above all in the winter of 201-200 BC, the land must have suffered under the war. This was the period of the counter-offensive launched by Scopas (see 5.5.2) and, immediately after that, of the conquest of the area by Antiochus III. Josephus[34] makes special mention of Samaria, Abila and Gadara. Even Judaea and Jerusalem were not spared all this.[35] The temple must have been badly damaged in this period.[36] This is evident from reports[37] that the then high priest Simon II later (see 6.3) had considerable restoration work carried out on the city and the temple. Furthermore, in a decree of Antiochus III[38] (see 6.2.1) contributions are asked for, among other things, the temple and city of Jerusalem. All this suggests considerable devastation. The scanty reports about the battle fought against the Ptolemaic garrisons in Jerusalem also point in this direction.[39]

There are indications that during the Fifth Syrian War there was a pro-Seleucid party in Judaea and Jerusalem. We have already recalled that most Tobiads chose the Seleucid side at this time (see 5.3). Furthermore, a fragment of Polybius preserved in Josephus[40] reports that the inhabitants of Jerusalem went over to Antiochus III. Daniel 11.14 also suggests this.

It is certain that for his part Antiochus recognized the privileges that Jerusalem and the Judaeans had enjoyed during Ptolemaic rule and moreover – for the moment – granted them a reduction in the taxes which they had hitherto had to pay.[41]

All this put an end to Ptolemaic rule, which had lasted for more than a century (301-198 BC). As had happened now for centuries, the land again came under the rule of new powers. After the Assyrians, the Babylonians, the Persians and the Ptolemies it was now the Seleucids from their centre of power in Antioch who exercised rule over Palestine. Like the previous rulers, the Seleucids, too, were ready to leave the spiritual authority of the high priest in Jerusalem undisturbed. This fitted in very well with their own interests. It was to emerge all too quickly how their own interests were paramount. The cries of joy with which many had greeted the Seleucids were all too soon to fall silent.

Chapter 6

The Beginning of Seleucid Rule
(198-175 BC)

6.1 *The general political situation*

6.1.1 *The time of Antiochus III (222-187 BC)*

Victory over the Ptolemies and the conquest of 'Syria and Phoenicia' did not put an end to the political aspirations of Antiochus III. His aim was to continue to extend the Seleucid empire to the north and west. We have seen (5.5.1) that Antiochus III had made a treaty with Philip V of Macedon even before the Fifth Syrian War, in which he promised to share with Philip the Ptolemaic possessions lying outside Egypt. Antiochus now wanted to put this treaty into effect.

In the meantime, however, a new power had appeared on the political scene, Rome. At about the time that Antiochus III conquered Palestine, the Romans had finally defeated Hannibal. This not only put an end to the Second Punic War (202 BC), but also considerably strengthened the power of Rome. The Romans now directed all their attention to Philip V, an old ally of Hannibal.

An occasion for a war against the Macedonians was soon found. On the basis of his treaty with Antiochus III, Philip was engaged in making himself master of the Ptolemaic possessions in the Aegean Sea. Some Greek cities called in the help of the Romans, who inflicted a decisive defeat on Philip in *c.* 197 BC. Although the Romans withdrew again from Greece some years later, very few Greek cities came well out of their 'liberation', which was accompanied by all kinds of conditions. Some of them now invoked the help of Antiochus III, who hitherto had remained neutral in the conflict.

Antiochus succeeded in landing in Greece with troops and occupying some of it, but he was driven out again in the following year (192 BC). The Romans then in turn landed in Asia Minor, where in 190 BC they inflicted a major defeat on the troops of Antiochus III at Magnesia (cf.Dan.11.18). After that Antiochus had no other choice than to make peace with Rome.

The peace concluded at Apamea in 188 BC was very damaging to him. Among other things he had to give up all the territory west of the Taurus, let his second son, later to become Antiochus IV Epiphanes, go to Rome as a hostage, and pay an indemnity of 15,000 talents. This tribute, unprecedented in ancient history, had to be paid in twelve annual instalments.[1]

It was this last condition in particular which was to have a great influence on political relations between the Seleucid empire and Judaea in the years to come.

The main task of Antiochus III was now to raise this annual payment. In fact he did not have the means to do so, and therefore attempted to get the money he needed by laying his hands on temple treasures. In antiquity temples were not only sanctuaries but also acted as banks, above all after the invention of coinage. For this reason Antiochus went to rob the temple of Bel in Elam. However, this action aroused the wrath of the population. They rebelled and killed Antiochus and those who were helping him with the robbery.[2] Thus 187 BC brought a sorry end to the ambitious rule of Antiochus III the Great (cf. Dan.11.19).

6.1.2 *The time of Seleucus IV (187-175 BC)*

Antiochus III was succeeded by his oldest son Seleucus IV Philopator. The position which this king came to inherit was far from enviable. During his reign his every policy was dominated by the question how the annual tribute imposed by the Romans at the peace treaty of Apamea was to be paid. This is also the context of his abortive plundering of the temple in Jerusalem (cf.6.5).

During his reign, Seleucus IV was also threatened by Ptolemy V of Egypt, who had aspirations to take over the territory of 'Syria and Phoenicia' which Egypt had lost. However, the death of Ptolemy in 181 BC put an end to this threat.[3]

The rule of Seleucus IV came to an end when he was murdered in 175 BC by his minister Heliodorus. However, Heliodorus did not succeed in seizing power. Antiochus IV Epiphanes, the brother of Seleucus IV, successfully prevented him from doing this.

6.2 *The measures taken by Antiochus III in favour of Judaea*

6.2.1 *The letter of Antiochus III to the governor Ptolemy*

All the signs are that after his victory over Ptolemy, Antiochus tried to treat his new subjects well with a lenient policy. A letter which he wrote to Ptolemy, the governor of Coele-Syria, was also meant to serve this end. This letter has been preserved for us by Josephus in his *Jewish Antiquities* (*AJ* XIII, 138-44). The authenticity of the document is still disputed.[4]

In this letter Antiochus first expresses his thanks to the Judaeans who supported him in his struggle against the Ptolemies. The king also gave orders aimed at encouraging as far as possible restoration work on the city and temple and the repopulation of Jerusalem. In addition, the members of the council of elders (the *gerousia*, see 3.4.2), the priests and the rest of the temple personnel were exempt from paying taxes and it was stipulated that the government of Judaea was to be in accordance with the ancestral laws.

In fact this letter contains little that is new. The stipulations in it largely guaranteed a continuation of the policy which had already been carried out since the time of Persian rule and was largely based on support for the priests.[5] Of course the letter provided support and reinforcement for the pro-Seleucid group in the temple city of Jerusalem. However, the favourable financial provisions in the letter seem soon to have been qualified, wholly or in part, as a result of the burden of the heavy payments to Rome which the Seleucids had to make after the peace of Apamea in 188.

6.2.2 *The degree about the ritual purity of the temple*

In addition to this letter Josephus reports a decree of Antiochus III in which aliens are not allowed to enter the sanctuary in Jerusalem and there is a prohibition against keeping unclean animals in the city or introducing them into it.[6] Those who break these regulations have to pay a very heavy fine to the priests. Despite a variety of problems, this document seems to fit well into this period.[7] However, the report by Josephus that the decree was proclaimed 'throughout the kingdom' is much exaggerated.

In his *Jewish War*,[8] Josephus reports that there was an inscription in the temple giving in Greek and Latin letters the prohibition against aliens entering the sanctuary. This inscription was certainly there in Roman times.[9]

It goes without saying that a prohibition against the introduction of unclean animals in Jerusalem and the keeping of them there was not conducive to trade in the city. This was not unwelcome to strict religious groups in Jerusalem, who were always afraid of contacts which arose above all through trade between Judaeans and Gentiles.

6.2.3 *The Hefzibah inscription*

An inscription has been discovered in the region of Hefzibah, west of Scythopolis (the ancient Beth-shean) in Galilee from the years 201-195 BC,[10] which contains a number of decrees of Antiochus III and Seleucus IV connected with 'Syria and Phoenicia'. In it we find regulations of Antiochus III which are particularly aimed at protecting the inhabitants of villages from the excesses of the Seleucid occupying forces. Seleucid soldiers are forbidden to have quarters in these villages or to drive the inhabitants out of their houses. Very strict penalties are imposed on those who break these regulations.[11]

This suggests that Antiochus II was not just concerned to secure the sympathy of leading groups, like those in Jerusalem; he also tried to win the favour of the country people.

6.3 *The high priest Simon II*

At the time when Judaea came under Seleucid rule, Simon II was high priest in Jerusalem. He held this office from about 220-190 BC.

Simon II was a son of Onias II, who had come into conflict with Joseph the Tobiad and after that had comparatively little influence (cf.5.1.2).

Simon must have been a much more powerful figure than his father. At least, in all probability he succeeded in gaining much more influence. At any rate, he is given high praise by Sirach (50.1ff.) as a very skilful political and religious leader.[12] This Simon is presumably the person who is described in Pirqe Aboth I.1 as 'the Just' and is mentioned there as one of the last of the 'Great Assembly' (cf.3.4.2). If this is correct, it is a further indication of the important position that Simon II had in Jerusalem at that time.

We do not know Simon's political attitude towards the Ptolemies. Certainly he saw at an early stage that it was important to have good relations with the Seleucids. The measures that Antiochus III took in connection with the temple in the decrees mentioned in 6.2.1, 6.2.2 suggest good relations with the high priest. Obviously Simon II also had personal responsibility for the implementation of the various regulations mentioned in it. At least, this is what Sirach 50.1ff. suggests.

All this also implies that Simon II and his followers in Jerusalem took pains to preserve their own religious forms. The content of the decrees mentioned above points very clearly in this direction. This fact also implies that Simon II and his followers were certainly not strongly influenced by Hellenism.

6.4 *The conflict within the Tobiad family*

Conflict arose within the Tobiad family even during the lifetime of Simon II. The cause of this conflict must be sought in the hostility between Hyrcanus, the eighth son of Joseph the Tobiad, and the rest of his sons. Hyrcanus was evidently anxious to occupy the same position of power as his father, and for this reason wanted to displace his brothers. They did not take to it very kindly.

To begin with, Hyrcanus seems to have been successful, thanks to his good contacts with the royal court in Alexandria. The change of power in Alexandria evidently turned the tide, for while the rest of the Tobiads sailed with the wind and courted the favour of the Seleucids, Hyrcanus remained faithful to the Ptolemies.[13] This pro-Ptolemaic attitude was presumably crucial in resolving the conflict, and in all probability they owed the continuation of their position in Jerusalem to it.

Hyrcanus, on the other hand, left Jerusalem and went to Transjordan, to his grandfather's stronghold in Ammanitis (see 5.2). There he succeeded in establishing an independent princedom.[14] He maintained it throughout the reign of Antiochus III and Seleucus IV, though his success must be attributed more to the flexible administration of these two kings than to the powers of Hyrcanus. From his base Hyrcanus among other things undertook forays against the Nabataeans.[15]

According to Josephus, this conflict was more than a family dispute: it produced a split in the people.[16] This gave rise to a pro-Seleucid group, to which the majority and most of the Tobiads belonged, and a pro-Ptolemaic group, in which we can put Hyrcanus and his supporters. The fact that Hyrcanus left Jerusalem indicates that the latter were in the minority.

6.5 *The struggle between Onias III and Simon the captain of the temple*

Simon II was succeeded as high priest by Onias III, who held this office between about 190 and 174 BC. From the information at our disposal it would appear that Onias III was a less strong personality than his predecessor. However, we should remember that in the time of Onias III the high priesthood was open to heavy attacks from the Tobiads and moreover suffered under the changed political circumstances resulting from the peace of Apamea (cf. 6.1.1). From that moment on the Seleucid kings were chronically in need of money. One of the consequences was, of course, an increase in the burden of taxation. Even Judaea was not spared this, as is evident from an allusion to Seleucus IV in Dan.11.20.

We have seen that in his attempts to pay the high indemnity to Rome Antiochus III did not stop short of plundering the temple of Bel in Elam (see 6.1.1). According to II Macc.3-4, an attempt was also made in the time of Seleucus IV to seize the temple treasure in Jerusalem.

According to II Macc.3.4 the occasion for this was a difference of opinion over the supervision of the market in Jerusalem between Onias III and a certain Simon. This Simon, a supporter of the Tobiads, was appointed by the king captain of the temple, a post which presumably meant that he was responsible for its finances.[17] It is not clear precisely what the difference of opinion over the market was about. It is possible that Simon wanted to do away with certain restrictions and that Onias rejected this because it would endanger the ritual purity of the market.

According to II Macc.3.5, the consequence of Onias' refusal was that Simon went to Apollonius, the then governor of Coele-Syria, and told him that there were great riches in the temple. He in turn informed Seleucus IV. It is understandable that because Seleucus was in great financial straits he then attempted to lay hands on this treasure. With that in view he sent his minister Heliodorus to Jerusalem.

When Heliodorus arrived in Jerusalem, Onias III told him that the money in the temple was the savings of widows and orphans and a contribution deposited by Hyrcanus, the son of Joseph the Tobiad who was in Transjordan. The rest of the account in II Macc.3.13-40 has a very legendary character, so that we do not know what happened next.[18]

However, it is striking that according to II Macc.3.11 Onias had business dealings with Hyrcanus. This could mean that the dispute with Simon also had a political background. Further support for the conjecture comes from the fact that because of his contacts with Hyrcanus,[19] Onias III tended towards a pro-Ptolemaic policy, while Simon and the rest of the Tobiads saw salvation more in a pro-Seleucid policy. Such an attitude on the part of Onias III would also be understandable in view of the general political situation (see 6.1). After the peace of Apamea the position of the Seleucids was still far from rosy, and this could have led to the thought that a return of Ptolemaic government was quite possible. However, it seems even more probable that Onias III was hostile to the Seleucids.

At all events, political opposition seems to have come to a climax in Jerusalem. On the basis of II Macc.4.3 we may assume that it was even accompanied by unrest and bloodshed. For the moment the party of Onias came out worst. Again through the intervention of Simon, Onias was forced to go to Antioch to give account of his actions there.[20] His mission failed because just as he arrived, Seleucus IV was murdered by Heliodorus, who in turn was driven out soon afterwards by Antiochus IV Epiphanes. This ushered in a new period for Judaea and Jerusalem and indeed for all Palestine.

Onias III never returned to Jerusalem. Some years later he was murdered in captivity in the region of Antioch.

6.6 *The situation in the rest of Palestine*

From the beginning of Seleucid rule Palestine was part of the administrative district of 'Syria and Phoenicia', which in addition to Palestine also included the southern part of Syria and Phoenicia.[21] The Apollonius mentioned in 6.5 was one of the best-known governors of the region.

It is unclear what the administrative division of Palestine was at this time. In addition to the temple state of Judaea, Samaria must certainly be seen as a separate administrative unit. However, it is problematic, for instance, whether Galilee was part of Samaria[22] or whether it is to be seen as a more or less independent entity.[23] Lack of further information leaves us in the dark here.

We also have very little information for this period about further events and the situation in this part of Palestine. According to Josephus,[24] to begin with, this part of Samaria was generally prosperous. On the basis of Sirach 50.25f. we may conjecture that at that time in Jerusalem, at least in certain circles, there was considerable opposition to the 'Samaritans'. Sirach called them 'the foolish people who live in Shechem'. Kippenberg[25] sees this statement as the earliest evidence of Jewish polemic against the 'Samaritans'. The inhabitants of the coastal plain are also ridiculed by Sirach in these verses.

In 6.4 we already saw that in this period an independent princedom came into being in Transjordan under the leadership of Hyrcanus. It is not impossible that other such miniature states came into being about this time, especially in this area.

6.7 *The work and position of Jesus Sirach*

6.7.1 *The work*

According to Sirach 50.27 the author of the book ('The Wisdom of Jesus Sirach') came from Jerusalem. Given that he must be counted as a wisdom teacher, we may assume that, like Koheleth (cf.4.4), he was an important figure. He calls himself a scribe (38.24). This term here has to some degree the later significance of the word.[26]

Since Sirach presupposes the death of Simon II (50.1ff.) and there is no trace in his book of the turbulent times which began with the accession of Antiochus IV Epiphanes, his work can be dated roughly in the time around 190 BC.[27]

The book begins with a prologue in which the grandson of Sirach acknowledges responsibility for the Greek translation of it which he made in about 135 BC on behalf of the Jewish Diaspora in Egypt. This is followed in 1.1-42.14 by a series of sayings, hymns of praise and instructions about the nature and origin of wisdom. Then in 42.13-43.33 we have praise of God's glory in creation and nature. Folowing this we find a section in 44.1-50.21 which is known as the 'praise of the fathers'.[28] The conclusion consists of a thanksgiving and a prayer by Sirach (50.22-51.21).

6.7.2 *Sirach's position*

It is clear that formal Hellenistic influences have not passed by Sirach. There are certain traces of them to be found in his work.[29] However, such influence must not be over-estimated. Even if Sirach could read Greek it is a different matter to assume that he had consideerable knowledge of Greek literature.

In terms of subject-matter we see that Sirach is very firmly opposed to Hellenism.[30] This opposition is expressed above all in his championship of the rule of the priests based on the Law of Moses.[31] He puts particular emphasis on the figure of the high priest. Among other things, this emerges from the fact that in the 'praise of the fathers' three times as much space is devoted to Aaron as to Moses (45.6-22),[32] while Phinehas, a descendant of Aaron, gets as much attention as Moses (45.23-25). The stress on the figure of the high priest is also evident at the end of the 'Praise of the fathers' (50.1-21) in a brilliant description of the high priest Simon II.

All this implies that, albeit in a cautious way,[33] Sirach takes up a particular position in the political difficulties in Jerusalem. In his perception of the dangers of riches (8.2,12) and in his description of the rich aristocracy which makes unheeding use of its power (9.13; 13.9-13), Sirach can only be thinking of the Tobiads.[34]

For all these reasons and because of his stress on the importance of the high priest, Sirach can best be described as a sympathizer with or supporter of the group around the high priest Onias III. Moreover, this attitude characterizes him as someone in whom the spirit of opposition to Hellenism begins to emerge. Sirach can thus be seen as a forerunner of later public opposition to Hellenism.

Chapter 7

The Prelude to the Revolt

7.1 *Antiochus IV Epiphanes (175-164 BC)*

Antiochus IV was a son of Antiochus III. After the peace of Apamea (6.1.1) he had been sent as a hostage to Rome. However, he was set free again in 177 BC in exchange for Demetrius, the son of Seleucus IV, whereupon he settled in Athens. A short time later Seleucus was murdered by Heliodorus (cf. 6.1.2). Antiochus IV, however, succeeded in rapidly removing Heliodorus from the political scene and himself seized power. Antiochus IV was not yet the legal successor of Seleucus IV. Seleucus' son had that position (cf. Dan.11.21).

Obviously all this happened with the tacit approval of the Romans. After the peace of Apamea, the real power in this part of the world rested to an increasing degree with Rome. Moreover, the successes of the Maccabees and the Parthians which are to be described in the following chapters must also be seen in this light. These successes could only be achieved through the diplomacy and political intervention of Rome.[1] The policy of Antiochus IV Epiphanes must also be seen in this context.

In the first instance Antiochus IV made attempts to restore the Seleucid kingdom in its old glory. The campaigns he undertook against Egypt served this end. These campaigns are also important for understanding the situation in Palestine and, in particular, because of the effect that they had on certain events in Jerusalem.

The first campaign took place in 170-169 BC. According to II Macc. 4.21 the occasion for it was the hostile attitude in Egypt towards the Seleucid king. This campaign was particularly successful. Antiochus IV was able to get as far as Alexandria. He then made a treaty with Ptolemy VI (180-145 BC) on very favourable terms which in fact made Ptolemy VI his dependent.

However, Ptolemy broke this treaty very quickly, so as early as 168 BC Antiochus had begun a new campaign against Egypt. This campaign again went very well to begin with. However, at that point the Roman Senate intervened; it was happy for Coele-Syria and Phoenicia to be in Antiochus' possession, but it would not allow the Seleucid ruler to get great power and influence in Egypt. An embassy from Rome told Antiochus shortly and sharply to leave Egypt.[2] Antiochus had no choice but to obey.

It hardly needs to be pointed out that this was a great humiliation to the Seleucid king. It also meant that a definitive end had now come to the position of power occupied for some time by the Seleucid kingdom in this part of the world.

Antiochus made a reputation not only in the political sphere but also in the sphere of religion. During his long stay in Rome and Athens (from 188-175 BC), Greek culture and religion in particular seem to have made a deep impression on him. All this was certainly significant for his religious policy. Two important innovations by Antiochus IV should probably also be seen in this light. In the first place he assumed the cult name *theos epiphanes* (the manifest god), and secondly he replaced the image of the traditional Seleucid Apollo with that of Zeus Olympius on the reverse of the Antiochene tetra-drachm.[3] All this clearly influenced later events in Palestine.

7.2 *The dispute over the figure of the high priest*

7.2.1 *The emergence of Jason*

After Onias III had gone to Antioch (cf.6.5), his brother Jason made an appearance, ostensibly as his representative.[4] However, soon afterwards Jason (the Greek form of the name Jeshua) obtained the permanent post of high priest from the king.[5] This presumably happened shortly after the accession of Antiochus Epiphanes. Jason voluntarily offered the king an increase in taxes and an extra single contribution (II Macc.4.7-8). He then, according to II Macc.4.9, offered the king more money if he would consent to the establish-ment of a sports centre (*gymnasium*) and a training centre (*ephebeia*) in Jerusalem to instil the Hellenistic spirit in young men. Moreover, he asked the king to regard the citizens of Jerusalem as 'Antiochenes'. This meant that the inhabitants of Jerusalem would enjoy the same privileges as those of Antioch.

Evidently this did not yet mean that from then on Jerusalem was to be seen as a Greek polis. It is also obvious that Jason could not take such initiatives without having a particular group behind him (cf. also I Macc.1.13f.). We cannot establish with any certainty who belonged to this party, but Hengel's view[6] that it consisted of the priests and well-to-do who held the *de facto* power in Jerusalem seems reasonable (see also II Macc.4.14). We even get the impression from I Macc.1.11 (cf. Dan.11.23) that there were a large number of such people. It goes without saying that the old clan of Tobiads belonged to the group.

This 'Hellenistically inclined' group very probably formed a more or less independent community within Jerusalem.[7] Such Greek communities (and other ethnic groups) existed elsewhere among the native population. For example, the Jews in Alexandria formed such a community there,

It is conceivable that landowners and merchants in Jerusalem were particularly sympathetic to this 'Hellenistic' movement, hoping that it would stimulate economic growth[8] and that the city would obtain the right to mint its own coins (a right which Antiochus IV had granted to a number of cities in the Seleucid empire).[9] On some coins the citizens of the cities which minted them are called 'Antiochenes', i.e. the very designation that Jason wanted to secure for the Hellenists in Jerusalem (see above).[10]

All this does not of itself imply that Hellenism in Jerusalem had already assumed a very radical form. It is equally possible that in the time of Jason there was no more than a tendency towards Hellenism.[11]

It is understandable that Antiochus IV, who, like his predecessors, was desperately in need of money, should have gratefully accepted Jason's offer. It is just as understandable that this development should have caused great scandal among particular groups in Jerusalem and in Judaea. For the moment these could probably not give much vent to their indigation. However, it would all too quickly become evident that there was already a spirit of opposition abroad.

Meanwhile, in 171 Jason's high priesthood had already come to an end. In that year Jason sent Menelaus, a brother[12] of Simon, the temple overseer mentioned in 6.5, to the king to pay the usual tribute. However, when Menelaus arrived in Antioch, for the promise of a payment of 300 talents more than Jason had sent, he managed to get Antiochus IV to appoint him high priest in Jerusalem.

In doing this Antiochus was treading on dangerous ground. While Jason could trace back his ancestry to the Zadokites, the only family from which the high priest might come, Menelaus, who came from another priestly family,[13] was a different matter. To nominate such a figure as high priest was in conflict with the tradition and raised the most enormous problems. This course of action shows that Antiochus IV was badly informed about the religious situation in Jerusalem.

At all events, in the meantime the result of all this was that the days of Jason as high priest were numbered. Jason understood this and also that his life in Jerusalem was no longer secure. So he fled as rapidly as possibly to Transjordan (cf. II Macc.4.26).

7.2.2 *Menelaus as high priest*

Menelaus held the office of high priest from about 172 to 162 BC. According to Josephus,[14] in contrast to Jason, he could rely on the support of the Tobiads. This account seems quite trustworthy. In the last resort Jason was still part of the Oniad family and was probably too moderate in his approach for the Tobiads. With the fall of Jason an end had now come to the dominant position which the Oniads had long held in Jerusalem.

In the meantime the high priesthood of Menelaus caused him a great many difficulties. The greatest problem with which he was confronted was how to pay the 300 extra talents he had promised to Antiochus IV. He did not succeed in getting the payment together. Although the king summoned him to explain why, he was evidently able to find an excuse. At all events, he continued to hold office as high priest.

While Menelaus was with the king, his brother Lysimachus had been appointed his replacement in Jerusalem. He did not hesitate to help himself to treasure from the temple, with the result that a raging mob killed him on the spot.[15] When three delegates from Jerusalem sought out Antiochus IV in Tyre to make a complaint about this, they were put to death on the orders of the king (II Macc.4.43-48).

Menelaus again got into difficulties when during an absence of Antiochus IV he was able to bribe Andronicus, his representative in Antioch, with some of the temple treasure to have Onias III murdered in captivity.[16] After his return Antiochus IV had Andronicus executed for this, but he left Menelaus completely untouched. In all probability, the reason why Menelaus again got off scot-free was the mutual financial concern which he shared with Antiochus.[17]

As can be imagined, all these events did not do Menelaus' position in Jerusalem any good. The resistance against him steadily increased. According to Josephus[18] there seems to have been a change in sympathy among the population over politics. In the time of Hyrcanus (cf. 6.4) the majority seems to have taken the side of the pro-Seleucid Tobiads. With the emergence of Menelaus the situation seems to have changed.

Such a change is quite understandable in the circumstances. While it had promised to be light at the beginning, the burden of taxation under the Seleucid government after the peace of Apamea in 188 BC was presumably greater than it had ever been in the time of the Ptolemies. Furthermore, in the religous sphere the Ptolemies were much more cautious and detached than someone like Antiochus IV Epiphanes.

The fall of Jason described in 7.2.1 can also be seen in this light. Jason was probably not only too moderate for the Tobiads, but may also have been suspected of having pro-Ptolemaic sympathies. His flight to what was (at least earlier) the pro-Ptolemaic stronghold of Ammanitis in Transjordan may point in ths direction. For that reason there is something to be said for the view that Menelaus was little more than an unwilling tool in the hands of the Tobiads.[19] At least that made his position as high priest undisputed. But the problems with which he was confronted continued. That will become clear in what follows.

7.2.3 *Jason's revolt*

II Maccabees 5.5ff. describes an attempt by Jason to regain the office of high priest by means of a revolt. According to II Macc.5.5 he went to Jerusalem with about a thousand men and caused a terrible blood-bath. Menelaus had to take refuge in a suburb of the city.

Josephus[20] also mentions a revolt by Jason. According to him the majority of the people were behind Jason. This majority consisted of pro-Ptolemaic Oniads,[21] who here joined forces with Jason against a pro-Seleucid minority.

Thus the picture painted by II Macc. is in some ways differnt from that of Josephus. However, Josephus does not give us any information about the revolt, but simply reports it as a fact.

The only certain conclusion that can be drawn on the basis of these two sources is that there was a revolt by Jason against Menelaus. Given Jason's earlier activity as high priest, when he certainly did not seem to be anti-Hellenistic, we may reasonably suppose that this was primarily a conflict between two rival Hellenistic groups.[22] However, it seems improbable that the majority of the population felt deeply involved. Presumably that is the reason why important sources like Daniel and I Maccabees are completely silent about this event. We are also in the dark about when the event took place. Some scholars have suggested 169 BC, immediately after the first campaign of Antiochus IV against Egypt;[23] others 168 BC, directly after his second campaign.[24]

One thing is clear, though: in this conflict Jason came off worst. According to II Macc. 5.7ff. he had to flee and could not find refuge anywhere. He did not even find sanctuary with Aretas, ruler of the 'Arabians' (which probably means the Nabataeans), or in Egypt. Finally he died in the land of the 'Lacedaemonians', i.e. in Sparta.

It is also unclear who drove Jason out of Jerusalem. Tcherikover[25] suggested a third group made up of the Hasidim (see 8.1.3), who formed a religious rather than a social movement. However, this view has no support in our sources. It seems more likely that Jason fled from the Seleucid troops.

7.3 *Antiochus IV's actions against Jerusalem*

7.3.1 *The plundering of the temple*

We have three reports of a plundering of the temple by or on the orders of Antiochus IV.

The first is in I Macc.1.20-24. This mentions the year 143 by the Seleucid chronology, i.e. 169 BC.[26] II Maccabees 5.15f. also mentions a plundering of the temple, in which Menelaus accompanied Antiochus IV as a guide. This plundering is said to have taken place after Antiochus' second expedition to Egypt and Jason's revolt. The king is supposed to have interpreted the revolt as a rebellion by Judaea (II Macc.5.11) and to have occupied Jerusalem at that time by force. Thousands of inhabitants are said to have been killed, with others being carried away as slaves. The plundering of the temple in 168 is supposed to be set against this background. Josephus also appears to have had the same date in mind in *AJ* XII, 248-50, when he mentions a plundering of the temple by Antiochus IV.

However, the question is whether this information suggests that the temple was plundered on two different occasions. Given that both in Dan.11.28-31 and in *AJ* XII, 246-50 (though this account is somewhat confused in Josephus), two visits by Antiochus IV seem to be mentioned, it would appear that we should suppose that on both occasions the temple was plundered. Since I Maccabees was Josephus' most important source for the period 175-134 BC,[27] he must have taken the information about the plundering of the temple in 168 BC from another source, perhaps the history of Nicolaus of Damascus.[28]

7.3.2 *Measures of Antiochus IV against Jerusalem*

Antiochus IV also took other measures against the city of Jerusalem, probably in close connection with the events just mentioned and his forced retreat from Egypt in 168 BC (see 7.1). The walls of the city were dismantled, and a heavily fortified citadel, the Acra, was set up over against Mount Zion. The Acra was not just a base for a garrison but at the same time a kind of Greek polis with its own institutions.[29] We find an account of the building of this Acra in both I Macc. (1.33) and Josephus (*AJ* XII, 251). In Josephus it is Antiochus himself who goes to Jerusalem, while in I Maccabees an official responsible for taxes is sent by the king with a great army against the city. This official is probably none other than the Apollonius mentioned in II Macc.5.24 (see also 6.5).

It is clear from these measures that Antiochus regarded something like Jason's revolt (7.2.3) as primarily a political dispute. So he treated it as such. Moreover, since the Romans had ruined his campaign against Egypt Judaea became all the more important to him because this area was now frontier territory. Antiochus must have been particularly concerned to maintain law and order there.

7.4 *The religious situation*

7.4.1 *The decree on religion*

I Maccabees 1.41 reports a decree which Antiochus IV is said to have promulgated to make 'all in his kingdom one people', stipulating 'that each should give up his customs'.

One would expect that there would be at least traces in non-Jewish sources of such a decree affecting everyone in the Seleucid empire (cf. also I Macc.1.51). However, this is not the case. Daniel 11 and II Maccabees also make no mention of any such decree for the whole of the Seleucid empire. The same thing also holds for Josephus. So we must infer that Antiochus IV never in fact promulgated a decree relating to all the empire. The only conclusion we can come to is that the decree concerned just Judaea. This also emerges from the fact that of the eleven verses which deal with the decree, only nine refer to Judaea, while just the beginning and the end refer to the Seleucid empire.

All this can only mean that there is no reason for supposing a general religious persecution in the Seleucid realm in the time of Antiochus IV. On the contrary, there are many indications that Antiochus was tolerant to local cults.[30] The only conclusion that we can draw from I Macc.1.41-51 is that there must have been a religious persecution in this period which was limited to the territory of Judaea (see 7.4.3). Bunge's theory that the Jews outside Judaea were also affected by the persecution[31] seems completely untenable.[32]

As for the background of the information in I Macc.1.41-51, there is much to be said for Lebram's view[33] that the author of I Macc. made an attempt here to put what is mentioned in Dan.11.36-39 in a broad historical framework.[34] At most one can say that the decree in I Macc.1.41-51 and the description in Dan.11.36-39 were influenced by events which were experienced as a more or less total religious persecution at a local level.[35]

7.4.2 *The 'Samaritans'' request*

According to Josephus, at this time the 'Samaritans' sent a letter to Antiochus IV (reproduced in *AJ* XII, 258-61) asking him to regard them as non-Jews and to exempt them from taxation. Moreover they asked for their temple on

Mount Gerizim to be allowed to bear the name Zeus Hellenios (or Zeus Xenios[36]). This request was accepted by Antiochus IV (see *AJ* XII, 262-3). The authenticity of the letter and the answer to it have been sufficiently demonstrated by Bickerman,[37] though a later Jewish revision is perhaps not entirely to be excluded.[38]

It is striking that in these passages in Josephus the name 'Samaritan' does not yet appear, nor does it in Sirach 50.26, so presumably it was still unknown at this time. Furthermore, this group was evidently still seen as part of Israel. This seems at least to follow from the fact that here in Josephus, as in II Macc.6.2, it is mentioned in the context of action directed against the Jews.[39]

However, the question is whether the request mentioned above came directly from the 'Samaritans' themselves. On the basis of a closer investigation of a variety of texts,[40] Kippenberg has come to the conclusion that this particular request was in fact made by a colony of Sidonians (cf. also *AJ* XII, 258 and 262), who had settled in Shechem at the time of the Seleucids. In this connection it does not seem coincidental that according to II Macc.6.2 the temple on Gerizim was named after 'Zeus Xenios' (the god of foreigners). Presumably these Sidonians, like the 'Samaritans', were not particularly well disposed to 'Hellenism'. One pointer in this direction is a report in II Macc.5.22f. that Antiochus IV left behind governors 'to suppress the people' both in Jerusalem and on Gerizim. Philip the Phrygian was governor of Jerusalem and Andronicus governor of Gerizim.

The correspondence mentioned by Josephus also seems to indicate that the religious group centred on Gerizim asked to be allowed to celebrate the sabbath undisturbed and that this request was also granted without further ado. This again indicates that there can hardly have been any large-scale religious persecution in the time of Antiochus IV, and confirms the view that what happened was merely an internal Jewish affair (see 7.4.3). The aim of the Samaritan letter was therefore in all probability to seek protection from the king against the all too active moves towards 'Hellenization' which were already being made by a Hellenistic group in Jerusalem, when, with the help of their Seleucid supporters, these were extending their activities even as far as Shechem and its environs.

7.4.3 *The background and character of the religious persecution*

In the preceding section we already noticed that there can be no question of a general religious persecution in the Seleucid empire in the time of Antiochus IV, but that it was principally limited to Judaea. This view has been demonstrated convincingly in a number of studies.[41]

The question now arises as to why Antiochus IV should have embarked on such a persecution in Judaea. In this connection much emphasis is placed on a remark by Tacitus[42] that Antiochus IV strove to do away with Jewish belief and introduce Greek customs. However, it would seem that here Tacitus has incorporated very anti-Jewish sources,[43] so that not too much weight can be put on this remark.

Daniel (11.30) connects the persecution with the disappointment of the king on his Egyptian campaigns. Here the stress falls (see v.30b) on the king's interest in those who 'forsook the holy covenant'. These people are without doubt the supporters of Antiochus IV in Jerusalem. At that time it was certainly very attractive, both politically and financially, for the king to favour this particular group in Jerusalem.

According to this view the Seleucid ruler will have taken a number of measures against the existing cult which in fact restricted the privileges formerly given by Antiochus III (cf.6.2). However, the measures should be attributed not so much to Antiochus IV as to those inclined towards Hellenism in Jerusalem.[44] From the Acra and under the direction of the high priest Menelaus, a number of changes were introduced in the sphere of the cult which angered a large proportion of the population. However, Menelaus and his followers were able to convince the king of their utility.[45] The aim of these changes was to give Jewish worship a more Hellenistic form. One means towards this end was the adoption of the name Zeus Olympius in place of the 'Lord of heaven', which had been usual since Persian times as a designation for God, and to set up a second altar, or perhaps a holy stone, on the existing altar of burnt offering in the temple of Jerusalem. This second altar or stone is referred to by Daniel (11.31; 12.11) as the 'abomination of desolation'.[46] Moreover, the cult was not limited to one place, but altars were erected in several places in Judah (cf. I Macc.1.54).

In connection with this, I Macc.1.47; II Macc.6.21; 7.1 report that the Judaeans were forced to sacrifice pigs. Such sacrifices were rejected among the Syrians, and the Greeks were not in the habit of offering pigs to Zeus as a sacrifice. As Bickerman rightly observes,[47] the sole aim of compelling the Jews to make this sacrifice was to attack the special character of the Jewish religion.

It follows from this that a Seleucid king would never have hit on the idea of introducing pigs as sacrificial animals. This fact is a further indication that almost all the incursions in the sphere of Jewish religion must be attributed to the Hellenists in Jerusalem, though they happened with the consent and even perhaps the support of Seleucid officials and soldiers.

We should not suppose that the persecution in Jerusalem and Judaea was on a large scale. Of course we might get this impression not only from I Macc. but also from II Macc., but the latter is noticeably dependent on the former.[48]

Josephus also suggests something of this kind (*AJ* XII, 253ff.), but his most important source is also I Maccabees.

However, we have seen (1.2.2) that I Maccabees was primarily written with the aim of demonstrating the legitimacy of the Hasmonaean dynasty and thus the attitude of Simon Maccabaeus and his followers to the high priest-king.[49] Since the Maccabees did not belong to the legitimate high-priestly family, the approach of the author of I Maccabees was to show them not only as deliverers of the people but above all as defenders of true religion. The greater the persecution that was described, the greater the prestige of the Hasmonaeans in this sphere. All this must have served as a motivation at least to call them high priests, despite their origin.

As a result of all this, I Maccabees and sources dependent on it like II Maccabees and Josephus cannot be cited as proof of a large-scale religious persecution in Judaea. Rather, we must assume that the persecution was only a limited one.[50]

7.5 *Apocalyptic*

It might be useful at this stage to give some information about the phenomenon of apocalyptic, which was to play an increasingly prominent role in the next period of Israelite history.

The word apocalyptic is connected with a Greek word which means 'unveil'. In theology it is used to denote the thought-patterns and imagery which appear in a number of Jewish writings between about 300 BC and AD 100.[51]

We already find the first literary products of apocalyptic in the Old Testament. Among them may be listed Isa.24-27 (the Isaiah apocalypse); Zech.12-14 and large parts of Daniel.

Opinions vary widely as to the origin of apocalyptic. It is usually seen as an offshoot of prophecy,[52] but wisdom[53] and the cult[54] have also been connected with its origin. Then we also have the view of Plöger[55] that conventicles of pious Jews are to a large degree responsible for the phenomenon. So it is obvious that there can be no question of a common view of the origin of apocalyptic. Presumably a number of influences were at work, since apocalyptic as such cannot be regarded as a homogeneous whole.

The heyday of apocalyptic falls in the period from *c.*165 BC on. A whole series of apocalyptic writings appeared at this time. In addition to Daniel, the most important of them are I Enoch, Jubilees, IV Ezra, the Testaments of the Twelve Patriarchs and (in the New Testament) the Revelation of John.

The most prominent characteristics of apocalyptic can be said to be pseudonymity, numerical symbolism, secret language, a doctrine of angels, references to the coming time of salvation and a division of history into periods.[56] That does not mean that all these characteristics appear in every apocalyptic writing.

Pseudonymity occurs where, in apocalyptic, visions are attributed to great figures from the past like Enoch, Moses, Isaiah and Daniel. By means of these visions these figures then make the secrets of history known to believers.[57]

Numbers always have symbolic value in apocalyptic. Thus the figure four usually serves to indicate totality. Numbers also give a point of reference, since everything is defined by them, like the duration of the world empires and the time that evil will rule over the world.[58]

As to secret language, names from the past are often used to denote contemporary rulers and lands. Thus for example Babylon is used in Revelation (18.2) for Rome. Animals often serve to denote individuals and peoples. The just are described as sheep or lambs (cf. Enoch 90.6-9; Matt.25.31ff.), and the four kingdoms in Dan.7 are described as beasts.

The figure of the angel comes increasingly to the fore in apocalyptic literature. Thus in Daniel there is mention of the angels Gabriel (cf.8.16) and Michael (12.1). These two figures prominent in Daniel belong among the four or seven archangels in other apocalyptic writings (cf. Enoch 9.1; also Tobit 12.15). In Daniel we do not yet have a developed angelology; that comes in the later post-canonical books.

History is divided into periods, as is evident in the account of the four world empires in Dan.7. After these comes the time of salvation (7.13). There is also a marked distinction between 'this (evil) world' and the 'new world to come'.

The 'world to come' will emerge after the downfall of 'this world', in which believers now live and are oppressed. In this expectation, which is expressed in visions, the coming Messiah becomes increasingly significant. This messiah is sometimes described as a national and sometimes as a heavenly figure. Two or three messianic figures are even distinguished in the Qumran community: a messianic king (from the house of David), a messianic priest (from the family of Aaron), and a prophet, who functions as forerunner of the messiah or as an Elijah redivivus.[59]

Apocalyptic movements most often come to the fore in times of oppression and persecution. However, the aim of apocalyptic is to give encouragement by stressing that all powers, even the greatest world empires, will not last and that eventually the kingdom of God, the time of salvation, will dawn. Therefore men are summoned to look closely at the past so as to be able to recognize the signs of the times in their own day. In this way they can face the future with confidence.[60]

7.6 *The literature from this period*

7.6.1 *The Book of Daniel*

By far the most important work from this period is the book of Daniel. It is almost unanimously accepted that the work was written about 167-164 BC.[61] From a literary point of view the book consists of a narrative section (chs.1-6) and an apocalyptic part (chs.7-12). Moreover, part has been transmitted in Hebrew and part in Aramaic.

Despite the complexity of this book, the majority of commentators believe that it is a literary unity.[62] Views differ over the milieu from which Daniel derives. Many scholars[63] think in this connection of the circles of the 'pious' (Hasidaeans or Hasidim). Lebram[64] thinks of priestly circles. His view is based not least on the fact that the cult occupies an important place in the book of Daniel. Presumably we need not distinguish these two views too sharply. The little information we have about the Hasidaeans in the books of Maccabees[65] at least suggests that the cult was very important for them.

The book of Daniel and especially Dan.7-12 must be seen as one of the most important apocalyptic writings. This work marked the beginning of the heyday of apocalyptic (cf.7.5).

Daniel gives us some idea of the tense situation that prevailed in Judaea about 165 BC. It is clear that the author knew the events of this time from personal experience. He depicted Antiochus IV Epiphanes as the great evildoer who was responsible for disaster coming upon city and land.[66] He does not have much respect for the Maccabees. Final deliverance will only come from God. In this respect even the Hasidaeans are only 'a little help' (11.34).

7.6.2 *The rest of the literature from this period*

The most important other writings from this period are a number of apocryphal and pseudepigraphical works.

Most important of the pseudepigrapha is I Enoch (Ethiopian Enoch). Some parts of the book, attributed to the Enoch mentioned in Gen.5.24, certainly come from this time, like the so-called Book of Watchmen or the angelological book (6-36) and the astronomical book (72-82). A number of fragments of Enoch written in Aramaic appear among the scrolls found near the Dead Sea.[67] Like Daniel, I Enoch, too, had a great influence on apocalyptic.[68]

Of the apocryphal books, mention must be made here of III Ezra and Judith. The former in some places recalls the book of Daniel, as in 4.40,58,[69] and may perhaps come from a rather later period than Daniel.[70] This is also true of the book of Judith,[71] which seems above all to have been written under the impact of events from the time of the Maccabees.

Chapter 8

The Maccabaean Struggle

8.1 *Background to the various groups*

8.1.1 *The supporters of Hellenism in Jerusalem*

In the previous chapter we saw how this group tried to make first of all the population of Jerusalem and later also the rest of the country, including Shechem, adopt Hellenistic culture. Their chief aim was to abolish the special status of Judaism.

Even after the events described in 7.2, for a long time the leadership of the group remained – at least in name – in the hands of Menelaus. An end to this came only in *c.*163/2 BC, when he was killed on the orders of Antiochus V.

We can begin by assuming that this group was relatively small.[1] However, its influence and authority was very great, because for the most part it consisted of the important upper stratum of the population, which had a considerable amount of influence and power, above all in the economic sphere (see e.g. 5.3).

All this means that, leaving aside religious conflicts, we certainly need to reckon with social and economic differences between the supporters of Hellenism and the rest of the population. As we have seen, in the meantime Menelaus had voluntarily raised the tribute due to the Seleucid king, which was already high (see 7.2.1). Of course this tax had to be paid by the people, and it was a burden which weighed heaviest on the shoulders of those who had least possessions. Such a development inevitably caused bitterness, and was certainly one of the most important motives for the outbreak of a rebellion. This conclusion must also be drawn from a letter attributed to Demetrius I (I Macc.10.26-45), in which he tries to secure the loyalty of Jonathan (cf.8.5). The letter first (I Macc.10.28-30) promises exemption from many high taxes. This fact is an important indication of the considerable role that economic factors played in the revolt.

8.1.2 *The Maccabees*

The members of the group which played by far the greatest part in the rebellion
are known as the Maccabees. This name is taken from the nickname 'the
Maccabaean' (presumably 'the hammer') given to Judas, the son of the priest
Mattathias, who rapidly became the leader of the revolt. At a later time this
family became known as the 'Hasmonaeans', derived from Hasmon, their
putative ancestor.[2]

The Maccabaean revolt began not in Jerusalem but in the country (cf. 8.2.1),
in Modein, where Mattathias and his family lived. This is an indication that
the old conflict between the rich upper class in Jerusalem and the peasant
population in the country[3] had again broken out fiercely. In the course of time
this conflict steadily increased. We have seen that in the time of Joseph the
Tobiad the great landlords preferred to live in Jerusalem. The burden which
this group, too, must have represented and the cost of their rich life-style was
passed on to the peasant population,[4] who in addition also had to give up part
of their harvest for the Seleucid king (cf. I Macc.10.30). It was this group
which played an important and often decisive role in the revolt, so it is not
surprising that their leaders belonged to the lower priestly class. They were
close to the ordinary people, while the powerful priestly families in Jerusalem
had allied themselves to the rich aristocracy there.

All this clearly indicates that the Maccabaean revolt must be seen primarily
as a peasant war. Bickerman also comes to this conclusion,[5] but in fact he sees
the war only as a religious war. Most emphasis is placed on this dimension in
the literature (Daniel; I & II Maccabees), but that is because only this aspect
was important to later generations and to Daniel. In reality (see above), social
and economic factors largely determined the character and course of the
revolt.

Of course the significance of religion in all this must not be understimated.
The country population was not only among the poorest, but also among the
most conservative parts of the people. For them, faithful as they were to
Yahwism, the idea of a process of Hellenization was in itself a scandal.
However, this attitude does not emerge so much among the Maccabees as
among the Hasidaeans, the group whom we shall consider next.

8.1.3 *The Hasidaeans*

The Hasidaeans (Greek) or Hasidim (Hebrew, meaning pious) are a group
which played a significant role during the revolt and obviously afterwards.
This group is mentioned by name for the first time in I Macc.2.42; 7.13; II
Macc.14.6.

In I Macc.2.42 they are mentioned as having joined the Maccabees shortly after the beginning of the revolt, and in 7.13 they are those who wanted to collaborate with the newly nominated high priest Alcimus. According to II Macc.14.6 Alcimus joined forces with the Maccabees. In I Macc.2.42 they are further described as a group of those who 'offered themselves willingly for the law'.

We can deduce from all this that the Hasidaeans took part in the rebellion for only a short time and that their main aim was to live on the basis of the Torah without any hindrance.

This gives the strong impression that even before the rise of the Maccabees the Hasidaeans must already have existed as a kind of party.[6] At the same time we can conclude from this that the Hasidaeans gave a central place to life according to the Mosaic law. As long as freedom of worship was at stake they took the side of the Maccabees, but as soon as this freedom was achieved, they withdrew at least a good deal of their military support.

The influence of this group was very great, both directly and indirectly. As we shall see later, there is a clear relationshp between the Hasidaeans and the Qumran community, the Pharisees and the Essenes. The influence of the group can also be seen in the earliest apocalyptic literature, for example in I Enoch 90.6-15, while the author of Daniel (see 7.6.1) was at least a sympathizer with the Hasidaeans.

8.2 *The beginning of the revolt*

8.2.1 *The emergence of Mattathias*

Both in I Maccabees (2.15ff.) and in Josephus (*AJ* XII, 268ff.), we are given an account of the way in which Mattathias rebelled in Modein against the command of Antiochus IV to offer sacrifice there in accordance with the royal command. Mattathias refused to obey the king, and when another Judaean was prepared to do so, he killed him and the king's representative. After this he fled into the hills with his five sons, John, Simon, Eleazar, Judas and Jonathan, along with other fugitives. This event marked the beginning of the revolt.

Troops from Jerusalem, probably for the most part the Seleucid occupying forces which supported Menelaus and his followers, were sent to track down the rebels.[7] One group, evidently Hasidaeans, was massacred on a sabbath because its members refused to offer any resistance on that day.[8] The result of this was that Mattathias and his followers decided from then on even to fight on the sabbath if they were attacked.[9] Another important consequence of this massacre was that the Hasidaeans – or at least many of them - now took the side of the Maccabees in the revolt. This brought considerable reinforcements to the movement.

Mattathias himself was hardly involved in this revolt. He died right at the beginning, which must have been about 166/165 BC.[10]

8.2.2 *The first successes of Judas*

After the death of Mattathias his son Judas became leader of the rebels. It is not clear why he took over this role and not, for example, the oldest son of Mattathias.

Judas mustered and organized his troops and waged a kind of guerrilla war. He soon proved very successful. He defeated an army under the leadership of Apollonius, and killed Apollonius. Seron, according to I Macc.3.13 'the commander of the Syrian army', also suffered a heavy defeat at the hands of the Maccabees. This happened at Beth-horon, about twelve miles north-west of Jerusalem.[11] These successes were due above all to the fact that there were only a few Seleucid troops in the country. Those there were belonged to the auxiliaries stationed in the Acra and elsewhere, who were in no way capable of coping with a guerrilla war in the hills. Moreover, the supporters of Hellenism seem to have underestimated the Maccabaean movement.

While these events were taking place, Antiochus IV was in the East, where he was concentrating all his attention on a war against the Parthians.[12] This shows that he had less interest in events in Judaea than sources like I Maccabees and Josephus suggest.

Only in the autumn of 165 BC did Judas's successes begin to cause some anxiety to the central government. Antiochus IV then gave his chancellor Lysias, his representative in the capital and at the same time the guardian of his son, orders to quash the revolt. Lysias then sent three Syrian generals, Ptolemy, Nicanor and Gorgias, to Judaea. However, they were defeated by Judas near Emmaus.

Immediately after this,[13] Lysias himself went with an army to Judaea. Going through Idumaea he advanced as far as Beth-zur, where he had an encounter with the Maccabees. According to I Macc.4.34f.; II Macc.11.1; *AJ* XII, 314, Lysias was defeated here,[14] but presumably the situation was rather more complicated. Some documents in II Macc.11 rather give the impression that circumstances forced Lysias and the Maccabees to negotiate. Lysias was compelled to return to Antioch by affairs of state (a serious illness of Antiochus IV).

We find the first document in which Lysias reports that he will intervene with the king in favour of Judaea in II Macc.11.17-21. Antiochus IV died in

164 BC, i.e. about the same time,[15] but his son and successor Antiochus V (164-162 BC) responded to the mediation of Lysias by giving the Judaeans full religious freedom. A letter from this king to Lysias to that effect is reproduced in II Macc.11.23-26. In a letter addressed directly to the Judaeans Antiochus V reports that he is granting an amnesty to all rebels who return home and giving the Judaeans permission to live according to their (Mosaic) laws. Otherwise the whole situation remained unchanged (see II Macc.11.27-33). Given the mediating role which is attributed to Menelaus in this letter, it must be authentic, since the author of II Maccabees elsewhere always puts ths high priest in an unfavourable light.

Another factor seems to have determined events after the defeat of Bethzur to a considerable extent, namely the intervention of Rome. At least we get this impression from a letter which is reproduced in II Macc.11.34-38.[16]

8.2.3 *The purification and reconsecration of the temple*

In close conjunction with the events mentioned above, the purification and rededication of the temple took place on 25 Kislev (about 15 December) 164 BC.

We have a letter about this purification of the temple in II Macc.1.10-2.18, addressed to the Jews living in the Diaspora. This is presented as a letter from Judas addressed to Aristobulus, a Jewish governor in Alexandria. At the very least, there is considerable doubt[17] as to whether this letter does in fact come from Judas.[18] However, contacts with Egypt seem possible in this period.[19]

The feast of Hanukkah is still celebrated annually in commemoration of the rededication of the temple. In one respect the inauguration of this feast represents a break with the past. Hitherto every feast was established upon the basis of a divine instruction given in the Old Testament. According to I Macc.4.59; II Macc.10.5-8 and *AJ* XII, 325, the feast of Hanukkah was initiated by Judas and his followers, i.e. on the basis of a human decision. This was common practice among the surrounding peoples, but it was a far-reaching innovation for Israelite tradition and implies that by his action Judas was introducing a Hellenistic custom into Judaism.

Neither Maccabees nor Josephus speaks of the eight-branched candlestick which is customary at this feast. Obviously the custom comes from a later time.

8.2.4 *New successes of Judas*

In 163 BC Judas laid siege to the Acra in Jerusalem. However, the siege was unsuccessful. Judas's guerrillas had neither the expertise nor the means to capture a fortress. Moreover, those besieged in the Acra had called on the

Seleucids for help, and in fact they soon appeared on the scene. Lysias again commanded the Seleucid army. In the meantime he had proclaimed himself regent of the young king Antiochus V and now in fact represented the supreme authority among the Seleucids.

Thereupon Judas had to break off his siege of the Acra. There was an encounter at Beth-zechariah, south of Bethlehem, between the troops of Lysias and those of Judas. Judas was defeated, and one of his brothers, Eleazar, was killed in the fight. Lysias conquered Beth-zur and advanced on Jerusalem, to which Judas had retreated. Now he in turn was besieged by the troops of Lysias.

This should have meant the end of the Maccabees, but as so often in the history of Israel politics on the world stage now proved decisive, even for a conflict on a very small scale. Lysias had to withdraw and the Maccabees again had their hands free. Strangely enough, they had the latest testament of Antiochus IV to thank for this. On his death-bed he had named another general, Philip, rather than Lysias, as regent for his son.

This Philip now went to Antioch to take over power there. On hearing news of this, Lysias wanted to break off the siege of the temple mount and return as quickly as possible to Antioch. Before doing so he made peace with the Judaeans, in fact restoring the situation to what it was before Antiochus' intervention.[20] According to Josephus[21] the Seleucids then took Menelaus with them to Antioch.

On his return to Antioch, Lysias soon managed to eliminate Philip, but his power did not last long. Demetrius I Soter (162-150 BC), who in the meantime had been sent as a hostage to Rome by his father Seleucus IV in place of his brother Antiochus IV (see 7.1), managed to escape from there in 163 BC and shortly afterwards killed Lysias and Antiochus V with the help of the army.

In the meantime Menelaus had been put to death. The new high priest, presumably nominated by Demetrius I, was Alcimus, a priest from the family of Aaron. By 162 BC, now that religious freedom was restored and a legitimate high priest had again been appointed, for many people, including the Hasidaeans, the aim of the struggle had been achieved.

A minor conflict seems to have developed in the meantime. According to Josephus,[22] Onias IV, a son of the former high priest Onias III, fled at this time to Egypt, where he had a temple built in Leontopolis along the lines of that in Jerusalem.[23]

8.3 *The situation after 162 BC*

The consequence of the events described above was that the Hasidaeans immediately detached themselves from the Maccabees. For them the aim of the struggle had been achieved. However, things were quite different for Judas and his followers. Although Judas, as leader of the opposition, must have been involved in the meeting with Lysias, he was clearly not completely satisfied with it. It is not clear precisely what his reasons were. It is possible that he and his followers got less power than they wanted. At all events, from now on the Maccabees clearly directed their struggle towards political power and freedom. Presumably they had already returned to their hiding places in the hill country by 162 BC in expectation of a new chance of success. This was not long in coming.

The new high priest Alcimus had come to Jerusalem with a Seleucid army under the command of Bacchides. There Bacchides, according to I Macc.7.13f., had sixty Hasidaeans killed. Of course this action did not help the reputation of the new high priest. In this situation Judas seems again to have occupied the temple mount in order to prevent Alcimus from exercising his functions as high priest. Thereupon Alcimus appealed for help to Demetrius I.

In response to this request for help, Demetrius I sent an army under the command of Nicanor to Judaea. However, this Seleucid army was defeated at Adasa, in the neighbourhood of Beth-horon, in 161 BC. Nicanor was also killed in this battle. The day of his death was declared a festival under the name of Nicanor's day.[24]

About the same time Judas must have sought to make contact with the Romans. There is an account of this in I Macc.8,[25] in which there is also a document (vv.23-28) with the conditions of the treaty that was made between Judas and Rome.[26] In I Macc.8 it is not said when this treaty was made. Chronologically it comes after the defeat of Nicanor, and there seems little against this.[27] Obviously the treaty was part of Roman policy, the ultimate aim of which was to put Judas in a position dependent on Rome. This process was crowned with success about a century later.[28]

According to II Macc.8.31f., at the same time Demetrius I received a letter from the Romans in which they announced their support for Judas.

Presumably, after these events Demetrius I quickly wanted to restore order in Judaea. To this end he sent an army there under the leadership of Bacchides. Bacchides defeated Judas in the neighbourhood of Jerusalem. Judas died in this action. The high priest Alcimus was restored to his office and for the moment was able to maintain his position with the support of Bacchides.

8.4 *Jonathan as leader of the Maccabees (161-142 BC)*

8.4.1 *The general political situation*

The next period is marked by increasing Roman influence. The Romans were able to develop their power and influence by resorting to the principle of 'divide and rule'. With this aim in view, they now in fact supported anyone and everyone with whom the Seleucids were having difficulties. Their dealings with the Maccabees mentioned in the previous section also fit in with this political policy.

This Roman policy also caused the greatest possible problems for Demetrius I when in 153 a civil war broke out in his kingdom between himself and Alexander Balas. The latter claimed to be a son of Antiochus IV and therefore to have a right to the throne. The situation became impossible for Demetrius I when in 153 the Roman Senate recognized Alexander's rights.[29]

Alexander Balas was able to hold on to the Seleucid kingdom until 145 BC. Thanks to the support of the Egyptian king Ptolemy VI (180-145 BC), Demetrius II (145-138 BC) then managed to regain the Seleucid throne. Alexander Balas fled to Arabia, where he was murdered.[30]

8.4.2 *The political situation in Palestine after the death of Judas*

It is clear that the Seleucids and the Hellenist party again had very firm control of Judaea and Jerusalem after the death of Judas. In order to consolidate this position, fortresses were built in various places in Judaea and Galilee. These included Jericho, Emmaus, Beth-horon, Bethel, Timnah, Pharathon, Tephon,[31] and above all the city of Jerusalem.[32]

For the first eight years after the death of Judas, Jonathan does not seem to have gained any foothold. This is evident, among other things, from the fact that he had to flee into the wilderness and take refuge first in the area of Tekoa and then in Transjordan. The only battle which is reported from this period is an act of vengeance against the Jambrite 'Arabians'[33] who had killed his brother John.[34]

During this time Jonathan lived in the same kind of conditions as David when he was fleeing from Saul (cf. I Sam.22ff.).[35]

From *c.*156 BC Jonathan resided in Michmash, a place north of Jerusalem, where according to I Macc.9.73 he 'began to rule the people'. He remained there with the approval of Bacchides, with whom he had more or less made peace. I Maccabees 9.23 (see also *AJ* XII,2) also indicates that the Maccabees had singularly little influence in this period.

All this changed in *c.*153 BC, as a result of the great political difficulties in the Seleucid empire.

8.4.3 *The social and economic situation after the death of Judas*

In *c.* 156 BC the high priest Alcimus died. We do not know how the government of Judaea was organized in the subsequent years. According to Josephus (*AJ* XX, 237) there was no high priest in Jerusalem in the years 159-152 BC.[36] It is argued that in fact the 'Teacher of Righteousness' known from the Qumran community (see 9.4.2) was high priest in Jerusalem for seven years.[37] He is said then to have been displaced by Jonathan. On the evidence that we have, this theory is hard to accept.[38]

Of the different groups in the country, hitherto we have heard only of the Hellenistic party, the Maccabees and the Hasidaeans. Although we have only vague information, there must have been other trends. The heyday of apocalyptic in this period (see 7.5) suggests that it derived from certain circles about which we are otherwise completely in the dark. As we shall see in the next chapter, the Sadducees, the Pharisees, the Essenes and the Qumran community now come into view.

As to the economic situation, we hear both in I Macc. (9.24) and Josephus (*AJ* XII,2-3) that there was a severe famine in the land. Both sources also give this as the reason why many people in the country went over to the Hellenist party. However, they do not explain further. It seems likely that many of the ordinary people and the country dwellers had originally taken the Maccabaean side in the hope that the Maccabees would help them to solve their economic problems. However, they gradually came to realize that this was not the Maccabees' most important concern. Obviously an author who was well disposed to the Hasmonaeans like the author of I Maccabees, and Josephus, who is dependent on him, would not bring out such a motivation. The view of Kreissig,[39] that the fortunes of the small farmers will have been improved by the Maccabees, must therefore certainly be ruled out as a general conclusion. I Maccabees 14.12, which he cites in this connection, 'Each man sat under his vine and under his fig tree, and there was none to make them afraid', serves more to glorify Simon the Maccabee than to indicate the actual situation, and can therefore hardly be used as evidence here.

8.4.4 *Jonathan's diplomatic and political successes*

From about 153 BC, Jonathan was able to exploit the difficulties in the Seleucid empire sketched out in 8.5.1 by supporting both Alexander Balas and Demetrius I in turn.

Because Demetrius I gave permission for Jonathan to raise troops in exchange for his help, Jonathan was able to occupy Jerusalem in 152 BC. However, when Alexander Balas sought an agreement with him, Jonathan asked for the high priesthood as the price of his help; thereupon Alexander Balas did in fact bestow this office on him (I Macc.10.18-20; *AJ* XIII, 45). This was again seen by many people as a break with an existing tradition, for while Jonathan was of priestly descent,he could not be regarded as a legitimate descendant of the Zadokites, who were regarded as the legitimate high-priestly family. For these reasons many people regarded the nomination of Jonathan as illegal.

The events described above certainly brought Jonathan personal success, but at the same time they made the internal situation much worse, by simply widening the gulf between different groups.

Not only did Jonathan take the office of high priest; according to I Macc.10.65 he was also appointed by Alexander Balas general and governor of a province, probably Judaea. This must have happened after the death of Demetrius I, when Alexander Balas had built up a good relationship with Ptolemy VI.

In the subsequent period Jonathan succeeded in extending his power considerably by being able to adapt at the right time to the various changes in the political sphere. His support of Alexander Balas gradually brought him into possession of an important part of the coastal plain. When Ptolemy VI again took the side of Demetrius II (145-138 BC) and dropped Alexander Balas, Jonathan managed to occupy the Acra. Soon afterwards Jonathan made an agreement with Demetrius II which confirmed him in all his offices and in addition gave him control over three districts of Samaria and exemption from a number of taxes. We find all this narrated in a letter of Demetrius II, reproduced in I Macc.11.32-37 and *AJ* XIII, 125-8. It is impossible to establish for certain how original this letter is, but there is much to suggest its authenticity.[40]

In a new battle for power in the Seleucid empire between Demetrius II and a certain Trypho, who wanted to put Antiochus VI, the son of Alexander Balas, on the Seleucid throne,[41] Jonathan managed to gain further advantages by supporting one or the other depending on circumstances. Thus in this period he captured the Acra and his brother Simon the stronghold of Beth-zur. At the beginning of 142 BC he was captured by Trypho through treachery and soon afterwards killed by him.

During his rule Jonathan clearly also sought other foreign contacts. According to I Macc.12.3-4 and *AJ* XIII, 163-5, with this in view he sent a delegation to Rome in order to renew friendship with the Romans. However, we have more detailed information about contacts with Sparta. I Maccabees

12.5-18 and *AJ* XIII, 166-70 mention a letter in which Jonathan among other things sought closer contacts with the Spartans. The authenticity of this letter is disputed,[42] and that goes even more for the letter to Onias III quoted in I Macc.12.20-23 (cf. also *AJ* XII, 225-7), which is probably the work of an admirer of the Oniads.[43] All this, however, does not exclude the possibility that there were in fact contacts with Sparta in the time of Jonathan.

8.4.5 *The consequences of Jonathan's policy*

We have seen that Jonathan was able to make very good use of the permanent struggle for power between the various claimants to the Seleucid throne. By making payments and providing soldiers he was in a position to gain increasing privileges. The result of this was not only that Jonathan increased in personal power and influence but also that the territory of Judaea expanded considerably.[44] Therefore we can regard Jonathan as the *de facto* founder of the Hasmonaean empire, the fruits of which Simon and his successors were later able to reap.

Another development was set in motion with Jonathan, totally different from those of the time of Mattathias and Judas. With him there was an assimilation to Hellenism which was unthinkable in the former period. The distinctive feature here is that Jonathan allowed a Seleucid pretender to the throne to bestow the office of high priest on him. In 161 BC Judas and his followers refused to recognize the nomination by the Seleucids of Alcimus, a priest from the family of Aaron, something that the Hasidaeans certainly seemed ready to do.

However, the event mentioned above is very typical of Jonathan and his later successors. Their eyes were fixed only on gaining power. Religious considerations were certainly not predominant for them. On the contrary – as so often in history – they tried to use religion to realize their own aspirations and secure a position of power. Religion played a much more important role in a number of groups which according to Josephus (*AJ* XIII, 171-3) already existed in the time of Jonathan. Since these groups became important later in history, we must now look at them more closely before again taking up the historical thread.

Chapter 9

The Origin and Development of Some Important Groups

9.1 *The Sadducees*

9.1.1 *Sources*

It may be presumed that we have no writings from Sadducean circles. Some works, like Jesus Sirach and I Maccabees, are sometimes attributed to a Sadducean author, but there must be serious doubts as to whether this is the case.[1]

We must therefore derive our information about the Sadducees from those who wrote about them. This means Josephus, the New Testament and rabbinic literature. However, the light that all this sheds on the Sadducees is very fragmentary and often also polemic in perspective. Thus in fact the Talmud only gives a summary of the heresies which were noted among the Sadducees.[2] Of course we should not be surprised at such an account, given that the rabbinic literature has been largely collected and edited from a Pharisaic standpoint (see 9.2.1). As for Josephus, it is well known that he himself was a Pharisee and so his views on the Sadducees are coloured accordingly.[3] Moreover, his account of the Sadducees, as of the Pharisees and Essenes, is aimed at making these groups understandable to Greek and Roman readers. This factor, too, needs to be taken into account in his description. Finally, we also have the New Testament. In it we find only sparse information about the Sadducees, and the main stress is on all their shortcomings.

This verdict on the sources does not of course mean that they do not give us any detailed information about the Sadducees, but it does warn us to approach and interpret the information they contain as objectively as posisble.

9.1.2 *The name*

The etymology of the name Sadducees is disputed. The texts which discuss the group do not give us a clear picture. The logical conclusion, therefore, is that over the course of time different possible explanations were advanced.[4] The most usual explanation is that there is an association with the name of the priest Zadok, who held office in Jerusalem in the time of David and Solomon.[5] Philologically, however, a connection between Zadok and the Sadducees is very uncertain,[6] though that need not mean that the Sadducees did not regard themselves as descendants of Zadok. As we shall see shortly, we also find a similar view in the Qumran community. Thus both groups laid claim to the legitimate priesthood (cf.Ezek.40.46).

The Sadducees were also referred to as Boethusians.[7] The name is derived from the high-priestly family of Boethus which came from Alexandria. This family came to the fore in the time of Herod the Great and was certainly the most powerful of the four families who provided the high priest in the Roman period.[8] The Boethusians were presumably related to the Sadducees.[9] At all events the terms Sadducees and Boethusians are used indistinguishably, and that even gives the impression that they are synonyms.[10]

9.1.3 *Origin and history*

It is impossible to say when the Saducean party came into being as an organized group or whether it ever existed as such. Apart from this question people are usually inclined to suppose a degree of continuity between the Zadokites of the Persian and Greek period and the Sadducees.[11] In view of what was known in a later period about the important position occupied by the Sadducees in priestly circles (cf. Acts 5.17; *AJ* XX, 199), this too seems very probable.

According to Josephus (*AJ* XIII, 173), the Sadducees, like the Pharisees and Essenes, already existed as a separate group in the time of Jonathan the Maccabee. Certainly from the time of John Hyrcanus (134-104 BC) down to AD 66/70 they played an important role in Jerusalem and Judaea, apart from a period during the brief reign of Salome Alexandra (76-67 BC). It is completely impossible to discover what place they occupied before that. Given their position and views as known from a later period, we may well suppose there to have been some affinity between the Sadducees and the supporters of Hellenism who dominated the city of Jerusalem at the beginning of the second century BC.[12] This does not mean that we should conclude that this last group already consisted of Sadducees.

Ernst Bammel's view is rather different.[13] He believes that one can only speak of a Sadducean party in the first century of our era; it arose as a result of a conflict with the Pharisees. Before that the Sadducees were priestly families brought to Jerusalem by Herod the Great to restrain the influence of the Hasmonaean priest-kings and there presented as legitimate sons of Zadok. The name Sadducee was an honorific name which these priests gave themselves.

9.1.4 *Characteristics*

Clearly the Sadducees were a specific class and indeed an upper stratum of well-to-do members of the society of their time.[14] In Acts 4.1 the Sadducees are mentioned in the same breath as the priests and the captain of the temple, while in Acts 5.17 they are identified as the party of the high priest. This last fact in particular indicates that the high-priestly circles often consisted of Sadducees.[15]

Given what has already been said, it is best to describe the Sadducees as a group of senior clergy and aristocracy, i.e. the classes with possessions. That is evident from their constant concern to preserve political and social stability in order to secure their economic interests. That is also why they constantly favoured a policy of cooperation with foreign rulers, though this does not mean that they were always prepared to collaborate. Given that unrest and turmoil arose all too easily around the temple, they made use of the services of temple police there.

The attitude I have just described implies that the Sadducees were interested in maintaining the *status quo*. As such they can be described as conservatives. Such an attitude was also expressed in their religious views. Here too they did not want any innovations. As is well known, they recognized only the written tradition as holy scripture and in contrast to the Pharisees would have nothing to do with an oral tradition which made new adaptations possible. Moreover they rejected the (Pharisaic) doctrine of the resurrection of the dead and the existence of angels and spirits.[16]

Closely connected with all this is the fact that the Sadducees were very hostile to messianic and apocalyptic movements which brought innovations and in this way threatened the *status quo*. For the same reasons they did not have much time for the message of the prophets.

All this does not imply that there were not different trends within the Sadducean movement. There doubtless were, but in the main the description given here applies to all the Sadducees.

9.2 *The Pharisees*

9.2.1 *Sources*

Our sources for the Pharisees are the same as those for the Sadducees (see 9.1.1), namely Josephus, the New Testament and the rabbinic literature. Although these sources are rather less fragmentary about the Pharisees and often not at all polemic (Josephus and the rabbinic literature), this does not meant that we always have information about the Pharisees at first hand. The works of Josephus were written about AD 75-100 and the New Testament about 50-90, and the regulations and teachings of the Pharisees before AD 70 were only written down by rabbis who lived in the first and second centuries.[17] The influence of the (later) Pharisees on rabbinic literature was enormous. After the fall of Jerusalem in AD 70 they were in fact the only group to survive. It was the Pharisees who guided Judaism through this catastrophe and gave it a new form and hope, especially in the religious sphere. In studying the rabbinic literature this factor must constantly be taken seriously. It is obvious that this applies primarily if we use this literature in order to get a picture of the Pharisees.

9.2.2 *The name*

The name Pharisee is derived from a word which in Hebrew and Aramaic means 'separated'. The question is in what direction this indication points. Most probably the designation is connected with a separation in which not all the people were involved.[18] At all events, the name must have been given them by a third party (opponents). In favour of this is the fact that the Pharisees are described by this name only three times in the Mishnah, and then it is attributed to a Sadducee.[19] The Pharisees themselves used terms which mean 'friend', 'scribe', or 'wise man'. In Jewish literature the preferred description of the Pharisees is 'wise men' or more often 'our wise men'.

9.2.3 *Origin and history*

In fact we know nothing for certain about the origin of the Pharisees. They are often associated with the Hasidaeans or Hasidim who at the beginning of the revolt fought side by side with the Maccabees.[20]

The Pharisees appear on the historical scene for the first time as a more or less independent group, like the Sadducees and Essenes, in the time of Jonathan, if at least this fact in Josephus (*AJ* XIII, 171) rests on accurate information. We have no other information about a still earlier period or about the origin of the Pharisees. Nor do we find any in the rabbinic traditions about the Pharisees. Neusner[21] has pointed out that these traditions go back at most fifty or eighty years to before the destruction of the temple in AD 70.

Presumably from about the beginning of the Christian era the Pharisees banded together in communities.[22] These were made up, for example, of the lower ranks of priests, craftsman, small farmers and merchants. This list already shows that support for the Pharisees, unlike that for the Sadducees, must rather be sought in the middle-class groups. The ordinary people were also fairly sympathetic towards them. Most scribes were also Pharisees, although the two categories should not be identified without further ado.

There were probably always only relatively few Pharisees in the strict sense of the term. Josephus (*AJ* XVII, 42) tells us that they numbered only about six thousand in the time of Herod the Great. However, their influence was usually much greater than one might expect from so small a number.[23] This influence later made itself felt above all through the significance which the school and synagogue acquired in Judaism and especially because the Pharisaic movement after AD 70 was the one dominant force in the existence of Judaism (cf. 9.2.1).

The Pharisees certainly cannot be regarded as a political party, although this does not mean that they had no concern for the political questions of their time.[24] We shall see in due course that in several periods their political influence and their concerns in this sphere were considerable. However, at a later period their main attention seems to have been directed more emphatically to religious matters.[25] Still, it is never possible to see a strict division between politics and religion among the Pharisees, as one would expect in the light of the Jewish and biblical traditions. Political questions were seen in the light of religion. Wellhausen's theory[26] that the Pharisees and Sadducees stood over against each other as the parties of church and state is also very questionable.

9.2.4 *Characteristics*

In contrast to the Sadducees, the Pharisees attached great importance not only to the written Torah but also to oral tradition.[27] In their view this tradition was handed down by word of mouth from generation to generation through Joshua, elders, prophets and teachers until it was set down in writing in the Mishnah.[28] They regarded it as a closer interpretation and further development of the written Torah (cf. Matt.5.21; 15.2).

In addition, they also differed from the Sadducees in believing, unlike them, in the resurrection and in the existence of angels and spirits (cf. Acts 23.8).

Whereas human freedom stood very much in the foreground for the Sadducees (*BJ* II, 164), for the Pharisees the emphasis lay both on divine omnipotence and providence and on human freedom and responsibility (*AJ*

XIII, 173). This is particularly sharply expressed in a remark attributed to R.Akiba in Aboth III.19: 'All is foreseen, but free will is given.' This reproduces a general view in Judaism,[29] although the personal responsibility and free will of the individual were often stressed less in apocalyptic groups than among the Pharisees.

As the centre party the Pharisees had far more divisions than the Sadducees. Thus a Pharisee was among those who founded what would later be the party of the Zealots or a group related to them (see 12.8.1). Another illustration is given by the well-known schools of Shammai and Hillel, founded at the beginning of our era; the views of the former were stricter than those of the latter. However, in later tradition the views of the school of Hillel seem to have gained the upper hand.

9.3 *The Essenes*

9.3.1 *Sources*

If we leave the discoveries in the wilderness of Judah out of account here, we must regard the Jewish authors Josephus and Philo as the earliest and most important sources for the Essenes. Alongside them mention must also be made of Pliny the Elder.[30] Perhaps with the exception of Josephus, these authors did not know the Essenes from their own experience. Thus they have taken the facts about the Essenes from other sources unknown to us. A group in Egypt related to the Essenes, the so-called Therapeutae, may possible have been known personally to Philo.[31]

We know nothing about Essene writings, unless we put those from the library of Qumran in this category.

The Essenes are never mentioned by name in rabbinic literature[32] nor in any of the writings of the New Testament which have come down to us.

9.3.2 *The name*

There is no unanimity over the meaning of the name Essenes.[33] It is often associated with an Aramaic word which means pious,[34] but any connection of this kind is very doubtful.[35] Another theory is that the name Essene is connected with a word that means 'healers'.[36] Reference is then made to the fact that in Philo they are also referred to as Therapeutae. However, this view, too, has not commanded general agreement. So we are in fact completely in the dark here.

9.3.3 *Origin and history*

The question of the origin of the Essenes is also very difficult to answer. The facts that we have about them give us no specific pointers in this direction. Hellenistic Jewish and other writers from antiquity[37] write about them as an existing group without going into detail about their prehistory. Starting from what Josephus tells us,[38] we can only say that the Essenes, like the Sadducees and Pharisees, already formed an existing group in the time of Jonathan.

It is often assumed that the Essenes are the spiritual descendants (from the pacifist side) of the Hasidaeans (see 8.1.3).[39] Among other things, their name would also point in this direction. However, this last theory rests on a very weak foundation,[40] so we must conclude that the question of the origin of the Essenes remains very obscure. The possible identification of the Essenes with the Qumran community will be discussed in the next section of this chapter.

The Essenes were certainly active in the Jewish community down to the end of the second temple in AD 70. This can be established on the basis of the facts that we have. Their numbers were probably always relatively small. Josephus and Philo speak[41] of four thousand in their time. According to Philo the Essenes lived in the villages of Judaea, where most of them worked as small farmers or craftsman. They avoided cities as far as possible because they regarded them as breeding grounds for injustice.[42] However, at another point Philo tells us that they did live in cities.[43] Neither Josephus nor Philo knows anything of Essenes living in the neighbourhood of the Dead Sea. Nor does the classical author Pliny the Elder.[44]

9.3.4 *Characteristics*

Here are some of the most important characteristics of the Essenes as they are described in different sources.

Essenes know no slavery[45] and avoid swearing oaths.[46] They usually wear white clothes and pay careful attention to rites of purification.[47] While they bring gifts to the temple, they reject animal offerings.[48] They observe the sabbath very strictly.[49] All possessions are held in common, and they reject luxury and private possessions.[50] Both Josephus and Philo, and also Pliny the Elder, tell us that the Essenes live celibate lives,[51] though Josephus also mentions a group of Essenes who allowed marriage.[52] Philo also tells us that the Essenes held pacifist views.[53] There were rules for a probationary period and rites of initiation before entry into the community.[54]

A number of these characteristics indicate the priestly character of the group. Some facts, like for example the difference of opinion over marriage, give the impression that the name Essenes is the collective name for a group in which not all were of the same opinion, but had many things in common.

It emerges from all this that the Essenes were a closed community in which there were several shades of opinion but in which abstinence, communal possessions and a sober life-style were the most prominent features. In contrast to the Sadducees and Pharisees we may note that the Essenes had virtually no interest in political matters.

9.4 *The Qumran community*

9.4.1 *Identification*

Very soon after the first discoveries in 1947 in the area of the Dead Sea it became clear that the writings found there must have belonged to a group which had spent a long time in this area. It was more difficult to identify the group in question. Most scholars think that the Qumran community consisted of Essenes or a group closely related to them.[55] There are also some who think the group was made up of Sadducees,[56] Pharisees,[57] or Zealots.[58] Very recently it has even been argued that the nucleus of the Qumran community was a group of conservative Judaeans who returned from Babylon to Palestine shortly after 165 BC.[59]

All these views show that the identification of the Qumran community is by no means a straightforward matter. The affinity with the Essenes is in fact their most striking feature, but that does not mean that we should immediately identify the group with the Essenes. Moreover, the community seems to have consisted above all of priests who presented themselves as 'sons of Zadok'. It seems best to see the group as largely consisting of priestly families (perhaps of a lower class) and in many respects showing great affinity to the Essenes.[60]

9.4.2 *Origin and history*

From archaeological evidence it has been established that the central buildings of the community settlement in the area of the Dead Sea were at Ḥirbet Qumran (about twenty miles north of Engedi). On the basis of the archaeological and literary material that has been discovered it can be assumed that the community lived there from about 150/140 BC – AD 68.[61] The settlement seems to have been abandoned from about 31 BC to about the beginning of our era as the result of an earthquake.[62] The living quarters of the community were again destroyed during the struggle against the Romans in AD 68.

One much-disputed question is the identity of the 'Teacher of Righteousness' who is mentioned in many of the community writings. Various attempts have been made to identify him with a particular figure, as for instance with Onias III, the high priest who succeeded Alcimus in about 159 BC (see 8.5.3), and with Jesus,[63] but without any convincing results. We could be more certain about his identity if we knew who was meant by his opponent, 'the godless priest' or 'the man of lies'.[64] There are also a great many different views about the identity of the latter. He has been directly identified with Jonathan, Simon, Alexander Jannaeus and Hyrcanus II.[65] Most recently there seems to be a consensus in favour of Jonathan, but there is considerably uncertainty all round. It is also a real possibility that the 'godless priest' could represent a number of figures.[66]

Thus the figure of 'the Teacher of Righteousness' remains anonymous.[67] His influence on the community was certainly very great, as is evident among other things from CH I,11; 1 QpHab XI.4-8 and 1QH V, 23-25. It is impossible to establish whether this teacher was also the founder of the community. There are often allusions to the fact that the 'Teacher of Righteousness' and his followers went into captivity to the 'land of Damascus' or 'the land of the north',[68] where they entered into a 'new covenant'. Some scholars[69] think that 'Damascus' here must be taken literally; others[70] think of Qumran, while yet others[71] suppose that this is an allusion to the Judaeans who were taken into captivity in Babylon in the time of Nebuchadnezzar.

CD I, 6ff. describes how the Qumran community came into being in the 'time of wrath', viz., in the three hundred and ninetieth year after the fall of Jerusalem in 586 BC (cf. Ex.4.5). Although this figure looks very symbolic, the end of this period (the beginning of the second century BC) can certainly be seen as the time when the community came into being.[72] Archaeological evidence also points in this direction. Excavations have indicated that Qumran was built and lived in very close to about 140 BC.[73] If the community settled here about this time, the group must certainly have came into being some decades earlier.

In about 100 BC the settlement seems to have been expanded considerably. Presumably as a result of an earthquake (see above), there was a time when it was uninhabited, but soon after the death of Herod the Great the group returned and rebuilt everything. This phase of the settlement finally came to an end when in about AD 68 the Romans destroyed the settlement and the whole complex of buildings belonging to it.

9.4.3 *Library*

Since 1947 a large number of Hebrew, Aramaic and Greek manuscripts or fragments of manuscripts have been found around Ḥirbet Qumran.[74]. It is almost universally accepted that all these writings formed the library of the Qumran community.[75] The manuscripts from a much later period which were found at Ḥirbet Mird (about six miles south-west of Qumran) and Wadi Murabbaʿat[76] (about twelve miles south of Qumran) cannot be included with them. The manucripts found in the valleys of Nahal Tseʿelim, Nahal Ḥever and Nahal Mismar, even more to the south, are yet further removed; for the most part they come from the period of AD 132-135. The same is true of the manucript finds from the citadel of Masada, the fortress known from the fight against Rome in AD 66-73.

Clearly the documents in the library of Qumran must have been written before AD 68. The earliest of them can be dated to the second century BC. Among the manuscripts that have been discovered there are biblical manuscripts, apocrypha, pseudepigrapha, pesharim (Bible commentaries), Targums and rules of the Order. To identify these manuscripts found in eleven caves of Qumran a particular system of abbreviations is used, the first two characters indicating the place where the manuscript was discovered. Thus 1Q denotes Qumran Cave 1. The following characters then give the content (p = pesher, commentary; ap = apocryphon and tg = targum) and the name of the manuscript in question, e.g. 1QpHab, 1QapGen, and 1Qtg Job. If a large number of manuscripts of the same book are found, this is indicated by a small superior letter. Thus 1QIs^a is the first Isaiah scroll from Cave 1 and 1QIs^b the second. If a manuscript cannot be identified, the indication of where it was found is followed by a figure in Arabic numerals, e.g. 4Q180.

The significance of these manuscript discoveries is enormous. In the first place they provide us with insight into and knowledge of the customs, the history and the faith of the Qumran comunity itself. Furthermore, they are important for studying Hebrew from the third century BC to the second century AD and for the history of the text of the Old Testament. Finally, the great importance of the literature for understanding the background to the New Testament needs to be stressed.

9.4.4 *Characteristics*

It is clear that the priests of the Qumran community were rivals of the priests from the Jerusalem temple. Whoever may be meant by the 'godless priest', he was certainly high priest in Jerusalem. The community regarded worship in Jerusalem as illegitimate, since the priests there did not observe the rules, at least as Qumran understood them.

The rules of the Order are the best source for the views of the community. The most important of these are 1QS 'Community Rule' (*serek* = rule) and

CD (= Covenant of Damascus), the 'Damascus Document'.[77] The first of these comes from about 90 BC and the second from about 30 BC. In addition, mention might also be made of the Temple Scroll (11Q Temple),[78] which can be roughly dated to the first century BC.[79] 1QM, the 'War Scroll', also provides useful information.

From the evidence at our disposal it looks as if the Qumran community regarded itself as the true Israel. This view means that the community made polemical attacks not only on the priests in Jerusalem but also on the Pharisees and Sadducees, who are referred to as Ephraim or Nineveh and Manasseh or No-Amon respectively.[80] The community even called itself Judah or Jerusalem (cf. CD VI.5).

The leadership of the community lay with a council consisting of twelve people who represented the tribes of Israel and three priests (see 1QS VIII, 1f.). Each group within the community, which had to consist of at least ten people, was led by an 'overseer'.

In order to be admitted to the community someone first had to undergo a probationary period of three years. After giving an oath he could then enter the community (cf. CD XV, 5-7). Very strict rules were observed within the community. Anyone who dishonoured the name of the LORD was cast out of the community, and the same went for those who rebelled against the rules of the community (cf. 1QS VI, 27-VII,2; 1QS VII, 17).

Great stress was laid on purity and ritual washings (see CD X, 10-13; XII, 12-14). Communal meals were also held regularly.

In contrast to worship in Jerusalem people in Qumran observed the solar calendar of fifty-two weeks known to us from I Enoch and Jubilees, according to which feasts fell on the same day of the week every year (cf.1QpH XI, 4-8).

These brief notes about the views held in Qumran must suffice here.[81] More detailed information can be found in numerous specialist studies on this material.[82]

Chapter 10

The Period of the Hasmonaean Priest-Rulers

10.1 *Simon (143/42-135/34 BC)*

10.1.1 *The international situation*

In 8.5.4 we saw that from about 145 BC Trypho made attempts to remove Demetrius II from the Seleucid throne and replace him with Antiochus VI, a son of Alexander Balas.

However, Trypho's real intentions soon emerged. In 142 BC he had his charge, the young king Antiochus VI, killed and put the crown on his own head.[1] But his reign did not last long. He was only able to hold power from 142 to 138 BC. In 138 he was driven from the throne by Antiochus VII Sidetes (138-128 BC), a brother of Demetrius II. The latter had been taken prisoner in the same year by the Parthian king Mithridates I (*c.* 171-138 BC), when he was trying to regain territory lost to the Parthians. Antiochus VII later made a similar attempt, but had just as little success.[2]

So we can see that the Seleucid empire was collapsing on all sides. Both the Parthians and the Maccabees were able to strengthen their position at Seleucid expense. In the long run the Seleucids lost all control over the territories of the Parthians and Judaea and its wider surroundings. However, it must be emphatically stressed that the Maccabees and Parthians did not gain this position and their independence by virtue of their own might. They owed their success to Rome, which had every interest in weakening the Seleucid empire. Moreover, the independence of Parthia and Judaea was only temporary, and only lasted as long as the Romans wanted it to.

10.1.2 *Freedom from taxation*

After the capture of Jonathan by Trypho (8.5.4), the leadership of the Maccabaean rebels came into the hands of Simon, the last survivor of the five brothers. In the dispute between Demetrius II and Trypho, Simon soon took the side of the former. However, he made it a condition that Demetrius II should give the people complete exemption from taxation. Demetrius had little option but to consent to this demand (cf. I Macc. 13.36-40; *AJ* XIII, 213). This happened in 143/2 BC. From that moment the Seleucid calendar was also abolished in Judaea. All documents and treaties were now dated according to the years of Simon (cf. I Macc.13.41; 14.27; *AJ* XIII, 214). This last practice was a formal confirmation of the independence that had been gained.[3]

The granting of freedom from taxes was an important milestone in the history of Judaea. In I Macc.13.41f. and *AJ* XIII, 213, this event is regarded as the end of oppression, and it clearly indicates that economic motives played a large role in the Maccabaean struggle.

An important factor in the Seleucid system of taxation was so-called state leasing, which was imposed by the aristocracy on the small farmers and the country population.[4] The disappearance of this state leasing was an enormous relief for the oppressed country-dwellers.

Rostovtzeff's view[5] that the Hasmonaeans took over the Seleucid system of taxation unchanged has been rejected out of hand by Kippenberg.[6] The Hasmonaeans made certain of income by raising a tithe, which was a very old custom,[7] a tax on the produce of the country and a levy consisting of one tenth of what had been sown.[8]

The abolition of the Seleucid system of taxation meant that the economic aim of the rebellion had been achieved. The Maccabees who had had so great a part in it now began to reap its fruits.

10.1.3 *Simon nominated high priest, general and leader*

In I Macc.14.28 (cf. also 14.41-43) we are told that a so-called 'great assembly' was summoned, composed of priests, leaders of the people and elders of the land. It is uncertain precisely what is meant by 'great assembly' here.[9] Clearly this is meant to be the same sort of gathering as those mentioned in I Kings 8.65 (cf. II Chron.7.8); Neh.5.7. In I Macc.14 it is said that this gathering praised Simon and his brothers greatly for all that they had done and resolved on, and also that Simon was to possess the hereditary title of high priest, leader and general (I Macc.14.25-49). Only one reservation is made. Simon and his descendants are to hold this title 'until a true prophet shall appear' (I Macc.14.41). This last reservation is seen as a compromise between the Maccabees and their following and those who found it difficult to accept that the 'Maccabees' should have a high-priestly function and, moreover, a hereditary one. Moreover, the concession had no political value.

In particular, the nomination of Simon as hereditary high priest was a great break with existing religious tradition. Until 152 BC, when Jonathan was nominated high priest by Alexander Balas (see 8.5.4), only the Zadokites were regarded as legitimate high priests. Although there is no specific mention of the fact, we can assume that at that time many people found it difficult to accept the nomination of Jonathan. It is understandable that a hereditary high priesthood involving Simon was now even more difficult to accept.

Be this as it may, the nomination of Simon as hereditary high priest, general and leader was endorsed by the decree of the 'great assembly'. According to I Macc.14.27, 48f., the words of this decree, given in I Macc.14.27-45, were engraved on copper plates which were set up in the sanctuary.

10.1.4 *Simon's relations with foreign powers*

Soon after the death of Jonathan, Simon sought contacts with Rome. His aim was to strengthen his position as an independent ruler, so good relations with Rome were very important. Therefore he sent a delegation led by Numenius there (I Macc.14.24). According to I Macc.15.15, 22f., the result of this mission[10] was that the Roman consul Lucius sent a letter to the kings of the surrounding countries in which the Romans guaranteed the independence of Judaea. The text of this letter is given in I Macc.15.16-21. Its authenticity is disputed. Josephus mentions a similar document, but dates it much later, in the time of Hyrcanus II (*AJ* XIV, 145-8). Presumably, however, it must be put in the time of Simon and therefore dated about 139 BC.[11]

Meanwhile, Antiochus VII Sidetes, the brother of Demetrius II, had come to power in the Seleucid empire (see 10.1.1). This king, who still had to deal with Trypho, began by confirming all the privileges which he had granted to Simon. According to I Macc.15.1-9, on this occasion Antiochus also granted Simon the right to mint his own coins. Josephus (*AJ* XII, 223-4) also relates the concessions that the Seleucid king made at the time.

This right to mint coins comprised the making of coins which were valid only in a particular city or district, in this case Jerusalem (I Macc.15.6). It is almost certain that Simon never made use of the privilege,[12] although against that it is argued that Simon indeed made use of his rights, but that his coins bore the name of Jerusalem rather than his own name.[13]

The attitude of Antiochus VII to Simon changed once he had driven out Trypho. He then felt strong enough to advance on Simon. He asked Simon to return the cities of Gadara (Gezer), from which Simon had driven out the pagan population in 142 BC,[14] Joppa (Jaffa) and the Acra in Jerusalem. Moreover, he asked for taxes from all the cities and places outside Judaea, or in lieu of that for a tribute of about a thousand talents of silver (I Macc.15.25-31). When Simon seemed only ready to pay a mere hundred talents for Gadara and Joppa, Antiochus VII sent his general Cendebaeus to Judaea. Simon, who was himself too old, put his sons Judas and John at the head of the army which went to meet Cendebaeus. Cendebaeus was killed, and the city of Ashdod, from which the Seleucids had fled, was burned (I Macc.16.8-10; *AJ* XIII, 226f.). During the lifetime of Simon, Antiochus VII did not make any further attempt to gain control of Judaea.

10.1.5 *The end of Simon*

Ptolemy, a son-in-law of Simon from Idumaea, who was district commander of Jericho, made an attempt to seize power from the Hasmonaeans. To this end he invited Simon and his sons Mattathias and Judas to a feast in Dok, the fortress he had built near Jericho. When they arrived, Ptolemy had them put to death. At the same time he had also sent men to the city of Gadara to murder John there. However, this last attack failed because John was warned in time. John immediately rushed to Jerusalem and was able to seize the city before Ptolemy arrived. So in fact Ptolemy's *coup d'état* had already failed.

Simon's violent end shows once again how turbulent and full of unrest the time of the Maccabees must have been. All those in the first generation of Maccabees lost their lives through violence. It is clear that the population in this period shared in the violence and unrest. That was also true of Simon's time. The report in I Macc.14.12 that in the time of Simon 'Each man sat under his vine and under his fig-tree, and there was none to make them afraid' says more about the exaggerated sympathy of the author of I Maccabees for Simon than about the real situation.

I Maccabees ends with the account of Simon's death (I Macc.16.11-22). For the rest of the history of the Hasmonaeans for the most part we only have the works of Josephus. The work mentioned in I Macc.16.24 about the history of John Hyrcanus I has not survived.

10.2 *John Hyrcanus I (135/34-104 BC)*

10.2.1 *The beginning of his reign*

On the basis of the honorific titles granted by the 'great assembly' (see 10.1.3), the third and last surviving son of Simon, Johanan, better known under his Greek (!) name John, was named his lawful successor, with the title John Hyrcanus.

John Hyrcanus first of all had to deal with Ptolemy, which he did quickly and successfully. After that, right at the beginning of his rule he had to cope with an invasion by Antiochus VII. Antiochus ravaged the whole land of Judaea[15] and besieged Hyrcanus in his capital, Jerusalem.[16] According to Josephus (*AJ* XIII,236) this took place in the first year of the rule of Hyrcanus (134 BC), but that is by no means certain.[17]

Lack of food in the beleaguered city forced Hyrcanus to come to terms with Antiochus VII. Among other things Hyrcanus had to pay five hundred talents of silver, break down the walls of Jerusalem, take part in a Seleucid campaign against the Parthians, and again recognize Seleucid sovereignty over Judaea.[18] The extreme moderation of these conditions seems above all to be due to the fact that Antiochus VII was also forced to break off the siege of Jerusalem as a result of an intervention by the Roman Senate.[19]

In fact at this time Hyrcanus seems to have had secret contacts with Phraates II, the king of Parthia.[20] In this period the Parthians also freed Demetrius II, the brother of Antiochus VII (see 10.1.1), to provide the latter with a rival. Antiochus VII died in 128 BC in battle against the Parthians, after which Demetrius II again ascended the Seleucid throne.

The campaign against the Parthians mentioned above was a failure. As a result of this, and through internal conflicts in the Seleucid empire, John Hyrcanus I was in a position to make Judaea independent again and to emerge as sovereign ruler. From 129 BC Hyrcanus no longer needed to bother about the Seleucids and could devote his full attention to Judaea and the surrounding area.

Moreover, the events described here show once again that Judaea could be independent only while the Seleucid empire was in difficulties, because it was occupied with internal problems or conflicts with foreign enemies. Rome was always behind the latter, either openly or in a disguised way.

10.2.2 *Conquests of John Hyrcanus I*

The rule of John Hyrcanus I was marked by a series of conquests in the area around Judaea. First Hyrcanus invaded Transjordan, where after a siege of six months he conquered the important city of Medeba on the Via Regis.[21] Medeba is also well known and mentioned often in the Old Testament (see e.g. Num.21.30; Josh.13.9). Scythopolis, the old Beth-shean, also seems to have been occupied in the time of John Hyrcanus.[22] This place west of the Jordan was an important crossroads.

Great emphasis must be placed here on two of John Hyrcanus' conquests, because they made an important mark on later history. First, Hyrcanus conquered Idumaea with its district capital Marisa.[23] He compelled the Idumaeans to be circumcised and to observe Jewish laws, as he did the inhabitants of other conquered areas. As a consequence of this the Idumaeans later thought of themselves as Jews (*BJ* IV, 270-84). So the Idumaean Herod the Great could claim to be a Jew, though we know that the Jews themselves, above all the leading circles in Jerusalem, regarded him as inferior (cf. *AJ* XIV, 403).

Even more decisive was the conquest and the subjection of the 'Samaritans' and the destruction of their temple on Mount Gerizim.[24] This event in particular made a great impression and created an unbridgeable gulf between Judaeans and 'Samaritans'. The traces of this are at least still perceptible down to the first century AD.[25] We do not know precisely when this event happened. On the basis of *AJ* XIII, 254 it is often assumed that it took place in the first years of Hyrcanus' government, namely in 128 BC.[26] Others tend to think more in terms of about 108 BC.[27] In the latter case the destruction of Shechem would then have taken place about the same time as that of Samaria.

As a result of all these conquests John Hyrcanus secured a kingdom which in broad outline was similar to that of Solomon. The degree to which in all this John Hyrcanus was purely pursuing political aims emerges from the fact that in his campaigns he did not employ a Judaean army, but made use of foreign mercenaries (*AJ* XIII, 249). Thanks to these troops and the weakness of the Seleucid empire he was able to achieve territorial expansions.

10.2.3 *Foreign contacts*

Like his predecessors, John Hyrcanus was concerned for good relations with Rome. Josephus mentions at least two resolutions which were passed about Judaea by the Roman senate in the time of the Hasmonaeans. The first (*AJ* XIII, 259-66) confirmed the treaty of friendship between Judaea and Rome and the second (*AJ* XIV, 247-255) was on the same lines.[28] However, both documents are concerned with the return of the fortresses of Joppa (Jaffa) and Gadara (Gezer) to John Hyrcanus. At that time both fortresses were in the possession of Antiochus. It is not clear which king is meant here. Both Antiochus VII Sidetes and Antiochus IX Cyzicenus are possibilities. With the former these documents would have to be dated about 132 BC and with the latter about 105 BC. The exact dating of the two documents mentioned by Josephus in this connection is, however, largely uncertain.[29]

John Hyrcanus wanted good relations not only with the Romans but also with the Ptolemaic court in Egypt.[30] He was also able to achieve this, probably above all because there were numerous Jews living in Egypt who had close contact with the court (cf. *AJ* XIII, 284-287). However, little is known about contacts between John Hyrcanus and these Judaeans. There is, though, a letter in II Macc.1.1-9 from the Judaeans in Judaea and Jerusalem addressed to the Jews in Egypt dating from 124 BC, calling for the celebration of the Feast of Tabernacles in the month of Chislev.[31]

Thanks among other things to these contacts with Rome and Egypt and also to the weak position of the Seleucids, in the time of John Hyrcanus Judaea was completely independent of the Seleucid empire.

10.2.4 *The domestic policy of John Hyrcanus*

In 10.1.4 we saw that Simon probably did not mint any coins. According to many scholars,[32] John Hyrcanus did. In fact a great many coins have been found on which the name Johanan appears, but they may well connected with Hyrcanus II (76-67 and 63-40 BC). On the basis of the information given by the finds of coins it is most probable that Alexander Jannaeus (103-76 BC) was the first Hasmonaean to have coins minted.[33]

John Hyrcanus' strong position in the political and military sphere, which, like David and Solomon at one time, he largely owed to his foreign mercenary troops,[34] could not relieve him of having to cope with enormous problems at home. One of the reasons for them was doubtless his plundering of the tomb of David, which is mentioned by Josephus (*AJ* XIII, 249). John Hyrcanus needed the proceeds of the robbery, three thousand talents of silver, to pay his foreign mercenaries. It is understandable that such tomb-robbing and plundering caused great offence in many quarters. Such action doubtless recalled the way in which the Hellenists and the Seleucids had acted in former times. One can also see many parallels in other respects between the early Hellenists and the Hasmonaeans. The latter had a government which can be increasingly described as Hellenistic. The hiring of pagan soldiers also fits into this context; it must have been a thorn in the flesh particularly for the 'pious' in Judaea.

According to Josephus (*AJ* XIII, 288-92), in the course of time a break developed between John Hyrcanus and the Pharisees. The latter wanted John Hyrcanus to surrender the office of high priest. Because of all this John Hyrcanus is said to have turned away from the Pharisees and made a closer alliance with the Sadducees (*AJ* XIII, 293-8).

We find a parallel story about this event in the Babylonian Talmud,[35] but Hyrcanus' son Alexander Jannaeus is mentioned here in place of John. However, the reading by Josephus is the correct one.[36]

10.3 *Some important literature from about 150-100* BC

As the title of this section indicates, here I shall limit myself to discussing a few of the most important works, restricting myself further to those which were written in Palestine. One exception to this is the Letter of Aristeas, which was written in Egypt.

The final redaction of I and II Maccabees, to which we have already devoted a good deal of attention in 1.2.2, must have taken place about 100 BC.

In addition to these important apocryphal or deutero-canonical works, mention needs to be made of the pseudepigraphical Jubilees. One name used for this book in the early church was the 'Little Genesis', because its content largely runs parallel to that of the first book of the Bible. The name Jubilees is taken from the division of the history narrated in this work into jubilee-year periods of forty-nine years (cf. Lev.25.8-13). The book as a whole has only come down to us in Ethiopic,[37] but among other evidence a number of Hebrew fragments found in the Qumran caves[38] indicate that it must go back to a Hebrew original.

A special feature of this book is that, like Enoch, it uses the traditional solar calendar,[39] which after the Babylonian captivity was gradually replaced in Palestine by the lunar calendar.[39] This last feature already shows that the book comes from a group which attached great importance to preserving old traditions. Therefore the author must have come from anti-Hellenist circles.

It is impossible to date the book exactly, but the final redaction must have taken place in roughly the period I have given above.[40]

Another important work from this period is the Letter of Aristeas. In form and content this work is not a letter but a narrative. The greater part of it is the account, or rather the legend, of the origin of the Greek translation of the Pentateuch. Above all through the action of Ptolemy II Philadelphus mentioned in 4.2.2, seventy-two translators, chosen from the twelve tribes of Israel, are said to have completed the work in Alexandria in seventy-two days. The whole Greek translation of the Old Testament was later called the Septuagint after the number of seventy(-two) translators mentioned here.

The legend of the origin of the Septuagint which appears here in the Letter of Aristeas cannot go back to a historical event. The language and background of the work show that it can only have been written about 100 BC. Its aim is rather to stress the legitimate character of the Greek translation by showing the miraculous way in which it came into being.

Chapter 11

The Reigns of the Hasmonaean Priest-Kings

11.1 *Aristobulus I (104-103* BC*)*

It had been the aim of John Hyrcanus I that his oldest son Aristobulus I should succeed him as high priest after his death and his widow take over the government of the country. However, Aristobulus had his mother and his brothers, other than Antigonus, whom he named his co-regent, put in prison. His mother died of hunger there, and shortly afterwards Antigonus was put to death on Aristobulus' orders. In this way Aristobulus himself took all power.

According to Josephus (*AJ* XIII, 301; *BJ* I, 70), Aristobulus was the first of the Hasmonaeans to take the title king. Strabo,[1] however, attributes this to Alexander Jannaeus. We should probably regard Josephus as the more reliable tradition. At all events there are no compelling reasons why he should have given this information unless there were some historical background.[2] In addition, it is striking that Strabo nowhere mentions Aristobulus I and therefore possibly knew nothing of his very short reign.

We do not know whether there was opposition to Aristobulus' taking the title of king. It is, however, certain that from the return from exile up to this time a majority in Judaea was against the restoring the monarchy.[3]

Aristobulus was regarded as a friend of the Hellenists (cf. *AJ* XIII, 318). The fact that he used a Greek name in place of his Hebrew name Judas already points in this direction, though of course all the Hasmonaeans did the same thing.[4] It is probably also above all because of this leaning towards Hellenism that Josephus (*AJ* XIII, 319) attributes a friendly and modest character to him. However, his activities (see above) hardly bear this out.

The most important event during the short reign of Aristobulus was his conquest of the greater part of Ituraea. The inhabitants of this area were forcibly circumcised.[5] The northern part of Galilee also belonged to the territory of Ituraea at this period,[6] and this was the part that Aristobulus I conquered. Otherwise, it can hardly be assumed that compulsory circumcision was imposed on the whole population of northern Galilee. Descendants of the old population of Israel must still have been living there. They, or at least some of them, may well have neglected the practice of circumcision. Aristobulus corrected this when he conquered them.

In 103 BC Aristobulus I suddenly died.

11.2 *Alexander Jannaeus (103-76 BC)*

11.2.1 *The beginning of his reign*

After the death of Aristobulus I, his brothers were freed from their captivity by his widow. This widow, who bore the name Alexandra Salome, married Alexander Jannaeus and appointed him king and high priest. Alexander was the third son of John Hyrcanus I and thus a brother of Aristobulus. The fact that Alexander Jannaeus married his brother's widow shows that he had little respect for Mosaic legislation, according to which a high priest was not allowed to marry a widow (cf. Lev.21.14). Moreover Alexander Jannaeus showed himself to be an unworthy high priest in every respect. He was concerned only with military conquests and with extending his own power.

Thus throughout his reign of twenty-seven years Alexander Jannaeus was constantly involved in wars, while constantly causing new conflicts in the domestic sphere. All this began very soon after his accession.

11.2.2 *The general political and social situation*

The successes which Alexander Jannaeus achieved in the military sphere are very closely connected with particular developments which took place on an international level.

First of all there was the situation in Egypt. At this time Cleopatra III was on the throne; she was nicknamed 'the red'. She did not much care for Egyptian nationalism and therefore had her son Ptolemy IX, who was very popular with the Egyptians, sent away in about 107 BC to Cyprus as military governor. For the same reason she also supported Alexander Jannaeus in his attempt to take control of Ptolemais and a number of other places (see 11.2.3) when Ptolemy IX came to their help.

Then there was the political and social situation in Rome. Political differences there led to a civil war around 88 BC. Thanks to the encouragement of the consul Sulla, the *optimates*, who supported a traditional policy under the direction of the Senate, were at that time able to get the better of the *populares*, who wanted to rule by means of a popular assembly. The result of this civil war, which was preceded by two decades of disturbances, was that in Rome people were far more concerned with domestic matters than with foreign affairs.

In this troubled situation, Mithridates VI, king of Pontus, with some help from Ptolemy IX, who was still on Cyprus, succeeded in conquering almost the whole of Asia Minor, the Greek islands and part of Greece. In 84 BC Sulla made peace with Mithridates on conditions which very much favoured the latter. Sulla was forced to do this because the growing influence of the *populares* in Rome forced him to return rapidly to the city. In 83 BC Sulla succeeded in regaining power in Rome.

The situation I have just outlined shows that almost throughout the reign of Alexander Jannaeus Rome had its hands full with the conflicts in its own land and the war with Mithridates. Above all because of this, Alexander Jannaeus was in a position to pursue his extensive expansionist policy.

11.2.3 *The first conquests of Alexander Jannaeus*

Very soon after becoming ruler in 103 BC, Alexander Jannaeus made an attempt to seize the important coastal city of Ptolemais (Acco). The inhabitants of Ptolemais called on Ptolemy IX for help, and shortly afterwards he landed south of Carmel with an army. Alexander then had to break off the siege of Ptolemais. There was a battle by the Jordan in Galilee between Ptolemy IX and Alexander Jannaeus, in which Alexander was defeated.

At that moment Cleopatra III, on whom Alexander Jannaeus had called for help, intervened. Ptolemy IX was defeated and forced to go back to Cyprus. Through the mediation of Hananiah, the Egyptian-Jewish commander of the Egyptian army, Cleopatra made a treaty with Alexander Jannaeus, which again left his hands free.[7]

Directly after that Alexander Jannaeus undertook a campaign in Transjordan, where he conquered Gadara and other places. He was also able to capture the city of Gaza by treachery, whereupon he had it plundered and razed to the ground. A short time beforehand Gaza had called on Aretas II, the king of the Nabataeans, for help, but it came too late.[8]

From this time on (*c.* 95 BC), Alexander Jannaeus had the whole of the coastal plain with the exception of Ashkelon under his control.[9] After that he had to turn all his attention to domestic problems. The matters which concerned him here were to take him eight years to deal with.

11.2.4 *Domestic conflicts*

In chapter 9 we looked at a number of important Judaean groups, some of which begin to come to the fore especially in the period described here. In

Judaea at this point we have the conservative group of the old priestly élite which may be said to have included not only the Hasmonaeans but also the Sadducees (cf.9.1), and the popular party of the Pharisees which in this period was certainly to be regarded as progressive (cf.9.2).

It was especially at this time that the Pharisees adopted an increasingly critical attitude to the Hasmonaeans. The break which had come about in the meantime between John Hyrcanus I and the Pharisees (see 10.2.4) increased enormously in the time of Alexander Jannaeus. The Pharisees were deeply offended by Alexander, since though he was high priest he was married to his brother's widow, which was forbidden by law (see 11.2.1). Moreover they were scandalized by the fact that a cruel warrior like Alexander Jannaeus should hold this sacred office.

The extent of the influence of the Pharisees and the unpopularity of Alexander Jannaeus is evident from an incident during the Feast of Tabernacles in *c.* 90 BC. When Alexander Jannaeus on this occasion deliberately went against the prescribed ritual by pouring holy water on the ground instead of on the altar, the people pelted him with the lemons which they had with them for the feast.[10] According to Josephus (*AJ* XIII, 373), the king thereupon had six thousand people executed.

Some years later Alexander Jannaeus was defeated in a campaign against Obodas I, king of the Nabataeans (*c.* 93-85 BC). When Alexander fled back to Jerusalem, open rebellion broke out against him. The civil war that ensued lasted six years. Fifty thousand Judaeans were killed in this war. Evidently the struggle did not go very well for the opponents of Alexander Jannaeus, since in *c.* 88 BC the rebels called in the help of the Seleucids.[11] Thereupon Demetrius III (95-87 BC) invaded the territory of Alexander Jannaeus with an army. To begin with, Demetrius had great successes and was also able to inflict a heavy defeat on Alexander Jannaeus at Shechem.

At that point many Judaeans again had a sense of national solidarity. In the last resort they preferred a bad Hasmonaean ruler to Seleucid domination. So a large number of Alexander Jannaeus' opponents again took his side. As a result of the changed circumstances Demetrius III was forced to leave the country again. Soon after that, Alexander Jannaeus succeeded in eliminating the other rebels and their leaders. After the struggle was over he had about eight hundred rebels crucified in Jerusalem.[12] Many of his opponents also went into exile. Alexander Jannaeus then largely had peace in his country, but not outside the frontiers of his kingdom.

This civil war and the campaign of Demetrius III are presumably also echoed in the writings of Qumran, at least if the Demetrius mentioned in 4QpNah2 is indeed Demetrius III.[13] In that case there would be an allusion to these events in 4QpNah 1-12. and the designation 'those who seek smooth things' in 4QpNah 3 could simply be the Pharisees. This passage would then show that the relationship between the Qumran community and the Pharisees was not particularly good at this time. However, this should not lead us to conclude that people in the community had a positive attitude towards Alexander Jannaeus. The way in which the crucifixion of his opponents (presumably for the most part Pharisees) by Alexander Jannaeus is condemned in 4QpNah 8 speaks volumes in this respect.

11.2.5 *The struggle against the Nabataeans*

Alexander Jannaeus' position in foreign affairs was also weakened by the civil war. This became clear when the Seleucid king Antiochus XII Dionysus (87-84 BC) was involved in a dispute with Aretas III (*c.*85-62 BC), the king of the Nabataeans. In his campaign against Aretas III, Antiochus XII went straight through Judaean territory, but Alexander Jannaeus hardly dared to defy him openly.

When a short time later Antiochus XII was killed in a battle against Aretas III, the rule of the latter extended far into Syria in the north and as far as Egypt in the south.[14] After this conquest Aretas III attacked Judaea. It soon became clear just how dangerous the situation was for Alexander Jannaeus. Aretas III advanced quickly and defeated Alexander at Adida, a place about four miles north-east of Lydda, controlling the route from Joppa to Jerusalem.[15] However, Alexander succeeded in making an agreement with Aretas III, the result of which was that the latter again withdrew from Judaea.[16] Thus the victory of Aretas seems to have been less decisive than appeared at first sight.

After these events Alexander Jannaeus controlled Judaea, Samaria and Galilee, part of Transjordan and the Philistine coastal region. In order to take possession of the whole of the territory east of Jordan he invaded Transjordan, where in *c.* 83-80 BC he succeeded in conquering a number of predominantly Greek cities.[17] Most of them were part of the Decapolis, which became particularly famous at a later stage.[18]

The inhabitants of these cities went over to Judaism, but not without putting up some resistance; only the people of Pella refused. For that reason their city was destroyed.[19] After this campaign Alexander Jannaeus returned home, where he was again enthusiastically greeted by many people because of the successes he had achieved.

11.2.6 *The end of Alexander Jannaeus*

Shortly before his death Alexander Jannaeus again went on the warpath in Transjordan. He died during the siege of the fortress of Ragaba[20] in 76 BC.

Shortly before his death, according to Josephus (*AJ* XIII, 400ff.), he had advised his wife Salome Alexandra to make peace with the Pharisees again. Alexander clearly saw that otherwise the situation in the country would be untenable.

After Alexander's death his corpse was brought to Jerusalem and there buried with the pomp and splendour befitting a king and high priest.[21] He had been king for twenty-seven years. In this period he had waged numerous wars and exercised a real rule of terror on at least part of his subjects, like the Pharisees. It goes without saying that all this had great and often catastrophic consequences for the country and the population.

11.3 *The political and economic consequences of the reign of Alexander Jannaeus*

In the previous section we saw that Alexander Jannaeus was involved for much of his reign in wars and that this resulted in a considerable expansion of his territory. All this happened especially in the years 103-95 and 83-76 BC.[22] Obviously these wars inflicted an enormous amount of suffering and damage. So they also led to the downfall of many cultural centres. In the so-called Hellenistic cities Greek culture was often eradicated root and branch. This was especially true of the coastal cities which flourished at that time, and the Hellenistic cities east of the Jordan.

In order to safeguard his kingdom, Alexander arranged for new fortresses to be build or already existing fortresses to be extended and strengthened. Among the latter can be included a fortress in the neighbourhood of Engedi.[23] The new fortresses certainly included Machaerus, in Transjordan east of the Dead Sea,[24] and Alexandrium in the area of the Jordan north of Jericho.[25] The well-known fortress of Masada is also regarded as the work of Alexander Jannaeus, though it is more probable that it was an initiative of Herod the Great.[26]

It is also evident that the civil war described in 11.2.4 inflicted great suffering on the land. Thousands died or fled the country. A situation of this kind was obviously not conducive to prosperity in the country. Great poverty and bereavement in many families was the sorry consequence, not to mention the vast destruction that was inflicted in the process.

However, the activity of Alexander Jannaeus must also have had its positive side for various aspects of the economy of the country. It was no coincidence that his first and prime aim was to capture the coastal cities. The possession of these cities meant that Judaea controlled connections with the sea, a situation which was particularly favourable for trade, and this must again have favoured the development of agriculture.

Minting coins was also important for trade. Quite apart from the question whether Alexander Jannaeus was the first Hasmonaean to have his own coins minted (see 10.2.4), it is clear that in his time the minting of individual coins increased. It is no coincidence that an anchor is engraved on some of them:[27] this indicates trade connections overseas. We do not know whether this trade had already developed to any degree in the time of Alexander Jannaeus. Given the constant conflicts in which he was involved, we must assume that it developed only after his death.

These coins are also instructive in another respect. A large number of them bear the title 'Alexander the king' (in either Hebrew or Greek). However, coins have also been found which were reminted; these now bear the title 'Jonathan (= Jannai) the high priest and the community of the Jews'. Some scholars see the new inscription as the result of a concession that Alexander Jannaeus had to make to the Pharisees after the civil war (11.2.4).[28] It has also been suggested that the coins come from opponents of Alexander in this war.[29] If all this is true, these coins would come from the last period of Alexander Jannaeus' reign. However, we cannot be certain about that.

11.4 *Messianism*

In the coming period of the history of Israel the expectation of the messianic time and of the messiah, which has a background in the Old Testament,[30] was to have an increasingly prominent place. It is for that reason that we must now pay some attention to this phenomenon.

Messianic expectations are directed towards the (coming) period of salvation in which God achieves his final goal with the people and the world and in which he makes use of particular figures like an anointed or Messiah. In the period described here messianic expectations were strongly determined not only by tradition but often also by the circumstances of the time. In no case can we speak of a uniform structure. Thus for a long time it has been inappropriate to speak in terms of *a* messiah.

The Book of Jubilees is one of the works that can be put in this context.[31] In addition, a book like the Psalms of Solomon (17.21-25) mentions a political messiah who will purify the city of Jerusalem of Gentiles (17.32-38). Israel will not only have independence but also extend to the ends of the earth. Sometimes in messianic expectation we also find more than one Messiah, as in the Qumran writings (see 7.5) and in the 'Testaments of the Twelve Patriarchs'.[32]

The majority of messianic expectations in this and later periods have a common feature. All are permeated by the notion that God will deliver his people and free them from whatever situation they are in. In this connection there is also a clear difference from the apocalyptic mentioned in 7.5. The apocalyptists were very pessimistic about the survival of the existing world. By contrast, in messianic expectation the hope was that the time of salvation would be realized in this world. So it is no coincidence that messianic expectations played a role in liberation movements like those of the Zealots and Bar Kochba ('Son of the star'). It is also precisely for these reasons that messianic movements flourished most in situations of need and times of oppression. Least of all should we be surprised that such movements found many supporters, especially in Galilee. The messianic expectation was the only hope of a human existence for the impoverished country population.

Chapter 12

The Downfall of the Hasmonaean Dynasty

12.1 *The international situation*

In this period international politics were increasingly dominated by Rome. Despite problems in Spain and Italy, where among other things a slave rebellion broke out in 74 BC, and another confrontation with Mithridates the king of Pontus (see 11.2.2), the Romans succeeded in putting things in order within a few years and even in considerably strengthening their position of power in Asia. The person who came in the fore here was the Roman general Pompey. He undertook a successful campaign in the East, where in about 66 BC he inflicted a decisive defeat on Mithridates.[1] A conflict with Armenia was also brought to a satisfactory conclusion. Tigranes, the king of Armenia, made peace with Rome. He remained in possession of his empire on condition that he restrained the increasing Parthian aggression from the East. The result was that Armenia became a kind of vassal state of Rome and at the same time functioned as a buffer between Rome and the Parthians. Sulla (see 11.2.2) had signed a treaty with the Parthians in 84 BC in which it was determined that the Euphrates should be the frontier between Rome and the Parthian empire;[2] this treaty was endorsed and renewed by Pompey.[3]

After dealing with these matters Pompey turned his attention to Syria, the former Seleucid realm. In 65 BC he sent Scaurus to Damascus to restore order there. The following year (64 BC), Syria became a new province of the Roman empire,[4] which soon included the greater part of Palestine. The high priest still had some authority, but he was under the strict control of the governor of Syria (cf. also Luke 2.2).

The Romans had never had so strong a position in the East. The Seleucid power had finally vanished from the political scene. The Roman empire extended as far as the Euphrates. Within this territory there were still some miniature states which were vassals of Rome, but almost everywhere else was under direct Roman supervision of Rome. It is clear that from now on the

Romans began to be extremely interested in Judaean affairs. The unpleasant fraternal dispute between the Hasmonaeans Aristobulus and Hyrcanus gave them good reason for this.

12.2 *Salome Alexandra (76-67 BC)*

In accord with the wishes of Alexander Jannaeus, his widow Salome Alexandra took over the rule of Judaea after his death. Of course she could not be high priest. She nominated her oldest son, whom the tradition portrays as a weak man, to this post.

Whatever may be the truth in the tradition in Josephus and the rabbis[5] that shortly before his death Alexander Jannaeus advised his wife to be certain to secure the favour of the Pharisees, the Pharisees certainly had great influence during her reign. Josephus says that during her reign they in fact had all the power in their hands.[6] According to a rabbinic tradition,[7] Simeon ben Shetaḥ, a brother of Salome Alexandra,[8] was their most important leader in this period.

A change also seems to have taken place in the composition of the *gerousia* (see 3.4.2) under Salome Alexandra, which favoured the Pharisees. Hitherto it had been made up of the heads of the leading families in Judaea and priests who were related to the high priest or had a very important function in the priestly hierarchy. Over the course of time these two groups had come to consist mainly of Sadducees. However, Salome Alexandra introduced a change by giving a third group, the scribes, a place in the *gerousia*. In this way the Pharisees, too, from then on had a voice in the assembly, since many of them were scribes.[9]

Under the influence of the Pharisees, many of those who had been imprisoned during the reign of Alexander Jannaeus were freed and countless fugitives returned to the country. However, when the Pharisees began to take vengeance on their former opponents, the fervent supporters of Alexander Jannaeus, opposition developed. A delegation of Sadducees supported by Salome Alexandra's younger son Aristobulus (see below) seems to have prevailed on her to keep them in check. That avoided civil war for the time being.[10]

All in all, the rule of Salome Alexandra may be said to have been a fairly peaceful time. In foreign affairs we are told of an expedition by Aristobulus against Damascus on behalf of the queen. However, this campaign came to grief.[11] The threat of an invasion by Tigranes, king of Armenia, against Judaea was warded off when in 69 BC Tigranes was defeated by the Romans under the command of Lucullus.[12]

For the moment there was also peace and quiet at home, but trouble was brewing. The ambitious Aristobulus wanted to take over power. To this end he secured the support of former friends of his father, who formed a group of rich and powerful figures.[13] Above all through their help he succeeded in occupying twenty-two important fortresses in Judaea shortly before his mother's death.[14] The Pharisees in particular looked askance at this development. They saw their newly secured position threatened by Aristobulus, through whose activity the Sadducees were again coming to the fore.

12.3 *Aristobulus II (67-63* BC*)*

After the death of Salome Alexandra it was already clear that Aristobulus had the strongest position. The legitimate successor of the dead queen was, however, Hyrcanus II, who already held office as high priest. A conflict between him, supported by the Pharisees, and Aristobulus II, supported by Sadducees, was therefore understandably soon in coming. There was a battle between the two sides near Jericho, which went completely against Hyrcanus II. He fled to the Acra in Jerusalem, but even there he soon had to yield to his brother. Aristobulus and Hyrcanus then made an agreement under which Hyrcanus handed over power to Aristobulus. However, this treaty allowed Hyrcanus his possessions and income.

In the account of this event it is not very clear whether Aristobulus was now king and high priest. In *AJ* XIV, 41,97 and *AJ* XX, 243f., Josephus says that Aristobulus was also high priest, but in *AJ* XIV, 6 and *BJ* I, 121 he says only that Aristobulus was king. However, taking *AJ* XIV, 7 into consideration, and given the fact that Hyrcanus nowhere gives the impression of being an ambitious figure (he is portrayed as a peace-loving character), it seems most probable that Aristobulus was given both offices under the treaty.[15]

At this moment, however, Antipater, the father of Herod the Great, appeared on the political scene. Antipater was the son of a rich Idumaean, also called Antipater, who had been nominated *strategos* (a kind of governor) by Alexander Jannaeus. This son, who perhaps held the office which was formerly his father's, tried to exploit the fraternal dispute between the two Hasmonaeans. He realized that he would get more influence and power under a government led by Hyrcanus than under that of the powerful and energetic Aristobulus. Antipater succeeded in persuading Hyrcanus to make a treaty with Aretas III (*c.*85-62 BC), the king of the Nabataeans. In it Hyrcanus promised Aretas III the land conquered by Alexander Jannaeus from the Nabataeans, while in turn Aretas III was to support Hyrcanus in the battle against Aristobulus.

Along with supporters of Hyrcanus, Aretas was able to defeat Aristobulus. After that, Aretas laid siege to Aristobulus in the temple of Jerusalem, where he had fled with his troops.[16] In this situation both Hyrcanus and Aristobulus turned to the Romans for help.[17]

12.4 *The intervention of Rome*

While the events described here were taking place in Judaea, the Roman general Pompey was busy with his successful campaign in Asia (66-62 BC); one of his generals, Scaurus, had captured Damascus for him in 65 BC (see 12.1). Soon after that he turned his attention to Judaea. At about that time delegations came from both Aristobulus and Hyrcanus to ask for his help. Both offered him gifts. On this occasion the Romans opted for Aristobulus. Presumably they did so because Hyrcanus had Aretas III as his ally, and the Romans did not want the Nabataeans on any account to gain too much influence in Judaea. Moreover, Scaurus commanded Aretas to retreat from Judaea, which he immediately did, because he dared not risk a war with Rome. On his retreat Aretas was attacked by Aristobulus, who inflicted heavy losses on the Nabataeans.[18]

In 63 BC Pompey himself arrived in Damascus. There not only delegations from Aristobulus and Hyrcanus but also representatives of the people of Judaea came to him. These last asked Pompey to abolish the Hasmonaean dynasty because they wanted to be ruled by priests.[19] Josephus also tells us that on this occasion Aristobulus offered Pompey a golden vine which was worth five hundred talents.[20] According to Strabo[21] this so-called *terpole*[22] came from Alexander Jannaeus and was later put in the temple of Jupiter Capitolinus in Rome.

At the time of this meeting Pompey did not make any decision, but promised that he would sort things out in Judaea as soon as he had dealt with the Nabataeans.[23] Aristobulus was least happy with the delay. He probably was all too well aware that after dealing with the Nabataeans the Romans would take the side of the weak Hyrcanus. So he established himself in the fortress of Alexandrium to make his position secure. This action aroused the wrath of Pompey, who immediately invaded Judaea. Aristobulus quickly surrendered, but most of his supporters refused. Pompey then went back to Jerusalem and besieged the city.[24] Hyrcanus and his followers opened the gates to the Romans, who were then able to occupy the city and the royal palace. However, a group of the supporters of Aristobulus, who had already been taken prisoner, occupied the temple. Only after a siege of three months did the temple fall into the hands of the Romans.[25] To the dismay of the pious, on this occasion Pompey entered the Holy of Holies.[26]

Pompey led Aristobulus and numerous Judaean prisoners through Rome in the triumphal procession by which he celebrated his return. When they were later freed, the latter formed the beginning of a great Jewish community there.[27]

12.5 *The reorganization of the Judaean state*

The intervention of Rome in fact meant the end of the Hasmonaean dynasty and of Judaean independence, which had lasted about eighty years. The fact that Pompey again established Hyrcanus as high priest did not do anything to change this. Judaea lost all the territory won by Alexander Jannaeus and a good deal of that conquered by Simon and Jonathan. This included all the coastal cities from Raphia to Dor and all the non-Jewish cities east of the Jordan.[28] All that was left of the former Hasmonaean kingdom was Judaea, Galilee, Idumaea and Peraea. Moreover, Jerusalem and Judaea had to pay tribute to Rome. In this way the same sort of situation came into being as formerly under Ptolemaic and Seleucid rule.

Presumably the founding of the federation of ten cities, called the Decapolis in the New Testament, also dates from this time.[29] All these cities were subordinate to the newly-established Roman province of Syria.

It is clear that the Romans found Hyrcanus a willing tool. Moreover, the *de facto* power came into the hands of Antipater, whose policy was particularly favourable to Rome.

At the beginning of the Maccabaean struggle Judas and his followers could not foresee that this would ultimately be the result of their calling on the Romans for help. A long period of Roman domination now began. This domination would in future hit the Jewish state harder than the Seleucids had ever done.[30]

12.6 *Hyrcanus II (63-40 BC)*

12.6.1 *The position of Hyrcanus*

The renomination of Hyrcanus II as high priest by the Romans gave the state of Judaea still an appearance of independence. Hyrcanus himself had hardly any influence on the course of events in Judaea. He had to pay tax to the Romans, and moreover was very strictly controlled by the Roman governor of Syria. Presumably as high priest Hyrcanus was allowed to levy a temple tax. Such a privilege would fit in with the tolerant attitude which the Romans always had towards Jewish reliigon.

Hyrcanus' position was somewhat strengthened when after the death of Pompey in 48 BC he and Antipater took the side of Julius Caesar, Pompey's opponent in the second Roman civil war. They supported Caesar with Jewish auxiliaries on his campaign in Egypt. As a reward, in 47 BC Hyrcanus received the title 'ethnarch of the Jews', which gave him a kind of political status. Perhaps this also meant that Hyrcanus was now seen as a representative of all the Jews, both those in Judaea and those in the Diaspora.[31] However, this cannot have meant much, since the central figure in Jewish politics was and remained Antipater.

12.6.2 *The role of Antipater*

In the previous section we saw (12.3) that Antipater's father had been appointed *strategos* of Idumaea by Alexander Jannaeus when he conquered the region. Now the roles were completely reversed. Antipater gave his sons Phasael and Herod (later Herod the Great) the task of governing Jerusalem and Galilee respectively.[32] The corner-stone of Antipater's policy was to maintain good relations with Rome and to keep himself and his sons in the public eye. Here he was almost completely successful. Above all his younger son Herod came into the limelight.

In 47 BC Herod made quite a reputation for himself by launching a fierce attack on a certain Ezechias (Hezekiah) who with his followers was waging a guerrilla war in the north of Galilee. Herod had him and his men put to death after a mock trial. This arrogant attitude brought Herod into conflict with the Sanhedrin, which called him to account for his action. Herod did not go there in the customary penitential dress but in purple, surrounded by an armed bodyguard. He was almost condemned by the Sanhedrin, but at the decisive moment Hyrcanus had the session of the Sanhedrin interrupted, probably on the orders of the Roman authorities, and advised Herod to leave Jerusalem.[33]

Herod thereupon wanted to attack Jerusalem, but he was restrained by Antipater and Phasael. Antipater rightly understood that a new civil war would do no good to his own position and that of his sons.[34] During his conflict with the Sanhedrin, Herod's position was considerably strengthened by his nomination as *strategos* of Coele-Syria, and probably also of Samaria, by Sextus Caesar.[35]

Antipater himself did not live long after these events. In 43 BC he was murdered by a certain Malichus, who was attempting to win more influence in Judaea at Antipater's expense. Soon afterwards this Malichus was killed on Herod's orders by assassins in the region of Tyre.

12.6.3 *Political and economic developments*

The first years after the conquest of Jerusalem by Pompey seem to have been relatively peaceful. After that the situation deteriorated considerably. This was particularly the case in the years after the death of Antipater.

The changed situation was closely connected with the fact that Cassius and Brutus, who wanted to restore the old republican traditions in Rome, were defeated in 42 BC at Philippi in Macedonia by the troops of the triumvirate of Octavian, Antony and Lepidus.[36] From this moment on the government of the Eastern provinces of the Roman empire fell into the hands of Antony. Soon after that (*c.*41 BC) a Jewish delegation appeared before Antony to complain about Phasael and Herod. Herod himself was able to neutralize these accusations by going straight to Antony. A new attempt by a Jewish delegation that same year to complain about the two Idumaeans also had no success. Phasael and Herod were even nominated tetrarchs of Judaea by Antony.[37] We do not know precisely what this function involved (see 14.2.1).

The period of Antony's government was a bad time for Palestine. Antony's ostentatious life-style demanded a good deal of money and to provide this his subjects had to endure very heavy taxes. Since the coming of the Romans these had not been particularly light anyway,[38] but now they were quite intolerable. The tumultous times which now dawned must certainly be seen in this light.

In 40 BC the Parthians began a large-scale invasion of the ancient Near East. On this occasion Antigonus, a son of Aristobulus II who was captured in 63 BC, offered them his services in exchange for their help in setting him on the Jewish throne. The invasion succeeded. Antigonus got a good deal of support, above all in Judaea and Galilee, presumably also because of the bad economic situation there.[39] The Parthians took Phasael and Hyrcanus II prisoner by a trick, and Herod was forced to flee. The ears of Hyrcanus II were cut off, thus making it impossible for him to be high priest (cf. Lev.21.17). He died later in Parthian captivity. Phasael committed suicide.

After these events Antigonus was installed king by the Parthians.[40] Dio Cassius[41] reports the accession of Antigonus, but wrongly calls him Aristobulus instead of Antigonus.

12.7 *Antigonus (40-37 BC)*

During his brief reign Antigonus also had coins minted. These coins had the usual inscription 'King Antigonus' (in Greek) on one side and 'Mattathias the high priest and the community of the Judaeans' on the other.[42]

In the meantime Antigonus was little more than a vassal of the Parthians and virtually completely dependent on them for his throne. This situation could not last long, because Rome would soon put things in order. In this connection Antigonus' most important opponent was Herod.

As early as 40 BC Herod was nominated king of Judah by the Roman Senate with the approval of Antony and Octavian; this was almost at the very moment that Antigonus took over the throne. So Herod had first to conquer his kingdom with the help of the Romans.

In 39 BC Herod was able to seize Joppa and the fortress of Masada, but a subsequent siege of Jerusalem failed because he did not have enough Roman help.[43]

When the Parthians were defeated by the Roman general Ventidius in 38 BC, Antigonus' power soon faded. In the same year Herod was able to conquer the whole of Palestine apart from Jerusalem with the aid of Ventidius' successor Sosius. Only the onset of winter prevented him from actually capturing Jerusalem.[44] He only managed that in the spring of 37 BC.

Jerusalem did not hold out long. It was soon occupied by the Romans, who fought side by side with Herod's troops. A fearful blood-bath followed. Antigonus was taken prisoner and beheaded in Antioch by the wishes of Herod and on the orders of Antony.[45]

Herod, who in the meantime had married Mariamne, a granddaughter of Hyrcanus II, now had control of his kingdom. Before we look more closely at him, we must first pay some attention to a group that was to be very influential in Palestine in the days to come, the Zealots.

12.8 *The Zealots*

12.8.1 *The rise of the Zealots*

According to Josephus,[46] in AD 6 a fourth philosophy arose alongside the Sadducees, Pharisees and Essenes. Judas, surnamed 'the Galilean',[47] is named as the founder of this group, along with the Pharisee Zadok. It is strange that this 'fourth philosophy' is not named by Josephus in *AJ* XVIII, 23ff.; *BJ* IV, 121ff., when the Sadducees, Pharisees and Essenes are. According to Hengel,[48] this may be because this group still had no name when it was founded, or Josephus did not think the designation 'Zealots' appropriate for the movement. It is certainly impossible to demonstrate that Josephus here identifies the 'fourth philosophy' with the Zealots.[49] Moreover Josephus uses the designation Zealots almost solely for a group which played an important role in the First Jewish War against Rome under the leadership of the priest Eleazar.[50]

This information in Josephus, our main and indeed almost our only source of information in this period, gives the impression that only during the First Jewish War did the Zealots come into the limelight as a group. However, we must remember that he is extremely tendentious, above all in his view of revolts against the Roman authorities. Especially in the *Jewish War* he is constantly concerned to praise the Romans, the victors in the First Jewish War. This attitude is presumably to be explained by the fact that during this war Josephus had problems with particular groups of rebels and himself went over to the Romans at that time. Josephus often calls rebels against Rome robbers, a terminology which, as we know, is also used in the New Testament.[51]

Apart from the two terms mentioned above we also find the designation *sicarii*, men armed with a *sica*, dagger. By these Josephus understands the followers of Judas the Galilean and his descendants.

It is generally thought that the groups above mentioned by Josephus are in fact the Zealots and that the Sicarii formed an extreme wing of them.[52] This group as a whole would then be identical with the 'fourth philosophy' founded by Judas the Galilaean, which therefore came into being about AD 6.

However, not everyone puts the beginning of this movement at this time. Kohler[53] sees its origins in the time of the Maccabees, and Klausner[54] suggests the Hasmonaean period. Driver[55] and Roth[56] identify the Zealots with the Qumran community. However, this last view has found hardly any following.

Alongside these views which put the origin of the Zealot movement around AD 6 or even earlier, in a very instructive article[57] Menken has defended the view that only from 66 BC onwards can we speak of a party of Zealots.[58] Earlier rebel movements would then have been connected with other groups, e.g. the followers of Judas the Galilaean and his successors with Sicarii.[59] On the basis of Josephus' terminology it is indeed hard to come to any other conclusion. The extremely sparse information in the other sources, like the New Testament and the rabbinic literature, do not give us any support here. One thing is evident: if there were in fact different groups, it must be said that, broadly speaking, these strove for the same goal. So in the long run the term Zealots can certainly be a collective name for a movement which, while it may have combined different groups, on the whole was governed by the same aims (see 12.8.3). This movement became stronger in the course of time and then finally disappeared from the scene after the first Jewish War.

12.8.2 *Terminology*

The word 'Zealot' denotes someone who has 'zeal for the honour and glory of God'. Here the great examples are the priest Phinehas (cf. Num.25.6-13) and the prophet Elijah (cf. I Kings 19.10,14). Phinehas is recalled in I Macc.2.26 and Sirach 45.23 and Elijah in Sirach 48.1-11. According to Hengel,[60] this zeal was an important characteristic of Jewish piety between the Maccabean period and AD 70 (or AD 135).

It follows from this that at the time which we are considering, the term 'Zealot' was understood as an honorific title. It is therefore conceivable that

Josephus does not like using this term of the rebels.[61] However, it is certain that many Zealots fought for the cause of their God with heart and soul. They wanted to acknowledge only him as their Lord; therefore they staked all on the liberation of Israel from the Roman oppressors; they were ready to give their lives for this and to realize the kingdom of God on earth by force of arms.[62] And that brings us to the aims of the Zealots.

12.8.3 *Aims*

The most important aim of the Zealot movement was, as I have said, the liberation of Israel. This idea of freedom was indissolubly connected with the feeling that God is king of Israel. As we shall see, the Zealot opposition was fiercest when this freedom was most threatened and attacked. A special characteristic of the Zealots was that they were prepared to die as martyrs rather than to bow to foreign rulers.[63] In particular the events at the fall of Masada in AD 73 are a vivid illustration of this.

What I have just said at least indicates that the activity of the Zealot movement was not governed by social factors.[64] As so often in the Bible, for the Zealots, faith, social concern and politics went hand in hand, as we shall see again in a later chapter.

Chapter 13

The Reign of Herod the Great
(37-4 BC)[1]

13.1 *The situation in the Roman empire in c.37-4* BC

13.1.1 *The rivalry between Antony and Octavian*

Antony (see also 12.6.3) began to behave more and more like a Hellenistic prince in the eastern part of the empire. His close relationship with Cleopatra of Egypt was a major factor here. This relationship was sealed by marriage in 36 BC. Antony's way of behaving was greatly disapproved of both by Octavian and in Italy generally. His marriage with Cleopatra was at the same time a repudiation of his wife Octavia, a sister of Octavian. A request by Antony for troops to fight against the Parthians was rejected in Rome.

An open conflict between Antony and Octavian was not long in coming. Pressure from Antony to drive Octavian out of Rome did not find any support. But when Octavian called on the Romans to send a punitive expedition against Antony his summons did find a response in Italy. The conflict between the two rivals was resolved at the battle of Actium in 31 BC.[2] Antony was defeated and had to flee with Cleopatra to Egypt, where they both committed suicide. Egypt became part of the Roman empire.[3] It goes without saying that all this considerably strengthened Octavian's position.

13.1.2 *Octavian as sole ruler*

After the death of Antony, Octavian soon took all power into his own hands. The Roman senate bestowed on him the title Augustus, the exalted one. This name, by which he is also known in Luke 2.1, had previously been reserved for gods. He was also given the honorific title *princeps civitatis*, 'the first of the citizens'. This term became the designation of the form of state which began under Augustus: the principate, the monarchical form of state in which the emperor was the first of the Roman citizens.[4] When Lepidus, who had previously formed a triumvirate with Octavian and Antony, died in 12 BC, Augustus was to all intents and purposes the undisputed ruler of the Roman empire.

The territorial expansion in the time of Augustus was enormous. For example, great tracts of territory in North Africa and Central Europe were conquered. However, in the East Augustus did not annex any more territory. In the last years of his rule his policy was above all concerned with consolidation.[5] It is because of this that his rule is usually described as a period of peace in the empire.

One of Augustus' most faithful servants in carrying out his policy was Herod the Great. In the rest of this chapter we shall be mainly concerned with him.[6]

13.2 *Herod's position*

13.2.1 *Characteristics*

Only in *AJ* XVIII, 130, 133, 136 does Josephus call Herod 'the Great'. Nor is this title found elsewhere in Josephus. Presumably the designation 'the Great' is used to distinguish him from his sons, who were also called Herod. Herod was not a 'great' man in the sense that he was an admirable ruler. His rule was characterized by the greatest possible cruelty, of which a number of examples are given in both Jewish and Christian literature, although that is not always very objective.[7] As we shall see, he did not even spare his own children. In this light even the well-known story of the massacre of the children in Bethlehem (Matt.2.16) is certainly credible.[8]

Herod's attitude is closely connected with his awareness that his rule over Judaea rested purely on oppression. The whole of his domestic policy was directed towards the preservation of his own life and rule. As far as that was concerned he mistrusted everything and everyone.

So as a statesman, Herod can be described as merciless. This is already evident, as we saw in the previous chapter (12.6.2), from his action against the rebels in Galilee and his attitude towards the 'Sanhedrin'.[9] His policy towards Judaism might be described as tolerant. Although under the influence of his court historian Nicolaus of Damascus[10] he favoured Hellenism, he presented himself to the Jewish community as a Jew. The coins minted on his orders have no image on them. Nor were statues placed on important buildings in Jerusalem. As far as possible he respected the views of the Pharisees, who were important in his time (but cf. also 13.5).

It would be wrong to judge Herod purely in negative terms. There were also positive features to his government.[11] For example, when the country was visited about 25 BC by a severe famine, Herod used all the gold and silver from his palace to buy corn in Egypt in order to provide the hungry population with food.[12]

Herod's foreign policy was quite different from his domestic policy. It was entirely based on the principle of maintaining his friendship with Rome, in all circumstances and at any price. Here he completely succeeded, although often he could hardly complain about his luck.

13.2.2 *Relations with Rome*

The vassal kings set up by Rome in certain areas were usually chosen from princes. Herod was an exception to this. Hereditary monarchies were not tolerated by the Romans. In specific instances investigations were made as to whether a son could follow his father.[13]

Herod's power was in many respects limited. A Roman vassal was not allowed to make treaties with other peoples or wage wars on his own. In time of war his duty was to help Rome with troops. Thus we know that in a campaign by Aelius Gallus in 25-24 BC against the Sabaeans in Arabia (which proved a failure), five hundred Jewish auxiliaries were also involved.[14]

Vassals were given limited rights to mint coins, to have their own army (a small one) and to raise taxes. They also had unlimited power of life and death over their subjects.[15]

The greatest crisis in Herod's relations with Rome came in 32-31 BC at the time of the civil war between Antony and Octavian (cf.13.1), from which the latter emerged as victor. As a protégé of Antony Herod risked being put in a dangerous position. However, luck was with him in that he had not been involved in this civil war; at the time Cleopatra had sent him, against his will, to fight against the Nabataeans. After the victory at Actium Herod resolved to pay a personal visit to Octavian, who at that time was on Rhodes. Without disguising his former friendship with Antony, Herod now offered Octavian his services. Octavian accepted them, and in addition gave Herod Cleopatra's possessions in Palestine.[16] When further extended in Samaria and Transjordan, Herod's kingdom soon became the same size as it was in the time of Alexander Jannaeus.[17] According to Josephus,[18] Octavian trusted Herod to such a degree that he ordered the procurators of Syria to use Herod as their advisor in all matters. However, this piece of information is extremely dubious.[19]

13.3 *Building works*

13.3.1 *In Jerusalem*

Without question Herod made a great impression with the many imposing buildings that were erected on his initiative. One of his most important projects was the rebuilding and expansion of the temple in Jerusalem. Work went on here for years even after the death of Herod. Only in AD 64, in the time of Agrippa, was it completely finished. This means that the temple only stood for six years after being completed. Not only tens of thousands of laity but also thousands of priests worked on the project. Priests had to do the work in places to which non-priests had no access. So here, too, Herod had to cope with religious sensibilities.

The splendour and size of this temple seem to have been proverbial. We have detailed descriptions of its extent and arrangement in Josephus[20] and in the Talmud.[21] The two descriptions largely agree.

In the temple an inscription was put up prohibiting foreigners (non-Jews) from entering the inner court: it stated that the penalty for transgressing this command was death.[22] According to Bickerman,[23] Zerubbabel had already put up a notice to this effect in the temple in 200 BC (see also 6.2.2).

As in the time of the temple of Solomon (see I Kings 7.1), even this temple in all its glory did not compare with the palace which Herod had built for himself in Jerusalem. The palace was built on a high hill in the west of the city and dominated the whole panorama of Jerusalem. The palace had three gates on the north side, Phasael, Hippicus and Mariamne. According to Geva,[24] Hippicus was on the site of the former 'gates of David'.

The citadel of Antonia, well known from the New Testament, and situated on the north-western corner of the temple mount, was another of Herod's buildings from this time. This citadel was particularly important from a military point of view. Herod also had an amphitheatre built in the immediate environs of Jerusalem.[25]

13.3.2 *Buildings outside Jerusalem*

Outside Jerusalem and Judaea, as I have already said, Herod behaved as a non-Jew. So in various non-Jewish cities he had temples built, mostly in honour of the Roman emperor.[26] He did so, for example, in Samaria and Caesarea. These two cities are to be seen largely as Herod's creation. He almost completely rebuilt the city of Samaria and renamed it Sebaste[27] in honour of Augustus. In about 22 BC he began to built a completely new port, which he called Caesarea.[28] Another city refounded by Herod was Antipatris.

It was presumably on the site of the city of Aphek, mentioned e.g in Josh.12.18.[29] These three places are typical non-Jewish cities. According to Broshi[30] the number of this sort of city increased from twelve to twenty-five in Herod's reign.

Excavations have also shown that in Jericho Herod built a great winter palace with a large garden, reservoirs and swimming baths on the remains of a Hasmonaean winter residence.[31]

Another important enterprise was the building, rebuilding or extension of a number of fortresses. Thus he strengthened the fortresses of Alexandrium, north of Jericho, Hyrcania in the wilderness of Judah about seven miles southeast of Jerusalem, Machaerus in the extreme south of Peraea, and Masada in the wilderness of Engedi (cf. I Sam.24.1), on the west coast of the Dead Sea, all of which had been built by the Hasmonaeans. He also rebuilt Anthedon, on the coast near Gaza,[32] which he called Agrippium[33] or Agrippias.[34] Two new fortresses were named Herodium in his own honour.[35] One was near the village of Tekoa, about six miles south of Jerusalem,[36] and the other in the hills facing Nabataean territory. However, the exact site of this last fortress is not known. A new fortress was also built at Jericho, which was called Cyprus after Herod's mother.[37]

13.4 *The social and economic situation*

13.4.1 *Taxation*

It is almost certain that Herod largely took over the system of taxation which existed in the time of the Hasmonaeans (cf. 10.1.2).[38] The burden of taxation became enormous under Herod's rule. He needed an vast amount of money; even more than the Hasmonaeans. The countless building works in his day (see 13.3) and the state which he developed must have swallowed up very great sums of money.[39] The only way in which he could get it was by raising taxes. That these taxes were unacceptably high is evident, for example, from the fact that directly after his death the Judaeans asked his successor Archelaus to reduce the high taxation;[40] this situation recalls events after the death of Solomon.[41]

We do not know precisely how high these taxes were. Nor do we have any information about how they were raised. However, it is certain that one way was to make rich aristocrats[42] who from the start had been supporters of Herod responsible for them;[43] another way particularly favoured was the use of a system of publicans which is known from the New Testament. In one form or another this institution goes back to the system of tax farmers which existed in the Ptolemaic period.[44] The publicans also had a contract from the authority for collecting direct taxes.

In one instance we know that Herod granted a remission of a third[45] of the taxes, but this was to stave off the threat of a rebellion. All this shows how heavy the taxes must have been.

We do not know whether or not Herod had a census in his kingdom in connection with the raising of taxes. According to Schalit,[46] he must have done something of the sort, probably in 20 and 14 BC. One of Schalit's arguments is that something of the kind is also reported of another client king, namely Archelaus of Cappadocia.[47] A considerable objection to this is that, for example, Josephus says nothing about such a census.[48] The census reported in Luke 2.1-2 could just as well have taken place in the time of Herod.[49]

13.4.2 *Poverty and riches*

Avigad[50] has established on the basis of archaeological investigations that there were great riches in Jerusalem in the time of Herod. Excavations in the suburbs of the city where the well-to-do then lived show this clearly. The houses there have reservoirs and splendid mosaic floors, which is certainly evidence of the great wealth and prosperity of the well-to-do citizens of Jerusalem in this period. Such an observation should not surprise us, given what was said in 13.4.2 about Herod's supporters.

However, these riches were limited to a particular small group of the population. Alongside that there was very great poverty in the country. The heavy taxation was a burden not so much for the rich supporters of Herod mentioned in 13.4.1 as for the country and peasant population. The fact that rebels against Roman (Herodian) authority could count on much support from this population[51] itself points clearly in this direction. Above all, Galilee constantly came to the foreground at that time. In this context we might recall the activites of Ezechias (Hezekiah) and his supporters in the time before Herod became king (see 12.6.2).

However, not all the well-to-do escaped Herod's demands for money. At all events, Josephus[52] describes how, shortly after the occupation of Jerusalem in 37 BC, Herod robbed the well-to-do to get money. Above all the former supporters of Antigonus, who were especially to be found in Judaea and Galilee, were the losers here. And Herod needed a good deal of money, not only to maintain his army and his famous capital but also to be able to give large gifts to his friends. We know, for instance, that at the beginning of his reign he gave large gifts to Antony and his staff.[53]

One advantage for the country was that for a great deal of Herod's rule (from *c.*31 to 4 BC) there was relative peace. Such a situation meant that the farmers could work without being troubled by war and violence. Given the severe burden of taxation this at least was a relief.

13.5 *Herod's religious policy*

We saw earlier (13.2.1) that Herod was very cautious over Judaism and Jewish customs and that he presented himself to Jews as a Jew. However, later traditions suggest that people did not respect him very highly in religious matters.[54] There were reasons enough for offence here. We may recall his contemptuous attitude towards the Sanhedrin (see 12.6.2). Another great source of offence was the golden eagle[55] which he had fixed to the gate of the temple. Herod would not have it removed, and when towards the end of his reign it was taken away as a result of a conspiracy led by the scribes Judas and Matthias, these suffered terrible punishment.[56]

Herod also nominated and deposed high priests at will. For high priests he chose people who were well disposed towards him and took little notice of existing traditions. This way of carrying on did not do much for the respect of this old institution. It can also be assumed that Herod's action widened the gulf between the people and the priests. Even apart from this, the reputation of the priests continued to sink in an uninterrupted decline.

Although in religious matters Herod took account of the views of the Pharisees, Josephus[57] says that he clashed with them when they refused to give an oath of allegiance to him and the emperor. This refusal clearly had a religious background.[58] It would have put too much emphasis on their obedience to a foreign (and indeed pagan) ruler. It is striking that in this case Herod did not have the Pharisees killed, as he did other offenders, but let them off or simply imposed a fine.

One reason for Herod's accommodating attitude to the Pharisees was doubtless that this group had great influence among the people. In addition, another factor may have played a role. This group gradually transferred its concern from political matters more towards the religious sphere. Such a shift cannot have ben displeasing to Herod. Politically he had nothing to fear from them. Another reason for his tolerant attitude towards the Pharisees may well have been that at the siege of Jerusalem in 37 BC the gates of the city were opened on the urgent advice of two Pharisees, Shemaiah and Pollio.[59] However, they did this not so much out of sympathy for Herod as from a sense that he was a divine instrument for punishing the apostasy of the people.[60]

It is clear that not all the Pharisees kept religion and politics apart. One striking figure here was, as we shall see in the next chapter, the Pharisee Zadok.

13.6 *Herod's action against his family*

Herod regarded the Hasmonaeans as a constant threat to his throne. That is evident from the fact that during his government he had all the members of this family put to death.

This might seem to be contradicted by Josephus' report[61] that in 40 BC Herod urged Antony to make Aristobulus, a grandson of Hyrcanus II, king over Judaea. However, this information in Josephus presumably comes from Nicolaus of Damascus, Herod's court historian, or from Herod's own memoirs, and was simply aimed at presenting Herod's attitude towards the Hasmonaeans in as favourable a light as possible.[62]

Herod's marriage to the Hasmonaean Mariamne, a sister of this Aristobulus, was an attempt to give his rule a kind of legitimacy. Clearly this marriage caused great problems and conflicts at court. The first came very soon.

At the beginning of his reign Herod had nominated a certain Ananel, an unknown figure, high priest. This was not to the taste of Alexandra, the mother of Mariamne, who wanted this office for her son Aristobulus (see above). With the help of Cleopatra, Alexandra got her way. However, when Aristobulus seemed to be enjoying great popularity among the people as high priest, in 35 BC Herod had him drowned by his underlings during a game in a bath.[63]

After this, executions followed in rapid succession. In 29 BC Mariamne was executed, as was her mother Alexandra a year later on grounds of treachery and conspiracy; here Salome, Herod's sister, played a malicious part.

In about 23 BC Herod sent Mariamne's two sons, Alexander and Aristobulus, to Rome to be brought up. After about five years they returned to Jerusalem, whereupon Herod arranged a wedding for them. Alexander took as wife Glaphyra, a daughter of Archelaus, king of Cappadocia, and Aristobulus married Berenice, a daughter of Salome, Herod's sister.

New intrigues in which again Salome and also Antipater, the son of Herod's first wife Doris, were involved, led to accusations against Alexander and Aristobulus. Despite attempts at reconciliation by Archelaus of Cappadocia and even Augustus, the two sons were executed on the orders of Herod. This happened in Sebaste, about thirty years after Herod's marriage there to Mariamne, their mother.[64]

Antipater also suffered the same fate in 4 BC, only a few days before Herod himself died.

This lack of compassion was characteristic of Herod's whole life. Obviously he could only maintain his authority over family and people by harsh and cruel action.

13.7 *Herod's end*

Herod died in 4 BC[65] after a terrible illness. It is unclear from the text in Josephus what this was,[66] since it is difficult to interpret what it is saying.[67] A funeral procession with great pomp and ceremony bore his body to the Herodium south of Jerusalem, which he had built, and there he was buried.

The direction of this funeral was in the hands of his son Archelaus, whom Herod had named as his heir shortly before his death. This last act was typical of Herod's character. His insecurity led him to nominate one heir after another. However, his testamentary disposition had no value until the emperor had given it his approval. In the following chapter we shall see how this raised some problems. First, though, we must pay some attention to the group which was closely allied to the dynasty of Herod.

13.8 *The Herodians*

In the New Testament[68] there is only one mention of the Herodians. These Herodians must be regarded as sympathizers with the Herodian dynasty and as favourable to Rome. It is not altogether clear whether this group already existed at the time of Herod the Great. In one passage,[69] Josephus speaks of 'followers of Herod'. According to Schalit,[70] this reference is certainly to a group which is known in the New Testament as that of the Herodians. Every strong personality, according to Schalit, manages to surround itself with such a group of followers. This conception seems to be closer than that which sees the Herodians as servants of Herod Antipas.[71]

In no way can the Herodians be regarded as non-Jews. Were that the case it would be inconceivable that the Pharisees could be paired with them, as happens in the New Testament passages where they are mentioned.[72]

It seems best to regard the Herodians as supporters of the dynasty of Herod. This group would then have been more or less active during both the time of Herod the Great and that of his sons.

The fact that in Luke 20.20, the parallel to Matt.22.16; Mark 12.13, the Herodians are not mentioned, need not be an argument against their historicity.

13.9 *Literature from the first century* BC

In an account of the most important literature from the first century BC originating in Palestine, a work like Jubilees, which appeared about 100 BC, must be regarded as a borderline case. However, this work has already been discussed in 10.3.

Some parts of the book of Enoch, which has already been discussed in 7.6.2, also come from this period. These include the 'Book of Admonitions' in chs.91-105, with the exception of the 'Ten Weeks' Apocalypse' which is included in 91.12-17 and 93.[73]

The Psalms of Solomon are another important work from this period.[74] These are eighteen psalms which have been preserved partly in Greek and partly in Syriac, but which very probably go back to a Hebrew original. In various respects they show agreements with the apocryphal psalms found at Qumran.[75]

In addition to these pseudepigraphical works there is also the apocryphal I Baruch. The author of the book purports to be Baruch, the secretary and friend of the prophet Jeremiah. The dating already shows that this is historically impossible.[76] There are some indications (see e.g. Baruch 1.1-14) that this work had a place in the liturgy of 9 Ab, when the destruction of the temple was recalled.

In addition to these literary works mentioned above we should also pay some attention to the Damascus Document, various fragments of which were found in the caves of Qumran (see 9.4.4). A good deal of this writing was in fact already known from two mediaeval manuscripts which were discovered in 1896.[77] The final redaction of the Damascus Document presumably took place in the first century BC, though a rather earlier dating of this work, or part of it, cannot be ruled out.[78]

The 'covenant' which is mentioned in the document is with a holy remnant. This holy remnant forms the true Israel, who observe the rules of the 'covenant' (cf. CD VI, 1ff.). The element of choice also plays an important role in the Damascus document. If this work was not written in the Qumran community, at all events it has many features which resemble the views of the community.[79]

Chapter 14

The Period from the Death of Herod the Great to Agrippa I (*c.* 4 BC to AD 41)

14.1 *Events after the death of Herod*

14.1.1 *Rebellions*

Immediately after the death of Herod a rebellion broke out in Jerusalem. This rebellion was a consequence of the execution of Judas and Matthias shortly before Herod's death (see 13.5). Their sympathizers now asked for Herod's advisors to be punished. Archelaus, who had been appointed by Herod as his successor, sent troops to put down the rebellion. This action failed in the first instance, after which Archelaus sent new troops who made a bloody end to the revolt.[1]

After the departure of Archelaus to Rome (cf.14.1.2), new unrest broke out in Judaea which was checked by Varus, the governor of Syria. Having restored order he returned to Antioch, but left behind in Jerusalem a legion under the command of Sabinus to keep the peace there. However, this peace did not last long. When Sabinus oppressed the people violently, new unrest broke out, This happened just about Pentecost, when there were many pilgrims in the city.[2] In Jerusalem even some of Herod's soldiers joined the rebels.[3] Revolts also broke out outside Judaea, in Galilee, under the leadership of Judas, a son of Ezechias (see 12.6.2), and in Peraea under Simon, a former slave of Herod.

As a consequence of these events Varus again returned to Palestine. Using forces including auxiliaries from the Nabataean king Aretas IV (*c.* 9 BC – AD 40),[4] he succeeded in defeating the rebels. After the revolt two thousand of them were crucified.[5]

All this shows that the period directly after the death of Herod certainly cannot be called a peaceful time.[6]

14.1.2 *Herod's testament*

While most of the events described above were taking place, the majority of Herod's family was in Rome in order to clear up the matter of Herod's testament. Three sons of Herod were present: Archelaus, the successor to the throne whom he had nominated; Herod Antipas, to whom he had assigned Galilee and Peraea; and Philip. These three argued for their interests in the presence of Augustus, who had to endorse the testament. Herod Antipas, supported by most of Herod's family, moreover pressed Herod to nominate him successor to the throne in place of Archelaus, in accordance with an earlier testament.

Meanwhile two further delegations came from Palestine to Rome. There was a Jewish one which asked that none of the family of Herod should be made king, but that the government should be entrusted to a high priest, and one from the Greek cities of Gadara, Hippus and Gaza, who asked to be incorporated into the Roman province of Syria.

After some heart-searching Augustus decided to endorse Herod's testament. The three cities with Greek names were incorporated into Syria: Archelaus got Judaea, Samaria and Idumaea; Herod Antipas got Galilee and Peraea; and Philip got Auranitis, Trachonitis and presumably Ituraea.[7] None of them was allowed to call himself king. Archelaus became ethnarch and the two others tetrarch (see 14.2.1).[8]

14.2 *The government of Palestine after the death of Herod*

14.2.1 *Judaea and Samaria*

As we have seen, Archelaus became ethnarch of this part of the country. The title ethnarch is higher than that of tetrarch, 'ruler of four', but lower than that of king, and was often given to a vassal.[9] Matthew (2.22),however, calls Archelaus king. Josephus also does this once (*AJ* XVIII, 93), but wrongly so. Of all the sons of Herod he most resembled his father in cruelty.[10]

The rule of Archelaus lasted only from 4 BC to AD 6. Complaints made by a delegation from Judaea and Samaria were taken seriously by Augustus. Archelaus was dismissed and sent to Gaul.[11] It is possible that Augustus' decision was also influenced by the way in which Archelaus' style of government threatened the peace and security of the important trade route from Syria to Egypt.[12]

The territory of Archelaus was now part of the Roman province of Syria and governed by a procurator.

The removal of Archelaus brought a decisive change in the existing situation.

Despite everything, both Herod and Archelaus, unlike the Roman procurators, had taken account of Jewish religion because of their knowledge of affairs in this area. The subsequent procurators Coponius (6-9), Marcus Ambibulus (9-12), Annius Rufus (12-15), Valerius Gratus (15-26), Pontius Pilatus (26-36), Marcellus (36-37) and Marullus (37-41) made mistake after mistake in this respect. There was also a constant threat of unrest, which sometimes could be defused by the spiritual leaders in Jerusalem but sometimes in fact erupted, albeit on a limited scale. The situation in Jerusalem was particularly tense at the time of the great feasts.

One of the greatest difficulties arose at the beginning of Roman rule. A census had to be taken when a country was incorporated into the Roman empire. This census took place in 6 or 7 BC under the direction of Quirinius, the legate of Syria.[13] A census of this kind included a registration of land as well as a kind of head count. The head count in particular provoked great religious objections (cf. II Sam.24.1ff.). The high priest of the time, Joazar, had the greatest difficulty in persuading the people to accept this census. Despite his efforts, a minority of the population rebelled. This group, which consisted of Zealots or a group related to them (cf.12.8.1), was led by Judas the Galilean. The revolt, in which Judas presumably lost his life, was put down by the Romans. However, the embers of rebellion continued to glow until there was a great conflagration in 66.

The best-known procurator of the period described in this chapter is Pilate.[14] In his time conflicts flared up. More than once he hurt Jewish religious sensibilities, among other things by putting up shields with the emperor's portrait on them in his palace in Jerusalem. The Jews, who saw this as a beginning of the imperial cult, protested to Tiberius, Augustus' successor. He gave Pilate orders to take back the shields to the residence in Caesarea.[15]

In some respects the Judaeans still enjoyed a degree of freedom. For example, Jews were exempt from military service in the Roman army. Relations with the Sanhedrin even seem to have improved compared with the period of Herod and Archelaus. It had much more power in domestic matters (cf. Matt.5.22). In the liturgical sphere, the Sanhedrin also made its influence felt in the Diaspora. The leadership of the Sanhedrin rested with the high priest, who as such was also regarded by the Romans as the representative of the domestic government. The Sanhedrin was also responsible for raising the direct taxes which had to be paid to the emperor (see 14.3.1).

14.2.2 *The territory of Philip (4 BC-AD 33/34)*

The areas assigned by Augustus (see 14.1.2) to Philip lay in the north and east of the country,[16] and were almost all inhabited by non-Jews. These were areas which had originally never been part of Old Testament Judah or Israel, and were only added to it at a later period.

Philip was regarded as the least important of Herod's heirs. He was certainly the most attractive. His behaviour was moderate, and he did not undertake great political activities in an ambitious way.[17] Like his father he seems to have been very interested in building work. Thus among other things he rebuilt and extended the old city of Panias at the source of the Jordan; to distinguish it from the well-known coastal place of the same name it was called Caesarea Philippi (cf. e.g. Matt.16.13). After Philip's death this kingdom was first added to Syria, and afterwards, in 37, was given to Agrippa I as his kingdom.

14.2.3 *The territory of Herod Antipas (4 BC-AD 39)*

Herod Antipas[18] had inherited a more important area from Herod than Philip (see 14.2.2). His tetrarchy is also important because it was principally the sphere in which John the Baptist (Peraea) and Jesus (Galilee) worked. Peraea was on the other side of the Jordan and was divided from Galilee, the other part of Antipas' kingdom, by the Decapolis and Samaria.

Herod Antipas most resembled his father in his behaviour, but he was less skilful. The judgment that Jesus passes on him is very unfavourable, in Luke 13.32 calling him 'that fox'.

Antipas was just as involved in building as his father and brothers. One of the most important places to be built on his initiative was the city of Tiberias, named after the emperor Tiberius (14-37), with whom Antipas was in great favour.

Herod Antipas was first married to a daughter of the Nabataean king Aretas IV. When he rejected this wife and married Herodias, the former wife of his brother Philip, he came into conflict with the Nabataeans, who inflicted a heavy defeat on him.[19] According to Josephus (*AJ* XVIII, 116ff.), some Jews saw this defeat as a divine punishment for the killing of John the Baptist. The authenticity of this passage is sometimes disputed, but most scholars regard it as genuine.[20] If it is, it is a supplement to what the Gospels tell us about John the Baptist in this connection. According to Matt.14.3-12 par., John was beheaded at the instigation of Herodias after Salome's dance.

After the death of Tiberius in 37 the power of Herod Antipas soon declined. Moreover, as a result of the intrigues of Herod Agrippa he fell into disfavour with Caligula, who in 39 banished him to Gaul.

14.3 *Social and economic conditions*

14.3.1 *Taxation*

Taxation fell into two categories: direct taxation and tolls. The Sanhedrin, under the supervision of the Roman procurator, was responsible for raising direct taxes. These taxes included a tax on the produce of the land[21] (*tributum soli*) and a poll tax (*tributum capitis*). The *tributum soli* had been paid to Rome since 63 BC. The *tributum capitis*, which provoked most opposition, had only to be paid after the annexation in AD 6 (see 12.2.1). The poll tax is the tax discussed in the question put to Jesus whether people should or should not pay tax to Caesar.[22] It was a particularly heavy burden on the population of Syria and Judaea, especially in about 17.[23]

Although the system of tolls, like most of the taxes mentioned above, already existed in one form or another in an earlier period,[24] we will not go further here into the figure of the person responsible for collecting it, the publican, since a good deal of attention is paid to him in the Gospels. Tolls included import and export taxes and also money for roads, ports and markets.[25] The raising of these taxes was farmed out by the Romans to entrepreneurs, who were usually rich men.[26] The real work of the tax farmers consisted in raising taxes through subordinates and other personnel. The tax-collectors mentioned in the New Testament are probably always the latter, except in the case of Zacchaeus (Luke 19.1-10). Thus Levi mentioned in Mark 2.14 is probably an ordinary publican. These belonged to a socially unprotected group and were usually very badly paid. It was almost inevitable that in such a situation there should be corruption.[27] So these people were often despised, not so much by the poor and the day-workers, since they usually did not have to pay any tolls, but by the well-to-do, who had to make use of their services. That Jesus is called a friend of publicans (Matt.11.19) implies that he was against such social arrogance.

14.3.2 *Landowners and leaseholders*

In a number of the parables of Jesus (see e.g. Matt.20.1-15; Mark 12.1-11) the characters are clearly large landowners. On the basis of the Mishnah and archaeological evidence Applebaum argues that land ownership increased markedly in the first century of our era. Whole villages often came to be owned by one landowner.[28]

The reason for this was that an increasing number of farmers were forced to sell their land as a result of sickness, drought and above all high taxation. These farmers and their sons then became day-workers. The new owners, the great landowners, themselves lived in the cities (often in Jerusalem) or went on travels (cf. Luke 16.1-8). They included many relatives of the high-priestly families and merchants. They usually left the supervision of their possessions to stewards. The real work was done by day-workers, slaves and leaseholders.[29]

It need hardly be argued that all this had a considerable influence on the social and economic situation in the country. In Judaea and Samaria and above all in Galilee agriculture was always the main mode of existence. The impoverishment of the farmers resulted in an enormous exodus from the country. Galilee was particularly affected by this because most of the villages were there. It has therefore been supposed that the designation 'Galileans' in Josephus usually means 'village dwellers'.[30]

In addition to the great landowners and the decreasing number of farmers there were also various kinds of leaseholders in the country. Some had to pay a fixed part of the harvest (often a half or a third) to the owner, while others paid a fixed sum in the form of 'money';[31] yet others cultivated a piece of ground and then later paid half of the harvest as their lease.[32]

The cost of the lease to be paid itself meant that these leaseholders had a hard life. In addition to their lease they also had to pay taxes (see 14.3.1). How difficult their existence often was is evident from a number of the parables of Jesus.[33]

14.3.3 *The position of the poor*

First mentioned in this category, which also included most leaseholders, come the day-workers. These were people who served a master for a fixed time, amounting to at least a day. As well as day-workers we hear of labourers, those who had a more fixed contract of service. In the period with which we are concerned here the situation of these two groups was far from rosy. Such men were often out of work, with all the consequences that followed. In the parable of the workers in the vineyard there seem to have been plenty of people standing around the market without work, for example at the eleventh hour (Matt.20.6f.). The circumstances of slaves were even more difficult. People could find themselves slaves if they were not in a position to pay their debts. Here the parable of the merciless servant is instructive. It suggests that there were two ways of paying a debt. The first was for the debtor to be sold, along with his wife, children and possessions (Matt.18.25); the second was for the debtor to be thrown into prison until his family had paid the debt.

Even in the time of Jesus many of his fellow-countrymen were slaves.[34] In addition there were also slaves of foreign origin, but it is not clear whether these were in the majority.[35] The fact that between 67 and 70 Simon bar Giora commanded the freeing of all (Jewish) slaves (*BJ* V, 108), suggests otherwise.

It is clear from the New Testament that in this period there were also a great many beggars in the country. As elsewhere, their position was very bad (see e.g. Luke 16.20).

14.3.4 *Competition and trade*

According to information given in Jewish literature there were more than forty different groups of craftsmen in Palestine at this period.[36] Many of them were connected with agriculture. Priests and scribes also practised a craft alongside their office (cf. e.g. Acts 18.3).

The craft was a profession which was often handed down from father to son. Sometimes there were families which had a particular skill at a craft (cf. m.Joma, III, XI) and kept it carefully within the family as a professional secret. Despite the very large difference in types of craft, the numbers of those involved was few in comparison to the many people involved in agricultural work.

From ancient times trade was carried on only by Phoenicians and later above all by Canaanites.[37] Hence the word Canaanite ultimately became synonymous with 'merchant'.[38] Gradually Judaeans and the inhabitants of Galilee and Samaria increasingly became involved in trade (cf. e.g. I Macc.14.5). In the time of Jesus it must have flourished.[39]

The development of trade was brought about by a variety of factors. The situation of Palestine on the important trade routes from Egypt to Mesopotamia[40] involved transit operations. In addition there was trade with Greek cities and above all with the Judaeans in the Diaspora. We should also remember the pilgrimages to Jerusalem, which doubtless encouraged trade. The markets in various cities were also important for the increase in trade. Archaeological investigations have demonstrated the important role played by the market in Jerusalem.[41] Alongside the products of the crafts, agricultural products were also very important objects of trade. Of course the tolls (see 14.3.1) which had to be paid were a disincentive.

14.4 *The religious situation*

14.4.1 *The temple*

The focal point of religious life at this time was still temple worship in Jerusalem. The temple was of great significance not only for Judaea and a wide area around,[42] but also for the Diaspora. This is clear, for example, from the temple tax of half a shekel a year paid by the Jews in the Diaspora,[43] and from their participation in pilgrimages. According to Safrai[44] tens of thousands of people came to Jerusalem for the three great festivals, from Judaea, Galilee and the Diaspora.

The daily sacrifice, which was offered morning and evening, was one of the most important cultic activities in the temple. We know very little about the temple liturgy[45] apart from the fact that sacrifices were offered regularly. It seems certain that the Psalms,[46] and also the blessing from Num.6.24-26, had a function in it.[47]

The temple had a key position not only in religious matters, but also in finance and the economy. Like all sanctuaries in antiquity,[48] it also functioned as a financial institution.[49] The many sacrificial animals that were needed, the payment of the temple tax and other gifts, the fact that the temple acted as a kind of bank, gave it a prominent position. The result of this was that the primary purpose of the temple as a 'house of God' often fell right into the background. Jesus' action against the money-changers and merchants in the temple forecourt (Mark 11.15-17) must be seen in this light.

14.4.2 *The synagogue*

There is a large literature on the question when and where the synagogue came into being.[50] Its origin must definitely be sought in the Diaspora, and in all probability in Babylon[51] or in Egypt.[52] The most probable time seems to be the third or second century BC.

In Palestine, the institution of the synagogue only developed fully after the destruction of the temple in AD 70 (see 17.3.3). According to the Gospels there were already synagogues in Palestine in the time of Jesus. Matthew and Mark mention synagogues only in Galilee, but Luke (4.44) also mentions synagogues in Judaea. Here some manuscripts have 'Galilee' instead of 'Judaea'[53] (see also 17.3.3).

Most investigations begin by stating that the reading of scripture and prayer were already the most important parts of the synagogue liturgy at a very early stage.[54] We find an earlier example of the later synagogue practice in Neh.8.1-8,[55] where we are told that Ezra read the Torah (which is what we must understand the text to refer to)[56] aloud to the people on New Year's Day.

It is hard to establish precisely on what days and on what occasions scripture reading (and exposition) had a fixed place in the synagogue liturgy. Originally, perhaps, it happened only on special occasions and feast days and later became a regular part of celebrating the sabbath. It was evidently common practice in the time of Philo.[57]

14.4.3 *The Sanhedrin*

The Sanhedrin can be seen as being in some sense a continuation of the Great Assembly and the *gerousia* (see 3.4.2). The name Sanhedrin came to be used from about 63 BC.[58] During the reign of Herod the Great it had hardly any influence. After the country was taken over by Rome the situation improved somewhat. One of the most important tasks of the Sanhedrin was to expound and apply the traditional law, and pronounce on secular and religious cases. It was also able to exercise some authority in Judaea in the political sphere. However, no important decision could be taken on any matter without the approval of the Roman procurator.

It is evident from the information in the New Testament and Josephus[59] that in the time of Jesus not only the senior priests but also scribes and elders had a place in it. The former were Sadducees, and the majority of the latter were Pharisees. We have no precise information about the numerical relationship between Sadducees and Pharisees there. However, in view of the fact that the high priest functioned as president and that the senior priests are always mentioned first, we must assume that at all events the Sadducees had the greatest power in the Sanhedrin. As we shall see in 14.5.3, this is also clear from the trial of Jesus.

14.4.4 *Spiritual leaders*

Having looked at the Sadducees and Pharisees in 9.1 and 9.2, we must now pay special attention to the priests and scribes.

As in ancient times, the high priest was the head of the priesthood. After the time of Herod the Great he was no longer the political leader of the people. However, he remained president of the Sanhedrin. This function, and the fact that the high priest was always chosen from one of the leading aristocratic families in Jerusalem, meant that he still had some influence in the political sphere. As had been customary from Persian times, the high priest was nominated by the foreign power in control, in this period the Romans. The best known high priest in the time of Jesus was Joseph surnamed Caiaphas,[60] who held this office from about 18 to 36.

The high priest was supported in the cult by priests who from Persian times had been divided up into twenty-four courses.[61] Each of these courses served in the temple for one week (from sabbath to sabbath). Thus Zachariah belonged to the course of Abijah (Luke 1.5; cf. I Chron.24.10). Each of the courses was in turn divided into 'father's houses', each of which did service in the temple on a particular day.[62] The leadership of these courses and 'fathers' houses' was in the hands of some prominent families in Jerusalem.[63] Members of these priestly families benefitted specially from the offerings brought to the temple. The priests of a lower grade usually lived in the country and had to earn a living, generally by engaging in a craft.

The main task of the priests was to offer sacrifices in the temple. They were helped here by Levites, who evidently also served as singers and musicians in the temple.[64]

One important group at this time was that of the *sop^erim*. The *soper* (originally scribe) was the man of the book, the scholar whose task it was to expound and study the message of God. We already hear of scribes in an earlier period (cf. Neh.8.2; Sirach 38.24-39.14), but only in the first century of our era; they come into prominence especially after the fall of Jerusalem in 70.[65]

In the time of Jesus the scribes still formed a group distinct from the Pharisees, though there was a great affinity between the two. Many scribes were also Pharisees, but not all of them. After AD 70 they and the Pharisees formed the group of rabbis.

In the period before 70 attention must be paid above all to the 'schools' of Shammai and Hillel. After 70 that of Hillel had a dominant position.[66] Shammai is usually thought to have been more conservative and Hillel more progressive. Hillel came from Babylon to Jerusalem as an adult, while Shammai spent his whole life in Judaea. Otherwise very little is known about them and their work. Many of their supposed views come from accounts by their followers from the time after 70 and it is far from certain that these are always authentic.[67] In Pirqe Aboth (m.Aboth I,II) Shammai and Hillel are the fifth and most famous pair of those who handed down oral teaching from the time of Moses to their own day.

14.4.5 *Religious life*

We know very little about the religious life of ordinary people. They were only very passively involved in temple worship. All the sacrificial actions were performed by priests, and the same was true of other ritual actions. Ordinary people were not even allowed to enter the sanctuary proper. Institutional and ritual elements were completely predominant. The rise of the scribes shows that there was a concern for another kind of religion in which a more personal involvement and concern for the spoken word were to the fore. In the New Testament we can also see this quite clearly from the appearance of Jesus.

It is often assumed that the observation of the regulations of the oral and written tradition was at the centre of many people's lives.[68] However, it cannot be demonstrated that this was true of many of the ordinary people, because most of the evidence comes from a later time. At all events, we should be doubtful whether there was a generally accepted orthodoxy at this period.[69]

The three great feasts in which pilgrims came to Jerusalem were like great meetings. However, here, too, only a small part of the population actually had any part to play. Most of them were not in a position to make that sort of journey.

14.5 *The ministry of Jesus*

14.5.1 *Chronology*

Roughly speaking, it may be said that Jesus was born and lived during the reigns of the Roman emperors Augustus (BC 27 = AD 14) and Tiberius (14-37).

We may sure that the beginning of the Christian era does not coincide chronologically with the birth of Jesus. This is because of a mistake of four years in the calculations made by the monk Dionysius Exiguus in the sixth century.

It is impossible to tell precisely from the Gospels when Jesus was born. Matthew (2.1) says 'in the days of King Herod', which would mean not later than 4 BC, the year in which Herod died. Luke (2.2) connects the birth with a census in the time of Quirinius, the legate of Syria. In that case Jesus would have been born in AD 6 or 7, when Judaea and Samaria came under the direct rule of Rome (see 14.2.1). Attempts have also been made to fix the birth year of Jesus with the help of astronomy in connection with the star mentioned in Matt.2.2. This has led to the birth year of Jesus being put at 7 BC.[70] So the evidence is not unanimous. That in Matt.2.1 agrees most with the corrected calculations of Dionysius Exiguus (see above), according to which Jesus must have been born in about 4 BC.

The same problems arise over the length of Jesus' ministry. The Synoptic Gospels mention one passover, which gives the impression that Jesus spent only one year going around preaching. By contrast, the Gospel of John mentions a passover three or four times,[71] and that suggests a longer period. Given that the evangelists have no more than a selection of the many stories which were in circulation about Jesus,[72] it is conceivable that the Synoptics were only interested in the one passover in Jerusalem which was so important in connection with the death and resurrection of Jesus. Consequently, a three-year activity on the part of Jesus seems more likely.[73] According to the tradition of the evangelists, Jesus spent most of this time in Galilee, particularly in the broader surroundings of Nazareth, 'his father's home'.[74]

We are also uncertain of the year and date of Jesus' crucifixion. He died on the day before the feast of the Passover (cf. Mark 15.4). According to Lev.23.6

the Passover had to be celebrated on 15 Nisan. It is usually assumed that Jesus was crucified and buried in April of the year 30 or 33.[75]

14.5.2 *Jesus and the various trends of his time*

The New Testament evidence suggests that Jesus most often engaged in discussion with the Pharisees and that he also agreed with them in his polemic against the Sadducees,[76] as for instance over the question of the resurrection.[77]

At the time of Jesus the Sadducees formed a small but powerful aristocracy (cf. also 9.1) who also occupied key positions in political matters. They do not seem to have had much contact with ordinary people and we do not know that they had any sympathy with the poor (cf.9.1.4). It is clear that here, too, Jesus was closer to the Pharisees, who enjoyed much respect and sympathy from the ordinary people.

All this does not alter the fact that more than once Jesus was critical of the Pharisees (see e.g. Matt.23.3-4, 27-28). However, it is striking that much of his criticism of the Pharisees also emerges in one way or another in the Talmud, which is certainly of Pharisaic origin. There is an instance in b.Sota 22b, where seven types of inauthentic Pharisee are criticized.[78] Jesus seems to have clashed with the Pharisees, for example, on the matter of divorce (Mark 10.2-12) and healing a lame man on a sabbath (Mark 3.1-6), though it is uncertain whether this was a clash with *all* Pharisees. It is striking that in none of the three Synoptic Gospels are the Pharisees mentioned in connection with the trial of Jesus (cf. 14.5.3).[79]

It has been stressed that both Jesus and John the Baptist must have had close connections with the Qumran community (see also 9.4).[80] However, there are also obvious differences between Jesus and the community of Qumran, and the same is true of John the Baptist. Moreover, any agreements with this group are primarily indirect.[81]

Jesus' relationship to the Zealots is problematical. Some scholars have constantly stressed that he had close relations with this group.[82] Others reject such a view out of hand.[83] It is in fact hard to imagine how Jesus could have been a supporter of violent resistance against the Romans, which is what the Zealots stood for. Different sayings of Jesus show that he believed that violence was not the way to realize the kingdom of God.[84] This does not rule out the possibility that many people in his day nevertheless regarded Jesus as a Zealot. Above all his Galilean background may have suggested such a view.

14.5.3 *The trial of Jesus*

As I have just said, nowhere in the Synoptic Gospels are the Pharisees connected with the trial of Jesus.[85] They are in the Gospel of John. There we read, for example, 'Pharisees' in 18.3,12 where Matthew has 'elders of the people' (26.47) and Mark 'scribes and elders' (14.43), while Luke has 'leaders of the temple and elders' (22.52). The fact that John has 'Pharisees' here presumably indicates a later interpretation which is again connected with the fact that this Gospel came into being later than the Synoptics.[86]

All this gives the impression that the Pharisees did not play a very active role in the trial of Jesus and were more sympathetic to him than is often assumed. The often protective attitude of the Pharisees to the first Christians also points in this direction.[87] When apostles are imprisoned by the Sadducean high priest, the Pharisee Gamaliel secures their freedom (cf. Acts 5.17-42). Josephus also reports[88] that when James the brother of Jesus was killed in 62 on the orders of a Sadducean high priest, the Pharisees complained to Agrippa II with the result that the high priest was deposed.

In addition to all this it is pointed out that in Mark 14.33-64 par. there can be no question of a trial along Pharisaic lines.[89] This could suggest that we should imagine the trial to have been a legal process implemented by the Sadducees, though we have no knowledge of such legal procedures.

Another question which has never been satisfactorily resolved relates to the authority of the Sanhedrin in matters involving the death penalty. It is often assumed that they did not have authority to impose this penalty,[90] but that is far from certain.[91] At all events it is a fact that Jesus was finally condemned to death by Pilate and executed by the Romans. So Dequeker[92] is right in saying that 'the responsibility of Pilate for the execution of Jesus was greater than the Gospels suggest; for understandable reasons, since they were written for a Roman public'.[93]

Closely connected with this is the question whether Jesus was condemned on political grounds. This view has in fact been put forward by some scholars.[94] I have already said (cf.14.5.2) that Jesus can hardly have been a Zealot. However, it is quite conceivable that the Roman authorities and the Sadducees, who were sympathetic to them, saw it as such, given his Galilean background, above all because in recent decades Galilee had been regarded as a cradle of rebel movements.

14.5.4 *The preaching of Jesus*

Between the activity of Jesus and the writing of the Gospels lies the preaching of the community which drew on traditions about him.[95] Despite this, we can certainly demonstrate some of the main features of the preaching of Jesus in the Gospels.

It is clear that Jesus did not develop any systematic teaching. His proclamation must primarily be understood as a message of salvation. Salvation is indissolubly bound up with an announcement of judgment. The proclamation of salvation and judgment indicates that the kingdom of God is near. Jesus' attitude towards the Old Testament must also be seen in this light. The coming of God's kingdom means the fulfilment, the complete establishment of Torah and prophets. Jesus himself shows that all this is being realized in his actions. This is evident among other things from his social concern with the masses 'because they were like sheep without a shepherd' (Mark 6.34), and with 'tax-collectors and sinners'.

Jesus' remarks in Luke 6.20f. (cf. Luke 6.24-26) are particularly important in this connection,[96] as are his words to John the Baptist in Matt.1.4-6 (cf. Isa.35.5f.; 61.1) and the parables. When Jesus speaks here about the poor he always means poor in the literal sense. For him the coming of the kingdom of God opens up new perspectives (Matt.11.4-6). It is significant that Jesus was called the 'hope of the poor'.[97] This aspect comes clearly to the fore in the earliest traditions about him.[98]

The preaching of Jesus about the coming kingdom of God does not offer any mirage, but a reality which is brought about in his own life and work. The central notion of a judgment on the actions of men and women in the preaching of Jesus is also to be explained in this light (cf. Matt.5.16). For this reason Jesus also calls his disciples and followers to follow him. The words with which he ends the parable of the good Samaritan are typical: 'Go and do likewise' (Luke 10.37). Of course the parables have a very important place in Jesus' proclamation of the coming kingdom of God. Anyone who takes them seriously will also understand their meaning.[99]

Finally, Koester[100] is right in stressing that Jesus' ethics are above all eschatological and not interim. The coming kingdom of God is a real event and puts Jesus' followers in a new situation. The Samaritan in the parable (Luke 10.29-37) does no more than what is needed in this situation, in the context of God's rule.

Chapter 15

The Period from Agrippa I to the Beginning of the First Jewish War (AD 41-66)

15.1 *The general political situation*

After the death of Augustus, during the period described in this chapter the Roman empire was governed by the emperors Tiberius (14-37), Caligula (37-41), Claudius (41-54) and Nero (54-68). None of these figures had the diplomacy and supremacy of Augustus. One result of this was that they had more difficulty in keeping in check the opposition to the sole rule of the emperor.

Tiberius, mentioned in the New Testament only in Luke 3.1, was far from popular in the Senate or among the people, although he courted the good will of the former, especially at the beginning of his reign. His greatest mistake in government was probably his supreme trust in Sejanus, the commander of the imperial bodyguard. In 31 Sejanus was imprisoned and killed when he began to take on imperial airs. Military successes in the time of Tiberius were repeated in Gaul, Germany and Armenia. However, these successes were mostly due to Germanicus, a nephew of the emperor.

Gaius, a son of Germanicus, better known by his nickname Caligula, 'little boots', succeeded Tiberius as emperor in 37. He achieved nothing in either the political or the military sphere. Soon after his accession his mind was impaired by an illness which made him take the most crazy decisions. One of them was to seek to be worshipped as a deity during his life. We shall see (15.2.1) that this also threatened to have consequences for the temple in Jerusalem.

The 'best emperor after Augustus'[1] was Claudius. During his reign the people of Gaul obtained the right to become senators.[2] Claudius made his mark above all in the legal sphere by beginning to set up an efficient administrative apparatus.[3]

Claudius was succeeded by Nero, who was notorious for his cruelty. He neglected both his administrative duties and foreign policy. There were countless conspiracies against him, the last of which (in 68) succeeded. Before he could be imprisoned, Nero committed suicide. During his reign there was the famous burning of Rome (in 64). Nero was suspected of being responsible. To shift suspicion he accused the Christians in Rome. This led to the first persecution of Christians there.[4]

15.2 *The reign of Agrippa I*

15.2.1 *Agrippa's relations with Rome*

Agrippa[5] (in Acts 12.1-23 called Herod), who was a grandson of Herod the Great and Mariamne, was friendly with Caligula. On being appointed emperor in 37, one of Caligula's first acts was to give Agrippa Philip's tetrarchy (see 14.2.2). When two years later Antipas was banished, Agrippa also got his territory (see 14.2.3). He also seems to have had a hand in the repudiation of Herod Antipas.[6]

At about the same time Caligula, wanting to be worshipped as a deity (cf.15.1) gave orders for a statue of himself to be put in the temple at Jerusalem. In 40/41 the Syrian governor Petronius went to Palestine to carry out the commission. However, when he arrived he did not go ahead with it because he saw that to carry it out would lead to a revolution. Thanks among other things to Agrippa's skilful policy and the fact that Caligula was murdered in 41, a conflict was avoided.[7]

After these events Agrippa again played an important role in Rome on the accession of Claudius. In gratitude Claudius appointed him king over the whole area which had previously been ruled by his grandfather Herod the Great.[8]

15.2.2 *Agrippa I as king of all Palestine (41-44)*

This decision by Claudius again detached Judaea and Samaria from the Roman province of Syria, so that it was no longer under the direct rule of Rome. In the meantime, Pilate's bad administration[9] had given way to the administrations of Marcellus (36-37) and Marullus (37-41), of whom we know little more than their names.

In contrast to Herod the Great, Agrippa seems to have found more sympathy among the leading groups in the land. It is not impossible that this was because, as the grandson of Mariamne, he was regarded as a more or less legitimate descendant of the Hasmonaean dynasty.[10] He also had the right approach. In Jerusalem he presented himself as a pious Jew who observed the law.[11]

It is evident that Agrippa only did this to keep his subjects in Jerusalem happy. Outside Jerusalem he acted as a patron of Hellenistic culture. He had statues of his daughters put up in Caesarea (*AJ* XIX, 357) and organized games there (*AJ* XIX, 343). The coins which he had minted also show his ambivalent attitude. Those minted in Jerusalem have no image, but those from other cities bear his image or that of the emperor.[12] His upbringing in Rome doubtless contributed to this attitude.

In his domestic policy Agrippa seems to have made some attempts to be rather less dependent on Rome. He wanted to build a new wall on the north side of Jerusalem. However, he could not finish the work because Rome prevented him.[13] He also held a conference in Tiberias with five Roman client-kings, clearly with the aim of producing a more independent policy. This conference also failed because Rome again intervened (*AJ* XIX, 338ff.).

Agrippa had rather more success in another sphere. Through his interventions at court he managed to persuade Claudius to grant important privileges to the Jews in Alexandria (*AJ* XIX, 279ff.), which were later extended to all the Jews in the Roman empire (*AJ* XIX, 288ff.). In the New Testament Agrippa is described as a persecutor of the first Christians. According to Acts 12.1-19 James, one of the sons of Zebedee (Mark 1.19), was killed on his orders and Peter almost suffered the same fate.

His reign lasted only a short time. He died in Caesarea in 44. According to Josephus (*AJ* XIX, 356), news of his death was received with joy in Sebaste (Samaria) and Caesarea. Evidently Agrippa I was less popular in non-Jewish circles than among the Jews, from whom we hear of no such expressions of delight (cf. also Acts 12.21-23).

15.3 *The whole of Palestine under direct Roman rule*

15.3.1 *The Roman procurators from 41-66*

After the death of Agrippa I, Claudius made the whole of Palestine a Roman province. This measure suggests that Agrippa did not have the full confidence of the Roman authorities, probably as a result of his attempts to carry on a more independent policy (see 15.2.2).

The first procurator to be nominated by Claudius was Cuspius Fadus (44-46). During his rule a prophet named Theudas appeared (cf. Acts 5.36) who persuaded many followers to go with him to the Jordan. Fadus scented danger and attacked the group with his cavalry, which resulted in a fearful bloodbath.

Fadus' successor was Tiberius Julius Alexander (46-48). He came from Alexandria and was a nephew of the famous philosopher Philo. In his time the land was afflicted by a famine (*AJ* XX, 10; cf. also Acts 11.27-29), and James and Simon, the sons of Judas the Galilean (see 12.8.1), were crucified (cf. *AJ* XX, 102). Like his predecessors, Alexander remained only a short time as procurator in Palestine. In 70 we find him back at the siege of Jerusalem, where he was an advisor to the Roman commander.[14]

After Alexander, Ventidius Cumanus became procurator (48-52). Under him unrest in the land increased, a situation which was largely due to the thoughtless action of Cumanus himself. The worst incident cost Cumanus his post. About 52 a conflict broke out between Galilaeans and Samaritans when a Galilean was murdered in Samaria. When Cumanus failed to do anything about this, conflict spread, and inhabitants of Jerusalem also became involved. Two 'Zealots', Eleazar and Alexander, then undertook a punitive expedition into Samaritan territory with a group of followers. The conflict was finally resolved by Claudius, who declared the Samaritans guilty and punished them. This action on the part of Claudius was largely due to the mediation of the man who was later to be King Agrippa II. Cumanus was relieved of his office and exiled.[15]

Antonius Felix (52-60) was nominated the new procurator. This Felix is the procurator mentioned in the New Testament, who held Paul in Caesarea as his personal prisoner.

The period of Felix's government was marked by an ongoing and increasing disquiet among the population. There were also constant attempts at rebellion.[16] Felix dealt with it not only very cruelly but also very untactically. The result was that the opposition to Rome steadily increased. All in all Felix was a very bad governor.[17] Acts 24.26 also gives some indication of his corrupt attitude.

In 60 Felix was removed from his post by Nero and replaced by Porcius Festus (60-62). Paul appealed to his Roman citizenship (Acts 25.11f.), so Festus sent him to Rome to answer there to the emperor.

Festus can be seen as a moderate and cautious governor. This is evident from his attitude to Paul and also his intervention in a conflict between Agrippa II and the priests in Jerusalem. These priests had had a wall built which deprived Agrippa of a view of the temple. Agrippa wanted to have the wall pulled down. Festus agreed with him, but at the same time he allowed the priests to send a delegation to Rome to put the question to Nero. Nero then decided in favour of the priests.[18]

The procurators Albinus (62-64) and Gessius Florus (64-66) who followed Festus are best known for their venality and greed. Under Albinus any prisoner could get his freedom for money, and Florus plundered whole cities and villages. The First Jewish War broke out under his rule, in 66.

15.3.2 *Agrippa II (c.49-92)*

Agrippa II was only seventeen years old on the death of his father Agrippa I in 44. According to Josephus,[19] Claudius' intention was that he should succeed his father on the latter's death, but Claudius' counsellors advised him against this (see also 15.3.1).

Like almost all the members of the household of Herod, Agrippa too was brought up in Rome. Even after the death of Agrippa I he remained there for some time. This period saw his mediation on behalf of the Jews in their conflict with the Samaritans (see 15.3.1).

In 49 Agrippa II was appointed king of Chalcis, a small kingdom in the Lebanon (*AJ* XX, 104). Here he was at the same time entrusted with the oversight of the temple in Jerusalem and was given the right to nominate the high priest there. Agrippa made much use of this right.

About 53, the territory of Agrippa was extended by the former tetrarchy of Philip (see 14.2.2), to which Abilene was added. Later Nero gave him another four cities with the surrounding territory, namely Abila and Julias[20] in Peraea and Tiberias and Tarichaea in Galilee.[21] This probably happened in about 54/55,[22] though the year 61 has also been suggested.[23] Freyne[24] conjectures that this assignation of territory was a personal gift of Nero and had nothing to do with the political strategy of Rome. This also seems most likely.

The private life of Agrippa II was looked on very unfavourably. Above all the fact that his sister Berenice often lived with him was a great cause of scandal.[25]

In the sphere of foreign policy Agrippa showed himself at all points a faithful vassal of Rome. Almost all the coins that he had struck bore the name and image of the Roman emperors ruling in his time.[26] In Acts we hear that he very soon made his mark on the new procurator Festus. Rome also supported him in the war against the Parthians.[27]

He managed to establish a good relationship with the Judaeans in domestic affairs. Rabbinic sources even say that he made serious enquiries about the law to the well known Rabbi Eleazar ben Hyrcanus.[28] However, we have seen that he also came into conflict with priests in connection with the building of a wall (15.3.1).

Agrippa II did everything possible to prevent the outbreak of the First Jewish War with Rome in 66. However, once it started he was completely on the side of the Romans. After that he seems to have acquired even more territory.[29]

In the further course of history we hear virtually nothing more about him.

He probably died in about 92, but we cannot be sure. Of course the whole chronology of his life is very uncertain and disputed.[30]

15.4 *The social and economic situation between 41 and 66*

The economic situation[31] got steadily worse in the period after 44. This was also largely due to the bad administration of most procurators, whose régimes were based on greed and corruption. Such a policy aroused opposition and therefore provoked disturbances. Obviously the attitudes of the higher authorities were reflected at a lower level. Thus, for example, far more tax was collected than was needed, because too much of it disappeared in the hands of intermediaries. All this fed anti-Roman feelings, especially among the groups which were already fiercely opposed to paying tax to the Roman emperor. Such groups saw their popular following steadily increase in this period.

Of the main areas in Palestine – Judaea, Samaria, Galilee and Peraea – Judaea and its capital Jerusalem were still by far the most important places in this period. The main priestly families lived there, the most prominent people and the rich landowners. The city owed this position to the fact that it was the most important religious centre and had a flourishing economic life. Other important cities in Judaea were Jericho, Jaffa (Joppa) and Jabneh.

Samaria had a special position. Geographically it formed a kind of bridge-head between Judaea and Galilee. The religion of the inhabitants of Samaria was not centred on Jerusalem. The Samaritans had a temple of their own as a religious centre. This temple was on Mount Gerizim, near Shechem. It is evident from the New Testament (cf.e.g. John 4.9) and other sources (see 15.3.1) that the relationship between Jews and Samaritans was particularly bad. However, Samaritans fought alongside Judaeans in the later struggle against the Romans.

The centre of Peraea was Gadora.[32] This area was relatively sparsely populated. Most people lived in the cities in the east and north, but these were typically Hellenistic places.

Despite the difficulties outlined in 14.3.2, Galilee seems still to have been a relatively prosperous place in the last decades before the First Jewish War. The main cities there were Sepphoris and Tiberias. The former seems even to have been friendly to Rome. Tiberias, which with its immediate surroundings belonged to Agrippa II (15.3.2), had the character of a Greek polis, though many Judaeans must have lived there at that time. Another important place in Galilee was Gabara, where Johanan ben Zakkai (see 16.3.3) lived and worked in the last years before 66.

We already noted earlier that there were important developments in Galilee.

Jesus spent a lot of time here and it was also the cradle of the anti-Roman movement. John of Gischala, one of the defenders at the siege of Jerusalem in 66-70, also came from there.

15.5 *The first Christian church*

15.5.1 *The community in Jerusalem*

The book of Acts (2.41) describes the origin of the first Christian church in Jerusalem. We have only very scanty information about the activities of this earliest community. The author of Acts (Luke) did not have the aim of writing 'history'. The first chapters of his book simply seek to stress that 'there is no salvation other than in Jesus Christ'.[33] It is clear that John, James and Peter were important figures in this community.[34]

In Acts 2.44f.; 4.32-37 (cf. also 5.1-11) we are told that the solidarity of the community was also expressed for a while in the common possession of goods, though the authenticity of the content of this passage is disputed.[35] However, it seems quite likely that the community should have taken such a step in this period,[36] not least because many instances of this kind of life-style can be demonstrated in antiquity.[37]

There is much to suggest that the community remained faithful to Jewish belief and therefore was also usually seen as a group within Judaism. Its members took part in temple worship (cf.Acts 3.1) and presumably also observed the other regulations that went with Jewish worship. Moreover, for some time the Roman authorities regarded the Christians as a stream within Judaism.[38]

Baptism and the eucharist (I Cor.11.23) must already have been celebrated in the Jerusalem community, but for want of further information we cannot say when and in what form.[39]

We may assume that in the first period the 'twelve disciples' formed the nucleus of the Jerusalem community. Despite the fact that we know very little about the earliest community in Jerusalem, it must be accepted that it was of very great significance. From it groups of people came into being everywhere who felt themselves to be united in belief in the risen Lord.

15.5.2 *The Greek-speakers in the Jerusalem community*

We have already noted often in previous chapters that in the course of time Jerusalem had become an important city. One of the consequences of this was that Greek speakers had also settled in the city, while the use of Greek also came into vogue in some Jewish circles. Evidently some of these people also joined the earliest community, and their presence there led to a conflict (cf. Acts 6.1).[40] Luke describes how in this situation seven men were appointed deacons from the group of Greek speakers (cf. Acts 6.3). We get the impression that the term deacon in this period was used primarily as a name for missionaries (cf. Acts 8.4ff.). One of these seven deacons, Stephen, was killed during a brief persecution (cf. Acts 7.57f.). Evidently this persecution was directed only against the Greek-speaking part of the community in Jerusalem, since figures like John, James and Peter continued with their work there undisturbed. The Greek-speaking members of the community, on the other hand, were driven out of Jerusalem.

The result of this was that Christian communities became established in other places. In Acts (7.14ff.) there is an emphatic reference in this connection to the activity of the deacon Philip, who preached the gospel of Christ in the city of Samaria. Others went, for example, to Antioch (Acts 11.19ff.), where later the name 'Christians' was used for the followers of Jesus.

15.5.3 *The death of James*

For a long time the leadership of the earliest community was in the hands of Peter, one of the apostles, and James, the brother of Jesus. James eventually came to have the most prominent place.[41] In the year 62, when after the departure of Festus (see 15.3.1) there was a short period without a procurator, this important leader of the community in Jerusalem was killed. We are told about this by Josephus in *AJ* XX, 200ff. According to his account James was summoned before the Sanhedrin on the orders of the high priest Annas II and then stoned on a charge of having broken the law. This action aroused opposition among moderate Jews and the Pharisees. They laid charges against Annas II to Agrippa II and the newly arrived procurator Albinus, and Annas was deposed by Agrippa II as high priest.

It is clear that there can be no question here of a normal trial. Rather, we get the impression that this was a brief witch-hunt in which other members of the community in Jerusalem were also taken prisoner.

15.5.4 *Flight to Pella?*

Eusebius describes in his Church History (III,5,3) how the Christians in Jerusalem fled to Pella in Transjordan in 66 BC, shortly before the Romans laid siege to the city. For a long time this report was almost universally regarded as accurate, and still is by some scholars.[42] However, in recent times it has been increasingly challenged.[43] Among other things, scholars point out the great distance between Pella and Jerusalem (about sixty miles), involving a journey through a region controlled by the Romans, and that in 66 Pella was plundered by Jewish partisans, which certainly would not have encouraged the Jewish Christians to settle there. It therefore seems most likely that the members of the earliest community in Jerusalem shared the fate of their fellow-citizens in the siege and after its capture by Titus in 70. All this does not exclude the possibility that individual members of the Jerusalem community like Johanan ben Zakkai (see 16.4.3) could have fled before or during the siege.

Chapter 16

The First Jewish War (66-74)

16.1 *The beginning of the struggle*

16.1.1 *Causes*

It is clear that the corrupt and bad government of various Roman procurators (see 15.2.2; 15.3.1) and the hatred of many Judaeans towards the Roman occupying forces was one of the immediate occasions for the outbreak of the struggle. In addition, social, economic, nationalistic and religious motives also played a part. No single one of these, however, can be said to have been the decisive cause of the war.[1] Social and economic factors (see 16.1.3) must be supposed to have been particularly to the fore, though the events between 66 and 74 certainly cannot be described as the culmination of a class struggle.[2] Still less can the hostility between Jewish and Greek communities be regarded as the fundamental cause of the dispute with Rome.[3] Rather, we must say that a combination of all these factors eventually led to the outbreak of hostilities. In this connection we must also be very cautious about the information in Josephus, since he describes the events very subjectively in what is in effect an apologia for his own position.[4]

A combination of events sparked off the war, beginning in Caesarea. This city had a mixed population of Jews and Greeks. When Greek inhabitants built on a piece of ground next to a synagogue, as a result of which the synagogue was partly blocked off, a conflict arose between the two population groups. The dispute was even referred to Nero, who in 61 decided in favour of the Greeks (cf. *AJ* XX, 184). After that, unrest continued in Caesarea, and in 66 this led to street fighting in the city.

At the same time the procurator Florus gave orders for seventeen talents to be taken from the temple treasury. This sort of thing had happened before, but not seemed provocative; now part of the population mocked Florus by holding a street collection for him. This made Florus so angry that he gave his soldiers orders to punish the population. However, the opposition to him was so great that he had to retreat to Caesarea, leaving behind only one cohort in Jerusalem and making the leaders of the city responsible for law and order (*BJ* II, 318ff.). They failed to keep it.

These events were the last straw for groups like the Sicarii and Zealots (but see 12.8.1), who had increased in number over the years,[5] and they began to fight against the Romans.[6] The majority of the population of Judaea and Galilee soon joined them, along with the Idumeaeans and in 67 also the Samaritans.

16.1.2 *Peace initiatives*

Not everyone was happy with this course of events. Agrippa II, who at this time was staying in Alexandria, rushed back to Jerusalem to mediate there. His attempt failed, above all because he had so little support from Florus.

Agrippa II was not the only one to try to settle the conflict. The high priest and the Sadducees, along with the Pharisees, who were satisfied that there were no hindrances to worship, and the supporters of the dynasty of Herod, did everything possible to restore peace. At a later stage the Pharisees do seem to have taken part in the struggle, though they were always only moderately enthusiastic about it.[7] However, for our information we are almost entirely dependent on Josephus,[8] who himself was a Pharisee and wanted to present the Pharisees to his readers, who were Romans, in as favourable a light as possible. Nothing is known about the attitude of the Essenes, but we may assume that in view of their character (cf.9.3.4) they kept out of the hostilities.[9]

In the meantime the Zealots had already conquered various fortresses, including Masada, and under the leadership of Eleazar, a son of the high priest, they occupied the temple and put an end to the offering of the daily sacrifice to the emperor.

In this situation, the groups who had tried to mediate in the conflict called for help from Agrippa II. He sent three thousand troops to eliminate the Zealots and their supporters. This attack failed completely and war with Rome became inevitable.

16.1.3 *The first successes*

Directly after this abortive intervention on the part of Agrippa II, the palaces of Agrippa, Berenice and the high priest were set on fire by the Zealots. The city archive was also burned to ashes. This last action was connected with the social and economic aims of the Zealots and their supporters – which were to achieve a redistribution of land[10] and do away with the discontent over the excessive disparity between the wealth of Jerusalem and the poverty of the rest of the country.[11] A few days later the fortress Antonia was captured, and soon afterwards the whole city was liberated from the Romans.[12]

Vigorous fighting also broke out in the rest of the country. There were particularly bloody scenes in cities with a mixed Jewish and Gentile population. Depending on which party was in the majority, the rest were often cruelly butchered.

After a long period of preparation the Roman governor of Syria, Cestius Gallus, began an expedition to Palestine in the autumn of 66. He advanced on Jerusalem, but soon afterwards had to retreat again. On his withdrawal the greater part of his army was annihilated in a pass near Beth-horon.[13]

The main result of this victory was that many people now joined the anti-Roman group. The first coins dated according to the years of the war must derive from this time.[14]

16.2 The battle in Galilee

16.2.1 Preparations

After the defeat of Gallus, measures were rapidly taken to offer resistance to the new campaign by the Romans which was a foregone conclusion. In the meantime the leading priests in Jerusalem realized that thy would lose their positions of importance if they did not come out against Rome. Many of them did precisely that. The Sanhedrin was now entrusted with executive power, while a popular assembly, which had had no significance under the client kings, was now reorganized as the supreme authority.[15] To begin with its leadership lay primarily with the upper class of priests and Pharisees.

This popular assembly entrusted Flavius Josephus, later to become a historian, with command of the troops in Galilee. Without doubt this was a very responsible and important post, because the first great attack of the Romans could certainly be expected there.

One of Josephus' first tasks was to strengthen the cities in Galilee. Those involved were Jotapata,[16] Tarichaea, Tiberias, Sepphoris and Gischala.[17] According to his own account, Josephus was able to mobilize 100,000 men and train them for battle (*BJ* II, 572ff.). Given the short time that he had, this figure seems exaggerated, to say the least. Moreover we get the impression that initially Josephus tried to keep his hands free, *vis-à-vis* both Rome and Agrippa II.

The Zealots, and above all their leader John of Gischala, probably had good reasons for suspecting Josephus of entering into negotiations with the Romans than preparing for a decisive battle. This mistrust even led to armed opposition to Josephus, who on his own account (*BJ* II, 614ff.; *Vita* 84ff.) only just escaped an atttempt on his life.[18]

Josephus says that there was further opposition in Galilee between the country population and the larger cities. The inhabitants of the countryside, who according to Freyne[19] are usually described in Josephus' *Vita* as 'Galileans', were more nationalistic than those of the cities, who were usually more well disposed to Rome.

All these factors were of great influence in preparing for the coming fight against the Romans. The differences which have been mentioned suggest that the preparation cannot have been very good.

16.2.2 *The Roman advance in Galilee*

Nero was in Greece when the war broke out in Palestine. He sent his general Vespasian to restore order there.[20] In 67, as soon as the weather allowed, he set out. There had already been some fighting before that, and the important city of Sepphoris had fallen into his hands.

With an army consisting of three legions supplemented by auxiliaries from, among others, Agrippa II and the Nabataean king Malchus II, Vespasian advanced into Galilee. At that moment, according to Josephus,[21] many of the Jewish troops took flight. Josephus himself retreated to Tiberias, while the main part of his army fled to the fortress of Jotapata. Shortly afterwards, Josephus also went there to take personal charge of its defence.

According to a detailed account in *BJ* III, 145ff., Jotapata was besieged by Vespasian for forty-seven days. Finally it fell into Roman hands through treachery. All the inhabitants were killed or taken into slavery, while the city itself and all its defences was razed to the ground. This happened in about June or July of 67. With the fall of Jotapata the Romans had regained one of the most important fortresses in Galilee. Josephus himself took refuge with about forty of his fellow-fighters in a cave. Josephus claims to have escaped with his life by a miracle and as a result of his forecast that Vespasian would become emperor (*BJ* III, 340ff.).[22] However, his account gives us the strong impression that he is simply disguising his treacherous defection to the enemy.

After the fall of Jotapata Tiberias pressed on with hardly a blow being struck against him and soon the Romans had also conquered Tarichaea, the fortress of Gamala in Gaulanitis, and Mount Tabor. By the end of 67 the Romans had the whole of Galilee under their control again. John of Gischala then fled with his supporters to Jerusalem.

16.3 *The course of the war in 68-69*

16.3.1 *The situation in Jerusalem*

After the rapid advance of Vespasian in Galilee there were bloody clashes in Jerusalem. The Zealots blamed the fiasco of the loss of Galilee on the old leaders and were also aggrieved that these were so ready to enter into negotiations with the Romans. So they did not rest until these leaders were eliminated. Leadership in Jerusalem now fell into the hands of the Zealots. However, they needed a helping hand from the Idumaeans to succeed in their coup.

A short time later, however, in the summer of 69, new difficulties arose. At that time another Zealot leader, Simon bar Giora, arrived; he and his followers had been driven out of Idumaea by Vespasian (see 16.3.2). Moreover, yet a third group of Zealots were active. This last group consisted of Jerusalem Zealots who had split from John of Gischala's party under the leadership of the priest Eleazar ben Simeon. This split took place shortly after the Idumaeans had left Jerusalem.

These three groups had vigorous disputes, although Josephus' account (*BJ* IV, 573f.) is highly coloured. However, between the disputes people were busy fortifying the city. The building of the most northerly or third wall, begun in the time of Agrippa I, was continued.[23] The minting of coins also continued in Jerusalem, during this time.[24] On the other hand we hear[25] that large stores of grain in the city were burned, an action which soon caused great problems for the defenders during the siege.

When the Roman troops were approaching Jerusalem, the city was in fact divided into three fortresses: Simon bar Giora held the upper city and a good deal of the lower city, John of Gischala the temple mount and Eleazar the inner forecourt of the temple. In this situation Titus prepared to encircle the city.

16.3.2 *Vespasian's further advances in 68-69*

According to Josephus,[26] to begin with Vespasian left Jerusalem alone, until the parties fighting there had exhausted one another. He first turned his attention to Peraea and it was not long before the whole of this area was in his hands. After that, Antipatris, Lydda, Jabneh (Jamnia) and the territory of Idumaea were conquered. Next he advanced through Samaria to Shechem, where the Samaritans who had begun the battle against Rome in 67 were defeated.[27] Jericho was also captured. By then the Romans had reconquered most of the country.[28]

At that moment, just as Vespasian was making preparations for an attack on

Jerusalem from Caesarea, where he had his headquarters, the news reached him that Nero had died on 9 June 68. From then on Vespasian had other things to worry about than Palestine, so he decided for the moment to suspend all activites.

However, he must later have regretted this, when Simon bar Giora made use of this *de facto* ceasefire to plunder the south of Judaea with a group of his followers and even attacked the city of Hebron.[29] Thereupon Vespasian launched another campaign against Judaea, Hebron being among the other places to be destroyed. Apart from Jerusalem and the fortresses of Herodium, Masada and Machaerus, Vespasian at that time had the whole of Palestine again under Roman rule.

Before he could begin an attack on Jerusalem, Vespasian was proclaimed emperor by the armies in the eastern part of the Roman empire, on 1 July 69. Directly after that he left Palestine and travelled through Antioch and Alexandria to Rome. His son Titus then took command of the Roman troops in Palestine.

16.4 *The flight of Johanan ben Zakkai*

The flight of Johanan ben Zakkai[30] from Jerusalem must have taken place in this period. There are various detailed accounts of this flight in the rabbinic literature.[31] All the versions agree that Johanan ben Zakkai left Jerusalem during the First Jewish War and received permission from Vespasian to settle in Jabneh.

The question is precisely when Johanan ben Zakkai left Jerusalem. Momigliano[32] assumes that we must read Titus for Vespasian in the rabbinic literature mentioned above and that the flight took place in 70. However, it seems to me more probable that we should put it in the period when Jerusalem was troubled by new internal disputes (see 16.3.1), about the time when the Idumaeans also left the city. It is known that a number of people fled at that time.[33] In that case Johanan ben Zakkai will have left Jerusalem in the early summer of 69. This dating comes close to that of Doeve,[34] who wants to put this flight between 15 May and 25 June 69.

At all events, the flight of Johanan ben Zakkai must be seen as one of the most important events of the First Jewish War. As we shall see in the next chapter, this simple event was of crucial significance for the later development of Judaism.

16.5 *The siege and fall of Jerusalem*

In early 70 Titus began the siege of Jerusalem. His followers included Josephus and the former procurator Tiberius Julius Alexander (see 15.3.1). Titus had in all four legions and auxiliaries for this siege.[35] The beginning of the siege fell some weeks before the Passover. At that very moment the various groups in Jerusalem were still engaged in a life-and-death struggle. When Eleazar opened the gates of the temple forecourt for those who came to celebrate the Passover, his group was attacked and overcome by that of John of Gischala.[36] From that moment on there were just two rival groups in the city.

The Romans began by attacking the northernmost wall. In military terms this side was always the most vulnerable part of the city to defend.[37] Only then did John and Simon stop their mutual dispute. Despite that, three weeks later the Romans had the whole of the inner city in their hands (*BJ* V, 299f.; 331ff.).

Meanwhile a pressing lack of food in the city made itself felt. That of course was disastrous to the morale of the defenders.

The focal point of the dispute now shifted to the temple mount with the citadel of Antonia and the upper city. When the defenders succeeded in destroying the entrenchments which the Romans threw up against the wall, Titus had a stone wall put round the whole city. This was done in three days.[38] Shortly after that the Romans were able to capture the citadel of Antonia in a night attack; it was then completely destroyed.[39]

A great blow to the morale of the besieged was the day when the offering of the daily morning and evening sacrifice had to be stopped.[40] From that day on the temple was only a fortress. At the cost of very severe losses Titus succeeded in gradually getting it into his hands. According to Josephus,[41] Titus wanted to spare the temple. This does not sound very plausible, since such an action would go against the usual military practices of the time.[42] Be this as it may, the temple went up in flames. This event is still recalled in the synagogue on 9 Ab (about August).

The fall of the temple did not, however, mean that the battle was over. John of Gischala and his supporters succeeded in escaping to the upper city and continued the fight from there. After the fall of the temple, according to Josephus there were negotiations between Titus and the besieged.[43] Titus offered them their lives, but they also wanted free passage to the wilderness, which Titus refused.

The struggle did not last much longer, not least because the besieged were exhausted through lack of food. Consequently the Romans soon succeeded in rapidly storming the upper city as well. That settled things, and after a siege of five months the Romans were again in full possession of Jerusalem.[44] Traces of the destruction which was inflicted at the time of the fight for the city and temple have come to light from various archaeological investigations over the course of time.[45]

After the fall of Jerusalem, 700 young men were taken to Rome to participate in the triumphal procession of Titus; others were put to work in mines in

Egypt or sold as slaves. To begin with, John and Simon managed to remain hidden in underground passages with some followers, but they were soon captured and also taken to Rome for Titus' triumph. After that, according to Josephus[46] Simon was put to death, while John spent the rest of his life in prison.

The city was almost completely destroyed. Only some few remnants still recalled the Jerusalem of the time of the second temple.

16.6 *The battle for the last fortresses (70-74)*

At the time of Titus' triumphal procession in Rome, which included not only a large number of prisoners but also the seven-branched golden candlestick and the table of the showbread from the temple, the fortresses of Herodium, Masada and Machaerus had not yet been captured. Titus delegated this task to Sextus Lucilius Bassus, who in 71 was nominated procurator of Judaea by Vespasian.

Herodium was probably conquered without too much difficulty as early as 71.[47] The siege of Machaerus took rather longer. However, here, too, the fighting did not last long because the defenders surrendered on the promise of free passage.[48] Archaeological investigations have confirmed the devastation that Bassus did there in 72.[49]

A short time after this Bassus died, and it was now the task of his successor Flavius Silva to conquer the last surviving fortress of Masada. He began on it in the early part of 73.

The leadership of the occupation of Masada was in the hands of Eleazar, a grandson of Judas the Galilean (see 12.8.1). Eleazar and his followers had been in Masada since 66 and they had not been idle. They had made the casemates as habitable as possible for their families,[50] and seen to good supplies of food and water to withstand a long siege. By contrast, the Romans had the greatest problems in providing food and water, because these had to be brought over a long distance. Moreover they had to conquer the citadel early in the season, since from May onwards the heat was almost unbearable.[51]

Silva began to build a wall of almost 4000 yards, further strengthened with a number of towers from which shots could be fired at the fortress.[52] The Romans succeeded in making a breach in the casemate wall by an earth wall. The defenders succeeded in making good the breach with wood, but the Romans were able to undo their work rapidly by setting fire to it. The fall of Masada was then only a matter of time.

Before things got that far, according to Josephus there was a drama in the fortress.[53] When the Romans entered Masada the besieged and their families seemed to have committed suicide.[54] Eleazar's call for this seems to be based on Deut.6.5.[55] According to Josephus (*BJ* VII, 406), the action even aroused the amazement of the Romans. Only two women and five children escaped.

As a result of excavations, in a small cave close to the top of the rock of Masada, twenty-five skeletons have been found which in Yadin's view[56] come from the last defenders of Masada. It is not completely clear in what year Masada fell, but the usual assumption is that it was in 73.[57] However, on the basis of two newly-discovered inscriptions,[58] the year 74 seems more likely.[59]

16.7 *Consequences*

Apart from the great devastation and the loss of countless human lives, the defeat by Rome also had major consequences in the field of religion, politics, and social and economic life. The significance of these consequences for the further history and development of Judaism cannot be put too highly,[60] though Noth goes too far[61] in talking of the end of the history of Israel.[62]

The devastation of the temple meant that the religious and national centre had been lost. This had consequences for both the mother country and the Diaspora. From now on there were no longer any pilgrimages to Jerusalem at the great festivals. However, the former significance of the temple as the centre of religious life must certainly not be overestimated. The existence of a community like that of Qumran shows that for a long time there had been those who did not regared the temple in that way.

Another consequence of the loss of the temple was that sacrifices were no longer offered.[63] However, it can legitimately be asked whether they could not have been offered in a different way after the destruction of the temple, as also happened after 587/6 BC.[64] Guttmann[65] rightly argues that one reason why sacrifice was not revived was that the Pharisees were against renewing the power of the Sadducean priests and the Romans did not want to appoint another high priest. We shall see in the next chapter how as a result religious life began to develop in other forms.

An additional but hurtful humiliation was that from now on the two-drachma temple tax on had to be paid to the temple of Jupiter Capitolinus in Rome as the *fiscus Judaicus*. However, the tax was abolished under the Roman emperor Nerva (96-98).

From a political perspective the defeat by Rome was the most far-reaching of all. Judaea now became an independent Roman province. This new status meant that there was a fixed army of occupation in the country; this was the tenth legion, which had also taken part in the war. The headquarters of these Roman troops was Jerusalem.

The social and economic consequences were equally disturbing. Various places including Jerualem were almost completely destroyed, while a number of areas were utterly depopulated. All this and the great loss of human life had a catastrophic effect on the country. Moreover, much of the land was taken over and given to Romans or favourites of the emperor. Thus, for example, Emmaus became a fortress of 800 war veterans (cf. *BJ* VII, 217).[66]

Chapter 17

The Period between the Two Wars with Rome (74-132)

17.1 *Political developments in Rome*

As we already saw in the previous chapter, in 69 Vespasian became emperor of Rome while on his campaign in Palestine. He ruled for ten years (69-79). His accession marked the beginning of the rule of the Flavian emperors. These emperors had quite a different background from their predecessors, as they had not come from patrician houses.

When Vespasian began his reign, the financial state of the Roman empire was extremely bad. This situation had come about above all because of the extravagant expenditure of Nero. By raising taxes Vespasian was able to solve the problem. The bad discipline in the Roman army was also improved during his rule.

His son Titus ruled for only a short time (79-81) and was succeeded by his brother Domitian (81-96). Domitian, the last of the Flavians, was something of a despot, but the rule of his successor Nerva (96-98) was very different. He had a much greater social concern. During the reign of Trajan (98-117) the so-called Quietus War (see 17.4) took place. This was a rebellion of Jews above all in the Diaspora, though Palestine itself did not remain untouched. After Nerva came Hadrian (117-38), who spent a good deal of time travelling round his empire; he was particularly fond of staying in Greece. The Bar Kochba revolt or the Second Jewish War took place in his reign (see ch.18).

Above all in the time of the emperors Trajan and Hadrian the Roman administrative apparatus was well organized. Prosperity was very great in the Roman empire in the period we shall now be considering. However, wealth can hardly be said to have been evenly distributed. For the most part it lay with the emperors and the senators.[1]

17.2 *The social and economic situation in Palestine*

At the end of the previous chapter (16.7) we already saw the social and economic consequences of the First Jewish War. It is understandable that these had an effect long after 70. Thus the destruction of the temple meant that an important social and economic centre was lost for the future. Here we need only think of the many Jews in the Diaspora who no longer came to Jerusalem for festivals, though some seem to have kept up these pilgrimages for a long time to come.[2] The destruction of the temple also meant the loss of an important financial institution to Jerusalem (cf.14.4.1). Moreover, the sacrificial worship had brought with it considerable economic activity (cf.14.3.4) which had now been completely lost.

The population structure underwent just as great changes. Before the outbreak of the war Judaea had been inhabited almost completely by Judaeans, while a mixed population had settled in Galilee[3] and especially in Transjordan. After the fall of Jerusalem, the tenth legion was stationed in the city and its wider surroundings. Along with their families, these Roman occupation forces made up another group in the area. The same thing also happened in other cities and villages. Moreover, all Jewish inhabitants were expelled from cities like Caesarea. And new cities were founded. For example, Vespasian had the city of Neapolis built,[4] close to the site of ancient Shechem.

Despite the widespread devastation and the greater poverty, there were people in Judaea who still had considerable riches even after the war.[5] In a later period these included Rabbi Tarfon,[6] Rabbi Eleazar ben Azariah[7] and Rabban Gamaliel II.[8]

After a number of years there may be said to have been a recovery of economic growth in both Judaea and Galilee. Slowly and ingeniously new modes of existence were worked out.[9]

There was a slump during the reign of Trajan, after his conquest of the Nabataean kingdom in 106. The Romans used this as a base to extend the important trade route along the old so-called Via Regis, the King's Way,[10] in Transjordan and breathe new life into it, with the result that trade increasingly took this route, to the detriment of the land west of the Jordan, which as a result lost it as a source of income.

17.3 *The rabbis and religious developments*

17.3.1 *The rabbis*

After the war with Rome all that remained of the various religious groups in Judaea were the Pharisees, though alongside them a number of figures from other groups of an earlier period also made their impression on developments in the time to come. However, the Pharisees managed not only to maintain themselves as a group but also to increase their influence considerably.

A development of this kind was not least due to the fact that the group rejected important concessions from the Romans in order to develop their activities in the religious sphere. This benevolent attitude on the part of the Romans gives the impression that the Pharisees, or at least some of them, had either stood aside or had acted very cautiously during the war against Rome after 66.[11]

The name 'Pharisees' gradually disappears after 70. The members of the group which began to play such an important role in the further development of Judaism are known as rabbis. The term rabbi, regularly used in Palestine, means 'my teacher'. However, the personal suffix 'my' in this title became as it were otiose, so that rabbi became a regular term for 'teacher'. The Babylonian teachers simply bore the title rab ('teacher'). The important leaders of rabbinic Judaism were later given the honorific title rabban, 'our teacher'.[12] The usual designation for (rabbinic) scholars was 'the wise'.

This new group of rabbis or wise men thus largely originated from the Pharisees. In addition to the Pharisees, mention should also be made of the scribes, who in a former period must have formed a separate group or class (cf. also 14.4.4), but later (perhaps even shortly before 70) were incorporated into the Pharisees.

One of the most important aims of the rabbis was to introduce reforms after the fall and destruction of the temple in 70 in order to overcome the consequences of the catastrophe of 70.[13] The temple had long been to a great extent the centre of religious life. After 70 the rabbis stressed the study and adaptation of scripture to the whole of daily life. They regarded themselves as those who handed on and mediated the oral tradition, which they did by a chain passing from generation to generation. This tradition was derived from Moses and went down to the rabbis of the generation living at the time.[14] The tractate Pirke Aboth, which gives the representatives of this chain of tradition, was also the most important document from which the rabbis derived their legitimacy as bearers of the tradition and teachers.

The function of the rabbi was not a ministry but a particular form of life, the goal of which was to live according to the aims of the tradition of the Torah and to teach others to do the same. The ideal situation was that the rabbi should also earn his own living by some other means.[15]

The most important rabbis from the period that we shall be considering here were Johanan ben Zakkai,[16] Eleazar ben Hyrcanus,[17] Ishmael ben Elisha, Gamaliel II, Akiba[18] and Tarfon.[19]

17.3.2 *Jabneh (Jamnia)*

After his flight from Jerusalem, Johanan ben Zakkai obtained the assent of Vespasian to begin a school for the study of the Torah in Jabneh, a place south of Jaffa. In the time to come this place became an important centre of rabbinic Judaism and remained so until 135. Under the leadership of Johanan ben Zakkai and his successor Gamaliel II (*c.*80-120) the foundations were laid here for rabbinic Judaism.[20]

We do not know how long Johanan ben Zakkai worked in Jabneh. It is said that at a particular moment he had to resign.[21] It seems very likely that he had to cope with opposition at Jabneh. Whether his flight from Jerusalem and his more or less pro-Roman attitude were contributory factors is not clear, but it seems reasonable to suppose that there were those who held these things against him.[22] Clearly not all rabbis followed Johanan ben Zakkai to Jabneh, but went to live in other places. Thus at a very early stage there also seem to have been rabbis in Tiberias, which was later to become an important rabbinic centre.[23]

In Jabneh the Beth Din ('court of judgment'), a continuation of the Sanhedrin, was also established, but we do not know the precise date. Nor is it certain whether Johanan ben Zakkai and Gamaliel II already bore the title *naśi'* ('president') of the Beth Din.[24]

The dispute between the schools of Hillel and Shammai, mentioned in 14.4.4, seems already to have been settled by the time of Gamaliel II. Moreover, in his day the Beth Din seems again to have acquired some political significance. Such a development is understandable. After a strict rule in the first years after 70 the Romans will gradually have allowed a degree of political freedom again.

Two other important matters from the time of Gamaliel II should also be singled out for mention. First, the establishment of the canon of the Old Testament. It is often assumed that this took place about 100 during a synod at Jabneh.[25] However, there are strong indications that nothing of the kind happened so early. Books like the Song of Songs and Koheleth were still disputed, as is evident, for example, from m.Yad.III, IV. Moreover, Schäfer[26] has given good grounds for supposing that the process of the formation of the canon ('canonical' meaning 'being appropriate for use in worship') only took place in the second century, perhaps under the influence of the events of 132-135. Moreover, this process already had a long prehistory, in which a marked Pharisaic and rabbinic influence is only perceptible in the final phase.[27] Secondly, we should note the origin of the *birkat ha-minim*, the so-called 'saying against heretics' (a euphemism for a 'curse on heretics') in the Eighteen

Benedictions. The view that this was primarily a curse on Christians, inspired above all by the church fathers,[28] is untenable.[29]

Gamaliel II probably died between 100 and 120. It is certain that he was not followed directly by his son Simeon ben Gamaliel II. It has been supposed that first Tarfon acted as president of the Beth Din.[30] Another view is that after about 120 and up to the Bar Kochba revolt in 132, other schools were dominant, above all that of Akiba in the neighbourhood of present-day Tel Aviv and that of Ishmael ben Elisha in the south of Judaea.[31]

17.3.3 *The new position of the synagogue*

Only after the destruction of the temple in 70 did the synagogue come to occupy an increasingly important place in Palestine. The earliest synagogues in Palestine date from the first century AD,[32] and primarily were to be found in Galilee (cf.14.4.2). Archaeological evidence indicates that the earliest known synagogue in the south is that of Masada.[33] This synagogue was used by the Zealots in the years between 66 and 73, but was perhaps also used by others at a rather earlier stage. After 70 a situation came about in which gradually every Jewish community, not just in the Diaspora but also in Palestine, had its own synagogue. In larger communities there were often more than one synagogue. These synagogues were always the centre of spiritual life. One important factor in this connection is that Judaism had the status of a permitted religion, *religio licita*, throughout the Roman empire. This status, which was already granted by Julius Caesar, meant that Jews everywhere in the world were free to live according to their own religious laws and regulations. Claudius later also granted the Jews exemption from military service for this reason. The *religio licita* which gave the synagogue jurisdiction over its own members was of the utmost significance for Judaism.[34]

17.4 *The so-called Quietus War (115-117)*

In 115-117 we hear of revolts of Jews in the Diaspora which began in Cyrene and spread from there to Cyprus, Egypt and Mesopotamia. These revolts took place while Trajan was occupied in a campaign against the Parthians.[35] We have very few pieces of information about the course of these revolts[36] and even then they are not always trustworthy.[37]

In Mesopotamia the revolt was put down by the Roman general Lucius Quietus, so that the revolts are known as the Quietus War. Quietus went to work in an extremely barbarous way and killed thousands of Jews. When the revolt had been put down, as a reward Quietus was nominated procurator of the province of Judaea as a reward.[38]

It is not completely certain whether these revolts also spread to Palestine. Some facts seem to point in this direction.[39] The most important reason for supposing that the war affected Jews in Palestine is that it is hard to imagine that they would have remained passive while their fellow-Jews in the Diaspora were involved in the struggle. Moreover the nomination of Quietus as procurator, mentioned above, is some indication that Palestine was not completely tranquil in the period between 115 and 117. For this reason it is assumed that the status of Judaea was also changed during the Quietus war and that it was then, rather than in 135, that it became a consular rather than a praetorian province and was given the name Palestine.[40] This change implies among other things that from then on two legions, rather than one, could be stationed there. Such reinforcement of the Roman occupying forces would certainly not have come about unless there had been a pressing need.

17.5 *The most important literature from Palestine between c.1 and 135*

In the schools which came into being in Palestine after the fall of Jerusalem in 70, the rabbis and their pupils occupied themselves with studying and interpreting the (written) Torah and the oral tradition (see 17.3.1). The collection of study material which came into being in this way is known as a *mishnah* (= teaching). Those who made such a collection are called the *tanna'im* (scholars). Johanan ben Zakkai, the founder of the school in Jabneh, is regarded as the first of these *tanna'im*. All these *mishnah* collections were later given the collective name Mishnah. The final reaction of the Mishnah, in which Jehuda ha-Nasi had a hand, took place about 200. These collections were first handed down by word of mouth, but presumably they already appeared as written collections in the period with which we are concerned.[41]

As for the New Testament, only the letters of James and Jude may be assumed with any degree of probability to have been written in Palestine.[42]

Apart from these works, I should also draw attention to some important pseudepigrapha which originated in Palestine at this time. These are the Ascension of Moses (between 4 BC and AD 30), the Life of Adam and Eve (before 70), IV Ezra 3-14 (c.95) and the *Paralipomena Ieremiae* (beginning of the second century). The last two works were clearly written under the impact of the fall of Jerusalem in 70. For example, the author of IV Ezra (3.34-36) protests against the devastation of Judaea and Jerusalem, not because Israel is innocent but because the sins of those who devastated it were far greater.[43]

Chapter 18

The Bar Kochba Revolt (132-135)

18.1 *Causes*

18.1.1 *The political background*

Hadrian (117-138) is known as an emperor who aimed at consolidating the frontiers of the Roman empire and not seeking to extend its territory any further. For this reason he also renounced the claims that Trajan had made to Parthia (cf. 17.4). This made areas like Syria and Palestine all the more important, because they came to be near to the eastern frontier of the Roman empire.

One of the great problems in Palestine was the relationship between the Jewish and Greek inhabitants. Here the Romans adapted their old principle of 'divide and rule' in order to keep peace in the area. Another way of achieving this end was to strengthen the Roman army in the province of Arabia (the land of the Nabataeans). One factor which probably played a part here was that in the past there had often been good contacts and alliances between Judaea and Parthia. The reinforcement of the occupying forces in the province of Arabia increased the barrier between these two countries.

On his journeys through the eastern part of his kingdom, in about 130 Hadrian had also visited Palestine, and there as elsewhere set up buildings in the Hellenistic style. This happened, among other places, in Caesarea and Tiberias. The predominantly Jewish city of Sepphoris was given the name Diocaesarea, the first letters of which indicate a connection with Zeus Olympius.[1] It is clear that a great many Jews were unhappy with these developments, and were even more so when Jerusalem and religious matters were involved (see 18.1.3).

18.1.2 *The economic situation*

There are indications that the economic situation in the country again deteriorated during Hadrian's rule (cf. 17.2). In particular the position of the leaseholders seems to have become steadily more wretched. In rabbinic sources[2] there is constant mention of landowners who oppress their lease-holders and even use violence. These landowners were often Romans or agents of the Romans or the emperor. According to Applebaum,[3] these facts are confirmed by leasing contracts which have been found in the caves of Murabba'at[4] and Nahal Ḥever.[5] These contracts relate to leasing agreements between Bar Kochba and other Judaeans during the period of the revolt. Evidently they refer to land which was taken by Bar Kochba from the then owners.

All this gives the impression that bad economic conditions were also a breeding ground for the revolt in 132-135. The feeling of being exploited obviously led to increasing tension. The sending of a Roman legion from Caparcotna to Sepphoris[6] may also indicate a tense situation. Evidently only one or two provocative actions by Rome were needed for the dam to break.

18.1.3 *Direct causes*

Dio Cassius (LXIX 12,1-2) gives as a cause of the revolt the fact that Hadrian planned to rebuild Jerusalem as a Graeco-Roman city with the name Aelia Capitolina. By contrast, the reason given in the *Historia Augusta*[7] is that Hadrian had forbidden circumcision. Moreover some sources[8] seem to allude to a promise by Hadrian to rebuild the temple, a promise which he later withdrew. However, the authenticity of these last texts is so disputed that they need not be considered further.[9]

As to the first two causes, many scholars think that both the prohibition of circumcision and the plan to rebuild Jerusalem are to be seen as consequences rather than as causes of the revolt,[10] in other words that these are measures which were taken after the revolt. There is evidence in Eusebius[11] which points in this direction in connection with the rebuilding. It is difficult to come to any conclusion here because the sources I have mentioned give us too little information. However, we have seen (18.1.1) that Hadrian had Hellenistic buildings erected in various part of his kingdom. His plan to found Aelia Capitolina certainly fits in with this. Since he visited Palestine in about 130, it seems natural that this plan should have come to the fore then. So the plan for Jerusalem must have been at least one of the causes of the rebellion.[12] We have less support for presupposing a prohibition of circumcision. At all events it is going too far to see it as one of the main causes of the revolt.[13]

In addition to all this another point needs to be considered. Schäfer[14] considers the possibility that there was a group of Jews in Palestine who actively supported Hadrian's Hellenistic policy and therefore were very much in favour of changing Jerusalem into the Roman colony of Aelia Capitolina. In that case

Hadrian will have made his plans exclusively in connection with this group and may later have been completely surprised by the opposition of the Jews who were faithful to the law. The revolt of 132-135 and the prelude to it would on this view show similarities in various respects to that against Antiochus IV Epiphanes in the time of the Maccabees. The positive attitude of the Jews who were well disposed to Rome would then be expressed in *Sibylline Oracles* V, 46-50, in which, according to Schäfer, Hadrian is highly praised.

There is a very real possibility that such a group of Jews favourable to Rome did in fact exist in Palestine. It would have been made up above all of those who profited from the Roman occupation. There is no occasion to suppose that they were large in number, but they will doubtless have had the sympathy of the many non-Jewish inhabitants of Palestine. Their influence must therefore not be underestimated. Thus the existence of this group may also have played into the hands of the rebels.

Looking back on this section we get the impression that perhaps a complex of factors influenced the revolt, among which the economic ones must certainly not be lost sight of.

18.2 *The figure of Bar Kochba*

18.2.1 *Name and origin*

Thanks to the discovery of a number of documents and letters in the caves of Murabba'at and Nahal Hever,[15] along with a number of coins,[16] we know a few things about the Jewish leader of the revolt in 132-135. He called himself Simon ben Kosiba, but in the Christian tradition[17] he is called Bar Kochba, which means 'son of the star' (see 18.3). In rabbinic literature he is called Ben or Bar Kozeba/Koziba.[18] This name was probably interpreted as 'son of the lie'.[19]

We have no reliable historical information of any kind about the origins of Bar Kochba.

18.2.2 *Title*

On many coins Bar Kochba is designated 'prince of Israel',[20] as he also is in documents [21] and one letter.[22] The title 'prince' (*nasi*) was used in Talmudic times after 70 for the president of the Beth Din or the head of the Jewish community in Palestine. Those who bore the title in this period were descendants of Hillel. There is some dispute as to what significance the title has in connection with Bar Kochba. Schäfer [23] conjectures that in the time of

Bar Kochba it was not yet associated with descent from Hillel, so that in the case of Bar Kochba it need not have this connotation. We do not find the title messiah or king for Bar Kochba either in documents and letters or on coins. However, while this may be the evidence in Rabbinic literature,[24] it is clear that messianic expectations were bound up both with the figure of Bar Kochba and with the revolt itself (see also 18.3).

18.2.3 *Bar Kochba as leader*

We have some information about Bar Kochba which gives us a vague impression of him as leader of the rebellion.

We find the most important material in the correspondence carried on by and with him.[25] Bar Kochba shows his authority not only in the military sphere but also in social, economic and religious matters. Clearly his leadership extended to all aspects of the people's life. On the basis of the documents that have been discovered containing leases (see 18.1.2) we must assume that Bar Kochba carried out land reforms.

The regulation of religious life has a prominent place in a number of letters. Matters discussed include the raising of tithes[26] and the Feast of Tabernacles.[27] The sabbath year also seems to be significant in the leases (cf. Mur 24B, 24C, 24D). The importance attached to religious life by the rebels also emerges in the designation 'the priest Eleazar' on a number of coins.[28] This could indicate that in addition to political power, the priesthood was also restored, perhaps even in the framework of a newly established sacrificial cult.[29] Be this as it may, Eleazar must be regarded as one of the leaders of the revolution, subordinate to Bar Kochba. An identification of him with Rabbi Eleazar ben Azariah or Eleazar of Modein, an uncle of Bar Kochba, cannot be substantiated.[30]

All this information about Bar Kochba gives the impression that he was the undoubted leader of the revolt.

18.3 *The role of Rabbi Akiba and the other rabbis*

According to rabbinic sources,[31] the famous rabbi Akiba regarded Bar Kochba as the 'star of David' which was expected on the basis of Num.24.17. In this connection Akiba also called him 'king Messiah'. With this interpretation Akiba was going back to the old traditions like those in Qumran (cf. CD VII, 18-20).

This positive attitude attributed to Akiba in connection with Bar Kochba seems to go against that of other rabbis – at all events the majority of them. The designation 'son of the lie' in rabbinic literature (see 18.2.1) suggests that the rabbinic authorities were very suspicious about Bar Kochba's enterprise. Now it may well be that these sayings were only written later and therefore after the revolt, when it was already evident to what a catastrophe this revolt had led, but despite this we do not get the impression that many rabbis were very enthusiastic about the revolt, although we really have no specific details of their attitude during the years 132-135. Granted, there are the lists of the 'ten martyrs',[32] on which some rabbis from about 135, including Akiba, are mentioned, but it is very uncertain how far these lists are historically reliable. On the whole the rabbis were not inclined towards revolution, so that in his sympathy for Bar Kochba, Akiba may be regarded as an exception. It therefore seems most probable that apart from Akiba and some followers, most rabbis kept as far from the revolution as they could.

The fact that Akiba's positive attitude is described so explicitly in the rabbinic literature also argues strongly for its historical authenticity. People might have preferred to keep quiet about such a misconception on the part of one of the most important rabbis in later times.

18.4 *The course of the revolt*

18.4.1 *The scene of the struggle*

The big question is whether the whole of Palestine was affected by this revolt. There is uncertainty over Galilee, Samaria and Transjordan. Dio Cassius (LXIX 13,1) speaks of 'all Judaea', but it is conceivable that here he meant the whole land.[33] On the other hand, on the basis of an investigation into information in the Talmud, Büchler[34] has indicated that the revolt was limited to Jerusalem and its wider environs. This view of Büchler's is largely shared by Schäfer, who after a thorough investigation of all the sources[35] comes to the conclusion that the revolt was limited to part of Judaea and at most a small part of Samaria. Others, however, think that the revolt must have spread much further.[36]

Presumably Judaea was the major scene of the revolt, but that does not mean that there were no disturbances and skirmishes with the Romans in the rest of Palestine in 132-135. A more passive attitude in Galilee might perhaps be explained by the fact that even before the outbreak of the revolt a strong Roman contingent was stationed there.[37] However, that does not mean to say that no Galileans fought on Bar Kochba's side (cf. Mur.43.4).

18.4.2 *The beginning of the revolt*

On the basis of the most important sources,[38] we must assume that the revolt began in early 132.[39] The coins from the time of the rebellion also seem to point in this direction. Three kinds of coins have been found, two kinds dated after the first and second year of the revolt respectively and a group of undated coins, most of which are regarded as coming from the third year.[40] So the duration of the revolt can presumably be put at about three years. Current Roman coins were also used for the striking of these coins, the oldest of which come from 131/132. These Roman coins must have been in circulation up to the beginning of the revolt. This gives an indication that the revolt began in 132.[41]

The rebels must soon have occupied a number of fortresses (including Herodium), strongholds and caves, which served as a kind of hiding place. This can be inferred from a report by Dio Cassius (LXIX 13,1-14,1) that in a later phase the Romans recaptured fifty important fortresses from the rebels. The city of Jerusalem may also have fallen into the hands of the rebels at a very early stage, though we have no solid information about this.[42] However, some contemporaries[43] report an occupation and devastation of Jerusalem. Had the city not been in the hands of the rebels, something of this kind would not have happened.

An open battle with the Romans was carefully avoided by Bar Kochba's troops. A fierce guerrilla war was waged against them from strategic positions.[44]

At the time when the rebellion began, Tineius Rufus was procurator in this area. He and his troops could not cope with the rebels, which was why to begin with Bar Kochba and his men were successful, above all thanks to the element of surprise. The result of this successful beginning was that Bar Kochba's following rapidly increased. However, it soon became evident that these successes could only be repeated because the Romans did not have enough troops in the country. This siutation would soon change.

18.4.3 *The further development of the struggle*

At a later stage of the rebellion Hadrian ordered one of his most famous commanders, Julius Severus, to put it down. Severus pursued the tactic of hunting down the rebels and blockading them when they hid in caves. In this way they were forced to surrender to the Romans through lack of food and the like. The burial places in the caves at Nahal Hever show the cruel scenes which must have taken place there.[45] In this way Severus was therefore able successively to eliminate the rebels.

We have no accurate information about the precise course of events in the fight between Bar Kochba and the Romans. The letters from the Murabba'at caves mentioned above suggest that the situation gradually got worse for Bar Kochba. The last phase of the campaign involved the occupation and capture of the fortress of Bethar. This place, not far from Jerusalem,[46] was, like Engedi, an important base for the rebels. Bethar must have been very easy to defend because the fortress was surrounded on three sides by ravines, while the fourth side was a kind of fortified ditch.[47]

When the city was finally taken by the Romans, there must have been some bloody scenes, though the later descriptions are probably somewhat exaggerated.[48] Bar Kochba and Rabbi Akiba must have been among the dead.

In Jewish tradition the fall of Bethar is dated on 9 Ab (m.Ta'an IV, VI), the day of the commemoration of the destruction of the first and second temples. However, this must be a theological symbol rather than a historical recollection.

The fall of Bethar was not the final end of the revolt. There are indications[49] that the Romans took more time to eliminate centres of resistance in the caves in the wilderness of Judah.

18.5 *Consequences of the revolt*

The Roman victory over Bar Kochba and his followers must have cost them dearly. This is to be concluded from the fact that in his account of this event to the Roman senate Hadrian left out the customary formula 'all is well with me and my legions' (Dio Cassius LXIX 14,3). Moreover Judaea had suffered so much from the revolt that to all intents and purposes an important province was lost to Rome.[50]

Even more serious were the consequences for the Judaeans themselves. Countless of them were killed in battle, while after the revolt many were sold as slaves. The story even goes that the number of Judaean slaves was so great that in the market in Hebron a Jewish slave did not cost much more than a horse.[51]

Jerusalem was now a completely Gentile city under the name of Aelia Capitolina. Judaeans were forbidden to enter the city on pain of death.[52] According to Dio Cassius (LXIX 2,1), a shrine to Jupiter was built on the site of the ruined temple, but this seems far from certain.[53]

In various rabbinic sources it is suggested that during and above all after the revolt there was a religious persecution in Palestine. Circumcision, the observance of the sabbath and the teaching of the Torah are said to have been forbidden. All we can demonstrate with any certainty is a prohibition of circumcision, since later under Antoninus Pius (138-161) the rescinding of such a prohibition is recorded.[54]

After this revolt an extremely hard and difficult time dawned for the Jewish people. Deprived of their political homeland, the Torah was the only bond that held them together. History has shown just how strong this bond has been over the course of time.

NOTES

Chapter 1   Introduction

1. For the use of this term see H.Jagersma, *A History of Israel in the Old Testament Period*, London and Philadelphia 1982, 2.

2. See n.1.

3. See also Jagersma, op.cit., 1f.

4. E.g. M.A.Beek, *Das Danielbuch*, Leiden 1935, differs.

5. For a detailed account of all this see e.g. J.C.H.Lebram, 'Perspektiven der gegenwärtigen Danielforschung', *JSJ* 5, 1974, 1-33, and K.Koch (ed.), *Das Buch Daniel*, EdF 144, Darmstadt 1980.

6. Thus F.Crüsemann, 'Die unveränderbare Welt. Überlegungen zur Krisis der Weisheit beim Prediger (Kohelet)', in W.Schottroff-W.Stegemann (eds.), *Der Gott der kleinen Leute* I, Munich 1979, 80ff.

7. See e.g. J.H.Charlesworth, *The Old Testament Pseudepigrapha*, New York and London 1983; G.W.Nickelsburg, *Jewish Literature between Bible and Mishnah*, Philadelphia and London 1981; J.A.Soggin, *Introduction to the Old Testament*, ²1980, 429-73; J.T.Nelis, 'Joodse literatuur uit de periode tussen Oude en Nieuwe Testament', *BH* 2b, Kampen 1983, 118-47.

8. Cf. e.g. K.D.Schunck, *1.Makkabäerbuch*, JSHRZ I, 4, Gütersloh 1980, 291f.; Nelis, op.cit., 125f.

9. See e.g. C.Habicht, *2. Makkabäerbuch*, JSHRZ I, 3, Gütersloh 1979, 185ff.

10. For more details on this question see e.g. J.T.Nelis, *I Makkabeeën*, BOT, Roermond 1972, 16ff.; id., *II Makkabeeën*, BOT, Bussum 1975, 17-34; J.R.Bartlett, *The First and Second Books of the Maccabees*, CBC, Cambridge 1973, 14ff.; 215ff.

11. See further Schürer I, 34-7.

12. Thus e.g. also M.A.Beek, *A Short History of Israel*, London 1963, 166. For *BJ* see also H.Lindner, *Die Geschichtsauffassung des Flavius Josephus im Bellum Judaicum. Gleichzeitig ein Beitrag zur Quellenfrage*, AGAJU XII, Leiden 1972; T.Rajak, *Josephus. The Historian and His Society*, London 1983, 78ff.

13. See further Lindner, op.cit., 135-41: R.Mayer-C.Möller, 'Josephus, Politiker und Prophet', in *Josephus-Studien* (FS Otto Michel), Göttingen 1974, esp. 271-3.

14. But cf. also H.F.Weiss, 'Pharisäismus und Hellenismus. Zur Darstellung des Judentums in der Geschichte des jüdischen Historikers Flavius Josephus', *OLZ* 74, 1979, 421-33.

15. Cf. Schürer I, 57f. But see also Rajak, op.cit., 233-6.

16. For this see e.g. E.Bickerman, 'Un document relatif à la persécution d'Antiochos IV Epiphane', *RHR* 114, 1937, 188-221; id., 'Ein jüdischer Festbrief vom Jahre 124

v.Chr. (II Macc.1.1-9)', *ZNW* 32, 1933, 233-54, and I. Gafni, 'On the Use of I Maccabees by Josephus Flavius', *Zion* 43, 1978, 81-95.

17. See H.St J.Thackeray, *Josephus, The Man and the Historian*, New York 1929, 100-24.

18. For further information about Josephus see e.g. Thackeray, op.cit.; Schürer I, 43-63; A.Schalit (ed.), *Zur Josephus-Forschung*, WdF 84, Darmstadt 1973; O.Betz-K.Haacker-M.Hengel (ed.), *Josephus Studien* (FS O.Michel), Göttingen 1974; S.J.D.Cohen, *Josephus in Galilee and Rome. His Vita and Development as a Historian*, Leiden 1979; and also especially H.Schreckenberg, *Bibliographie zu Flavius Josephus*, ALGHJ I, XIV, Leiden 1968, 1979; Rajak, op.cit., and L.H.Feldman, *Josephus and Modern Scholarship (1937-1980)*, Berlin and New York 1984.

19. In this connection see F.Jacoby, *Die Fragmente der griechischen Historiker* I-III, Berlin-Leiden 1923ff.; T.Reinach, *Textes d'auteurs grecs et romains relatifs au Judaïsme*, Hildesheim 1963; M.Stern, *Greek and Latin Authors on Jews and Judaism* I-II, Jerusalem 1974, 1980.

20. See A.M.A.Hospers-Jansen, *Tacitus over de Joden (Hist.5,2-13)*, Groningen 1949.

21. For this group see also 9.4.

22. There is a good survey in e.g. G.Vermes, *The Dead Sea Scrolls. Qumran in Perspective*, London 1977, 142ff.

23. In this connection see also C.J.den Heyer, 'Het Ontstaan en de Ontwikkeling van het Nieuwe Testament', in A.F.J.Klijn (ed.), *Inleiding tot de studie van het Nieuwe Testament*, Kampen 1982, 12ff.

24. For more detail on this literature see e.g. G.F.Moore, *Judaism in the First Centuries of the Christian Era* I, Cambridge, Mass. 1958, 125-78; Schürer I, 68-118; J.Maier, *Geschichte der jüdischen Religion*, Berlin and New York 1972, 122ff.; and H.L.Strack-G.Stemberger, *Einleitung in Talmud und Midrasch*, Munich 71982.

25. Cf.e.g. B.Jongeling, 'Een Aramees boek Job uit de bibliotheek van Qumran', *Exegetica* (Nieuwe reeks 3), Amsterdam 1974, 12ff.

26. See H.Lichtenstein, 'Die Fastenrolle. Eine Untersuchung zur jüdisch-hellenistischen Geschichte', *HUCA* 8-9, 1931/32, 257-31, and J.Derenbourg, *Essai sur l'histoire et la géographie de la Palestine*, Paris 1867, 439-46.

27. For the significance of the archaeology of Palestine see further e.g. H.J.Franken and C.A.Franken-Battershill, *A Primer of Old Testament Archaeology*, Leiden 1963; F.Crüsemann, 'Alttestamentliche Exegese und Archäologie. Erwägungen angesichts des gegenwärtigen Methodenstreits in der Archäologie Palästinas', *ZAW* 91, 1979, 177-93; E.Noort, *Biblisch-archäologische Hermeneutik und alttestamentliche Exegese*, Kamper Cahiers 39, Kampen 1979; and C.H.J.de Geus, 'De ontwikkeling van de Palestijnse archeologie en haar betekenis voor de bijbelwetenschap', *BH* 1, 94-109. Accounts of recent excavations can regularly be found in journals like *BA, IEJ, PEQ, RB* and *ZDPV*.

28. See Schürer I, 6-16, and the literature given there.

29. Cf. F.M.Cross, 'The Discovery of the Samaria Papyri', *BA* 26, 1963 = *BAR* 3, 227-39, and P.W. and N.Lapp, *Discoveries in Wadi ed-Daliyeh*, AASOR 41, Cambridge, Mass. 1976.

30. The papyri which are significant for Palestine can be found in *CJP* I, nos.2a, 2b, 2c, 2d, 4, 5. Cf. also P.W.Pestman (ed.), *Greek and Demotic Texts from the Zenon Archive*, I-II, Leiden 1980, esp. no.32.

31. See Y.Yadin, *Masada*, London 1966.

32. See Y.Yadin, *Bar-Kokhba. The Rediscovery of the Legendary Hero of the Last Jewish Revolt against Imperial Rome*, London 1971. Cf. also *DJD* II, 119ff.

33. *Hist* III, 9.

34. M.Noth, 'Die Geschichte des Namens Palästina' (1939), *ABLA* I, Neukirchen-Vluyn 1971, 294-308.

35. See C.H.J. de Geus, 'Idumea', *JEOL* 26, 1979-1980, 53-74; W.Schottroff, 'Die Ituräer', *ZDPV* 98, 1982, 125-52.

Chapter 2   The Beginning of the Hellenistic Period

1. For this see the detailed account in e.g. J.G.Droysen, *Geschichte des Hellenismus* I, Hamburg 1836; W.W.Tarn and G.T.Griffith, *Hellenistic Civilization*, London [3]1952; R.Bichler, *Hellenismus. Geschichte und Problematik eines Epochenbegriff*, Impulse der Forschung 46, Darmstadt 1983.

2. Cf. A.H.M.Jones, *The Greek City from Alexander to Justinian*, Oxford 1940.

3. See G.J.D.Aalders, 'De Hellenistische wereld', *BH* 2b, Kampen 1983, 97.

4. Cf. P.Grimal, *FWG* 6, p.18.

5. See H.Bengtson, *FWG* 5, p.292.

6. Bengtson, op.cit., 305.

7. Ibid., 303.

8. For this see the outstanding survey in J.P.Levy, *L'économie Antique*, Que sais-je? 1155, Paris 1969, 45ff., and also M.Cary, *A History of the Greek World, 323-146 BC*, London 1972, 287-306.

9. Defended by K.Elliger, 'Ein Zeugnis aus der jüdischen Gemeinde im Alexanderjahr 332 v.Chr.', *ZAW* 62, 1950, 63-115, esp. 107-10, and M.Delcor, 'Les allusions à Alexandre le Grand dans Zach.ix.1-8', *VT* 1, 1951, 110-24.

10. *AJ* XI, 325ff.

11. b.Yoma 69a.

12. *AJ* XI, 321-5.

13. See F.M.Cross, 'Aspects of Samaritan and Jewish History in Late Persian and Hellenistic Times', *HTR* 59, 1966, 201ff.

14. See in M.Stern, *GLAJJ* I, Jerusalem 1974, 448.

15. See in H.G.Kippenberg, *Garizim und Synagoge*, Berlin and New York 1971, 46.

16. Thus e.g. F.M Cross, 'The Discovery of the Samaria Papyri', *BA* XXVI (1963) = *BAR* 3, 236f.; G.E.Wright, *Shechem*, London 1965, 181; M.Stone, *Scriptures, Sects and Visions*, New York 1980, 27. But cf. also Kippenberg, op.cit., 46f.; R.J.Coggins, *Samaritans and Jews. The Origins of Samaritanism Reconsidered*, Oxford 1975, 107f.; P.Schäfer, *Geschichte der Juden in der Antike*, Neukirchen-Vluyn 1983, 21.

17. Thus S.H.Horn, 'Shechem. History and Excavations of a Palestinian City', *JEOL* 18, 1964, 305f.; G.E.Wright, op.cit., 173; K.Jaroš-B.Deckert, *Studien zur Sichem-Area*, OBO 11a, Göttingen 1977, 47ff.; R.T.Anderson, 'Mount Gerizim: Navel of the World', *BA* 43, 1980, 218; J.Negenman, *Geografische gids bij de bijbel*, Boxtel 1981, 302.

18. See Coggins, op.cit., 110; B.Reicke, *The New Testament Era*, London 1969, 30.

19. The name 'Samaritans' only comes into use later and is therefore strictly speaking

incorrect here, as also in H.Jagersma, *History of Israel in the Old Testament Period*, London and Philadelphia 1982, 207f. In the period described here they are referred to, for example, as Shechemites.

20. As in Jagersma, op.cit., 208.

21. See *AJ* XI, 342.

22. See also V.Tcherikover, *Hellenistic Civilization and the Jews*, Philadelphia 1961, 42ff.; Kippenberg, op.cit., 56; and Schäfer, op.cit., 20.

23. See Kippenberg, op.cit., esp. 57; Coggins, op.cit., esp. 97.

24. See also M.Delcor, 'Le temple d'Onias en Egypte', *RB* 75, 1968, 188-203; Coggins, op.cit., 112; D.E.Gowan, *Bridge Between the Testaments*, Pittsburgh ²1980, 167. G.Fohrer, *History of Israelite Religion*, London 1973, 368, differs.

25. Thus e.g. Kippenberg, op.cit., 59ff.

26. Thus e.g. Coggins, op.cit., 164.

27. See e.g. Gen.12.6f; 33.18-20; Josh.24; I Kings 12.

28. See A.Alt, *Der Stadtstaat Samaria*, Berichte über die Verhandlungen der Sächsischen Akademie der Wissenschaften zu Leipzig. Phil.hist.Klasse. Band 101, Heft 5, 1954 = *KS* III, 301.

Chapter 3 The Period of the Diadochi (c.323-301 BC)

1. Cf. Diodorus Siculus XVIII, 28, 3-4.

2. Cf. Diodorus Siculus XIX, 93, 2.

3. Cf. Diodorus Siculus XIX, 93, 5-7.

4. Cf. P.Grimal, *FWG* 6, p.59.

5. Cf. e.g. O.Plöger, *Das Buch Daniel*, KAT XVIII, Gütersloh 1965, 155; M.Delcor, *Le livre de Daniel* (SB), Paris 1971, 222; A.Lacoque, *Le livre de Daniel*, CAT XVb, Neuchâtel-Paris 1976, 159.

6. Cf.E.Bickerman, *From Ezra to the Last of the Maccabees*, New York ⁶1975, 46f.

7. *Contra Apionem* I, 186-9.

8. Thus also P.Schäfer, *IJH*, 570.

9. Cf. Y.Meshorer, *Jewish Coins of the Second Temple Period*, Tel Aviv 1967, 36.

10. For the Nabataeans see e.g. J.R.Bartlett, 'From Edomites to Nabataeans: A Study in Continuity', *PEJ* 111, 1979, 53-66.

11. Cf. Diodorus Siculus XIX, 94-5.

12. Cf. Diodorus Siculus XIX, 110, 1-3.

13. See Schürer II, 146 and n.324.

14. Cf. *contra Apionem* I, 208-11; *AJ* XII, 4-6.

15. Cf. *AJ* XII, 7.

16. Cf. Letter of Aristeas 12-13.

17. Thus F.M.Abel, *Histoire de la Palestine* I, Paris 1932, 31.

18. Thus e.g. V.Tcherikover, *Hellenistic Civilization and the Jews*, Philadelphia-Jerusalem 1961, 56f.; M.Hengel, *Jews, Greeks and Barbarians*, London and Philadelphia 1980, 19.

19. See A.Schalit, *König Herodes. Der Mann und sein Werk*, Berlin 1969, 187ff.

20. See M.Hengel, *Judaism and Hellenism* I, London 1974, 20f.

21. See Schürer II, 200ff.

22. Cf. Aboth I.1.

23. *AJ* XII, 142.

24. See also in Diodorus Siculus, LX, 3,5 and on this Stern, *GLAJJ* I, 28.

25. For this question see Stern, op.cit., 31; cf. also G.Alon, 'Par'irtin. On the History of the High Priesthood at the End of the Second Temple Period', in *Jews, Judaism and the Classical World. Studies in Jewish History in the Times of the Second Temple and the Talmud,* Jerusalem 1977, 48ff.

26. *AJ* XI, 347.

27. Thus e.g. Abel, op.cit., 41.

28. On this see J.T.Nelis, *I Makkabeeën*, BOT, Roermond 1972, 211f.; M.Hengel, *Judaism and Hellenism* II, 50 n.124.

29. *AJ* XII, 43; 57. Cf. also the fact that the Simeon mentioned in Luke 2.25 is regarded as 'righteous', i.e. just.

30. Cf. m.Aboth I,2; b.Yoma 39a,b; b.Menahoth 109b.

31. See Schalit, op.cit., 190 and n.150.

32. See S.Freyne, *Galilee from Alexander the Great to Hadrian (323 BCE to 135 CE)*, Wilmington, Delaware 1980, 25.

33. See e.g. B.van Elderen, 'Nieuwtestamentische geografie', *BH* 1, Kampen 1981, 68ff.

34. See S.T.Parker, 'The Decapolis Reviewed', *JBL* 94, 1975, 437-41.

35. For all these cities see now M.Rostovtzeff, CAH VII, 192.

36. *AJ* XIII, 364.

Chapter 4   The First Half-Century of Ptolemaic Rule (301-246 BC)

1. See M.Hengel, *Judaism and Hellenism* I, London 1974, 18.

2. See M.Rostovtzeff, in CAH VII, 113ff.; H.G.Kippenberg, *Religion und Klassenbildung im antiken Judäa. Eine religionssoziologische Studie zum Verhältnis von Tradition und gesellschaftlicher Entwicklung*, Göttingen ²1981, 79.

3. Cf. C.Préaux, *L'économie royale des Lagides*, Brussels 1939, 297ff.; Rostovtzeff, CAH VII, 136ff.

4. Cf. J.P.Lévy, *L'économie antique*, Que sais-je?, no.1155, Paris 1969, 53f.

5. See W.Clarysse, 'Egyptian Estate-Holders in the Ptolemaic Period', in E.Lipiński (ed.), *State and Temple Economy in the Ancient Near East* II, Louvain 1979, 731ff.

6. See the *Chronicle of Jerome*, ed. R.Helm, GCS 47, 127f.

7. See J.Negenman, *Een geografie van Palestina*, Palaestina Antiqua 2, Kampen 1982, 108ff.

8. Cf. *EAEHL* I, p.15.

9. See Schürer II, esp. 121ff., 142ff.

10. See *EAEHL* I, p.253. For the last-mentioned cities see also A.Alt, 'Galiläische Probleme', *KS* II, Munich 1964, 384ff.

11. See Schürer II, 155f.

12. Cf.M.Stern, in H.H.Ben-Sasson, *Geschichte des jüdischen Volkes* I, Munich 1978, 233ff.

13. Polybius V 86, 10.

14. Thus A.Kasher, 'First Jewish Military Units in Ptolemaic Egypt', *JSJ* 9, 1978, 57-67.

15. Cf. Kippenberg, op.cit., 78ff.

16. Cf. Kippenberg, op.cit., 78-82, 93.

17. Cf.M.Rostovtzeff, *The Social and Economic History of the Hellenistic World* I, Oxford 1941, 278ff.

18. In this connection see *CPJ* no.6.

19. See *AJ* XII, 169f.

20. See Rostovtzeff, CAH, 130.

21. Cf. Kippenberg, op.cit., 79.

22. Edited e.g. by P.W.Pestman, *Greek and Demotic Texts from the Zenon Archive*, Papyrologica Lugduno-Batava XX A and B, I,II, Leiden 1980, and see also *CPJ* nos.1-16.

23. *CPJ*, nos 4,5.

24. See the Letter of Aristeas, 84ff., and Diodorus Siculus, XL 3.

25. See Rostovtzeff, CAH VII, 193.

26. Thus too Hengel, op.cit., 24.

27. See also F.Crüsemann, 'Hiob und Kohelet', in *Werden und Wirken des Alten Testament* (FS Claus Westermann), Göttingen 1980, 392, and also the literature mentioned in nn.90,91.

28. Cf. e.g. J.P.M.van der Ploeg, *Prediker*, BOT, Roermond-Maaseik 1953, 8ff.; H.W.Hertzberg, *Der Prediger*, KAT XVII, 4-5, Gütersloh 1963, 45ff.; A.Lauha, *Kohelet*, BKAT XIX, Neukirchen-Vluyn 1978, 3. We find a completely different view in C.F.Whitley, *Koheleth. His Language and Thought*, BZAW 148, Berlin and New York 1979, who thinks in terms of about 152 BC.

29. In this connection see Crüsemann, op.cit., 386, and the literature listed in n.69 there.

30. For all this see now also Crüsemann, 'Hiob und Kohelet', and id., 'Die unveränderbare Welt. Überlegungen zur "Krisis der Weisheit" beim Prediger (Kohelet)', in W.Schottroff and W.Stegemann, *Der Gott der kleinen Leute* I, *Altes Testament*, Munich 1979, 80-104, and the criticism of it by D.Michel, 'Qohelet-Probleme. Überlegungen zu Qoh 8,2-9; 7.11-14', *Theologica Viatorum* 15, 1979/80, 81-105.

31. See n.27.

Chapter 5   The Second Half-Century of Ptolemaic Rule (246-198 BC)

1. Cf. P.Grimal, *FWG* 6, p.157.

2. Thus e.g. M.Hengel, *Jews, Greeks and Barbarians*, London and Philadelphia 1980, 29; cf. also p.147 n.42.

3. Cf. Grimal, op.cit., 154.

4. Cf. W.W.Tarn, CAH VII, 719.

5. *AJ* XII, 159.

6. For the arguments see M.Hengel, *Judaism and Hellenism* II, London 1974, 179 n.76.

7. *AJ* XII, 159.

8. *Contra Apionem* II, 48.
9. Thus B.Mazar, 'The House of Tobiah', *Tarbiz* 12, 1941, 122 (in Hebrew). See further on the Tobiads e.g. A. Büchler, *Die Tobiaden und die Oniaden im II. Makkabäerbuch und in der verwandten jüdisch-hellenistischen Literatur* (1899), Hildesheim 1975; although on some points this is dated, it still has much useful information. Cf. also B.Mazar, 'The Tobiads', *IEJ* 7, 1957, 137-45, 229-38; V.Tcherikover, in A.Schalit, *The World History of the Jewish People*, Vol.6: *The Hellenistic Age*, Jerusalem 1972, 96ff.
10. *AJ* XII, 160-236.
11. See e.g. Tcherikover, op.cit., 98.
12. Cf. *CPJ*, nos. 2d, 4,5.
13. *CPJ*, no.2d and cf. also *AJ* XII, 233.
14. Se O.Plöger, 'Hyrkan im Ostjordanland', in *Aus der Spätzeit des Alten Testaments*, Göttingen 1971, 92ff.
15. *AJ* XII, 175ff.
16. Cf. M.Hengel, *Judaism and Hellenism* I, London 1974, 269.
17. Cf. *AJ* XII, 180-5.
18. Hengel, *Judaism and Hellenism*, 53.
19. Cf. *AJ* XII, 200.
20. Cf. *AJ* XII, 168.
21. Cf. *AJ* XII, 185-6; also *CPJ*, no.5.
22. Cf. *AJ* XII, 187ff., 206.
23. See Grimal, op.cit., 172 and Tarn, op.cit., 772ff.
24. Cf. Polybius V,34 and Tarn, op.cit., 727.
25. Cf. Polybius V, 58-61,2.
26. Cf. Polybius V, 40,1-3; 61,3-62,6.
27. Cf. Polybius V, 71, 11,12.
28. Thus e.g. Büchler, op.cit., 65f.; Hengel, *Judaism*, 8. M.Stern, *GLAJJ* I, 112f., differs.
29. For Joppa see B.Lifhitz, 'Beiträge zur palästinischen Epigraphik', *ZDPV* 78, 1962, 82f. and for Marisa F.J.Bliss and R.A.S.Macalister, *Excavations in Palestine during the Years 1898-1900*, London 1902, 62ff.
30. Cf. F.M.Abel, *Histoire de la Palestine* I, Paris 1952, 82.
31. Hengel, *Judaism and Hellenism* I, 269.
32. Cf. P.Jouguet, 'Les Lagides et les Indigènes', *RBPH* 2, 1923, 419-45, and also Abel, op.cit., 84.
33. Polybius XVI, 22a, 6.
34. In a report in *AJ* XII, 136, taken from Polybius.
35. Cf. *AJ* XII, 129-30, 139.
36. Cf. *AJ* XII, 141.
37. See Sirach 50.1. Cf. *AJ* XII, 141.
38. Cf. *AJ* XII, 138-44.
39. Cf. *AJ* XII, 133 and also Stern, op.cit., 134.
40. Cf. *AJ* XII, 136.
41. Cf. *AJ* XII, 138ff. and also 6.2.1.

Chapter 6 The Beginning of Seleucid Rule (198-175 BC)

1. See F.M.Abel, *Histoire de la Palestine* I, Paris 1952, 104.
2. Cf. Diodorus Siculus XVIII, 3; XXIX, 15; Strabo, *Geographica* VII, 223.
3. See Abel, op.cit., 105.
4. See E.Meyer, *Ursprung und Anfänge des Christentums* II, Stuttgart 1925, 127 n.21; E.Bickerman, 'La Charte séleucide de Jérusalem' (1935), *Studies in Jewish and Christian History* II, Leiden 1980, 44-85; A.Alt, 'Zu Antiochos' III. Erlass für Jerusalem', *ZAW* 57, 1939, 283-5.
5. Cf. H.Jagersma, 'The Tithes in the Old Testament', *OTS* XXI, Leiden 1981, 126f.
6. *AJ* XII, 145f.
7. Cf.E.Bickerman, 'Une proclamation séleucide relative au temple de Jérusalem' (1937), *Studies in Jewish and Christian History* II, Leiden 1980, 86-104.
8. *BJ* V, 194. Cf. also *AJ* XV, 417.
9. Cf. Acts 21.26ff.; Philo, *Leg. ad Gaium*, 31; and above all, E.Bickerman, 'The Warning Inscriptions of Herod's Temple' (1947), *Studies in Jewish and Christian History* II, Leiden 1980, 210-24.
10. See Y.H.Landau, 'A Greek Inscription found near Hefziba', *IEJ* 16, 1966, 54-70.
11. Cf. Landau, op.cit., 66 n.15.
12. See e.g. G.A.te Stroete, 'Van Henoch tot Sion', in *Vruchten van de Uithof (feestbundel voor H.A.Brongers)*, Utrecht 1974, 120-33.
13. See *AJ* XII, 197-202, 213-20; also Abel, op.cit. 107; M.Hengel, *Judaism and Hellenism* I, London 1974, 272.
14. Cf. Hengel, op.cit., 272 and *AJ* XII, 229-36.
15. Thus at least Josephus in *AJ* XII, 229ff. Cf. also O.Plöger, 'Hyrkan im Ostjordanland' (1955), in *Aus der Spätzeit des Alten Testaments*, Göttingen 1971, 90-101.
16. *AJ* XII, 228f.
17. Cf. Abel, op.cit.; V.Tcherikover, *Hellenistic Civilization and the Jews*, Philadelphia and Jerusalem ²1961, 464f. n.10; Hengel, op.cit., 25.
18. On this see E.Bickerman, 'Héliodore au temple de Jérusalem' (1939-44), in *Studies in Jewish and Christian History*, Leiden 1980, 159-91.
19. Thus e.g P.Schäfer, *Geschichte der Juden in der Antike*, Stuttgart 1983, 51f.
20. Cf. Tcherikover, op.cit., 156ff.
21. Cf. II Macc.10.11; Strabo, *Geographica* XVI 2,2, 34, and also J.T.Nelis, *I Makkabeeën*, BOT, Roermond 1972, 95.
22. Thus S.Freyne, *Galilee from Alexander the Great to Hadrian (323 BCE to 135 CE)*, Wilmington and Notre Dame 1980, 33.
23. Thus A.Alt, 'Galiläische Probleme' (1940), *KS* II, Munich ³1964, 404 and n.3. Cf. also *AJ* XII, 154, 175.
24. *AJ* XII, 156.
25. H.G.Kippenberg, *Garizim und Synagoge*, Berlin and New York 1971, 74 and n.70.
26. See now H.Stadelmann, *Ben Sira als Schriftgelehrter. Eine Untersuchung zum*

Berufsbild des vor-makkabäischen Sofer unter Berücksichtigung seines Verhältnisses zu Priester-Propheten- und Weisheitslehrertum, WUNT 2,6, Tübingen 1980.

27. Cf. Hengel, op.cit, 131; G.Sauer, *Jesus Sirach*, JSHRZ III, 5, Gütersloh 1981. T.Middendorp, *Die Stellung Jesu Ben-Siras zwischen Judentum und Hellenismus*, Leiden 1972, 141.

28. See E.Janssens, *Das Gottesvolk und seine Geschichte*, Neukirchen-Vluyn 1971, 16ff.; te Stroete, op.cit., 120-33.

29. Cf. e.g. Middendorp, op.cit., 7-34.

30. For this see e.g. A.Sisti, 'Riflessi dell'epoca premaccabaica nell'Ecclesiastico', *RivBib* 12, 1964, 215-56; Hengel, op.cit., 138f.

31. Middendorp, op.cit. For this material see now especially P.C.Beentjes, *Jesus Sirach en Tenach*, Nieuwegein 1981.

32. For this passage see Beentjes, op.cit., 176-86.

33. Thus Hengel, op.cit., 134.

34. See also J.C.H.Lebram, *Legitimiteit en Charisma. Over de herleving van de contemporaine geschiedschrijving in het jodentom tijdens de 2ᵉ eeuw v.Chr*, Leiden 1980, 7.

Chapter 7   The Prelude to the Revolt

1. For this see M.Rostovtzeff, CAH VII, 160.

2. Cf. Polybius, XXIX 27.8; Livy, XLV 12.4ff. For the relationship between Rome and the Ptolemies see also H.Heinen, 'Die politische Beziehungen zwischen Rom und dem Ptolemäerreich von ihren Anfängen bis zum Tag von Eleusis (273-168 v.Chr.)', *ANRW* I, 1, Berlin – New York 1972, 633-59.

3. See J.G.Bunge, 'THEOS EPIPHANES. Zu den ersten fünf Regierungsjahren Antiochos IV Epiphanes', *Historia* 23, 1974, 57-85.

4. Cf. V.Tcherikover, *Hellenistic Civilization and the Jews*, Philadelphia and Jerusalem ²1961, 466 n.17, and also II Macc.4.29.

5. See *AJ* XII, 238.

6. M.Hengel, *Judaism and Hellenism* I, London and Philadelphia 1974, 277.

7. Cf. E.Bickerman, *The God of the Maccabees*, Leiden 1979, 39.

8. Thus Hengel, op.cit., 279.

9. See J.A.Goldstein, *I Maccabees*, AB, New York 1976, 115 n.75.

10. See also Goldstein, op.cit., 115f.

11. Thus F.Millar, 'The Background to the Maccabean Revolution; Reflections on Martin Hengel's *Judaism and Hellenism*', *JJS* 29, 1978, 1ff. Cf. also the review of *Judaism and Hellenism* by J.C.H.Lebram in *VT* XX, 1970, esp. 505.

12. See II Macc.4.23. According to Josephus, *AJ* XII, 238, however, he was a brother of Onias III and Jason. But this is wrong, see Schürer I, 149 n.30.

13. The reading in II Macc.3.4 that he came from Benjamin is wrong. See C. Habicht, *2.Makkabäerbuch*, JSHRZ I, 3, Gütersloh 1979, 210 n.4b.

14. See *AJ* XII, 239ff.

15. Thus II Macc.4.39-42.

16. See II Macc.4.32-38; also Dan.11.22b.

17. Thus Bickerman, op.cit., 43.

18. See *AJ* XII, 239.

19. See also Hengel, op.cit., 280.

20. See *AJ* XII, 239-40.

21. See *AJ* XII, 229.

22. Thus also Tcherikover, op.cit., 187-90; E.Bickerman, op.cit., 46.

23. Thus e.g. F.M.Abel, *Histoire de la Palestine* I, Paris 1952, 119; Schürer I, 150ff.; T.Fischer, *Seleuciden und Makkabäer*, Bochum 1980, 257.

24. Thus e.g. Hengel, op.cit., 11, 280f.; Bickerman, op.cit., 45.

25. Op.cit., 187-9, followed e.g. by Goldstein, op.cit., 122.

26. The chronology is still disputed. See the literature mentioned in J.C.H.Lebram, 'König Antiochus im Buch Daniel', *VT* XXV, 1975, 737 n.3, and now also K.Bringmann, *Hellenistische Reform und Religionsverfolgung in Judäa. Eine Untersuchung zur jüdisch-hellenistischen Geschichte (175-163 v.Chr.)*, Göttingen 1983, 15ff.

27. Cf. Schürer I, 50.

28. Cf. Tcherikover, op.cit., 392ff.

29. Cf. Bickerman, op.cit., 47.

30. Cf. Polybius XXVI 1,11 and see also O.Mørkholm, *Antiochus IV of Syria*, Classica et Mediaevalia, Copenhagen 1966, and Bickerman, op.cit., 79.

31. J.G.Bunge, 'Die sogenannte Religionsverfolgung Antiochus IV Epiphanes und die griechischen Städte', *JSJ* 10, 1979, 155-65.

32. Cf. also J.C.H.Lebram, *Legitimiteit en Charisma*, Leiden 1980, 26 n.44.

33. Lebram, *Legitimiteit*, 16, 26 and also 'König Antiochus', esp. 754-61.

34. J.G.Bunge, 'Die Feiern Antiochos IV Epiphanes in Daphne in Herbst 166 v.Chr.', *Chiron* 6, 1976, 64ff. does this, but in order to connect I Macc.1.41-51 with a procession of Antiochus IV in Daphne. For this see e.g. the criticism by K.Bringman, op.cit., 35.

35. Cf. also Hengel, op.cit., 286f.

36. According to II Macc.6.2, Zeus Xenios, see below.

37. Cf. E.Bickerman, 'Un document rélatif à la persécution d'Antiochos IV Epiphane' (1937), *Studies in Jewish and Christian History* II, Leiden 1980, 105-35. Cf. also A.Alt, 'Galiläische Probleme' (1940), *KS* II, Munich ³1964, 398 n.2 and A.Schalit, 'Die Denkschrift der Samaritaner an König Antiochus Epiphanes zu Beginn der grossen Verfolgung der jüdischen Religion im Jahre 167 v.Chr. (Josephus, *AJ* XII, 258-64)', *ASTI* 8, 1970/71, 131-83.

38. See H.G.Kippenberg, *Garizim und Synagoge*, Berlin-New York 1971, 79.

39. Cf. Kippenberg, op.cit., 76.

40. Ibid., 80ff.

41. See Hengel, op.cit., 286f.; Bickerman, *God of the Maccabees*, 83f.; Bringman, op.cit., 103.

42. *Hist.* V.7.4.

43. See A.M.A.Hospers-Jansen, *Tacitus over de Joden*, Groningen 1941, esp. 156.

44. See the literature mentioned in n.41.

45. See II Macc.13.3 and especially *AJ* XII, 384.

46. See e.g. M.Delcor, *Le livre de Daniel*, SB, Paris 1973, 175-7, 201.

47. *The God of the Maccabees*, 88f.

48. Cf. K.Toki, 'The Dates of the First and Second Books of Maccabees', *AJBI* III, 1977, 69-83.

49. Cf. also Lebram, *Legitimiteit*, 17.

50. Cf. also Bickerman, *God of Maccabees*, 54.

51. C.J.den Heyer, *De messiaanse weg* I, Kampen 1983, 148.

52. Thus e.g. H.H.Rowley, *The Relevance of Apocalyptic*, London 1961, 13; D.S.Russell, *Between the Testaments*, London and Philadelphia ²1963, 93ff.; T.C.Vriezen, *The Religion of Ancient Israel*, London 1967, 266.

53. Thus G.von Rad, *Old Testament Theology* II, Edinburgh and New York 1965, 306ff. For this view of von Rad and also the views of the authors mentioned in n.52 see R.Wilson, 'From Prophecy to Apocalyptic. Reflections on the Shape of Israelite Religion', *Semeia* 21, 1981, 79-95, but he fails to recognize that there is a direct line from prophecy or wisdom to apocalyptic.

54. Thus P.A.H. de Boer, *Het oudste Christendom en de Antieke Cultuur* I, Haarlem 1951, 444-78.

55. O.Plöger, *Theocracy and Eschatology*, Oxford and Philadelphia 1968.

56. See e.g. D.S.Russell, *The Method and Message of Jewish Apocalyptic*, London and Philadelphia 1964; also J.M.Schmidt, *Die jüdische Apokalyptik*, ²1976, 277ff.

57. For this see e.g. I. Willi-Plein, *Das Geheimnis der Apokalyptik*, *VT* XXVII, 1977, 62-81.

58. See further e.g. den Heyer, op.cit., 150.

59. For details see e.g. A.S.van der Woude, *Die messianische Vorstellungen der Gemeinde von Qumrân*, Assen 1957, and also E.M.Laperrousaz, *L'attente du Messie en Palestine à la veille et au début de l'ère chrétienne*, Paris 1982, 75-333.

60. See also M.Noth, 'The Understanding of History in Old Testament Apocalyptic', in *The Laws in the Old Testament*, Edinburgh 1966 reissued London 1984, 194-214; G.I.Davies, 'Apocalyptic and Historiography', *JSOT* 5, 1978, 15-28, and above all also den Heyer, op.cit., 149ff.

61. Cf. K.Koch, *Das Buch Daniel* (EdF 144), Darmstadt 1980, 8ff. Fischer, op.cit., 140, differs; he thinks in terms of 160/159 BC.

62. Cf. Koch, op.cit., 59-61.

63. See e.g.Plöger, op.cit., 17; Hengel, op.cit., 176; A.Lacocque, *Le livre de Daniel* (CAT XVb), Neuchâtel-Paris 1976, 20ff. Delcor, op.cit., 15ff., assumes this for the second part of Daniel.

64. J.C.H.Lebram, 'Apokalyptik und Hellenismus im Buche Daniel. Bemerkungen und Gedanken zu Martin Hengels Buch über Judentum und Hellenismus', *VT* XX, 1970, 523f.

65. See 8.1.3.

66. See Lebram, 'König Antiochus'.

67. Cf. J.T.Milik, *The Books of Enoch: Aramaic Fragments of Qumran Cave 4*, Oxford 1976.

68. See M.A.Knibb, *The Ethiopic Book of Enoch*, Oxford 1979.

69. See e.g. J.M.Myers, *I & II Esdras*, AB, New York 1974, 52f.

70. Cf. Myers, op.cit., 8-15.

71. See N.Poulssen, *Judith*, BOT, Roermond 1969, 8f. According to E.Zenger, *Das Buch Judith*, JSHRZ I, 6, Gütersloh 1981, 431, however, this book was not written before 150 BC.

Chapter 8   The Maccabaean Struggle

1. See M.Hengel, *Judaism and Hellenism* I, London 1974, 56.
2. Cf.*AJ* XII, 265. But cf. also I Macc.2.1 and J.A.Goldstein, 'The Hasmonaeans: The Dynasty of God's Resisters', *HTR* 68, 1975, 53-8. In the Talmud the term 'Hasmonaean' is used exclusively, see e.g. b.Sabbat 21b.
3. Cf. Neh.5.1-13 and on it my *History of Israel in the Old Testament Period*, London and Philadelphia, 1982, 205.
4. See H.Kippenberg, *Religion und Klassenbildung im antiken Judäa*, Göttingen ²1982, 81.
5. E.Bickerman, *The God of the Maccabees*, Leiden 1979, 90f.
6. Thus also e.g. O.Plöger, *Theocracy and Eschatology*, Philadelphia and Oxford 1968; L.Finkelstein, *The Pharisees*, II, Philadelphia ³1966, 573; Hengel, op.cit., 181. H.A.Brongers, 'De chasidim in het Boek der Psalmen', *NTT* 8, 1954, 297, and others differ.
7. Cf. I Macc.2.31-32; *AJ* XII, 272.
8. Cf. I Macc.2.33-38; *AJ* XII, 274.
9. Cf. I Macc.2.41; *AJ* XII, 276.
10. See J.T.Nelis, *I Makkabeeën*, BOT, Roermond 1972, 90; J.A.Goldstein, *I Maccabees*, AB, New York 1976, 13ff.
11. Cf. I Macc. 3.13-26 and on it B.Bar-Kochva, 'Seron and Cestius Gallius at Beit Huron', *PEQ* 108, 1976, 13ff.
12. See I Macc.3.31 and e.g. also F.M.Abel, *Histoire de la Palestine* I, Paris 1952, 136f.; J.A.Goldstein, *I Maccabees*, 252.
13. The events which now follow are put in I Macc. and II Macc. in a different order. I describe them in the generally accepted order. For these problems see A.Penna, 'Le spedizioni di lisa nella versione Peshitta', *Studii Biblici Franciscani Liber Annuus* 13, 1962/63, 93-100; P.Schäfer, in J.H.Hayes and J.Maxwell Miller, *Israelite and Judaean History*, London and Philadelphia 1977, 564ff.
14. Cf. also S.Wibbing, 'Zur Topographie einzelner Schlachten des Judas Makkabäus', *ZDPV* 78, 1962, 159ff.
15. Cf. also Polybius XXI.9, and D.Mendels, 'A Note on the Tradition of Antiochus IV's Death', *IEJ* 31, 981, 53-6.
16. See e.g. O.Roth, *Rom und die Hasmonäer*, BWAT 17, Leipzig 1914, 8. T.Fischer, 'Zu den Beziehungen zwischen Rom und den Juden im 2.Jahrhundert v.Chr.', *ZAW* 86, 1974, 90-3; id., 'Rom und die Hasmonäer. Ein Überblick zu den politischen Beziehungen 164-37 v.Chr.', *Gymnasium* 88, 1981, 139ff.
17. Thus B.Z.Wacholder, 'The Letter from Judah Maccabee to Aristobulus: Is 2 Maccabees 1:1b-2:18 Authentic?', *HUCA* 48, 1977, 89-133.
18. See Nelis, op.cit., 51ff.
19. For contacts with Egypt in this period see e.g. M.A.Beek, 'Relations entre Jérusalem et la diaspora égyptienne au 2ᵉ siècle avant J.C.', *OTS* XI, Leiden 1943, 119-43.
20. Cf. I Macc.6.58ff.
21. *AJ* XII, 383.
22. *AJ* XIII, 383.
23. See M.Delcor, 'Le temple d'Onias en Egypte', *RB* 75, 1968, 188-203;

R.Hayward, 'The Jewish Temple of Leontopolis: A Reconsideration', *JJS* 33, 1982, 429-43.

24. Cf. I Macc.7.26-50; *AJ* XII, 402-12.

25. Cf. also *AJ* XII, 417ff. and Diodorus LX, 2.

26. For this treaty cf. Roth, op.cit., 3ff.; T.Fischer, *Seleukiden und Makkabaër*, Bochum 1980, 105ff.

27. See Roth, op.cit., 10; Fischer, op.cit. (n.26), 108. J.G.Bunge, *Untersuchungen zum zweiten Makkabäerbuch*, Bonn 1971, 660 n.59a and Schäfer, op.cit., 589, differ.

28. See the literature mentioned in n.16.

29. See Polybius, XXXIII, 18, 6ff.

30. For all this see I Macc.11.1-19; *AJ* XIII, 103-19.

31. For this location see H.Donner, *Einführung in die Biblische Landes- und Altertumskunde*, Darmstadt 1976, 109f.; A.Schalit, *König Herodes. Der Mann und sein Werk*, Berlin 1969, 196f.; Schürer I, 175 n.15.

32. Cf. I Macc.9.50; *AJ* XIII, 15.

33. See Nelis, op.cit., 175.

34. See I Macc.9.35f.; *AJ* XIII, 11. Cf. also *BJ* 1, 47.

35. See Jagersma, *History*, 96f.

36. In *AJ* XII, 414, 419, 434, however, Josephus states that Judas succeeded Alcimus; this is impossible because Judas had already been killed in 161 BC. Moreover, according to an early rabbinic tradition Mattathias and all his sons were high priests, but cf. J.Derenbourg, *Essai sur l'histoire et la géographie de la Palestine, d'après les Thalmuds et les autres sources rabbiniques*, Paris 1867, 58.

37. Thus H.Stegemann, *Die Entstehung der Qumrangemeinde*, Bonn 1971, 250f. This theory has been taken over with some qualifications by J.G.Bunge, 'Zu Geschichte und Chronologie des Untergangs der Oniaden und des Aufstiegs der Hasmonäer', *JSJ* 6, 1975, 1-46, and in part also by J.Murphy-O'Connor, 'Demetrius I and the Teacher of Righteousness (I Macc.X, 25-45)', *RB* 83, 1976, 400ff.

38. For this see e.g. H.Burgmann, 'Das umstrittene Intersacerdotium in Jerusalem 159-152 BC', *JSJ* 11, 1980, 135-76.

39. H.Kreissig, *Wirtschaft und Gesellschaft in Seleukidenreich*. Schriften zur Geschichte und Kultur der Antike 16, Berlin 1978, 112.

40. See Nelis, op.cit., 202.

41. Cf. I Macc.11.54ff.; *AJ* XIII, 131ff., and Diodorus XXXI, 2.4a.

42. See H.Wilrich, *Urkundenfälschung in der hellenistisch-jüdischen Literatur*, Göttingen 1924, 23-7, and also F.M.Abel, *Les Livres des Maccabées*, Paris 1949, 231-3.

43. Thus rightly Nelis, op.cit., 212. Goldstein, op.cit.(n.10), 455ff., differs.

44. Cf.A.Alt, 'Galiläische Probleme' (1940), *KS* II, Munich 1964, 389f.

Chapter 9   The Origin and Development of Some Important Groups

1. For this see e.g. J.LeMoyne, *Les Sadducéens*, Paris 1972, 67ff.; H.Mulder, *De Sadduceeën. Deconfessionalisering in bijbelse tijden*, Amsterdam 1973, 13f.

2. For a survey see J.Wellhausen, *Die Pharisäer und die Sadducäer*, Göttingen ³1967, 56ff.

3. See in *AJ* XIII, 173; XVIII, 16f.; *BJ* II, 164-6.

4. For a survey see Le Moyne, op.cit., 159-63, and H.Mulder, op.cit., 16-24.

5. See H.Jagersma, *A History of Israel in the Old Testament Period*, London 1982, 104 and 243 n.62.

6. See Le Moyne, op.cit., 163 and n.11.

7. See e.g. b.Sukkah 43b.

8. Cf. J.Jeremias, *Jerusalem in the Time of Jesus*, London ⁴1979, 154f., 193f.

9. See Schürer II, 409 n.16; also Le Moyne, op.cit., 113-15.

10. Cf. Le Moyne, op.cit., 335.

11. Ibid., 388.

12. Thus also E.M.Smallwood, *The Jews under Roman Rule from Pompey to Diocletian. A Study in Political Relations*, Leiden ²1981, 17.

13. E.Bammel, 'Sadduzäer und Sadokiden', *ETL* 55, 1979, 107-15.

14. Cf. e.g. *AJ* XIII, 298; ARNa I.5.

15. See also M.Stern, 'Aspects of Jewish Society: The Priesthood and Other Classes', in S.Safrai and M.Stern, *The Jewish People in the First Century* II, Assen 1976, 610f.

16. See further e.g. D.Flusser, 'Josephus and the Sadducees and Menander', *Immanuel* 7, 1977, 61ff.

17. See J.Neusner, *The Rabbinic Traditions about the Pharisees before 70*, Parts I, II, III, Leiden 1971.

18. Thus Schürer II, 396. According to K.Schubert, *Die jüdischen Religionsparteien in neutestamentlicher Zeit*, SBS 43, Stuttgart 1970, this relates to their separation from the Hasidaeans.

19. See m.Hag II, 7; m.Sotah III,4; Yaddayim IV, 6-8.

20. See e.g. E.Lohse, *The New Testament Environment*, London 1976, 77f.; P.R.Davies, 'Hasidim in the Maccabaean Period', *JJS* 28, 1977, 127-40; Schürer II, 400.

21. Neusner, op.cit.

22. Neusner, op.cit., Part III, 318, speaks in this connection of a 'society of table fellowship'.

23. For this see M.Smith, 'Palestinian Judaism in the First Century', in M.Davis, *Israel: Its Role in Civilization*, New York 1956, 67-81.

24. Cf. also G.Alon, 'The Attitude of the Pharisees to Roman Rule and the House of Herod', in *Jews, Judaism and the Classical World*, Jerusalem 1977, 18-47.

25. J.Neusner, *From Politics to Piety*, New York 1979.

26. Wellhausen, op.cit., 94.

27. Cf. *AJ* XIII, 297 and e.g. also J.Maier, *Geschichte der jüdischen Religion*, New York 1972, 20-3.

28. Cf. m.Aboth I, 1ff. and also E.Bickerman, 'La Chaîne de la tradition pharisienne', in *Studies in Jewish and Christian History* II, Leiden 1980, 256-69.

29. Cf.Sirach 15.1-20; 36.10-15; Ps.Sol.9.4.

30. There is a full survey in A.Adam and C.Burchard, *Antike Berichte über die Essener*, Berlin ²1972. See also C.Burchard, 'Die Essener bei Hippolyt', *JSJ* VIII, 1977, 1-41, and D.Graf, 'The Pagan Witness to the Essenes', *BA* 40, 1977, 125-9.

31. Cf *De Vita contemplativa*, 1ff., and also *Quod omnis probus Liber sit*, 75ff.; *Hypothetica* 11.1ff.

32. Cf. S.Wagner, *Die Essener in der wissenschaftlichen Diskussion vom Ausgang des 18. bis 20. Jahrhunderts*, BZAW 79, Berlin 1960, 114-27.

33. Cf.G.Vermes, *Post-Biblical Jewish Studies*, Leiden 1975, 1-9; E.M.Laperrousaz, *L'Attente du Messie en Palestine à la veille et au début de l'ère chrétienne*, Paris 1982, 47.

34. Thus e.g. F.M.Cross, *The Library of Qumran*, New York 1961, 51 n.1; M.Hengel, *Judaism and Hellenism* I, London 1974, 175.

35. See Schürer II, 559.

36. Thus e.g. Vermes, op.cit., 19ff.

37. See n.30.

38. *AJ* XIII, 171.

39. Thus e.g. by W.Bousset, *Die Religion des Judentums*, Tübingen [3]1926, 457; Hengel, op.cit., 175; B.Reicke, *The New Testament Era*, London 1969, 170.

40. See also 9.3.2 and Schürer II, 257.

41. *AJ* XVIII, 21, and *Quod omnis probus Liber sit*, 75.

42. *Quod omnis probus Liber sit*, 76.

43. *Hypothetica*, 11.1.

44. *Naturalis Historia*, V.7.

45. Cf. *AJ* XVIII, 21 and *Quod omnis probus Liber sit*, 79.

46. Cf. *BJ* II, 135.

47. *BJ* II, 123 and 149-50.

48. *Quod omnis probus Liber sit*, 75, and cf. *AJ* XVIII, 19.

49. Cf. *BJ* II, 147.

50. See *AJ* XVIII, 20; *BJ* II, 120 and *Hypothetica* 11.4.

51. See *AJ* XVIII, 21; *BJ* II, 120-21; *Hypothetica*, 11.14-16, and *Naturalis Historia* 73.

52. *BJ* II, 160-61.

53. See *Quod omnis probus Liber sit*, 78.

54. Cf. *BJ* II, 141.

55. Thus e.g. A.Dupont-Sommer, *The Essene Writings from Qumran*, Oxford 1961, 39-67; M.Black, *The Essene Problem*, London 1961; J.P.M.van der Ploeg, *Vondsten in de woestijn van Juda*, Utrecht and Antwerp 1970, 61; F.M.Cross, 'The Dead Sea Scrolls and the People who Wrote Them', *BARev* 3, 1977, 1, 23-32, 51; G.Vermes, *The Dead Sea Scrolls. Qumran in Perspective*, London 1977, 125-30.

56. Thus e.g. R.North, 'The Qumran Sadducees', *CBQ* 17, 1955, 164-80. Cf. also R.Eisenman, *Maccabees, Zadokites, Christians and Qumran*, Leiden 1983, esp. 19ff.

57. Thus e.g. C.Rabin, *Qumran Studies*, Oxford 1957, 53ff.

58. Thus e.g. C.Roth, *The Historical Background of the Dead Sea Scrolls*, Oxford 1958.

59. Thus J.Murphy-O'Connor, 'The Essenes in Palestine', *BA* 40, 1977, 100-24. This view has been strongly challenged by M.A.Knibb, 'Exile in the Damascus Document', *JSOT* 25, 1983, 99-117.

60. The influence of the priest in the community was very great, especially as there is also mention among the community of a priest Messiah, see 7.5.

61. Cf. Cross, op.cit. (n.34), 57ff., 63; R. de Vaux, *Archaeology and the Dead Sea Scrolls*, London 1973, 5,18; J.Maier and K.Schubert, *Die Qumran Essener*, Munich and Basle 1973, 28f.

62. E.M.Laperrousez, *Qumran, L'établissement essénien des bords de la Mer Morte*, Paris

1976, 44ff., 93ff., differs; he thinks that the settlement was uninhabited between 67 BC and the beginning of the reign of Herod the Great.

63. For a full survey of the various views see Vermes, op.cit., 160. There is quite a different view in B.E.Thiering, *Redating the Teacher of Righteousness*, Sydney 1979, 212ff., who argues that there is enough evidence to suggest that John the Baptist is this Teacher. According to J.Starcky, 'Les Maîtres de Justice et la chronologie de Qumrân', in M.Delcor, *Qumrân. Sa piété, sa théologie et son milieu*, Louvain 1978, 249-56, the designation 'Teacher of Righteousness' does not denote a historical figure but a function.

64. One and the same person can also be indicated by these two figures, cf. Vermes, op.cit., 150; also B.E.Thiering, 'Once More the Wicked Priest', *JBL* 97, 1978, 191-205.

65. See the survey in Vermes, op.cit., 161, and also in W.H.Brownlee, *The Midrash Pesher of Habakkuk*, Missoula 1979, 95-8.

66. Thus A.S.van der Woude, 'Wicked Priest or Wicked Priests? Reflections on the Identification of the Wicked Priest in the Habakkuk Commentary', *Essays in Honour of Yigael Yadin*, *JJS* 33, 1982, 349-60.

67. See also Vermes, op.cit., 160.

68. See CD VI, 4-5; VII, 13-19; and also 1QpHab XI.6.

69. Thus e.g. J.T.Milik, *Ten Years of Discovery in the Wilderness of Judaea*, London 1957, 58f., 113f.

70. Thus e.g. R.North, 'The Damascus of Qumran Geography', *PEQ* 87, 1955, 34-48.

71. Thus e.g. I.Rabinovitz, 'A Reconsideration of Damascus', *JBL* 73, 1954, 11-35; A.Jaubert, 'Le pays de Damas', *RB* 75, 1958, 214-48.

72. See Vermes, op.cit., 147f.

73. See de Vaux, op.cit., 5, 18.

74. For a survey see Cross, op.cit.; Vermes, op.cit., 45-86; J.A Fitzmyer, *The Dead Sea Scrolls. Major Publications and Tools for Study*, Missoula 1977, 11ff.

75. K.H.Rengstorf, *Hirbet Qumran und die Bibliothek vom Toten Meer*, Stuttgart 1961, who sees these as the remains of the temple library which was brought there shortly before the fall of Jerualem in AD 70.

76. See *DJD* II.

77. English texts are easily available in G.Vermes, *The Dead Sea Scrolls in English*, Harmondsworth 1970.

78. Edited by Y.Yadin, *The Temple Scroll*, Jerusalem 1977 (in Hebrew)., See also J.Maier, *Die Tempelrolle vom Toten Meer*, Munich 1978; B.Jongeling, 'De Tempelrol', *Phoenix* 15, 1979, 84-99.

79. Cf. Maier, op.cit., 9f.; Jongeling, op.cit. 89. J.Milgrom, 'The Temple Scroll', *BA* 41, 1978, 105-29, himself thinks that a dating around the middle of the second century BC cannot be ruled out.

80. See D.Flusser, 'Pharisäer, Sadduzäer und Essener im Pescher Nahum' (1970), in K.E.Grozinger et al. (ed.), *Qumran*, WdF CDX, Darmstadt 1981, 134ff.

81. See also 7.5 and 8.5.3.

82. See C.Burchard, *Bibliographie zu den Handschriften vom Toten Meer*, BZAW 76, Berlin 1957; id., II, BZAW 89, Berlin 1965; W.S.Lasor, *Bibliography of the Dead Sea*

Scrolls 1948-1957, Pasadena 1958; B.Jongeling, *A Classified Bibliography of the Finds in the Desert of Judah 1958-69*, Leiden 1971.

Chapter 10   The Period of the Hasmonaean Priest-Rulers

1. See 1 Macc.13.31f.; *AJ* XIII, 218-22; Diodorus XXXIII, 28.
2. See T.Fischer, *Untersuchungen zum Partherkrieg Antiochos' VII im Rahmen der Seleucidengeschichte*, Tübingen 1970, and also 10.2.1.
3. Cf. G.F.Moore, *Judaism in the First Centuries of the Christian Era* I, Cambridge, Mass. 1958, 55 n.3. According to J.C. van der Kam, 'II Maccabees 6,7a and the Calendrial Change in Jerusalem', *JSJ* 12, 1981, 52-74, the Seleucid calendar was introduced in the time of Antiochus IV to replace the old priestly calendar.
4. See H.G.Kippenberg, *Religion und Klassenbildung im antiken Judäa*, Göttingen ²1982, 84ff.
5. M.Rostovtzeff, *The Social and Economic History of the Hellenistic World*, Oxford 1941, 1000, 1577f.
6. Kippenberg, op.cit., 91 n.71.
7. See H.Jagersma, 'The Tithes in the Old Testament', *OTS* XXI, Leiden 1981, esp.122ff.
8. Cf. *AJ* XIV, 203.
9. See S.W.Baron, *A Social and Religious History of the Jews* I, Philadelphia ²1952, 367f., and *Encyclopaedia Judaica* 15,629f. According to S.B.Hoenig, *The Great Sanhedrin*, New York 1953, this will already have been the Sanhedrin, but this view is incorrect; see 3.4.2.
10. See e.g. J.T.Nelis, *I Maccabeeën*, BOT, Roermond 1972, 246.
11. Thus e.g. F.M.Abel, *Histoire de la Palestine* I, Paris 1952, 267; Nelis, op.cit., 247; P.Schäfer, in *IJH*, 595. For detailed comments on this letter see J.A.Goldstein, *I Maccabees*, AB, New York 1976, 493f.
12. See B.Kanael, 'The Beginning of Maccabees Coinage', *IEJ* 1, 1950, 170-5; Y.Meshorer, *Jewish Coins of the Second Temple Period*, Tel Aviv 1967, 42f; Schürer I, 190f.
13. Thus W.Wirgin, 'History from Coins', *PEQ* 104, 1972, 104-10.
14. See R.Reich, 'Archaeological Evidence of the Jewish Population at Hasmonean Gezer', *IEJ* 31, 1981, 48ff.
15. Thus Josephus, *AJ* XIII, 236f.
16. See *AJ* XIII, 237ff.; Diodorus XXXIV/XXXV 1,1-5.
17. See Schürer I, 202f. n.5.
18. Cf. *AJ* XIII, 245ff. and Diodorus XXXIV/XXXV 1, 1-5.
19. Cf. *AJ* XIII, 259ff. and also J.C.H.Lebram, 'Eerste ontmoetingen tussen Rome en de Joden', *Phoenix* 26, 1980, 94ff.; T.Rajak, 'Roman Intervention in a Seleucid Siege of Jerusalem?', *Greek, Roman and Byzantine Studies* 22, 1981, 65-81.
20. For this see M.Pucci, 'Jewish-Parthian Relations in Josephus', *The Jerusalem Cathedra. Studies in the History, Archaeology, Geography and Ethnography of the Land of Israel* 3, 1983, 13-25.
21. Cf. J.Negenman, *Een geografie van Palestina* (Palaestina Antiqua 2), Kampen

1982, 119-333. Cf. also G.Foerster, 'Concerning the Conquest of John Hyrcanus in Moab and the Identity of Samaga', *Eretz-Israel* 15, 1981, 353-5 (in Hebrew).

22. Cf. also G.Fuks, 'The Jews of Hellenistic and Roman Scythopolis', *Essays in Honour of Yigael Yadin, JJS* 33, 1982, 407ff.

23. Cf. *AJ* XIII, 255-258; *BJ* I, 63 and also G.Horowitz, 'Town Planning of Hellenistic Marisa: A Reappraisal of the Excavations after Eighty Years', *PEQ* 112, 1980, 95ff.

24. Cf. *AJ* XIII, 255-258; *BJ* I, 63. It is uncertain whether Megillat Ta'anit 22 also relates to this event. Cf. J.Derenbourg, *Essai sur l'histoire et la géographie de la Palestine, d'après les Thalmuds et les autres sources rabbiniques*, Paris 1867, 72.

25. See e.g. John 4.9, and also J.J.Collins, 'The Epic of Theodotus and the Hellenism of the Hasmonaeans', *HTR* 73, 1980, 91-104.

26. Thus e.g. Schürer I, 207; D.E.Gowan, *Bridge Between the Testaments*, Pittsburgh ²1980, 168; B. Reicke, *The New Testament Era*, 66; A.S. van der Woude, in *BH* IIB, 57.

27. Thus e.g. E.Campbell Jr, 'Excavations at Shechem', *BA* 23, 1960, 102ff.; G.E.Wright, *Shechem. The Biography of a Biblical City*, New York and Toronto 1965, 172, 184; P.R.Ackroyd, *AOTS*, 351; D.S.Russell, *The Jews from Alexander to Herod*, Oxford 1967, 63.

28. For these two documents see Schürer I, 204f.

29. See Schürer I, 204ff.; T.Fischer, *Seleukiden und Makkabäer*, Bochum 1980, 64-77. For the first mentioned document see also J.C.H.Lebram, 94ff.

30. Cf. M.Stern, 'The Relations between Judaea and Rome during the Rule of John Hyrcanus', *Zion*, 1961, 1-22.

31. For this letter see E.Bickerman, 'Ein jüdischer Festbrief vom Jahre 124 v.Chr. (II Macc.1.1-9)' (1933), in *Studies in Jewish and Christian History* II, Leiden 1980, 136-58.

32. Thus B.Kanael, 'Ancient Jewish Coins and their Historical Importance', *BAR* 3, 1970, 281ff.; A.Ben-David, 'When did the Maccabees begin to strike their First Coins', *PEQ* 104, 1972, 93-103; U.Rappaport, 'The Emergence of Hasmonean Coinage', *AJSR* 1, 1976, 171-86; B.Daraq and S.Kedar, 'When did the Hasmonaeans begin Minting Coins?', *Qadmoniot* 15, 1982, 29-32 (in Hebrew).

33. Thus Meshorer, op.cit., 56-9, cf. also 43ff.; Schürer II, 603ff.

34. See H.Jagersma, *A History of Israel in the Old Testament Period*, London and Philadelphia 1982, 101, 108.

35. See b.Qidd.66a.

36. See Derenbourg, op.cit., 80 n.1, 95 n.1; Schürer I, 214 n.30; cf. also b.Ber.29a. M.S.Keller, 'Alexander Jannaeus and the Pharisee Rift', *JJS* 30, 1979, 202-11, differs.

37. In this connection see also W.Baars and R.Zuurmond, 'The Project for a New Edition of the Ethiopic Book of Jubilees', *JSS* 9, 1964, 67-74.

38. See e.g. *DJD* I, 82-4; *DJD* III, 77-79, 96-98, and A.S.van der Woude, 'Fragmente des Buches Jubiläen aus Höhle XI (11QJub)', in J.Jeremias and H.Stegemann, *Tradition und Glaube* (FS K.G.Kuhn), Göttingen 1971, 140-6.

39. See also n. 3 and e.g. E.Vogt and H.Cazelles, 'Sur les origines du calendrier des Jubilées. Note sur le calendrier du Déluge', *Biblica* 43, 1962, 202-16; S. van Mierlo, *De oude kalender bij de Hebreeën en zijn verband met de lijdensweek*, Kampen 1963, 9f. and above all J. van Goudoever, *Biblical Calendars*, Leiden 1961, 62ff.

40. See G.L.Davenport, *The Eschatology of the Book of Jubilees* (SPB XX), Leiden 1971; K.Berger, *Das Buch Jubiläen*, JSHRZ II, 3 (Unterweisung in erzählender Form), Gütersloh 1981.

Chapter 11   The Reigns of the Hasmonaean Priest-Kings

1. XVI 2, 40.
2. See also M.Stern, *GLAJJ* I, 307.
3. For this see D.Mendels, 'Hecateus of Abdera and a Jewish *patrios politeia* of the Persian Period', *ZAW* 95, 1983, esp. 104, and the literature mentioned there.
4. See also 10.2.1, 10.2.4.
5. Thus Schürer I, 218. Cf. also *AJ* XIII, 319. S.Freyne, *Galilee from Alexander the Great to Hadrian (323 BCE to 153 CE)*, Wilmington and Notre Dame 1980, 43f., differs.
6. See *BJ* I, 76; Schürer I, 217f.; W.Schottroff, 'Die Ituräer', *ZDPV* 98, 1982, 134.
7. Cf.*AJ* XIII, 324ff.; *BJ* I, 86; and also G.Barkay, 'A Coin of Alexander Jannaeus from Cyprus', *IEJ* 27, 1977, 119-20.
8. Cf.*AJ* XIII, 354ff.; *BJ* I, 87.
9. See M.Stern, 'The Political Background of the Wars of Alexander Janna', *Tarbiz* 33, 1963/4, 325ff.; Schürer I, 134-221.
10. Cf.*AJ* XIII, 372ff. and also J.Derenbourg, *Essai sur l'histoire et la géographie de la Palestine, d'après les Thalmuds et les autres sources rabbiniques*, Paris 1867, 98.
11. Cf.*AJ* XIII, 375f.
12. Cf.*AJ* XIII, 380.
13. Thus e.g. J.M.Allegro, 'Further Light on the History of the Qumran Sect', *JBL* 75, 1956, 92; Y.Yadin, 'Pescher Nahum (4QpNahum) erneut untersucht', *IEJ* 21, 1971, 1ff. H.H.Rowley, '4QpNahum and the Teacher of Righteousness', *JBL* 75, 1956, 192, differs. For more detail on this question see M.Burrows, *More Light on the Dead Sea Scrolls*, London 1958, 201-3.
14. See F.E.Peters, 'The Nabateans in the Hawran', *JAOS* 97, 1977, 263-77.
15. See J.Negenman, *Geografische gids bij de bijbel*, Boxtel 1981, 171.
16. Cf.*AJ* XIII, 392.
17. Cf.*AJ* XIII, 393f. and *BJ* I, 104f.
18. See S.T.Parker, 'The Decapolis Reviewed', *JBL* 94, 1975, 437-31, and B. van Elderen, 'Nieuwtestamentische geografie', *BH* I, Kampen 1981, 68f.
19. Cf.*AJ* XIII, 397.
20. For the situation, etc., of this fortress see F.M.Abel, *Géographie de la Palestine* II, Paris ³1967, 427.
21. Thus *AJ* XIII, 406.
22. See Stern, op.cit (n.9), and also the survey by Josephus in *AJ* XIII, 395-7; also most recently Schürer I, 228 n.31.
23. See B.Mazar, *AOTS*, 227.
24. For the situation of the fortress see *BJ* VIII, 165-70.
25. See Abel, op.cit., 241f.
26. See Y.Yadin, *Masada*, London 1966, 15f.; *EAEHSL* III, esp.805f.
27. See Y.Meshorer, *Jewish Coins of the Second Temple Period*, Tel Aviv 1967, 118f.
28. See Meshorer, op.cit., 59.

29. Thus D.Jesselsohn, 'Hever Yehudim – A new Jewish Coin', *PEQ* 112, 1980, 11-17.

30. For this see J.Klausner, *The Messianic Idea in Israel from Its Beginning to the Completion in the Mishnah*, London 1956, 7-243; S.Mowinckel, *He That Cometh*, Oxford 1956; H.Cazelles, *Le Messie de la Bible*, Paris 1978; C.J. den Heyer, *De messiaanse weg* I, Kampen 1983.

31. See G.L.Davenport, *The Eschatology of the Book of Jubilees*, Leiden 1971, esp. 77.

32. See Test.Simeon VIII, 1-2 and also den Heyer, op.cit., 202ff.

Chapter 12 The Downfall of the Hasmonaean Dynasty

1. See e.g. E.Will, *Histoire politique du monde hellénistique* II, Nancy 1967, 419-34, and P.Grimal in *FWG* 7, p.148.

2. See Grimal, op.cit., 136. M.Grant, *The History of Ancient Israel*, London 1984, 221, differs.

3. Cf. Livy, *Ab urbe condita* C, and Dio Cassius XXXVI 45,3.

4. For this see also H.J.W.Drijvers, 'De Provincia Syria. Grieks Romeinse beschaving in het Nabije Oosten', *Phoenix* 26, 1980, 73ff.

5. See 11.2.6 and also J.Derenbourg, *Essai sur l'histoire et la géographie de la Palestine, d'après les Thalmuds et les autres sources rabbiniques*, Paris 1867, 96-101.

6. Cf. *AJ* XIII, 409. Cf. also *BJ* I, 111.

7. m.Hag.II, 2. But cf. J. Neusner, *The Rabbinic Traditions about the Pharisees before 70*, I, Leiden 1971, 110ff., esp. 141.

8. Thus b.Ber, 48a.

9. Cf. F.M.Abel, *Histoire de la Palestine* I, Paris 1952, 240, and Schürer I, 230.

10. Cf. *AJ* XIII, 410ff.

11. Cf. *AJ* XIII, 418 and *BJ* I, 115-16.

12. Cf. *AJ* XIII, 419-21; Strabo XVI 2,8.

13. Cf. e.g. *AJ* XIII, 427f., and also W.H.Buehler, *The Pre-Herodian War and Social Debate*, Bonn 1974, 40,53.

14. Cf. *AJ* XIII, 427.

15. Thus also Abel, op.cit., 248.

16. Cf. *AJ* XIV, 19-21.

17. Cf. *AJ* XIV, 30.

18. Cf. *AJ* XIV, 29-33.

19. Thus Josephus in *AJ* XIV, 40f., and also Diodorus Siculus in XL, 2.

20. Cf. *AJ* XIV, 34ff.

21. Cited by Josephus in *AJ* XIV, 35f. For this see K.Albert, *Strabo als Quelle des Flavius Josephus*, Würzburg 1902, 27ff.

22. For this see K.Galling, 'Die *terpole* des Alexander Jannäus', in J.Hempel and L.Rost (eds.), *Von Ugarit nach Qumran, FS O.Eissfeldt*, BZAW 77, Berlin ²1961, 49-62, and also H.E. del Medico, '*Zahab parwayim*. L'or fructifère dans la tradition juive', *VT* 13, 1963, 169-83.

23. Cf. *AJ* XIV, 45.

24. Cf. Dio Cassius XL 4,1.

25. Cf. *AJ* XIV, 58ff.; *BJ* I, 145-51 and also on this campaign Dio Cassius XXVIII, 14, 2 and Strabo XVI, 2,40.

26. See Ps.Sol 2,8 and also Tacitus, *Histories* V,9.

27. Cf. Philo, *Leg. ad Gaium* 155 and also E.M.Smallwood, *The Jews under Roman Rule*, Leiden ²1981, 2.

28. Cf. *AJ* XIV, 75f. and *BJ* I, 155f. See also G.Alon, 'The *Strategoi* in the Palestinian Cities during the Roman Epoch', in *Jews, Judaism and the Classical World*, Jerusalem 1977, 458ff.

29. See 11.2.5 and n.18 of that chapter; also H.Bietenhard, 'Die syrische Dekapolis von Pompeius bis Traian', *ANRW* II, 8, Berlin and New York 1977, 220-61.

30. Cf. V.Burr, 'Rom und Judäa im 1.Jahrhundert v.Chr. (Pompeius und die Juden)', *ANRW* I, 1, Berlin and New York 1972, 875-86; also B.Lifhitz, 'Jerusalem sous la domination romaine. Histoire de la ville depuis la conquête de Pompée jusqu'à Constantin (63 a.C.- 325 p.C.)', *ANRW* II, 8, Berlin and New York 1977, 444ff.

31. Thus e.g. M.A.Beek, *A Short History of Israel*, London 1963, 191.

32. Cf. *AJ* XIV, 158 and *BJ* I, 203.

33. Cf. *AJ* XIV, 159ff.

34. Cf. *AJ* XIV, 181-4.

35. *BJ* I, 213. But cf. *AJ* XIV, 180 and A.Schalit, *König Herodes. Der Mann und Sein Werk*, Berlin 1969, 46 n.154.

36. See Grimal, op.cit., 217ff.

37. *AJ* XIV, 302ff., 324ff.

38. See H.G.Kippenberg, *Religion und Klassenbildung im antiken Judäa*, Göttingen ²1982, 110ff.

39. Cf. *AJ* XIV, 342, 412 and 450. However, for Galilee see also E.Loftus, 'The Anti-Roman Revolts of the Jews and Galileans', *JQR* 68, 1977, 78ff.

40. Cf. *AJ* XIV, 303-69; *BJ* I, 248-373.

41. Dio Cassius, XLVIII 26,2.

42. See Y.Meshorer, *Jewish Coins of the Second Temple Period*, Tel-Aviv 1967, 60-3.

43. Cf. *AJ* XIV, 394ff.; *BJ* I, 290ff.

44. Cf. *AJ* XIV, 451ff., *BJ* I, 328ff. and also Dio Cassius XLVIII 41,4-5.

45. Cf. *AJ* XV, 8ff.

46. *AJ* XVIII, 9, 23 and *BJ* II, 118.

47. But cf. *AJ* XVIII, 4.

48. M.Hengel, *Die Zeloten*, Leiden and Cologne 1976, 92.

49. Cf. also G.F.Moore, 'Fate and Free Will in the Jewish Philosophers according to Josephus', *HTR* 22, 1929, 373.

50. In *BJ* IV, V. See e.g. *BJ* IV, 224f.; V, 5ff.

51. Cf. Luke 10.30 and J.T.Nielsen, *Het evangelie naar Lucas* I, PNT, Nijkerk 1979, 317f.

52. Thus e.g. S.W.Baron, *A Social and Religious History of the Jews* II, Philadelphia ²1952, 46-8; S.G.F.Brandon, *Jesus and the Zealots*, Manchester 1967, 26ff.; Hengel, op.cit., esp. 411.

53. K.Kohler, in *Jewish Encyclopaedia* XII, 1907, 639f. Cf. also W.R.Farmer, *Maccabees, Zealots and Josephus*, New York 1956.

54. Cf. J.Klausner, *Jesus of Nazareth*, 274.

55. G.R.Driver, *The Judean Scrolls – The Problem and a Solution*, Oxford 1965.
56. C.Roth, *The Dead Sea Scrolls – A New Historical Approach*, New York 1965.
57. M.Menken, 'De "Zeloten" ', *Vox Theologica* 45, 1975, 30-47.
58. Menken, op.cit., esp. 33ff. Cf. also T.Rajak, *Josephus. The Historian and his Society*, London and Philadelphia 1983, 86ff.
59. Menken, op.cit., 34.
60. Hengel, op.cit., 151ff.
61. Cf. also M.de Jonge, *Jezus, inspirator en spelbreker*, Nijkerk 1971, 101.
62. De Jonge, op.cit., 102.
63. Cf. *AJ* XVIII, 4ff.
64. See S.Applebaum, 'The Zealots: The Case for Revaluation', *JRS* 61, 1971, 155-70, and also H.Kreissig, *Die sozialen Zusammenhänge des judäischen Krieges*, Berlin 1970.

Chapter 13 The Reign of Herod the Great (37-4 BC)

1. There is another view e.g. in W.E.Filmer, 'The Chronology of the Reign of Herod the Great', *JTS* NS 17, 1966, 183-98, which dates the reign of Herod from 38 to 2 BC.
2. For this see Plutarch, *Vita Antonii*, LXI, 1-3.
3. For more details about these events see P.Grimal, in *FWG* 7, 226-9, and H.M.Beliën and F.J.Meijer, *Een geschiedenis van de oude wereld. Historisch overzicht*, Haarlem 1980, 264-6.
4. Cf. Beliën and Meijer, op.cit., 268.
5. Cf. Grimal, op.cit., 230ff.
6. A.Schalit, *König Herodes. Der Mann und sein Werk*, Berlin 1969, is a thorough study of the life and work of Herod. For further details see e.g. also M.Stern, 'The Reign of Herod and the Herodian Dynasty', in *CRINT* I, 216-307.
7. For a survey see Schalit, op.cit., 648ff.
8. Thus e.g. Schalit, 248f. n.11, and cf. also J.T.Nielsen, *Het Evangelie naar Matthëus* I, PNT, Nijkerk ³1978, 52 n.31.
9. For a detailed portrait of Herod see Schalit, op.cit., 605-10.
10. For him see B.Z.Wacholder, *Nicolaus of Damascus*, Berkeley and Los Angeles 1962.
11. Cf. Schalit, op.cit., 674f.
12. Cf. *AJ* XV, 305ff.
13. Cf. J.Gagé, 'L'Empéreur romain et les rois', *Revue Historique* 221, 1959, 221-60.
14. Cf. *AJ* XV, 317 and Strabo XVI, 4,23.
15. Cf. Schalit, op.cit., 146ff.
16. Cf. *AJ* XV, 187ff.; *BJ* I, 386ff.
17. Cf. *AJ* XV, 217.; *BJ* I, 396.
18. *AJ* XV, 360.
19. Cf. Schürer I, 319 n.122 and also *BJ* I, 399.
20. Cf. *AJ* XV, 380ff.; *BJ* V, 181ff.
21. Cf.b.Middoth 34a-37b. See further e.g. also R. de Vaux, 'Le temple de

Jérusalem', in *BeO*, Paris 1967, 312ff. A.Schalit, op.cit., 372-97; D.M.Jacobson, 'Ideas concerning the Plan of Herod's Temple', *PEQ* 112, 1980, 33-40.

22. Cf. *AJ* XV, 417.

23. E.Bickerman, 'The Warning Inscriptions of Herod's Temple', in *Studies in Jewish and Christian History* II, AGJU IX, Leiden 1980, 222ff.

24. H.Geva, 'The "Tower of David" – Phasael or Hippicus?', *IEJ* 31, 1981, 57-65.

25. Cf. *AJ* XV, 417. For excavations relating to the time of Herod the Great in Jerusalem see e.g., J.L.Blok-v.d.Boogert, 'Israëlische opgravingen langs de muur van de tempelberg', *Phoenix* 20, 1974, 345-50; id., 'Recente opgravingen op de westelijke heuvel van het oude Jerusalem', *Phoenix* 22, 1976, 70; *EAEHL* II, 604-8; M.Broshi, 'Along Jerusalem's Walls', *BA* 40, 1977, 12f.; B.Mazar, 'Herodian Jerusalem in the Light of the Excavations South and South-West of the Temple Mount', *IEJ* 28, 1978, 230-7.

26. Cf. *AJ* XV, 280ff.; *BJ* I, 407.

27. Cf. *AJ* XV, 292f.; *BJ* I, 403; Strabo XVI, 2.4.

28. Cf. *AJ* XV, 331f.; XVI, 136ff. Archaeological excavations seem to confirm the information in Josephus, see e.g. R.Bull, 'Caesarea Maritima: The Search for Herod's City', *BA Rev* 8.1, 1982, 25-40; R.L.Hohlfelder, 'Caesarea beneath the Sea', *BA Rev* 8.1, 1982, 42-7, and id. *et al.*, 'Sebastos, Herod's Harbor at Caesarea Maritima', *BA* 46, 1983, 133-43. For the significance of Caesarea see especially L.I.Levine, *Caesarea under Roman Rule*, SJLA 7, Leiden 1973; B.Lifhitz, 'Césarée de Palestine, son histoire et ses institutions', *ANRW* II, 8, 490-518.

29. Cf.M.Kochavi, 'The History and Archeology of Aphek-Antipatris: A Biblical City in the Sharon Plain', *BA* 44, 1981, 75-86.

30. M.Broshi, 'The Cities of Eretz-Israel in the Herodian Period', *Qadmoniot* 14, 1981, 70-9.

31. Cf. E.Netzer, 'The Hasmonean and Herodean Winter Palaces at Jericho', *Qadmoniot* 7, 1974, 27-36, and id., 'Recent Discoveries in the Winter Palaces of Second Temple Times at Jericho', *Qadmoniot* 15, 1982, 21-9.

32. Cf. Schürer II, 1979, 104.

33. Thus according to *BJ* I, 416.

34. Thus according to *BJ* I, 87.

35. See *BJ* I, 419.

36. For this fortress see E.Netzer, *Greater Herodium*, Qedem Monographs of the Institute of Jerusalem 13, Jerusalem 1981.

37. For all these fortresses see also F.M.Abel, *Géographie de la Palestine* II, Paris 1967, 172, 242, 350, 371; *EAEHL* II, 502-10 (Herodium) and III, 792-816 (Masada). Also Schalit, op.cit., 341ff., and Y.Tsafrir, 'The Desert Forts of Judaea in Second Temple Times', *Qadmoniot* 8, 1975, 41-53.

38. Cf.Schalit, op.cit., 271.

39. Cf. J.Jeremias, *Jerusalem in the Time of Jesus*, London [4]1979, 124f.

40. Cf. *AJ* XVII, 205, 308 and *BJ* II, 85f.

41.Cf I Kings 12.1-4 and on this H.Jagersma, *A History of Israel in the Old Testament Period*, London and Philadelphia 1982, 127f.

42. Cf. *BJ* III, 55f. and on it H.G.Kippenberg, *Religion und Klassenbildung im antiken Judäa*, Göttingen [2]1982, 116.

43.Cf. *AJ* XIV, 450.

44. See F.Herrenbrück, 'Wer Waren die Zöllner?'. *ZNW* 72, 1981, 178-94.

45.Cf. *AJ* XV, 365.

46. Schalit, op.cit., 274ff.

47. See Schalit, op.cit., 276 n.439.

48. See Schürer I, 416ff.

49. Thus also Schürer I, 420ff. J.T.Nielsen, *Het evangelie naar Lucas* I, PNT, Nijkerk 1979, 67ff., differs.

50. N.Avigad, 'How the Wealthy Lived in Herodian Jerusalem', *BA Rev* 2,4, 1976, 23-35.

51. Cf. e.g. *BJ* I, 153.

52. Cf. *AJ* XV, 5.

53. Cf. *BJ* I, 358.

54. See e.g. b.BB 3b-4a and the Ascension of Moses 6.2.

55. See Schalit, op.cit., 734.

56. Cf. *AJ* XVII, 149ff.; *BJ* I, 648ff.

57. *AJ* XV, 368ff.; XVII, 42.

58. See Schürer I, 394ff.

59. For these two figures see e.g. Schalit, op.cit., 768-70.

60. Cf. also *AJ* XV, 3-4.

61. *AJ* XIV, 386f.

62. Cf. also Schalit, op.cit., 689f.

63. Cf. *AJ* XV, 50ff.; *BJ* I, 435ff.

64. Cf. *AJ* XVI, 361ff.; *BJ* I, 538ff.

65. See also n.1.

66. *AJ* XVII, 168ff.; *BJ* I, 656.

67. See Schalit, op.cit., 638ff., and especially D.J.Ladouceur, 'The Death of Herod the Great', *Classical Philology* 76, 1981, 25-34.

68. See Matt.22.16; Mark 3.6; 12.13.

69. *AJ* XIV, 450; also *BJ* I, 319 and 351.

70. Schalit, op.cit., 479f. and n.1127.

71. Thus Bickerman, 'Les Hérodiens', *RB* 47, 1938, 184ff.

72. Thus also rightly Schalit, op.cit., 479.

73. See e.g. R.H.Charles, *The Apocrypha and Pseudepigrapha of the Old Testament In English*, II, *Pseudepigrapha*, Oxford 1913, 163-281; J.H.Charlesworth, *The Old Testament Pseudepigrapha*, New York and London 1983, 5-90.

76. See also Charles, op.cit., 625-52.

75. See e.g. J.A.Sanders, *The Psalms Scroll of Qumran Cave 11*, DJD IV, Oxford 1965.

76. See Charles, op.cit., I, *Apocrypha*, 569-95.

77. Published by S.Schechter, *Documents of Jewish Sectaries, Vol.I: Fragment of a Zadokite Work*, Cambridge 1910.

78. See now P.R.Davies, *The Damascus Covenant. An Interpretation of the 'Damascus Document'*, JSOT Suppl.Series 25, Sheffield 1983, esp. 202ff.

79. For a survey of the various studies of the Damascus Document see H.Bardtke, 'Literaturbericht über Qumran VIII. Teil', *TR* NF 39, 1974, 189-221; Davies, op.cit., 5-47.

Chapter 14   The Period from the Death of Herod the Great to Agrippa I
(c. 4 BC to AD 41)

1. Cf. *AJ* XVII, 206f.; *BJ* II, 1ff.

2. For the pilgrimages to Jerusalem see S.Safrai, *Die Wallfahrten im Zeitalter des Zweiten Tempels*, Neukirchen-Vluyn 1981.

3. Cf. *AJ* XVII, 250ff.; *BJ* II, 39ff.

4. The name of this king and of his family appear on an inscription found in' Petra, cf. N.I.Khary, 'A New Dedicatory Nabataean Inscription from Wadi Musa', *PEQ* 113, 1981, esp. 21.

5. Cf. *AJ* XVII, 271ff.; *BJ* II, 56ff.

6. H.Guevara, *La resistencia Judia contra Roma en la época de Jésus*, Meitingen 1981, differs.

7. According to Luke 3.1 Philip ruled over Trachonitis and Ituraea.

8. For this division see *AJ* XVII, 317ff.; *BJ* II, 93ff.

9. Cf. Strabo XVII, 1,13.

10. Cf. also Matt.2.22; *AJ* XVII, 342; *BJ* II, 111.

11. Cf. *AJ* XVII, 342f.; *BJ* II, 111f.

12. Cf. P.Winter, *On the Trial of Jesus*, Berlin and New York [2]1974, 13ff.

13. Cf. *AJ* XVIII, 26; Dio Cassius LV, 27.6.

14. For a detailed account of him see J.P.Lémonon, *Pilate et le gouvernement de la Judée, Textes et monuments*, Paris 1981.

15. For the significance of this city see now K.Beebe, 'Caesarea Maritima: Its Strategic and Political Significance to Rome', *JNES* 42, 1983, 195-207. In the excavations there an inscription has also been discovered with the name of Pilate, see K.R.Veenhof, 'Nieuwe Palestijnse Inscripties', *Phoenix* XI, 2, 1965, 260.

16. For the situation of these areas see Schürer I, 336-8 n.2. For Ituraea see especially W.Schottroff, 'Die Ituräer', *ZDPV* 98, 1982, esp.132.

17. Cf. *AJ* XVIII, 106f.

18. For a detailed account see H.W.Hoehner, *Herod Antipas*, Cambridge 1972.

19. Cf. *AJ* XVIII, 114 and also G.E.Wright, 'Herod's Nabataean Neighbor', *BA* 41, 1978, 123.

20. For the problems see Schürer I, 346 n.24.

21. Cf. H.Kippenberg, *Religion und Klassenbildung im antiken Judäa*, Göttingen [2]1982, 125.

22. See Mark 12.14 par.

23. Cf. Tacitus, *Annals* II, 42 and also E.M.Smallwood, *The Jews under Roman Rule from Pompey to Diocletian*, Leiden [2]1981, 160.

24. Cf. F.Herrenbrück, 'Wer waren die "Zöllner" ', *ZNW* 72, 1981, 189 n.66; 191. See also 5.3.

25. Cf. M.Stern, 'The Province of Judaea'. in *CRINT* I, 1, 133 and L.Schottroff-W.Stegemann, *Jezus van Nazareth – de hoop van de armen*, Baarn 1982, 24.

26. Cf. Herrenbrück, op.cit.,184.

27. Cf. Luke 3.13 and b.Sanh 25b.

28. See S.Applebaum, 'Economic Life in Palestine', *CRINT* I, 2, 631-700 and also Josephus, *Vita* 47, 58.

29. Cf. Kippenberg, op.cit., 152.

30. Thus e.g. J.R.Armenti, 'On the Use of the Term Galileans in the Writings of Josephus Flavius', *JQR* 72, 1981/82, 45-9 and L.H.Feldman, 'The Term Galileans in Josephus', *JQR* 72, 1981/2, 50-2.

31. See J.T.Milik, *DJD* II, 122f.

32. See Applebaum, op.cit., 659; Kippenberg, op.cit., 147.

33. See e.g. Mark 12.1-12 and M.Hengel, 'Das Gleichnis von den Weingärtnern Mc.12,1-12 im Lichte der Zenonpapyri und die rabbinische Gleichnisse', *ZNW* 59, 1968, 1-39.

34. See H.L.Strack and P.Billerbeck, *Kommentar zum Neuen Testament aus Talmud und Midrasch* IV, 2, Munich 1969, 698, also J.Klausner, *Jesus of Nazareth*, London, 1925, 182f. and J.Helderman, 'De vrijkoop in het Nieuwe Testament met name in Mc 10:45 par', *Vox Theologica* 34, 1964, 90f. S.Safrai, 'Home and Family', *CRINT* I, 2, 751 differs.

35. Thus M.Stern, 'Aspects of Jewish Society: The Priesthood and other Classes', *CRINT* I, 2, 628.

36. Cf.S.Krauss, *Talmudische Archäologie* II, Leipzig 1911, 253-311; Klausner, op.cit., 177; Applebaum, op.cit., 576, 680-5; *AJ* XX, 54.

37. See H.Jagersma, *History of Israel in the Old Testament Period*, London and Philadelphia 1982, 120, 137.

38. See M.Elat, 'The Monarchy and the Development of Trade in Ancient Israel', in E.Lipiński (ed.), *State and Temple Economy in the Ancient Near East* II, Louvain 1979, 529, and also Hos.12.8.

39. See e.g. Matt.22.5; Luke 19.13-15; Josephus, *Vita* 70ff.

40. Thus e.g. F.Buhl, *Die sozialen Verhältnisse der Israeliten*, Berlin 1899, 7f.

41. See e.g. E.Otto, *Jerusalem – die Geschichte der Heiligen Stadt*, Stuttgart 1980, 147.

42. Cf. S.Safrai, 'The Temple', in *CRINT I*, 2, 865-9.

43. Cf. Safrai, op.cit., 880.

44. Ibid., 898.

45. See P.Billerbeck, 'Ein Tempelgottesdienst in Jesu Tagen', *ZNW* 55, 1964, 1-17 and Schürer II, 292ff.

46. Cf. J.Maier, 'Tempel und Tempelkult', in J.Maier and J.Schreiner (eds.), *Literatur und Religion des Frühjudentums*, Gütersloh 1973, 380, and the literature mentioned in n.25.

47. See m.Ta'anit IV, I and VII, II. Cf. also Luke 1.22.

48. See the different contributions in Lipiński, op.cit.

49. See V.Tcherikover, *Hellenistic Civilization and the Jews*, Philadelphia and Jerusalem ²1961, 155ff.

50. See S.Krauss, *Synagogale Altertümer*, Hildesheim ²1966, 2ff.; K.Hruby, *Geschichtliche Entwicklung einer Institution*, Zurich 1971, 21ff.; J.Gutman (ed.), *Ancient Synagogues: The State of Research*, Chico 1981, 1ff; L.I.Levine (ed.), *Ancient Synagogues Revealed*, Jerusalem 1981; M.Dothan, *Hammath Tiberias. Early Synagogues and the Hellenistic and Roman Remains*, Jerusalem 1983.

51. Thus e.g. C.H.Kraeling, *The Synagogue. Part I of Final Report VIII on the Excavations at Dura Europos*, Yale and London 1956, and Schürer II, 426.

52. Thus e.g. Hruby, op.cit., 19; M.Hengel, 'Proseuche und Synagoge', in *Tradition und Glaube* (FS K.G.Kuhn), Göttingen 1971, 158ff.

53. Cf. J.T.Nielsen, *Het evangelie naar Lucas* I, Nijkerk 1979, 147.

54. Cf. P.Schäfer, 'Der synagogale Gottesdienst', in J.Maier and J.Schreiner (eds.), *Literatur und Reliigon des Frühjudentums*, Gütersloh 1973, 391; J.J.Petuchowski, 'The Liturgy of the Synagogue: History, Structure and Contents', in W.S.Green (ed.), *Approaches to Ancient Judaism* IV, Chico 1983, 1-64, and also Luke 4.16ff.

55. Cf. Hengel, op.cit (n.52), 165 n.30.

56. See C.Houtman, 'Ezra and the Law', *OTS* XXI, Leiden 1981, 91-15.

57. Cf. Schäfer, op.cit., 394.

58. Cf. *AJ* XIV, 167 and also John 11.47; Acts 22.30.

59. See Schürer II, 212.

60. For a list of high priests at this time see Schürer II, 230.

61. For this see H.G.M.Williamson, 'The Origins of the Twenty-four Priestly Courses; A Study of 1 Chronicles XXIII-XXVII', in J.A.Emerton (ed.), *Studies in the Historical Books of the Old Testament*, SVT XXX, Leiden 1979, 251-68.

62. See also Schürer II, 247ff.

63. Cf. J.Jeremias, *Jerusalem in the Time of Jesus*, London ⁴1979, 181ff.

64. Cf.H.Gese, 'Zur Geschichte der Kultsänger am zweiten Tempel' (1963), in *Vom Sinai zum Sion*, Munich 1974, 147-58.

65. See P.A.H. de Boer, 'De godsdienst van het Jodendom', in J.H.Wassink, W.C.van Unnik and C. de Beus (eds.), *Het oudste Christendom en de antieke cultuur*, I, Haarlem 1951, 484ff.; Schürer II, 322ff.

66. See J.Neusner, *The Rabbinic Traditions about the Pharisees before 70*, I and III, Leiden 1971, pp.184-340 and 255ff. respectively. Also Schürer II, 363f.

67. See Neusner, op.cit., I,II, III and also A.J.Avery-Peck and J.Neusner, 'Die Suche nach dem historischen Hillel', *Judaica* 38, 1982, 194-214.

68. Thus S.Safrai, 'Religion in Everyday Life', *CRINT* I, 2, 793-84.

69. See L.L.Grobbe, 'Orthodoxy in First-Century Judaism: What are the Issues', *JSJ* 8, 1977, 149-53; N.J.McElency, 'Orthodoxy in Judaism of the First Christian Century. Replies to David E.Aune and Lester L.Grobbe', *JSJ* 9, 1978, 83-8.

70. Cf. J.Finegan, *Handbook of Biblical Chronology*, Princeton 1964, 238ff.

71. See e.g. A.F.J.Klijn, *De wordingsgeschiedenis van het Nieuwe Testament*, Utrecht and Antwerp ³1971, 59.

72. Cf.e.g. John 20.30; 21.25. For the traditions about Jesus see introductions to the New Testament and A.F.J.Klijn, *Wat weten wij van Jezus van Nazareth*, 's Gravenhage 1962; G.Vermes, *Jesus the Jew*, London and Philadelphia 1973; id., *Jesus and the World of Judaism*, London and Philadelphia 1983; and now especially E.P.Sanders, *Jesus and Judaism*, London 1985.

73. D.Flusser, *Jesus*, London 1969, 16f., and W.Schneemelcher, *Das Urchristentum*, Stuttgart 1981, 45, differ.

74. See e.g. Schneemelcher, op.cit., 56f.

75. For this problem see Smallwood, op.cit., 168 n.82 and also J.van Goudoever, *Biblical Calendars*, Leiden 1961, 161, 223ff.

76. H.Baarlink, *Anti-Judaisme in hed oudste Evangelie*, Kampen 1979, 16, rightly stresses that this indicates a common basis to Jesus and the Pharisees.

77. See Matt.22.23-33; Mark 12.18-27; Luke 14.20,27-40 and cf. also m.Sanh. XI, 1.

78. According to Flusser, op.cit., 54, the seven 'Woes' of Jesus in Matt.23.13-35 must be seen in this light. For the problems of this pericope cf. also K.Schubert, *Jesus im Lichte der Religionsgeschichte des Judentums*, Vienna 1973, 5ff.; W.S.Duvekot, *Kunnen wij Jezus kennen?*, Kampen nd., 125f.

79. For the relationship of Jesus to the Pharisees. cf. also H.Merkel, 'Jesus und die Pharisäer', *NTS* 1967/68, 194-208 and U.Luz, 'Jesus und die Pharisäer', *Judaica* 38, 1962, 229-46.

80. Thus e.g. by A.Dupont-Sommer, *The Essene Writings from Qumran*, Oxford 1961, 371ff.

81. For this material see also e.g. Schubert, op.cit., 105ff; K.Maier and K.Schubert, *Die Qumran-Essener*, Munich 1973, 124ff.; G.Vermes, *The Dead Sea Scrolls. Qumran in Perspective*, London 1977, 212ff.; J.H.Charlesworth (ed.), *John and Qumran*, London 1972.

82. Thus e.g. by S.G.F.Brandon, *Jesus and the Zealots*, Manchester 1967; P.Lehmann, *The Transfiguration of Politics: Jesus Christ and the Question of Revolution*, New York and London 1975.

83. See e.g. M.Hengel, *Was Jesus a Revolutionist?*, Philadelphia 1971; M.de Jonge, *Jezus. Inspirator en spelbreker*, Nijkerk 1971, 107ff.; Schubert, op.cit., 111ff.; Winter, op.cit., 69.

84. Cf. e.g. Matt.5.38f.; 26.52.

85. For this trial see e.g. J.Blinzler, *Der Prozess Jesu*, Regensburg ^{2}1960; H. van der Kwaak, *Het proces van Jezus*, Assen 1969; Winter, op.cit.,; J.Imbert, *Le procès de Jesus*, Que sais-je? 1896, Paris 1980, and also Lémonon, op.cit., 173-203.

86. Cf.e.g.Klijn, op.cit. (n.71), 72f.

87. Thus Flusser, op.cit.,56; Merkel, op.cit., 196f. differs.

88. *AJ* XX, 199-203 and see D.M.Rhoads, *Israel in Revolution 6-74 CE. A Political History based on the Writings of Josephus*, Philadelphia 1976, 92.

89. See S.Rosenblatt, 'The Crucifixion of Jesus from the Standpoint of Pharisaic Law', *JBL* 75, 1956, 315-21, and Schubert, op.cit., 142ff.

90. Thus Blinzler, op.cit., 109ff.; van der Kwaak, op.cit., 47f.; Imbert, op.cit., 33ff.

91. See Winter, op.cit., 127ff.; Schürer II, 221ff.; Lémonon, op.cit., 74ff.

92. L.Dequeker, *Geschiedenis van het Jodendom en het Zionisme*, Louvain 1982, 31.

93. Cf. also H.Koester, *Introduction to the New Testament* II, Philadelphia and Berlin 1984, 76. E.g. G.J.D.Aalders, *Het Romeinse imperium en het Nieuwe Testament*, Kampen 1938, 128ff., differs.

94. See n.82.

95. See Klijn, op.cit., 36.

96. For this passage see Schottroff-Stegemannn, op.cit., 37f. and C.H.Lindijer, *De armen en de rijken bij Lukas*, 's-Gravenhage 1981, 48ff.

97. Cf. Schottroff-Stegemann, op.cit.

98. Cf. Schottroff-Stegemann, op.cit., 37ff., and Lindijer, op.cit.

99. For the parables see e.g. J.Jeremias, *The Parables of Jesus*, London and New York ^{3}1972, and E.Linnemann, *Parables of Jesus*, London and New York 1966.

100. Koester, op.cit., II, 80ff.

Chapter 15   The Period from Agrippa I to the Beginning of the First Jewish
War (AD 41-66)

1. Thus H.M.Beliën and F.J.Meijer, *Een geschiedenis van de Oude Wereld. Historisch overzicht*, Haarlem 1980, 286.

2. Cf. Tacitus, *Annals* III, 23-25.

3. See Beliën and Meijer, op.cit., 304, and also H.Koester, *Introduction to the New Testament* I, 310f..

4. Cf. Tacitus, *Annals* XV,44.

5. For him see also S.Perowne, *The Later Herods. The Political Background of the New Testament*, London 1958, 58ff.

6. See *AJ* XVII, 252, but cf. Schürer I, 352 n.41.

7. See *AJ* XVIII, 261ff.; *BJ* II, 184ff., Tacitus, *Histories* V,9,7 and P.Bilde, 'The Roman Emperor Gaius (Caligula)'s Attempt to Erect his Statue in the Temple of Jerusalem', *Studia Theologica* 32, 1978, 67-93.

8. See *AJ* XIX, 265ff.; *BJ* II, 206ff.

9. See J.P.Lémonon, *Pilate et le gouvernement de la Judée, Textes et monuments*, 1981, 137ff.

10. Thus e.g. Koester, op.cit., I, 397.

11. See *AJ* XIX, 331; m.Bikk.III, IV, though it is not certain whether here in the Mishnah the reference is to Agrippa I or II.

12. See J.Meyshan, 'The Coinage of Agrippa I', *IEJ* 4, 1954, 186-200; Y.Meshorer, *Jewish Coins of the Second Temple Period*, Tel-Aviv 1967, 78-80, 138-41.

13. See also E.W.Hamrick, 'The Third Wall of Agrippa I', *BA* 40, 1977, 18-23 and E.M.Smallwood, *The Jews under Roman Rule from Pompey to Diocletian. A Study in Political Relations*, Leiden ²1981, 561f.

14. Cf. *BJ* V, 45; VI, 237.

15. See *AJ* XX, 118ff.; *BJ* II, 232ff. According to Tacitus, *Annals* XII, 54, however, at this time Cumanus was openly procurator of Galilee while Felix was governor of Samaria and perhaps also Judaea. For this difference between Josephus and Tacitus see Schürer I, 459 n.15.

16. See *AJ* XX, 160ff.; *BJ* II, 254ff.

17. Cf. also Tacitus, *Histories* V, 9; *Annals* XII, 54.

18. See *AJ* XX, 189ff.

19. See *AJ* XX, 360ff.

20. The former Bethsaida, cf. Schürer II,171f.

21. See *AJ* XX, 159; *BJ* II, 252.

22. Thus e.g. M.Stern, 'The Reign of Herod and the Herodian Dynasty', in *CRINT* I, 301 n.3 and S.Freyne, *Galilee from Alexander the Great to Hadrian (323 BCE to 135 CE)*, Wilmington and Notre Dame 1980, 77.

23. Thus e.g. by Schürer II, 573 n.8 and P.Schäfer, *Geschichte der Juden in der Antike*, Stuttgart 1983, 129.

24. Op.cit., 77.

25. See *AJ* XX, 145.

26. See Meshorer, op.cit., 143-53.

27. Tacitus, *Annals*, XIII, 7.

28. Cf. J.Derenbourg, *Essai sur l'histoire et la géographie de la Palestine, d'après les Thalmuds et les autres sources rabbiniques*, Paris 1867, 252-4.

29. See *BJ* VII, 96ff.

30, For details see Smallwood, op.cit., 572-4.

31. Cf. also S.Applebaum, 'Judaea as a Roman Province: The Countryside as a Political and Economic Factor', *ANRW* II, 8, 355-96.

32. For this place see F.M.Abel, *Géographie de la Palestine* II, Paris 1967, 154, and also Schürer II, 134.

33. See W.Schneemelcher, *Das Urchristentum*, Stuttgart 1981, 86ff.

34. See e.g. Gal.2.9.

35. See Schneemelcher, op.cit., 91ff.

36. See J.Jeremias, *Jerusalem in the Time of Jesus*, London ⁴1979, 130 n.19.

37. See H.J.Klauck, 'Gütergemeinschaft in der klassischen Antike, in Qumran und im Neuen Testament', *RQ* 1, 1982, 47-79.

38. See Smallwood, op.cit., 217 and especially B.Reicke, *The New Testament Era*, London , 245f.

39. Cf. Schneemelcher, op.cit. 95f.

40. According to N.Walter, 'Apostelgeschichte 6.1 und die Anfänge der Urgemeinde in Jerusalem', *NTS* 29, 1983, 387, this group consisting of Hellenists from the Diaspora was responsible for the foundation of an independent organization of the followers of Jesus.

41. E.g. by the time of Acts 15.13ff.

42. Thus e.g. by Schürer II, 498; Reicke, op.cit., 212; Koester, op.cit., II, 200, but see his hesitation on 315.

43. Thus e.g. by H.Mulder, *Geschiedenis van de palestijnse kerk*, Kampen nd, 43ff.; Smallwood, op.cit., 298 n.18, and Schneemelcher, op.cit., 52, 164.

Chapter 16   The First Jewish War (66-74)

1. Cf. also D.M.Rhoads, *Israel in Revolution 6-74 BC*, Philadelphia 1976, esp. 150ff.

2. As H.Kreissig, *Die sozialen Zusammenhänge des jüdischen Krieges*, Berlin 1970, does.

3. U.Rappaport, 'The Relations between Jews and non-Jews and the Great War against Rome', *Tarbiz* 47, 1978, 1-14.

4. Thus also rightly P.Bilde, 'The Causes of the Jewish War according to Josephus', *JSJ* 10, 1979, 179-202, and see also T.Rajak, *Josephus. The Historian and His Society*, London 1983, esp.78ff.

5. See M.Hengel, *Die Zeloten*, Leiden and Cologne 1976, 349ff., and R.A.Horsley, 'Banditry and the Revolt against Rome AD 66-70', *CBQ* 43, 1981, 409-32.

6. Cf. also J.A.Soggin, *A History of Israel. From the Beginnings to the Bar Kochba Revolt AD 135*, London 1984, 327.

7. Cf.C.Roth, 'The Pharisees in the Jewish Revolution of 66-73', *JSS* 7, 1962, 63ff.

8. See e.g. *BJ* II, 411.

9. See also K.Toki, 'Der literarische Character des Bell.Jud.II, 151b-153', *AJBI* 7, 1981, 53-69.

10. Thus also P.Schäfer, *Geschichte der Juden in der Antike*, Stuttgart 1983, 136.

11. Cf. also M.Goodman, 'The First Jewish Revolt: Social Conflict and the Problems of Debt', *Essays in honour of Yigael Yadin, JJS* 33, 1982, 417-27.

12. Cf. *BJ* II, 449ff. and also Meg.Ta'an. 14.

13. Cf. M.Gischon, 'Cestius Gallus' Campaign in Judaea', *PEQ* 113, 1981, 39-62.

14. See L.Kadman, *The Coins of the Jewish War of 66-73 CE*, Corpus Nummorum Palestinensium III, Jerusalem 1960, and Y.Meshorer, *Jewish Coins of the Second Temple Period*, Tel Aviv 1967, 88f.

15. See C.Roth, 'The Constitution of the Jewish Republic of 66-70', *JSS* 9, 1964, 295-319.

16. For this place see F.M.Abel, *Géographie de la Palestine* II, Paris 1967, 366.

17. Cf. *BJ* II, 573f. and *Vita*, 188.

18. For the disputes between Josephus and John of Gischala see now also U.Rappaport, 'John of Gischala: From Galilee to Jerusalem', *Essays in Honour of Yigael Yadin, JJS* 33, 1982, 479ff.

19. S.Freyne, 'The Galileans in the Light of Josephus' Vita', *NTS* 26, 1979/80, 397-413.

20. Cf.*BJ* II, 558; III, 1ff. and Dio Cassius LXIII 22,1.

21. Cf.*BJ* II, 127ff.

22. For this see A.Schalit, 'Die Erhebung Vespasians nach Flavius Josephus, Talmud und Midrasch. Zur Geschichte einer messianischen Prophetie', *ANRW* II,2, Berlin and New York 1975, 208-27.

23. Cf. G.Schmitt, 'Die dritte Mauer Jerusalems', *ZDPV* 97, 1981, 153-70.

24. Cf. Meshorer, op.cit., 90.

25. Cf.*BJ* V, 25f. and Tacitus, *Histories*, V, 12.

26. *BJ* IV, 366f.

27. Cf.*BJ* III, 307ff.

28. A road was probably made between Caesarea and Scythopolis in this period, cf. B.Isaac, 'Milestones in Judaea, from Vespasian to Constantine', *PEQ* 110, 1978, 47. But see also J.Negenman, *Een geografie van Palestina*, Kampen 1982, 130.

29. Cf.*BJ* IV, 503ff. and on this O.Michel, 'Studien zu Josephus', *NTS* 14, 1967/68, 402-8.

30. For this event see in more detail e.g. S.J.Salderini, 'Johanan ben Zakkai's Escape from Jerusalem. Origin and Development of a Rabbinic Story', *JSJ* 6, 1975, 189ff.; J.W.Doeve, 'The Flight of Rabban Yohanan ben Zakkai from Jerusalem', in *Uebersetzung und Deutung (feestbundel voor A.R.Hulst)*, Nijkerk 1977, 50f., and P.Schäfer, 'Die Flucht Johanan b.Zakkais aus Jerusalem und die Gründung des Lehrhauses in Jabne', *ANRW* II 19,2, Berlin and New York 1979, 43-101.

31. See e.g. b.Git.56a-b, ARNa 4, ARNb 6, Midrash Rabba Lam.I, 31 and Midrash Mishle 15.31.

32. A. Momigliano, CAH X, 861.

33. Cf.*BJ* IV, 377ff.

34. Doeve, op.cit., 58.

35. Cf. *BJ* V, 41ff. and Tacitus, *Histories*, V, 1.

36. Cf. *BJ* V, 41ff. and Tacitus, *Histories*, V, 12.

37. See M.Ottoson, 'Fortifikation och Tempel. En studi i Jerusalem topografi', *Religion och Bibel* 38, 1979, 26-39.

38. Cf. Luke 19.43 and *BJ* V, 499ff.
39. Cf. *BJ* VI, 68ff.
40. Cf. *BJ* VI, 94 and m.Ta'an IV, VI.
41. Cf. *BJ* VI, 241 and 254ff.
42. See also E.M.Smallwood, *The Jews under Roman Rule from Pompey to Diocletian. A Study in Political Relations*, Leiden ²1981, 325.
43. *BJ* VI, 343ff.
44. For the siege and fall of Jerusalem see also Dio Cassius LXV, 4-7.
45. See. e.g. *EAEHL* II, 607-10; E.Otto, *Jerusalem – die Geschichte der Heiligen Stadt*, Stuttgart 1980, 163f., and A.S.Kaufman, 'The Eastern Wall of the Second Temple of Jerusalem Revealed', *BA* 44, 1981, 108-15.
46. *BJ* VI, 433f.
47. Cf. *BJ* VII, 163 and *EAEHL* II, 509ff.
48. Cf. *BJ* VII, 190ff.
49. See S.Loffreda, 'Le terme erodiane di Macheronte', *Bibbia e Oriente* 23, 1981, 105-14.
50. See Y.Yadin, *Masada*, 140ff., 164ff. and also A.N.Zadoks and Josephus Jitta, 'Judea in Romeinse tijd: Masada en Herodion', *Hermeneus* 42, 1970, 43f.
51. See Yadin, op.cit., 212ff.
52. See I.A.Richmond, 'The Roman Siegeworks of Masada Israel', *JRS* 52, 1962, 142-55, and Yadin, op.cit., 226ff.
53. *BJ* VII, 319ff.; thus also Yadin, op.cit., 224ff.
54. Or in any case part, see S.J.D.Cohen, 'Masada, Literary Tradition, Archaeological Remains, and the Credibility of Josephus', *Essays in honour of Yigael Yadin, JJS* 33, 1982, 385-405.
55. Thus I.Jacobs, 'Eleazar ben Yair's Sanction for Martyrdom', *JSJ* 13, 1982, 183-6.
56. Yadin, op.cit., 193ff.; Smallwood, op.cit., 338, differs.
57. Thus e.g. F.M.Abel, *Histoire de la Palestine* II, Paris 1952, 42 and N.G.Yoss, 'Massada', *Conscience et liberté* 24, 1982, 40ff.
58. See W.Eck, 'Die Eroberung von Masada und eine neue Inschrift des L.Flavius Silva Nonius Bassus', *ZNW* 60, 1969, 282ff. and id., *Senatoren von Vespasian bis Hadrian*, Munich 1970.
59. Thus also e.g. Soggin, op.cit., 331, but cf. B.Reicke, *The New Testament Era*, London 1969, 289f.n.24.
60. Thus righly Schäfer, op.cit. (n.10). For the consequences of the fall of Jerusalem see now also H.Mulder, *De verwoesting van Jerusalem*, Amsterdam 1977, 59ff.
61. M.Noth, *History of Israel*, London ²1960, 447.
62. Thus rightly R.Rendtorff, 'Das Ende der Geschichte Israels' (1972), *GS* I, Munich 1975, 272.
63. According to I Clem.41.2-3 and Diognetus 3, however, this continued to exist. See also Schürer I, 501f.
64. See H.Jagersma, *History of Israel in the Old Testament Period*, London and Philadelphia, 184.
65. A.Guttmann, 'The End of the Jewish Sacrificial Cult', *HUCA* 38, 1967, 137-48.
66. See also B.Isaac, 'Judaea after 70', *JJS* 35, 1984, 44-50.

Chapter 17 The Period between the Two Wars with Rome

1. Cf e.g. H.M.Beliën and F.J.Meijer, *Een geschiedenis van de Oude Wereld. Historisch Overzicht*, Haarlem 1980, 301-3; H.Koester, *Introduction to the New Testament* I, Berlin and Philadelphia 1982, 322ff.

2. Cf.b.BB 75b.

3. Cf. S.Freyne, *Galilee from Alexander the Great to Hadrian (323 BCE to 135 CE)*, Wilmington and Notre Dame 1980, 101ff.

4. Cf. *BJ* IV, 449.

5. See A.Büchler, *The Economic Conditions of Judaea after the Destruction of the Second Temple*, London 1912. But cf. also S.Applebaum, 'Economic Life in Palestine', in *CRINT* I, 2, 697.

6. Cf.b.Ned.62a.

7. Cf.b.BM V, VIII.

9. See S.Zeitlin, *The Rise and Fall of the Judaean State. A Political, Social and Religious History of the Second Commonwealth* III, Philadelphia 1978, 238ff.

10. See e.g. Num.20.17 and J.Negenman, *Een Geografie van Palestina*, Kampen 1982, 118ff.

11. See also J.Neusner, *A Life of Yohanan ben Zakkai. Ca.1-80 CE*, SPB 6, Leiden ²1970, 166ff.

12. Cf. Schürer I, 325ff.; G.Stemberger, *Das klassische Judentum. Kultur und Geschichte der rabbinischen Zeit*, Munich 1979, 83, and P.Schäfer, *Geschichte der Juden in der Antike. Die Juden Palästinas von Alexander der Grossen bis zur arabischen Eroberung*, Stuttgart 1983, 147.

13. Cf.C.Thoma, 'Auswirkungen der jüdischen Krieges gegen Rom (66-70/73 n.Chr.) auf das rabbinische Judentum', *BZ* 12, 1968, 30ff., 186f.

14. See W.Bacher, *Tradition und Tradenten in den Schulen Palästinas und Babylons*, Berlin 1966, 25ff.

15. Cf. Stemberger, op.cit., 88-90.

16. For him cf. Neusner, op.cit.

17. For him see J.Neusner, *Eliezer ben Hyrcanus. The Tradition and the Man* I, II, Leiden 1973.

18. For him cf. S.Safrai, *The Life and Teaching of Rabbi Akiva Ban Yosef*, Jerusalem 1970 (in Hebrew).

19. For him see J.Gereboff, *Rabbi Tarfon, the Tradition, the Man and Early Rabbinic Judaism*, Missoula 1979; G.F.Willems, *Rabbi Tarfon. Le père de tout Israël (env.50-135 ap.J.C.)*, Brussels 1983.

20. See J.Neusner, 'The Formation of Rabbinic Judaism. Yavneh (Jamnia) from AD 70 to 100', in *ANRW* II, 19,2, Berlin and New York 1979, 3-42.

21. Cf. also Neusner, op.cit. (n.11), 225.

22. Thus Neusner, op.cit., 215, and Schäfer, op.cit., 154. But cf. also G.Alon, 'Rabban Johanan B.Zakkai's Removal to Jabneh', in *Jews, Judaism and the Classical World*, Jerusalem 1977, 269ff.

23. See H.T.de Graaf, *De Joodsche Wetgeleerden in Tiberias van 70-400 n.C.*, Groningen 1902.

24. Cf. Schäfer, op.cit., 154f.

25. Thus e.g. Zeitlin, op.cit., 203, and D.Barthélemy, in *Le canon de l'Ancien Testament*, Génève 1984, 25ff.

26. P.Schäfer, 'Die sogenannte Synode von Jabne', *Judaica* 31, 1975, 54-64.

27. See M.Smith, *Palestinian Parties and Politics that Shaped the Old Testament*, New York 1971.

28. See Schürer II, 462f. n.164.

29. See D.J.van der Sluis et al., *Elke Morgen Nieuw. Inleiding tot de Joodse gedachtenwereld aan de hand van het Achttiengebed*, Neukirchen-Vluyn 1978, 258ff., and also Schäfer, op.cit. (n.12), 154.

30. Thus G.Alon, 'The Patriarchate of Rabban Johanan Ben Zakkai', in *Jews, Judaism and the Classical World* (n.22), 321ff., and Willems, op.cit., 14.

31. Cf. e.g. Stemberger, op.cit., 18; Schäfer, op.cit. (n.12), 155.

32. See e.g. E.M.Meyers, 'Ancient Synagogues in Galilee: Their Religious and Cultural Setting', *BA* 43, 1980, esp. 100.

33. Y.Yadin, *Masada*, London 1966, 181ff.

34. Cf.A.M.Rabello, 'The Legal Condition of the Jews in the Roman Empire', *ANRW* II, 13, Berlin and New York 1980, 662-762.

35. Cf. F.A.Lepper, *Trajan's Parthian War*, Oxford 1948.

36. Cf. A.Fuks, 'The Jewish Revolt in AD 115-117', *JRS* 52, 1962, 98-104, and also M.Pucci, *La rivolta ebraica al tempo di Traiano*, Pisa 1981.

37. Cf. CPJ, nos.435-450, and Dio Cassius, LXVIII, 32,1-3.

38. Cf. E.M.Smallwood, *The Jews under Roman Rule from Pompey to Diocletian*, Leiden ²1981, 550.

39. Cf. Smallwood, op.cit., 424ff.

40. See M.Avi-Yonah, 'When Did Judaea become a Consular Province?', *IEJ* 23, 1973, 209-13. M.Grant, *History of Ancient Israel*, London 1984, 246, differs and suggests 135.

41. See H.L.Strack and G.Stemberger, *Einleitung in Talmud und Midrasch*, Munich ⁷1982, 127ff.

42. See A.F.J.Klijn, *De wordingsgeschiedenis van het Nieuwe Testament*, Utrecht and Antwerp 1971, 166, 177.

43. Cf. also M.E.Stone, 'Reactions to the Destruction of the Second Temple', *JSJ* 12, 1981, 200ff.

Chapter 18   The Bar Kochba Revolt (132-135)

1. See B.Lifhitz, 'Sur la date du transfer de la legio VI Ferrata en Palestine', *Latomus* 19, 1960, 110f., and P.Schäfer, *Der Bar Kokhba-Aufstand*, Tübingen 1981, 48 n.80. Schürer II, 176, differs.

2. See S.Applebaum, *Prolegomena to the Study of the Second Jewish Revolt (AD 132-135)*, Oxford 1976, 10ff.

3. See Applebaum, op.cit.,14.

4. See Mur. 24A-F.

5. See Y.Yadin, 'Expedition D – The Cave of the Letters', *IEJ* 12, 1962, 249ff. n.42.

6. See Lifhitz, op.cit., 110f.

7. HA Hadr.14, 2.

8. BerR 64,10 and Barnabas 16.4.

9. See Schäfer, op.cit., 29ff.

10. Thus e.g. H.Mantel, 'The Causes of the Bar Kokhba Revolt', *JQR* 58, 1968, 224ff., and Schäfer, op.cit., 38ff., 195ff. Schürer I, 537; E.M.Smallwood, *The Jews under Roman Rule from Pompey to Diocletian*, Leiden 1981, 431; and J.A.Soggin, *A History of Israel. From the Beginnings to the Bar Kochba Revolt, AD 135*, London 1984, 335, differ.

11. *HE* IV, 6, 1-4.

12. Cf. also A.Oppenheimer, 'The Bar Kokhba Revolt', *Immanuel* 14, 1982, 11.

13. As does M.D.Herr, 'The Causes of the Bar Kokhba War', *Zion* 43, 1978, 1-11.

14. Schäfer, op.cit., 46ff.

15. See e.g. Y.Yadin, *Bar Kokhba. The Rediscovery of the Legendary Hero of the Last Jewish Revolt against Imperial Rome*, London 1971, 28ff., 128ff., *DJD* II, 124ff., and cf. also J.A.Fitzmyer, *The Dead Sea Scrolls. Major Publications and Tools for Study*, Missoula, Montana 1977, 48.

16. See Y.Meshorer, *Jewish Coins of the Second Temple Period*, Tel-Aviv 1967, 92ff.

17. See e.g. Eusebius, *HE* IV, 6, 2.

18. See e.g. b.BQ 97b and b.Sanh 93b.

19. Thus e.g. Schäfer, op.cit., 52. But cf. M.A.Beek, *A Short History of Israel*, London 1963, 214, who rightly rejects such a view.

20. See Meshorer, op.cit., 94ff.

21. Thus *Mur* 24b, 24c, 24e and 24i.

22. Cf. Yadin, op.cit (n.15), 124.

23. Schäfer, op.cit., 73.

24. Cf. b.Sanh 93b and j.Ta'an 68d.

25. These letters are written in Aramaic, Hebrew or Greek.

26. See Yadin, op.cit., 129, and also W.J.van Bekkum, 'Enkele brieven uit de period van Bar-Kochba (132-135 n.Chr.)', in K.R.Veenhof (ed.), *Schrijvend Verleden*, 123 n.7.

27. See Yadin, op.cit., 128ff.; van Bekkum, op.cit., 123 no.10.

28 See Meshorer, op.cit., 159ff.

29. Thus e.g. J.Maier, *Grundzüge der Geschichte des Judentums in Altertum*, Darmstadt 1981, 107.

30. Cf. Schäfer, op.cit., 173ff.

31. See P.Schäfer, 'Rabbi Aqiva und Bar Kokhba', in *Studien zur Geschichte und Theologie des rabbinischen Judentums*, AGJU 15, Leiden 1978, 65-121; id., 'Rabbi Aqiva and Bar Kokhba', in W.S.Green (ed.), *Approaches to Ancient Judaism* II, Chico 1980, 113-30.

32. See e.g. G.F.Willems, *Rabbi Tarfon. Le Père de Tout Israel (env.50-135 ap.J.C.)*, Brussels 1983, 101ff.

33. Thus e.g. Smallwood, op.cit., 442.

34. A.Büchler, 'Die Schauplätze des Bar Kochba Krieges und die auf diesen bezogenen jüdischen Nachrichten', *JQR* 16, 1903/04, 143-205.

35. Schäfer, op.cit. (n.2), 103ff.

36. Thus e.g. Schürer I, 545; Applebaum, op.cit., 35; Smallwood, op..cit., 442f.

37. See also Oppenheimer, op.cit., 69f., and the literature mentioned in his nn.35, 36.

38. Cf. Dio Cassius LXIX 12,2 and also the sources mentioned in Schäfer, op.cit.(n.2), 18ff.
39. Milik, *DJD* II, 125ff., differs.
40. See Schäfer, op.cit (n.2), 85ff.
41. Cf. Meshorer, op.cit., 92ff., 159ff., and also B.Kanael, 'Notes on the Dates Used during the Bar Kochba Revolt', *IEJ* 21, 1971, 39-46.
42. Cf. Schäfer, op.cit (n.2), 78ff.
43. Justin Martyr, *Dialogue with Trypho*, 108,3; Appian, *Bellum Syriacum* 50.
44. Cf. Dio Cassius LXIX, 12,3 and also A.Kloner, 'Underground Hiding Complexes from the Bar Kokhba War in the Shephelah', *BA* 46, 1983, 210-21.
45. Cf. Yadin, op.cit. (n.15), 60-5.
46. Cf. F.M.Abel, *Geógraphie de la Palestine* II, 276.
47. Yadin, op.cit., 193.
48. Schäfer, op.cit., 178f.
49. See Applebaum, op.cit., 53ff.
50. Cf. Dio Cassius LXIX, 14,2.
51. Cf. Corpus Christianorum, Series Latina LXXIV, 307, and LXXVa, 851.
52. Thus Justin Martyr, *Dialogue with Trypho*, 16, and Eusebius, *HE* IV, 6,3.
53. See Schürer I, 554 n.186.
54. Cf. *Digesta Justiniani* XLVIII 8, 11, 1.

CHRONOLOGICAL TABLES

I. The Time of Alexander the Great and the Diadochi

The campaigns of Alexander the Great in the Near East (*c.* 333–323 BC)
The struggle between the Diadochi (*c.* 323–301 BC)

II. Ptolemaic Rule (*c.* 301–198 BC)

Ptolemies		Seleucids	High Priests in Jerusalem	
Ptolemy I Soter 323–283 BC		Seleucus I 312–280 BC	Onias I Simeon I Eleazar	
Ptolemy II Philadelphus 283–246 BC	First Syrian War 274–272 BC	Antiochus I 280–261 BC	Manasseh	Zeno's journey 261–258 BC
	Second Syrian War 260–253 BC	Antiochus II 261–246 BC	Onias II	
Ptolemy III Euergetes 246–221 BC	Third Syrian War 246–241 BC	Seleucus II 246–226 BC		Joseph the Tobiad
		Seleucus III 226–223 BC		
Ptolemy IV Philopator 221–204 BC	Fourth Syrian War 221–217 BC	Antiochus III 223–187 BC	Simeon II *c.* 220–190 BC	
Ptolemy V Epiphanes 204–180 BC	Fifth Syrian War 202–198 BC			

III. The Rule of the Seleucids (*c.* 201–142 BC)

Ptolemies		Seleucids	High Priests in Jerusalem	
Ptolemy V 204–181 BC	Defeat by Rome at Magnesia 188 BC	Antiochus III 223–187 BC	Onias III *c.* 190–174 BC	Conflict with Simon, the captain of the temple

Ptolemies		Seleucids	High Priests in Jerusalem	
Ptolemy VI 181–145 BC		Seleucus IV 187–175 BC		
	Campaigns against Egypt, 170–168 BC	Antiochus IV Epiphanes 175–164 BC	Jason 175–172 BC	
		Antiochus V 164–162 BC	Menelaus 172–162 BC	Judas the Maccabee
		Demetrius I 162–150 BC	Alcimus 162–159 BC	Jonathan 161–142 BC
			Intersacerdotium 159–152 BC	
		Alexander Balas *c.* 150–145 BC	Jonathan 152–142 BC	
Ptolemy VII 145 BC		Demetrius II *c.* 145–138 BC		
Ptolemy VIII 145–116 BC		Antiochus VI *c.* 145–142 BC		
		Trypho *c.* 142–138 BC		

IV. The Time of the Hasmonaeans (142–63 BC)

Ptolemies		Seleucids	Hasmonaeans
Ptolemy VIII 145–116 BC		Antiochus VII 138–28 BC	Simon 142–135/34 BC
	Conquest of Idumaea and subjection of the 'Samaritans'	Demetrius II 128–125 BC	John Hyrcanus 135/34–104 BC
Ptolemy IX 116–107 BC	Conquest of Ituraea great expansion of territory	Antiochus IX 119–95 BC	Aristobulus I 104–103 BC
Cleopatra III 107–101 BC		Demetrius III 95–87 BC	Alexander Jannaeus 103–76 BC
Ptolemy X 101–88 BC		Antiochus XII *c.* 86–84 BC	
	Hyrcanus II high priest 76–67 BC		Salome Alexandra 76–67 BC
	Syria becomes a Roman province in 64 BC		Aristobulus II 67–63 BC
	Pompey conquers Jerusalem in 63 BC		

V. The Period from *c.* 63 BC to 4 BC

Rulers in Rome	Some Roman Governors in Syria	Authorities in Palestine	
Triumvirate Pompey, Crassus and Caesar, 60–53 BC	Scaurus, 65–62 BC Gabinius, 57–55 BC	Antipater, procurator *c.* 55–43 BC	Hyrcanus II, high priest 63–40 BC
	Crassus, 55–53 BC		
Caesar, dictator 45–44 BC	Cassius, 53–51 and 44–42 BC	Hyrcanus II, ethnarch 47–40 BC	
Triumvirate of Antony, Lepidus and Octavian, 43–36 BC		Phasael governor of Judaea and Herod of Galilee, 43–40 BC	
		Antigonus, king and high priest 40–37 BC	
Octavian (Augustus) sole ruler 27 BC–AD 14		Herod, king 37–4 BC	
			Aristobulus III, high priest in 35 BC
			Boethus, high priest *c.* 24–4 BC

VI. The Period between 4 BC and AD 44

Roman emperors	Judaea & Samaria	Galilee & Peraea	North Transjordan
Augustus 27 BC–AD 14	Archelaus, ethnarch 4 BC–6	Herod Antipas, tetrarch 4 BC–AD 39	Philip, tetrarch 4 BC–AD 34
	Procurators: 6–41 Coponius, 6–9 Ambibulus, 9–12		
Tiberius 14–37	Rufus, 12–15 Valerius Gratus 15–26		
	Pilate 26–36		Under Syrian rule 34–37
	Marcellus 36		
Caligula 37–41	Marullus 37–41		Agrippa I king 37–44
Claudius 41–54	Agrippa I king 41–44	Agrippa I king 40–44	

VII. The Period from 44–66

Roman emperors	Procurators in Palestine		
Claudius 41–54	Cuspius Fadus 44–46	Emergence of Theudas c. 45	
	Tiberius Alexander 46–48	Famine c. 46	c. 49–92/93 Agrippa II
	Ventidius Cumanus 48–52	Conflict between Galileans and Samaritans in c. 52	c. 49 King of Chalcis c. 53 enlarged with the addition of the former
	Felix 52–60		tetrarchy of Philip
Nero 54–68		Arrest of Paul in Jerusalem, 58	and in c. 54/55 with parts of
	Festus 60–62		Galilee and Peraea
	Albinus 62–64	Death of James, 62	
	Florus 64–66		

VIII. The Period from 66–135

Roman emperors	Important Events in Palestine	
Nero 54–68	First Jewish War 66–72	Vespasian conquers Galilee (67), Peraea and part of Judaea (68)
Galba 68–69		
Otho, Vitellius 69		
Vespasian 69–79	Bassus, governor c. 71–73	Siege and fall of Jerusalem 70
	Silva, governor c. 73–81	Fall of Masada 74 Period of Jabneh c. 74–132 Johanan ben Zakkai c. 74–80
Titus 79–81		
Domitian 81–96		Gamaliel II c. 80–120
Nerva 96–98		
Trajan 98–117	Quietus, governor c. 117	Quietus War 115–117
Hadrian 117–38	Bar Kochba revolt 132–135	Fall of Bethar 135

INDEX OF MODERN SCHOLARS

Mantel, H., 196 n.10
Mayer, R., 162 n.13
Mazar, B., 168 n.9, 180 n.23, 184 n.25
McElency, N. J., 188 n.69
Medico, H. F. del, 181 n.22
Meijer, F. J., 183 nn.3, 4, 190 nn.1, 3, 194 n.1
Mendels, D., 173 n.15, 180 n.3
Menken, M., 103, 183
Merkel, H., 189 nn.79, 87
Mershorer, Y., 165 n.9, 178 n.12, 179 n.33, 180 n.27, 28, 182 n.42, 190 nn.12, 26, 192 nn.14, 24, 196, 197 n.41
Meyer, E., 169 n.4
Meyers, E. M., 195 n.32
Meyshan, J., 190 n.12
Michel, D., 167 n.30
Michel, O., 192 n.29
Mielo, S. van, 179 n.30
Milgrom, J., 177 n.79
Milik, J. T., 172 n.67, 177 n.69, 187 n.31, 197 n.39
Millar, F., 170 n.11
Miller, J. Maxwell, 173 n.13
Möller, C., 182 n.13
Momigliano, A., 192 n.32
Moore, G. F., 163 n.24, 178 n.3, 182 n.49
Mørkholm, O., 171 n.30
Mowinckel, S., 181 n.30
Mulder, H., 174 nn. 1, 4, 192 n.43, 193 n.60
Murphy- O' Connor, J., 174 n.37, 176 n.59
Myers, J. M., 172 nn.69, 70

Negenman, J., 164 n.17, 166 n.7, 178 n.21, 180 n.15
Nelis, J. T., 162 nn.7, 10, 166, n.28, 169 n.21, 173 nn.10, 18, 174, 178 nn.10, 11
Netzer, E., 184 nn.31, 36
Neusner, J., 72, 175, 181 n.7, 188 nn.66, 67, 194
Nickelsburg, G. W., 162 n.7
Nielsen, J. T., 182 n.51, 183 n.8, 185 n.44, 188 n.53
Noort, F., 163 n.27
North, R., 176 n.56, 177 n.70

Noth, M., 164 n.34, 172 n.60, 193 n.61

Oppenheimer, A., 196 nn.12, 37
Otto, E., 187 n.41, 193 n.45
Ottoson, M., 192 n.37

Parker, S. T., 166 n.34, 180 n.18
Penna, A., 173 n.13
Perowne, S., 190 n.5
Pestman, P. W., 163 n.30, 167
Peters, F. E., 180 n.14
Petuchowski, J. J., 188 n.54
Ploeg, J. P. M. van der, 167, 176 n.55
Plöger, O., 53, 165 n.5, 168 n.14, 169 n.15, 172 nn.55, 63, 173 n.6
Poulssen, N., 172 n.71
Préaux, C., 166 n.3
Pucci, M., 178 n.20, 193 n.36

Rabello, A. M., 195 n.34
Rabin, C., 176 n.57
Rabinovitz, I., 177 n.71
Rad, G. von, 172 n.53
Rajak, T., 162 nn.12, 15, 163 n.18, 178 n.19, 183 n.58, 191 n.14
Rappaport, U., 179 n.32, 191 n.3, 192 n.18
Reich, R., 178 n.14
Reicke, B., 164 n.18, 176 n.39, 179 n.26, 191 nn.38, 42, 193 n.59
Reinach, T., 163 n.19
Rendtorff, R., 193 n.62
Rengstorff, K. H., 177 n.75
Rhoads, D. M., 189 n.88, 191 n.1
Richmond, I. A., 193 n.52
Rosenblatt, S., 189 n.89
Rost, L., 181 n.22
Rostovtzeff, M., 80, 166, 167, 170 n.1, 178 n.5
Roth, C., 103, 174 nn.26, 27, 176 n.58, 183 n.56, 191 n.7, 192 n.15
Roth, O., 173 n.16
Rowley, H. H., 172 n.52, 180 n.13
Russell, D. S., 172 nn.52, 56, 179 n.27

Safrai, S., 175 n.15, 186 n.2, 187, 188 n.68, 194 n.18
Salderini, S. J., 192 n.30
Sanders, E. P., 188 n.72

INDEX OF NAMES

INDEX OF BIBLICAL REFERENCES

MAPS

1. The Near East in the Time of the Ptolemies and the Seleucids

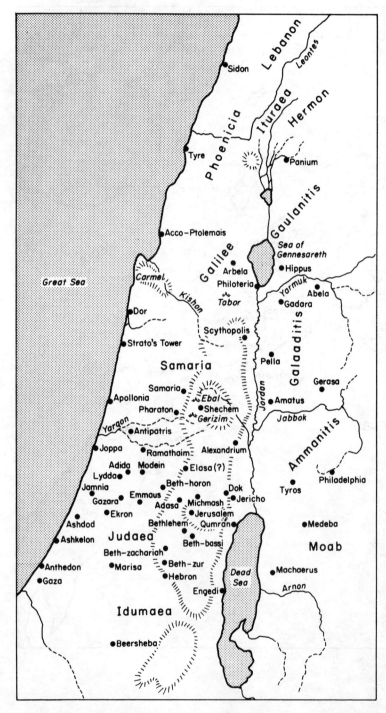

2. Palestine in the Time of the Ptolemies and the Selucids

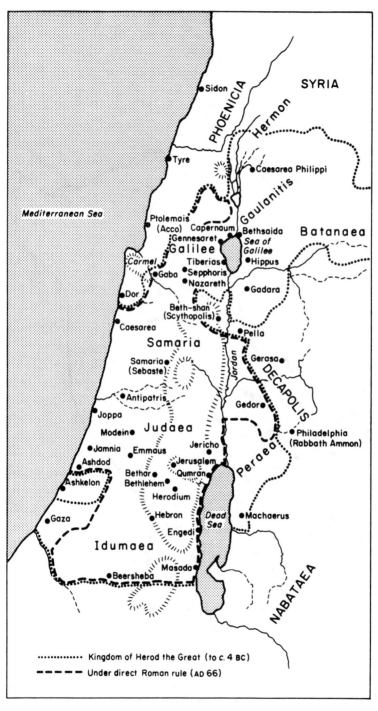

3. Palestine in Roman Times

Kingdom of Herod the Great (to c. 4 BC)
Under direct Roman rule (AD 66)

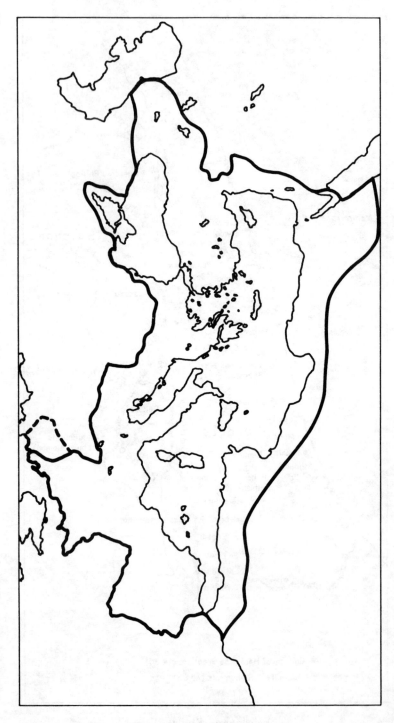

4. The Roman Empire